The Making of Global Capitalism

The Making Of Global Capitalism

The Political Economy of American Empire

by Leo Panitch and Sam Gindin

VERSO

London • New York

To Melanie and Schuster

First published by Verso 2012

3 5 7 9 10 8 6 4 2

Verso
UK: 6 Meard Street, London W1F 0EG
US: 20 Jay Street, Suite 1010, Brooklyn, NY 11201

www.versobooks.com

Verso is the imprint of New Left Books

ISBN-13: 978-1-84467-742-9

British Library Cataloguing in Publication Data
A catalogue record for this book is available from the British Library

Library of Congress Cataloging-in-Publication Data
Panitch, Leo.
The making of global capitalism : the political economy of American empire / by Leo
Panitch and Sam Gindin.
p. cm.
Includes bibliographical references and index.
ISBN 978-1-84467-742-9 (hbk. : alk. paper) – ISBN 978-1-84467-945-4 (ebook : alk. paper)
1. Capitalism--United States. 2. Finance—United States. 3. United States—Foreign
economic relations. 4. United States—Foreign relations. 5. International finance.
6. Globalization—Economic aspects. I. Panitch, Leo. II. Title.
HB501.G463 2012
330.12'20973—dc23
2012021104

Typeset in Bembo by Hewer Text UK Ltd, Edinburgh
Printed and bound in the US by Maple Vail

Contents

Preface

This book is about globalization and the state. It shows that the spread of capitalist markets, values and social relationships around the world, far from being an inevitable outcome of inherently expansionist economic tendencies, has depended on the agency of states—and of one state in particular: America. Indeed, insofar as the relationship between the American state and the changing dynamics of production and finance was inscribed in the very process that came to be known as globalization, this book is devoted to understanding how it came to be that the American state developed the interest and capacity to superintend the making of global capitalism. In this respect, this is emphatically *not* another book on US military interventions; it is about the political economy of American empire. In this quite distinctive imperial state, the Pentagon and CIA have been much less important to the process of capitalist globalization than the US Treasury and Federal Reserve. This is so not just in terms of sponsoring the penetration and emulation of US economic practices abroad, but much more generally in terms of promoting free capital movements and free trade on the one hand, while on the other trying to contain the international economic crises a global capitalism spawns.

The book has itself been a long time in the making. Indeed, it might be said that its origins go all the way back to the close friendship we forged when we were undergraduates together in the early 1960s. This took root in many common interests but especially important was our mutual awareness of how much historical materialism helped us understand the world. We soon came to appreciate this not in terms of unyielding economic laws and the development of a so-called monopoly capitalism, but rather because it revealed how continuing competition and class conflict, and the contradictions to which they gave rise, not only determined but also were determined by the actions of capitalist states. This perspective proved invaluable as we went on to work, one in academe, the other in the union movement—always drawing strength from this enduring friendship over five decades.

It was just over a decade ago that we set out to produce this book, a project in good part made possible by research funds from the Social Science and Humanities Research Council of Canada, and by the respective positions we held since 2001 as the Canada Research Chair in Comparative Political Economy and the Packer Visiting Chair in Social Justice at York University. It seems invidious to single out for thanks here only some colleagues and staff in the remarkable intellectual community that is York's political science department. It was there that many of our ideas were generated, and that research reports were first presented and debated, especially at the empire seminar series. The discussions with students in the Globalization and the State graduate course were also extremely helpful. For their especially important contributions to the research teams of graduate students that made our work on this book so productive, particular thanks are due to Martijn Konings, Travis Fast, Ruth Felder, Eric Newstadt and David Sarai; Scott Aquanno, Brad Bauerly, Aidan Conway, Tom Keefer, Adam Schachhuber and Sean Starrs; as well as Khashayar Hooshiyar, Frederick Peters and Angie Swartz.

Apart from stimulating interactions with so many of our colleagues at York whose work overlaps with ours, this book has also benefited from discussions over the years with Giovanni Arrighi, Patrick Bond, Dick Bryan, Vivek Chibber, Jane D'Arista, Gerard Dumenil, Peter Gowan, John Grahl, David Harvey, Ursula Huws, Gretta Krippner, Michael Lebowitz, Jim O'Connor, Fran Piven, Lukin Robinson, William Robinson, Chris Rude, Ellen Russell, Susanne Soederberg and Thomas Sablowski—among others too numerous to mention. We are above all appreciative of all the contributions that our dear friend Colin Leys made to this book: his close reading, generous praise, sharp criticism and insightful suggestions for each chapter were invaluable. The comments on the manuscript from Greg Albo, Scott Aquanno, Doug Henwood, Martijn Konings, Donald Swartz and Alan Zuege were also very rich, as were those from Adam Hilton and Justin Panos in the course of helping us prepare the final manuscript. The strong interest of Sebastian Budgen and Jake Stevens in publishing the book, and the thorough work of Mark Martin and their other colleagues at Verso in preparing it for publication, also deserve special mention here, as does the creative effort of Anne Sullivan in publicizing it.

Finally, we are grateful for the support of our wives and children over the decade that went into the making of this book. Long before we started working on it, Melanie Panitch and Schuster Gindin often used to say we really should have married each other. There were no doubt times over the past decade they wished we had, but in fact it was their love and encouragement that nourished us each day, even while their impatience to have it over with prodded us on. It is to them this book is dedicated.

Leo Panitch and Sam Gindin
Toronto, May 2012

Introduction

By the beginning of the twenty-first century, capitalism truly encompassed the world. The fashionable discourse of "globalization" vaguely spoke to this, yet cogent explanations of what had brought it about were in short supply. This was in good part due to the mistaken notion that, in going global, capitalist markets were escaping, by-passing or diminishing the state. This was seen to be true of all states, even the most powerful among them, including the American state.[1] In showing that the making of global capitalism cannot be understood in these terms, this book seeks to transcend the false dichotomy between states and markets, and to come to grips with the intricate relationship between states and capitalism.

In contrast with those who have emphasized the marginalization of states, our argument is that states need to be placed at the center of the search for an explanation of the making of global capitalism. The role of states in maintaining property rights, overseeing contracts, stabilizing currencies, reproducing class relations, and containing crises has always been central to the operation of capitalism. Far from multinational corporations (MNCs) finding it most convenient to have a world "populated by dwarf states or by no states at all," they depend on *many* states to see to it that these things are done.[2]

The American state has played an exceptional role in the creation of a fully global capitalism and in coordinating its management, as well as restructuring other states to these ends. Although there has also been a certain renewed fashionability of the term "empire" to designate the United States, the imperial practices of the American state are usually presented as accompanied by economic decline and explained in terms of fending off challenges from rival states.[3] The reality, however, is that it was the immense strength of US capitalism which made globalization possible, and what continued to make the American state distinctive was its vital role in managing and superintending capitalism on a worldwide plane.[4]

The insights of an Adam Smith or a Karl Marx into capitalism's DNA have often led people to imagine that globalization is no more than an inevitable outcome of capitalism's structural tendencies to expansion. Yet the spread of capitalism throughout the world was not the automatic result of the operation of any historical "law"; it was brought about by human agents and the institutions they created, albeit under conditions not of their choice. It has become quite commonplace to praise Marx in particular for recognizing that capital's competitive drive led it to "nestle everywhere, settle everywhere, establish connections everywhere," so that "in place of the old local and national seclusion and self-sufficiency, we have intercourse in every direction, universal inter-dependence of nations." Rarely quoted, however, has been Marx's no less perceptive insight that, while national barriers are "constantly overcome," so are new ones "constantly posited."[5]

The globalizing tendencies of capitalism may have seemed close to being realized by the end of the nineteenth century when, as Karl Polanyi wrote, "only a madman would have doubted that the international economic system was the axis of the material existence of the human race."[6] Yet the first half of the twentieth century—punctuated as it was by inter-imperial capitalist rivalry, world war, economic crisis and state protectionism—painfully suggested that, far from being inevitable, the very processes of capitalist globalization produced such morbid symptoms for humanity, and therefore such counter-tendencies, as to render the realization of a global capitalism quite unlikely. As Philip McMichael has argued, globalization is "immanent in capitalism, but with quite distinct material (social, political and environmental) relations across time and time-space . . . Globalization is not simply the unfolding of capitalist tendencies but a historically distinct project shaped, or complicated, by the contradictory relations of previous episodes of globalization."[7]

That capitalism's globalizing tendencies were revived after 1945 through the postwar "golden age" had a great deal to do with the way the capitalist states of Europe and Japan were restructured under the aegis of the American state. And although the economic turmoil of the 1970s demonstrated that capitalist crises were by no means a thing of the past, the degree of integration between the advanced capitalist states led them—in contrast to the 1930s—to promote the acceleration of capitalist globalization, rather than retreat from it. This soon included helping to turn the formerly Communist countries, as well as those of the third world, into "emerging market states." What the first great economic crisis of the twenty-first century, which began with a crisis in American finance in 2007, will eventually bring remains to be seen; but particularly notable is the strength of the interstate commitment—now extended from the G7 to the G20—to avoid protectionism, and the cooperation with the American state in containing the crisis so as to keep capitalist globalization going.

States in the Making of Global Capitalism

How global capitalism came about, and the nature of the American empire that superintends it today, are the central themes of this book. But before outlining them, a few general points must be made about states and capitalism, and about empire and imperialism. In the work of most economists, capitalism is seen as virtually synonymous with markets. In this framework, globalization is essentially the geographic extension of competitive markets, a process dependent on the removal of state barriers to this, and the overcoming of distance through technology. Political scientists, for their part, have usually understood that markets are not natural but had to be made, and that states are fundamental actors in this process; however, they rarely probe deeply into the ways this process has been shaped by the intersections of capitalist social relations and the dynamics of capital accumulation.

The mutual constitution of states, classes, and markets has been the main focus, of course, of political economists working within a historical–materialist framework. But they have often been hampered by Marxism's inclinations to analyze the trajectory of capitalism as derivative of abstract economic laws.[8] The conceptual categories Marx developed to define the structural relationships and economic dynamics distinctive to capitalism can be enormously valuable, but only if they guide an understanding of the choices made, and the specific institutions created, by specific historical actors. Building on earlier attempts to develop a theory of the capitalist state along these lines, it is this approach that guides this study of the role of the American state in the making of global capitalism.[9]

One of capitalism's defining characteristics, compared with pre-capitalist societies, is the legal and organizational differentiation between state and economy. This is not to say there was ever anything like an actual separation between the political and economic spheres of capitalism. The distinction between *differentiation* and *separation* is so important because as capitalism developed states in fact became more involved in economic life than ever, especially in the establishment and administration of the juridical, regulatory, and infrastructural framework in which private property, competition, and contracts came to operate. Capitalist states were also increasingly major actors in trying to contain capitalist crises, including as lenders of last resort. Capitalism could not have developed and expanded unless states came to do these things. Conversely, states became increasingly dependent on the success of capital accumulation for tax revenue and popular legitimacy.

It is one thing to say that capitalism could not exist unless states did certain things, but what states do in practice, and how well they do them, is the outcome of complex relations between societal and state actors, the balance of class forces, and, not least, the range and character of each state's capacities. Capitalist states have developed varying means of promoting and orchestrating capital accumulation, as well as anticipating future problems and containing them when they arise, and this has often been embodied in distinct institutions with specialized expertise. It is in these terms that we should understand the "relative autonomy" of capitalist states: not as being unconnected to capitalist classes, but rather as having autonomous capacities to act on behalf of the system as a whole. In this respect, capitalists are less likely to be able to see the forest for the trees than officials and politicians whose responsibilities are of a different order from that of turning a profit for a firm. But what these states can autonomously do, or do in response to societal pressures, is ultimately limited by their dependence on the success of capital accumulation. It is above all in this sense that their autonomy is only relative.

Capitalism's development was inseparable from the deepening of economic ties within particular territorial spaces, and indeed from the process through which formerly pre-capitalist states constructed and expanded their borders and defined modern national identities.[10] The differentiation between state and economy, which was a key aspect of the distancing of political rule from the class structure in capitalism, eventually allowed for the organization of class interests and their representation vis-à-vis opposing classes and the state. As capitalists, farmers, and workers developed distinctive institutions, the arbitrary authority of states was constrained, but the capacities of states were at the same time generally enhanced. One aspect of this was the establishment of the rule of law as a liberal political framework for property, competition, and contracts. Another was the establishment of specialized agencies to facilitate accumulation through regulating markets. Yet another was the establishment of liberal democracy as the modal form of the capitalist state, although this was not realized in any stable fashion even in the advanced capitalist states until the second half of the twentieth century.

As part of the differentiation between economic and political spheres, particular capitalists extended their range of activity beyond the territorial boundaries of their respective states. Insofar as states often encouraged and supported capitalists in doing this, there was always a specifically national dimension to processes of capitalist internationalization. And as the interaction with foreign capital affected domestic social forces, this in turn contributed to generating that combination of inside and outside pressures through which states came to accept a certain responsibility for reproducing capitalism internationally. As we shall see below, it is mainly in this sense that we can properly speak of the "internationalization of the state."[11]

It is therefore wrong to assume an irresolvable contradiction between the international space of accumulation and the national space of states. Rather, when looking at the role that states have always played on the international economic stage, we need to ask how far their activities have been consistent with extending capitalist markets internationally—and also consistent with the actions of other states. Some states have played a much greater role than others in this respect, of course, and in the making of global capitalism none has been greater than that of the American state.

Capitalism and Informal Empire

The age-old history of empires as involving the political rule over extended territories was fundamentally affected by the differentiation between state and economy under capitalism. Before the late eighteenth century all empires had combined economic control with military and political control. It fell to Britain, where the differentiation between economy and state was most advanced, to develop a conception of empire based as much on economic expansion and influence—the "imperialism of free trade"—as on the military and political control of overseas territories.[12] This prototype of an "informal empire" did not of course mark the end of territorial expansion, military conquest, and colonialism. Well into the twentieth century, international capitalist competition was still accompanied by formal imperial rule, and a tendency to dangerous inter-imperial rivalry. Nonetheless, by the late nineteenth century, even at the height of the scramble to extend old-fashioned formal empires, the development of capitalism had gone so far that, when capital expanded abroad, it was increasingly looked after by other states that were themselves spawning capitalist social orders.

The analysis of the international dimension of capitalism, and the insight that the export of capital was transforming the role of the state in both the capital-exporting and importing countries, was the most important contribution of theorists of imperialism writing at the beginning of the twentieth century. But the link these theorists made between the export of capital and the inter-imperial rivalry of those years was problematic, and would become even more so over the years from 1945 onwards. The problem was not only that the classical theories of imperialism saw states as merely acting at the behest of their respective capitalist classes, and thus did not give sufficient weight to the role of pre-capitalist ruling classes in the inter-imperial rivalries of their own time. It was also that they treated the export of capital itself as imperialist, and thus their theories did not really register the differentiation between the economic and political spheres in capitalism, or the significance of informal empire in this respect. This was itself a product of the failure, as Colin Leys once noted, to "disentangle the concept of imperialism from the concept of capitalism."[13]

Although this was perhaps not surprising, given the conjuncture in which these theories were formulated in the run-up to and during World War I, their tendency to directly associate the new export of capital with the old history of imperialism (as the extension of rule through armed conquest of territories), led them to mistakenly conclude that this fusion defined the historical terminus of a mature capitalism. Moreover, the notion of "finance capital" (extrapolated far too generally from the monopoly trusts formed between industrial and financial firms at the turn of the century in Germany) was a hindrance to understanding the much looser relationship between production and finance that increasingly became the norm, along American lines, through the course of the century. But most problematic of all was the attempt to explain the export of capital in terms of the saturation of domestic markets in the major capitalist countries. This failed to recognize the long-run implications of the growth of working-class organizations for the dynamics of capitalism. In the "golden age" after 1945, domestic markets were anything but saturated; profits were realized through expanding working-class consumption, yet capital exports continued, driven by quite different factors, as the export of capital itself was transformed over the twentieth century in the context of the international integration of production through multinational corporations and the extensive development of international financial markets.[14]

On the basis of the changes capitalism had undergone by mid-century, the American state was not only uniquely placed but uniquely capable, for reasons related to its institutional capacities as well as class structure, to relaunch capitalist globalization after its interruption by world war and economic depression.[15] This was a crucial moment in the historical differentiation between the economic and political in the making of global capitalism. In the passage from Britain's only partially informal empire to the predominantly informal American empire, something much more distinctive had emerged than Pax America replacing Pax Britannica. The American state, in the very process of supporting the export of capital and the expansion of multinational corporations, increasingly took responsibility for creating the political and juridical conditions for the general extension and reproduction of capitalism internationally.

This was not just a matter of promoting the international expansion of US MNCs. That state actors explained their imperial role in terms of considerations of universal rule of law was not mere dissembling, even if they always also cast an eye to whether this would benefit US capitalism. As with the informal regional empire that the US established in its own hemisphere at the beginning of the twentieth century, a proper understanding of the informal global empire it established at mid-century requires a scale of analysis that can identify not only the domestic but also the international role of the American state in setting the conditions for capital accumulation. It also requires a very different understanding of the roots of US empire than those advanced by critical historians who linked the American state's "Open Door" policy too directly to its own capitalists' needs for exports due to over-accumulation at home (or even to businessmen's belief in that need).[16] As Chapter 1 shows, economic crisis and class struggle at the time of the so-called closing of the US frontier in the 1890s contributed to the imperial posture of the American state at the turn of the century. But American capitalists invested abroad through the ensuing decades not because of the lack of opportunities at home, but to take advantage of additional opportunities.

It is incorrect, however, to try to explain US imperial practices in aid of commercial interests merely in terms of capitalists imposing them on the American state. The danger with this type of interpretation is that it exaggerates the extent to which capitalists' consciousness of their interests was always so fixed and clear. It also often leads to drawing far too rigid distinctions between internationally oriented and domestically oriented elements of the US capitalist class. The tensions, as well as synergies, between the American state's role vis-à-vis its own society and its growing responsibilities for facilitating capital accumulation in the world at large cannot be reduced to the lobbying of various "class fractions."[17]

Most crucially, such an interpretation gives insufficient weight to the relative autonomy of the American state in developing policy and strategic directions and bringing about political compromises among diverse capitalist forces—and between them and other social forces. This lack of attention to institutional capacity is also evident in Charles Kindleberger's highly influential argument that the Great Depression (and by implication perhaps even the world war that followed it) could have been avoided had the US state been willing to step into the "hegemonic" role that Britain could no longer play as underwriter of the system. This puts too much emphasis on US "reluctance" and too little on its institutional incapacity to manage the international system until the changes it underwent during the New Deal and World War II.[18] Despite the US already having become the leading industrial power and banker to the world by the end of the Great War, and despite the internationalist inclinations of many Republicans as well as Democrats in office, it was only through the crucible of the 1930s and 1940s, as Chapter 2 shows, that the American state developed sufficient institutional capacity to take the helm in a project for making capitalism global.[19]

The American Empire and the Internationalization of the State

The most important novelty of the relationship between capitalism and imperialism that World War II set in train was that the densest imperial networks and institutional linkages, which had earlier run North–South between imperial states and their formal or informal colonies, now ran between the US and the other major capitalist states. The creation of stable conditions for globalized capital accumulation, which Britain had been unable to achieve (indeed hardly even to contemplate) in the nineteenth century, was now accomplished by the American informal empire, which succeeded in integrating all the other capitalist powers into an effective system of coordination under its aegis.

The significance of this can only be fully appreciated with a proper understanding of what it meant in terms of the internationalization of the capitalist state. The creation of new international institutions in the postwar era did not amount to the beginnings of a proto-global state; these institutions were constituted by national states, and were themselves embedded in the new American empire. National states remained primarily responsible for reorganizing and reproducing their respective countries' social relations and institutions of class, property, currency, contract, and markets. But they were now "internationalized" in a different way than they had been before. Now they too had to accept some responsibility for promoting the accumulation of capital in a manner that contributed to the US-led management of the international capitalist order. The American state did not so much dictate this to other states; rather it "set the parameters within which [the others] determined their course of action."[20]

At the same time, while the policies of the new imperial state continued to reflect pressures coming from domestic social forces, including pressures to represent US capitalists' interests abroad, the state responded to these pressures in a way that redefined the American "national interest" in terms of the extension and defense of global capitalism. Domestic tensions with respect to its international role were reflected in heated debates, and even conflicting definitions of institutional responsibilities, within the American state. These tensions were eased by the fact that the accumulation strategies of the dominant sections of the US capitalist class were themselves increasingly global. That said, the state's actions in support of global capitalism were not merely dictated by American capitalists, even if their growing international interests and connections structured the range of options open to the state in its international role. Moreover, the capacity to generate coherent international policies in the face of the conflicts and compromises inside the American state, as it took on the central responsibility for global capitalism while remaining the nation-state of the USA, was never achieved once and for all. Nor was policymaking ever centered in any singular state "brain." It was only in the context of dealing with specific problems thrown up by an international capitalism, and of the accompanying shifts in the hierarchy of US state agencies, that key actors inside the American state struck the compromises and developed the common tactics to produce the kind of policy cohesion that allows us to speak in terms of the American state's imperial strategies.

Apart from its importance as the world's leading capitalist economy, what added to the legitimacy of the informal American empire was the cachet that liberal-democratic ideas and the "rule of law" lent to the US abroad, even if this did not always provide credibility to the claim that American military interventions were all about human rights, democracy and freedom. And just as the liberal democratic project of reconciling formal equality of citizenship with the inherently unequal social relations of capitalism obscured the realities of class, so did the attempt to reconcile national self-determination and the formal equality of states with the inherently asymmetric inter-state relations in a capitalist world economy likewise obscure the new realities of empire.

Many US administrative, legal and constitutional forms were imitated in other states, but this was always mediated and refracted by the specific balance of social forces and the institutional make-up of each of them. Their politics were never a direct reflection of American economic penetration of their economies. Nor did other states become merely passive actors in the American empire; "relative autonomy" characterized the internationalization of these states as well. It was relative autonomy within the American empire that allowed other governments to pressure US governments to carry out their pre-eminent responsibilities in the management of global capitalism in ways that would not simply reflect the political and economic pressures to which American political actors were subject at home. But in doing so, these other governments recognized, usually explicitly, that the US alone had the capacity to play the leading role in the expansion, protection, and reproduction of capitalism.

The US-led postwar order is usually presented in terms of "the victory of the interventionist, or welfare, economy over the market economy," which allowed states to cushion their populations from external disruptions in the context of "the movement towards greater openness in the international economy."[21] But what the notion of this so-called "embedded liberalism" obscures is that the social welfare reforms were structured so as to be embedded in capitalist social relations. They facilitated not the "decommodification" of society, but rather its increasing commodification through full employment in the labor market and through the consumer demand that the welfare state made possible.[22] The social reforms of the welfare state were extremely important in terms of employment and income security, education and social mobility, and they strengthened working classes in many respects; but at the same time these reforms were limited by the way they were linked to the spreading and deepening of markets amid the relaunching of global capitalism.

Chapter 3 shows that, contrary to what is often supposed, it was precisely the concern to lay a stable basis for the spreading and deepening of global financial markets that was embodied in the 1944 Bretton Woods agreement—and the IMF and World Bank that were established under its auspices. In effectively putting the capitalist world on the dollar standard, that agreement reflected the recognition on all sides of the immense size, depth, liquidity, and openness of US financial markets, and it ushered in the steady expansion of the financial sector both in the US and internationally.[23] The considerable power that bankers retained within the American capitalist class and the institutional intertwining of the US Treasury and Federal Reserve with Wall Street were registered in the American state's abandonment of its capital controls after the war. The controls that other capitalist states maintained represented not the defeat of international finance, but rather a pragmatic conjunctural response to postwar economic realities. Most US political actors regarded these controls as temporary arrangements. The explicit long-term goal of the American state was to create the material and legal conditions for the free movement of capital throughout the world. Precisely because these conditions were so successfully fostered in the advanced capitalist countries during the Bretton Woods era, those years should be understood as "the cradle of the global financial order that eventually emerged."[24]

One key feature of this transformation was the deeper incorporation of the American working class despite its considerable militancy immediately after World War II. As Chapter 4 shows, another of its crucial aspects, for which there was no historical precedent, was the extent to which US governments supported the revival of potential economic competitors— through low-interest loans, direct grants, technological assistance, and favorable trading relations—so that they could sell their products to the US. A pattern was thereby set for the economic integration of all the leading capitalist countries, and continues to this day. This laid the basis for the spread of US MNCs, whose growing strength and reach in turn reinforced the imperial capacities of the American state. The increasing flow of investment from Europe and Japan to the US further deepened the shift from "soft" integration based on lower tariffs to "hard" integration in the shape of cross-border networks of production. This did not mean that trade had become less important, but it was now structured by a broad range of MNCs that were more and more dependent on the regular flow of cross-border inputs and outputs. This increased pressures on states to support the "constitutionalization" of free trade and capital movements through both bilateral and multilateral agreements that effectively protected the assets and profits of MNCs around the world.[25]

As capitalist states increasingly sought to attract foreign investment, their policies became more oriented to offering equal treatment to *all* capitalists, independent of their nationality, which was precisely what the American state had pressed for. MNCs came to depend on equal national treatment by many states; and these states were also internationalized in the sense of coming to take on more and more responsibility for creating and strengthening the conditions for non-discriminatory accumulation within their

borders. This eventually included legal and regulatory changes that facilitated the development of their own MNCs along the lines pioneered by the
American state. This did not spawn a "transnational capitalist class," loosened from any state moorings or about to spawn a supranational global state;
"national capital," in the shape of firms with dense historic linkages and
distinct characteristics, did not disappear.[26] Nor did economic competition
between various centers of accumulation. But the interpenetration of capi-
tals did largely efface the interest and capacity of each "national bourgeoisie"
to act as the kind of coherent force that might have supported challenges to
the informal American empire. Indeed they usually became hostile to the
idea of any such challenge, not least because they saw the American state as
the ultimate guarantor of capitalist interests globally.

The dense linkages binding these states to the American empire were
also institutionalized, of course, through NATO and the hub-and-spokes
networks of intelligence and security apparatuses between Washington
and the other capitalist states. The containment of Communism, whether
in the Cold War in Europe or the very hot wars in East Asia, was largely
about ensuring that as many of the world's states as possible would be
open to the accumulation of capital. As Bacevich has put it: "US grand
strategy during the Cold War required not only containing communism
but also taking active measures to open up the world politically, cultur-
ally, and, above all, economically—which is precisely what policymakers
said they intended to do."[27] They made this quite clear, moreover, as is
now widely accepted among historians, "well before the Soviet Union
emerged as a clear and present antagonist."[28] This was not, as has often
been suggested, an extension of the old Open Door policy.[29] That earlier
policy had been conceived as securing equal treatment for American
products and businessmen within the rival capitalist imperial spheres of
influence, whereas the central strategic concern of those who planned the
new American empire during World War II was to do away with discrete
capitalist spheres of influence altogether. Their prime goal was to "alter
the character of the capitalist core."[30]

The new relationship between capitalism and empire established at this
time should not be understood in terms of the old "territorial logic of
power" long associated with imperial rule merely becoming fused with the
"capitalist logic of power" associated with "capital accumulation in space
and time."[31] The US informal empire constituted a distinctly new form of
political rule. Instead of aiming for territorial expansion along the lines of
the old empires, US military interventions abroad were primarily aimed at
preventing the closure of particular places or whole regions of the globe to
capital accumulation. This was part of a larger remit of creating openings for
or removing barriers to capital in general, not just US capital. The maintenance and indeed steady growth of US military installations around the

globe after World War II, mostly on the territory of independent states, needs to be seen in this light, rather than in terms of securing territorial space for the exclusive US use of natural resources and accumulation by its corporations.[32] For instance, US interventions in the Middle East—from the overthrow of Mossadegh in Iran in 1953 to the overthrow of Saddam fifty years later—cannot be understood simply in terms of keeping US gas prices low or winning exploration contracts for American companies. Such narrow concerns would not themselves "merit the intense level of US intervention in the region . . . Rather, America ensures that oil flows from the Persian Gulf are available to fuel international trade and economy as part of its global superpower responsibilities."[33]

The fact that the US could also plausibly present itself as anti-imperialist (in the old sense of the term) was based on its general encouragement of postwar decolonization and its promotion of an open and inclusive world capitalism. Of course, both the legacy of the old imperialisms, and the vast imbalance between the size of the Marshall Plan and Third World development aid, reproduced global inequalities between the new states and the advanced capitalist ones. Critical use of the term "imperialism" now became ever more loosely associated with core-periphery relations, dependency, and unequal exchange, with little focus on what distinguished the US from other empires. All the advanced capitalist countries might continue to benefit from the North–South divide, but any interventions abroad by them had to be either American-initiated or at least have American approval. The American state arrogated to itself the sole right to intervene against other sovereign states (which it repeatedly did around the world), and largely reserved to its own discretion the interpretation of international rules and norms. Its global reach and responsibilities made it not so much *primus inter pares* as qualitatively distinct from the other advanced capitalist states. (The Soviet Union was of course an entirely different matter, and insofar as it also played an imperial role in the postwar era, it did so in a very different way, precisely because it was not a capitalist state.)

Economic Crisis and the Illusion of Hegemonic Decline

By the 1960s, alongside the activities of MNCs abroad, the international operations of US management, legal, accounting, and consultancy firms also facilitated the making of global capitalism under the aegis of the American empire. This was further enhanced when the City of London switched its international allegiance from sterling to the dollar, and became by the 1960s the Eurodollar satellite of Wall Street. But, together with the appearance of US balance of payments deficits due to the flow of imports from Europe, as well as increased US foreign direct investment (FDI from here on) in Europe, this raised severe problems for the dollar's fixed exchange rate, even though the US Treasury bond market still served as the foundation for all calculations of value in the global capitalist economy. As Chapter 5 shows, it became the remit of the international nexus formed by the staffs of the US Treasury and Federal Reserve with those of the finance ministries and central banks of Europe and Japan to try to cope with the dollar's problems. In the end they failed to do so within the Bretton Woods framework. That failure was ultimately due to the contradictions produced by the success of the "golden age" in producing near full employment by the 1960s. Growing worker militancy in the advanced capitalist countries, and assertions of economic nationalism in the Third World, combined to deepen the "crisis of the dollar." This was a situation that proved confusing to all the main actors—including the Americans.

Many observers thought that the policy tensions among states around the time of the breakdown of Bretton Woods were a sign of challenges to American hegemony, and the clear beginnings of its decline.[34] As usual, the most prominent US political scientists were picking up the unease of American policymakers themselves, who, having "encouraged as a deliberate act of American policy" the growth of the US's main trading partners in the postwar era, were by the 1960s speaking privately in terms of "trying to make the decline of the United States in the world respectable and orderly."[35] In many respects, the expectations of US international relations "realists" were similar to those of Marxists who continued to expect a resurgence of inter-imperial rivalry.[36] Yet, as Nicos Poulantzas was one of the few to understand clearly at the time, this failed to appreciate the depth of the incorporation of other advanced capitalist states into the new American empire. As he put it just when the first serious postwar capitalist economic crisis was unfolding, in the early 1970s, there was "no solution to this crisis, as the European bourgeoisies themselves are perfectly aware, by these bourgeoisies attacking American capital . . . The question for them . . . is rather to reorganize a hegemony that they still accept."[37]

American "structural power" (to employ Susan Strange's term) was actually enhanced in the wake of the jettisoning of Bretton Woods, although this was not widely recognized until long after the dust from the crisis of the 1970s had settled.[38] It was only well into the 1990s, for instance, that Peter Gowan could plausibly present an account of the Nixon administration's 1971 decision to detach the dollar from gold as a "Faustian bid for world dominance" designed to give the US "monocratic power over international monetary affairs."[39] Yet despite its insights, this interpretation not only downplayed the importance of the links between New York and Washington *throughout* the postwar period; it also overplayed the coherence and clarity with which US policymakers responded to the crisis. In fact, the American state had embarked on an uncharted voyage through the "stagflationary" crisis decade of the 1970s.

But what was most significant was that this crisis did not produce anything approaching the kind of inter-imperial rivalry to which earlier capitalist crises had given rise. As Chapter 6 shows, the institutional infrastructure for the internationalization of the state built by the US, Europe, and Japan in trying to save Bretton Woods would lead in the 1970s to the creation of the G7, and would be crucially important in guiding the passage of international capitalism through the crisis. The fears of overwhelming currency instability once gold was demonetized "along with copper, nickel, silver, not to mention wampum and clam shells" (as Kindleberger once sarcastically put it[40]) proved unfounded, not least due to the development of currency derivatives by US financial markets. The development of derivative markets provided risk-insurance in a complex global economy without which the internationalization of capital via trade and FDI would otherwise have been significantly restricted.

In 1978 a scarcely noticed US law formally repealed the century-old Coinage Act, which had obliged the American state to convert dollars into gold coins or bullion. That this act was passed without any fanfare reflected the fact that "nobody seriously thought of the dollar in terms of its gold equivalent any longer."[41] But this certainly did not mean that no one any longer thought about the dollar's substantive value. On the contrary, the issue was now not just one of fluctuating exchange rates, or the US balance of payments, or even the price of Treasury bonds; the dollar's growing centrality as the measure of value in the global circuits of capital after the collapse of Bretton Woods made the American state's responsibility for sustaining capitalist confidence in the dollar more critical than ever. What had really sapped this confidence was the inflationary threat which full employment had given rise to, especially as this was associated with increasing labor militancy and popular pressures for greater social expenditure, economic planning, and controls over investment.

It was only when class discipline was eventually imposed inside the advanced capitalist economies that an exit from the crisis of the 1970s was found.[42] Amid a run on the dollar at the end of the decade, as Chapter 7 shows, the stage was finally set for the policy, introduced by the US Federal Reserve under Paul Volcker in 1979, which imposed that discipline. The "Volcker shock," as the Fed's draconian increase in interest rates became known, was designed to establish a permanent anti-inflation parameter which would guarantee that the dollar, backed by Treasury bonds, would provide a reliable anchor for international finance. This was accompanied by a broader neoliberal turn in the US, and its subsequent near-universalization as almost all the world's states, soon including Communist ones, opened themselves up to free trade and the free movement of capital, and promoted the spread and deepening of capitalist social relations.

The common tendency to analyze these developments in terms of the key tenets of neoliberal ideology as articulated by Reagan or Thatcher, or for that matter by Milton Freidman or Alan Greenspan, is a classic case of failing to see the wood for the trees. It misses the continuities between their prescriptions for free markets and the long-term goals already articulated by the American state at the time of the relaunching of global capitalism in the postwar era. And it fails to register the growing contradictions within the postwar class compromise, as the realization of near full employment and growing social expenditures took place alongside rapidly increasing commodification and ever-deepening capitalist social relations. Neoliberalism involved not only the restructuring of institutions to ensure that the anti-inflation parameter was enforced, but also the removal of barriers to competition in all markets, and especially in the labor market. Breaking the inflationary spiral involved, above all, disciplining labor. By accomplishing this, it secured the confidence of industrial as well as financial capital. Despite the Reaganite rhetoric in which neoliberal practices were enveloped ("government is not the solution, government is the problem"), it was the state that was the key actor. The mechanisms of neoliberalism—understood in terms of the expansion and deepening of markets and competitive pressures—may have been economic, but neoliberalism was essentially a *political* response to the democratic gains that had been previously achieved by working classes and which had become, from capital's perspective, barriers to accumulation. It was only on the most stylized and superficial reading that the state could be seen to have withdrawn. Neoliberal *practices* did not entail institutional retreat so much as the expansion and consolidation of the networks of institutional linkages to an already globalizing capitalism.

In understanding both the trajectory and the contradictions of capitalism in the second half of the twentieth century, it is very significant that the new period of financial competition, growth, and innovation was spawned not in the era of neoliberalism during the reactionary 1980s under the imprint of Reaganism and Thatcherism, but rather, as we shall see, during the heyday of Keynesianism in the radical 1960s, under the imprint of Kennedy's Camelot and Johnson's "Great Society." The ever-increasing importance of the Treasury and Federal Reserve within the American state was directly related to this, as well as to the further explosion of global finance in the 1980s, at the center of which were the large US international banks. Apart from being the key vehicle for the diffusion of American policy abroad through the liberalization of regulations on capital flows, financial markets also contributed in crucial ways to the renewal of the American empire. It was not so much that the American state "exploited" its power to secure favorable treatment from financial markets; rather, overseas central banks and private investors, whether structurally dependent on the US or attracted to the safety and returns in US financial markets, had a strong interest in moving funds to the US. As capital markets everywhere became increasingly internationalized, the US could take advantage of the depth and breadth of its financial markets to supplement its trade in goods with its international financial services. This is why US trade deficits no longer led to a crisis of the dollar.

Nevertheless these trade deficits, combined with the manifest effect of economic restructuring in industrial shutdowns and layoffs, fomented further widespread angst about "American decline."[43] An insistent theme of more critical analysts was that the new age of finance was a symptom of the failure to resolve the profitability crisis of the 1970s.[44] In fact, the weakening of labor provided American capital with competitive flexibility, and the explosion of finance contributed to the restoration of general profitability, both through the disciplinary impact of the "shareholder value" precepts it sponsored within firms and through the allocation of capital across firms. Firms restructured key production processes, outsourced others to cheaper and more specialized suppliers, and relocated to the US south—all as part of an accelerated general reallocation of capital within the American economy. Amid the bravado and almost manic competitiveness of Wall Street, pools of venture capital were made available for the high-tech firms of the "new economy."

By the late 1980s these transformations in production laid the basis for US exports to grow faster than those of all other advanced capitalist countries. Moreover, the American economy's unique access to global savings through the central position of Wall Street in global money markets allowed it to import freely without compromising other objectives. Despite very high rates of growth in the newly industrializing countries of the global south—the so-called NICs—the US proportion of world production remained stable, at around one-fourth of the total, right into the twenty-first century. In terms of the strength of American capitalism, there were indeed really two golden ages—the quarter-century up to the crisis of the 1970s (approximately 1948–73) and the quarter-century following the resolution of that crisis (approximately 1983–2007).

Many people initially expected that the Western European and East Asian "varieties of capitalism," characterized by "strong states" with "coordinated market economies," would provide an alternative to the allegedly "weak" type of Anglo-American states that were fully subjected to free market ideology and practice.[45] Even apart from the wildly erroneous designation of the American state as "weak," this view failed to recognize how far the increasingly transnational orientation of the leading sectors of capital in Europe and Asia necessarily involved greater ties with American capital. As Chapter 8 shows, the heady enthusiasm that attended the Common Market's completion in the 1960s soon gave way to "Eurosclerosis." The first steps towards a common European currency, in 1979, were seen by many as the battering ram for a challenge not only to the dollar but also to

US imperial hegemony. But the persistent inability to develop adequate mechanisms for transfers from surplus countries to deficit countries within the EU, together with the defeats suffered by the Left in the 1980s, reinforced Europe's economic dependence on the US as "consumer of last resort," and made "delinking" European capitalism from American capitalism virtually impossible.[46]

A similar mistake was commonly made in relation to Japan. The massive flow of Japanese capital to the US in the 1980s gave rise to widespread predictions that Japan would displace the US as capitalism's hegemonic power. But this reflected a fundamental misconception, namely that foreigners' purchases of US financial assets were all about compensating for the US trade deficit. Rather, as foreign capital was keen to invest inside the giant US economy and foreign states were eager to stabilize their currencies at competitive levels, both were attracted by deep US financial markets and their broad array of products and services. In practice, the flow of Japanese funds into US private assets and securities as well as Treasury bonds had the effect of reinforcing the American empire, not of turning the US into a supplicant debtor. It validated the dollar's role as the global currency and gave the Federal Reserve enormous leeway in setting interest rates, while permitting not only a large trade deficit but also the fiscal deficits that came with Reagan's policy of tax cuts combined with increased military spending. And, by no means least important, it enabled the Treasury and Federal Reserve to play an indispensible role as the world's firefighters-in-chief, turning on the taps of liquidity to douse the repeated crises that were an inevitable consequence of the increasingly volatile global financial system.

Consolidating Capitalism and Containing Crises

The extension of capitalism as a global project through the final quarter of the twentieth century was intimately related to the development of the new mechanisms of international coordination sponsored by the renewed American empire. As Chapter 9 shows, the practice of neoliberalism reinforced the material and ideological conditions for international legal rules guaranteeing free trade and for the national treatment for foreign capital in each social formation. This was exemplified by NAFTA, European Economic and Monetary Union, and the WTO, as well as by the bilateral investment treaties promoted by the US Trade Representative. In addition to the G7's role in forging a consensus first among finance ministries and then among heads of state, the Bank for International Settlements re-emerged as the major coordinating agency for central bankers, while the IMF became the vehicle for imposing neoliberal "structural adjustments" on Third World economies.

None of this could, in fact, go very far, or be very stable, without a much deeper process of capitalist state-building, or what the World Bank called developing "effective states."[47] Moreover, far from neoliberal legal rules finally creating a crisis-free world order, as the proponents of free trade promised, periodic interruptions in accumulation now more than ever took place on a global plane. The intensified competition characteristic of neoliberalism, and the hyper-mobility of financial capital, aggravated the uneven development and volatility inherent in this global order. In fact, although global financial markets were increasingly important for mediating the integrated production circuits of global capitalism, they also vastly increased the likelihood of currency and bank crises.

So the consolidation of capitalism through the last decades of the twentieth century did not bring a new plateau of global stability. Instead, this global financial volatility left the developing countries of Asia, Africa, and Latin America increasingly dependent on the crisis-management role of the US empire, as Chapter 10 shows. In the 1990s, at the same time as the US was called upon to act as the global policeman against human rights violations by "rogue states,"[48] so was it also expected to put out financial conflagrations around the world. In the wake of the 1997–98 Asian financial crisis, with the US Treasury now explicitly defining its role in terms of "failure containment" rather than "failure prevention," the cover of *Time* pictured Alan Greenspan of the Federal Reserve and Robert Rubin and Lawrence Summers of the US Treasury beneath the banner "THE COMMITTEE TO SAVE THE WORLD."[49] Conjured up here was an image of the American state as a global "executive committee of the bourgeoisie" (as Marx famously called the capitalist state). In advance of the creation of the G20 at the initiative of the US Treasury in 1998, Summers himself paraphrased the opening words of the *Communist Manifesto*: "[A] spectre is haunting the world's governments: that of the global capital market whose advances they cannot resist, whose sudden rejections they cannot survive . . . We need systems that can handle failure because until the system is safe for failure, we will not be able to count on success."[50]

Those at the pinnacle of the American state clearly shared Paul Volcker's view that both the volatility embedded in the globalization of finance *and* the US global role in containing the crises this produced were "a price we pay for the enormous advantages, the indispensable advantages, of open and competitive financial markets. It's part and parcel of the process of 'creative destruction.'"[51] Even as they bore responsibility for managing crises, they were determined that such changes as were introduced to the regulatory "architecture" of international financial markets should not get in the way of the "indispensable advantages" the markets offered for making more and more of the world capitalist.

As Chapter 11 shows, by the millennium all the elements of "globalization"—the transformations in the global division of labor, the development of competitive networks of production, and a new financial architecture to facilitate accelerated financialization—were implicated both in the US economy's continuing centrality in global capitalism and in the successful integration into it of the huge and fast-growing Chinese economy. At the beginning of the twentieth century the *Communist Manifesto*'s prediction that the bourgeoisie would soon "batter down all Chinese walls" was, despite the Open Door policy, still very far from being realized.[52] Half a century later, when the American informal empire was still at an early stage of expansion beyond its own hemisphere, the US was primarily concerned that China's Communist revolution should not have any domino effects in Asia. Three decades later, however, when the Chinese Communist elite made its historic determination that the most promising path to development passed through capitalism, this coincided with a new stage in the informal American empire's drive to realize a fully global capitalism.

The failure to grasp the centrality of the American empire to capitalist globalization led many commentators to predict that China's entry into it marked a fundamental "re-Orientation" of the global capitalist order.[53] Concerns over American dependence on external finance shifted from Japan to China, while fears that persistent US trade deficits reflected a "hollowing out" of the American economy were revived and intensified. But the US trade and credit "imbalances" were actually indicative of the extent of China's integration into the American-led global capitalist order. US imports from China provided low-cost inputs for businesses and cheap consumer goods for workers, while China's march to capitalism at home was characterized by the largest inflow of foreign capital and technology as well as the greatest export dependence of any late developer in history.

The New Crisis

The foreign reserves that not only China but other export-oriented developing states invested in US Treasuries were explicitly designed to prevent any recurrence of the vulnerability to capital outflows that South Korea and the other East Asian NICs had experienced in 1997–98. But the financial volatility that attended an increasingly integrated global capitalism was nevertheless preparing the ground for the first great capitalist crisis of the twenty-first century. If the financial crisis that began in 1997 deserved to be called the Asian Crisis, because of where it emanated from, the global crisis that started a decade later, in 2007, deserves to be known as the American Crisis. This is the subject of Chapter 12.

The nature of this crisis cannot be grasped if it is not first understood how not only labor but also capital—and not least finance—were strengthened in the postwar Keynesian era, how that determined both the causes and the outcomes of the 1970s crisis, and how the particular resolution of that crisis in turn set up the conditions for the American and global crisis three decades later. The failure to recognize this obscures the fundamental differences between the 1970s crisis and the present one in terms of the degree of working-class strength; the transformations in finance, technology, and the international division of labor; and key institutional changes that have occurred within and among states. By the 1980s and 1990s the greater mobility of financial capital across sectors, space, and time (especially via derivatives)—that is, financial capital's quality as general or "abstract" capital—greatly intensified domestic and international competition at the same time as it brought a much greater degree of financial volatility. Thus, while the phenomenal growth of financial markets since the 1980s led to over-leveraging and excessive risk-taking, this was tolerated and in fact encouraged for reasons that went far beyond the competitive dynamics and power of finance itself. It was accepted because financial markets had become so crucial to the domestic and global expansion of capitalism in general.

Despite the sheer tenacity of the view, going back to the theories of imperialism a century earlier, that overaccumulation is the source of all capitalist crises, the crisis that erupted in the US in 2007 was not caused by a profit squeeze or collapse of investment due to general overaccumulation in the economy.[54] In the US, in particular, profits and investments had recovered strongly since the early 1980s. Nor was it caused by a weakening of the dollar due to the recycling of China's trade surpluses, as so many had predicted. On the contrary, the enormous foreign purchases of US Treasuries had allowed a low-interest-rate policy to be sustained in the US after the bursting of the "new economy" stock bubble at the beginning of the new century. While this stoked an even greater real-estate bubble, after a brief downturn economic growth and non-residential investment resumed. Indeed, investment was growing significantly in the two years before the onset of the crisis, profits were at a peak, and capacity-utilization in industry had just moved above the historic average.

It was only *after* the financial meltdown in 2007–08 that profits and investment declined. The roots of the crisis, in fact, lay in the growing global importance of US mortgage finance—a development which could not be understood apart from the expanded state support for home ownership, a long-standing element in the integration of workers into US capitalism. Since the 1980s, wages had stagnated and social programs had been eroded, reinforcing workers' dependence on the rising value of their homes as a source of economic security. The decisive role of American state agencies in encouraging the development of mortgage-backed securities figured prominently in their spread throughout global financial markets. The close linkages between these markets and the American state were thus crucial both to the making of the US housing bubble and to its profound global impact when it burst, as mortgage-backed securities became difficult to value and to sell, thus freezing the world's financial markets. But crucially important in explaining why the financial crisis turned into such a severe economic crisis was that the collapse of housing prices also undermined workers' main source of wealth, leading to a dramatic fall in US consumer spending. The bursting of the housing bubble thus had much greater effects than had the earlier bursting of the stock-market bubble at the turn of the century, and much greater implications for global capitalism in terms of the role the US played as "consumer of last resort."

In true imperial fashion, the US fully shared its problems with the rest of the world. Given the role of US financial assets and consumer spending in global capitalism, illusions that other regions might be able avoid the crisis were quickly dispelled. But the centrality of the American state was at the same time made clearer than ever. Its key role in global crisis management was confirmed as the crisis unfolded, from the US Federal Reserve directly bailing out foreign banks and providing other central banks with much-needed dollars, to the Treasury's coordination of stimulus policies with other states. The enormous demand for US Treasury bonds right through the crisis reflected the extent to which the American state continued to be regarded as the ultimate guarantor of value, and demonstrated how much the world remained on the dollar standard. Even while international tensions surfaced, what was so striking when the G20 leaders were gathered together to meet for the first time in late 2008 in Washington, DC was the consensus on avoiding protectionist measures.

The establishment of the G20 was not a matter of shifting effective deci-sion-making powers from the national to the international level, much less from the American state to an international body. The G7 had never been about this in any case, and US hegemony within it was even further enhanced by the turn of the century. But it did symbolize the growing importance, and at the same time the difficult challenge, of integrating the leading developing states into the management of the global capitalist system under the aegis of the American empire. As we argue in the Conclusion, the severity of the first great crisis of the twenty-first century clearly exposed how far all of the world's states are enveloped in capitalism's irrationalities. Yet it was especially notable that the fissures the crisis produced did not take the form of conflicts between capitalist states, but of social conflict within them. The significance of the fact that the political fault-lines of global capi-talism run within states rather than between them is, we suggest, replete with implications for the American empire's capacity to sustain global capi-talism in the twenty-first century. It is also pregnant with possibilities for the emergence of new movements to transcend capitalist markets and states.

I

PRELUDE TO THE NEW AMERICAN EMPIRE

The DNA of American Capitalism

The role that the United States came to play in the making of global capitalism was not inevitable, but nor was it accidental. The American empire did
not appear from nowhere. But comparing it with empires of the past—
usually beginning with Rome's, and ending with Britain's—tends to miss
precisely what is distinctive about the American empire. When the new
Republic of the United States was founded, the term "empire" was quite
often used to describe it—George Washington was not the only Founding
Father to do so when he spoke of it ambitiously as "a rising empire"—but
proponents of American power gradually ceased to use the word.[1] Unlike
previous empires, the new American empire was primarily built without
colonies. The early articulation of dynamic capitalist development at home
with the Monroe Doctrine abroad involved building the continental territorial expansion of the republic directly into the American state structure,
while at the same time trying to contain, and finally sweep out, the colonies
established in the Western hemisphere by the European powers. This laid
the foundation, despite the few colonies the US took over from Spain at the
beginning of the twentieth century, for the eventual global reach of the
informal American empire.

Writing a few years before World War I, Karl Kautsky observed, "the
United States shows us our social future within capitalism."[2] Insofar as this
turned out to be true, it was because of the way American capitalism and its
worldwide appeal—"the attractive power of US models of production and
culture"—emerged out of "the particular matrix of its own social history."
As Perry Anderson goes on to say, the "unencumbered property rights,
untrammeled litigation, the invention of the corporation" that distinguished
the US in the nineteenth century was part and parcel of the US's remarkable economic dynamism in the twentieth, leading to "what Polanyi most
feared, a juridical system disembedding the market as far as possible from ties
of custom, tradition or solidarity, whose very abstraction from them later
proved—American firms like American films—exportable and reproduc-
ible across the world, in a way that no other competitor could quite match."
Combined here were, on the one hand, the invention in the US of the

modern corporate form, "scientific management" of the labor process, and assembly-line mass production; and on the other, Hollywood-style "narrative and visual schemas stripped to their most abstract," thereby not only appealing to and aggregating successive waves of immigrants, but ensuring that US consumption patterns were widely emulated abroad. But the role of the state in this could not be ignored: "The steady transformation of international merchant law and arbitration in conformity with US standards is witness to the process."[3]

An appreciation of how centrally US capitalism figures in the general development of capitalism in the hundred years before World War II is key to understanding what impelled the American state to assume its new imperial role. But we also need to understand what made it *capable* of "conjugating" (to borrow Anderson's apt term) its "particular power with the general task of coordination" in the making of global capitalism. Anderson's view is that US constitutional structures lacked the "carrying power" of its economic and cultural ones, being "moored to eighteenth century arrangements";[4] while Michael Hardt and Antonio Negri, in sharp contrast, see the US constitution as having conferred a new kind of "network power" well adapted to the creation and management of globalization.[5] While this is an important insight, it underplays not only the considerable power the US Constitution gave the federal state to police the regime against insurrection, to make war, to promote trade, and especially to expand the Union territorially, but also the room it provided for the federal state to superintend the development of an informal empire.

Abundant land and resources and access to large foreign pools of British capital and European labor privileged capitalist development in the US, but it is the way in which these came to be combined through its distinctive class relations, first in the independent commodity-producing farm economy and then in the modern corporate economy, that lies at the roots of the uniquely dynamic nature of American capitalist development.[6] Pivotal to this was the American state. Though often characterized as particularly weak and "laissez-faire," its activism sustained the conditions for the successes of US capitalism, and imprinted those successes with its own distinctive characteristics. Although he could not have imagined what this would actually look like two centuries later, it thereby fulfilled Thomas Jefferson's boast that "no constitution was ever before as well-calculated for extensive empire and self-government."[7]

The Dynamic Economy

A key characteristic of American economic development was the use of leading-edge technologies to deepen domestic capital accumulation through intensive growth, while an unprecedented extensive growth was facilitated by the state's expansion of the territory within its sovereign control (from Ohio to Texas to California to Oregon), as well as by widening access to both proximate and far-flung international markets in a variety of ways. The small-scale family farming which engaged most white citizens, as independent commodity producers, in competitive commercial agriculture spawned a process of agro-industrialization, first in the Northern Atlantic states and then, and especially, in the new Midwest states. Once the farmers were "let loose on a fertile plain," this system of agriculture "quickly generated huge surpluses for disposal elsewhere, revolutionized production methods across a wide range of agro-processing industries, and . . . built an immense urban system to support and sustain the bare bones of production."[8] Moreover, as early as the 1850s workers in the new cities and towns became significant mass consumers of standardized goods, adding another key element in the distinctive socio-economic matrix of American development: a relatively high-wage proletariat. The fact that by mid-century wages in the US were more than double those in Britain contributed strongly to pulling in the vast pools of labor that were simultaneously being pushed out by unemployment in Europe.[9]

In fact, an industrial working class had begun to emerge in the US by the time de Tocqueville wrote *Democracy in America*, and he already discerned tensions emerging between it and the "new oligarchy" of factory owners.[10] The shortage, and the mobility, of skilled labor was a key background factor here, reinforced by the bargaining power that an abundance of land and the possibility of starting a family farm gave to workers in the labor market, at least initially. By placing limits on the degree of exploitation employers could impose, in spite of the high rate of immigration of new workers, this spurred more capital-intensive production; it also provided levels of income that allowed some craftsmen to start their own factories, and forced factory owners to promote the development of labor-saving innovations in machine technology and factory organization. Two other factors reinforced this trend. One was the system of protective tariffs that, in spite of Northern merchant and Southern planter opposition, was in place from the 1820s onwards. Another was the initiation and coordination by the federal government, acting through the War Department's federal armory, of new production methods using interchangeable parts, precision gauges, specialist machines operated by relatively unskilled labor, and management control information systems—the "American System of Manufacturing" so much admired in Europe by the middle of the nineteenth century.[11]

After the defeat of the plantocracy in the Civil War, the vast inland domain stretching to the Pacific provided unparalleled space for industrial capitalism's expansion in what was already emerging as the largest domestic market in the world. Outside of the core Southern states (which until after World War II remained primarily a low-wage, staples-producing region), American capitalist growth in the last third of the nineteenth century—building directly on the previous phase of agro-industrialization—was both qualitatively and quantitatively spectacular. Until the mid 1890s, industrial growth was more or less internally financed, while financial capital concerned itself with the sale of securities to fund the public debt (which had grown enormously during the Civil War), and with handling the inflow of foreign capital that funded the extension of the railway system and the telegraph lines along every track—"probably the largest and most sustained construction program in world history to that time."[12] By 1890, railroads—the first really big US businesses—accounted for half of all capital nation-wide, and they had greatly stimulated further industrial production, as well as the emergence of the first bond-rating agencies, S&P and Moody's. At the same time, the massive over-investment in railroads, and the crises this spawned, led financial capital to turn increasingly towards the development of securities markets to raise funds for manufacturing industry, whose growth had by then begun to outstrip its capacity to fund all its own capital requirements.

The tremendous concentration and centralization of capital that took place in this period (almost 30 percent of the companies that made up the Fortune 500 list in the 1990s were founded between 1880 and 1910)[13] established a distinctive pattern of accumulation. Many of these large corporations had emerged out of capitalist firms that had begun small and then diversified and competed to build nation-wide markets. In the last three decades of the nineteenth century, capital invested per worker almost tripled—a fact made all the more impressive in light of the enormous population growth at the time, including the more than 15 million immigrants who entered the country between 1870 and 1913. The result was that, whereas in 1870 US productivity was some 14 percent lower than the UK's, by the end of the century it was 7 percent greater, and by 1913 it was 20 percent greater still, and more than twice that of France and Germany. The US share of world production, already 23 percent in 1870, reached 30 percent by 1900 and 36 percent by 1913. This was more than the UK and Germany combined, and not far from the share the US would hold in 1950.[14]

In spite of high tariffs which limited competition from abroad, the country's increasingly large firms remained intensely competitive with one another within the giant domestic market; to characterize the US economy of this time as uncompetitive or "monopoly" capitalism is a mistake. These firms' relationship with the financial sector was fundamentally different from that of companies in countries with the kind of centralized banking systems that initially funded and then came to control industrial firms.[15] This was in good part the legacy of the farmers' populist struggles against bank concentration. Moreover, the institutions created to organize and run the sale of agricultural produce (the commodity "exchanges"), with the state playing a crucial role in setting the legal framework for this, would eventually give birth to today's financial derivatives markets.[16] The links between US industry and finance were increasingly mediated by the stock market and the investment banks that handled the corporations' sale of their own stocks and bonds.

The huge strength and expansive dynamism of the US economy was momentarily obscured by an economic crisis that began in 1893, leading to severe unemployment and falling agricultural prices, prompting intense worker militancy and farmer populism, and seeming to confirm Frederick Jackson Turner's thesis, articulated in the same year, on the dark consequences of "the closing of the American frontier." Corporate leaders and business economists argued vociferously that the domestic market was no longer able to sustain the enormous productive capacity of the corporations or provide sufficient outlets for the capital they had accumulated. Their claims were, of course, soon to prove wildly wrong. By 1898 the recession had ended and home markets continued to dwarf exports. The frontier may have been filled territorially, but accumulation within it was only in its very early stages when Turner identified its "closing."[17]

Ironically, these misleading American business notions of surplus capital also went on to influence the development in Europe of the theory of "finance capital"—the institutional combination of industry and banking under the dominance of the latter to limit competition at home while aggressively advancing it abroad.[18] Yet this theory seriously misinterpreted the kind of capitalism developing in the United States. The merger boom at the turn of the century (epitomized by J.P. Morgan's takeovers in the steel industry) proved quite short-lived.[19] To be sure, the tremendous growth in the industrial bond and stock markets (their combined value rose from $500 million in 1893 to $7 billion in 1903) created a huge new intermediary role for New York investment banks, in particular, and was accompanied by the growth of interlocking directorships across finance and industry. Nevertheless, the generally decentralized and fragmented nature of American finance remained, and, as Konings has shown, it was largely because of this feature that the US financial system "held together by intricate networks of domestically grown institutional relations . . . [and] a complex set of linkages between banks and the stock market . . . was marked by capacities for liquidity creation and a degree of dynamism that had never been available to British banks."[20] Although this distinctive kind of financial intermediation would leave the US economy more prone to financial crises and initially limit the international role of the dollar, it would prove important for the eventual global dominance of US finance.

American capital had in fact begun to invest and accumulate abroad long before the 1890s, although the banks played a very small part in this, at least until World War I. Even before the Civil War, the US had become the world leader in machine tools, guns, reapers, and sewing machines (all already linked with mass production), and the decades after the war spawned a new communications revolution worldwide with the telegraph, the telephone, the phonograph, and the microphone. With the completion of the continental railway and the new communications technology, American companies had moved from local, state, or regional sales to marketing their products nation-wide, and soon also began marketing and producing internationally too. As Mira Wilkins has demonstrated, "the American companies with national sales plans and unique products . . . discovered the attractions of doing business abroad and were the first to be successful in undertaking such activities."[21] Singer, Edison, Westinghouse, Eastman Kodak, General Electric, National Cash Register, Otis Elevator, and International Harvester—not to mention Standard Oil—were among the first multinational corporations, spreading the inventions, technologies, and commodities of the American industrial revolution abroad.

The evolution of the corporate form as a legal personality evolved earlier and more fully in the US than anywhere else, and this laid the basis for the modular twentieth-century corporate form, and the multinational corporation.[22] The remarkable explosion of mergers in the late nineteenth century was especially closely associated with legal innovations at the state level allowing for incorporation "for any lawful business or purpose whatever"— and, ironically enough, also as a way of avoiding federal anti-trust legislation advanced by populist forces antagonistic to "Big Business." As Thomas McCraw notes, "[N]othing like this sudden concentration of economic power had occurred anywhere in the First Industrial Revolution . . . [nor] had it happened during the Second Industrial Revolution in any country besides the United States."[23] In the period 1897–1904, over 4,200 firms were combined into 257, and by the end of that period 318 American companies owned some 40 percent of the entire nation's manufacturing assets. But the intense competition that nevertheless prevailed proved that the concentration of capital was not synonymous with a monopoly capitalism that negated competition.

With the institutional crystallization of American capitalist class power in the modern corporation, and the defeat of the late-nineteenth-century challenges that had emerged from what was then the most militant industrial working class in the world, as well as from the radicalized farmers' movement, US capitalism entered the twentieth century having demonstrated a remarkable capacity to integrate and subsume under its hegemony not only small business but also professionals, middle class strata, and working class consumers.[24] And it was on this basis that the US developed the key industrial innovations that came to be known as "Taylorism" and "Fordism"—which together reorganized mass production in such a way as to make a high-wage proletariat compatible with and actually functional to industrial capitalism.

The international impact of American capital as it expanded abroad was phenomenal. In *The American Invaders*, published in 1901, a British journalist reported, "these newcomers have acquired control of almost every new industry created over the past fifteen years . . . the telephone, the portable camera, the electric street car, the automobile, the typewriter, passenger lifts in houses, and the multiplication of machine tools. In every one of these save the petroleum automobile, the American maker is supreme."[25] Indeed, by the beginning of the twentieth century, it was impossible to speak of the international spread of capitalism without speaking of the spread of "Americanization"—so much so that another perceptive British journalist, William Stead, also writing in 1901, saw in America's capitalist development "the greatest political, social, and commercial phenomenon of our time.'[26]

The Active State

The American state had of course also undergone massive change alongside the dynamic development of the economy. Territorial expansion had taken place through the addition of new states, not colonies, and produced such a great "plurality of interests" that, as Madison had hoped, the masses for the most part showed little common motive or capacity to come together to challenge the ruling classes.[27] This territorial expansion took place largely through the displacement or extermination of the native population, and the blatant exploitation not only of the black slave population but also of debt-ridden subsistence farmers. Yet not the least difference between these lay in the space it gave white farmers to infiltrate the frontier in a "chaotic and headlong process" that sustained, and often invited, the expansion that occurred through purchase and conquest by the federal government. After establishing settlements as facts on the ground—regardless of native treaty rights, or imperial French or Spanish ones—they agitated for their incorporation by the federal government as new states.[28]

And state "rights" within the federation meant a lot.[29] They were strong enough to eventually produce a civil war; and it was self-government at this level that lay at the heart of the localist democracy that commentators from Hegel and de Tocqueville to Marx all noted as so distinctive of the American state.[30] But this does not mean that the federal government was unimportant—far from it. As Charles Bright points out, it "maintained the currency, funded the national debt, collected the customs, registered patents and—what was most important—assisted in the transfer of public land and natural resources to private hands and thereby played a key role in the conversion of the vast continental inheritance for commercial exploitation."[31] And the whole political system was held together by two nation-wide party networks of locally based patronage and logrolling machines, and by the federal customs, land and post offices through which national revenues were distributed, votes mobilized and alliances main-tained.[32] This state played from the start a very active role in the growth of American capitalism.[33] Apart from protective tariffs, there was a host of federal, state, and city public works infrastructure projects, and widespread financial aid directly provided to new industries. Legislation in all jurisdic-tions was lenient on businesses declaring bankruptcy, and harsh on workers resisting exploitation. As "haphazard and uncoordinated" as all this often was, it nevertheless added up, as McCraw says, to "a reasonably coherent formula that today would be called an import-substitution but still market-conforming and entrepreneurially-oriented strategy for rapid economic growth."[34] It was through this active state that "laissez faire" was enthroned by mid-century. The courts proved especially important in promoting the conversion of inactive land to competitive developmental use, rejecting feudal legal principles imported from English common law, facilitating the rapid growth of commodity and labor markets, and countering what capi-talists saw as the dangerous tendencies of local democracy.[35] After the Civil War the doctrine of "due process" (articulated in the Fourteenth Amendment to protect the rights of freed slaves) was exploited to secure the crystallization of capitalist power in the legal form of the modern corporation, and to redefine the old concept of "takings" in the Fifth Amendment (that is, confiscation of land by the state for public use) so as to constrain the use of taxation or regulatory powers that might have the "consequence" of lowering the market value of corporate assets or expected profits.[36] (By the last decades of the twentieth century, this would have significant implications for the way property rights would come to be defined in international trade and investment agreements advanced by the US, and international law more generally.)

Yet by the late nineteenth century this "state of courts and parties"—and not least the patronage system that allowed, as Engels said, "two great gangs of political speculators" to exploit state power[37]—was in many respects increasingly dysfunctional for American capitalism, and a movement for reform found growing support within the capitalist class.[38] Some important elements of a more modern state had already begun to take shape during the Civil War, not least with the US Treasury's establishment of an income tax and the nation-wide marketing of Treasury securities. The national banking system established after the war "effectively brought the Treasury into a central position within the New York money market," so that by 1875 "63 per cent of the investment portfolios of the New York national banks was made up of Treasury securities, and the Treasury increasingly played an active role in providing liquidity during frequent periods of stringency and financial crises."[39] In the wake of the political fallout from the economic crisis of the 1870s, further important steps were taken to improve the state's capability, especially through the establishment in the 1880s of the Interstate

Commerce Commission and the introduction of the merit principle for appointments to the civil service.

In the absence of the kind of traditional state bureaucracy that oversaw late-nineteenth-century capitalist development in Europe and Japan, the legal profession came to play an especially important role in this modernization of the American state. The large law firms that arose alongside the new corporations acted as broker-dealers not only with Wall Street and London investment houses, but also with governments at all levels—even to the point of drafting "the documents they needed to build governance and capital structures to settle the rights, duties, and discretionary authority of the participants in the enterprise and [having] them approved by a legislature or a court."[40] At the same time, the scandals that tainted many a legal reputation in the era of the "robber barons" reinforced moves to professionalize the bar and the law schools, and lawyers took the lead in advancing Progressive reforms in the name of "legal and administrative science." Thus, while acting to squeeze the interests of their clients through every possible loophole that the law allowed for, lawyers simultaneously advanced the notion of the rule of law as "a tool for the efficient management of the social order in the public interest." And in what has been called the "institutional schizophrenia" that links lawyers to the state as "double agents," the practice was born (often followed by capitalists in the twentieth century as well) of taking time off from the private firm to engage in public service. In US business and legal circles, and in the political culture more broadly, it came to be accepted (and remains so to this day) that is it is "appropriate for lawyers in one role to do the utmost to undo their accomplishments in the other."[41]

What above all drove the modernization of the state was the remarkable political coalescence of business and political elites in response to intense and widespread class conflict. In the last quarter of the nineteenth century the organization and militancy of US workers had often made them seem to be in the vanguard of international class struggle. This was highlighted, after the formation of the Knights of Labor in 1869, by the Great Railway Strike of 1877 (essentially the first nation-wide strike in US history), and by the movement for the eight-hour day in the 1880s. The infamous Haymarket events of May 1886, and the death sentences imposed on seven strike leaders, triggered the international solidarity protests that culminated with the first congress of the new socialist parties associated with the Second International, calling on workers everywhere to join in an annual one-day strike on May 1. These struggles by American workers reached their peak in the early 1890s, when the dramatic strikes that marked the first attempts at industrial unionization in steel, rail, and metal mining briefly threatened to coalesce with farmer radicalism, before the strikes were broken through severe state repression.[42] The capitalist class regrouped through the formation of a wide variety of local civic, social, and cultural organizations, as well as through powerful new national institutions like the National Association of Manufacturers (formed to stimulate US exports, as well as being an active anti-union organization). The most important expression of this regrouping was a new alliance between business and the Republican Party that was forged in the run-up to the 1896 election. It was an alliance founded on an explicit recognition that "a system based on private property needs class-conscious leadership just as much as a revolutionary movement."[43]

The Republicans' historic victory over Bryanite populism in the 1896 election ushered in two key developments in the American state. The first was an extensive revision of electoral rules that tightened the eligibility to vote and incidentally weakened the old party machines.[44] The decline in voting participation that ensued not only partially insulated the state from democratic pressures—especially from the black underclass—but also contributed to the difficulties of building a mass socialist party in the US at the very time when the socialist parties of Europe were succeeding in mobilizing workers into electoral participation. This would come to play no small part in the high regard in which "the American capitalist system" was held by capitalist classes abroad. And it would be reinforced by the crucial role the judiciary continued to play, not only in upholding the new electoral exclusions, but (as epitomized by the famous *Lochner* decision of 1905) protecting property rights against trade unions and reforms to labor standards and conditions—a factor in further moderating labor militancy. After the defeats of the 1890s, the workers' political energy was channeled into the American Federation of Labor's pragmatic craft and business unionism.

Second, the executive capacities of the American state were strengthened. This was seen at the state and municipal levels, where technocratic practices adopted in the name of "efficient administration" increasingly restricted the local power of the old party machines. It was also seen at the federal level as business, especially under successive Republican administrations after 1896, accepted the extension of state regulation along the lines pioneered by the Interstate Commerce Commission in the 1880s. Capitalists increasingly came to terms with the fact that, as Kolko put it, "the political structure was the only place to find a unifying mechanism and establish a legally binding common denominator and rules for conduct."[45] Even while the corporations sought and obtained juridical protections from interferences with their autonomy in the market, they had also been searching since the 1870s for ways to limit destructive price competition. But the self-policing of prices without state sanctions proved frustratingly unstable, while at the same time giving rise to populist enthusiasm for trust-busting. This set the stage for business's acceptance of the regulatory reforms advanced by the Progressive movement, and by the new professional classes that the burgeoning capitalist economy had called into being. The new regulatory state apparatuses were structured so as to be insulated from democratic pressures, and their range of options was prescribed so as not to generally disturb the structures of power in the regulated industries. While price competition and entry of new firms was limited, other forms of competition associated with new products, technologies, and services, as well as the free movement of capital across the economy, were promoted, and this was underwritten by the Treasury's central position in the money market. Even though some leading Progressives had often been critical of capitalists in general, and bankers in particular, the main—and by no means unintended—effect of their regulatory reforms was to provide state-backed solutions to some of the contradictions of the new patterns of capitalist accumulation, and it certainly enhanced the capacities of the American state.

Internationalizing the American State

The Progressive era (lasting well into the second decade of the new century) also saw the beginnings of the internationalization of the American state, which initially involved above all a new promotional role, as well as a new policing role, in relation to "the American capitalist system" beyond its borders. This included taking greater responsibility and trying to develop greater capacity for overseeing and managing an increasingly international capitalism—even though that created some tension, or even contradiction, with domestic social forces. Central to the "promotional state" was the "internationalization of the tariff"—converting it from a purely protectionist mechanism (and the federal government's main source of revenue) into a lever for bargaining with other states to "assist in the expansion of US exports through selective reductions in duties on raw materials . . . while changing the policies and actions of other countries through manipulations of the tariff."[46] This change had been inaugurated, with considerable bipartisan support, by the McKinley Tariff Act of 1890. Its further development after 1896 culminated in the bargaining flexibility allowed by the establishment of minimum and maximum tariff duties under President Taft in 1909. This flexibility was far more important than the increase in current tariff duties which the Republicans also imposed, and was the practical basis of the Open Door policy that the American state now made central to its whole international posture, with not only Latin America but also China increasingly in its sights. The Open Door's central objective of securing "equality of opportunity" in foreign markets was now seen as a very "serious problem of statesmanship," as the State Department's newly created Bureau of Foreign Commerce put it in 1899.[47] The establishment of the Department of Commerce and Labor in 1903, with special agents assigned "to report on worldwide markets for specific American goods," further carried forward this development of the America state's "promotional capacity."[48]

A more dramatic dimension of the new internationalization of the American state came after its quick victory in the war with Spain in 1898, which led to the creation of an American sphere of influence across the whole of Central America and the Caribbean, creating a colony in Puerto Rico, and separating Panama from Columbia (and building the Panama Canal as a de facto US project), as well as tethering Cuba with the Platt Amendment.[49] Closely connected to this, and especially to the policy of the Open Door, was the development of US naval power and its policing of sea routes not only in the Caribbean Basin but also in the Pacific, through the annexation of Hawaii, the establishment of a naval base in Guam, the creation (always designated as merely temporary) of a colony in the Philippines—and the repeated deployment of the Marines to keep all this going.[50] Before 1898 the weak US navy had undertaken numerous gunboat interventions, but these had been far less important than British naval power in defending the formal sovereignty of the new states that had emerged out of the former Spanish and Portuguese empires, and also in protecting the expansion of the United States to the Pacific coast. So long as expansion to the Pacific had continued to uncover vast natural resources—from timber and gold to oil—it had largely precluded any serious imperial temptation for a southerly expansion into Central America. But by the last decades of the nineteenth century the growing penetration of American capitalists in Central America, largely to secure resources for import to the US, inevitably led to increasing demands for a US naval presence there—demands that were also advanced by "ambitious naval officers," as well as by conservative politicians concerned with "steering American minds away from domestic ills."[51]

So the American state now came increasingly to be seen, and to see itself, as one of the "Great Powers." Yet it was acutely aware that it had entered into a world not of its own making. The promotional and imperial roles it was now adopting were not just a manifestation of the growing weight of American capital in the world economy, but were also a reaction to the restructuring of the international trade and political regime that accompanied the long-drawn-out demise of what Polanyi called "the free trade episode" of 1846–79, during which Britain had been able—very much to the benefit of US capitalism—to practice free trade unilaterally, with the aid of the surpluses guaranteed by its formal empire, above all in India. The new global economic regime was more than ever subject to the gold standard in international finance, with the Bank of England's management of gold-sterling exchanges and the City of London's deep and liquid discount markets at its epicenter. Indeed, rigid commitment to the gold standard, which the American state now adopted as the foundation for the dollar and for international transactions (acquiring for the next three decades, as Charles Beard put it, "some of the characteristics of a fetish, a sacred thing") was part and parcel of proving before such company that the US state was "sound" and "responsible."[52]

But it was also a world increasingly defined by the imperial rivalries resulting from the "catch-up" capitalist development policies pursued by European (and increasingly the Japanese and Russian) states which still bore many of the traces of their pre-capitalist ruling classes and state forms.[53] Their new territorial colonizations were supplemented by spheres of influence extending from formal "protectorates" to the informal but more or less exclusive privileges that were presumed to belong to a Great Power by virtue of its dominant commercial or industrial interests in any given territory. The "internationalization of the tariff" was in this context a general phenomenon whereby all other European powers had already begun to accommodate themselves to British pressures for an "Open Door" by means of trade agreements that promised nondiscriminatory tariffs in their respective spheres of influence, well before this also became the centerpiece of American economic diplomacy. The US was by no means challenging the division of the world into these spheres of influence, except in insisting on having its own; nor did it oppose "the maintenance within colonial possessions of a tariff system" or other "regulations for the obstruction of trade"; but it did now take the lead in insisting that these restrictions be applied "equally as against all nations" so that they give "no preferences in favor of the proprietary country."[54]

Another dimension of the internationalization of the US state, which it again shared with other "Great Powers," was the need to participate in various new forms of international state coordination that the tremendous growth in trade and capital flows had called into being. This increasingly involved trying to bring a common set of norms, and more ambitiously the "rule of law," to bear on international competition—in other words, to reinforce the capitalist "law of value." This was already seen with the negotiations that led to the Universal Postal Union, established in 1874, and the International Union for the Protection of Industrial Property, created in 1883.[55] A crucial aspect of this was to have states commit themselves to extending to foreign capital the same legal protection for property rights in patents and trademarks enjoyed by domestic capitalists. But these bodies were hardly sufficient to meet the challenges that were already being thrown up by the globalization of capitalism. Although "levels of trade and investment among the capitalist states remained high and colonies never became fully exclusive," colonial policies did increasingly tend towards greater exclusivity: "Where colonies, under whatever flag, had so far been open to the capital of any country, they now (around the turn of the century) became the preserves of the colonizing power."[56]

The reasons for this were well captured by an American political scientist, Paul Reinsch (later appointed by Woodrow Wilson as ambassador to China), who in a number of works at the time addressed the question of why "the pressure for extended political control is much stronger at present than it ever was in the days of purely commercial colonization." He found the answer in the fact that foreign investment in mines, forests, plantations, railways, and manufacturing enterprises involved "a far more intimate connection with the territory and the population than do purely commercial dealings." Foreign investment required that "titles to property in land must be secure; there must be no fear of violence or of revolutions of government. Orderly methods of administration, a sound system of banking and currency—all these are prerequisites to a safe and paying investment in foreign or colonial regions."[57] And whereas, in the imperialism of the Roman type, the problem might have been solved by bringing all administration under the rubric of a singular world empire, in the prevailing conditions of "modern national imperialism," which not only recognized the separate existence of national states but even embraced the claim that "the national state is . . . a necessary condition of progress," the answer increasingly had to be found in rival capitalist empires policing the world in the name of good government. "Governments in many parts of the world are too unstable, too corrupt to admit of safe investments being made under them," Reinsch wrote:

> Civil courts in these backward lands are often ruled by favoritism or bribery, so that the property of the foreigner is not secure. From this naturally arises the demand that stable, responsible government be established so as to make possible the development of resources, even against the will of the inhabitants, where they stubbornly oppose all industrial progress . . . In this way, the real needs of the expanding human race are united with the self-interest of capitalism to form a lever for expansion.[58]

Albeit still replete with notions of superior and inferior races, this perspective recast the white man's "civilizing" burden in explicitly capitalist terms. And this was the perspective shared by those engaged in founding an American empire at the turn of the century, far more than was the case with any of the other Great Powers—whose leaders regarded with no little cynicism American protestations that its imperial practices should not be called imperial. But this self-image had some real traction at a time when the other empires were far from ready to countenance a world of nation-states, least of all when it came to their own colonies. The American state's own "founding myth" determined that its empire would be an informal one, not only leaving it free to appear as a champion of "national liberation" against colonialism, but also ensuring that the annexation of Hawaii and the establishment of colonies in Puerto Rico and the Philippines were seen to be, as in fact they eventually proved to be, "a deviation . . . from the typical economic, political and ideological forms of domination already characteristic of American imperialism."[59] Of course, the main business was that of establishing the political conditions for capital accumulation in what was now defined as the American sphere of influence. In this it was following what the British had sometimes done with their own informal empire, but whereas in the British Empire this still was more the exception than the rule, for the American empire it was taken as the modular form—including, as Emily Rosenberg says, by the

> new professionals, business managers and government officials, all of whom championed the global spread of market exchange [as] part of an expansive vision of an American civilizing mission and the inevitability of market-driven progress. Its supporters came not just from the Eastern-based business and professional elite but also from small-town Main streets, mid-level managers, and aspiring professionals throughout the country. Their faith that fiscal stabilization and economic expansion would bring social progress marked a broad cultural movement that would help shape the national and international order for the new century.[60]

The US justified its taking over of the supervision of customs houses and the collection of taxes on alcohol and tobacco in countries within its sphere of influence, and asserted substantial control over state expenditures through private American "financial advisors" to ministries of finance, "minimizing the danger of default and securing the integration of new and potentially risky areas."[61] The US also went to great lengths to ensure that the states within its sphere adopted the gold standard. This was advanced to secure monetary stability and foster foreign investor confidence, to simplify transactions for American companies doing business in the region, and to encourage countries to hold their gold balances in New York (and in some cases even to adopt the US dollar as their currency).[62]

At the same time, the legal foundations were being laid for the American informal empire. Strenuous efforts were made to establish trademark protection (the forerunner of today's concern for "intellectual property rights') that would apply in all of the states of the region. Most important, the due process doctrine evolved in the American courts was employed as a standard to measure, and if necessary object to, laws made by Latin American governments which had "an allegedly confiscatory effect upon property."[63] The early State Department view on expropriation was folded into a discourse on the protection of the right to private property in the legal systems of the "civilized nations." In a bald assertion of the universality of American law and constitutional principles, Elihu Root, Theodore Roosevelt's secretary of state and one of the founders of the Permanent Court of International Justice and the International Court of Justice, equated the protection of American capital with the extraterritorial enforcement of property rights in general. From Root's perspective, all governments had a legal duty to afford foreign investors a "minimum standard of treatment" equivalent to what they would be afforded in the United States.[64]

Although Theodore Roosevelt's "Corollary to the Monroe Doctrine" in his 1904 address to Congress was full of talk about the need for the "great civilized nations of the present day" to employ force against the "recrudescence of barbarism," it also explicitly rejected colonialism and guaranteed that states within the American sphere of influence would be independent and sovereign. Within this sphere, Roosevelt insisted, it fell to the US, as part of its "general world duty" given the absence of a regime of "international law" and other means of "international control" (such as the conventions adopted at the Hague Peace Conference of 1899), to serve as an "international police," with the purpose of establishing regimes that know "how to act with reasonable efficiency and decency in social and political matters," and to ensure that each such regime "keeps order and pays its obligations."[65]

As Thomas McCormick has recently written, the colonies and protectorates the US informal empire acquired through this practice "were principally important as means to a more important end—the economic penetration of heavily populated, emerging market areas such as Mexico and China."

> While still economically weak, such countries had the potential to become major profit makers for goods and capital if their politics could be stabilized in the hands of propertied regimes hospitable to foreign capital, if a modern railroad system could be built that would produce an integrated national market rather than fragmented local ones, if their agriculture could be commercialized and their mining mechanized so they could export and earn enough to pay for increased imports of foreign goods, and if, in like vein, they could develop cruder forms of labor-intensive manufacturing whose semifinished exports could not only earn foreign exchange but be fabricated into higher value products in core country factories . . . Rather than opting for exclusive trading privileges in spatially constrained spheres, the great powers would compete on an equal playing field where all would pay the same trade tariffs and railroad rates.

As McCormick goes on to point out, what would ultimately distinguish the American Open Door policy from Britain's was most evident in terms of "the effort to expand it from a commercial concept to a financial one as well—an open door for investment in railroads, mines, bank loans, and the like"—which led to its funneling investment and loans through the China Consortium of international bankers established in 1912. "In other words, informal empire, as a means of penetrating China, would be done collectively by the United States, Europe, and Japan—a kind of G-7 approach."[66]

The actual practice of this informal empire was, of course, replete with contradictions, as was clearly seen in the Mexican and Chinese revolutions, as well as the rivalries which led to World War I. Moreover, the occasions for the exercise of US "police power," even if undertaken in the name of a "world duty" to protect the rule of law and property rights in general, were all too often triggered by the complaints of a particular US capitalist. And for all its trumpeting of the Open Door policy in other powers' spheres of influence, the American state frequently tended to close the door to their trade in its own. Moreover, in what was an early symptomatic indication of the American insistence on preserving its own sovereignty while advancing internationalization, the US refused to be bound by the Central American Court of Justice (which it had taken the lead in establishing in 1907) to adjudicate regional inter-state disputes. Above all, while its imperial role was rationalized in terms of bringing freedom and good government, the US ended up supporting local dictators and landed bourgeoisies, thereby fossilizing social structures, blocking economic development, and creating the conditions for continued political instability and revolts.[67] The result was that, despite the repeated American military interventions in Cuba, Haiti, Nicaragua, Panama, and the Philippines, not a single one of these countries spawned a liberal democracy.[68]

Far more successful in this respect was the type of informal imperialism practiced north of the US border. The first US multinational corporations had established branch plants to jump over the Canadian tariff barrier and get access to a rich domestic market which, in terms of social structure and political regime, resembled the American Midwest. Whereas in 1812 Jefferson had seen conquering Canada as the only way of preventing "difficulties with our neighbors," exactly a century later President Taft could celebrate the "greater economic ties" that were making Canada "only an adjunct of the USA."[69] US economic penetration of Canada had the added advantage of "providing access to unfettered trade within the British Empire which could look like part of the scaffolding of a new world order, all the more as American capital had a growing stake in it."[70] Yet the latitude that even Canada could claim within the American informal empire was demonstrated in 1911 when Canadian voters (spurred by fears of annexation) rejected a free trade agreement with the US, and when Canada immediately entered into World War I in support of Britain, while the US initially stayed out.[71] It was nevertheless a mark of the status of Canada as a "rich dependency" within the American empire that Canadian banks were virtually unique internationally in utilizing the dollar as a reserve currency, and maintained large external balances in New York as a source of liquidity and to cover the massive flow of goods and capital across the border. This would presage the type of relationship that would develop between the American empire and so many other capitalist countries, including the most advanced, before the twentieth century had run its course.

Yet it was precisely the fact that the dollar and New York as a financial center still lacked such status internationally that indicated the limitations of the American imperial role before World War I. In spite of the international prominence of US industry by this time—accounting for a third of world production, with exports surpassing Germany and France and matching those of the UK—"the US was the only major industrial nation whose currency did not function as an international medium of exchange, unit of account or store of value."[72] This was only partly a legacy of its past reliance on the City of London to finance foreign trade; it also reflected the long tradition of farmer populism that had blocked the creation of a central bank and the emergence of a more centralized inter-state branch banking system. Whereas European central banking had its roots in "haute finance" far removed from the popular classes, the dependence of American small farmers on credit had made them hostile to a central bank that they recognized would serve bankers' interests. The tremendous accumulation of the post-bellum decades drew on the considerable liquidity and flexibility of a commercial paper market that knitted together the decentralized banking system, but which also gave rise to bank panics and financial crisis in 1873, 1884, 1890, and 1893 that were seen as a "curiosity in other countries." Even with the defeat of domestic inflationary forces in the 1896 election and the subsequent full embrace of the gold standard, so long as the US lacked a central bank which could help make its financial markets more stable and more resilient, "the essential prerequisites for internationalizing a national currency" were still missing.[73]

The contradictions this posed came to a head in the great financial crisis of 1907—a year punctuated by a Wall Street stock market crash, an 11 percent decline in GDP, and accelerating runs on the banks.[74] At the core of the crisis was the practice of trust companies to draw money from banks at exorbitant interest rates and, without the protection of sufficient cash reserves, lend out so much of it against stock and bond speculation that almost half of the bank loans in New York had questionable securities as their only collateral. When the trust companies were forced to call in some of their loans to stock market speculators, even interest rates that zoomed to well over 100 percent on margin loans could not attract funds. European investors started withdrawing funds from the US, and European central banks were reluctant to provide the liquidity to stem the bleeding. As they had done in the early 1890s, both the US Treasury and Wall Street once again had to rely on J.P. Morgan to try to mobilize and dispense sufficient liquidity to calm the markets. It was, however, a long and fraught process that was only resolved when, with $25 million put at his disposal by the Treasury, Morgan called together Wall Street's bank presidents and demanded they put up another $25 million "within ten or twelve minutes"—which they did.[75]

"From the ashes of 1907," as Chernow's biography of Morgan put it, "arose the Federal Reserve System: everyone saw that thrilling rescues by corpulent old tycoons were a tenuous prop for the banking system."[76] The Federal Reserve was founded not only to supervise the creation of money, liquidity, and credit, and not only to allay Wall Street fears that regulation by the Treasury might subject the banks to undue political pressures, but also to relieve the Treasury of its sole, precarious responsibility for managing domestic financial crises.[77] Paul Warburg (who was the key banking figure in drafting the legislation that created the Fed in 1913) saw most clearly that the US needed a central bank that could guarantee a domestic system of interbank discount market loans through its lender-of-last-resort function. But that was not all. He also clearly recognized that this "foundation on which our own financial edifice is erected" would at the same time make "our paper part and parcel of the means of the world's international exchange."[78] Although the Fed's corporatist and decentralized structure of regional Federal Reserve boards reflected the compromise the final Act had made with populist pressures, its main effect was actually to cement the "fusion of financial and government power."[79] This was so not only in the sense of the Fed's remit as the "banker's bank" domestically, but also—and not least, given the close ties between the Federal Reserve Bank of New York and the House of Morgan—in terms of the way the internationalization of the dollar underwrote the internationalization of the American state.

The New York congressman and Wall Street lawyer, John DeWitt Warner, had boasted in 1898: "Today, there are no more worlds to find. Upon us is the responsibility never laid before on a people—building the world's capital for all time to come."[80] Indeed, when the tendency of nineteenth-century capitalist globalization to spawn inter-imperial rivalry came to a tragic climax with the start of the Great War among the European powers in August 1914, American capitalists were in a position to treat this as an immense opportunity. New York's financiers and industrialists, as Burrows and Wallace's monumental history of the city concludes, "would steadily expand New York's imperial outreach, their efforts reaching an apotheosis during the First World War, when the United States was transformed from a debtor to a creditor nation and its leading metropolis began to replace London as the fulcrum of the global economy, emerging as heir presumptive to the title of Capital of the World."[81]

2

American State Capacities:
From Great War to New Deal

In the context of the breakdown of the old order that World War I represented, it was not only Woodrow Wilson's internationalist rhetoric but also
the determining role of US finance and industry in the war's outcome that
presaged the pre-eminent role the US would come to play in global capitalism. As the loans provided to the Allied European states funded their massive
imports of US munitions, food, raw materials, and manufactured goods
during the war, US exports doubled. The same financiers who had been the
conduit for London portfolio capital coming into the US now took the lead
in engineering the conversion of the most indebted country of the nineteenth century into the greatest creditor of the twentieth, while the "fusion
of financial and government power" coincided with growing international
confidence in the dollar.

During the Wilson administration, the federal state's powers were considerably enhanced by the establishment of the Federal Trade Commission
(the most powerful regulatory body established since the Interstate
Commerce Commission in the 1880s) and the passage of the Income Tax
Act (making the ability to secure revenues much less dependent on tariffs),
while the Departments of State and Commerce improved their promotional capacities on behalf of business. Yet, in sharp contrast to what would
be the case during World War II, when it came to lending substance to
Wilson's ideas for remaking the postwar world, the "few and comparatively
inexperienced officials" charged with this lacked any "real conception of
effective organization for so comprehensive a program."[1] Even more important than the problems this caused in the Paris peace negotiations was what
it meant inside the American state itself. The Senate's refusal to allow the
US to join the League of Nations highlighted the American state's limited
capacity to realize Woodrow Wilson's ambitions for reviving a liberal international order on a more secure and legitimate basis.

Yet, contrary to the misleading terms of so much political and academic
commentary, the expansive dynamism of American capitalism meant that,
by the 1920s, "isolationism" was not an option for the American state. Thus
when, shortly after World War I, President Coolidge referred to "our interests all over the earth," he was already articulating the American imperial

notion that, because "the fundamental laws of justice are universal in their application," the US practice of protecting "the rights of private property under the due process of law should apply to wherever its citizens might go." As secretary of commerce from 1921 to 1929, Herbert Hoover argued that US investment abroad "not only increases our direct exports but builds up the prosperity of foreign countries and is a blessing to both sides of the transaction." Whatever was going on under the Republican administrations of the 1920s, isolationism was hardly the right word for it. "The 1920s were the most economically expansionist decade in American history" to that point, and US governments were extremely active in encouraging "this private internationalist impulse."[2]

It was not isolationism, but the intractability of the problems now associated with trying to make the world of the 1920s run on nineteenth-century economic liberal lines, and the inadequacies of American state capacities to make it do so, that confounded this strategy. Although it now oversaw the world's leading capitalist economy, and was active not only in fostering US capital's overseas expansion but also in promoting postwar European recovery and integration, the American state's limited capacities were clearly revealed by the practices of the US Federal Reserve and Treasury in the aftermath of the 1929 crash. It would take the Depression, the New Deal and World War II to bring about those changes in the American state that would allow it to play the critical role it did in the successful relaunching of capitalism's globalizing trends.

From Wilson to Hoover: Isolationism Not

Woodrow Wilson had come to office determined to increase the relative autonomy of the American state from American capital by refusing to give unconditional government backing to particular capitalist interests in Central America—harboring, as he did, "a deep-seated suspicion of any business that violated his notion of an open, liberal order."[3] But his administration was nevertheless soon embroiled in even more problematic interventions than before. American intervention in the wake of the Mexican Revolution, for example, was once again justified in terms not of protecting American oil interests but rather of assisting the Mexicans to follow constitutional procedures, to elect "good men" and create "a stable, law-abiding society." The moral contradictions of this were graphically captured in the statement by Wilson's ambassador to London that US interventions in Mexico would be justified even if this meant staying "for 200 years . . . and shoot[ing] men for that little space till they learned to vote and to rule themselves."[4]

In fact, despite US leadership in the development of military hardware (from rifles, revolvers and machine guns through the nineteenth century to military aircraft during the Great War), the type of informal empire the US had established by the early twentieth century did not require extensive occupying forces. Its advocacy of this type of empire as a model for other empires reinforced its aversion to joining in a renewed arms race, although it did develop enough naval capacity after 1900 to back up its economic ambitions in South America and, to a lesser extent, the Far East. The US had entered the Great War with little advanced military buildup, and even after the mobilization of 1917 the traditional aversion to a standing army asserted itself yet again when the war ended. The Navy had grown tenfold, from 50,000 men in 1913 to half a million in 1918, but was back down to 86,000 by 1922.[5] This meant that the US was in no position militarily to dictate to the rest of the capitalist world, and this especially mattered in terms of Japan's ambitions in the Far East. The American state's increased coercive powers were in fact mainly applied at the end of the war to the violent repression of industrial militancy and socialist politics at home.

Wilson's commitment to freer trade (which had been embodied in the 1913 Underwood Tariff reductions contingent on reciprocity from other countries) had been frustrated by the onset of war in 1914. And two years later, the US's own entry into the war—shortly after Wilson's re-election in 1916 on an antiwar platform—had also abruptly ended his program of Progressive reforms. Yet with Wilson's definition of the war as a global campaign for liberal democracy rather than an inter-imperial conflict, and with the unions' integration into wartime corporatist structures at home and propaganda activities abroad, this appeared to validate the claim of the American Federation of Labor's president Samuel Gompers, when he was sent to address European labor leaders, that America was more "an ideal" than "a country."[6] Wilson's advocacy of a "peoples' war" for self-determination and his calls for a "peace without victory" and no secret treaties filled the vacuum created by the collapse of the Socialist International in 1914. The US became, as Arno Mayer has shown, a "powerful beacon of hope" for European Social Democrats, from Kautsky and Bernstein in Germany to the Webbs and MacDonald in Britain.[7] This inaugurated the informal alliance between US Democratic administrations and Social Democratic parties in Europe that would later be consolidated during the New Deal, reinforced in the post–World War II era, and renewed yet again under the rubric of the "Third Way" at the end of the century.

Wilson's promise to help establish the economic conditions that would lay the basis for social-democratic reform after the war—and offset the need for revolutionary change—appeared to be grounded in the expectation that even the victorious allies could be forced "to our way of thinking because by that time they will . . . be financially in our hands."[8] But expectations that the US "way of thinking" had much to do with substantial social reform were dashed at the Paris peace talks. Wilson's sordid compromises with the

leaders of the victorious old empires—allowing them to retain their colonies, and even to extend their "spheres of influence," while unanimously
turning their face against the Bolshevik revolution in Russia—exposed how
little the Fourteen Points he had brought to Paris were capable of transcending the old contradictions. In putting forward the Monroe Doctrine as
the model for the League of Nations and its principles,[9] Wilson revealed the
extent to which his main goal was to get the other victorious Great Powers
to adopt in their spheres of influence a more informal style of imperialism,
along US lines. At the same time, the concerns of Wilson and his advisers at
the Paris talks not to tie the US "to the shaky financial structure of Europe"
and to preserve the US's "freedom of action" led them to reject Keynes's
proposals for the cooperative financing of postwar reconstruction.[10]
Together with their refusal to cancel the massive debt that the Allies owed
the US at the end of war, this effectively condemned social-democratic
reformist politics in Europe to failure in the interwar period.

   In short, the American state failed to play the coordinating role that
could have sustained capitalist economic stability after World War I. The
lack of coherence in Wilson's own project was itself largely rooted in the
American state's inability even to conceive the kind of new political framework for international capital accumulation and social reform that could
have sustained economic stability in Europe after the war. The corporatist
War Industries Board, established in 1917 to run the war economy, which
heralded the "dollar-a-year men who came from the business community
into government . . . as America's answer to the bureaucratic statism of
Europe" actually reflected the limited capacities of the state.[11] And as we
have already seen, when the Federal Reserve was finally established as the
US central bank in 1913, far from this being the great Progressive victory
over the unaccountable big financiers, the main elements of the Federal
Reserve Bill had already been prepared by the Morgan and Rockefeller
interests during the previous Taft administration.

   To be sure, William McAdoo, Wilson's Treasury secretary, saw the
Federal Reserve Act's provisions allowing US banks to establish foreign
branches as laying the basis for the US "to become the dominant financial
power of the world and to extend our trade to every part of the world."[12]
But in terms of state capacity, the Fed was "a loose and inexperienced body
with minimal effectiveness even in its domestic functions."[13] As for the
Treasury itself, despite having set up the Foreign Loans Office (the department's first subdivision dedicated to international affairs), it had no ambition
to displace the New York bankers in international financial diplomacy
when in 1917 it became the major source of international credit; nor did it
play an active role in coordinating international economic recovery and
monetary stability after the war. Indeed, the clearest measure of the
Treasury's limited ambitions was that, while promoting the 1919 Edge Act

to loosen antitrust laws, so that bankers could form syndicates to finance American trade abroad, it simultaneously restricted its own loans to foreign governments and suspended export credits to Europe.[14]

Notably, however, despite all this, as well as the Senate's rejection of the League of Nations,[15] the three Republican administrations of the 1920s were in fact all "centrist internationalist," and cooperated with the League "almost as fully as the member states."[16] They provided active support for the measures that both central and private bankers now advanced to give top policy priority to currency stability, balanced budgets, and a return to the gold standard by all capitalist states.[17] Even in refusing to cancel the war debts—and encouraging private loans and investments abroad as the means of providing dollars to repay the interest on the debts and fund the purchase of US exports—they were only following in the tracks Wilson had himself already trodden at the end of the war. Nor were they the captives of the least competitive elements of American capital, as has often been suggested. American business generally was not averse to extending considerable loans to Germany and turning over the British and French debts in order to support American exports to these countries; this was supported by the AFL, although they were not always so enthusiastic about US direct investment in Europe.[18] Even the increase in tariff rates under the Fordney-McCumber Act of 1922 was less an expression of US isolationism than a means of coping with the devaluations which European states were wont to undertake in order to increase exports to the US. The Republican administrations made sure, moreover, that all of Congress's tariff bills of the 1920s, which in any case did not go back to the levels of the nineteenth century, remained linked to the Open Door reciprocity and non-discrimination principles of the 1913 Underwood Tariff.

By the mid 1920s manufactured goods exports were double what they had been before the war, and from 1922 to 1928 total exports grew almost 50 percent faster even than domestic GDP, which grew in real terms by 40 percent.[19] The dollar became the major reserve currency in the world financial system, albeit still sharing the stage with sterling, and to a lesser extent the franc. Moreover, the flow of private American capital to Europe after World War I was considerably greater than immediately after World War II.[20] The US Department of Commerce itself claimed that the rapidity with which the US acquired foreign assets through the 1920s was "unparalleled in the experience of any major creditor nation in modern times."[21] Over the decade of the 1920s, the book value of total American foreign direct investment increased by 129 percent in manufacturing, and 95 percent overall. In Latin America, US investment finally exceeded Britain's, and because so much of this involved owning the region's manufacturing as well as resource industries, rather than just providing loans through portfolio investment, US capital's penetration was far deeper. But it was now growing as fast in Europe as in Canada and Latin America. General Motors took over Vauxhall in the UK in 1925, and its purchase of Opel in 1928 completed the "virtual division" of the German auto industry between GM and Ford.[22]

All this was closely linked to the organizational innovations that American companies introduced in both production and consumption, including the development through the 1920s of a considerable degree of decentralization within large and vertically integrated corporations. These organizational changes were especially important in the new mass-production industries, where factory productivity grew by 75 percent; in the capital goods sector (machine tools and electrical equipment such as generators, transformers, and motors); and, especially, in the household goods sector (washing machines, refrigerators, electric stoves, vacuum cleaners). With productivity increasing much faster in the US than in other capitalist countries, this generated sufficient profits to allow for all the investment abroad even while domestic industrial production also grew rapidly.

In the iconic automobile industry, which had become the new growth hormone for the whole economy, US plants were producing over 80 percent of all the cars made in the world by the end of the 1920s (not even counting the cars made by American multinational auto manufacturers in Canada and Europe); 20 percent of all American steel production, 80 per cent of all rubber, 75 percent of all plate glass, and 65 percent of all leather were consumed in the making of cars. The price of a car had fallen by over three-quarters in the two decades after 1909, and this opened the way to mass consumption of a kind not yet seen anywhere else in the world. At the end of the 1920s there were close to 30 million cars in the US, and the number of drive-in gas stations had increased from 12,000 in 1921 to 143,000 by 1929. By this point, one in five Americans owned a car, and 60 percent of these cars were bought on credit. In 1927, Edwin Seligman's *The Economics of Instalment Selling* captured the ethos of Fordism in the new mass consumer age. He extolled credit-based marketing for not only increasing spending but ensuring that a "family with car payments to make would be forced to work hard to make the payments."[23] The overall explosion in demand for consumer durables also transformed the retail sector with the aid of a massive advertising industry, whose expenditures at the end of the 1920s were five times what they had been before World War I.

The impact of this abroad was seen in the international emulation of the "American Standard of Consumption," and this was as true for cultural products as for industrial goods.[24] In 1928 the US Department of Commerce proudly published a document called "World Markets for American Motion Picture Films," which showed that by the mid 1920s Hollywood was supplying 85 percent of the pictures shown in foreign theaters.[25] And it was, notably, the Department of Commerce that took charge of reconciling the vast complex of business interests through a multitude of public-private conferences, inquiries, and committees operating in accordance with Secretary Hoover's corporatist notion of an "associative state." The staff of the Bureau of Foreign and Domestic Commerce grew five-fold, to 2,500; the head of the Division of Regional Information saw the department's role as promoting "the aggressive expansion policy" of American corporations; and Hoover's top aid in the department described its general objective as "the internationalization of business."[26]

But even as its promotional capacities continued to grow, the American state in the 1920s also made a virtue of having private capitalists represent the United States in international negotiations. Restoring international economic stability and prosperity required the "healing power" that only came with the assistance of "private finance and commerce," Hoover wrote in 1921 to Benjamin Strong, the president of the New York Federal Reserve.[27] It was presumed that businessmen, rather than politicians or bureaucrats, "possessed the flexibility and technical expertise required to stabilize markets"; on these grounds, American delegations to the postwar international financial conferences relied on private bankers, and especially the House of Morgan, to represent the US internationally.[28] At the same time, the practice of imposing private "financial advisers" to guide the budgetary, monetary and customs policies of foreign states as a condition of receiving American loans, which had been adopted in Latin America at the beginning of the century, was now extended to China, Columbia, Chile, Poland, Germany, South Africa, Ecuador, Bolivia, Turkey, the Dominican Republic, Peru, and Iran.[29]

The Federal Reserve encouraged private bankers' solutions to the problems of reparations and debt-servicing (the Dawes Plan, the Young Plan), up to and including the establishment of the Bank of International Settlements at the beginning of the 1930s, even as the world economy collapsed about their ears.[30] But this should not obscure the American state's direct participation in the fraught management of international capitalism in the 1920s. Its main agent in doing so was the Federal Reserve Bank of New York, working closely with the Bank of England. Although 40 percent of the world's gold reserves were in the Fed's vaults and only 20 percent in the Bank of England's, the City of London was still the linchpin of the international financial system. Together the central banks of the US and the UK sought to coordinate a modicum of postwar monetary stability and prepare for a return to the gold standard. They participated directly in foreign-exchange markets through buying and selling currencies, as well as through the loans they made to foreign governments to sustain their currencies, on condition that they reduced budgetary deficits and the public debt. But even with the re-establishment of the gold standard in 1925–26, there was no way back to the kind of discipline that the Bank of England had famously overseen in the nineteenth century. The development of working-class unions and parties and the spread of mass suffrage rendered problematic government passivity in the face of the deflation that outflows of capital were now supposed to bring about in order to correct trade deficits "automatically." Moreover, since unemployment caused by deflation increasingly provoked popular resistance, proclamations by governments that they would adhere to the gold standard no longer evoked confidence from capital itself.[31]

This contradiction between capitalism and democracy was aggravated by the uncertainties created by the shift in the hierarchy of capitalist states, as the US replaced Britain as the world's creditor, as well as by the seemingly never-ending negotiations over World War I reparations payments.[32] There were tariff adjustments to allow for European imports to the US, but these "were never low enough for the continental countries to manage their balance of payments without serious deflationary consequences"; and the private bank loans that were encouraged and indeed orchestrated by the American state certainly "helped the Europeans to make ends meet until 1929," but they were not structured in such a way as "to guarantee reproductive investment."[33] In this context, speculation on exchange rates became more common, and economies were consequently left more vulnerable to destabilizing capital outflows. After 1926 the Federal Reserve kept US interest rates low, in order to support sterling following Britain's return to the gold standard; yet the main effect of low interest rates was to shift funds from bonds to further speculation in already overheated US stock and real-estate markets. Then, when in 1928 the Fed undertook a relatively modest interest-rate increase to dampen this down, it triggered a massive diversion of funds away from foreign loans, with immediate deflationary effects abroad. Finally the sudden bursting of the stock and real-estate market bubbles in October 1929 more or less completely cut off the flow of US credit that had kept the rickety international financial system going through the 1920s.[34]

On the eve of the 1929 New York stock market crash, the American economy accounted for no less than 42 percent of global industrial production—far more than Britain's share even at its peak in 1870.[35] That said, the development of the US domestic economy was itself highly uneven. This was true not only regionally, and especially as regards the South, but also sectorally: some industries, such as agriculture and textiles, remained notoriously vulnerable to any downturn in prices. Even within each industry, the dynamic modern corporation still coexisted through the 1920s with small and weak firms that had not yet adopted the new productive systems and technologies.[36] Moreover, the new mass consumption was rendered fragile, especially given the absence of public income-support programs, by growing income inequality and the gap between real wages and increasing productivity. The easy credit, economic growth, and technological advances of the 1920s obscured these problems. But with the onset of the Great Depression they became magnified—especially as it became clear that, although the US now dominated the world economy, neither American business nor, even more significantly, the American state, had the capacity to end the crisis, and prevent it from reversing capitalist globalization.

The Great Depression and the New Deal State

One of the reasons "there exists no general agreement" about the causes of the Great Depression is because its magnitude placed it "in a league of its own in capitalist history."[37] The attempts to find its causes in domestic over-production, underconsumption, profit rates, weaknesses of the banking system, and the uneven development of new industries and technologies are all relevant; but they cannot convincingly explain why the economic collapse was so deep, why it lasted so long, and why it spread so far. Nor can these features of the Depression be explained just by the breakdown in international trade which, however important, was not on a scale that could account for the depth of the crisis (in 1929, total American exports were only 4 percent of GDP). Flows of capital were a more significant factor, but outflows of short-term capital from some countries do not explain the stunning collapse in real domestic production everywhere. Yet whatever the continuing disagreements about its causes, what is absolutely clear is that, as economies moved in a recessionary direction, this was severely aggravated by the deflationary policy response of the capitalist states. The fundamental reason for this policy response, especially given the democratic changes in class and political relations that had occurred since the heyday of the gold standard in the nineteenth century, was to try to compensate for capital's loss of confidence in the absolute commitment of governments to monetary stability and the protection of bondholders.

Given the growing degree of international economic interdependence in trade and finance, and the sensitivity of the whole interwar order to developments in the US, the American crisis of 1929 affected the rest of the capitalist world in a way that no crisis in any other country could have done. In spite of the US state's financial strength, as measured in its gold reserves, its options were now also constrained by the crisis of the gold standard. With financial capital speculating as to whether the US would be next to go off the gold standard and devalue the dollar, it was hardly surprising that the Federal Reserve further raised interest rates, thereby severely aggravating the economic downturn at home and abroad. As Ingham has pointed out, a convincing indicator of the inability of the Fed to make a useful contribution to containing the international crisis was that it was unable to prevent the failure of a third of all domestic American banks.[38] And if the

American state was unable to set the framework for other states' economic policies at the beginning of the 1930s, neither was it yet able to channel domestic class forces in a way that was consistent with any such framework.

The Great Depression brought capitalism's tendencies towards globalization to a standstill; indeed, the globalizing trajectory that had been made so problematic by World War I, but which had nevertheless continued through the 1920s, was now reversed. By 1932 world trade had fallen to one-third of its 1929 level, and both short- and long-term term international credit had dried up. Britain itself went off the gold standard in 1931, and forty more countries soon followed. One state after another adopted a series of ad hoc measures in defense of their national economies, through exchange controls, devaluations, and import restrictions of every description. Partly in response to the Smoot-Hawley Bill of 1930, which took US tariffs back to late-nineteenth-century levels, Britain adopted a system of imperial trade preferences that confined a third of the world's trade within the sterling bloc; and Germany, paralleled in many ways by Japan, turned resolutely to an increasingly autarkic as well authoritarian capitalist regime that allocated scarce capital resources administratively, especially for militarist purposes.

By the time Franklin Delano Roosevelt was inaugurated as president in March 1933—the day before the Nazis were given full powers to govern by decree in Germany—American exports had fallen to one-third of their 1929 level, and the net outflow of US direct investment was the lowest on record. Manufacturing production had been cut in half, domestic investment had fallen by 90 percent, 5,000 banks had gone out of business, farm incomes had fallen by four-fifths, and 25 percent of the US labor force was unemployed. In the crucial auto industry, production had fallen by two-thirds, and only half of the 450,000 workers employed in 1929 were still at work. State and city governments, still carrying the primary responsibility for the distribution of public services and benefits, as they had done throughout the nineteenth century, were completely overwhelmed by demands for "relief." Protests by the unemployed, starting with the million that took part in the demonstrations of March 1930, had continued right through the 1932 election year.[39] These were often led by Communists, whose influence would soon also increase significantly in the African-American community as well as among students and intellectuals, while new populist leaders like Huey Long catalyzed a more traditional distrust of the rich and powerful. While Roosevelt's electoral platform had been vague enough to avoid any necessary implication of a radical programmatic departure from Hoover, his inaugural address reflected the atmosphere of social protest, and even legitimated many of the radical sentiments behind it—not least by intoning that "the rulers of the exchange of mankind's goods have failed," and that the "practices of the unscrupulous money changers stand indicted in the court of public opinion." Finding a solution to the Depression depended on "the extent to which we apply social values more noble than mere monetary profit."[40]

What distinguished the new Democratic administration from its Republican predecessors was above all the sense that the American capitalist system could not be restored by trying to reconstruct it with capitalists themselves acting as the main agents of the state. That practice obscured problems which were rooted in the very industrial, financial and class structures of modern capitalism, and left the American state with insufficient relative autonomy or capacity to attend to them. At the same time, the New Dealers' hopes of what government could achieve were "in many ways more modest than [those of] some earlier reformers," as Alan Brinkley has noted.

> There was, they realized, no "master plan" by which capitalism would become a just, stable, self-regulating system, and no cooperative or associational scheme that would create a smoothly functioning, ordered, and harmonious whole out of the economy's clashing parts. No antitrust strategy could create a small-scale, decentralized economy free from the influence of large combinations. The state could not, liberals had come to believe, in any fundamental way "solve" the problems of the economy. But the very limits of their ultimate ambitions made their vision of government more aggressive and assertive than those of many of their progressive predecessors. The inevitability of constant conflict and instability in a modern capitalist economy was all the more reason for government to become an active regulatory force.[41]

Central to FDR's brand of American liberalism was the notion that states needed to undertake from time to time a fairly broad agenda of regulatory and social reform to forestall revolutions and wars. Writing to a friend in 1930 he said there was "no question in my mind that it is time for the country to become fairly radical for at least one generation. History shows that where this occurs occasionally, nations are saved from revolutions."[42] This was, of course, to be what he liked to call a "sane radicalism," one inspired by his favorite maxim: "Reform if you would preserve." His admiration for the type of municipal social-democratic reformism in Europe that had cleared the slums and built the public housing of Red Vienna could be defended on this principle as having "probably done more to prevent Communism and rioting and revolution than anything else in the last four or five years." But what reform might mean in the American context was cast in vague and general enough terms to appeal to the moderate elements of the labor movement, the Democratic Party's Southern political oligarchs in Congress, the liberal lawyers and economists now brought into the state apparatus, and—given FDR's equally strong commitment to balanced budgets—significant elements of business too.

Such liberal consequentialism, rather than idealism, underpinned Roosevelt's international orientation as well: relations between states also needed to be reformed to prevent revolutions and wars. He was troubled, as Wilson had been earlier, by the lack of state autonomy indicated by American interventions in Latin America that had seemingly been undertaken at the behest of specific American capitalists, and this was reflected in his concern that the 1924 Democratic Party platform should address the issue of making a "definite effort to end the hate and dislike of America now shared by every other civilized nation in the world" because of these interventions. But a *Foreign Affairs* article Roosevelt wrote in 1928 showed that he thought that the US interventions in places like Santo Domingo, Haiti, and Nicaragua had "accomplished an excellent piece of constructive work, and the world ought to thank us." If, despite this, "the other republics of the Americas . . . disapprove our interventions almost unanimously," it was because such interventions should be taken "in the name of all the Americas and only in cooperation with other republics."[43] It was, he argued, mainly the absence of a multilateral framework for US intervention that caused such international resentment.

While showing no enthusiasm for free trade, which like the Republicans he saw as a political impossibility, through the 1920s Roosevelt had been an enthusiast for trade competition, and he derided "those materialists who assert that all wars are caused by economic and trade rivalries." He increasingly took the view that it was unemployment at home that led to militarism abroad, and his frustration with the London Economic Conference of June 1933 reflected the fact that, during its preparatory stages, his calls for "a synchronized international program" to deal with unemployment directly had been ignored and virtually kept off the table at the conference itself. There were considerable hopes and even expectations in the run-up to the Conference that the US was ready to assume the mantle of world capitalist economic leadership.[44] These were dashed by Roosevelt's famous telegram in the midst of the conference deriding "the old fetishes of so-called international bankers," and proclaiming that "the sound internal economic situation of a nation is a greater factor in its well-being than the price of its currency."[45] Immediately praised by Keynes, Roosevelt had here telegraphed internationally the priorities of the New Deal.

Roosevelt's inauguration address had already signaled these priorities by indicating that, while he would "spare no effort to restore world trade by international economic readjustment . . . the emergency at home cannot wait on that accomplishment." One of his first moves was the suspension of the dollar's convertibility into gold—thereby breaking with the Federal Reserve's stubborn clinging to the gold standard under Hoover. So frightened were the bankers themselves by the domestic situation at the time of Roosevelt's inauguration that they made no objection to the sweeping emergency authority he immediately secured from Congress to deal with the banking crisis, granting the Treasury extensive powers, including the power to buy up all private gold bullion and certificates as well as to provide liquidity to the banks. As Charles and Mary Beard noted, "With an alacrity suggesting spontaneous combustion, excited Representatives and Senators rushed the draft through the two houses and placed it on the President's desk before the end of the day. Neither Lincoln in 1861 nor Wilson in 1917 had been granted such drastic powers with so little haggling and bickering." The reason, as the Beards also noted, was of course that the emergency legislation "drove no money changers from the temple. On the contrary it gave the support of public credit to bankers while establishing the supremacy of the Federal Government over gold."[46]

The passage a few months later of the Glass–Steagall Act to regulate the domestic banking system by separating commercial banks from investment banks (thereby barring the latter from using deposits to speculate on securities) was widely seen as delivering "the *coup de grace* to the House of Morgan."[47] But this was by no means unpalatable to all the bankers. If anything, it signaled the victory of those on Wall Street, such as the Rockefellers, who since the end of World War I had looked to making New York the world's financial center directly, instead of gradually expanding American financial influence in London. As early as the 1928 election, Chicago bankers, and even some major New York investment houses, had been "enraged by the House of Morgan's use of the New York Fed to control American interest rates for the sake of international objectives" (in other words, keeping US interest rates low to protect sterling under the revived gold standard). In this context, and in light of Morgan's close ties with the Republican administrations of the 1920s, some of these bankers had shifted their support to the Democratic Party.[48]

Under the framework established by the 1933 and 1935 Banking Acts, a compartmentalization of the institutions handling different kinds of financial risk was created: securities firms and investment banks could channel long-term financial investment into capital formation; the insurance industry could underwrite risk for both companies and individuals; commercial banks could use the funds from deposits to provide commercial loans for working capital; and savings and loans companies ("thrifts") could act as the repository for household savings to finance home mortgages. This compartmentalization provided institutional shelter for investment bankers and allowed them to focus single-mindedly on capital markets, securities, and financing the international projects of US oil and utility companies. And the commercial banks welcomed the imposition of interest-rate ceilings on deposits (known as Regulation Q), since it reduced competition and guaranteed the banks a steady supply of cheap funds, while federal deposit insurance made panic runs on the banks less likely and so freed up a greater share of bank reserves for making loans. These measures thus allowed for low-cost loans to industry and at the same time ensured bank profitability.

Roosevelt was more tentative and less innovative in addressing the crisis in industry. Given his utterly conventional commitment to balanced budgets, his attention was entirely directed to regenerating corporate profits by limiting "destructive price competition." This approach proved quite successful in the case of agriculture.[49] But the limited capacity of the state in relation to industry was immediately revealed when the National Industry Recovery Act (NIRA) reverted to the corporatist model introduced in World War I. A National Recovery Administration (NRA) was established to oversee industrial self-regulation through a system of codes drawn up by the trade association in each sector. In a concession to labor, each code was required to establish minimum labor standards and collective bargaining rights, but its implementation was left to the discretion of the trade association itself.[50]

This failed as a solution to the crisis, not least because by "controlling most of the information about industrial operations on which the NRA codes and their enforcement would have to be based," private firms constructed loopholes so as to escape the labor standards and cut back production while keeping prices high; while the "NRA apparatus, itself thoroughly permeated by conflicting business interests, was unable to resolve disputes in an authoritative fashion."[51] The experience with the NIRA "foreshadowed the trend for the executive branch of the state apparatus to organize and reorganize departments and decision-making centers that would eventually circumvent conflicting interests."[52] But for the time being, especially without increased wages or public expenditures on the scale needed to generate effective demand and restore profits (which fell by three-quarters in 1934), the promised economic recovery did not materialize.

Nor did labor peace. The bitter class conflict that took off in 1934 ranks in American history only with that of the early 1890s, the main difference being that in the mid thirties the government was much less willing, and business much less able—despite employing corporate armies of industrial "detectives"—to repress industrial militancy. After 1934 "the number of strikes annually never fell below 2,000 and every upturn in the business cycle and tightening of the labor market stimulated greater unrest."[53] Moreover, the 20 percent growth in union membership in 1934 was registered in the increased voter turnout, which reinforced the Democrats' triumph in the midterm elections of that year, described by the *New York Times* as "the most overwhelming victory in the history of American politics."[54]

But it was at this point hardly clear what exactly the New Deal could achieve. By the time the Supreme Court (using the precedents that had sustained its brand of laissez-faire liberalism since the post-bellum era) invalidated the NIRA in 1935, "support for the NRA had substantially eroded, even within the New Deal itself."[55] As the administration stumbled towards what has become known as the Second New Deal, it used the 1935 Banking Act to expand the powers of the Federal Reserve's central board, so that it could be more than a lender of last resort and a passive regulator of credit creation. It was now given the capacity to conduct discretionary monetary policy by varying reserve requirements and selective credit controls, with a view to affecting not just the solvency of the banks but also the performance of the economy. Yet this left the Fed still considerably dependent on the information and expertise coming from the private banks.

This was all the more the case with the Securities and Exchange Commission and the system of regulation it put in place in 1935, whereby private firms—whose skills, personnel, and information the regulatory bodies relied on—were invested with regulatory privileges. "A regulatory world was created populated by a network of public and semi-public bodies, individual firms and professional groups like accountants. This regulatory world functioned largely independently of the competitive arenas of democratic politics."[56] Thus, just when the NIRA and its system of state-sanctioned industrial self-regulation was struck down by the Supreme Court, a new type of mutual embeddedness of state and finance was being established in the financial sector. As a Wall Street publication, the *Annalist*, put it at the time: "The large aggregates of financial capital stand to benefit in the long run from the new regime—the elimination of competitive methods, [the] close welding together of the private banking with the governmental financial apparatus, the increase of control and co-ordination—all are elements of strength of the future of financial capitalism."[57]

From New Deal to Grand Truce with Capital

It was, of course, not so much the administration's financial reforms as its labor and social legislation that came to symbolize the "Second New Deal." Although long advanced by liberal reformers, the 1935 National Labor Relations Act was only passed in response to what Senator Wagner himself, in introducing the Bill associated with his name, called "the rising tide of industrial discontent." The Wagner Act legalized unionization campaigns, collective bargaining and the right to strike, and established quasi-juridical procedures for securing recognition and settling disputes. The Social Security Act of the same year founded the American welfare state with its national provisions for unemployment and retirement benefits. To be sure, given the state's responsibilities for mediating class conflict *and* its dependence on capital accumulation, the Wagner Act also constrained labor militancy in various ways (not least by setting strict conditions for when the right to strike could be legally exercised), while the Social Security Act (in any case funded by regressive taxation) reinforced the discipline of the labor market with its limited benefits and the many conditions it established for eligibility. But this cannot gainsay the fact that both measures were substantial reforms, born out of class struggle from below. Business opposition to these reforms at the national level coalesced with local opposition to what the Works Projects Administration was doing as well as to the massive Tennessee Valley Authority project (attacked for the dangerous example that public ownership in this sector might set for Latin American states whose public utilities were owned by American corporations).

Above all, "business opposition to the Wagner Act was probably more unified than [its] response—positive or negative—to any other piece of New Deal legislation."[58] The influential revisionist interpretation of the New Deal that presents even the Wagner Act as part of the class project of capital-intensive corporations—seeing the latter's support for company unions in the 1920s as foretelling their acceptance of the legalization of independent industrial unionism in the mid 1930s[59]—is very hard to sustain in light of this. In the auto industry, "GM spent nearly a million dollars on labor spies between January 1934 and June 1936 alone" in fighting the CIO unionization drive that Wagner's Bill legitimated, while Ford recruited "the world's largest private army, and established the most extensive and efficient espionage system in American industry" as part of what the new National Labor Relations Board (NLRB) would call Ford's "war on unionism." The National Association of Manufacturers, "dominated by some of the nation's largest industrial interests during the Roosevelt years, attacked the Bill relentlessly"; indeed, one contemporary source called the business campaign against the Wagner Bill "the greatest ever conducted by industry regarding any Congressional measure."[60]

Roosevelt himself offered virtually no support to the Wagner Bill, in face of unified business opposition to it. Nevertheless, his signing of the Wagner Act helped generate the higher voter turnout that led to his landslide re-election in 1936. "In the auto centers, workers often shut down their lines and crowded their windows to cheer him. In Flint, with a dues-paying UAW membership of but 136, over 100,000 lined the streets . . . Half a million lined the streets from Hamtramck to Detroit and more than 250,000 gathered at City Hall Square to hear Roosevelt lash the auto magnates."[61] Nor could the synergy between political enthusiasm and industrial militancy be overlooked when the historic Flint sit-down strike began within weeks of the 1936 election. American capital certainly did not overlook the power of the sit-down strike—GM's president, Alfred Sloan, described it as "a dress rehearsal for Sovietizing the entire country"—especially as 247 more of them, involving 200,000 workers, spread across the country through 1937. Union recognition was extracted from General Motors, Chrysler, and US Steel, and overall union membership increased in 1937 alone from 4 million to 7 million, with little help from an NLRB that was only just becoming functional. Despite the financial support which elements of big business had given the Democrats in the 1936 election (while still in their vast majority supporting the Republicans), by 1937 hostility to Roosevelt pervaded the whole capitalist class. They blamed him as much as, or more than, the Communists for the leftward shift in public opinion.[62]

Having secured the key legislative achievements of the Second New Deal, yet chastened by the defeat of Roosevelt's "court-packing" bill in Congress, "the White House and most of the President's key advisers were ready to smooth over frayed relations with big business."[63] Roosevelt was in any case following his own and his Treasury Secretary Henry Morgenthau's inclination for balanced budgets by cutting public works and relief spending in 1937–38.[64] The ensuing "recession within the Depression" only highlighted the extent to which the New Deal had not slain the economic dragons of stagnation and unemployment. As investment dropped off in the fall of 1937, both Roosevelt and Morgenthau recoiled at this new "loss of business confidence." Despite the administration's repeated proclamations that "we are going to continue on a capitalist basis" and that it intended "to foster the full application of the driving force of private capital," fears of an "investment strike" further weakened Roosevelt's support in Congress.[65] This was reinforced by the results of the 1938 midterm election, where the effects of the cutbacks and the recession were measured in significant Republican gains.

By this time, "virtually nowhere on the political landscape were there vigorous grassroots movements of the sort so common in the mid-1930s . . . attacking concentrated wealth and corporate power."[66] This was partly due to the support for Roosevelt entailed in the "popular front" strategy of the Communist left. The new industrial unions of the CIO, moreover, found themselves considerably weakened by layoffs in the newly organized industries during 1938 and by internal divisions between radicals and reformists within the CIO, alongside continuing tensions with the old craft unions of the AFL. Corporate counteroffensives, were now reinforced by court rulings that interpreted the Wagner Acts provisions very narrowly, had particularly dampening effects on the sit-down strike strategy.[67]

This shift in the balance of class forces effectively ended the reforms of the New Deal's second phase. Nevertheless, a transformation in the capacities of the American state had been effected which the halting of the New Deal's momentum did not undo. Even though Roosevelt's attempt to give the White House more direct control over the budget and the bureaucracy was defeated by Congress in 1938, the New Deal had given the administrative branch of the government "its greatest infusion of potential power in peace time history."[68] Federal civilian employment almost doubled; and the seventeen new administrative agencies created by the New Deal were as many as had been set up in the previous three decades.[69] The federal state's new capacities were not only bureaucratic but also fiscal, insofar as they met Roosevelt's preoccupation with balancing the budget while at the same time "acquiring and sustaining independent sources of revenue that enlarged executive discretion."[70] These enhanced capacities did not signify a dichotomy of purpose and function between state and capitalist actors, since they were mainly oriented to working with regulated industries to stabilize or rejuvenate private markets and stimulating private capital accumulation. They were most strongly institutionalized in the area of financial regulation, where a "network of public and semi-public bodies, individual firms and professional groups" existed in a symbiotic relationship with one another, more or less insulated from democratic pressures.[71] The NRA had failed to develop this type of private-public synergy in the case of industrial regulation, but the Reconstruction Finance Corporation certainly did so, using its creditor relationships with banks, loan associations, and railroads to funnel "enormous sums of money into a stagnant economy," using "governmental resources to prop up the economic order without altering patterns of ownership or control."[72]

With these new state capacities in place, the White House organized—through meetings Roosevelt held with leading bankers, industrialists and moderate trade union leaders—what it called a "grand truce" with capital during the first months of 1938. This truce did not spell a return to the Republican strategy of the 1920s; on the contrary, the policy initiative was now taken by "economists and lawyers operating within the Roosevelt administration," who replaced the price-fixing and corporatist productivism that had inaugurated the New Deal with a turn to Keynesianism.[73] It was very significant that the Treasury, hitherto the bastion of balanced budgets throughout the New Deal, finally accepted that deficit public spending was required to stimulate demand and investment. Yet the fact that the actual steps taken before the war in this direction were "small and tentative—an augury of the halfhearted way in which Americans would embrace Keynesianism for most of the next forty years"[74]—was also significant. Indeed, it was crucial for making the truce with capital possible. The embracing of fiscal stimulus by the White House and the Treasury was tempered by the use of reassuringly conservative language: for example, a Keynesian fiscal policy was explicitly likened to the land grants made to homesteaders and to railway and mining companies that had stimulated capitalist development in the nineteenth century.[75]

This serves as an important reminder that, while the New Deal marked a crucially important moment in the development of American state capacities, its continuity with the historic role of the US state as a handmaiden of private accumulation must not be overlooked. Roosevelt's 1938 Executive Reorganization Bill, designed to enhance the planning and coordination capacities of the executive branch, suffered defeat in Congress in the face of a right-wing populist mobilization against such a "dictatorship" that was eventually supported by the US Chamber of Commerce—although, notably, not by most large corporations or banks. The "watered-down" bill, passed in 1939, "provided the basis for administrative reorganization in the years during and following World War II," and this would prove very important in creating the "conditions that were necessary for the expanded reproduction of capital."[76]

The US state now had a central bank, a largely merit-based professional civil service, a well-staffed Treasury, and a broad range of economic and financial regulatory agencies; and with US entry into the war it would also quickly establish an unrivaled, and permanent, military-industrial complex. Its capacity to act as a Great Power would then be no longer in question. But the distinctive interdependence between the state and capital, and the deep historic orientation of the US state towards the promotion of capitalism, would prove critical for the specific way it would play its emergent role as the manager of capitalism on a world scale. It is especially important to bear this in mind when we turn to consider how, with the onset of World War II, "US state capacities shifted towards realizing internationally-interventionist goals versus domestically-interventionist ones."[77]

II

THE PROJECT FOR A GLOBAL CAPITALISM

3

Planning the New American Empire

In May 1942 the editors of *Fortune, Time,* and *Life* magazines jointly published a statement entitled "An American Proposal," the product of a series of "Roundtable" discussions between prominent businessmen held under *Fortune*'s auspices since late 1939.[1] It began with the premise that "America will emerge as the strongest single power in the postwar world, and . . . it is therefore up to it to decide what kind of postwar world it wants." The momentous implications of this proposition had been recognized at the very first Roundtable. Its primary interest, it had declared, was in "the longer-range question of whether the American capitalist system should continue to function if most of Europe and Asia should abolish free enterprise"; the priority of "the next peace" was "to organize the economic resources of the world so as to make possible a return to the system of free enterprise in every country."

The "Proposal" recognized that the old Open Door strategy would be inadequate to spread the "area of freedom" throughout the postwar world. While the "ultimate goal" remained "universal free trade," it was "no longer an immediate political possibility," primarily because of "the uprising of [the] international proletariat" which was "the most significant fact of the last twenty years." For this reason, realizing the ultimate goal of universal free trade first of all required remaking the world's states so that not only tariffs, but also "subsidies, monopolies, restrictive labor rules, plantation feudalism, poll taxes, technological backwardness, obsolete tax laws, and all other barriers to further expansion [could] be removed." It was necessary, the authors of the "Proposal" declared, to replace "a dead or dying imperialism" with an American empire of a new kind:

> a new American "imperialism," if it is to be called that, will—or rather can—be quite different from the British type. It can also be different from the premature American type that followed our expansion in the Spanish war. American imperialism can afford to complete the work the British started; instead of salesmen and planters, its representatives can be brains and bulldozers, technicians and machine tools. American imperialism does

not need extra-territoriality; it can get along better in Asia if the tuans and
sahibs stay home . . . Nor is the US afraid to help build up industrial rivals
to its own power . . . because we know industrialization stimulates rather
than limits international trade . . . This American imperialism sounds very
abstemious and high-minded. It is nevertheless a feasible policy for
America, because friendship, not food, is what we need most from the rest
of the world.[1]

Yet the "Proposal" was by no means a case of capitalists imposing an
agenda on the state. "Responsibility for leadership" and the US's "great
economic strength" that had thrust such responsibility upon it—these were
terms being widely employed inside the Roosevelt administration since
1939 to refer to what would be the American state's unique role after the
war in enabling the internationalizing dynamic of capitalism to operate
once again.[2] The main contribution of the "Proposal," as its Preface recognized, was to help in establishing "some agreement among ourselves on
what we are prepared to do and to undertake."[3] It was primarily an exercise
in building public, and especially business, support for the strategy already
being developed inside the state.[4] That its role was going to be very different from that played by any of the imperial powers in the past was also
coming to be recognized outside the US. "Let there be no mistake about
it," the *Economist* wrote in July 1942, "the foreign policy put forward by the
American administration is revolutionary. It is a genuinely new conception
of world order."[5]

Those who were involved in planning the new imperial project were
certainly aware of how difficult it would be to realize it—all the more so
because the exact impact of the Depression and the war on the structures of
US capitalism and the state, let alone the balance of international forces, was
by no means yet clear. It was a project necessarily cast in terms of finding
solutions to problems the American state had already been forced to
confront, and had previously lacked the capacity to resolve. Dean Acheson,
seen by many as the leading architect of postwar American strategy, began
his famous autobiography, *Present at the Creation*, with the observation that
the period "was one of great obscurity to those who lived through it. Not
only was the future clouded, a common enough situation, but the present
was equally clouded . . . The significance of events was shrouded in ambiguity. We groped after interpretations of them, sometimes reversed lines of
action based on earlier views, and hesitated long before grasping what now
seems obvious."[6] Yet a growing conviction was certainly developing within
the American state that, as one of Acheson's biographers puts it, "only the
US had the power to grab hold of history and make it conform."[7] Intimations
of Fukuyama's infamous "end of history" thesis fifty years later, proclaiming
the triumph of a global capitalism in the image of the US, are already

unmistakable here—but as the basis for a project yet to be launched, as opposed to one already accomplished.

Internationalizing the New Deal

The internationalizing tendencies of capitalism which had formerly developed within the framework of the old imperial spheres of influence had been halted by the protectionism of the 1930s. This simultaneously negated the Open Door strategy that had officially defined American policy since the turn of the century. Even more ominously, the "living space" demanded by the Nazi regime was increasingly seen by those who guided the United States into World War II as meaning "dying space for American private enterprise and for capitalism as an integrated world system."[8]

This kind of thinking had been very clearly articulated by Dean Acheson in a speech at Yale University in November 1939.[9] The nineteenth-century world economy, during which American capitalism had flourished under the aegis of British-secured free trade and British naval power, had, he said, long been in an "obvious process of decline," and it was now clear that it "probably cannot be reestablished in anything approaching its old form, if at all." By the 1930s the profound impairment of the old system had finally produced a global situation wherein, with "credits unavailable, markets gone, and with them the means of obtaining the price of needed new materials, with populations pressing upon restricted resources, the stage had been set for the appearance of the totalitarian military state." In this new context, any "realistic American policy" would have to be not only "prophylactic" but "therapeutic." So, in addition to calling for massive support for the Allies in the war against fascism, Acheson proffered a long-term US imperial cure that involved "making capital available in those parts of Europe which need productive equipment" after the war, on condition that "exclusive or preferential trade arrangements" were removed—all to the end of "a broader market for goods made under decent standards" sustained by "a stable international monetary system." But this would depend, among other things, on the US being "willing to accept the minor limitations which come from assuming some responsibility for making possible a world of order."

The emphasis Acheson gave to trade arrangements reflected the continued commitment of many in the State Department to the Open Door strategy. The passage of the 1934 Reciprocal Trade Agreements Act had shown that the New Deal's domestic priorities did not entail a turn to isolationism.[10] The most tenacious advocate of this position was Secretary of State Cordell Hull, who "consistently maintained . . . that the alternative to radicalism was freer trade to restore employment and production." If Roosevelt's inclination was that "it is time for the country to become fairly radical for at least one generation," Hull's almost fanatical devotion to free trade was based on the belief that "the question of the survival or disappearance of free enterprise" at home depended on a liberal order of international trade.[11] But more important than the fact that the 1934 Act had turned US trade policy back in the direction of the Open Door was that, for the first time, Congress now delegated its constitutionally embedded tariff-making authority to the president (subject to Congressional renewal every three years). This had involved institutionalizing in trade policy the executive's greater relative autonomy from particular capitalist interests, with the effect of insulating the state "from unwanted protectionist pressures after the disastrous consequences of the 1930 Smoot-Hawley Tariff Act."[12]

As we have seen, while tariffs had once primarily served to limit imports and generate federal revenues, since the 1890s they had been "internationalized," in the sense of also coming to be used as a bargaining chip to open new markets—but this had been much constrained by log-rolling amendments so long as Congress had to approve each trade agreement. The Act granted the executive branch authority to raise or lower tariffs by as much as 50 percent from the 1930 levels; but, motivated by the goal of using tariffs more as a lever to expand US exports than as a means of preventing imports, this authority was used to launch a Reciprocal Trade Agreements Program, the "primary object" of which, in the eyes of the interdepartmental Committee on Trade Agreements, chaired by the State Department, "was to reduce tariff barriers rather than drive a sharp bargain."[13]

In fact, the reciprocal trade agreements signed in the 1930s with Britain, France, the Netherlands and Canada (as well as with three Latin American states) had done little to replenish foreign trade during the Depression. But their negotiation reflected the very different economic relationship that existed, on the one hand, between the US and these capitalist countries, which "made little effort to interfere with international movements of capital," and on the other with fascist Germany, Italy and Japan, which exercised strong capital controls.[14] The former's linkages to the American economy in the 1930s prefigured their eventual subsumption in the informal American empire after World War II. This was most clearly seen in the enormous flow of gold into the US and the purchase by foreigners of US stocks and Treasury bills right through the New Deal. And this indicated the extent to which capitalists abroad regarded the US as "the safest country in the world and the dollar the soundest currency."[15]

The enhanced role of the US Treasury during the Depression was very important in this respect.[16] The need to finance New Deal projects meant that the federal debt grew considerably; with relatively few other profitable options, financial capital at home and abroad gravitated to the "quality" debt that Treasury bills represented. The US Treasury bill market, to which the value of the dollar was now effectively tied, thus became essential to the revival of Wall Street. Concerns that the inflow of capital from abroad would increase the value of the dollar and have inflationary consequences were allayed by the Treasury's commitment to balanced budgets and to sterilizing the impact of the capital inflows. The alternative of using exchange controls to stop the inflow, as some economists in the Treasury suggested, was opposed by more senior Treasury officials, as well as by New York bankers who were determined to replace London as the world's leading financial center.[17] This too reflected the "mutual embeddedness" of the Treasury and Wall Street, despite Secretary Morgenthau's occasional use of disparaging rhetoric about "money changers."[18]

It was also significant that the most important planning for the postwar world took place in the Treasury, and led straight to Bretton Woods. In contrast with the State Department—whose "moralistic, pacifist and laissez-faire" orientation to free trade during the 1930s reflected a bureaucracy that, as Acheson himself said, "had no ideas, plans or methods for collecting the information or dealing with the problems"[19]—the Treasury had brought some of the country's brightest young economists on board. They included not only those who had engineered the turn to Keynesianism in 1938, but also people who provided an alternative international economic policy to the State Department's.[20] The growing importance of the Treasury in the state apparatus was registered in its taking over of responsibility for international financial negotiations not only from private financiers like the House of Morgan, but also from the State Department and the Federal Reserve, whose subordinate status vis-à-vis the Treasury was clearly reaffirmed during the Depression.

Before the US entered the war, the State Department under Cordell Hull often seemed more preoccupied by the fear, as one senior official put it, that "a war lasting two or three years, or which may run on for even a longer time will place the people of Europe in such a terrible position as to produce revolutionary movements looking towards communistic policies."[21] This perspective explains the initial attempts of the US to put itself forward as an arbiter of a peace agreement whereby the Nazi regime, together with the other European states, would agree to limit armaments and lower trade barriers—only be to greeted by Hitler's blunt rebuff to the American emissaries in 1940 to the effect that "unrestricted trade could not cure every problem in the world."[22] After the Nazi blitzkrieg across Western Europe in the spring of 1940 had put paid to such peace efforts, Roosevelt himself still sought to mobilize business behind US support for the Allies on free-trade grounds: it was "naïve to imagine that we could adopt a totalitarian control of our foreign trade and at the same time escape internal regimentation of our internal economy."[23] The priority the State Department gave to the removal of tariff barriers—even called "lunatic" by Keynes[24]—was more understandable from the perspective of winning Congressional and business support for Lend-Lease and preventing isolationist opinion from looking too closely into what would be entailed in the vaguely defined "new international responsibilities" the American state was embracing for the postwar world. But once the issue of entering the war was settled, and with business less fearful of a postwar depression and more confident that emerging state capacities would be an asset for capital rather than a threat, the State Department began to take seriously a much broader agenda for remaking the postwar world.

This in fact sustained what the prevailing view had been in the US Treasury all along. The recognition that full employment and economic growth after the war would depend more on accumulation at home than exports abroad did not negate the Treasury's strong support for liberalizing trade relations; but it took the view that trade could only be liberalized on the basis of an international monetary arrangement that would also allow for economic growth and domestic accumulation in other countries. Those planning Bretton Woods could draw on their experience in fashioning the 1936 Tripartite Monetary Agreement between the US, France, and Britain (subsequently joined by Belgium, the Netherlands, and Switzerland) whereby the US Treasury used the Exchange Stabilization Fund—which it had been given in the legislation that codified in 1934 the US's going off the gold standard—to manage the franc's devaluation in a way that avoided competitive depreciations of other currencies. In the process it initiated close contacts between the various finance ministries, coordinating intervention in currency markets on a daily basis.[25]

The seeds for establishing a multinational institution through which the Treasury could coordinate such activity were sown in the plans developed in 1938–39 for an Inter-American Bank to promote currency stabilization and economic development. Moreover, as early as April 1940, Alvin Hansen (who had led the shift to Keynesianism in the Treasury) had proposed to the Council on Foreign Relations' economic planning group the establishment of an international monetary fund to anchor the free convertibility of currencies in a system of international payments based on the American dollar.[26] Harry Dexter White, who became head of the Treasury's newly created Division of Monetary Research in the mid 1930s, could draw on all this experience when he was charged, only a week after Pearl Harbor, with developing the Treasury's plan for what Morgenthau called a "New Deal in international economics."[27]

The Path to Bretton Woods

The British Empire may have been acquired in a fit of absentmindedness, but the American empire that emerged after World War II was the product of considerable planning. The blueprints for the postwar international order drawn up by US wartime policymakers sought to graft "the philosophy, substance, and form of the New Deal regulatory state onto the world," recapitulating many of its legal and administrative forms in "virtually every issue area, ranging from the Food and Agricultural Organization to the projected International Trade Organization."[28] But above all, these blueprints were infused with a liberal conception of the rule of law, and also reflected the projection abroad of the New Deal's "grand truce with capital."

Widespread business concerns about the wartime planning of the domestic economy were quickly mollified by hard proof that such planning would be based on that truce. In the words of Henry Stimson, the leading Republican recruited to the administration to cement the truce with capital in the run-up to US participation in the war: "[I]f you are going to try to go to war, or prepare for war, in a capitalist country, you have to let business make money out of the process or business won't work."[29] Those advisers within the New Deal administration who had a more directive and interventionist conception of planning were either increasingly marginalized, or they adapted themselves to working closely with the "dollar-a-year" corporate executives brought in by their thousands to run the war agencies—whereas the few union leaders similarly recruited quickly accepted the role of subordinate partners.[30] By the beginning of the war, "democratic planning" was already being presented as a technique that did "not require totalitarian control of the means of production, for it begins by research and ends in the consulting chamber . . . [T]he planners are not the bosses, nor are they rubber stamps of the bosses; they merely act as advisers."[31] They were the custodians of an economy owned by the capitalists.

The plans evolved for the postwar economic order reflected this, too. The questions that concerned the planners ranged very broadly: How to develop a new international monetary order built around the dollar while also addressing the need for European economic integration? How to ensure that the decolonization of the old empires would not jeopardize the security of oil and other resources? How to counter the popularity of radical nationalist, socialist, and communist forces in war-torn Europe and elsewhere? And at the same time, even though it was taking on these "profound new responsibilities in connection with practically all vital problems of world affairs," the state of the new American empire remained the state of the American social formation. As the State Department's history of wartime planning went on to say, "the staff at all times sought to consider problems from the standpoint especially of the long-run national interest of the United States."[32] And how the "national interest" was defined necessarily reflected the grand truce with capital. The question for the planners was how to make the American national interest, as determined by the domestic balance of social forces and the state's own relative autonomy from them, compatible with the broader tasks that the American imperial state was now assuming.

The plan Harry Dexter White developed for the Treasury, which laid the foundation for Bretton Woods, was fundamentally predicated on there being "no advantage in achieving a pseudo stability by clinging to restrictive measures that seriously hamper international economic life."[33] The plan addressed what needed to be done in three overlapping and interacting areas: first, securing both currency convertibility and exchange rate stability as a condition of reviving international trade; second, allowing for some degree of flexibility for governments in the face of the deflationary implications of balance-of-payments deficits; and third, providing the huge amounts of capital that the European economies would need for reconstruction. But the overarching concern was that the American state should be able to limit its own liability for funding all of this, while at the same time ensuring that, even in the absence of the old gold standard, financial discipline could be imposed on other states.

The historic significance of the Bretton Woods Agreement is that it institutionalized the American state's predominant role in international monetary management as part and parcel of the general acceptance of the US dollar as the foundation currency of the international economy. Whereas the plans evolved for the United Nations, especially the composition of the Security Council, still bore significant traces of the old Great Power "spheres of influence," the Bretton Woods framework was designed to avoid this, and to establish a general system of rules for mediating the international and national economic responsibilities of all states. It was thus laying the foundations, as White put it, for "new instrumentalities that will pave the way for a high degree of coordination and collaboration among the nations in economic fields hitherto held too sacrosanct for multilateral sovereignty."[34]

At one level, this simply referred to the fact that the kind of global program for international monetary stability the Treasury was planning would be far more difficult, if not impossible, to bring into being through bilateral arrangements than through a multilateral agreement. But it had a more profound meaning as well. Unlike the Open Door's contingent and bilateral non-discrimination treaties across the old spheres of influence, the key objective of what the US was now proposing was to bind all states to a new rule of law in the international economy. It was true that, in contrast to the automatic discipline imposed by the gold standard, the "multilateral sovereignty" created through these new agreements was designed to give the states involved greater autonomy to pursue national economic policies. But they would simultaneously be subscribing to new constraints and responsibilities within the reconstructed international financial system. And the asymmetry of power embedded in these arrangements meant that embracing "multilateral sovereignty" would implicitly require member-states to embrace the new American empire.

It was hardly surprising, therefore, that White summed up the Treasury's plan as follows: "We in this country should face the fact that the success of international monetary co-operation will depend primarily on the participation and leadership of the United States. The dollar is the one great currency in whose strength there is universal confidence." He went on to add a crucial corollary, however:

It is not enough to establish international agencies. We must also make possible the successful functioning of such agencies through the right domestic policies after the war . . . Full employment in this country will provide additional foreign exchange resources to other countries . . . facilitate the reduction of high tariffs and of exchange and trade restrictions and . . . encourage the resumption of foreign investment by Americans.[35]

The Treasury thus recognized that the new international agencies were not necessarily the most important element of the new imperial project, but in classic New Deal fashion it nevertheless devoted enormous attention to their legal and administrative forms. The early drafts of the White Plan conceived the World Bank in terms of the need for an international public agency to supply Europe with large-scale and long-term public loans at very low rates of interest. This was because it was "futile to look to the private investor to supply more than a small part of the capital needed for the more urgent postwar reconstruction needs. The risks of loss seem to him too great and the prospects of profit too small." This classic justification for state activity in a capitalist market society was presented by White as advantageous to private capital itself in the long run, since both the replacement of and the controls on private capital flows were to be only temporary: after "the prospects of currency stability are improved and restrictions on dividend and interest withdrawals removed, private capital will doubtless flow in increasing volume to areas in need of capital."[36]

Even so, in the course of the Treasury's planning process the World Bank's role was redefined so that direct lending was "to remain secondary"; its main role became to "encourage private capital to go abroad for productive investments by sharing the risks of private investors and by participating with private investors in large ventures." At the same time, its mandate was expanded to include "development" (read: capitalist development), not just "reconstruction."[37] This famously turned the Bank's purpose away from European reconstruction and towards arranging and guaranteeing loans from private capital for economically underdeveloped regions. In fact, one of the reasons for this was a concern to get Latin American states to join the International Monetary Fund—reflecting Roosevelt's long-standing belief that at the end of World War I the Senate had failed to recognize that the US could have controlled the League of Nations with the votes of the Latin American states lined up with its own. Basing voting power in the World Bank and the IMF on the size of each country's subscription of gold, national currency, and government securities would give the US a veto on all important decisions, and, together with the Latin American states, a clear majority. The implication of this concentration of voting power was evident in the proposal that no member country would be allowed "to default on its external obligations . . . without consent of the Fund," nor adopt any "monetary or banking or price measure or policy . . . which, in the opinion of a majority of the member votes, would bring about sooner or later a serious disequilibrium in the balance of payments."[38] On such vital issues, the US would in practice be able to decide.

As to what matching restrictions would be imposed on financial capital, it was of course significant that White's plan, while insisting that the overall goal was "to reduce the necessity and use of foreign exchange controls," permitted states to maintain them.[39] And although it was never on the cards that the US itself would impose them, White's early drafts had contemplated, as a "far-reaching and important requirement," that the US would be prepared to cooperate in policing the capital controls of other countries. Without such cooperation, White reasoned, the control of capital by other states would be "difficult, expensive and subject to considerable evasion." But even while he proposed this, White had recognized that certain of his proposals would "not stand the test of political reality"—and there was no chance whatever that this one, in particular, could. It was already much weakened in the revised July 1943 plan, and by the time of the US-UK Joint Statement of April 1944 setting the final framework for the Bretton Woods Agreement, it was effectively a dead letter. Capital controls were not prohibited, but absent the crucial cooperation of the American state, they could not really be effective in the long run.

Although the American and British Treasuries famously collaborated closely as the plans evolved, the relationship was such that "the British proposed, the Americans disposed," as Keynes's biographer has put it.[40] Indeed, this reflected an asymmetry of power that would characterize the international financial order into the twenty-first century. This is not to say that the joint planning undertaken by the two Treasuries was an empty exercise: far from it, it was crucial for both the effective organization and the legitimation of the new "multilateral sovereignty" that defined the new American empire.[41] The US Treasury attached considerable importance to the extensive negotiations over the relative merits of White's and Keynes's plans, since "Britain was seen as a kind of bridge between the United States and the rest of the world."[42] The joint planning process substantiated the shift from sterling to the dollar as the core international currency. Keynes's plan for a postwar Clearing Union with an entirely new international currency issued by the Fund (designed to record trade transactions and allow overdraft facilities to extend credit on easy terms to countries experiencing balance-of-payments deficits) was rendered still-born; the US Treasury insisted instead on a subscribed Fund that states could only draw on under much tighter conditions than Keynes's plan envisaged. The Joint Statement hammered out between the two Treasuries in advance of Bretton Woods was thus largely framed in American terms, securing "discipline" on Britain's part and "limited liability" on America's.[43]

Yet however arduous the negotiations often were, the remarkable relationship between the two Treasuries prefigured the general nature of the postwar linkages that would develop between American state institutions and those of the former Great Powers in the emerging US empire. Keynes himself would speak both privately and publicly in terms of the historic novelty of British civil servants' "trying to make good economic bricks for the world after the war" with their American counterparts, and having "much the same relations with them as if we were all members of a single office in Whitehall."[44] Yet the fact that they were not actually members of the same office, but still located in distinct state structures embedded in their respective social formations was not without its problems. This was especially evident when Keynes defended the Joint Statement in the British House of Lords with a triumphant claim that it would allow Britain to govern the value of sterling with independent domestic policies and interest rates "without interference from the ebb and flow of international capital movements or flights of hot money." Keynes was, in fact, under no illusions about the limits the Joint Statement placed on Britain's policy autonomy; he had only signed it because, he acknowledged, "our post-war domestic policies are impossible without American assistance," and because "the Americans are strong enough to offer inducements to many or most of our friends [in the sterling area] to walk out on us." But his misleading representation of the Joint Statement for his domestic audience in the UK—greatly exaggerating what he had won from the Americans (in order, as he later admitted, "to save the Fund from political extinction at Westminster")—simultaneously sent a very different message to Wall Street, and thus had the exact opposite effect in Congress from the one he intended it to have in Parliament, revealing how the close ties between the two Treasuries also created tensions within their own states.[45]

Meanwhile the balance of class forces inside the UK was shifting, and would soon result in the first majority Labour Government in history. Insofar as its nationalization of the Bank soon proved to have remarkably little effect in displacing the City of London from the center of capitalist power in Britain, this had something to do with the fact that the domestic balance of forces inside the US was moving in the opposite direction. The

New Deal at home had meant corporatist regulation and suppression of competition among financial institutions, but not the suppression of financial capital as a powerful force in American society; it had never extended to controls over the international movement of capital, and the bankers were determined these should not be introduced through the back door of the International Monetary Fund. By the time many of America's leading capitalists entered the government during wartime, the bankers' adamant opposition to postwar controls over capital movements being introduced through an international treaty was well understood. White was no doubt well aware of this when his initial plan spoke in terms of certain proposals not meeting the test of "political reality," and this was reinforced by the Republican victories in the 1942 midterm elections, and by Congress's further evisceration, by 1943, of many domestic New Deal programs and agencies.[46]

The quick disappearance of White's proposals for cooperative support for capital controls revealed the Treasury's sensitivity to the interests and renewed power of financial capital. In their negotiations with the British, US Treasury officials constantly cited what Congress would or would not accept, but, as was proved when Congress voted overwhelmingly to endorse Bretton Woods once the Treasury had gotten the bankers onside, it was the latter's truculence much more than that of Congress that that needed to be overcome. Indeed, when Keynes at one point complained that the White plan was "written in Cherokee," he was told that "the reason it's written in Cherokee is because we need the support of the braves of Wall Street and this is the language they understand."[47]

Wall Street's opposition to the IMF (they had no problem with the World Bank, now that it was geared to underwriting the risks of private investors) was based on an array of concerns. To be sure, even the New York bankers were pragmatic enough to see that most countries—with the key exception of the US—would continue to require capital controls after the war. But they never relinquished their view that such controls should be only temporary. In the narrowest of terms, the handling of the capital that flowed into New York during the Depression had been profitable, and they were keen to see this resume after the war. More broadly their concerns related to their ambition to replace London as the world's international financial center.[48] But above all Wall Street's opposition reflected the concern that New Deal–type economists and technicians ensconced in permanent international institutions might have even greater autonomy from them than those in the Federal Reserve and the Treasury (especially since the Treasury clearly wanted the Fund to displace the Bank of International Settlements, which had been created by the bankers themselves).[49] Moreover, given the Keynesian provenance of the Fund and the Bank, it was hardly surprising that bankers would be anxious lest full employment rather than price stability might become the priority for governments. Their anxiety about the inflationary implications of full employment was by no means an idle concern, and would indeed prove to be—as Michal Kalecki and Joan Robinson also predicted at the time—the central contradiction of Keynesianism in the postwar era.

If there was ever a case where the advantages of relative autonomy were manifest, allowing a capitalist state to act on behalf of capital but not at its behest, it was in the extensive public campaign the US Treasury undertook to get the Bretton Woods agreement endorsed by Congress over the bankers' opposition. In "one of the most elaborate and sophisticated campaigns ever conducted by a government agency in support of legislation," the Treasury presented Bretton Woods as a "good business deal for the United States" as well as "the symbol for a new kind of cooperation."[50] The Treasury argued that Wall Street's portrayal of the Fund as a vehicle for capital controls was substantially incorrect. Its official "backgrounder" to the Bretton Woods Agreement emphasized that it "would be incorrect to assume that most capital exports are prohibited under the Fund's provisions" and that a "careful examination of the fund proposal will reveal that most capital exports can probably take place freely, and only in a minority of cases will exchange restrictions have to be imposed."[51] This was in fact the way the Treasury expected the Fund to operate—and the way it actually did.[52]

Even so, passage by Congress was not assured until the Treasury struck a last-minute agreement with the representatives of the American Bankers Association and leading Wall Street banks whereby the Treasury agreed to various amendments in a compromise Bill which set up mechanisms such as the National Advisory Council, to ensure that US representatives to the Fund would act in such a way as to impose greater conditionalities on governments that were given access to its resources. This effectively amounted to ensuring that the IMF would incorporate what, ever since 1868, the London-based Corporation of Foreign Bondholders had been doing insofar as it had "functioned like the IMF in some respects and even practiced a weak version of conditionality."[53] On this basis, the House of Representatives eventually passed the Bretton Woods Agreement Act by 345 votes to 18—"only a declaration of war gets a vote like that," Acheson noted.[54]

This victory in Congress publicly symbolized the immense managerial capacities that the key executive agencies of the American state had developed by the end of World War II—in sharp contrast with their weak capacities (as marked by the Senate's defeat of Woodrow Wilson on the League of Nations) at the end of World War I. Indeed, the importance of these new capacities for bringing other states into the orbit of the new American empire had already been much in evidence at the Bretton Woods conference itself, where the commission responsible for creating the Fund was chaired and tightly controlled by White. Even though Keynes oversaw the commission and subcommittees responsible for the Bank, "they had American rapporteurs and secretaries, appointed and briefed by White," who also arranged for "a conference journal to be produced every day to keep everyone informed of the main decisions." At White's disposal were "the mass of stenographers working day and night [and] the boy scouts acting as pages and distributors of papers"—all written in a "legal language which made everything difficult to understand [amid] the great variety of unintelligible tongues." This was the "controlled Bedlam" the American Treasury wanted in order to "make easier the imposition of a fait accompli." The conference ended with Keynes's tribute to a process in which forty-four countries "had been learning to work together so that 'the brotherhood of man will become more than a phrase.' The delegates applauded wildly. 'The Star Spangled Banner' was played."[55]

Laying the Domestic Foundations

"If it is true that our prosperity depends on that of the world, it is true also that the whole world's economic future hangs on our success at home."[56] Henry Stimson in this way captured the understanding which had developed inside the American state that, whereas the Open Door was predicated on US exports, the most important foundation of the new American empire was the unleashing of domestic consumer demand. But this is far too narrow a reading of what now transpired. What was really crucial to the postwar foundations of global capitalism was the deepening of commodification, alongside and even through the consolidation of the welfare state.

The containment of the New Deal through the wartime truce with business largely predetermined the nature of the industrial reconversion that took place at the end of the war. This had been foreshadowed in the summer of 1942 by the formation of the Committee on Economic Development (CED), which incorporated the *Fortune* Roundtable. The main concern of the CED was that planning for the postwar era should be guided by "a conservative version of Keynesian theory [to] promote growth in the private rather than the public sector."[57] Led by Studebaker's Paul Hoffman, the corporate executives who founded the CED had many ties with the business, labor, and government representatives on the wartime planning agencies, and especially with the Department of Commerce. To this end, by June 1945 it had organized 2,800 local groups across the country, involving over 50,000 businessmen, making freely available to them experts in industrial management, product design, advertising, and sales. The CED's goal was (as its bylaws put it) to "avoid the real perils of mass unemployment or mass government employment" after the war by helping private industry and commerce to develop conversion plans for "maximum employment and high productivity in the domestic economy." This was the model that Hoffman would later export to Europe in his capacity as the Marshall Plan administrator, and it would prove much more important than the export of commodities for the postwar American empire's capacity to penetrate the state policymaking apparatuses of the other capitalist countries of Europe.

As one CED research study put it in 1945, "foreign trade is offered time and again as sovereign remedy to relieve the affliction of excess capacity through getting rid of the surplus abroad. Attempting to solve the problem of 'overproduction' by selling abroad more than we are ready to buy is, of course, quite the ultimate in economic folly."[58] Exports, however important they were to particular sectors like agriculture and oil, would remain until 1970 only at the 5 percent level of GDP that had been reached in 1929.[59] This was simply too small to sustain the American economy, and postwar Europe, with its focus on rebuilding public and private infrastructure necessarily implying consumer austerity, could not import enough consumer goods to solve the US's postwar demand problem, even with American aid paying for such imports.[60]

The 10 million US soldiers brought back into the civilian economy after World War II were the equivalent of 20 percent of the 1945 workforce; by this measure, it was a demobilization two-and-a-half times greater than at the end of World War I. And given that 45 percent of American GDP consisted of military production at the war's end, it was hardly surprising that many economists feared that "V-J Day meant major depression and mass unemployment."[61] But in the event the corporations managed reconversion, even if it occurred in a rather haphazard fashion, with remarkable ease—aided as they were by the selling off at fire-sale prices of state-owned defense production plants (mostly to the private corporations that had been entrusted with running them during the war).

A crucial factor here was that the concentration of capital and the restructuring of production during both the Depression and the war, and the build-up of new technological opportunities, facilitated corporate planning. The 1930s had seen major innovations in synthetic rubber, aeronautics, and electrical machinery and equipment, as well as in electrical power generation, communication services, transportation, distribution, and civil engineering.[62] All this had a great deal to do with the fact that corporate research and development had reached a new stage of maturity in the 1930s; expenditures on these activities more than doubled in real terms, and the number employed in them tripled. Although public investment during the Depression had not stimulated sufficient demand, it had very significant impacts on the supply side in terms of construction technologies and building the infrastructure (highways, bridges, roads, housing) for the postwar automobile-driven suburbanization. And this is not even to speak of the transformation of the United States into the great military power it finally became during World War II—with enormous imperial implications for the rest of the century and beyond. The doubling of productive capacity during the war—and the seven-fold increase that was achieved in machine-tool production—involved many goods and components that could be readily converted to civilian production (from military trucks and airplanes to cars, civilian aircraft, and household appliances). The transition was further aided by easy access to investment funds from banks with wartime savings to lend at low interest rates.

By the beginning of 1947 the President's Report to Congress proudly announced that "profits in most lines of industry and business have been highly rewarding."[63] But since real disposable income had fallen between 1945 and 1947, and increased government expenditures on civilian items compensated for only 11 percent of the decrease in the military budget, the question arose of how the economy's enormous productive capacity could be sustained. The problem was aggravated by business-inspired Congressional amendments to the 1946 Employment Act that not only removed any reference to "full employment," but watered down its provisions so as to ensure that government promotion of "maximum employment, production and purchasing power" would only be undertaken "in a manner calculated to foster and promote free competitive enterprise."[64] This effectively guaranteed that even though the federal state's taxation capacity had increased enormously during the war, public spending would not play the kind of role that Keynesians had imagined would be required to sustain effective demand. American reconstruction in the postwar years was therefore bound to be heavily dependent on private consumer spending. Rising working-class incomes were the main mechanism through which this demand could materialize, but wage increases were also seen as threatening economic stability through their effects on price inflation and corporate profits. A resolution of the contradiction between the need for mass consumption and the fear of worker militancy only finally emerged out of a combination of direct state intervention to limit union strength, government-encouraged private consumption through interest-rate ceilings and mortgage guarantees, and the crucial subsequent "settlement" between capital and labor in industry.

The unions' trading-off of the right to strike in return for recognition during the war was followed by a doubling of their membership, but this went along with the suppression of the radical union culture of the mid 1930s. Labor's "marriage to the Democratic Party and the warfare state" thus yielded institutional gains that "advanced the union movement's internal bureaucratic deformities."[65] Whether this would last was put into question by an explosion of strikes in 1945–46.[66] At General Motors 225,000 workers walked off the job; 175,000 electrical workers and 800,000 steel workers soon did the same; and these actions were followed by national strikes in railroads and mining. The 1946 rail strike was ended by President Truman threatening to send in the army to run the railroads. The 1947 Taft-Hartley Act constrained union solidarity by banning secondary picketing and reinforcing state right-to-work laws. Moreover, the anti-Communist "witch-hunt" was already well in train by this time, especially in relation to the labor movement. Taft-Hartley included a provision that required officers of local, national, and international unions to file an affidavit swearing they were not members of the Communist Party. By 1949 Communist-led unions were being expelled from the AFL and CIO, while anti-Communist rhetoric was used to repress or at least marginalize rank-and-file militancy in the trade unions generally.

Alongside the stick came the carrot. Although wage incomes had decreased significantly in the first year after the war, by 1950 they had increased on average by 25 percent, despite the brief recession of 1949. The consumption possibilities this provided were supplemented not only by people spending wartime savings but also by their taking advantage of low interest rates and government provision for secure mortgages. The $72 billion growth in personal consumption between 1945 and 1950 (an increase of 60 percent) was more than enough to offset the decline in defense expenditures of $69 billion.[67] And the consumption boom had ideological as well as economic effects. With investment in residential housing rising eleven-fold in the five years after the war, William J. Levitt, who supervised the building of the paradigmatic working-class suburb, Levittown, declared in 1948 that "no man who owns his own house and lot can be a communist."[68]

But the most important event in resolving the contradiction between the need for private consumption and the dangers posed by wage militancy was the 1950 "Treaty of Detroit." When General Motors, the largest manufacturing company in the world, and the UAW, the most prominent union in the country, institutionalized the "Fordist" link between mass production and mass consumption through this path-breaking collective agreement, they went far beyond anything that Henry Ford ever imagined. By tying company-level wage increases to estimates of national productivity increases, and building in inflation protection through a cost-of-living index, they implicitly accepted that collective bargaining would not disturb the existing distribution of income. The Treaty also centralized power within the union. As the focus of collective bargaining shifted to the negotiation of company-wide wage and benefit increases, and as the union accepted management's control over production at the shop-floor level, local rank-and-file power was undermined. Since the New Deal labor law allowed for the right to strike during the term of a collective agreement, the Treaty's requirement that authority for this in any plant had to be secured from the national union leadership further institutionalized a corporatist relationship between top company and union leaders, and the loss of local autonomy. The commitment of the union leadership to this type of corporatist "productivism" was seen in the initial five-year term of the 1950 agreement, designed to guarantee the company a long period of "labor peace." This did become the focus of membership discontent, leading the UAW president Walter Reuther to get GM to reopen the agreement after three years (which became the norm from that point on). But in all other respects the Treaty held, including the groundwork it laid for privately negotiated healthcare, pension and other benefits that allowed the strongest unions to take care of their members, rather than secure universal public provision from the state.

The Treaty of Detroit, followed by similar agreements throughout the auto sector and other industries, was key to the resolution of the dilemma US capital had faced at the end of the war. The organized American working class would now become the backbone of a high-wage and high-consumption proletariat, but its unions were no longer prepared to challenge capital's right to manage production, let alone question the "capitalist system" along the lines often heard in the 1930s. Reuther now welcomed GM's high profits on the grounds they were "the goose that laid the golden egg," thereby confirming GM chairman Alfred Sloan's prediction that collective bargaining would prove to be an "irresistible force against encroachments on the competitive system of enterprise."[69] Looking back from the vantage-point of the early sixties, Sloan observed that

it is more than seventeen years since there has been an extended strike over national issues at General Motors. To those of us who recall the violent and crisis-ridden atmosphere of the mid-1930s, or the long ordeal of the great postwar strike wave of 1945–46, the record of the past seventeen years seems almost incredible. And we have achieved this record without surrendering any of the basic responsibilities of management.[70]

Fortune magazine had been right in July 1950 when it heralded the Treaty of Detroit with a headline that read "GM may have paid a billion for peace, but it got a bargain."

What was good for General Motors was now good for the world. The Treaty of Detroit epitomized what was meant by the term "productivism," which under the Marshall Plan also became the model for the export of American labor relations to Europe, and it gave enormous legitimacy to what the US was doing there. The appeal of the American model was powerfully reinforced by the contrasting realities the settlement highlighted between European austerity and American consumerism. What the Europeans were seeing across the Atlantic was a society in which auto production (having completely ceased during the war) by 1950 had reached 6.5 million units a year—some three-quarters of global production—and led the way to automobiles being "*the* key manufacturing industry for most of the middle decades of the twentieth century."[71] With the enormous expansion of the American highway system in the mid fifties, cars led the way to suburbia and shopping malls, and reinforced the boom in consumer products; and this in turn brought to fruition the product innovations and new production technologies that had been building since the twenties, but whose application had been largely frustrated by the Depression and the war.

To some extent the US was reviving "old industries" that Europe would soon revive too; but it was also developing new areas of leadership which had emerged out of war production. Commercial aircraft were one critical example (the first jet aircraft went into civilian service in 1957). Synthetic petroleum-based products contributed to the development of the American chemical industry, and the government-sponsored development of penicillin and other therapeutic drugs drove expansion in the pharmaceutical industry. The electronics industry became an integral part of the postwar military-industrial complex, and by the end of the 1950s new firms—as opposed to the established firms that dominated other sectors—were leading the civilian applications that were the foundation of the later revolutions in computing and telecommunications (the "integrated circuits" so crucial to these were patented in 1959).[72]

Meanwhile, financial institutions of various types not only participated in the rapid growth of industry across the country but also found ways to encourage and take advantage of rising consumerism to draw in the working classes, especially through state-backed mortgage securities and consumer loans. The tens of thousands of union-negotiated health insurance and pension plans established between 1949 and 1952 spread rapidly thereafter (and were also adopted by other firms to avoid unionization), providing lucrative profits for the rapidly expanding private insurance industry. International portfolio investment recovered slowly after the war, but New York's investment banks, far from suffering from their exclusion from commercial banking under the New Deal financial legislation, "were able to create and mould [their] business free from the restraints of the traditional slow-moving commercial banking culture. Put simply the US investment banks wrote the rules while everyone else . . . was busy trying to work out what investment banking was all about."[73] All this meant that Wall Street investment banks became unrivaled in the role they played (and the fees they earned) in international capital-intensive infrastructural "project financing" and in the placement of corporate, state, and World Bank bond issues.[74]

Although interest rates were low over this period, rising volumes supported bank profitability. Over the decade of the 1950s the average growth in profits was 40 percent higher in banking than in manufacturing (8.8 percent versus

6.2 percent).[75] The postwar economic boom and the financial bull market of the 1950s provided the space, within the framework of the New Deal and Bretton Woods regulations, for American finance to further deepen its markets at home, expand abroad, and lay the basis for the explosion of global finance that occurred in the last decades of the twentieth century.

Bankers had considerable influence in the Treasury under the Truman administration[76]—which, insofar as it still reflected any "lingering New Deal suspicion of Wall Street," expressed it in an antitrust suit launched by the Justice Department in 1947 against the investment houses that handled 70 percent of Wall Street underwriting. When this suit failed in the courts a few years later, it was seen as a "watershed in the history of Wall Street" that not only firmly closed the door on the old tensions between the bankers and the state, but also "finally freed the Street of its image as the home of monopoly capitalists . . . the investment bankers finally proved they were vital to the economy."[77]

Acceptance of this was institutionally crystallized inside the state, in an Accord reached between the Federal Reserve and the Treasury in 1951. Until the Accord, the New York Fed, acting as the Treasury's agent, had unilaterally dictated the price at which government securities were sold (this was seen on Wall Street as running the market "with an iron fist"). But now the Fed took up the position long advocated by University of Chicago economists and set to work successfully organizing Wall Street's bond dealers into "a self-governing association that would set minimum capital standards and assure low trading spreads," to the end of supporting "a free market in government securities" with "sufficient depth and breadth" so that dealers could take speculative positions, and thus allow market forces to determine bond prices.[78] The Fed's Open Market Committee would only intervene by "leaning against the wind" to correct "a disorderly situation" through its buying and selling of Treasury bills. Financial capital's hostility to inflationary policies thus became "an essential ingredient in the monetary policy process," as decreases in demand for government bonds "revealed the market's concern that inflation could rise." It was a measure of how far the Accord had consolidated the strength of Wall Street that "within a very short time, the Treasury invited the dealer community to advise on its financing." And insofar as the financial sector still had any lingering concerns that Keynesian commitments to the priority of full employment, and the use of fiscal deficits to that end, might prevail in the Treasury, they were allayed by the autonomy the Accord gave the Fed: "the pursuit of macro-economic stabilization and price level stability [had become] the rationale for central bank independence."

The Accord was designed to ensure that "forces seen as more radical" within any administration would not be able to implement inflationary monetary policies.[79] The roots of "monetarism"—understood not in the sense of policy determined by arcane measures of money supply, but in the sense of giving macroeconomic priority to "manipulating short-term interest rates to control aggregate demand and inflation"—thus really need to be located not in the 1970s but in the 1950s, during the supposed heyday of the Keynesian era. When William McChesney Martin, the Fed's chairman from 1951 to 1970, told the Senate Finance Committee in 1958 that an increase in interest rates "served as an indication to the business and investment community that the Federal Reserve rejected the idea that inflation was inevitable," he was indeed, as Robert Hetzel says, "reflecting views on monetary policy that foreshadowed those of Volcker and Greenspan."[80]

These developments in the Treasury and the Federal Reserve could not but critically affect the new American imperial project. But also important was the change that occurred in the outlook of the State Department. The priority given in postwar economic policy to securing the domestic foundation for capital accumulation effectively ended its fifty-year obsession with the Open Door policy.[81] In its representation of US economic interests, the State Department's role now shifted towards securing adequate natural resources to sustain domestic accumulation, and creating conditions abroad that would attract US foreign direct investment and ensure its security. And yet more important was the broader role it would now play in taking responsibility for the reconstruction of the other core capitalist states, promoting the decolonization of their former empires, and trying to ensure that both of these historic developments occurred in a manner consistent with their integration into global capitalism under the aegis of the new American empire.

4

Launching Global Capitalism

The mutual exhaustion of the old capitalist empires, the devastation of the European economies, and the weak political legitimacy of their ruling classes by the end of World War II created an unprecedented opportunity which the American state was now ready and willing to exploit. But the preceding thirty-year crisis had so gravely jeopardized capitalism's future, in the face of both Soviet Communism and the strength of the Left in labor movements, that more than just an American-led postwar restoration of European economies was at stake. The resumption of accumulation primarily rested on the reconstruction of capitalist states which had to find resources both for public infrastructure and private investment, while also dealing with urgent popular demands for security and consumption—at a time when the desperate need for food, raw materials, and capital goods came up against the inability to access the dollars to pay for such imports.

Such a project now depended on the unique capacity of the American imperial state. The most crucial dimension of this in postwar Europe was the space it afforded the European capitalist states to develop internal economic coherence, deepening their domestic consumer markets and expanding their export capacity. This occurred alongside regional economic integration, but the gradual institutionalization of the Common Market was not intended to be, and did not become, the basis for a new inter-imperial rivalry based on a European super-state. Rather, it was a key mechanism, in Alan Milward's apt formulation, for the "European rescue of the nation-state."[1] But this was strongly encouraged by American policymakers, and what was in fact taking place was the American rescue of the European capitalist state.

The Marshall Plan's achievements in this respect would later be called "history's most successful structural adjustment program"—one which permitted Europe's welfare states to be "built on top of and . . . not supplant or bypass the market allocation of goods and factors of production."[2] US policymakers repeatedly spoke, as Allen Dulles did in 1947, of their "desire to help restore a Europe which can and will compete with us in the world markets."[3] The economic rationale for this was that it would enable Europe to buy "substantial amounts of our products," and it was hoped that this would eventually entail not only exports from the US but also production by US corporations within Europe. In fact, in the first decade after the war, US banks and multinational corporations were not much inclined to invest in Western European countries (two-thirds of US foreign direct investment still went to the informal empire within its own hemisphere).[4] American capital was above all engaged in the massive reconversion program at home, and US FDI was concentrated on ensuring that natural resources—above all oil—would be available "for ourselves and our allies."[5]

In this context, the leading role in influencing the nature of European postwar reconstruction fell not to American capital but to the American state. With Europe accounting for only 13 percent of US FDI, what Susan Strange called America's new "imperial bureaucracy" was thus not initially involved so much in sustaining American corporate interests further afield as in anticipating and creating the conditions for their "invasion" of Europe that really only took off in the late 1950s.[6] For the European capitalist classes seeking to re-establish themselves after the war, the predominance of the US was crucial, making adherence to the informal American empire indispensable. Yet it was not so much an imposition as it was "imperialism by invitation."[7] American power and resources were used by European elites to install policies that would have been impossible to pursue on the basis of the domestic alignment of forces.[8]

This was, however, no easy matter, because the postwar constellation of class and ideological forces in Europe was so different from that in the US. The strength and initial radicalism of European labor movements in the early postwar years, on the one hand, and, on the other, the strength of both financial and industrial capital in the US, constituted the crucial matrix that determined European capitalist classes' accommodation to the new imperial relationship. The particular manner in which American labor came to be integrated at home, and its active cooperation with the state and capital in spreading this example abroad, played an important role in accommodating European labor to a new configuration of capitalist class forces which did not so much involve weakening European labor as inflecting it towards an emulation of American "productivism." This was achieved by the political reorganization of European bourgeoisies and the integration of Catholic trade unions into the Christian Democratic parties that came to govern most of continental Europe in the 1950s—and also by the orientation of European Social Democracy towards the type of welfare state and economic planning that would be consistent with the revival of capitalist markets.

US policymakers recognized that there was a "variety of forms free societies may take," in Henry Stimson's phrase.[9] But the meaning of "free society" was explicitly framed within a conception of the state's role in the economy that did not depart significantly from the explicitly capitalist way in which "democratic planning" had already come to be defined in the US itself by 1939, after the New Deal's "grand truce" with capital. The postwar British Labour Government—the first social-democratic majority government in a core capitalist country—articulated an almost identical approach to democratic planning that "turned away from direct control by public administration and toward indirect control by manipulation of the market . . . compatible with private ownership, competition and profit-making."[10]

Insofar as this became the dominant framework for state intervention, it was largely a product of domestic political and class compromises. Yet these compromises were inseparable from the way in which the American state structured the reconstitution of European states. Of course these states could not and did not become replicas or branches of the American state—and this was all the more true outside Western Europe, where integration of states into the US informal empire took a qualitatively different form, not only in Japan but also in oil-producing states of the Middle East, as well as elsewhere in the "Third World."

Evolving the Marshall Plan

As we saw in the previous chapter, the key condition Wall Street had set for calling off Congressional opposition to the Bretton Woods Agreement Act was the creation of the interdepartmental National Advisory Council (NAC) to oversee the making of US international economic policy. And in the immediate postwar period, as the Treasury and State Department were each going through significant changes in both personnel and orientation, the NAC in fact proved more effective and more independent from Congress, as Keynes quickly recognized, "than is usually the case with such Washington Committees."[11] What political economists later called the "embedded liberal" norms of Bretton Woods were little in evidence as US policymakers played the central role in shaping the World Bank and IMF. By insisting on reviewing World Bank loans as well as installing conservative bankers in its executive directorships, the NAC ensured that the Bank would be "a permanent international institution that promoted corporatist collaboration between private international investors, member government officials and economic technicians under the leadership of New York's financial community." And the decisions taken at the NAC played a no less formative role in relation to the IMF, ensuring that "the US conception of the conditional use of IMF resources was . . . officially established as IMF policy," and establishing the "practice of holding confidential consultations" to set out the fiscal and monetary steps states would need to take to satisfy the conditions set for the receipt of IMF loans.[12]

But in the postwar years neither of these institutions came to play the major role intended by their founders or portrayed by their admirers today. In the absence of the major intervention represented by the Marshall Plan, the overwhelming economic dominance of the US would have led to balance-of-payments crises in Europe that the newly formed IMF clearly could not handle; "fixed" exchange rates would have had to be repeatedly adjusted; beggar-thy-neighbor trade policies would have been revived. The Bank and the IMF did not, therefore, become the key agencies for "internationalizing" European states. As a prestigious contemporary report by leading US policymakers and academics noted, "universal inter-governmental agencies play a peripheral or waiting part," while American programs and government agencies "occupy the center of the stage."[13]

The fundamental American policy orientation throughout what is often called—somewhat misleadingly—the "Bretton Woods era" was that currency and capital controls should be transitional, not permanent.[14] All the essential questions of policy informing the intergovernmental negotiations that defined the era were cast in terms of facilitating this transition, beginning with the condition that US negotiators attached to the 1945 British loan requiring sterling to be made convertible within one year (rather than the five years allowed for in the Bretton Woods negotiations). This was indicative of just how short both Washington and New York initially expected the transitional period for the removal of controls might be.

The rhetorical bravado of the kind occasionally heard from politicians like Morgenthau, about "driving the usurious money lenders out of the temple of international finance," should never have been taken too seriously. The facts spoke clearly enough: even the New Deal had not included controls over the international movement of capital; the idea that the American state might cooperate in policing the capital controls of other states was quickly abandoned during the war; a wave of capital flight from Europe immediately after the war was received by Wall Street with open arms. And this was matched by the reluctance of European states, and especially the British, to confront their own capitalist classes by nationalizing and repatriating their extensive holdings of assets in the US economy. But the continuation of this correlation of short-term interests between European and American capitalists, and the fact that the latter engaged in virtually no private investment in Europe in the years immediately after the war, threatened to undermine the reconstruction of viable capitalist states in Europe.

Thus, despite Truman's concern to secure "the return of our foreign commerce and investments to private channels as soon as possible,"[15] it was left to the American state itself to address the economic crisis that engulfed Europe in 1947. The Marshall Plan was conceived in this context for quite pragmatic reasons, not because of a new enthusiasm for the normative framework outlined at Bretton Woods.[16] A shift in responsibility for the central aspects of international economic policy from the Treasury to the State Department was important here. Whereas the Treasury's autonomy from Wall Street was diminished after the war, as reflected in both its domestic economic policy (balanced budgets) and international policy (removal of controls), the State Department's autonomy was enhanced, as the main responsibility for international economic policy was transferred to it both from the Treasury and from the NAC and its Treasury-provided staff. Notably, Cordell Hull's obsession with free trade as the necessary alternative to radical New Deal policies at home no longer held sway in the State Department. In his famous speech at Baylor University in March 1947, Truman had trumpeted: "We are the giant of the economic world. Whether we like it or not, the future pattern of economic relations depends upon us." As part of this, he expressed his commitment to "the achievement, not of free trade, but of freer trade" at the first multilateral trade negotiations about to begin in Geneva, so long as the outcome of these negotiations conformed with "our devotion to freedom of enterprise," since that was "part and parcel of what we call American."[17]

There was, however, a marked lack of enthusiasm in the administration, and especially in the State Department, for the Charter negotiated at Geneva for the International Trade Organization that was supposed to complement the IMF and World Bank in a new triumvirate of international economic organizations. When the Truman administration decided not to ask Congress to endorse the ITO, this reflected not just the difficulty of overcoming protectionist Congressional opposition at the time, but also the discontent of the administration—and even of the most internationally oriented US capitalists—with the Charter proposed for the ITO. As the US Council of the International Chamber of Commerce put it, the ITO Charter was "a dangerous document" because of the provisions for economic development and full employment it appeared to institutionalize permanently.[18] Essentially this amounted to the Charter's failure to provide sufficient openings and protection for US foreign investment—something which would become a central element in the multitude of bilateral trade treaties signed by the US government in the 1950s.

The negotiations had been handled by the State Department's main enthusiast for free trade, Will Clayton, the undersecretary of state for economic affairs (although he was much more preoccupied with developing the Marshall Plan in response to the economic crisis in Europe). In the end Clayton was quite content to go no further than the commercial chapter of the ITO negotiated in Geneva, known as the General Agreement on Tariffs and Trade. Not only was it, as Clayton's biographer put it, "the most sweeping trade agreement—in terms of tariff reduction and the number of goods and countries involved—in the history of the industrial world";[19] it also allowed for flexibility in both bilateral and multilateral negotiations, where "the procedures of negotiation preserved the political advantage of the rich countries and permitted American dominance."[20] As a commercial trade agreement not encumbered by the proposed charter for the ITO, the GATT set out long-term liberalizing goals, and set ground rules for non-discriminatory treatment of national and international investors while leaving ample scope for the type of temporary trade restrictions that were agreed with the British in the summer of 1947.[21]

US trade policy, which would henceforth no longer go under the name of the Open Door, remained primarily "shaped by domestic influences" rather than an "embedded" international regime.[22] But those influences were themselves increasingly structured by the way the American state had been internationalized and the responsibility it took upon itself for developing capitalism on a global scale after World War II. In the postwar period, the institutional restructuring introduced in the 1934 Trade Act was rendered much more significant than it could have been during the Depression, as successive administrations pursued "a general process of trade liberalization with only exceptional treatment to 'special' cases" (which were left to the play of "industry-specific pressures" in Congress).[23] And now that it was recognized, even in the State Department, that accumulation at home was only marginally dependent on exports, trade strategy was determined above all by the commitment to ensuring that what Truman called "the future pattern of economic relations" internationally would be conducive to the expansion of "free enterprise" in ways that would eventually allow for the free movement of capital. In the interim, however, this explicitly involved selectively opening up the massive US market even to states that protected their own markets, whether through tariffs, subsidies, or undervalued exchange rates. Of course, it was a policy that was constantly subject to pressures from, and compromises with, protectionist lobbies that enjoyed Congressional support, but these pressures and compromises did not deflect the American state's strategic orientation towards trade policy, which was now applied to Europe under the Marshall Plan—and soon, in a different way, to Japan, South Korea, and Taiwan.

The uppermost concern was the one Acheson had expressed in 1939—namely that the US capitalist system could not survive if the core European countries took a different path. But now the concern was not with stopping the spread of fascism, but rather preventing indigenous Communist and left-socialist political forces from increasing their considerable popular support, and getting them removed from postwar coalition governments, especially since general elections were impending across much of Western Europe in 1947–48. Together with reports arriving in the State Department of severe economic crises across Western Europe in the winter of 1947, the challenge posed by the European Left, coming to a head with Greece at this time, prompted both the formulation of the Truman Doctrine on the containment of Communism and the creation of the Marshall Plan.[24] At a State Department meeting in May 1947, Clayton emphasized that the initiative behind the plan should "come—or, at any rate, appear to come—from Europe. *But the United States must run the show.* And it must start running it now." According to Acheson's account of the meeting, "On this main point there was no debate."[25]

Since the US insisted on confining Marshall Aid to Western Europe, and was especially committed to reconstituting an economically viable West German state, the Truman Doctrine was designed to avoid making it look as if it was the US rather than the USSR that was responsible for dividing Europe.[26] It heralded the new geopolitical and military links that came to bind the core capitalist states to the American empire. These links would soon be institutionalized—not only through NATO, but also through the hub-and-spokes network that linked other states' intelligence and security apparatuses to those of the US. But American policymakers recognized that in Europe it was domestic left-socialist or Communist forces, whose popular support was likely to be increased in the context of the economic crisis, that were the main problem. This was made very clear in 1947 by George Kennan, who as director of the State Department's Policy Planning Staff was the primary author of the containment doctrine, when he said that US policy in Europe should "be directed not to the combating of communism as such but to the restoration of the economic health and vigor of European society."[27] And even the National Security Council's 1950 master document on the strategy of containment, NSC-68, stated that the "overall policy at the present time may be described as one designed to foster a world environment in which the American system can survive and flourish . . . a policy which we would probably pursue even if there were no Soviet threat."[28]

Alan Milward has demonstrated that the Marshall Plan funds were not as crucial to European recovery as was claimed at the time, and by some historians subsequently, nor as significant for furthering American exports and capital investment.[29] Yet even if the funds provided were not much greater than the relief aid given from 1945 to 1947, the three-year advance commitment of funds that the Marshall Plan gave Europe in 1948 was much more effective in sustaining economic recovery than relief aid—not least to offset the capital that until this point had been escaping European controls and heading to New York. Such "offsetting financing" had been discussed at Bretton Woods, but was rejected there in favor of capital controls.[30] Yet at a time when the new International Monetary Fund had insufficient resources to play much of a role, the provision of such offsetting finance was in a certain sense what the Marshall Plan now amounted to.

To the extent that Marshall Plan funds eased the consumption-investment

tradeoff and the balance-of-payments constraint, they also reduced tendencies to deflation and helped overcome specific bottlenecks critical to both
growth (transportation, raw materials, components) and shortages of basic
necessities (food, oil). In the pivotal years 1948 and 1949 Marshall Plan
assistance amounted to an estimated 15 percent of the combined gross
domestic capital formation of the UK, Italy, and France, while for
Germany it was over 25 percent.[31] Equivalent funds might of course have
been "found" without Marshall Plan assistance, but that would have
required either radical state intervention against domestic capital or even
more austerity for the working class. The former was precisely what the
Marshall Plan was determined to prevent; the latter risked further radical-
izing workers and undermining the fragile legitimacy of both capital and
states in Europe.

The bilateral pacts which each government had to sign with the US to
obtain Marshall Plan funds required them "to agree to balance government
budgets . . . restore internal financial stability . . . and stabilize exchange
rates at realistic levels." The recipient states were allowed to be "committed
to the mixed economy. But the US insisted that market forces be represented more liberally in the mix." Crucial here as well was that "for every
dollar of Marshall Plan aid received the recipient country was required to
place a matching amount of domestic currency in a counterpart fund to be
used only for purposes approved by the US government."[32] W. F.
Duisenberg, the first head of the European Central Bank, looking back in
1997 on the occasion of the fiftieth anniversary of the Marshall Plan, notably
celebrated its functions in this respect as "similar to the approach followed
in later years by the International Monetary Fund in its macroeconomic
adjustment programs."[33]

The American Rescue of European Capitalism

The Marshall Plan's success in stabilizing Western European finances should
not obscure its broader strategic significance—the economic, political,
ideological, and military dimensions of the American rescue of European
capitalism were intertwined and inseparable. John J. McCloy, the prestigious Wall Street lawyer who moved from the US Control Commission in
postwar Germany to become president of the World Bank in its formative
years from 1947 to 1949, summed it up as follows:

> The prevailing lack of confidence in European currencies is perhaps most
> dramatically reflected in the flight of capital now going on. The causes, of
> course, are both political and economic. There can be no financial stability
> in the absence of sound financial policies, but there can also be no financial
> stability without confidence on the part of the people in the political future

of the country. This explains why the problem of military guarantees has such direct and vital economic implications.[34]

What the American state was signaling with the Marshall Plan was its commitment to underwriting the European states as *capitalist* states, while at the same time making it possible to secure cooperation from labor in the process. Thus, while trade unions bore the immediate burden of the imposition of wage restraint and incomes policies, they were also attracted by the Marshall Plan's explicit promotion of a "social contract" for labor peace and improved productivity. In this way, economic growth—making the pie bigger, as it was often put—assumed priority over the redistribution of income and wealth.

The postwar balance of class forces in Europe meant that labor could not be repressed as it had been before, which made it all the more important that financial discipline should be reinforced. The commitment to this varied from country to country. This was especially seen in the determination with which the Bundesbank and the Ministry of Finance in Germany espoused neoliberal monetarist policies (at the time called "ordoliberalism") throughout the postwar period. "Whereas the rest of Europe read Keynes many West Germans read Friedrich von Hayek."[35] Notably, "the strong market orientation of US officials led them to secure important posts for 'ordoliberals' and provide institutional support for their ideas."[36] And the Bank of England—even after its nationalization by the postwar Labour government—continued to represent the interests of the City of London, often in alliance with a Treasury increasingly obsessed with restraining union wage power under conditions of high employment.[37] Meanwhile, the Bank of International Settlements (BIS), that orthodox club of central bankers, was conscripted, now with the strong backing of the US Treasury, as the vehicle for running the European Payments Union mechanism in the late 1940s.[38]

As early as 1948 Per Jacobsson, who had effectively run the BIS since its inception and would later be appointed to head the IMF, reassured American policymakers that something he called "neo-Liberalism . . . has begun to gain ground" in Europe: price controls were "being replaced by ordinary financial control, involving balancing of budgets, curtailment of credit through an increase of interest rates, and cessation of the intervention by the central banks in support of government bonds." But this success in terms of financial discipline was, he insisted, only really important as a signal of a profound change that had occurred in the balance of political forces: "Non-Socialist parties have a majority in Denmark, Holland, Belgium, Luxembourg, Eire, France, Switzerland, Italy, Iceland, Greece, Portugal, Austria and Turkey—thirteen out of the Sixteen Nations. And in 1947–48, the elections have generally strengthened the non-socialist majority," he reported. "Only in Great Britain, Norway and Sweden is there now a Labour majority in Parliament." And with respect to the latter he went on to quote the *New Statesman and Nation* of February 21, 1948: '[S]ocialist remedies which many propounded two years ago or even twelve months ago, have been ruled out by events."[39]

Nevertheless, coming to terms with popular forces in postwar Europe required balancing the need for financial restraint, in order to accommodate the priorities of rebuilding the social infrastructure and allowing room for private investment, with the need to address the high expectations of farmers and workers—the former concerned with prices and the latter with wages. It might seem that in these respects the American state made compromises that undermined the liberal objectives it had set for itself: European development came with social and industrial policies, barriers to free trade, and trade discrimination against the US. But this would be to take too idealized a view of the American imperial project. "Liberalization" was a process; pragmatic compromises were part of making progress within the overall project. Moreover, this was not just a matter of "two steps forward, one step back." Interventionist domestic policies and regional trade protection from US exports were not contrary but essential to the imperial project's long-term success.

Also essential to the success of the project was marginalizing the most radical impulses in the labor movement and channeling the expectations and demands of workers and farmers towards making gains within the boundaries of a growing capitalism. A great deal has been written on the isolation of Communist unions and parties, including the role played by the the AFL and CIO in establishing, with CIA funding, non-Communist— and anti-Communist—unions.[40] But no less crucial was the consolidation of the "politics of productivism" among the majority of European workers, "superseding class conflict with economic growth."[41] This was in fact the crucial condition both for the distinctive development of the European welfare states and for the regional integration of their economies, which culminated in the European Common Market.

The productivity councils that emerged during the Marshall Plan were especially important in identifying productivity with "modernization." But most influential was the example of labor relations and working-class conditions in the US itself. This was communicated through formal exchanges and visits by trade unionists to American factories, homes, and shopping centers, and also—and in the long run perhaps more importantly—through the informal dissemination of American culture and the trans-Atlantic contacts of immigrant families, friends, and visitors. It is hardly surprising that, to workers who had suffered through the Depression and the war, the tangible and immediate gains that appeared to be obtainable from "responsible" unionism seemed more attractive than alternatives that held out the prospect of more chaos in the short term, and distant and uncertain promises in the longer term. Moreover, European social-democratic parties progressively ceased to provide the leadership, education, and confidence needed for mobilization towards a socialist alternative. In fact, their leaders' statist notions of "socialism" identified calls for greater democratization of the state and economy more as problems for their parties than as opportunities.[42]

But the success of the strategy for incorporating the working classes depended on having the material ability to transform European economies.[43] And for this it seemed that at least three basic problems needed to be overcome which Marshall Plan funds, even with the disciplinary conditions attached to them, could not solve. The first problem was how to mobilize long-term capital for investment without jeopardizing the distributional compromises so essential for the fragile peace with popular forces. Second, although the American market was open to them, European companies did not (in general) have the capacity to compete there with US firms.[44] Third, even reconstruction and larger regional markets could not in themselves overcome the technological—and institutional—advantages of American business. For all these problems Marshall Plan dollars offered only short-term relief. These were American problems as much as European ones. An uncompetitive Europe would not be able to pay for, and therefore absorb, American exports, and this therefore risked extending Europe's status as an expensive ward of the US.

As it turned out, Europe's accumulation problem was overcome in spectacular fashion: investment as a share of GDP through the 1950s surpassed every previous peak for European countries.[45] Absolutely crucial to this was the American endorsement—some would say orchestration—of European regional economic integration. This started with the radical currency devaluations implemented by the European states relative to the dollar after the 1948–49 recession in the US had drastically reduced American imports from Europe.[46] This realignment of currencies set the stage for the shift in the balance of trade between the US and Europe that took place over the course of the 1950s. The most critical institutional reform in making this viable was the European Payments Union (EPU), which came into effect in 1950. It was Paul Hoffman, the American businessman now heading the Economic Cooperation Administration (ECA), the agency responsible for carrying out the Marshall Plan's Economic Recovery Program, who aggressively intervened in 1949 to press for the formation of a European Payments Union, arguing that "nothing less than the integration of the Western European economy" would do, and that, absent such integration, "a vicious cycle of economic nationalism would again be set in motion."[47]

The principle behind the EPU was simple. The American dollar, which had become the primary means of exchange even in trade between European countries, could not, because it was in short supply in Europe, accommodate increased trade—and this led to a highly restrictive system of bilateral trade relationships. This was overcome by the EPU, which allowed each European state to use its own currency to pay for imports from other European states.[48] By allowing national room for maneuver in economic policy, the EPU was especially important for industrial reconstruction and sustained accumulation in the context of a process of regional economic integration centered very much on the West German economy. Of course, European elites played the main part in the actual running of the EPU, as well as in the formation of the European Coal and Steel Community (ECSC) in 1951, and the negotiations that led to the Treaty of Rome in 1957. Yet the catalytic role of the US in European integration should not be underestimated. The American state's strong encouragement of European economic integration was crucial, as was its acceptance of what it always saw as temporary and transitional barriers to selected US exports and investments while the European Common Market was being constructed.

There was thus no fundamental contradiction between the "European rescue of the nation-state" and the American rescue of European capitalism. It was precisely because the American state so clearly understood the importance of economic integration to the strengthening of Europe's nation-states, and because these stronger states were a condition for expanded liberalization, that US policymakers were usually so determined in their support for the process that led to the European Common Market. Moreover, the centrality of Germany within the regional economy was quite consistent with the special role played by the American state. In its formative years "the FRG represented the almost ideal type of a penetrated system. American hegemony and the Marshall Plan crucially conditioned its integration into regional and global regimes of liberalized trade and payments."[49] Even the initiatives towards European integration that France took via Jean Monnet owed much to American encouragement. While accepting that Monnet's "political inspiration was quite different from the Americans'," Perry Anderson rightly insists that Monnet's "direct line to Washington was the source of his strength as an architect of integration. American pressure, in the epoch of Acheson and Dulles, was crucial in putting real force behind the conception of 'ever greater union' that came to be enshrined in the Treaty of Rome."[50]

The postwar recovery of European capitalism also involved the adoption of forms of production and accumulation which had been developed earlier in the US—large firms, competing with each other across a large "domestic" market—and which now made possible the development in Europe of the US-style productivist labor relations discussed above. And this was accompanied by the completion in Europe of the second industrial revolution (electronic machinery, chemical processes, and mass–consumer goods industries). Europe's rapid and sustained growth through the 1950s was clearly based on very high levels of investment, albeit building on an industrial base that was not as totally devastated by the war as is often thought.[51] No less crucial was the shift of labor from agriculture to industry—and, especially in the case of Germany, the additional supplies of labor coming from the east. The demand stimulus that resulted from social programs won through pressure from below was crucial too: farmers had price supports, unemployed workers had income, and retirees could continue to consume.

To all this must be added the role played by the American technology and related productive and managerial systems which were now transferred to Europe on an historically unprecedented scale. In contrast with the immediate postwar years, when the priority was rebuilding collapsed infrastructure and overcoming the bottlenecks in production and distribution networks, by the early 1950s—when consumer demand was growing and competition was being restored—"micro" issues of quality and productivity came to the fore, and with them the adoption of specific American technologies. The European Productivity Agency was "an institution and a productivity campaign initially conceived by the Americans" that was successfully Europeanized. It included managerial retraining seminars, "pilot plant" projects, consultancy programs, and thousands of visits to American industries by European managers, technicians, and trade unionists. It was through the national productivity centers it coordinated, which were composed of European businessmen focused on quite specific industrial problems, that technology was most effectively disseminated.[52]

The organizational and ideological relations that went with "productivism" could be presented as merely using the advantages of "technology" to facilitate the substantiation of shared capitalist common sense, and doing so in a way that did not undermine national sovereignty. The most important transfers of technology occurred in steel, chemicals, retail and distribution, and above all in the automobile sector, which, apart from its key role in promoting the dream of mass consumption and providing the organizational structure for its achievement, was directly linked to production in machinery and tooling, steel, rubber, glass, textiles, and chemicals such as paints and fluids. General Motors and Ford had already been an influential presence in Europe for some two decades (especially in Germany and the UK), but the American influence now took on a new dimension. Volkswagen, which passed GM-OPEL as Germany's leading automotive producer in 1952 and became Europe's largest motor-vehicle producer by the mid 1950s, based its entire strategy on a "systematic technological transfer from the US," as well as getting into the US market via American-style advertising and distribution.[53] All this meant that the evolution of the European industrial system "was unmistakably towards the structural model originally pioneered by the USA."[54] But with the United States accounting for almost half the world's industrial production at the beginning of the 1950s, and with its leadership and dynamism so clear, what was being imported seemed to be not so much "American" productive systems as generic "modern" technology.

This was especially important in relation to the decartelization of European industry. A primary concern of the Marshall Plan administrators had been to use the added influence that the US occupation of Germany provided to turn it into, as Hoffman put it, "the kind of free competitive economy which we have in the United States."[55] The American concern with European traditions of cartelization was articulated in terms of the inefficiencies of non-competitive production, but a deeper cause for anxiety was the relationship between cartelization and lack of access for American capital. Firms coming together to set prices necessarily required state-supported barriers to entry such as tariffs, limits on direct investment, and "private interests being provided with political influence" (as an American-influenced section of the Schuman Plan put it).[56] Despite no little friction between the American administrators of the Marshall Plan and their European counterparts, the foundations were established for the legal codes limiting cartelization that were introduced in the 1950s.

It was highly significant, moreover, that under the aegis of the US, German capital—especially with the imposition of an anti-cartel competitive framework—had already fully embraced what would later be called neoliberalism, and indentified "internationalization," with the closest of ties to the US, as central to its postwar rehabilitation. While the rest of Europe increasingly exported to Germany in the 1950s, Germany increasingly exported to the US.[57] By contrast, the UK, clinging to the imperial preference system and sterling's place within it, and resistant to American pressures to join in European integration, proved more intractable—despite (or perhaps because of) the "special relationship." Yet with the City of London pressing for the removal of currency controls in order to regain its place as a leading financial center, the way was being paved for the role the UK soon came to play as one of the main conduits of the American financial penetration of Europe.[58]

"The Rest of the World"

In his 1936 State of the Union Address, President Roosevelt used the phrase "The rest of the world—Ah! there is the rub" to express his frustration that states in Europe were not following the example of the US's "good neighbor" policy in its own hemisphere. The American state's intense postwar focus on Europe, which marked the displacement of the old "good neighbor" trope with the Marshall Plan, ran the risk of implying that it did not attach equivalent importance to the potentials of Asia, Latin America, and

Africa.[59] Yet its primary focus on Europe was also reflected in its commitment "to supply friendly nations as well as ourselves" with resources, leading it to assume increasingly global responsibilities.[60]

This meshing of the American state's particular and universal responsibilities was nowhere clearer than in relation to oil. Entering the war, the US was by far the world's greatest oil producer; in 1940, it accounted for two of every three barrels produced in the world, while Middle East production then accounted for only 5 percent.[61] Over 85 percent of the oil used in Europe by the Allies during the war came from the US. After the war, three seismic and interrelated shifts occurred in the relationships between the US, Europe, and the Middle East. First, by extending, especially through the special relationship it established with the Saudi Arabian ruling class, the foothold the US had previously obtained in Middle East oil production under the "Red Line Agreement" of 1928, the American state assumed responsibility for overseeing the international oil companies' control of "the richest prize in the world in the field of foreign investment."[62] Second, the source of European oil supplies was shifted, so that by 1950, 85 percent of Europe's oil was coming from the Middle East.[63] This preserved American oil for American needs—by the late 1940s, American consumption of oil was already outrunning domestic production—while also securing from the Middle East the oil Europe needed for its reconstruction. Third, the nature of postwar economic growth in both the US and Europe led to an explosion of demand for oil. A mobile suburban car culture; the expansion of trucking for mass production and distribution; the growth of commercial aviation; new industries in chemicals, plastics, and fertilizer—all this required more oil, cheap oil, and above all secure oil. Before the war, some 90 percent of European energy came from coal, and even though the security of oil as an energy source rested on the creation of trusted regimes in the Middle East, oil was seen as "more politically reliable" than coal because "many coal miners belonged to communist unions."[64]

The relationship between the American state and US oil companies in this process thus already epitomized "globalization": US companies producing abroad for markets abroad. And it was already clear by the time of the Marshall Plan that American policy in this sector could no longer be characterized as simply sustaining the interests of American oil companies. Amy Myers Jaffe's summary of US oil policy captures this very well:

American policy in the Persian Gulf is not designed . . . simply to keep the price of US gasoline cheap or to make sure that American companies get handsome oil exploration contracts. Neither of these goals would likely merit the intense level of US intervention in the region . . . Rather, America ensures that oil flows from the Persian Gulf are available to fuel international trade and economy as part of its global superpower responsibilities. More simply put, the physical oil needs of the US economy can certainly be met fully by protecting oil flows closer to home, from Canada, Mexico, South America, the North Sea and Africa. But the United States must consider the health of the overall global economic system since a massive shortfall of oil elsewhere would not only affect the price of oil everywhere but almost certainly collapse the global economic system.[65]

The truth of this observation could already be seen in the relationship the US established with Europe after the war. Since oil was "the largest single item in the dollar budget of most of the Marshall Plan countries," its US administrators "kept up constant pressure on the companies to lower their prices and thus lower the dollar costs of 'oiling' European recovery"; the critical issue became how to "balance the US interest in European recovery with the interests of US oil companies."[66] Similar issues were already familiar in the informal empire the US had forged in its own hemisphere earlier in the century. In 1939 a National Planning Association study argued that "the investment program in Latin America in the future should not be concentrated on the further specialization of raw materials, but rather should be focused on the development of industries making goods which Latin Americans need." This was only one of a plethora of reports that culminated in the emphasis placed by the interdepartmental Executive Committee on Economic Foreign Policy in 1944 on the "fostering and encouraging of sound industrialization" in Latin America.[67] As an official history of the role of the CIA in Brazil in the immediate postwar period put it, "the United States assumed, out of self-interest, responsibility for the welfare of the world capitalist system."[68]

Unlike in postwar Europe, however, it was private US capital rather than the state that took the lead in Latin America. Belgium and Luxembourg received more official American aid between 1945 and 1950 than all the Latin American states combined.[69] In this context, and as part of its turn away from the Open Door, the US accepted restrictions on free trade as long as American corporations had non-discriminatory access for direct investment.[70] For manufacturing corporations FDI was, of course, an alternative to free trade for reaching foreign markets. In 1955, for example, 94 percent of the output of American MNCs in Latin America was sold locally. It is today largely forgotten that US foreign economic policy in the 1950s actually supported Import Substitution Industrialization (ISI) as a development model, and that this was underwritten by the Federal Reserve's endorsement of greater national control over monetary policy in the Third World. To a significant extent this also implied temporarily living with— even if not endorsing as permanent—protective tariffs and capital controls.[71]

Indeed, as Maxfield and Nolt have shown in case studies in Latin America, Asia, and the Middle East, ISI became development orthodoxy in the 1950s,

and was often introduced on the initiative of US policymakers and businessmen who were assertive participants in the restructuring of other countries'
policies and laws to create favorable infrastructural, fiscal, and property-
rights conditions for foreign investment. Although the UN Economic
Commission for Latin America (ECLA) and its executive secretary Raul
Prebisch were often the targets of US hostility for expressing a nationalist
reaction to liberalism, a report in 1951 by the US representative to the
Organization of American States indicated that American officials were
"much impressed with the work of ECLA and . . . especially with Dr
Prebisch [who] is in a position to bring home to Latin American officials
economic truths which they would not accept on the basis of any statement
made by US representatives."[72] This should not be taken to mean that the
US–ECLA relationship was ever anything but tense; yet by the 1950s this
was not about ISI itself, but the specifics of how it was applied and of
American participation within it. Like European reconstruction, ISI cannot
be understood in terms of states versus markets or the "balance" between
them. The issue was the role of states in *making* markets and *shaping* market
relationships. In the Philippines the US believed that, in order to overcome
the government's inefficient and limited implementation of ISI, "it had to
attain a degree of control over Philippine economic life unprecedented
even during the colonial period"; and in Turkey, far from opposing state
intervention, US policymakers desired "government coordination of trade,
credit, and monetary and fiscal policies to provide an environment to attract
private investment."[73]

In early 1949 *Fortune* magazine had applauded Truman's inaugural address
for its focus on the Third World, enthusing that a "rebirth of international
capitalism through the medium of the American businessman, who alone
has the strength to bring about such a revolution, is the last, best, visible
hope of establishing a new world economy."[74] But, whereas the correlation
of class forces in the US and Europe led to a successful postwar dynamic of
reconstruction, development, and integration into a liberalizing global capitalism, in the Third World this dynamic largely failed to arise. The imports
of machinery and equipment that ISI required could only be paid for by
exports of labor-intensive consumer goods. But the American state lacked
sufficient autonomy from domestic class forces to generally open the market
to such imports; nor could it force American capital to invest adequately in
the Third World. Moreover, the American state's capacity to penetrate the
social formations of most Third World states was limited by their relatively
underdeveloped capitalist institutions and social relations. In the aftermath
of the emergence of Newly Industrializing Countries and the "Asian miracle," it is easy to forget that, at the end of the 1950s, as Benedict Anderson
observes, "the income accruing to the Indonesian state was not much bigger
than that of a large American university," while the Philippines had not

recovered from being "trampled to rubble by the Japanese and American Armies" and Thailand was still "a sleepy, rice-exporting country which . . . had no effective nationwide system of primary education."[75]

Between the First and Third Worlds, Japan was in a category of its own: it was neither part of the underdeveloped world nor part of the capitalist core. Japan had been an imperial power, but with the American occupation Japan became an effective "ward" of the US, and its postwar revival signaled a return to "semiperipherality as a permanent second-rank economic power."[76] Prospects for integrating Japan into the type of larger regional economic bloc that was being constructed in Europe were severely limited by the low level of Southeast Asian economic development, as well as by the lingering French and British imperial role there. And Japan, with its large population, confined space, and unfavorable topography, was even more dependent than Europe on external sources of food and raw materials. Even by the end of the 1950s, after a decade of breakneck industrial growth, its overall productivity and living standards were still only about half those of Europe.[77]

Under the US occupation, and with the support of a conservative capitalist class and state bureaucracy that had survived the war largely intact, the main social bases of Japanese fascism—the military and large landowners— were purged. Yet in spite of the initial US goal of breaking the industrial-financial power of the Zaibatsu and introducing legal reforms to allow for "free trade unions," US policy began shifting to an accommodation with Japan's business elite, including reversing its support for an independent labor movement. By 1950, with the defeat of the militant Toyota workers' union, the Japanese labor movement was essentially smashed as a social force, disappearing into company unionism as suddenly as it had emerged anew in the short-lived postwar liberalization.[78] In contrast to Europe, this meant that the revival of Japanese capitalism would depend less on the development of its internal market than on exports. As an important 1955 report by US policymakers put it, "it is probably valid to conclude that during the next decade, it would be politically tolerable to apply the major parts of the proceeds of Japanese growth to purposes other than consumption, with increases in consumption the residual claimant. The opposite is more nearly true of Western Europe."[79] This in turn carried implications for tighter internal austerity, greater labor control, and a more limited welfare state, and all this was indeed already reflected in the policies of the American occupation authorities from 1949 onwards.[80]

In this regard the American state played a critical role on a number of fronts. The US provided security for Japanese resource needs, especially oil, as well as continually reinforcing—with ever greater purpose and determination as the Chinese Communists emerged victorious—the US military's strength in the region. American procurements during the Korean War were Japan's equivalent of the Marshall Plan; in 1952–53 they accounted for over two-thirds of Japanese commercial exports.[81] The US regularly intervened to push the reluctant Europeans and other OECD members to ease restrictions on Japanese imports and provide access for Japan to their former spheres of influence, culminating in the US-sponsored admission of Japan to the OECD in 1962. Over the period 1952–64, Japan ran a cumulative trade deficit with the US in goods and services of $6.5 billion, essentially financed by American military expenditures of $6.2 billion.[82]

The nature of Japan's integration into the informal American empire was thus considerably different from that of Europe. There seemed little potential in the 1950s for Japan to serve as a platform for regional markets. Nor was the ground laid in Japan, as it was in Europe, for an influx of American industrial and financial capital. By allowing Japanese economic reconstruction through export surpluses and portfolio capital loans used to purchase US technology, the American state was taking responsibility for Japan becoming the capitalist pole around which US strategy in Southeast Asia could pivot. This involved the encouragement of a form of mercantilism that kept foreign capital out in favor of direct state support for domestic capitalists whose corporate expansion was based on the asymmetric opening of US markets alongside the relative closure of their own. Although this would become the model for Taiwan and South Korea, no other part of the Third World would be so successfully integrated in this fashion into the American empire. But even the successful integration of Europe and Japan, as we shall now see, was hardly a process without contradictions.

III

THE TRANSITION TO GLOBAL CAPITALISM

5

The Contradictions of Success

The Broadway hit of 1961 was *How to Succeed in Business Without Really Trying*. If this title seemed to epitomize the vast expansion of the activities of US multinational corporations at just this time, it belied the fact that this had actually been the product, as we have seen, of a very concerted effort on the part of the American state. Towards the end of the 1950s, with the reconstruction of Europe's physical and social infrastructure and the establishment of mass markets, supplier networks and favorable investment policies, US foreign direct investment came pouring into Europe. This was a novel experience: "Europeans had grown used to complaining that the United States was draining Europe of funds, and Americans had grown used to stressing the lack of investment opportunities in Europe, the inconvertibility of European currencies, and so on."[1] What US corporations had been unwilling to do for more than a decade after the war, they did in spades by the end of the 1950s—not least to retain their market shares vis-à-vis increasingly competitive European companies. American MNCs—including American banks—now became strong and dynamic elements inside most European countries.

By the time full currency convertibility in Europe was achieved in 1958, it might have been expected that the Bretton Woods framework would finally come into its own in mediating international economic relations in a way that reconciled currency stability with capital mobility, as had always been the US goal. In practice, however, serious contradictions in that framework immediately began to reveal themselves. The first of these was that growing trade competition from Europe and the growth of US private investment in Europe combined to produce severe pressure on the dollar. A second and related contradiction emerged as US financial capital, having been nursed back to health under the regulatory framework of the New Deal, increasingly strained against the limits of that framework at home, and also found new outlets through the overseas expansion of MNCs and the opportunity this gave to internationalize US banking. The vast cross-border flows of private capital this now involved were bound eventually to undermine the Bretton Woods system of fixed exchange rates.

And a further, much more profound contradiction had arisen—one that overlapped with and to a considerable extent really underlay the others. The realization of Keynesian "full employment" objectives by the 1960s clearly brought to the fore the old question of how capital and the state were to cope with the demands made by working classes no longer restrained by the fear of involuntarily conscription into the reserve army of labor. The achievement of near full employment within all the advanced capitalist states spurred the growing militancy of a new generation of workers who drove up wages, challenged managerial prerogatives, and forced a steady increase in social expenditures—all of which not only made it very difficult for capitalist states to resolve international economic imbalances through domestic austerity policies, but generated growing worries about price stability, productivity and profits. Because this was not a zero-sum game, and capital was also strong by virtue of its having been restored to health so effectively, the contradiction became intense amid rising inflation and class conflicts.

Moreover, alongside this new balance of class forces in the advanced capitalist countries, the success of postwar decolonization of the old empires, so much encouraged by the new American empire, stoked the rise of economic nationalism in the "Third World" that challenged the international norms for the mutual interstate protection of capitalist property. The sangfroid with which the *Fortune* editors had proclaimed in 1942 that the new American empire would not be "afraid to help build up industrial rivals to its own power ... because we know industrialization stimulates rather than limits international trade" was not much in evidence by the late 1960s. By the time the US in 1971 hesitatingly ended the dollar's link to gold, it was already clear that neither clinging to nor jettisoning the Bretton Woods system offered a long-term solution to this accumulating set of contradictions.

Internationalizing Production

The American state's capacity to assume such a central role in the making of global capitalism was closely related to, and augmented by, the growing international predominance of American corporations. This was itself associated with the shift over the course of the second half of the twentieth century in capitalism's international fulcrum from trade linkages across national spaces of accumulation to the development of transnational productive spaces characterized by the crisscrossing and straddling of borders via networks of production internal to, or closely linked to, multinational corporations.

The specifically American leadership in the development of the modern corporate form by the beginning of the twentieth century—not least in its administrative capacities for simultaneous decentralization and centralization—was crucial to the evolution of its global offspring, the multinational corporation. "In becoming national firms," as Stephen Hymer noted in his path-breaking work on the MNC, "US corporations learned how to become international."[2] That the multinational corporation has become the institutional expression of the "globalization of production" might seem an obvious consequence of capitalism's tendency to concentration and central-ization, and of its drive to "nestle everywhere, settle everywhere." Yet the extension of national corporations into multinational networks of produc-tion did not necessarily flow from capital's international ambitions and pressures. It was far from inevitable that this would lead to more foreign direct investment as opposed to international loans and trade, or that foreign states would accommodate such territorial penetration. Approaching this development in purely abstract terms hinders identification of the imperial role of the American state as an essential ingredient in establishing the conditions for the expansion of MNCs and their crucial role in the making of global capitalism. Though MNCs had made their modern appearance at the end of the nineteenth century, and their importance, led by investments abroad on the part of US corporations, was accelerated in the 1920s, their further development was essentially put on hold for some three decades.

The determining factor behind the explosion of US FDI by the late 1950s lay in the realization by MNCs that the capitalist reconstruction of the European states and their economies had succeeded in establishing the key structural conditions for economic growth and profitable investment. Its timing was associated with the onset of a recession in North America in 1958, but more fundamentally by the formation of the European Community in the Treaty of Rome a year earlier, soon followed by full currency convertibility. US MNCs could now use FDI to jump the EC tariff barrier and have access to the whole European market, while facing no exchange-rate problems in repatriating their profits. US corporations' experience in producing and selling in a continent-wide market at home meant, as an Olivetti executive noted, that "American business has been very quick to grasp the profound meaning of the European integration movement, antici-pating its potentials . . . very much ahead of European competitors."[3] Ford and General Motors, which had been in Europe since the 1920s, had under-stood this especially quickly. This was the basis for Servan-Schreiber's famous lament that, while "Common Market officials are still looking for a law which will permit the creation of European-wide businesses, American firms, with their own headquarters, already form the framework of a real 'Europeanization.'"[4] With the Common Market in place, and with US MNCs able to locate anywhere and sell into all the European countries, their competitive strength was reinforced and nationalist strategies to limit the penetration of US capital were thwarted. Rather than trying to limit the penetration of US capital, European governments competed for American investment, offering special treatment for foreign capital; and they in turn set up tax policies and labor relations regimes more favorable to all capital—domestic and foreign—within their borders.[5]

In 1950 the value of manufacturing trade was still only half that of the global trade in resources; by 1973 it was two-thirds greater. International trade during the 1960s grew 40 percent faster than GDP; but this was outstripped by FDI, which increased twice as fast as GDP.[6] It was significant that manufacturing FDI—as opposed to FDI in resource-extraction and utilities—grew fastest, tripling between 1955 and 1965, and growing two-and-a-half times faster in Europe than in the rest of the world. By the early 1960s twice as much US FDI went to Europe as to Latin America, reversing the historical pattern. Whereas in the mid fifties Europe had received only about a quarter of US manufacturing FDI, by 1966 its share had risen to over 40 percent. By then, the 9,000 US subsidiaries in Europe were not only three times more numerous than a decade earlier, but also on average much larger. With retained earnings accounting for 50 percent of their investment, and with borrowing on European capital markets accounting for another 30 percent, this meant only 20 percent involved an outflow of capital from the US itself.[7]

Although there was widespread emulation of the American corporate model well before the mass arrival of US MNCs, it was the latter development that really drove the competitive self-transformation of European firms. By the end of the 1960s the proportion of firms in the main European countries with US-style corporate share ownership had increased more than threefold, and the adoption of multidivisional administrative structures (allowing centralized investment planning to be combined with decentralized production and distribution) had spread to about 40 percent of the largest firms in France and Germany.[8] These changes encompassed technology and systems of work organization as well as corporate administration, and were an important element in the completion of Europe's "second industrial revolution." US consultancy firms, which first crossed the Atlantic mainly to service US MNCs, quickly became a primary vehicle for spreading the American business zeitgeist. In the course of a few years during the middle of the 1960s, the three dominant US consulting firms doubled their size, and the European profits of McKinsey, the most prominent of the three, grew at an astonishing 69 percent annually (indeed a new verb, "to McKinsey," referring to the complete restructuring of a corporation, entered the lexicon).[9] As business management started to emerge as a university subject in Europe in the 1960s, and new institutions were established (or old ones modified) to focus on this new subject, "the structure, content and pedagogical methods of European management courses were reshaped in line with the new American orthodoxy."[10]

The stage was thus set for the implantation of American capital as a class force inside European social formations, whereby US MNCs' "economic expertise, social norms, and cultural habits [tied] the recipient economies into the broader social totality out of which the investment [had] come."[11] While the European social formations all retained distinctive characteristics, the evolution of their economies "was unmistakably towards the structural model originally pioneered by the USA."[12] The effect this had on the European capitalist classes was profound. Taking Germany as an example, companies like GM, Ford, and IBM became intimately linked with the German capitalist class through the webs of suppliers, banks, distributors, and industrial customers, not to mention the influence of the social ties that developed among them. US and German-based auto companies had a joint interest in getting lower prices from German steel companies, a common concern to counter any protectionist tendencies among smaller German companies, and a general aversion to union wage demands that they perceived as inflationary. Moreover, as German (and other European) firms became more concentrated in the form of large US-style corporations, they also increasingly became oriented to becoming multinational enterprises themselves, including the establishment of a presence in the US. European FDI in the US, marginal before the 1960s, reached a level equal to a third of US investment in Europe by the end of that decade.

Thus, as US corporations penetrated the home space of European corporations, so did the latter become more able and indeed eager to compete with the former inside the US market. From this time on, the growth of European companies in the US was increasingly interpreted as signifying a decline in the material base of US hegemony. But this missed the fact that, as increased competition took the form of two-way cross-border and cross-Atlantic networks of integrated production, European capitalists forged ties with American capitalists both within Europe *and* within the US, which actually reinforced the material foundation of American imperial hegemony. European capitalists no longer constituted "national bourgeoisies" inclined towards anti-American sentiments, let alone towards reviving inter-imperial rivalries. Europe's leading capitalists, as acute observers of such diverse ideological perspectives as Raymond Aron and Nicos Poulantzas already recognized by the early 1970s, were becoming "Canadianized."[13]

From the late 1950s through the 1960s, the expansion of US MNCs was in good part driven by the goal of expanding sales in developed consumer markets, not by the search for resources or cheap labor. On the other hand, while Europe was of great importance to US MNCs because of its potential as a market, Japan, as we saw in the previous chapter, was not, and little effort was made to get the Japanese state to remove restrictions on FDI. Nevertheless, Japanese firms bought and adapted US technology, and increasingly came to emulate US MNCs as they embarked on their own FDI—tentatively until the mid 1970s, but much more confidently thereafter. The deepening of integrated international production came in stages, of course. The lowering of tariffs within Europe at the end of the 1950s had supported GM and Ford's desire to *sell* across Europe, but the actual integration of their production did not occur until later, in part because of ongoing national concerns within Europe to protect the status of each country's own industry. As a study for the United Nations noted, "The process of regional integration started in the 1960s in North America with the free flow of vehicles and components between the United States and Canada while in Europe, Ford and GM began to integrate their operations in the 1970s."[14] What was distinct about the Canadian–US Auto Pact in 1965 was that, unlike Third World national policies to protect or build an auto industry, this agreement accommodated Canadian concerns to retain "safeguards" for production in Canada while moving to take advantage of cross-border specialization and economies of scale (it was not until the late 1970s that Mexico moved towards significant integration into US production).

The increasing interest on the part of US MNCs to produce in many Third World economies was counteracted in the 1960s by the growing economic nationalism that accompanied decolonization and the more general assertion of national sovereignty in the Third World. The standard set down by US Secretary of State Cordell Hull in 1938 that "no government is entitled to expropriate private property, for whatever purpose without provision for prompt, adequate, and effective payment" was accepted by all the advanced capitalist states, and codified in the OECD's adoption in 1961 of the binding *Code of Liberalization of Capital Movements*. But the "Hull Rule," as this principle was known, was increasingly rejected by developing states. The central theme of a speech by US Treasury Secretary Henry Fowler to the International Chamber of Commerce in 1965 was that the experience of US MNCs in Europe showed that "a vast area of potential conflict" could be minimized provided that host states applied "equal treatment under the law for foreign and domestic enterprises," and thus exorcised "the spectre of state confiscation and state operation of competitive units." The role of the US and European governments and international agencies, Fowler insisted, was

> to bring home to governments and people . . . the truth that the multinational corporation cannot and will not play its proper role in developing countries in an institutional environment that accepts state confiscation or state operation of competitive units on an unrestricted basis . . . [This] depends primarily on the willingness of potential host countries to forego voluntarily as a matter of national policy the exercise of the extremes of nationalism, even though within the bounds of national sovereignty.[15]

The widespread disputes over the expropriation of foreign capital, even apart from Cuba, pitted the US against many Third World states from Brazil to Ceylon in the early 1960s. (Notably, Germany at this time inaugurated the modern bilateral investment treaty for investor protection, signing more than forty such treaties in the 1960s.) A US Supreme Court ruling in 1964 that it would not examine the validity of a foreign expropriation of property in the absence of an explicit treaty signed by the states in question spurred the negotiation of the *Convention on the Settlement of Investment Disputes between States and Nationals of Other States* (1965). This established the International Center for the Settlement of Investment Disputes (ICSID) as an arm of the World Bank dedicated to the conciliation of investor-state disputes and to drafting treaties, model clauses, and model laws to stimulate "a larger flow of private international capital into those countries which wish to attract it."[16] The motivation for founding the ICSID was not so much to set down new substantive principles of international law as to provide a "neutral forum" to "depoliticize" and "delocalize" investment-related disputes by giving the states and private parties involved in them some "impartial" direction in selecting among and applying the relevant rules of law.

The ground was being laid here for the international state and legal foundation of what subsequently became known as global neoliberalism. But for the time being the main action in relation to FDI and the internationalization of production remained very much a North American–European affair.

Internationalizing Finance

Another crucial moment in the transition to global capitalism was the City of London's deeper integration into the American empire through the creation of the Eurodollar market. From the time that Keynes led the wartime Lend-Lease negotiations right through to Britain's resistance to the formation of the European Payments Union, the British state had been engaged in a rearguard action to save sterling as a world currency. Throughout the postwar period the Bank of England, despite having been nationalized in 1946, "continued to depend for direction and leadership upon the City's small merchant banking community"; it had not only been anxious to end capital controls and free the City from detailed banking regulation, but also articulated the fervent belief of British "merchant" (i.e. "investment") bankers that the Keynesian commitment to full employment had "prevented London from re-establishing its position as the world's international financial centre."[17] But when sterling was made convertible in the mid 1950s, and its weakness was fully exposed after the Suez debacle (a run on the British pound was aggravated by the US preventing the IMF from lending to the UK, leading to the temporary closure of the City's external sterling loan market), London's merchant bankers—the financial praetorian guard of the old empire—made a bold move to switch allegiance to the US dollar. Employing an accounting loophole in the exchange control regulations, and facilitated by the Bank of England without either approval or oversight by the UK Treasury, the City created a completely unregulated international market for the dollar.[18]

London's Eurodollar market exploded at a time when capital controls were being eased in Western Europe, when the need for financing of increased trade and FDI was becoming pressing, and when the dollar famine in Europe was turning into a dollar glut.[19] For its part, the US government, in the face of its new balance-of-payments problem, was increasingly reluctant to accept the massive outflow of dollars that resulted from foreigners borrowing on Wall Street. Moreover, in the context of currency convertibility, the system of fixed exchange rates made it necessary for Western European governments to have their central banks hold dollar reserves available for possible intervention in foreign exchange markets to maintain the value of their currencies. By the early 1960s they were the main holders of the $3 billion in Eurodollar deposits in London; another large share was held by US corporations. The latter were directed there by their US banks, which could offer higher rates for short-term deposits in London, due to the continuation of New Deal "Regulation Q" ceilings on the interest banks could pay on deposits at home. These banks then imported funds from the Eurodollar market to expand their domestic US operations. The London Eurodollar market, therefore, did not threaten but complemented New York's role as the world's financial center. In fact, American commercial banks quickly came to dominate London's Eurodollar market, so that as early as 1962 the nine most active of them already took most Eurodollar deposits. Furthermore, when in 1963 the Eurobond market was launched in London to tap these dollar deposits, and Eurodollar bond issues rapidly rose from $148 million in 1963 to $2.7 billion in 1970, New York's investment banks moved in to dominate this market too.[20]

The Americanization of the Eurodollar and Eurobond markets was accompanied by the entry of American banks into Europe more generally. Before the war, the branches of American banks had acted mainly as diplomatic outposts for their home offices (as late as 1960 there were only 131 foreign branches of American banks, compared with some 3,600 foreign branches of British banks).[21] But during the 1960s American bank branches became significant financial actors inside Europe. This involved the export of American banking techniques and expertise as US commercial (i.e. deposit, or "high street") banks, which had been barred since the New Deal from investment banking activity at home, started to conduct in Europe the full range of activities requested by their American clients. Like the management consultant firms discussed above, they too were soon wooing European companies, and providing a broad range of services to them as well as to US MNCs.

But none of this could have happened without the way American finance had been developing at home. The dramatic expansion of US domestic financial markets in the 1950s, including an unparalleled degree of integration from coast to coast that culminated in major mergers between New York commercial banks, contrasted starkly with the situation in Europe throughout most of that decade. By the time European countries had recovered sufficiently to restore convertibility, the American financial system had already gone through almost two decades of domestic growth—propelled by industrial recovery, heavy government lending, and the steady integration of ever more layers of the American population into the financial system. In this sense, the origins of the changes that took place in Europe from that time on are best understood not so much in terms of a sudden re-emergence of "global finance," but rather as part of a process through which the postwar growth of American finance assumed international dimensions. The externalization of American practices and institutions, which by the 1960s had begun to create an integrated system of expanding financial markets, would characterize capitalist globalization for the rest of the century—and beyond.

Yet to see this move abroad merely as a means of escaping restrictions at home would be to miss the extent to which US banks were strengthened after the war, even under the New Deal regulations. This had been especially facilitated by the Federal Reserve's shift to running monetary policy through the New York banks' "market-making" in Treasury bonds. As US financial markets became internationalized, the Treasury–Fed–Wall Street money market nexus would become increasingly central to the operation of global finance, and the US domestic securities market would become the most significant international bond market, based on the volume of US Treasury securities it made available to foreign investors. The full achievement of the central role that would ultimately be played in global capitalism by US Treasury bonds depended on the removal of exchange and capital controls abroad, but it depended first of all on the growth of US domestic financial markets. The liquidity of the Treasury bond market was used to extend the geographical and institutional reach of the money market, and also had the subsequent effect of enabling the large banks to invent new financial instruments, such as certificates of deposit, which competed directly with Treasury bills.[22]

The American dollar's role as an internationally secure store of value made "Yankee" bonds (foreign bonds issued in dollars in New York) especially attractive assets—so much so that between 1955 and 1962 they totaled one-and-a-half times the amount of foreign bonds issued in the principal European countries combined. This was a key factor in turning what had been an American dollar shortage in Europe into a dollar glut by the early 1960s.[23] Amid a wave of takeovers and mergers, US banks built on the development of certificates of deposit to establish the securitization of commercial banking—in other words, to encourage customers to shift from depositing money in a bank to buying a tradable financial asset from it. This transformed the role of commercial banking from that of direct credit intermediation (taking deposits from and loaning money to particular customers) to that of mediating the depersonalized interactions of lenders and borrowers in the securities markets.

But as the US financial sector expanded, it increasingly ran up against the 1930s banking regulations. It was not that financial capital had done badly under the New Deal regime, but it had outgrown it through the increasing involvement of both corporations and states in financial markets, and by the deeper penetration of financial relations into the whole society. With the development of the unregulated Eurodollar market and the international expansion of US banks as well as non-financial MNCs, the field of operations of American finance now extended far beyond what was envisaged in the New Deal's regulatory regime. Facilitated by technological innovations in communications, the internationalization of US finance took the form of a competitive push abroad across the full range of financial services, which then rebounded back home in the form of intensified domestic competition. All this strained against the compartmentalization laid down in the Glass–Steagall Act, and was particularly manifested in mounting pressure to remove price controls on brokerage fees for investment banks, as well as the limits on the interest commercial banks could pay on deposits.

The move abroad by US finance was in fact part and parcel of a long process whereby Wall Street would gradually bring the Eurodollar market home, as "the very same practices, strategies and techniques that drove the international expansion of American finance also laid the foundation for its continued domestic expansion."[24] And what this clearly portended was the process of international regulatory arbitrage which would soon become so central to the making of global capitalism, in which less onerous regulations in one financial center (in this case London's Eurodollar market) would be exploited to undermine stronger regulations in another (in this case the US's own New Deal banking regulations).

By the early 1960s, with the securitization of commercial banking and the enormous expansion of investment banking already in train (including Morgan Stanley's creation of the first viable computer model for analyzing financial risk), the erosion of the New Deal's watertight financial compartments was well underway. The creation of bank holding companies (53 in the 1950s, 291 more in the first half the 1960s, and 891 more between 1966 and 1970) was undertaken explicitly to enable banks to develop the legal and market potential to span commercial, investment, insurance, and mortgage functions. The regulation of the new holding companies was assigned to the Federal Reserve, effectively making the Fed a sponsor of the process.

At the same time, the Treasury's Office of Comptroller of the Currency, the traditional regulator of national banks since the 1860s, encouraged a growing concentration in the US's traditionally decentralized commercial banking system by overseeing the growth in the number of local branches attached to large and diversified national banks from 5,296 in 1960 to 12,366 in 1970.[25]

All this was reinforced by the greater incorporation of workers into financial markets as savers as well as borrowers. A dramatic expansion of national interbank credit card networks that had emerged by the mid 1960s was spurred by the new opportunities that computers had opened up.[26] The proliferation of employer-sponsored pensions plans reflected the strength of unions in collective bargaining in the 1960s: fortified by tax advantages for both corporations and workers, pension plan coverage was extended from a fifth of the private sector workforce in 1950 to almost half by 1970 (with even higher coverage in the public sector).[27] Institutional fund managers began to test their strength as powerful new players in the stock market and large owners of corporate assets by challenging the "Regulation Q" interest ceilings and the fixed brokerage fees administered by the corporatist network of regulators and securities dealers through which the older, more established financial institutions had fortified themselves against competition in the 1930s.

This had nothing whatever to do with "pension fund socialism."[28] On the contrary, it had the effect of making the investment banks even more ambitiously competitive and eventually more powerful, both at home and abroad. And the incorporation of workers into the financial system through pension funds further contributed to breaking down the New Deal's compartmentalization of finance, insofar as commercial banks were similarly driven to compete more broadly when faced with the massive volumes of consumer credit that unregulated non-financial firms were providing—so much so that by the early 1970s there was less consumer credit coming from the three largest banking companies than from either the three largest manufacturing firms or the three largest retailers.[29] In a word, both domestically and internationally the baby had outgrown its New Deal–era incubator.

To understand the 1960s properly, and the role of the "baby-boomers" in it, it must not be forgotten that matching the rise of the radical new Left in sociology and history departments of US universities was a new generation of MBAs, "bright and ambitious students . . . paying more attention to business strategy, product development, marketing, and costs, the stuff of business-school curricula."[30] The members of the 1960s generation who were recruited into the expanding financial sector were also oriented to "changing the system," albeit in a very different way from their more radical counterparts—and as it turned out they were rather more successful at it. Some of them also went into the regulatory agencies, adding to the agencies' prestige and confidence. But the agencies were no longer as unchallengeable as before, since economists, lawyers, and accountants now commonly intervened in regulatory debates.

The new breed of regulators themselves did not necessarily call for greater public control, since "the essential feature of the American regulatory system . . . its fusion of the public and private spheres" ensured that not only the financial institutions but also the regulatory agencies themselves became subject to the contradictory pressures that had emerged in the 1960s.[31] Although the SEC itself proved largely immobile until the "big bang" it detonated in the mid 1970s, which wiped away many of the New Deal restrictions on investment banks, other regulatory agencies in the 1960s were among "the most enthusiastic destroyers of the regulatory structure." Thus, while the Treasury's Office of the Comptroller of the Currency underwent considerable expansion, gave a good deal more autonomy to its regional bank examiners, and established its own Research Division staffed by professional economists, the OCC under Kennedy's appointee James J. Saxon became at the same time one of "the main sources of regulatory innovations designed to circumvent restrictions of competition." As early as 1962 an important OCC report contended that maintaining interest-rate ceilings on bank deposits contradicted the "free market" in government bonds that had been permitted since 1951 under the Treasury-Fed Accord.[32]

For its part, the Justice Department by 1968 had also "put the full weight of its institutional prestige, and of anti-trust ideology behind the public critique of the anti-competitive character" of the New Deal regulatory system, and secured very broad support for this, "from Chicago-style efficient market theorists to leading Keynesians like Samuelson."[33] This broad reaffirmation of faith in the virtues of competition in the financial sector, even among those who supported the growth of the state and its regulatory agencies, was also an important foretaste of the subsequent neoliberal turn of the American state in the making of global capitalism.

Detaching from Bretton Woods

Given how much it was the internationalizing of the New Deal that was responsible for the Bretton Woods framework, it was hardly surprising that the two should have been beset by contradictions at the same time. The internationalization of production as well as finance by the 1960s increasingly made it difficult to distinguish between "productive" and "speculative" capital flows. The IMF and World Bank, which had not been able to play much of a role in addressing the dollar shortage of the previous period, found that new problems once again overwhelmed their capacities. Insofar as they played any significant role, it was at the grace of the US Treasury and Federal Reserve, which were in any case mainly concerned to establish new arenas for cooperation with the central banks and finance ministries of the "G10" advanced capitalist states (Belgium, Canada, France, Germany, Italy, Japan, Sweden, Switzerland, the UK, and the US).

In the face of the build-up of dollar surpluses in Europe, the central policy dilemma for both the American and the European states became how to maintain the system of fixed exchange rates that revolved around the dollar without jeopardizing both economic growth and the momentum towards liberalized trade and capital flows. This dilemma had already been registered in the "dollar crisis" of 1960 that roiled both the outgoing Eisenhower and the incoming Kennedy administrations. As the US presidential election approached, speculation on the private gold market in London pushed the price to $40 an ounce. This forced Kennedy to pledge to maintain the value of the dollar at $35 an ounce in order to reassure European central bankers that any commitment to a more Keynesian growth strategy would not endanger monetary stability. This became the central issue of international finance during the 1960s, with significant effects on the American state itself.

In the past the Fed had "paid almost no attention to international conditions in the formulation of the country's monetary policy";[34] but by 1960 "the US Government relied increasingly on the Federal Reserve System, and on the New York Fed in particular, to play critical roles in managing the international monetary system."[35] It was significant that the Fed's active engagement in international economic policy in the 1960s took place through giving a larger role to the international network of central bankers whose very displacement had been the original goal of Keynes and White when they set out on the path to shifting responsibility for international finance to elected governments at Bretton Woods. The Federal Reserve Bank of New York now became more closely involved with the Bank for International Settlements, which as we saw in the previous chapter had been resurrected to play the central role in overseeing the European Payments Union. After the EPU was wound up, with the implementation of exchange convertibility in 1958, the BIS found a new role for itself as the arena where the central bankers, not just of Europe but of all the advanced capitalist states, came together to work out the politics of international finance. As David Andrews has insightfully put it: "Allowing the central banking community to return to prominence created a more conducive regulatory environment for the progressive liberalization of capital movements."[36]

This involvement of the Fed with the BIS included its staff participating from December 1960 in the central bankers' monthly meetings in Basel. The US Treasury had formerly opposed this, but now quietly approved, since it did not amount to any diminution of the Treasury's role in international finance. To the contrary, that role was enhanced, highlighted by the movement of key personnel from the State Department to the Treasury.

Douglas Dillon, the prominent Wall Street Republican investment banker who became Kennedy's new Treasury secretary, oversaw the conversion of the OEEC in 1961 into the OECD, which gave the US and Canada permanent membership in the most important European economic policy forum. Robert Roosa, widely considered the foremost US expert on international financial issues, was moved from vice president of the New York Fed to undersecretary for monetary affairs at the Treasury. He brought with him the young Paul Volcker, who would later occupy the same position in the Nixon administration, before President Carter appointed him chairman of the Federal Reserve at the end of the 1970s.[37]

The Treasury was the pivot of the "Quadriad" that brought it together with the heads of the Federal Reserve, the Council of Economic Advisers, and the Office of Management and Budget in the White House, as well as a wider range of interagency councils and staff groups that regularly met "to facilitate the exchange of views and the coordination of policy."[38] It was also the pivot of the creation of a new institutional infrastructure for the internationalization of the advanced capitalist states, as the Treasury shifted "from a passive role to an active role in international transactions involving dollars and gold"—a shift explicitly designed to ensure that, in Dillon's words, "the US should continue as banker for the rest of world."[39] This started in early 1962 when, at the Treasury's initiative, the G10 was unofficially designated a "club of countries that had assumed special responsibilities for the system." Finance ministry and central bank officials from these countries began to meet as frequently as every six weeks under the auspices of the OECD, in "an intimate setting where senior officials with responsibility for their governments' policies would frankly review economic and political developments within their countries, consider the implications for international markets, explain their own policies, and even hint at future policy plans." As Paul Volcker further noted:

> These people were not politicians; they mainly had long careers in government. They all had an unusual sense of commitment and common purpose, and they built up a reserve of mutual trust that paid off later in an ability to reach quick decisions. Occasionally they would . . . prepare a formal letter for transmission to one government or another, typically in support of appropriately restrictive policies that might be politically unpalatable. It would be written in close consultation with the officials from the recipient country, who felt it would be useful at home to have a message of international concern and support delivered to the head of their government.[40]

The concrete measures adopted in light of such discussions to deal with the top item on the agenda in the early 1960s on which the endangered fixed-rate currency exchange system depended—the defense of the dollar—were both "permanent" and "temporary." The General Agreement to Borrow and IMF Special Drawing Rights were permanent; the London gold pool to stabilize the official price at $35 an ounce, and the issuance of "Roosa bonds" by the Treasury to guarantee against a devaluation of the dollar, were designed as temporary. Roosa called all of these the "rings of outer and inner defenses for the dollar and the system."[41] In fact, in the decades to come, long after fixed rates had been abandoned, the "swap networks" that the US Treasury and Federal Reserve developed at this time to coordinate interventions by the advanced capitalist states in foreign exchange markets would become central to achieving the much broader goal of defending the system of global capitalism in the face of economic and financial crises.

As far as the Kennedy administration was concerned, while coordinating international interventions to stabilize the dollar was certainly necessary, the more fundamental solution to the problem lay in promoting US firms' export competitiveness amid freer trade. It was on this premise that the US administration enacted the domestic Keynesian stimulus recommended by the new Council of Economic Advisers. The 1962 Trade Expansion Act gave the administration the authority to negotiate a 50 percent across-the-board reduction in tariffs, and created the Office of the Special Trade Representative in advance of the opening of the 1963–67 Kennedy GATT Round. It also effectively introduced one of the most important changes in US foreign aid policy by requiring that food aid in the form of agricultural exports be treated as loans to be paid for in US dollars. As the percentage of US agricultural exports that was outright food aid decreased from some 35 percent in the early 1960s to around 5 percent by 1970, this was a powerful inducement to Third World countries to turn to foreign direct investment and export-oriented development strategies in order to try to secure dollars to pay off food loans.[42]

The initial hope was that these measures, taken together, would solve the dollar problem by as early as the mid 1960s.[43] Yet the impact that foreign direct investment was having on the growing US balance-of-payments deficit proved too great to be ignored. A 1961 proposal to end the deferral of tax on the foreign profits of American MNCs was universally opposed by business.[44] The Treasury then turned instead to securing the passage of the 1963 Interest Equalization Tax (IET), designed to tax capital outflows. Such an intervention into what were already increasingly integrated capital markets was bound to run into all kinds of problems. Since, as Volcker explained, "short-term capital flows were too numerous and served too many essential purposes, such as financing exports, to make a transactions tax feasible," the IET exempted foreign borrowings of less than three years' maturity, as well as all lending to American subsidiaries. By the time the legislation made its way through international negotiations that exempted

Canada as well as Japan, it offered "a neophyte Treasury deputy undersecretary" like Paul Volcker "a very good lesson about how difficult, messy,
and arbitrary controls can be."[45] The controls did dissuade Europeans from
borrowing funds in the US, but at the same time encouraged the even more
rapid entry of US banks into the Eurodollar markets—not least to attract
dollar funds back to the US. This did help the balance of payments, but at
the cost of undermining domestic interest ceilings and making the management of monetary policy at home much more difficult.

Insofar as there was a long-term American strategy to deal with this, it
was to further open and deepen European capital markets. In fact, the
Treasury's support for the Eurodollar market in London reflected its belief
that the capital outflow from the US was caused by the insufficient liberalization of domestic capital markets across Europe. Securing this was seen as
the most necessary next step in the making of global capitalism. The
Treasury especially used the Working Groups established under the OECD's
1961 Code of Liberalization of Capital Movements to push for further liberalization.[46] Since the complete opening, let alone deepening, of European
capital markets could not be brought about in the short term, the Treasury
soon moved beyond the interest-equalization tax to the voluntary controls
on capital outflows it introduced in 1965. This was not designed to stop US
MNCs' expansion abroad, but rather to force a shift in the locus of financing for this expansion to European capital markets.

The effect of these policies was to encourage the further development of
integrated international financial markets. But they also aggravated speculation against the dollar in view of the prevailing assumption, both in those
markets and among economists, that only the achievement of US trade
surpluses could make the dollar secure. Charles Kindleberger was one of the
few economists who understood as early as the mid 1960s that the new
developments in FDI and financial flows meant that the US international
accounts needed to be conceived not in terms of trade and its imbalances
but in terms of the role of the US as "the world's banker."[47] So long as
capital markets in Europe were "much less well organized . . . and just plain
smaller than in the United States," the dollar reserves and accounts held by
foreign central banks as well as private actors (whether in London or New
York) could be seen as the equivalent of short-term bank deposits, while
US FDI and long-term bonds denominated in dollars could be seen as the
equivalent of bank loans which would generate income over time. And
rather than see their currencies appreciate relative to the dollar, the European
countries were more likely to hold on to dollar assets, and even buy more
(as would also prove to be the case with Japan, and eventually China too),
whether the peg to gold was maintained or not.

By 1969 even Robert Roosa had come rather close to publicly embracing this understanding of the US role in globalizing capitalism.[48] But whereas

the implication of Kindleberger's argument was "to let gold go," Roosa still reflected the reluctance of the Kennedy, Johnson *and* Nixon administrations to take this route. The main reason for this was the belief that to do so would be seen as a narrowly nationalist move, and thus strike a blow to the hegemonic role the US had played in the launching of global capitalism. Yet, as Kindleberger argued, such a move could "reasonably be interpreted as internationalist. It would enable the United States to preserve the international capital market."[49] This would indeed prove to be the case, especially as the further expansion of capital and securities markets in subsequent decades would attract not only short-term but even long-term capital to the US. For this to occur, however, the American state would be required, as we shall see in the next chapter, to provide the kind of ironclad guarantee against inflation that only came with the Federal Reserve's Volcker shock at the end of the 1970s.

What made such a guarantee so long in coming was the fact that behind the tensions over the dollar and the management of balance-of-payments accounts lay a set of deeper contradictions arising from both the successes of, and yet at the same time the changing balance of class forces within, all the advanced capitalist countries. As capitalism outgrew the cradle of Bretton Woods it ran up against the labor militancy as well as the popular social movements that attended the full employment conditions of the 1960s. The fact that labor markets in Europe had turned tighter by the early 1960s laid the basis for considerable class conflict over distribution, which later intensified and led to the strike explosion that occurred across Europe at the end of the decade.

In the early 1960s, when US unemployment was still relatively high, the Treasury thought wage and price inflation in Europe would allow US exports to increase sufficiently by mid-decade to ameliorate the balance-of-payments problems.[50] But the cumulative impact of Kennedy's Keynesian-inspired tax cuts, Johnson's Great Society social programs, and the ramping up of the Vietnam War led to a spike in growth and lowered the unemployment rate in 1966 to below 4 percent for the first time since the Korean War. Now US inflation rates also began an inexorable rise, and US corporations began to feel the effect of greater competitive pressures on their profits when they tried to compensate for labor militancy by raising prices.

In fact, every advanced capitalist state now had to deal with this central problem of class relations, as governments were more and more drawn to containing inflationary pressures by wooing trade unions into corporatist arrangements for wage restraint.[51] The first key instance of this was in the UK when—as part of its defense of sterling, and strongly urged on by a US government which feared that speculative pressures would spill over to the dollar—the British Labour government turned its incomes policy (initially promoted as one element in overall economic planning) into a statutory wage freeze. Even with considerable cooperation from the union leadership, this defense proved futile in the face of hostility from British bankers to any sort of planning and the growing openness of the City of London to international finance. This finally led, in late 1967, to the devaluation of the pound.[52]

In Germany, strikes under full-employment conditions heralded renewed class conflict for the first time since the war—the head of Germany's largest union, IG Metall, called the employers' use of lockouts "class warfare waged from above."[53] The Bundesbank's traditional opposition to Keynesianism—underscored by its concern that the Social Democrats (in government from the mid 1960s) would go too far in this direction in exchange for union wage restraint—made it especially wary of the inflationary implications of US policies that might "subordinate the pursuit of price and exchange rate stability to other goals."[54] Sustaining the mark–dollar exchange rate and containing inflation at home amid the massive trade surpluses generated by Germany's export-led growth strategy required the Bundesbank to engage in massive purchases of dollars, yet by the end of the decade it was forced to revalue. In France, where low union density and Communist strength in the labor movement ruled out cooperation on incomes policies, de Gaulle tried to return to the gold standard as a way of imposing austerity at home—which had the added attraction, for him, of undermining the dollar internationally. In the end this led nowhere: in May 1968, when he granted a huge wage increase in order to derail a general strike and seduce labor away from the revolutionary ambitions of the students, he effectively acknowledged that the gold standard would have denied him the flexibility to do this. Before long, even the French state "stopped daydreaming about a return to gold."[55]

But the focal point for the handling of the class contradictions besetting all the advanced capitalist states lay in the US itself. The panic over the dollar at the time of the 1960 US election was not unrelated to the long steelworkers' strike that had only ended at the beginning of that year. The price and wage guidelines that accompanied the somewhat Keynesian inclinations of the new Kennedy administration had little long-term effect in dampening worker militancy—the annual total of days lost to strikes more than tripled from the first to the second half of the decade. Meanwhile President Johnson's Great Society programs (explicitly designed to dampen racial and class conflict) brought about a doubling of public social expenditures between 1963 and 1969, increasing even faster than military expenditures.[56] Both the domestic and the international pressures at work as US inflationary pressures increased were clearly revealed with the brief eruption in 1966 of the first financial crisis in the US since World War II. "Regulation Q" ceilings on what banks could pay to attract deposits had stayed above average market interest rates from 1933 to 1965. As the banks strained harder against the ceilings—and when the Federal Reserve did not raise them sufficiently to keep up with the rate of inflation but instead imposed higher reserve requirements on the banks—the New York bond market seized up for a two-week period in August 1966.

The alleged problem was the Federal Reserve's apparent "lack of independence" from what were seen as the Keynesian proclivities of the Treasury and Council of Economic Advisers; but what the banks were really upset about was that the Fed was showing signs of excessive independence from Wall Street. Indeed, the Fed's action was partly a response to pressure from small banks that relied on "Regulation Q" ceilings to allow them to compete against the big commercial banks for deposits. To be sure, the Fed's reluctance to tighten monetary policy too much was important in supporting the Treasury's role in facilitating—through the relatively low interest it needed to pay on Treasury bonds—the cheap funding of the Vietnam War and the Johnson administration's Great Society expenditures. It was only after President Johnson made very public and very explicit assurances that the Federal Reserve's autonomy would not be compromised that the crisis ended, with the Fed further guaranteeing the New York banks "unhindered access to the Eurodollar market in competing for funds."[57] It also ameliorated the big banks' displeasure by applying "Regulation Q" ceilings to savings and loans firms as well as banks (albeit at a higher level that still protected their deposits from too much big bank competition). But all this indicated the extent to which the Fed was by now "pursuing several, often incompatible, objectives simultaneously."[58]

The inability to stem the inflationary pressures and balance-of-payments deficits of the mid 1960s, combined with the impact on US gold reserves of the British devaluation in late 1967, finally pushed the Johnson administration into imposing statutory controls on the outflow of capital in 1968, for the first time since World War II. Once again, not only the Chicago School but also many Keynesian economists vociferously opposed this on the grounds that it undermined the liberal international economic order that Bretton Woods had been designed to foster. Writing in the *Wall Street Journal*, John Kenneth Galbraith declared: "[T]he fruits of great strenuous private efforts and of the most carefully conceived public policy extending over the last several decades are about to be extinguished."[59] Although Galbraith complained of the weakness of American business in failing to stop the controls program, Wall Street's reaction to them (like that of the central bankers in Europe) was to demand instead higher American interest rates to cope with the problem, and these were indeed instituted in the Fed by 1969, as we shall see in the next chapter.

The argument has been made in retrospect that the US government's adoption of capital controls at this time proves that "finance was clearly weak" in the 1960s.[60] This is extremely misleading. Not only does this fail to address the growing material strength and international reach of US financial capital (as shown in its very high profits in the latter half of the 1960s despite the move from voluntary to mandatory capital controls); it also fails to put this in the context of the trajectory of the longer-term development of policy and further strengthening of finance in the subsequent decades. In fact, the Treasury certainly regarded the controls as only a temporary measure, and administered them in such a way as to allow for massive exemptions (their main effect, once again, was to deepen the insertion of US corporations and banks into the Eurodollar market). This aspect of the controls program actually led the new Republican administration, despite Nixon's vociferous opposition to it in the 1968 election campaign, to keep the controls program going into the early 1970s.

But in the face of the huge amounts of private foreign debt and volatile short-term capital movements that resulted from the ever more substantive integration of European and American capital markets, the balancing act involved in trying to maintain fixed exchange rates became increasingly difficult. Just as the temporary US capital controls were a response to the strength of finance as speculation built up around possible adjustments in interest rates to cope with the emergence of simultaneous recessionary and inflationary pressures in both Europe and the US, so coordinated central bank interventions to protect fixed exchange rates became more and more onerous. The basis was laid for the dollar crisis of August 1971 and the final abandonment of the Bretton Woods system.[61]

And just as the US Treasury had been central to the establishment of new forums and mechanisms for the international management of the "dollar crisis" within the Bretton Woods framework, so was it now central to that framework's dismantling. This did not involve withdrawing from the multilateral management of the contradictions and tensions in the Bretton Woods institutions, but rather bringing into play—as the US inexorably moved towards breaking the dollar's link to gold—all the links the Treasury and the Fed had developed with other states' finance ministries and central banks. Inside the Treasury itself, the fate of Bretton Woods appeared to come to rest in the large hands of Paul Volcker. He had left the Treasury for three years to do the obligatory stint on Wall Street required of senior civil servants in the American state's financial apparatus, and now, despite being a Democrat, he was recruited to take on the post of undersecretary of the Treasury for monetary affairs under Nixon, where from 1969 to 1971 Volcker "for all practical purposes *was* Treasury."[62]

When in August 1971, after two years of trying to "muddle through," the Nixon administration finally terminated the dollar's link with gold, the decision was tentative and uncertain. It reflected a Treasury policy stance on international monetary reform which often appeared "schizophrenic"—as was indeed epitomized by Volcker, who "could never quite make up his mind . . . [S]ome days he would lean one way and some days another."[63]

There was so much reluctance to detach from Bretton Woods precisely because it had been the framework in which unprecedented economic success had been achieved, both at home and globally. Moreover, as a 1969 report on "Basic Options in International Monetary Affairs" issued by the key interdepartmental committee chaired by Volcker put it, "The available funding for our deficits has permitted the United States to carry out heavy overseas military expenditures and to undertake other foreign commitments, and to retain substantial flexibility for domestic economic policy." So while seeking "a substantial degree of US control" of the intense, often secret negotiations with France, Germany, and the UK during the crisis (even Japan at this time was kept out of the "inner circle" of the G10), Volcker was careful not to play this up too much: "[I]n the interests of facilitating international harmony the appearance of US hegemony should not be sought."[64]

What was mainly at stake for the US was its ability to attract foreign capital to cover its deficit while also continuing to export capital and encourage other states to allow for this. This would indeed prove a crucial condition for the continuation, and indeed acceleration, of a globalizing capitalism under the auspices of the US empire for the rest of the century. But, as we shall see, the factors determining whether this would prove possible were to be found in domestic class relations and the state's attempt to cope with their effects, rather than in the twists and turns of international negotiations. Between the first and second halves of the decade, as the average inflation rate increased from 1.3 percent to 5.1 percent, domestic class tensions increasingly overlapped with pressures from abroad for US "economic discipline"—even though the average US inflation rate for the decade as a whole was actually no higher than in the main European countries and Japan. What was expected of the US, precisely because the dollar and Treasury securities were now so central to international calculations of value, was that US inflation would be kept lower than in the other advanced capitalist states. The Bretton Woods fixed exchange rate system finally had to be abandoned because it became more and more of a drag on the American state's capacity to navigate between its domestic and imperial responsibilities.

6

Structural Power Through Crisis

There was no little irony in Richard Nixon's intoning, in 1971, of the phrase Milton Friedman had coined in 1965—"We are all Keynesians now"—just as the crisis of Keynesianism was becoming most visible.[1] By the early 1970s the contradictions that the successes of the 1960s had produced came to a head. In the midst of a crisis of corporate profitability and financial instability, the simultaneous rise of both inflation and unemployment ("stagflation") confounded any consistent application of fiscal and monetary policy not only in the US, but in all the advanced capitalist states. There was also a "fiscal crisis of the state": public expenditures systematically outran revenues, as governments tried to cope with many of the increased costs of capital accumulation and of social services, as well as the growing costs of legitimating and policing an inherently inegalitarian social order.[2] The class conflict underlying the crisis of Keynesianism was seen not only in the industrial militancy of the period, but also in the rise of new social movements that fueled rising social expenditures. If "in the 1950s Keynesianism seemed to have erected a decisive barrier to the advance of socialism," as Keynes's biographer Robert Skidelsky would later put it, "the subsequent identification of Keynesianism with a disproportionate growth in the public sector accompanied by growing labor militancy was crucial in destroying the psychological or *expectational* function of the Keynesian revolution—the belief that it would make the world safe for capitalism and capitalists."[3]

The crisis of Keynesianism also coincided with a crisis of US imperial power in relation to the Third World. To be sure, the fact the revolutions in Cuba and Vietnam did not have a "domino effect" was in good part due to US support for the dictatorships that emerged in Asia and Latin America (the first epitomized by the mass annihilation of Indonesia's Communists in 1965, the latter by the military coup in Chile against the Allende government in 1973), as well as to the opportunities given by the Vietnam War to several East Asian capitalist countries to kick-start their export drive into US markets. Nevertheless, the growth of economic nationalism, which Treasury Secretary Fowler had identified in 1965 as the main threat to global capitalism, was increasingly unmistakable: the average number of expropriations of foreign investments per year in Third World countries increased from eight in the first half of the 1960s to seventeen in the second half. And when such expropriations jumped to an average of fifty-six per year between 1970 and 1975, the regime of international property rules of which the US had been "the principal guarantor" in the postwar period looked very shaky indeed.[4]

In this situation it was hardly surprising that the breakdown of Bretton Woods appeared to signal not only the "downfall of the dollar" but the "end of multilateral liberal internationalism," the "erosion of US hege-mony" and even the return of "interimperial rivalry."[5] Such apocalyptic interpretations were misplaced. What was particularly significant, especially in the context of the challenge from the Third World coinciding with the crisis of Keynesianism, was actually the further integration of European, Japanese and American capital, as well as intensive cooperation between the European and Japanese states and the American state. In this context, it was a mistake to see the economic relations between the major capitalist states at this time in terms of US pro-market ideas clashing with European and Japanese interventionist ones.[6]

What was also not understood by those who saw the decline in the US share of global GDP from 35 percent in 1950 to 27 percent in 1970 as evidence that the material base of US hegemony had already disappeared, was that the project for a global capitalism was always predicated on reviving the other capitalist economies and their capitalist classes.[7] Moreover, although the European and Japanese economies had certainly narrowed the gap with the US on various indicators, the notion that they had "caught up" was mislead-ing; the US economy was not standing still in terms of technological leadership, as the computer revolution was soon to prove. This was also the case with the derivatives revolution in the financial sector in the 1970s.

The continuing predominance of the dollar in the new era of flexible exchange rates could not have been realized without the increased role played by the American state, and its restructuring to accommodate this role. What was evident here was that, just as the process of market deregulation to promote greater competition was beginning to be registered across the world's financial centers, an increasing involvement in international financial activi-ties was also being undertaken and coordinated among the advanced capitalist states. The US Treasury's efforts, in particular, to sustain and develop a common purpose and solidarity along these lines among the finance officials of the core advanced capitalist states was also related, as we shall see, to its successful efforts in turning back the challenge that Third World economic nationalism posed at the time for the IMF and World Bank. But this did not involve—as so many misinterpreted the emergence of the G7 as represent-ing—the dawn of a new trilateral capitalist order *displacing* the US's postwar hegemony. On the contrary, the G7 was essentially "a vehicle for providing support and endorsement for US-generated initiatives and ideas."[8] Nevertheless, it was a measure of the severity of the crisis of the 1970s that it took a whole decade to realign the balance of class forces both domestically and internationally so as to exit the crisis in a way that left the American-led globalizing dynamic of capitalism not only intact, but strengthened.

Class, Profits and Crisis

It is generally agreed that a crucial factor in the crisis of the 1970s was a decline in manufacturing rates of profit. During the 1950s there had been a gradual decline in profitability from the very high levels of the immediate postwar years, but American capitalism's "success story" had especially been registered in a profit spike from 1964 to 1966. By 1970, however, the US rate of profit was already down 40 percent from the high level of the mid 1960s, and, more significantly, a third below the average of the period from the mid 1950s to the mid 1960s.[9] (In Europe, where there was no comparable profit spike in the mid 1960s, profits continued a steady downward trend from their very high postwar rates.) The response of corporations was to increase their rate of investment: the amount of capital invested by non-financial US corporations grew at the historically high rate of 4.3 percent (adjusted for inflation) per year between 1967 and 1973, compared with an average of 3.1 percent over the years 1949–66.[10]

The vigorous corporate investment strategies this represented were designed to increase productivity so as to cope with competitive and inflationary pressures. But the productivity gains secured were not commensurate with the level of capital investment undertaken, resulting in falling "capital efficiency" (see Figure 6.1). The consequence was that, far from sustaining the spurt in profits achieved in the mid 1960s, the decline in profits was aggravated. This was also true in Europe, where the rate of investment was even higher than in the US.[11]

This decline in output per unit of capital, which was a crucial element in the "profit squeeze" in this period, alongside the pressures of rising wages and increased competition, was closely linked to class conflict in the workplace.[12] Working classes in the advanced capitalist countries were not strong enough (nor always inclined) to stop the technological and managerial reorganization of work that accompanied the high rate of investment, but they were nevertheless capable of a degree of resistance that impeded the optimal implementation and utilization of the new investments.[13] A new generation of workers, sharing the anti-authoritarianism of a rising counter-culture, rejected both the dreariness of their jobs and the pace of work, and thus posed a barrier to capital efficiency. This was above all manifested in the US autoworkers' rebellion against their "gold-plated sweatshops." "There is a new breed of workers in the plant who is less willing to accept corporate

decisions that pre-empt his own decisions," the UAW president Walter
Reuther noted, while also acknowledging that union leaders were themselves perplexed by "a different kind of worker than we had twenty-five or
thirty years ago."[14] In both Europe and the US there was an explosion in the
number of strikes over the reorganization of work, including what this
meant in terms of speeding up production lines and managerial abuse of
overtime as well as other unilateral reversals of past practice, all of which
had further implications for health and safety.[15] That so many of the work
stoppages were local and "unofficial" or "wildcat" reflected the workplace-
based nature of the frustrations.

Figures 6.1: Capital Efficiency (GDP/Capital Stock)

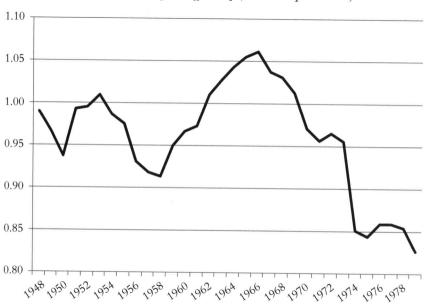

Source: US Bureau of Economic Analysis, NIPA Table 1.15 and Fixed Assets Accounts Table 1.1
(net private non-residential capital stock).

Corporate concern with workplace control was indicated by an explosion of articles in business journals and speeches at business forums that
addressed the integration of workers into the production process and also,
most notably, by the not-uncommon practice of offering higher wages as
a trade-off for workplace peace. Beyond trying to win worker cooperation through higher compensation (including not only wage increases but
also increases in benefits—which unions increasingly emphasized in
collective bargaining), corporations tried to develop buffers that minimized the impact of disruptions, such as larger inventories and deliberate

excess capacity—measures that came, however, with higher overall capital costs.[16] In general, the capital costs incurred in the investment drive of the late 1960s and early 1970s could not yield the kind of productivity growth that would be achieved by the widespread application of computerization to industry in the 1990s. This was not only because of worker resistance, but because the type of investments that were possible at the time still mainly involved variations on the technological paradigms developed for industry in the 1930s and 1940s, and by the 1960s these had reached their limits in terms of new productivity growth.

No less significantly, while productivity failed to rise fast enough, workers were generally able to prevent capital from compensating for this at the expense of wages and benefits, despite some concessions by union leaders (such as some large US unions forgoing cost-of-living adjustments in the 1968 bargaining round). The rank-and-file militancy that had emerged with full employment in the early to mid 1960s, together with the increased consumption expectations fostered by the burgeoning advertising industry, had reached new heights by the end of the 1960s. Whether wage demands were chasing inflation or causing it probably varied from country to country, and from economic quarter to economic quarter; the crucial point is that worker resistance was a significant factor in preventing the restoration of both higher profit rates and a higher profit share of national income. This increase in the worker share and the rapid increase in the social expenditures during this period, in addition to the limits worker militancy placed on further productivity improvements (see Table 6.1) makes it clear that what happened to profits cannot be understood apart from the heightened class struggles of the late 1960s and early 1970s.[17]

Table 6.1: Productivity and Compensation 1965–73

Percentage Annual Average Growth	
Productivity (Business Sector)	2.5
Real wages	1.5
Real compensation (CPI)*	2.5
Real compensation (PPI)**	3.1
*Adjusted by Consumer Price Index ** Adjusted by Producer Price Index	

Source: Economic Report of the President, 2005, Tables B-49, B-47, B-65. "Compensation" refers to wages plus benefits.

It was a measure of the contradictions involved that attempts by the American state to rein in inflationary pressures at this time only compounded the problem. The fiscal restraint introduced in 1968 put a brake on Johnson's "Great Society" initiatives even before the end of his administration. But the hope that this would obviate a turn by the Federal Reserve to higher interest rates was dashed by a rate of inflation that, by the end of 1968, had risen above 5 percent. In this context, the inauguration of Nixon, who was explicitly committed to lowering inflation even at the expense of allowing unemployment to rise above 4 percent, allowed the Fed to give top priority to defeating what its chairman, William McChesney Martin, called the "credibility gap over our capacity and willingness to maintain restraint."[18] Indeed, in going so far as to raise "the ghost of overkill" by increasing its key funds rate to 9 percent by the beginning of 1970, and touching off the first recession in a decade, the Fed seemed ready to do what in fact it would only do a decade later with the Volcker shock. But on this occasion it quickly and drastically reversed direction: its funds rate was reduced through the course of 1970 by five full points.

The monetarists' explanation of this volte-face as being due to the Fed's lack of autonomy from the Nixon government and its short-term electoral calculations would leave a powerful ideological imprint, expressed as a generalized clarion call for "central bank independence"—a call that would become the touchstone for the restructuring of all states in the context of capitalist globalization. Yet what this episode really demonstrated was how trapped central banks had become by precisely the rapid development of financial markets which they had encouraged. With the realization that a tightening of monetary policy was having the effect of inducing a financial crisis, the central bank's role as lender of last resort to keep the financial system afloat trumped the commitment to monetary restraint. Indeed, the deep structural relationship between the Fed and Wall Street could not but be affected by the new volatility of financial markets—all the more so since major non-financial corporations were also increasingly embedded in those markets. In a development not unlike what would happen on an even larger scale in the 1990s, the trading of shares in the New York Stock Exchange, fueled by the new mutual fund industry, gave rise to a degree of asset inflation that more than matched the price inflation of the late 1960s, and bore little relation to actual or potential earnings from stocks.

This was taking place, moreover, as the debt of corporations rose steeply through the latter half of the decade. Neither the massive capital investments by corporations in the late 1960s nor the wave of mergers at the time were funded by retained earnings, or by bank loans, but by raising funds through the commercial paper market. It was already a symptom of the contradictions the New Deal banking regulations were running into, given inflation and the expansion and internationalization of finance by the 1960s, that the "Regulation Q" limits on the interest banks could pay on deposits were leading large depositors to secure higher returns by investing in the rapidly expanding market for commercial paper. What was involved here was the massive issuance of short-term corporate bonds by both financial and non-financial companies, some of which had "very high debt-to-equity ratios and income flows of dubious quality."[19] Their widespread take-up reflected little capacity on the part of the financial markets to distinguish good paper from bad (it was not until 1971 that Moody's bond-rating agency began to grade commercial paper). This meant that when the Fed deliberately changed the financial markets' entire risk structure by dramatically increasing short-term rates throughout 1969 and into 1970, the "ghost of overkill" ceased to be ghostly, and in June 1970 claimed the largest bankruptcy in US history to date, when Congress refused Nixon's attempt to secure a $200 million dollar bailout for Penn Central Transportation Company, the country's sixth-largest corporation, and its largest owner of real estate.

As Penn Central's bankruptcy loomed, and as it also became clear that Goldman Sachs had continued to sell the company's commercial paper even while being well aware of its difficulties, fears spread that other corporations, from Chrysler to IBM, might similarly be unable to raise the cash to turn over their debt.[20] What made the situation worse was that such "blue chip" companies were unable to obtain credit from the commercial banks to cover their loans, because the shift to securitization had produced a massive drop in the banks' liquidity even as their profits and dividends climbed through the 1960s.[21] The *Wall Street Journal* went so far as to warn that a Penn Central insolvency would likely have domino effects that would turn "the present severe strain on the cash resources of banks and corporations into a liquidity crisis, draining the flow of money and credit and plunging the nation into a depression."[22]

It was in response to this "serious threat to financial stability" that Martin's newly appointed successor as chair of the Fed, Arthur Burns, oversaw a shift from what he described as "the policy of extreme restraint followed in 1969" to one designed to meet "the precautionary demands for liquidity" generated by the commercial paper crisis. He did so by opening the "discount window" through which banks could borrow directly from the Fed to meet temporary shortages in cash reserves, and by suspending "Regulation Q" ceilings on the interest they were allowed to pay on their large certificates of deposit. The Fed thus poured liquidity into the banking system not to overcome a bank panic, as had been its traditional remit, but—as would become all too familiar in later decades—in order to defuse a "disruptive liquidity crisis" in a particular non-bank market.[23] It was this conflict within monetary policy, more than the concern to ensure the re-election of Nixon (as Burns's critics alleged), that led to the Fed's about-face in 1970.[24] As Burns himself put it, "the financial community was reassured that the Federal Reserve understood the seriousness of the situation, and that it would stand ready to use its intellectual and financial resources, as well as its instruments of monetary policy, to assist the financial markets through any period of stress."[25]

Notably—if unsurprisingly, given that the Fed's prime concern was to get the large banks to furnish cash to corporations that were unable to sell their corporate bonds—the relaxation of "Regulation Q" ceilings was not extended to the small deposits of the savings and loans companies. Coming at a time when they were subject to intense new competition from Real Estate Investment Trusts, which were offering investors short-term securities at high rates of return, this threatened to shift capital away from the savings and loans companies into the interbank money market, dramatically curtailing their capacity for long-term mortgage lending.[26]

This was especially significant given that one major response to the urban riots of the mid 1960s, drawing on the long-standing identification of home-ownership as contributing to social stability, had been to answer the cry of "Burn, baby, burn," with "Build, baby, build," as one prominent mortgage banker put it.[27] The extension of mortgage credit to marginalized communities—rather than the renewal and massive extension of public housing—would become the central means of coping with inequality in the decades to come. The basis for the subprime crisis needs to be dated all the way back to this moment. It was in this context that Fannie Mae (the Federal National Mortgage Association, semi-privatized in 1968) stepped in to underpin the mortgage market by creating the first secondary mortgage securities. Domestic and foreign investors who were not interested in coping with the details of specific mortgages could now invest in these new universalized paper (but asset-backed) commodities. Moreover, given their backing by the government, these securities now served the needs of investors such as the rapidly growing private pension funds, which looked to long-term safe investments.[28]

Insofar as policy was conducted with an eye to electoral calculations under the Nixon administration between 1970 and 1972, it was to be seen not in the Fed's interest-rate policies but in a roughly $3 billion increase in private housing subsidies, alongside a $7 billion expansion in the federal ownership of mortgages.[29] The roots of the massive expansion of mortgage finance in subsequent decades, leading to the housing bubble and subprime crisis of the first decade of the twenty-first century, go back to this original intertwining of public and private financial institutions in the inflationary conditions of the early 1970s.

A further contradiction in those years was that the Fed's abandonment of its "policy of extreme restraint" against inflation in order to cope with the commercial paper crisis took place in the midst of a strike wave that involved one out of every six unionized workers. Even as unemployment rose through the year, nation-wide strikes by 133,000 General Electric workers in January 1970, 152,000 federal postal workers in March, 110,000 truckers in May, 355,000 General Motors workers in September, and 360,000 railroad workers in December were interspersed with protracted local strikes by construction workers, teachers, coalminers, rubber workers, longshoremen and—with the most direct impact on Wall Street—42,000 New York taxi drivers.[30] The strikes were mostly about recouping income lost to inflation, but Arthur Burns regarded them, and the successful postal workers' strike in particular, as nothing less than "an insurrection against the Government." He especially identified public sector trade unionism and welfare programs (which he saw as a subsidy to strikers) as the reason why "at a time when unemployment was rising prices continued to advance at an undiminished pace and wages rose at an increasing pace."[31]

While lamenting "the difficulties of pursuing independent monetary policies in a world of high capital mobility," the Fed was still determined to play a role in safeguarding the value of the dollar by stopping any attempt to "'buy' low levels of unemployment by tolerating inflation."[32] With the commercial paper crisis having foreclosed the continuation of a tight money policy, Burns became the leading advocate of incomes policy, with the strong support of Paul Volcker at the Treasury. Steadfastly resisted for over a year by a Republican White House influenced by "free market" ideology, wage and price controls were nevertheless adopted as part of the package that accompanied Nixon's announcement of the end of the dollar's link to gold at Camp David on August 15, 1971.[33] The controls were temporarily effective in restraining both wages and prices: the president's 1973 Economic Report boasted that the US anti-inflation policy was "the marvel of the world." Their removal later that year came when Europe and Japan had accepted that it was impossible to return to fixed exchange rates, but it was also in good part due to growing capitalist complaints, despite their initial support for the program, about bureaucratic intervention.

Given what was now a prolonged profit squeeze amid sharply reduced productivity, sufficient investment was not forthcoming to bring the crisis to an end by renewed growth. When, on top of this, the tremendous OPEC-induced spike in energy prices of late 1973 sparked a recession, the profit squeeze turned into a global economic crisis. Its severity in Europe as well as the US, in sharp contrast to the preceding golden-age decades, is clearly demonstrated in Table 6.2.

But there was a more profound aspect to the crisis than was measured by such statistics. Within the US itself, the rise of the environmental movement at the same time as the shop-floor worker rebellion was registered in a battery of legislative impositions on corporations in the areas of occupational health and safety and industrial pollution. This climate of activism also generated new consumer-protection campaigns, including the 1968 Truth in Lending Act and the 1970 Fair Credit Reporting Act. This considerably burdened the regulatory agencies (the Treasury's OCC, for instance, had no personnel specializing in consumer issues until this time), and the number of federal regulatory personnel increased in 1970–75 from under 10,000 to over 50,000.[34] The Treasury's First Deputy Comptroller of the Currency, Justin Watson, lamented: "Consumer activists are running around the country literally trying to tear down banks and business."[35] Yet when castigated for not preventing banking crises in this period, it was notable how much such regulators intoned words almost identical to those of Greenspan in the face of the 2007–8 crisis. Thus the comptroller of the currency, James E. Smith, told the *Wall Street Journal* at the time of Franklin Bank's failure in 1974: "We haven't been as sensitive as we should have been to large institutions. Maybe we were unduly secure that a major bank that had prospered for many years couldn't develop big problems."[36]

Table 6.2: Economic Indicators US and Europe, 1950–73 and 1973–79

		US	UK	Germany	France	Italy	Average (unweighted)
GDP	1950–73	2.2	2.5	5.0	4.1	4.8	3.7
	1973–79	1.9	1.3	2.6	2.6	2.0	2.1
INFLATION	1950–73	2.7	4.6	2.7	5.0	3.9	3.8
	1973–79	8.2	15.4	4.7	10.7	16.3	11.1
UNEMPLOY-MENT RATE	1950–73	4.8	2.8	1.9	2.0	4.9	3.3
	1973–79	6.5	4.6	3.1	4.2	6.0	4.9
PRODUCTIVITY	1950–73	2.6	3.1	6.0	5.1	5.8	4.5
	1973–79	1.1	2.9	3.7	3.0	2.5	2.6
INVESTMENT	1950–73	4.0	3.9	6.1	4.5	5.1	4.7
	1973–79	3.0	3.2	4.1	4.5	4.2	3.8

Source: Compiled from Andrew Glyn et al., "The Rise of the Golden Age," in Stephen A. Marglin and Juliet B. Schor, eds., *The Golden Age of Capitalism: Reinterpreting the Postwar Experience*, Oxford: OUP, 1990, p. 47, Table 2.6; and from the data appendix to Philip Armstrong, Andrew Glyn, and John Harrison, *Capitalism Since World War II*, London: Fontana, 1991. Investment here is non-residential capital stock.

Amid strong union support for legislation that would put limits on US MNCs moving abroad, a 1975 Harris poll found that only 15 percent of Americans had "a great deal of confidence" in corporate leaders—in contrast to 55 percent a decade earlier.[37] The sense among capitalists themselves that their "golden age" was over has been well captured by Robert Rubin, who recalls one of the old partners at Goldman Sachs telling him at the time "that we junior partners would be unlikely to ever do as well financially as the older partners had because there would never be another period as good as the one that had just passed."[38] Nelson Rockefeller, in the Annual Report of the Chase Manhattan Bank, stated that "it is clear to me that the entire structure of our society is being challenged."[39] A prominent corporate lawyer who was later to be appointed to the Supreme Court wrote to the head of the US Chamber of Commerce that "it was time for American business to apply their great talents vigorously to the preservation of the system itself."[40]

This was hardly surprising given that the crisis of Keynesianism in the US coincided with the anti–Vietnam War mobilizations, the explosion of African-American frustrations in urban riots, and the radicalization of black workers and unemployed youth. This formed the background to the emergence of a "new left" inside the Democratic Party in the early 1970s, seeking to make it more representative of the social movements and to extend state regulation of business. Even reformist calls to heal the divisions through new corporatist institutions were made in terms of the need for the type of national economic planning that the New Deal had never yielded. Not surprisingly, therefore, the joint call issued in 1975 by Robert Roosa (now an investment banker), Wassily Leontief (the eminent economist), and Leonard Woodcock (Reuther's successor at the UAW) for a "US Office of National Economic Planning" aggravated business fears.

These fears were intensified by developments abroad—particularly what was being proposed inside Europe's major social-democratic parties. The language of "class," "capital," "exploitation," "imperialism," and "transformation," which had become marginalized within these parties, was again disturbing parliamentary elites. This was associated with "new left"-inspired socialist strategies based on a growing sense that the postwar reforms would be eroded if they could not be transcended by a radically democratized state and a fundamental shift in class power. Sweden's powerful LO union federation advanced the famous Meidner Plan for the gradual takeover of the country's big private corporations by wage-earners' funds; German unions turned towards investment planning ("Strukturpolitik") and the extension of co-determination; in France a push for workers' self-management and bank nationalization led to the French Socialists' "Programme Commune" with the Communist Party. But from the perspective of the American state, perhaps the most disturbing development of all, given the key role of the City of London in global financial markets and sterling's role as the de facto first line of defense for the dollar, was the British Labour Party's adoption of a radical Alternative Economic Strategy just before its election in early 1974, after a miners' strike had brought down the Conservative government of Edward Heath.[41]

The fears of US capital were aggravated further still by the support for national economic planning increasingly voiced in the Third World. This seemed especially significant amid the wave of nationalizations in the petroleum industry in the mid 1970s and the sharp hike in oil prices. The danger this appeared to pose for the global capitalist project was rather spectacularly underscored in 1974 by the passage in the UN, by 120 votes to 6, of the Charter of Economic Rights and Duties of States, which declared that each state has the right to "nationalize, expropriate or transfer ownership of foreign property under the domestic law of the nationalizing State and by its tribunals."[42] However often UN resolutions had previously recognized the rights of states to control their own natural resources, the breadth of support for the 1974 Charter's targeting of foreign capital was something the American state, as the US ambassador to the UN Daniel Moynihan said at the time, "seemingly could not understand, much less control."[43] The link between the American state and the fate of capitalism was never clearer than when, on July 14, 1975, the cover of *Time* magazine simply posed the question: "Can Capitalism Survive?"

Transition through Crisis

"It's our dollar but your problem." This glib remark by Nixon's Treasury secretary, John Connally, to European finance ministers in 1971 shortly after the US effectively ended the Bretton Woods system was immediately belied by the increased attention the US gave to international economic coordination throughout the 1970s. While detaching the dollar from gold decreased one set of perceived restrictions on the US (the threat of some countries choosing gold over dollars), it at the same time *expanded* not only the international status but the responsibilities of the Federal Reserve and the US Treasury. What was essentially happening was a transition from the fixed exchange rates designed to foster capitalist reconstruction under the Marshall Plan and the European Payments Union, to the establishment of the legal, institutional and market infrastructure that would sustain capitalist globalization amid floating exchange rates anchored by a US dollar–Treasury bill standard. As President Ford's Treasury secretary, William Simon, put it when the IMF finally ratified the new monetary order (five years after the fact):

> This is of major interest to the United States, not only because gold is an inherently unstable basis for the monetary system but because it is inevitably linked to a fixed exchange rate system. Gold never really served fully the purpose for which it was intended under the Bretton Woods System—regulator of liquidity, enforcer of discipline. It couldn't because of its own rigidities, and its international monetary role has been dying from natural causes, as its domestic role did.[44]

The international adoption of the US dollar–Treasury bill standard gave the American state distinct "seigniorage" advantages, as the reward for being held responsible for securing and validating confidence in the dollar. This was all the more remarkable in that this expansion of responsibilities took place even amid Watergate—perhaps the greatest crisis of the presidency in US history.[45] And the results were seen as the dollar continued rising from late 1973 to early 1975 through the most serious economic crisis since the 1930s. As Paul Volcker noted, "traders and investors were reminded that the United States, after all, was still a relative bastion of strength and stability and a safe haven in troubled times."[46] The lead taken by the Treasury and Fed in preventing bank failures during this period from turning into an international financial conflagration also goes very far to explaining why, despite all the initial fears that the move to floating exchange rates would undermine the financing of world trade, an internal Treasury memorandum was able to note in 1976 that "businessmen have found that the difficulties of operating under floating rates were not as great as many of them had anticipated."[47]

The pragmatic, tentative, and uncertain steps the US had taken in approaching the decision to go off gold were replicated in successive rounds of G10 and IMF meetings to attempt to revive a fixed exchange rate system. When Volcker proposed during the IMF's Interim Committee negotiations in 1972 that an "indicator system" be adopted, "whereby a country's deviation from an established norm of international reserves would trigger application of 'graduated pressures' on the offending country to impel it to take the necessary steps towards adjustment, European participants objected to the automaticity implied in the plan . . . [They] were unwilling to accept automatic interference in their own policies."[48] Thus, when in early 1973 the US prevailed on the Japanese and European states to embrace a system of floating exchange rates, this decision, as Volcker put it, "was not taken out of any general conviction that it was a preferred system. It was simply a last resort when, by general assent, the effort to maintain par values or central rates seemed too difficult in the face of speculative movements of capital across the world's exchanges."[49]

Just as Volcker also explains the US imposition of an import surcharge in August 1971 as a bargaining counter to secure currency revaluation and agricultural tariff reductions from the Europeans (a tactic that would again and again be deployed as part and parcel of the US push for "free trade"),[50] so were the Europeans' calls for capital controls mainly tactical. Indeed, Volcker himself thought the Europeans had not pushed the option of extending capital controls nearly as much as they should have.[51] Those among the German political elite who were in favor of the temporary use of capital controls were in fact the most conservative and monetarist and the least oriented to the guiding principles of Bretton Woods; German

Keynesians (above all the social democratic finance minister, Karl Schiller) were at one with US economists like Galbraith and Kindleberger in viewing capital controls as antithetical to liberal internationalism.[52] In fact, among the nine leading industrialized countries, by 1973 Germany's financial system was already the most liberalized.[53]

The fact was that, by this time, the degree of financial interpenetration among the leading capitalist states was such that controls would have had to be very extensive—and they could only have been imposed against the strong opposition of the most powerful sections of the European and Japanese capitalist classes. Eric Helleiner, who sees the Americans as imposing free-market ideology on European states more inclined to cooperative capital controls in this period (although they too he admits were unwilling to even consider "the option of rigid, comprehensive exchange controls"), nevertheless observes that their capitalist classes wanted "an open financial system" and saw New York and London as "the most attractive international markets for private and public investors." By 1973, once the European states had embraced the new system of flexible exchange rates, it was only temporary controls for balance-of-payments purposes that they were prepared to have included in new IMF guidelines, in sharp distinction from controls "applied for economic and social reasons." Not surprisingly, Helleiner concludes the "unique depth and liquidity of US financial markets ensured that private investors, if given the freedom to invest globally, would continue to underwrite US deficits through their holding of attractive US assets."[54]

Yet in a conjuncture in which both the domestic and the international balance of forces made it very difficult indeed simply to turn off inflationary pressures, the American state itself would have to be anything but laissez-faire with respect to the stability of currency markets. Although Treasury Secretary Simon (who as the young millionaire bond dealer at Salomon Brothers had acquired a reputation as "one of the greatest traders ever") expounded neoliberal nostrums about the need for a small state more loudly than anyone else in the cabinet, he was fully aware how intertwined were Wall Street and "big government." He knew very well that it was New York State's bond sales that gave Salomon Brothers "more business than any other institution in the world"; that its trading inventory in government bonds was the basis for its ability to secure loans from banks; and, above all, that his firm "could take a degree of comfort from the fact that the Federal Reserve Bank of New York knew everything that was going on."[55] It was not really surprising, then, that Simon made it very clear in his first address to the annual meeting in Washington of the IMF and World Bank in 1974 that "we do not believe in an attitude of laissez faire, come what may. If there is a clear need for additional international lending mechanisms, the United States will support their establishment."[56]

The growing centrality of the American state's role in global capitalism through the 1970s showed that whatever problems and frictions US balance-of-payments deficits might produce, they did not have the same implications for the US as they would for any other state. As a paper prepared for the Federal Reserve of Boston in 1971 put it: "This asymmetry appears to be appropriate, for it corresponds to an asymmetry in the real world."[57] Far from necessarily representing a diminution of American power, the outflow of capital from the US and the balance-of-payments deficits that had so concerned economic and political elites through the 1960s had actually laid the basis for further dollar-based credit expansion and financial innovation both domestically and internationally in the 1970s. This is what Jeremy Seabrooke later would aptly term the "diffusion of power through the dollar."[58] Indeed, one could also speak of the *concentration of US power through the dollar*, as more and more capital flowed into the US in the wake of the demise of Bretton Woods.

The capacity to achieve this, however, still rested not only on the international activities of the American state, but also on the material base of the American empire at home. And this was, in fact, by no means depleted, in spite of the accumulating contradictions that produced the crisis of the 1970s. For example, US expenditure on research and development at this time was about four times that of the countries of Western Europe combined.[59] In the newly developed business computer market (with the personal computer market, initially fully dominated by the US, still to come), US firms supplied one-third of the computers in Japan, half of those in the UK and France, and more than three-quarters of those in West Germany. And given that three-quarters of the computers in use worldwide were located in the US, this meant that in the early 1970s over 90 percent of the global market was in the hands of US firms.[60] Moreover, the US also retained its competitive advantage in agriculture. Alongside the enormous expansion of US agricultural production (with corn production and the high-fructose revolution at its core, and agricultural productivity continuing to outpace that of non-farm industries though the 1970s), the US not only benefited from high commodity prices, but saw its overall agricultural exports increase between 1972 and 1980 by more than 300 percent.[61]

This technological lead reflected a distinctive American combination of supporting factors: the military-industrial complex; university research serving private innovation; early access to venture finance, alongside secure property rights; a base of skills in engineering, optics, chemistry, and metallurgy, as well as sales; and the mobility of managers across firms and regions, which helped to disseminate and further commercialize the new technology. The direct role of the American state itself was especially important: agencies from the Pentagon to the Department of Health ensured that "government funding and infrastructure played a key role in such technologies as computers, jet planes, civilian nuclear energy, lasers and ultimately bio-technology."[62] European capital now flowed to the US (where half of all global total FDI was located by the end of the 1970s), not so much to avoid protectionist measures as to have access to the wide range of research, productive, financial, and sales capacities that were constitutive of the richest market in the world.[63]

The significance of all this was recognized in an April 1973 memorandum prepared for Treasury Secretary George Shultz by Bill Casey, who had just moved from chairing the SEC to become undersecretary of state for economic affairs (he would later become Reagan's CIA director). Casey argued that "the dollar's problem comes from a failure to properly assess the solid assets which lie below the surface . . . The US is still dominant in computers, photography, pharmaceuticals, medical technology, aerospace, nuclear power, home building, heavy industrial machinery, off shore drilling utility operations and so on."[64] Moreover, the balance-of-payments accounts did not register the $90 billion in book value of American foreign direct investment or the operations of over a hundred American banks and 250 brokerage offices overseas. Although the US could, Casey observed, wipe out its trade deficit by a 25 percent increase in its exports, achieved through an export-oriented business strategy, a devalued dollar, and US government pressure on other countries to open their markets, this would "appall our trading partners." So, in direct contrast to the State Department's traditional position for so much of the twentieth century, Casey presciently argued that "trade need no longer be the only source of major gains in our balance of payments." It was precisely because the US could instead make "securities an export" that it had

> such a large stake in the creation of better capital markets and in a better interrelationship of capital markets around the world. Fortunately know-how is one of our great assets and the securities markets of the world are becoming increasingly internationalized . . . With the announcement that controls on the export of capital are to be phased out, it is vital for our talented financial community to unleash itself.[65]

Casey was not alone in expecting that the removal of capital controls and the devaluation of the dollar would themselves bring about "a substantial shift of activity back to New York" from the Eurodollar markets. But he insisted that this would need to be sustained by amending the Federal Reserve's regulation on banks so that they could "competitively bid for foreign deposits," while Nixon's tax deductions on pensions would "give an enormous lift to our rate of capital formation." All this would allow US financial institutions, Casey insisted, "to take the leadership in the developing global securities market" as long as there was also extensive action by other states to establish "common rules of the road in the various capital markets."[66]

At first the signs seemed to indicate that the state would retreat further from regulation of the financial sector. The 1971 Report of the Hunt Commission, appointed by Nixon to study how to "improve the functioning of the private financial system," had already been oriented to move "as far as possible towards freedom of financial markets and equip all institutions with the power necessary to compete in such markets."[67] And in August 1973 Nixon, arguing that "the public is better served by the free play of competitive forces than by the imposition of rigid and unnecessary regulation," proposed to Congress the gradual elimination of interest-rate ceilings.[68] This would in fact be delayed until 1980, but with the famous "big bang" it delivered to Wall Street in 1975, the SEC dramatically shifted away from its long-maintained support for the cartel-like structures of brokers, investment banks, and corporate managers that had dominated the capital markets since the 1930s. Congressional investigations attracting considerable media attention had provided the pension and mutual funds and insurance companies, supported by retail-oriented investment banks like Merrill Lynch, with a forum to make their case for the abolition of fixed rates on brokerage commissions on Wall Street.

What was notable, however, about the amendments to the Securities Acts that ushered in this foundational instance of "deregulation" was that this did not amount to reducing the power of the state. On the one hand, the SEC removed barriers to price competition and market entry, but, on the other, it acquired more powers—not only to intervene in the structures of self-regulation, so as to enforce competitive market structures, promote market transparency, and target insider practices, but also to set limits to the debt-to-capital ratios of investment banks. Whether such powers were actually used extensively or not, as Michael Moran's insightful study shows, "the financial services revolution" was accompanied by "the growing codification, institutionalization and juridification of the system of regulation, in the effort to either prevent scandals and crisis or to manage the consequences when they have happened."[69]

Indeed, the sheer density of both public and semi-public regulation in US domestic financial markets meant that institutional reform in this sector became a key dimension of capitalist strategies for innovation and the construction of competitive advantage. This could especially be seen when, immediately after the collapse of the Bretton Woods system of fixed exchange rates, the Chicago Mercantile Exchange—the world's central futures market in livestock long after the slaughterhouses were gone from Chicago—gave birth to the financial derivatives revolution by inventing a futures market in currencies. According to the head of the CME, Leo Melamed, who initiated the process in 1971 with the help of Milton

Friedman, this could not have been done without "the cadre of traders who left the known risks of the cattle, hog and pork belly pits for the unknown dangers of foreign exchange"—although it also took plenty of "planning, calculation, tenacity and arm-twisting" on his part.[70] The Chicago Board of Trade, which was also still the world's center of futures trading in wheat, corn, and soya even though grain was no longer stored in Chicago, soon followed by launching a futures market in US Treasury securities. The key role state regulation played in the process was indicated by the creation in 1974 of the Commodity Futures Trading Commission (CFTC) to regulate derivatives in a way that facilitated their development. Melamed recognized that the CFTC would be "beneficial to the growth of our markets. Our plans relating to new financial instrument futures were ambitious and could be greatly assisted by a federal stamp of approval."[71]

State agencies like the CFTC were keen to promote the spreading and hedging of risk, including by the many non-financial corporations that invested in derivatives to protect themselves from volatile commodity prices, floating exchange rates, and fluctuating interest rates. This determined the explicit "Why not?" approach that the CFTC adopted in allowing space for self-regulation and innovation in derivatives markets—an approach sealed in 1978 by the Treasury's conclusion that the exchange of derivatives on the US debt that the New York Fed brought to the bond markets would, by allowing for some hedging of risk, help stabilize and increase the holdings of US Treasury bonds.[72] It was on this foundation that the internationalization of the derivatives markets took off in the next decade. It was institutionalized with the opening of the London International Financial Futures Exchange in 1982, on the occasion of which Melamed noted: "It was necessary first to convince the world financial community that financial futures were a necessary adjunct to the management of risk. It took years of late nights and early mornings, an incalculable amount of traveling, unceasing gospel spreading, arm twisting and ear bending."[73] It was on this, as much or more than on risk-modeling equations provided by Nobel Prize–winning economists, that the derivatives revolution was built.[74]

The derivatives revolution was crucial to the stabilization of currency markets in the wake of the end of fixed exchange rates, and was also intimately linked to the internationalization of the US bond market, which was occurring at the same time as the development of the separate Eurodollar bond market. In 1970 foreign private investors already held almost 10 percent of US Treasury securities. The aggregate value of these holdings was 50 percent higher than that of all Eurobonds, and indeed was boosted by the enhanced institutional capacity for the global distribution of Treasury securities, which was facilitated by US investment banks operating in the Eurobond market. By 1980 foreigners held over 21 percent of US Treasuries, and over the previous decade their aggregate value had increased seven-fold.[75] The financial uncertainty that followed the collapse of the fixed exchange rate system, amid the volatility of commodity prices and rising short-term interest rates, actually enhanced the attractiveness of Treasury bills for international investors, who recognized the depth and liquidity of the US bond market despite all the hand-wringing about declining US power and economic strength. This was accompanied, moreover, by the immediate growth (by some 230 percent) of New York's "Yankee" bond market (where foreign governments and corporations issued securities in US dollars) after the removal of capital controls in 1974. The Yankee bond market did not in the long run retard the growth of the Eurobond market: the two financial centers, with US banks operating as central agents in both of them, continued to grow together through the 1970s.

In addition to the creation of agencies like the CFTC to facilitate the development of new financial instruments so crucial to globalization, an interdepartmental Council on International Economic Policy was established, along the lines of the National Security Council in order to pull together "domestic economic developments and our broad foreign policy objectives."[76] It was headed by the secretary of the Treasury, which in this period considerably advanced its claims to play, right across the policy spectrum, "a leading role in the international as well as the domestic sphere."[77] This was facilitated by the 1974 Trade Act's provision for a "fast track procedure," whereby Congress would only vote to accept or reject international trade agreements without the possibility of introducing amendments to negate trade-offs made in the inter-state negotiations. With very few exceptions, the Treasury's consistent and effective opposition to the use of countervailing duties in relation to investigations of unfair trading practices by other states through the crisis of the 1970s permitted it not only to fend off the implementation of domestic protectionist measures, but to use the threat of these as a lever for the liberalization of foreign markets, including in relation to what were increasingly being identified as "non-tariff barriers" associated with other states' domestic regulations.[78]

As an internal Treasury memo on export policy and exchange rates put it in 1975, "a policy of international interdependence is politically unacceptable except where job losses through imports are offset by creating jobs in expanding export industries." It especially stressed that, although the US enjoyed a comparative advantage not only in financial services but in those sectors where technology was most advanced, the examples of aircraft, computers, nuclear reactors, and synthetic materials showed that "the staggering cost of technology has reached levels that must be recovered from sales in excess of those that the domestic market can absorb." Such economies of scale "would reduce unit costs in the US, and ultimately prove anti-inflationary."[79] Yet this was a long-range strategy. The more immediate challenge that the Treasury still confronted, if the dollar's new role as the anchor of global capitalism was to be made secure, was its incapacity to cope with the continuing impact of domestic inflationary pressures on global financial markets. Neither monetary restraint by the Fed, nor Nixon's prices and incomes policy package, nor trade policy, had resolved this problem.

Facing the Crisis Together

When Ford took over the presidency in 1974, with William Simon as Treasury secretary and Alan Greenspan as chair of the Council of Economic Advisers, monetarists seemed as baffled as Keynesians about how to respond to the simultaneous rise in unemployment and inflation. At the high-powered Financial Conference on Inflation that Simon and Greenspan immediately organized in September 1974, monetary policy received very little criticism due to the broad consensus that the Fed "had no choice but to validate the rise in prices if it wished to avoid compounding the recession" by correspondingly loosening the money supply.[80] It was because the necessity of expanding credit was unquestionable that most of the participants, including Alan Greenspan, concentrated on fiscal policy and argued instead for public expenditure cuts in areas like health insurance and welfare.

But a stance in favor of regressive cuts in state expenditure ruled out securing union support for wage restraint at a time when, moreover, inflationary pressures were coming not just from rising wages but also from rising agricultural, metal, and paper commodity prices, even before the oil-price explosion of late 1973. Besides, the demise of US wage and price controls at this time met with strong business approval: "Initially business people had supported controls enthusiastically. However, by 1973, they had become more concerned about the bureaucratic control that came with them than with labor union militancy."[81] This confirmed the Treasury's view, articulated by Volcker, that "keeping controls for any length of time would be impossible in the kind of open economic and political system we want in the United States."[82]

That this had nothing to do with any general laissez-faire principle could be seen in how quickly the state reacted to the collapse in October 1973 of the US National Bank of San Diego—the largest US bank failure since the Depression. The USNB had been heavily involved in the Real Estate Investment Trusts created by the banks to compete with the savings and loans sector, which, after over-stimulating construction in 1972, was especially hard hit by the 1973 recession. The OCC and Federal Deposit Insurance Corporation (FDIC) responded "dramatically in a carefully coordinated sweep by 165 national bank examiners and 292 FDIC officials who took possession of the bank and its branches."[83] And both the Fed and the

OCC were by this time also closely monitoring the even larger Franklin National Bank, which had followed its Wall Street rivals to London in the early 1970s and was deeply involved in foreign exchange speculation. Actively playing the role of lender of last resort—through 1974 the Federal Reserve Bank of New York lent Franklin $1.7 billion—US regulators delayed closing Franklin as long as they could out of "concern that a failure of a bank of Franklin's size might cause a general scramble for liquidity."[84]

What was especially significant was that, even by the mid 1970s, the concern that certain banks were "too big to fail" was not confined to what the effect of their failure would be in US financial markets. Much of the Fed's intervention involved purchasing foreign currencies on Franklin's behalf, assuring foreign creditors they would be paid—and even extending its lender-of-last-resort function to Franklin's London office, on the grounds that "the failure of Franklin to perform on such a volume of international commitments would lead to a crisis of confidence in foreign exchange markets and possibly to an international banking crisis."[85]

The grounds for such fears were real enough. The UK's 1973 "secondary banking" crisis, which was also due to the collapse of a real-estate bubble, "threatened some of the biggest financial institutions with the real risk of collapse."[86] Moreover, a broad range of European banks were revealing major losses amid the volatility in short-term capital flows that were initially triggered by both floating currencies and the recycling of petrodollars. This came to a head in June 1974, when the Bundesbank allowed Bankhaus I.D. Herstatt of Cologne, one of Germany's largest private banks, to collapse. Apart from the Bundesbank's traditional obsession with a tight monetary policy, this was justified in terms of avoiding "moral hazard'—that is, "to teach speculators, as well as banks dealing with speculators, a lesson."[87] But in contrast to the carefully managed Franklin crisis that the Fed and OCC were engaged in, the consequence of the Bundesbank's action was that the Herstatt crisis immediately spilled over to the international interbank lending markets, including nearly collapsing the New York clearing house, CHIPS, which connects the dozen or so largest US banks with major banks around the world in processing payments among them primarily related to foreign exchange transactions. Since CHIPS (in contrast to the Federal Reserve's clearing system for US banks, Fedwire) did not guarantee payments nor settle net debits and credits for each bank until the end of each day, this meant that when the Bundesbank allowed Herstatt to close down, the world's major banks "suddenly discovered themselves to have sold millions of deutschemarks for, in effect, an empty suitcase."[88]

The Herstatt crisis marked a turning point. It was the Bundesbank that was taught a lesson in the internationalization of the state. By the end of the year it had agreed to assume responsibility for paying off Herstatt's creditors, giving foreign banks preference over German banks and corporations. More broadly, it was drawn into supporting the US position that "a firm and explicit commitment must be given to the marketplace that central banks would provide lender-of-last-resort assistance to banks operating in the Euromarkets."[89] After this, bank regulators in different countries kept in close contact with one another, even sharing private phone numbers as well as information, so as to be able to act in a concerted way as a collaborative team of "firefighters" to deal with international financial crises.[90] At the initiative of the Fed in the summer of 1974, this practice was gradually institutionalized, with regular meetings of the G10 central bankers at the Bank of International Settlement's headquarters in Basel, Switzerland.

The "Concordat" that the Basel Committee on Banking Supervision arrived at in 1975—whereby the home state of an international bank was responsible for the solvency of its international branches, while the host state was responsible for the supervision of all banks on its terrain—involved considerable expansion and restructuring of state regulatory functions. The role of the Basel committee was to allow member-states "to learn from each other and to apply the knowledge so acquired to improving their own systems of supervision, so indirectly enhancing the likelihood of overall stability in the international banking system."[91] The Bank of England now offered, for the first time in its history, "formal and public instruction" to all banks operating in the City of London to "tighten up their internal control systems" on their branches' foreign exchange operations; the US Treasury's Comptroller of the Currency created a Multinational Banking Department which oversaw the international activities of all US banks, with the aid of a permanent London office and a staff of traveling examiners; and the Bundesbank established a Liquidity Consortium Bank, with the participation of the German banking industry, to perform lender-of-last-resort functions.[92]

The liberalization of finance and the volatility that came with accelerated competition and capital mobility were accompanied by a "reregulation" that required *greater* state intervention and cooperation.[93] Nurturing ties between US Treasury staff and other countries' finance ministry officials was also critical to this. Notably, the very settings where senior officials of the advanced capitalist states had met together during the decade-long effort to save Bretton Woods now provided the venues for establishing the legal and institutional framework for floating currencies. The most intimate of these settings were the private dinners attended only by US, UK, German, and French officials during G10 meetings (even the Japanese were not invited, let alone the officials from those smaller countries in the G10 whose attitudes the US Treasury resented as reflecting "the most conservative European views").[94] It was at one of these meetings in the White House library in the spring of 1973 that the framework was established for the G7—as the meetings of finance ministry officials and heads of state became known when they were expanded to include Japan, Italy, and Canada in the following few years.

This new venue for "discourse construction, the promotion of shared causal and normative beliefs, mutual endorsement [and] suasion" was one in which the officials involved "often had more common ground and shared understandings than with colleagues at home."[95] The first Rambouillet summit, in 1975, endorsed a text that Simon's deputy, Edwin Yeo (also a former banker), had initially hammered out with French Finance Ministry officials, in consultation with senior IMF staff, to the effect that a stable system of exchange rates would primarily be the product of "market forces" reacting to clear evidence of domestic price stability. The mandate of the IMF was to be extended to allow for its "surveillance" of the commitment of individual states to policies designed to secure such market discipline. The concept and the practice of IMF surveillance would carry a heavy load in the making of global capitalism for the next quarter-century.

The Nixon administration's famous hostility to the IMF and World Bank had contributed to marginalizing their role in the key decisions that determined the fate of Bretton Woods. Yet a more sober appreciation of the utility of the international financial institutions to the making of global capitalism had soon prevailed in Washington. An internal US Treasury memorandum of May 1973 stated, "[T]he strategic significance of the IFIs (International financial institutions) to the US lies in their role as a major instrument for achieving US political, security and economic objectives with particular respect to the developing nations," stressing in particular the IFIs' alignment with "a western market-oriented framework."[96] The IMF's "Committee of 20" (made up of the finance ministers and heads of the central banks of the twenty states that composed the IMF's executive board) was formed in 1973 precisely because the G10 was, as Volcker put it, "seen as too much of a rich man's club to provide legitimacy for fundamental reform of the international monetary system."[97]

When, at its 1976 Jamaica meeting, the C-20 finally produced the amendment to the IMF's Articles of Agreement that was needed to legitimize the new system of floating exchange rates, it was clear that the US had succeeded not only in blocking proposals for IMF backing for temporary capital controls, but also in explicitly redefining the purpose of the international monetary framework as being to facilitate the international exchange of capital as well as of goods and services. Bill Simon was described in the US press as having come back from Jamaica with "everything except the kitchen sink," and proudly told a group of Republican Congressmen: "We have succeeded in persuading the world to agree on what is essentially a US view of the operation of the exchange system under the IMF Articles."[98]

A number of leading Third World countries also adopted this view. This was of course very much related to their growing involvement with Wall

Street, especially in the wake of the explosion in oil prices and the removal of US capital controls. The Treasury itself played a significant role not only in encouraging Saudi Arabia, in particular, to purchase US Treasury bills and other long-term securities and equity (after the Saudis had initially been burned by undertaking speculative short-term investments), but also in encouraging New York banks to channel petrodollars to major "market-oriented" developing states such as Brazil, Mexico, and South Korea.[99] How far any of these parties needed such encouragement is an open question, but there is no doubt that the profits to be made in the "channeling of such very large sums of money from foreign lenders to foreign borrowers," as Simon put it, did improve the mood of New York's bankers.[100]

An internal Treasury document noted in the summer of 1975: "Private bankers in the US and abroad do appear to be going through a period of renewed confidence in contrast to their demoralized state after the difficulties of Herstatt and Franklin National last summer." In fact, New York bankers now "stressed the difference between LDC rhetoric in, e.g., the UN, and their reasonableness in, e.g., dealing with banks. There is need to discount the rhetoric."[101] The bankers' confidence came from first-hand experience. Since the early 1970s US banks had "emerged as the primary source of balance of payments financing [and] the prime source of funds for public and private infrastructure investments."[102] Private capital had moved into the void as the Nixon administration went beyond what had already been done in the 1960s to cope with the US balance-of-payments problem, by no longer offering grants and long-term credits to Third World states. The aggressive promotion of agricultural exports to replace food aid was also reinforced by the new authority granted to the executive by the 1974 Trade Act. At the same time the penetration of the US agricultural model in the Third World significantly contributed to the transformation of peasant agriculture into export-oriented and FDI-developed agribusiness.[103] The process went well beyond the transformation of agriculture, as McMichael has pointed out; through the course of the 1970s, "the international division of labor had been remade if not reversed. The third world's exports included more manufactured goods than raw materials and the first world was exporting 36 per cent more primary commodities than the third . . . [T]he third world share of agricultural exports fell from 53 to 31 per cent between 1950 and 1980."[104]

Moreover, the increased FDI and commercial bank lending that this entailed was no longer endangered by expropriations of foreign property by Third World states (which reached a high of eighty-three in 1975, and declined to an annual average of only sixteen in the last three years of the decade). This is not to say there was no concern about the long-term ability of Third World states to repay the massive debts they were accumulating. But while over half of the financing of current account deficits of Third

World countries came from private banks, the fact that most of the remainder consisted of "official" loans from the IMF and the World Bank and other international lending agencies reduced this anxiety, since "it seemed impossible to default on commercial banks while still hoping to receive official assistance . . . [S]tate and private finance were intertwined in the developing world."[105]

What was to be avoided at all costs, as Simon privately put it, was any "dilution of conditionality of IMF credit power. Private providers of credit to LDCs rely heavily on IMF conditionality to change the policies of countries that have wandered from the reservation in terms of conduct of their affairs."[106] At the October 1976 IMF meeting Simon made it clear what "wandering from the reservation" meant. It was not just about the "avoidance of the use of controls over international trade and payments, long a basic objective of the Bretton Woods system . . . [I]t also applies as much or more to governmental action to restrict the operation of market forces through the exchange rate mechanism." As opposed to relying on "transfers of wealth which can only be one time in nature," or foreign aid which could only "supplement" more decisive policies, development required "removing unnecessary and burdensome government controls, not . . . imposing additional barriers and impediments to market forces."[107]

But the most important reason to prevent any unconditional finance for Third World countries was the poor example it would set for the advanced capitalist economies themselves: "How ironic it would be if we reflated with great care domestically and blew our opportunity to grope toward price stability by creating massive amounts of international finance."[108] Indeed, the immediate context of Simon's comments was the crisis just then engulfing the British state: a severe run on sterling, prompted by the scale of the fiscal deficit, had forced the government to seek a loan from the IMF. The relentless pressure that the US Treasury, as well as the banks in the City of London, now brought to bear on Britain to accept the severe conditions attached to the provision of funds must be understood in this context: getting a Labour government to make a definitive break with Keynesianism would set a crucial example for the US itself.[109]

As his government was negotiating the IMF loan, British Prime Minister Callaghan told the 1976 Labour Party conference that the Keynesian commitment to full employment was over: "We used to think you could spend your way out of a recession, and increase employment by cutting taxes and boosting Government spending . . . Now we must get back to fundamentals." When the delegates responded by turning to socialist fundamentals rather than capitalist ones, passing a resolution calling for the nationalization of the major banks and insurance companies, Callaghan called President Ford, hoping to use the delegates' resistance as a lever to try to soften the IMF conditions, and playing on US fears that if his left-wing cabinet minister Tony Benn's "alternative economic strategy" were adopted "it would call into question Britain's role as an Alliance partner."[110] But the US did not let up. Bill Simon flew to London himself in the last days of the IMF negotiations with the UK to meet secretly with Bank of England and UK Treasury officials and steel their will to get the Labour cabinet to accept the IMF's terms.[111] It was the first time—at least since the late 1940s, when the Marshall Plan was tied to policies of social and financial discipline—that IMF conditionality was imposed on a major capitalist state.

Given that a sterling crisis had been a repeated fact of life in the UK in the postwar era, the Labour government elected in 1974 could hardly have escaped yet another one in the context of the deep crisis of Keynesianism in the 1970s. The government had clung to its old Keynesian and corporatist practices, in spite of the fact that before the election the party had embraced the Alternative Economic Strategy. On taking office the government did not have to wait to be apprised by the governor of the Bank of England of the City of London's monetarist views; their widespread coverage in the financial press meant that they were on the new ministers' breakfast tables every morning. Inflation was seen as being due to deficit financing of excessive public expenditure, with the latter having the further effect of soaking up resources that would other-wise go to private investment and private consumption. The monetarists' message was clear: the Keynesian perspective was passé—at best irrelevant, at worst counterproductive. In the face of successively more intense runs on sterling, climaxing in the IMF crisis, the Labour cabinet's turn to scaling back the welfare state, confronting industrial militancy, and dismantling capital controls was so thorough that, for the first few years of her 1979–83 govern-ment, Margaret Thatcher could claim she was only following Labour's policies.[112]

The Labour government's final explicit rejection of Keynesianism in 1976 was a defining moment in the politics of globalization. London's role, along-side New York's, at the center of international finance, meant that Britain was expected to share with the US the responsibility for managing the crisis of the 1970s and winning the confidence of financial capital. William Rogers, who had been Nixon's secretary of state, later explained the American state's perspective on the crisis: "We all had a feeling it could come apart in a quite serious way . . . It was a choice between Britain remaining in the liberal financial system of the West as opposed to a radical change of course. I think if that had happened the whole system would have begun to fall apart. So we tended to see it in cosmic terms."[113]

The role the Treasury and Fed played in the 1976 British crisis was indeed crucial, but it was played in concert with UK Treasury and Bank of England officials. While the State Department favored a gentler handling of such a key Cold War ally, the US Treasury was unrelenting. Edwin Yeo, Simon's undersecretary, later described how he, along with Scott Pardee of the New

York Federal Reserve, had "sweated blood" to get the Labour leadership to renege on their social-democratic ideology and so clearly distance themselves from their own party base. The Americans could not directly tell the British what to do, but, as Yeo later said, they "put up the money for the bait"—in other words, they offered a rescue that hooked the UK economy into IMF conditionality in order to secure the financial and political discipline on which they believed the global capitalist system depended. For the US to work in this way to get international agencies like the IMF to force countries to adopt certain policies was "traditional rather than innovative; what was more unusual was that the pressure in this case was being put on a rich, industrialized country, and the US made no attempt to dissemble."[114] But the real significance of the triumph of monetarism in Britain in the late 1970s was the class alignment that went with it. In accepting the need to give priority to fighting inflation, industrial capital accepted that a finance-led accumulation strategy was in its interests too.[115] Even more significant was the way previously militant industrial workers in Britain, frustrated with the effects of inflation and taxation on their income, acquiesced in these policies, especially in a context where so little was done to dissuade them that "in the face of the crisis there appeared to be no 'practical' alternative."[116]

Yet what ultimately mattered most would be what happened within the US itself: until the senior partner applied the same kind of monetarist discipline and secured the same kind of class alignment at home, it would not work in a lasting way anywhere else.

IV

THE REALIZATION OF GLOBAL CAPITALISM

7

Renewing Imperial Capacity

A two-page advertisement in *Fortune* magazine in March 1976 by Phillips Petroleum was headlined: "It's time American Industry took a stand for Free Enterprise." The text went on to say: "It's gone past the point where an isolated business is under attack. The system itself is in danger. And if we don't stand up for it, who will?"[1] In fact, US capitalists had already embarked on a series of political mobilizations, including through the creation of new business associations and policy-planning organizations, which strengthened their "ability to act as a class, submerging competitive instincts in favor of joint, cooperative action."[2] American MNCs and international bankers also led the way in bringing together the elites of the advanced capitalist countries in 1973 to form the Trilateral Commission, dedicated to preventing the abandonment of liberal internationalism. Their mood was captured by Samuel Huntington's report for the Commission, which saw "the crisis of democracy" in terms of a "demand overload."[3] Yet, faced with continuing wage pressure from US workers to catch up with inflation, and a Democratic Party legislative agenda that reflected pressure from new social movements, it took the full decade of the 1970s before the shift in the balance of class forces was effected that crystallized the turn to neoliberal discipline.

The decade of crisis appeared to come full circle when President Carter appointed Paul Volcker, who oversaw the US Treasury's response to the dollar crisis of the late 1960s, to chair the Federal Reserve at the end of the 1970s. What was now required to resolve the dollar crisis, said Volcker, was to "discipline ourselves," by which he meant that the Fed had to discipline *itself* to see through a policy of pushing interest rates to such "painfully high" levels—the substance of the so-called Volcker shock—as would prove that beating inflation trumped all other policy goals.[4] By the end of the 1970s most industrial sectors of capital had come to accept the need to give priority to fighting inflation and defeating labor, and agreed that the strengthening of financial capital this would involve was in their own interest. This was crucial for the new age of US finance that took off in the 1980s, as well as for making the US Treasury bonds that covered the Reagan administration's fiscal deficits seem as good as gold (indeed, since they paid interest, better than gold).[5] All this led to the development of the "active international market in financial claims as a whole" that best defines global finance.[6]

But the question lingered as to whether the new age of finance would aggravate rather than resolve the profitability crisis of US industry. Many critics at the time insisted that high interest rates would not only block economic growth but further expose US industry's vulnerability to competition from Europe and Japan. In fact, the shift in the balance of class forces in favor of capital promoted restructuring of the US economy so as to lay the basis for overcoming the crisis of corporate profitability. The way in which the crisis of the 1970s was resolved was decisive for realizing the project for a global capitalism under US leadership in the final two decades of the twentieth century.

The Path to Discipline

In 1972 the CEOs of the largest US corporations formed the Business Roundtable and launched the most extensive organizational campaign of private capital since the formation of the Committee on Economic Development in the early 1940s, while at the local level small and mid-size businesses flocked to the Chamber of Commerce, increasing its membership four-fold. The immediate catalyst for this was the introduction of a new set of regulations on worker, environmental, and consumer protection, stimulated by a militant labor movement, as well as by new social movements, that affected all industries and produced a reaction that involved "the organization of diverse business interests into a *unified* political front on major issues."[7]

This was much in evidence when so-called internationalist and protectionist capitalist interests were brought together to defeat the Foreign Trade and Investment Act of 1973, backed by the AFL–CIO, which would have put in place import quotas and restrictions on US corporations' export of capital abroad. A similar coalition of US capitalists actively joined in the administration's extensive mobilizing campaign in 1973 to ensure passage of the 1974 Trade Act, which established a new trade policy advisory committee system under the Office of the Special Trade Representative that was largely composed of representatives from firms in each major sector, and soon became "the principal vehicle for translating capitalist interests into coherent trade policy positions."[8] The state's role as organizer of the capitalist class was especially important for developing a "new coalition of supporting political forces" behind a free-trade strategy since, as Fred Bergsten (a policy advisor to Kissinger and later assistant secretary for international affairs at the Treasury during the Carter administration) pointed out at the time, constituencies such as the auto industry that had supported "the essentially free trade approach of the last thirty-five years have either reversed their positions or become relatively ineffective."[9]

Meanwhile Wall Street had already also "stood up" in its own back yard. In the face of the fiscal crisis that engulfed New York City in 1975 (the same year in which the "big bang" introduced more competition in the securities markets), bankers moved decisively to take advantage of the difficulties the city had in selling its municipal bonds to restructure its class and state relations. This was done with the strong encouragement of the US Treasury, whose own crucial loans to New York City at the end of 1975 were provided on terms that were explicitly intended, as Treasury Secretary Simon told a Senate hearing, to be "so punitive, the overall experience so painful, that no city, no political subdivision would ever be tempted to go down the same road."[10] While municipal unions were conscripted to invest their pension funds in New York City's bonds, committees dominated by bankers framed the loan conditions on the basis of the policies that later became widely identified with neoliberalism—a concept of fiscal rectitude that rejected higher taxes and instead cut social programs, froze wages, and privatized public services and assets.[11]

Many of New York's Democratic Party elite were complicit in imposing this early structural adjustment program, and this appeared to reinforce what Alan Greenspan saw at the time as a remarkable emerging consensus among Republican and Democratic leaders on economic policy—"a convergence of attitudes between the liberal left and the conservative right . . . looking to restrain inflation, cut deficit spending, reduce regulation, and encourage investment."[12] But it was by no means clear that the new Carter administration would sustain this elite consensus. During the 1976 election campaign Carter had surrounded himself with Keynesian economic advisors, and explicitly endorsed their view that "until you get the unemployment rate down below five percent there is no real danger of escalating inflationary pressures," as well as their call for corporatist wage and price guidelines to deal with inflation. In a speech to the AFL-CIO, Carter had condemned the Ford administration for using "the evil of unemployment to fight inflation."[13] Meanwhile, a successful month-long Ford strike towards the end of the election campaign yielded real wage gains to workers in the "Big Three" auto companies, alongside a major victory on reduced work-time as a progressive way to deal with layoffs. All this seemed to confirm labor's continuing political and economic strength.

Once the Democrats were in office, however, the extensive capitalist mobilizations against the consumer protection and labor law reforms on the legislative agenda led to "a massive outpouring of 'grassroots' opposition by state and local interests."[14] In fact, the rise of a new populism on the right (most prominently expressed in the Proposition 13 tax revolt in

California), combined with Democratic pledges to restrain deficits, put not only organized labor but also the broader social movements on the defensive.[15] Labor suffered another major defeat with the passage of the Airline Deregulation Act in October 1978, which it correctly saw would have the effect of driving down airline workers' wages and benefits through the removal of price controls, as well as leading to the concentration of the industry once price competition had driven out small carriers. The Act's leading sponsor in the Senate was Edward Kennedy, and in fact Carter himself had put deregulation of the transportation industries near the top of his legislative agenda.

The most significant indicator of the changing political balance of class forces lay in the fate of the labor-backed Humphrey-Hawkins Equal Opportunity and Full Employment Bill, to which the administration—in order to win over Democratic "moderates" in the Senate and assuage business critics—attached provisions specifying that it should not encourage inflation or "employee migration from the private to the public sector."[16] Those endorsing the bill faced the seemingly insurmountable task of overcoming the "fears of expansive government, increased taxes, and, especially, the acceleration of inflation." Unsurprisingly, the Humphrey-Hawkins Bill's ambitious proposal for "nationally coordinated economic planning to bring about full employment" was countered by those "entrenched interests that opposed planning—interests that were aggressively re-organized in the 1970s."[17] By the time the bill was passed, in October 1978, as the Full Employment and Balanced Growth Act, the promise of access to work for all was gone, and it was stipulated that for fiscal deficit reasons no new job-creation programs could be started before the end of 1980.

This reflected a pragmatic accommodation to the developing "supply-side" consensus in Washington policy circles, which lay behind cuts in the top capital gains tax rate by over 40 percent and the reduction of corporate tax rates, while social security taxes were increased. Amid this consensus the Democrats' Keynesianism increasingly looked threadbare and confused.[18] The federal deficit as a share of GDP fell from 4.2 percent in 1976 under Ford to 2.7 percent under Carter in both 1977 and 1978, and 1.6 percent in 1979. Yet since US growth rates in this period nevertheless exceeded those of most of the other advanced capitalist countries, thereby widening US trade deficits, the Carter administration's lingering Keynesian commitments were increasingly focused on using the new G7 architecture to launch a joint "locomotive" strategy for economic expansion. Although this was reluctantly agreed to by Japan and Germany at the 1978 Bonn Summit, the response of the financial markets to seeing the US trying to turn the G7 away from its initial policy of fostering monetary restraint was a sustained assault on the dollar. Elaborate Fed and Treasury interventions in foreign exchange markets that were coordinated with the European central banks and the Bank of Japan counteracted this only temporarily.[19]

Carter's famous July 1979 "crisis of confidence" speech, lamenting the end of an era when "the phrase 'sound as a dollar' was an expression of absolute dependability," was made in the context of the failure of these interventions, as well as by the rise in oil prices triggered by the Iranian revolution.[20] It was effectively an admission that the joint international stimulus strategy had proved unviable. As this strategy had been intended to compensate for the state's inability to overcome the growing contradictions of Keynesianism at home, it further exposed the impact high inflation (which had reached double-digit levels even before the oil crisis) was having on both finance and industry. Persistent negative real interest rates upset the role of the financial system in mediating between savers and investors, and wreaked havoc on the traditional relationship between the costs of long-term versus short-term lending. And when, after a short recovery from the depths of the 1973–75 recession, profit rates resumed their fall, it created further doubts about industry's ability to renew the equity capital it needed for investment, turn over its bank loans, and underwrite consumer finance. Just as Carter made his 1979 speech, the threatened bankruptcy of Chrysler—unable to meet its debt obligations to no fewer than 180 banks—was especially sobering for *all* US capital. The "crisis of confidence" Carter was talking about, however much it was highlighted by the rapid depreciation of the dollar in international currency markets, was above all a crisis of *business* confidence.

The main contribution Carter made to restoring business confidence was to appoint Paul Volcker, with his "strong reputation" in financial circles for "soundness" and a "commitment to financial stability," as chair of the Federal Reserve.[21] If Volcker had seemed unable to "quite make up his mind" when (as we saw in Chapter 5) he was seen "for all practical purposes" as *the* Treasury during the Nixon administration's attempt to manage its own dollar crisis, by the end of the 1970s he was singularly determined to save the dollar by squelching inflation permanently. Although Volcker was never a monetarist, as economists narrowly understood that term, after he left the Treasury for the New York Fed in the mid 1970s he had increasingly articulated Wall Street's call for the Federal Reserve to adopt an unwavering anti-inflationary commitment to monetary discipline. This was the new "comprehensive symbol," as he put it in 1978, of the Fed taking on the central "role in stabilizing expectations [that] was once a function of the gold standard, the doctrine of the annual balanced budget, and fixed exchange rates."[22] In the wake of the sharp rise in unemployment in the 1974 crisis, the Fed's main achievement in securing the confidence of the financial markets had been to render "toothless and compromised" a multitude of Congressional attempts to challenge its independence.[23] But financial markets had been incensed when Carter's first appointee as chair of the Fed, William Miller, continued publicly to express a preference for Keynesian-style incomes policies, rather than monetarism, to address inflationary pressures.[24]

What the Volcker shock entailed in policy terms, as he later admitted, was not "very fancy or very precise."[25] It ostensibly involved a change in procedure from announcing a target interest rate (and then selling or buying the quantities of Treasury bills through its "open market operations" to reach it) to targeting the money supply (and then forcing banks to bid against each other for the funds they needed to maintain their reserves with the Fed). The Fed's embrace of restrictive monetary targets may have been, as Krippner puts it, a "political cover" to avoid direct responsibility for the resulting high interest rates,[26] but the impact on the economy was clear enough: what was really significant about the conduct of monetary policy under Volcker "was not the money targeting but the austerity."[27] A new and increasingly invariant ethos for monetary policy, designed above all to "break inflationary expectations," was in its formative stages during this period: "the change in objective was much more important and more dura-ble than the change in procedures."[28] Volcker himself made it perfectly clear that he was prepared to embrace austerity—"and stick to it," as he told the American Bankers Association three days after he announced the new policy in early October 1979.[29]

And stick to it he did, sustained by the public show of unanimous support he secured from the Fed's governors and Open Market Committee, as the federal funds rate reached previously unheard-of levels.[30] Carter's presidency ended with the federal funds rate at 19.1 percent; and with the interest rate still at this level six months into the Reagan presidency, the US was plunged into the deepest economic downturn since the 1930s. US inflation, aggravated by the sharp rise in oil prices at the time, had stood at over 12 percent at the end of 1979, and was still almost 10 percent at the end of 1981. The back of inflation was finally broken when unemploy-ment (which initially rose only slowly from its 1979 level of 6 percent) reached double digits in the fall of 1982. It was at this point, exactly three years after it had been launched, that Volcker let it be understood that the "shock" was finally over: the Fed's "policy objective" had at last changed to monetary "easing."[31] Even when growth finally resumed in 1983, infla-tion came down to just over 3 percent and more or less remained there for the rest of the century.

But the ability to stick to a policy of state-induced austerity for as long as three years was based on much more than Volcker's personal determina-tion. As we saw in the last chapter, previous attempts by the Fed to raise interest rates dramatically had run up against what McChesney Martin had once called the "ghost of overkill." This was usually understood as meaning that the Fed drew back from raising rates too high to accommodate the democratic opposition to high unemployment. In fact, when the Fed drew back it was because it was itself caught up in financial capital's own contradictory relationship to monetary discipline. Despite financial capitalists being the most vocal constituency for monetary restraint, they recoiled in horror at the instability that the imposition of high interest rates actually caused in financial markets. In 1969–70, as we have seen, once the financial system proved unable to accommodate the high-interest-rate policy that produced the commercial paper crisis and the collapse of Penn Central, the Fed had quickly pumped liquidity back into the system. US policymakers were subsequently haunted by the fear that this would happen again. Shortly before becoming head of the Council of Economic Advisors under Ford in 1974, Alan Greenspan warned in a private memo to the Treasury's Bill Simon that a tight monetary policy would have particularly dire effects, especially since the size and range of the US mortgage market meant that the nature of "our peculiarly American thrift institutions places the crisis threshold far lower than any country in the world." He notably added that that "the Federal Reserve's response would be immediate and massive support for the thrift institutions"—which could, of course, only negate the initial monetary restraint.[32]

What, then, allowed Volcker to go beyond what he himself called the earlier "hesitations and false starts"?[33] Crucial to the change was the broadening and deepening of financial markets through the 1970s. This reflected the enormous growth in international finance that followed the removal of US exchange controls in 1974, which was further spurred by the British and Japanese liberalizations in the midst of the Volcker shock. But it also reflected the development of new derivatives markets that allowed for the spreading and hedging of risk, a more extensive commercial paper market, and the development of new securitized instruments including money-market mutual funds.[34] The latter provided an escape hatch from the New Deal "Regulation Q" controls on how much interest banks and thrifts could pay on deposits, and so reduced the sensitivity of housing finance to high interest rates—although this meant that the Fed needed to push interest rates higher still to secure austerity.[35] These changes would not have been enough to prevent the kind of scenario that Greenspan had feared back in 1974, if the Volcker shock had not been quickly followed by the passage of the Depositary Institutions Deregulation and Monetary Control Act (DIDMCA) in early 1980; this Act finally accomplished what Nixon had proposed in 1973: the phasing out of "Regulation Q" ceilings. It also removed state usury laws that limited the interest banks could charge on loans, and gave more flexibility to thrifts by broadening their ability to engage in consumer and commercial lending.[36]

Although the previous deregulation in airlines, trucking, and railways appeared to suggest that "banking's time had arrived,"[37] the Depositary Institutions Deregulation and Monetary Control Act revealed by its very title the futility of seeing things in terms of a dichotomy between regulation and deregulation. Besides mandating greater regulatory cooperation between the Federal Reserve, the Treasury's Office of the Controller of the Currency (OCC), and the Federal Deposit Insurance Corporation (FDIC), the Act—"the most massive change in banking laws since the Depression"—widened the state's regulatory remit over the whole banking system.[38] All deposit institutions were now required to hold reserves with the Fed, and new rules were established for more uniform reporting to regulators, and for extended federal deposit insurance coverage. And it was this joint supervisory capacity that allowed the Fed, working more and more closely with the OCC and the FDIC, to sustain the Volcker shock by undertaking selective bailouts of those banks that were deemed "too big to fail." This included the largest bailout in US history to that point, that of First Philadelphia Bank (whose roots went back two centuries to the first private bank in the US). The regulators feared that if the bank "collapsed slowly, in the manner of Franklin National [in 1973–74], it might provoke a crisis of confidence in the banking system."[39]

The Fed's autonomy with respect to the financial system, and the detailed information it had about its precise workings that was unavailable to anyone else, was decisive in terms of the flexibility and persistence it needed to act. As Chris Rude has put it: "Contrary to the beliefs of certain populists, therefore, the Fed did not act in the interests of the banking system when it imposed austerity under Volcker because it was held captive by its member banks. The Fed was able to use austerity to promote the general interests of the larger US financial institutions because they were subject to its supervisory and regulative authority."[40] Yet the Fed's autonomy could not have been sustained without support from the White House and leading members of Congress—not to mention the Treasury, which Volcker all along saw as the real "center of gravity."[41]

Underlying this was a broad class alignment between finance and industry. This encompassed not only Wall Street but also small savers, since high inflation had eroded support for the old New Deal ceilings on the interest paid for bank deposits, as could be seen in the American Association of Retired Persons and "Gray Panthers" lobbies, which called for the phasing-out of the "Regulation Q" ceilings.[42] And the new class alignment also encompassed not only most industrialists, who were by now more than ready to endorse the bankers' traditional hostility to Keynesianism, but even the AFL-CIO leadership who, as Volcker pointedly noted at the time, had in September 1979 reached a "National Accord" with the Carter administration that went so far as to give "top priority" to the "war on inflation."[43] All this allowed the Fed to claim in its 1979 Report that no internal opposition existed within the US to its "new approach to central banking."[44]

Fundamentally, the Volcker shock was not so much about finding the right monetary policy as shifting the balance of class forces in American society. Inflationary "expectations" (the economists' buzz word at the time) could not be broken without shattering aspirations of the working class and its collective capacity to fulfill them. The defeat of the working-class militancy of the previous decade had culminated politically in the failed attempt to secure the state's commitment to full employment in the Humphrey-Hawkins Act. A bone that labor was thrown when the Act was passed in 1978 required the chair of the Fed to make annual reports to Congress on its objectives for the year ahead. Nothing symbolized labor's defeat more vividly in the following years than Volcker using his "Humphrey-Hawkins testimony" to make the monetarist case that low inflation was the Fed's overriding target, even at the expense of unemployment, and that this was the principal means of ultimately reaching high employment.[45]

But it was a Democratic Congress's imposition on labor of what was effectively a "structural adjustment program"—in the conditions attached to the loan guarantees Congress gave Chrysler in 1979 to prevent its bankruptcy—that signaled the most important factor in sustaining the Volcker shock. Whereas there had been an explosion of labor militancy in the strike wave that erupted in the wake of the Fed's 1969–70 "policy of extreme restraint," a decade later the acquiescence of the UAW in the "reopening" of its collective agreement, to make wage concessions and allow for the outsourcing of production to non-union plants, now became the template for the spread of similar concessions throughout US industry. The union strategy that had informed collective bargaining in the auto industry had always been based on extending unionization in the sector, and removing wages from competition through "pattern bargaining" (in other words, negotiating agreements covering all the major firms). Against the backdrop of heightened competition from Japan (aggravated by high interest rates as well as the increases in oil prices) and the political defeat of the Democrats' full-employment policy response to the recession of 1973–75, the threatened bankruptcy of Chrysler exposed, as Kim Moody has noted, the lack of any union plan for "dealing with large-scale business failure."[46] But if pattern bargaining in the auto industry was ended with Chrysler, it was soon perversely restored as similar concessions were granted to GM and Ford—and rank-and-file resistance was broken as unemployment reached 24 percent in that industry in the early 1980s.

The appeal of Ronald Reagan's tax cuts to the Democrats' working-class constituency, followed by the explicit class war from above undertaken by his administration after the 1980 election (through cutbacks to welfare, food stamps, Medicare, public pensions, and unemployment insurance), was a major factor in turning this initial defeat of labor in the iconic auto sector into an historic shift in the broader balance of class forces. With workers desperate to hold on to their jobs, by the end of 1982 "major concessions had been negotiated in airlines, meatpacking, agricultural implements, trucking, grocery, rubber, among smaller steel firms, and in public employment."[47] Anti-union appointments to the Department of Labor and the National Labor Relations Board had immediate effects in checking union organizing drives and sustaining employers' bad-faith bargaining tactics. But, as Alan Greenspan subsequently reflected, in discussing Reagan's legacy, "perhaps the most important, and then highly controversial, domestic initiative was the firing of the air traffic controllers in August 1981 . . . his action gave weight to the legal right of private employers, previously not fully exercised, to use their own discretion to both hire and discharge workers."[48] The strike by PATCO (the Professional Air Traffic Controllers Organization), which had actually endorsed Reagan in the 1980 election campaign) was broken not only by the permanent dismissal of 12,000 controllers, but by military personnel being brought in to run the airports, while many of the strike leaders were arrested and led away in chains.[49] Notably, Volcker himself thought that the breaking of PATCO did "even more to break the morale of labor" than had the earlier "breaking of the pattern of wage push in the auto industry."[50]

The "contradictions of success" that had erupted with worker and social-movement militancy in the mid 1960s were thus finally resolved in the early 1980s. The imposition of class discipline to break the great inflation and the wage militancy of US labor strongly confirmed the American state's commitment to property, the value of the dollar, and the inviolability of its debt. The way in which this was achieved—high interest rates, a deep recession, and the liberalization of markets—also laid the basis not only for the new age of finance, but also for the restructuring of US industry.

The New Age of Finance

In the words of a subsequent Congressional study, the 1980s were "undoubtedly the most turbulent years in US banking history since the Great Depression."[51] The contradictions of the New Deal regulatory framework, brought to a head by the Volcker shock, had opened further space for the spread of neoliberalism's deregulatory ideology. But the creation of "freer markets" necessarily involved "the reformulation of old rules and the creation of new ones."[52] The systemic risk inherent in the more competitive, integrated, and volatile financial markets of the 1980s quickly proved that reliance on "market discipline" produced its own severe contradictions, and actually required more, not less, state intervention.

Perhaps the most dramatic instance of the contradictions of market discipline was seen in the fate of the savings and loan industry after the Volcker shock; the S&L crisis had only been temporarily postponed by the 1980 DIDMCA legislation. And despite the "spirit of deregulation" that imbued the subsequent 1982 Garn–St. Germain Act, which was designed to aid the S&L industry by loosening the rules on what thrifts could invest in, it simultaneously allowed the FDIC to provide direct assistance to a failed bank if "severe financial conditions exist which threaten the stability of a significant number of insured banks possessing significant financial resources."[53] While it would have been much cheaper to have closed out the industry in 1980 (the delay only "increased the eventual costs of the crisis," as the FDIC later put it), the impact that this would have had on the housing market would have made it politically impossible to sustain the Volcker shock. The number of S&L insolvencies accelerated into the hundreds through the mid 1980s, amplified by the notorious shady characters and practices that were now allowed into an industry that had previously been structured to perform a type of public service. This overwhelmed the ability of the state agencies created during the New Deal to regulate the "peculiarly American thrift institutions" that were supposed to integrate the working class into the American Dream. Although the resolution of the crisis was avoided in an exemplary bipartisan manner until after the 1988 election, the final cost to the state, after winding up the old agencies and passing responsibility for the S&L debts to a new Resolution Trust Corporation, was over $160 billion.[54]

The center of gravity in housing finance shifted to the mortgage-backed securities market, facilitated by the Secondary Mortgage Market Enhancement Act of 1984, for which Wall Street had lobbied intensely. The development of the mortgage-backed securities market had already begun in the early 1970s, with the aid of the federal mortgage agencies; and by a decade later, as Alan Greenspan later said in celebrating the "resiliency" of the mortgage-credit market, "the greater institutional diversity in the sources of mortgage finance played a key role in maintaining the uninterrupted flow of mortgage credit during the then-biggest financial debacle since the Great Depression—the S&L crisis of the late 1980s."[55]

By the time the dust had settled at the end of the 1990s, thrifts accounted for only 5 percent of total US financial assets—down from 20 percent in 1980. Alongside the S&L collapse, there was an enormous concentration in commercial banking: over 4,500 independent banks (36 percent of all banks) closed between 1979 and 1994.[56] To limit the worst effects of the carnage, the takeover of small regional banks by large national banks was encouraged at the state level, thus finally producing the "true interstate banking system" which the Fed and the Treasury's OCC had strongly encouraged by, among other things, facilitating the spread of technological and marketing innovations such as the networks of automatic teller machines (ATMs) shared by the banks. The resulting concentration was such that the share of deposits held by the top ten banks almost doubled, reaching 37 percent by the end of the 1990s.[57] But there was, overall, a massive decline in the proportion of total financial assets held by commercial banks.

It was really the Wall Street investment banks, as the key intermediaries in the trading of these assets, that led the way into the new age of finance, obtaining cheap cash by selling Treasury bonds to commercial banks on immediate repurchase terms ("repos") and investing the cash in making markets for securities that paid a higher return (thereby creating more and more business for credit-rating agencies in grading risk on securities). The commercial paper market, which as we saw in Chapter 6 had already become a major alternative to bank loans for the short-term funding of corporations, exploded in the 1980s, with investment banks earning massive fees as the intermediaries in this market (see Table 7.1).

Table 7.1: Growth of Financial Instruments 1980–1999

MONEY MARKET FUNDS (SHORT-TERM CAPITAL)			
	1980 ($ billions)	1999 ($ billions)	CHANGE %
US TREASURY BILLS	216	653	202
CERTIFICATES OF DEPOSIT	317	837	164
COMMERCIAL PAPER	122	1,258	931
REPURCHASE AGREEMENTS	57	308	440
MISC	115	275	139
TOTAL	827	3,331	303

CAPITAL MARKETS (LONG-TERM CAPITAL)			
	1980 ($ billions)	1999 ($ billions)	CHANGE %
CORPORATE STOCKS	1,601	19,871	1,141
RESIDENTIAL MORTGAGES	1,106	4,996	352
CORPORATE BONDS	366	2,021	452
US GOVT SECURITIES	407	2,473	508
US GOVT AGENCY SECURITIES	193	1,241	543
STATE/LOCAL BONDS	310	1,425	360
BANK COMMERCIAL LOANS	459	1,367	198
CONSUMER LOANS	355	1,370	286
COMMERCIAL/FARM MORTG	352	1,109	215
TOTAL	5,149	35,873	597

Source: This table is adapted from Frederick S. Mishkin, *The Economics of Money, Banking and Financial Markets*, Boston: Addison-Wesley, 2000, Tables 1 and 2, pp. 26, 29.

The investment banks responded to the 1970s regulatory changes which had opened up competition in stock-market brokerage by shifting their operations more towards underwriting, deal-making in mergers and acquisitions, and creating new financial commodities and markets. The Fed's 1979 change of procedure to using fluctuating interest rates to implement its monetary policy meant that bond prices (which move inversely with interest rates) fluctuated more than ever. The banks then responded to the increased volatility in interest rates that accompanied Volcker's monetary policy by shifting further to trading in bonds, commercial paper, and other securities. This was also crucial to turning investment banking into a much more speculative business. "Had Volcker never pushed through his radical change the world would be many bond traders and one memoir the poorer," Michael Lewis noted in his famous 1989 book *Liar's Poker* on "the golden age of the bond man" on Wall Street: "A Salomon salesman who had in the past moved five million dollars' worth of merchandise through the traders' books each week was now moving three hundred million dollars through each *day*.'[58]

The main purveyors of the new financial instruments, not only on Wall Street but globally, were the rising firms since the 1960s such as Salomon Brothers and Goldman Sachs, which displaced old established ones like Dillon Read and Kuhn Loeb. They were the principal conduits for the massive inflow of capital from abroad, assisted by the removal in 1984 of the final remnnant of the tax penalties introduced in the 1960s to protect the dollar. At the same time, the US investment banks not only greatly expanded their operations in the City of London, but also spread out into the European continent, and beyond. In addition to underwriting the bonds that covered the growing indebtedness of US federal, state, and municipal governments, and facilitating the privatization of state assets at home and abroad, they were also at the center of the burgeoning commercial paper, corporate bond and stock markets of the 1980s. With the top five firms dominating in each of these markets, the return on equity for the large investment banks exploded to 48 percent between 1980 and 1984, before stabilizing over the following two decades at just below 20 percent.[59] It was the new bankers of the 1960s generation, such as Goldman Sachs's Robert Rubin, who now hired the economists, mathematicians, and engineers (the "quants") who modeled risk with sophisticated computer programs—and thus, as Charles Ellis says in his history of Goldman Sachs, "deliberately and conscientiously transformed the bond business from the old business of making judgments and taking risks on interest rates and bond maturities . . . to a business that concentrated on managing spreads and arbitrages in deliberately crafted portfolios across markets and between different types of securities all over the world."[60]

But the action was not confined to Wall Street's investment banks. The large US multinational commercial banks were also now fully engaged in what Gillian Tett has described as the "years of bold innovation that made high-risk trading and aggressive deal-making the gold standard of the Street [where] a 'kill or be killed' ethic prevailed."[61] She notes that, shortly after Salomon Brothers engineered the first major derivative bond swap between IBM and the World Bank in the early 1980s, J.P. Morgan used its City of London operations to circumvent the Glass-Steagall Act and allow its clients to take advantage of the explosion of derivatives markets. By the early 1990s, after also pioneering the development of credit default swaps, half of Morgan's trading revenues came from derivatives contracts. But Morgan was only one of eight US banks that by then accounted for over 50 percent of interest-rate and currency swaps worldwide, as well as 90 percent of US bank derivatives activity; and there was a similar concentration of derivatives activity in the US investment banking sector.[62] This concentration was closely related to the highly complex information and risk-management systems that were required to allow the risk on bonds with different interest-rate and currency structures to be traded without any bonds actually changing hands.

The derivatives activities of these banks were crucial to the making of global capitalism because they could, as Bryan and Rafferty put it, "blend together (or make transmutable) different forms of capital, [and] create a market of conversion between fixed and floating rate loans, and between different currencies."[63] While this certainly involved extensive leveraging and speculation, it met the hedging needs not only of financial institutions (which exchanged 40 percent of all swaps among themselves), but also of the many corporations seeking protection from the rapidly evolving vulnerabilities associated with global trade and investment. Moreover, there was also a pronounced shift from the earlier standardized commodity and currency derivatives on organized exchanges, such as the Chicago Mercantile Exchange, to over-the-counter (OTC) bilateral contracts that banks fashioned themselves. Following the recession of the early 1980s, these custom-made derivative products supplemented Wall Street's fresh knack for tapping pension funds and rendering them into the loans that leveraged the corporate takeovers, mergers, and restructurings that Reagan's tax allowances encouraged. The practice developed in the 1970s by the Bank of America, among others, of "slicing and dicing" mortgage loans and selling them to institutional investors, was applied to corporate bonds and loans in the 1980s, and to credit default swaps in the 1990s.[64]

What had initially led Wall Street's investment banks to sell mortgage-backed instruments that "looked and tasted" like safe bonds was the desire to gain access to the large investor base represented by institutional investors such as pension funds and insurance companies: "If there was a master plan, it was to meet the needs of our institutional investor clients," noted Laurence Fink, at the time Wall Street's leading player in this arena.[65] The 1970s had seen the introduction and tightening of minimum funding requirements for pension funds, while new tax breaks for individual contributions to retirement savings plans had launched a massive explosion of mutual funds. Both developments sharply increased the demand for new hedging instruments, such as mortgage-backed and other derivative securities, to protect the pension and mutual funds' investments in bonds, equities, and real estate. By the beginning of the 1990s, four out of every five pension funds were using derivative products.[66] There was no little irony in the extent to which the growth of pension funds—one of the main products of US workers' ability to secure retirement benefits under the class compromise in the postwar era—should have become one of the central pillars of the neoliberal financial order that accompanied the defeat of American trade unionism in the 1980s.

It was highly significant that, in the new age of finance, the Federal Reserve came into much greater prominence. As a Fed paper later exulted: "In the early 60s, the Federal Reserve was little known outside of the financial services industry and university economics departments. Twenty years later Fed Chairman Paul Volcker was one of the most recognized names in American public life."[67] In fact, not only investors on Wall Street but businessmen everywhere increasingly seemed more attuned to the decisions of the Federal Reserve than Soviet managers were to Gosplan's. Just as the Fed discovered, in its monetarist moment, that the range and diversity of liquid financial instruments that were now available made the money supply almost impossible to define and control,[68] it also discovered that this very range and diversity left financial markets extremely sensitive to the Fed's interventions in setting the interest rate for federal funds. Since this was the foundation of the calculation of risk on all other financial instruments, the Fed "increasingly became the fulcrum on which the US economy turned"—though this political role was often obscured, since Fed officials would "present their activities as the product of 'market forces' while at the same time continuing to regulate the economy."[69]

As early as mid 1982, Volcker "clearly began to shift to an explicit interest rate target," and this policy was continued by Alan Greenspan when he succeeded Volcker in 1987.[70] But it took until 1994 before the Fed's Open Market Committee—finally sufficiently confident its operations in the markets could always bring about its target rate—came to announce its interest-rate decisions publicly and in advance (at this point financial commentators started referring to it as the "Open Mouth Committee"). But the New York Fed's reports in the 1980s had already noted the close relationship between the chair of the Fed's public speeches and movements in the market towards the desired federal funds rate. Newstadt is correct to read this as bringing the Fed and financial markets even closer together: "beyond clear social proximity, the Fed was in the process of developing a functional proximity" to financial capital[71]—and this was true not only nationally, but also internationally.

Aside from its monetary policy role, the Fed was on what it described as "a learning curve" about how innovations in financial instruments and the blurring of lines between banks and non-banks would affect its supervisory and regulatory functions. The largest US commercial bank holding companies, long engaged in investment banking activities abroad, had by the early 1980s begun moving into a range of brokerage, insurance, financial counseling, tax-planning, and other such services at home (with ad hoc Fed approvals of such boundary crossings consistently upheld by Supreme Court rulings).[72] Thus, although the New Deal's Glass-Steagall Act was not formally repealed until the end of the 1990s, by the mid 1980s Fed reports recognized that the transformations in banking and finance were "simply too powerful to be overcome by a regulatory or legislative regime based on the past." But while insisting that regulation along the old New Deal lines was now "impractical politically and substantively," the reports also stressed the need for more extensive, although radically different, powers.[73] The basic point of departure, as the New York Fed's 1986 Report put it, was that "[t]here are public interest considerations associated with the banking and financial system that call for a higher degree of official supervision and regulation than is needed in other kinds of business enterprise."[74]

The widespread notion that the transformation of US finance was primarily due to deregulation is misleading, even though the volume of deregulation rhetoric was certainly pitched even higher during Reagan's presidency than its already considerable level under Carter.[75] Indeed, the US financial markets remained "among the most heavily regulated sectors of the American economy."[76] The supervisory burdens of the regulatory agencies actually increased through the course of the 1980s. The number of OCC bank examiners, having declined in the first half of the decade from some 2,300 to 1,800, had by the end of the 1980s returned to its 1979 peak, while the OCC's expenditures grew 25 percent faster than the banking system's assets.[77] But, given the transformations in finance that had taken place, and that the regulatory agencies had encouraged, these regulatory and supervisory functions could not ward off the long series of financial crises that became characteristic of the new age of finance.

This meant that the Fed's function as lender of last resort was increasingly called upon. The role it played in sustaining the Volcker shock was extended in subsequent years to bailing out failing banks that stood as strategic nodes in the international circuits of capital. Troubled small banks which could not be safely merged with larger ones were closed by the Fed and the Treasury, and their depositors paid off by the FDIC, while the large banks were bailed out—thanks to their importance not only for the US economy but also for the international clearing-house system, whose hundreds of billions of dollars of daily interbank payments greased the wheels of global capitalism. The pattern of letting banks that were too small to matter go under, while acting as lender of last resort to save the ones that were "too big to fail" was set in 1982, when Volcker bluntly told the Federal Open Market Committee (FOMC): "If it gets bad enough, we can't stay on the side or we'll have a major liquidity crisis. It's a matter of judgment as to when and how strongly to react. *We are not here to see the economy destroyed in the interest of not bailing somebody out.*"[78]

The "moral hazard" tightrope that the state had to walk in this respect was nothing compared with the practical hazard involved in figuring out whether allowing even a small bank to collapse might have systemic effects. This was vividly demonstrated in the summer of 1982, when the decision to close a small Oklahoma bank, Penn Square, immediately endangered Continental Illinois, the sixth-largest commercial bank in the US, which then immediately turned to the international interbank market for its funding. The Fed and OCC's attempts to help Continental improve its asset and liability management proved to be in vain, and finally, in May 1984, with "the liquidity of the whole banking system" at stake according to the Treasury, the most ideologically free-market-oriented Republican administration since the 1920s nationalized the bank and bailed out its creditors.[79] It was when the Treasury's comptroller made it clear during Congressional hearings on Continental Illinois that the uninsured creditors of the eleven largest US commercial banks would be treated in the same fashion that the term "too big to fail" came into widespread usage.[80]

In fact, these banks had already been effectively bailed out, albeit much more indirectly, in 1982, when the high interest rates of the Volcker shock produced, as an unintended side-effect, the Third World debt crisis. The Treasury and Fed began meetings to address the likely inability of Mexico to meet the payments on its loans from both Wall Street and other foreign banks, and this led to their secretly launching a rescue operation explicitly designed to bail out the banks that held Mexico's debts—and then conscripting the British, Japanese, and Swiss central banks into the operation too.

What concerns us here, however, is the changing role of the American state in relation to the new domestic contradictions that emerged after the Volcker shock. By the time Volcker was replaced by Alan Greenspan, in 1987, "the Great Inflation was over" and "markets recognized it was over."[81] But just as the "demons of the 1970s—high inflation, oil shocks, bitter labor disputes, stagnation—seemed to be receding, banished by liberalized markets, monetarism, Reaganism, Thatcherism, and by the vogue for aggressive financial management,"[82] a stock market crash confronted Greenspan with a stark new contradiction: the inherent volatility of the new age of finance. It was under Greenspan that the Fed's lender-of-last-resort role now came to play a much more systemic function than ever before.

The exorcism of the demons of the 1970s was registered in the stock market. The Dow Jones index, having stayed more or less flat throughout the crisis of the 1970s, almost tripled in the five years after monetary policy began to be eased in the summer of 1982. But on October 19, 1987, promptly dubbed "Bloody Monday," it fell by almost a quarter (by far the largest one-day stock market decline in its history, including 1929's Black Thursday). This was aggravated by the computerized "program trading" and the derivatives on stock market indices that had been developed to manage risk.[83] As an important study by the US Government Accounting Office (GAO) put it a decade later, the speed and extent of the collapse could only be understood in terms of the way "the increased linkages between the equities markets and the futures markets could change the character of a financial crisis . . . The primary concern of federal officials was that the system for allocating credit would be halted, and the financial system would stop functioning."[84]

But what was no less remarkable than the suddenness and scale of the crash was the immediate, decisive, and coordinated state response to it. In the GAO's words: "The readiness of federal officials to manage the market crash largely depended upon the availability of information that federal agencies had routinely collected, the existing communication networks among the agencies, and the ability of the agencies to influence the behavior of market participants and their creditors."[85] Although the Fed hardly had the time even to consult the previously developed written plan outlining potential responses to a range of financial crises, it immediately took the lead in response to the frantic calls from the chief executives of the New York Stock Exchange and the Chicago Mercantile Exchange. It instructed them to stay open, and followed this with a statement issued before the opening of financial markets on the following day declaring its "readiness to serve as a source of liquidity to support the economic and financial system." This promise itself "contributed significantly towards supporting market sentiment," but it was backed up by the New York Fed's market operations, which pushed the federal funds rate down, and by personal telephone calls to senior Wall Street bankers to assure them of "a continuing supply of credit" so that they would continue their lending to securities dealers (on October 20 Citicorp's margin lending soared to $1.4 billion from a normal level of $200–$400 million).[86] As a *Wall Street Journal* report put it: "The banks were told to keep an eye on the big picture—the global financial system on which all their business ultimately depends. A senior New York banker says the Fed's message was, 'We're here. Whatever you need, we'll give you.'"[87]

The turnaround was stunning. The Dow Jones index immediately resumed its unprecedented climb, and by 1999 the price of corporate equities had increased twelve-fold over their level in 1980. The upward drive was sustained by the Fed's "continuing injection of reserves to buoy liquidity in financial markets."[88] In sharp contrast to his predecessors, the room through the 1990s that Greenspan had for doing this without compromising the Fed's anti-inflation priority was due to the earlier defeat of labor in the 1980s: a relaxation of monetary policy no longer spawned much wage pressure. The Fed certainly watched this very closely and exercised continuing vigilance against general price inflation, but this was matched by its continuing laxity on asset-price inflation. This did not mean that it was unconcerned by the increased likelihood of further finan-cial crises. On the contrary, as the New York Fed's annual reports in the years after the 1987 crash make very clear, it saw what was happening in financial markets as a double-edged sword, expanding the range and cheapening the costs of financial transactions while at the same time producing such a massive increase in market volatility as to make financial crises more likely.

The Fed's concerns were registered internationally in the importance it attached to the BIS negotiations at Basel on international capital adequacy standards for banks; while on the domestic side it was already expressing some anxiety by 1991 that the expanding securities-based mortgage market would allow even local banks and mortgage brokers to pass risk on to others, and thus relax prudential standards in their loan operations.[89] Examiners were not only placed in all the major banking institutions, but the Fed also broadened its daily monitoring efforts to include investment banks and other securities dealers, and prepared measures to extend its emergency lending powers to them.[90] The deepening coordination with other regula-tory agencies that this required had in fact been institutionalized immediately after the 1987 crash with the creation in March 1988 of the President's Working Group on Financial Markets. Regularly bringing together the most senior officials from the Treasury, the Fed, the Securities and Exchange Commission, and the Commodities Futures Trading Commission, it was seen among insiders on Wall Street as acting as a mere cover for what was dubbed the "plunge protection team."[91]

"It is in our national interest for the US banking and financial system to be seen as the bedrock of the international banking and financial system," the president of the New York Fed, Gerald Corrigan, told the New York State Bankers' Association in 1992—adding that this goal "will only be reached if the global marketplace sees US institutions as the unquestioned leaders in financial and managerial strength." For this very reason, he insisted, what the bankers regarded as the "regulatory over-kill" response to the turbulence of the 1980s would not be lightly abandoned in the 1990s.[92] In a typical example of the "double agent" roles traditionally played by so many of Wall Street's key players as they switch from acting for the banks to acting for the state and back again (see Chapter 1), Corrigan went to work at Goldman Sachs after leaving the Fed, and soon became co-chair of the Derivatives Policy Group, "whose goal was to convince legislators that the bankers themselves were in the best position to understand these complex instruments and manage their risks."[93] What was clearly involved here was the state walking the tightrope of allowing volatile financial markets to flourish while at the same time managing and containing the inevitable financial crises that volatile financial markets spawned.

The ability to walk this tightrope for no less than two decades after the 1987 crash was, in fact, crucial to Wall Street's increasing ability to act as a vortex drawing in capital from around the world. Yet at the same time there was considerable anxiety about the future among US economic, political, and intellectual elites.[94] The very high unemployment, and the devastation of whole industrial and agriculture regions—let alone the growing imbalance between imports and exports that came with the rapid appreciation of the dollar relative to other currencies—had certainly generated enormous pressure for protectionist measures. But the strong commitment of the leading US MNCs to open international markets, alongside the heightened laissez-faire rhetoric of the Reagan revolution, ensured that protection was largely limited to the imposition of selected temporary import quotas. And the threat of these measures was used in negotiations with other countries to drive the free trade agenda, which the US Trade Representative pursued with considerable autonomy from Congress. This allowed for administrative compromises in the face of industrial and popular pressures that gave the USTR room to present US trade restrictions as selective, temporary, and transitional measures for the purpose of securing agreements to further open markets abroad, and to ensure that capital controls did not stand in the way of foreign direct investment flowing into the US, as well as out of it.

The strategy of using Congressional protectionist pressures as a lever for opening foreign markets to US goods and services, and gaining greater US access to global savings, eventually proved highly successful. Its immediate results could be seen in the Canada–US Free Trade Agreement and in the foreign direct investment that poured into the US in the 1980s. The Treasury also used the threat of protectionism as leverage in pressing to secure a coordinated inter-state intervention in currency markets that would bring about the devaluation of the dollar, which was arranged in the 1985 Plaza Accord. Nevertheless, anxiety about the underlying vulnerability of the US economy persisted. It was especially feared that any significant financial disturbance, let alone one of the order the 1987 crash, would trigger an even deeper recession than that of the early 1980s, and that under these conditions protectionist sentiment might carry the day and derail the long-term strategy. The stock market's rapid recovery—thanks to the state intervention engineered, ironically enough, by Ayn Rand's disciple at the Fed, Alan Greenspan—helped to allay some of the worry. It also certainly helped to elect Reagan's vice president, George H. W. Bush, one of Washington's most practiced imperial stalwarts, to the presidency in 1988. But if the spirits of the proponents of global capitalism were raised even higher by the ignominious collapse of the Communist world in the following year, the stubborn persistence of the US trade deficit, combined with the 1990–91 economic recession, again brought to the fore troubling questions about whether Bush's New World Order was running on air.

The Material Base of Empire

"It's the economy, stupid" was the slogan that got Bill Clinton elected in 1992. Yet the Clinton administration was then the beneficiary of an upsurge in US productivity through the 1990s that had its roots in the class realignment and industrial restructuring of the previous decade. After the brief recession of the early 1990s, this led to an economic expansion of unprecedented length, during which unemployment dropped to almost 4 percent, its lowest in thirty years. By the beginning of the new millennium, mainstream economists had begun to refer to the whole period after the mid 1980s as the "Great Moderation," while pundits in the *New York Times* asked "what word but 'empire' describes the awesome thing that America is becoming?"[95] But if the angst-ridden 1980s thesis of "American decline" by then looked quite overblown, it was equally misleading to describe the subsequent period in the self-satisfied terms of economic stability. The defining characteristic of the period was neither decline nor moderation, but *restructuring*. It was through the accelerated volatility of finance and an extraordinary degree of economic disruption and social dislocation that the domestic material base of the American empire was reconstituted.

The profitability crisis into which US capitalism had fallen between 1968 and 1982 came to an end. Although profits did not return to the stratospheric levels they had reached during the 1940s—their growth had steadily slowed down in the 1950s, before the brief spike of the mid 1960s—after 1982 both the rate of profit and the share of profits in GDP moved on an upward trend (see Figure 7.1).

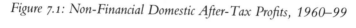

Figure 7.1: Non-Financial Domestic After-Tax Profits, 1960–99

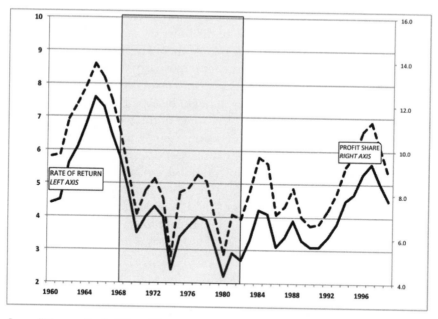

Source: "Note on Profitability of Domestic Nonfinancial Corporations 1960–2000', *Survey of Current Business*, September 2002, Table 1. Available at bea.gov/scb.

   In fact, the mass of real non-financial corporate profits—a strong indicator of capital's capacity to accumulate—doubled between 1983 and 1999.[96] If we include the "hidden profits" contained in the notoriously accelerating salaries, benefits, and bonuses that corporate managers paid themselves in the latter period, the upturn in profits is even more dramatic.[97] By contrast, real private-sector wages were, in spite of a short upswing at the end of the century, lower in 1999 than in 1968. Real hourly compensation (which includes benefits) rose between 1983 and 1999 at a yearly average of only 0.6 percent—while CEO salaries increased by 650 percent.[98] Since the annual growth in productivity averaged 2 percent over this period, the lag in workers' compensation was significant. This was especially so in manufacturing, where real productivity gains per hour increased at an annual rate of 3.5 percent between 1983 and 1999—higher even than during the so-called "golden age."[99] From the late 1960s through the 1970s, investments did not lead to commensurate increases in labor output per hour, and profits were negatively affected. After the early 1980s, however, this pattern was reversed; capital investments combined with work reorganization and labor layoffs led to more than proportionate increases in productivity, the upturn in profits cited above, and the uptick in growth (see Figure 7.2).[100]

Figure 7.2: Real Growth in GDP, Non-Residential Investment, and Productivity

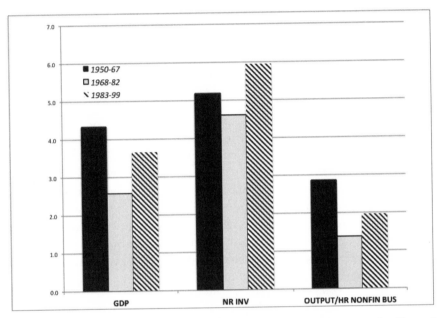

Source: US BEA, NIPA, 1.1.3; US Bureau of Labor, Productivity. Available at data.bls.gov/ cgi-bin/dsrv. (Non-financial business includes services as well as manufacturing.

After the crisis decade, real investment increased between 1983 and 1999 by an annual average of 6.0 percent—a rate of growth that was even greater than in the so-called "golden age" from 1950 to 1967.[101] The strength of investment was often obscured by structural and technological changes in the economy, such as the greater weight in the economy of services, since these are generally less capital-intensive, and by the growth of research and development expenditures, which are not treated as investment in the US National Income and Product Accounts.[102] Especially important in this regard was what the shift to greater reliance on computerized equipment and software in industry meant in terms of investment. It not only meant a reduction in the size of factories, and therefore in the amount of capital that was needed to put into physical structures; it also meant, with the unit costs of information technology falling so dramatically in this period, that much more capital could be bought per dollar of expenditure. As a consequence, measures of investment as a share of GDP that failed to reflect accurately the fall in equipment prices failed to capture what was going on with real investment. From 1950 to 1982, the price index for nonresidential investment rose at an average annual rate of 4.1 percent, approximately the same as GDP; but from 1983 to 1999, the price of investment goods was essentially flat, increasing over the *entire* period by less (3.8 percent) than it had formerly increased *each year*, while the GDP price index increased by 57 percent.

The common periodization of the years since 1950 into an era of rapid growth until 1973 followed by a period of significantly slower growth since then, is rather misleading. Indeed, Maddison's examination of historical US growth rates reveals that the period 1973–98 ranked in per capita growth behind 1950–73 but higher than any other period since 1820, including 1870–1913, when the US emerged as a leading capitalist power (see Figure 7.3). Moreover, if we follow the contours of the historical account presented here, we can see that the second half of the twentieth century really falls into three periods, starting with the "golden age" from 1950 to 1967, whose contradictions gave rise to the extended crisis of 1968–82, which was then followed by the recovery of profits, productivity, investment *and* overall economic growth from 1983 to 1999. The successes of US capitalism that came with the restructuring undertaken in this period were also subject to contradictions, as we shall see in subsequent chapters; but it is very important to understand that they were not the same contradictions that gave rise to the crisis of the 1970s.

Figure 7.3: GDP Per Capita Growth 1820–1998

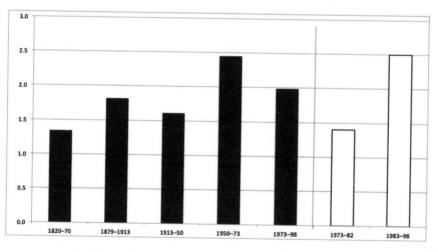

Source: Angus Maddison, *The World Economy: A Millennial Perspective*, Paris: OECD, 2001, Table A1-D, p. 186, and Appendix C, Table C1-c, p. 279.

The sheer scale of the restructuring that took place in the 1983–99 period is, in fact, astonishing. The Fortune 500 list of the largest US corporations had changed very little over most of the twentieth century.[103] This changed dramatically over the last two decades, which saw the emergence of entirely new products, technologies, and industries; at the same time the annual average rate of business failures rose to twice the already high rate of failures seen during the crisis decade from 1973 to 1982.[104] The merger wave that began in the 1980s tended to increase corporate concentration even as the arrival of new entrants—overseas as well as American firms—renewed competition in many markets and prevented anything resembling industrial stasis. Meanwhile, American corporations remained leaders in strategic manufacturing industries and services such as computer hardware and computer services, and the US was the location of about half of the world's research and development in this period.

The established corporate giants also often moved into new areas of production while reorganizing the labor process in their core businesses and shifting production from urban centers to rural communities, where land and labor were cheaper. The number of workers employed in durable manufacturing industries like auto and steel actually increased by 8.7 percent in the Great Lakes region in 1983–99, but this paled in comparison to the 27 percent increase in the south-east, much of it in what previously had been rural areas.[105] Yet many of the jobs in non-durable manufacturing (such as textiles and leather) that had previously moved to the southern states for lower wages continued their travels, to Mexico and Asia. Managerial mobility further contributed to the dispersion of the new technologies, while the weakness of unions gave American capitalists a flexibility in relation to all these changes that was envied by capitalist classes elsewhere. All this helps to explain why, in spite of the weaknesses of particular companies, and even of entire sectors that had previously been especially important in the US economy, the proponents of free trade and financial liberalization had the confidence to stress that the positive effects of "creative destruction" would ultimately outweigh the negative.

Four specific transformations were especially important in this restructuring of the economy and social relations in the US, each with particular implications for the making of global capitalism. The first of these was the relationship between industry and finance. A much larger share of total corporate profits now went to the financial sector: between 1960 and 1984, the financial sector's share of domestic corporate profits averaged 17 percent; from then through 2007 it averaged 30 percent, peaking at 44 percent in 2002.[106] In this context, there was an enormous increase in dividends paid to stockholders: dividends as a share of the profits of nonfinancial corporations averaged a steady 32 percent between 1960 and 1980; they then rose sharply, and averaged almost 60 percent between 1981 and 2007.[107] The new age of finance was often portrayed as diverting corporate funds from potentially productive investment to speculative activity, forcing corporations to look for high immediate rates of return rather than longer-term growth in order to maximize "shareholder value."[108] The new age of finance certainly did involve enormous speculation, and was accompanied by much economic irrationality. Yet, as was proved in the following decade's remarkable productivity growth in manufacturing, amid an expansion of unprecedented length, it is a mistake to see the dominance of finance in terms of speculation displacing productive activity.

The greed that lay behind the assertion of shareholder value, and that drove so many of the corporate mergers and industrial closures, should not blind us to the way in which the broadening and deepening of US financial markets, including their ability to attract so much capital from abroad, expanded the availability of relatively cheap credit for US firms. This was seen not only in the enormous growth of the commercial paper and corporate bond markets, but also in what has been called the "financialization" of nonfinancial corporations.[109] Without this usually becoming the foundation for their central activities or even their profits, large corporations increasingly engaged in financial arbitrage themselves, using both the credit subsidiaries they had developed to attract consumers and their own bond and equity portfolios. As for the impact of financial discipline on corporate governance, this was not so much imposed on managers as used by them to facilitate and accelerate restructuring within firms and across industries.[110] Moreover, the massive reallocation of capital that was involved in restructuring the US economy would have been inconceivable without the role financial markets played not only in pushing so-called "inefficient" firms out of business, but also in supporting risky but innovative startups through the US's unique venture capital markets, whose disbursements grew tenfold in the 1980s alone.[111] The development of derivatives products was also important, not only for limiting exchange-rate and interest-rate risks for corporations but also for assessing and comparing alternative accumulation strategies across both space and time; risk management, like transportation and marketing, should not necessarily be seen as a drain on the productive sectors of the economy, even if it does increase systemic volatility.

The second transformation—the one most associated with the thesis of US decline—occurred in the core industries that had fueled American economic dynamism in the postwar era. The old labor-intensive sectors like shoes, textiles, food, and beverage had seen a sharp contraction well before the 1980s, but it was rising imports and the corresponding loss of jobs in steel, auto, and machinery that occasioned alarm about the state of American manufacturing. Employment in the automobile sector fell by a quarter of a million jobs between 1979 and 1983, and by the end of the 1980s foreign-based producers had captured almost half of the US car market (up from less than 20 percent before the first energy crisis, in 1973). Steel employment had also been falling through the 1970s, but between 1980 and 1984, amid bankruptcies, closures, and layoffs that often devastated entire communities, it was cut in half (a decrease of some 200,000 jobs), and continued to fall thereafter. And the machinery sector—emblematic of the US economy's advanced economic status in construction equipment, turbines, precision tools, and so on—experienced a considerable contraction in its historically large trade surpluses.

But more was going on here than the word "decline" could adequately capture. By the end of the century, a major restructuring had occurred within these industries. In the auto industry there were eighteen assembly plant closures between 1988 and 1999, but thirteen new plants also opened, while the sixty-six auto-parts plants that closed over these years were more than offset by 184 new parts plants. Moreover, the number of plant expansions greatly exceeded the number of downsizings.[112] The direct foreign investment flowing into domestic US auto production, primarily from Japanese companies, expanded rather than diminished the US industrial base. The spatial relocation of the industry involved not only Japanese (as well as some German and South Korean) corporations concentrating their production in the states of the US south, but also saw GM and Ford opening plants there (they also opened plants in the midwest states, sometimes just a few miles away from where old plants had closed).

This was accompanied by the reorganization of plants everywhere in the US to facilitate "lean" production and outsourcing. The emulation of Japanese firms in this respect was enhanced by the possibility of outsourcing to non-union plants, decreases in transportation and communication costs, and the logistical coordination enabled by computerization. Outsourcing was also directly promoted by the state, as was seen when federal loan guarantees to Chrysler were made conditional on it. Alongside the relocation and reorganization of production, the "Big Three" US auto companies responded to foreign competition by shifting output towards truck and SUV production in the 1990s, where they retained a strong competitive advantage. This too was at least indirectly promoted by the state, whose commitment to low interest rates and low energy prices sustained the market for such expensive and fuel-hungry vehicles. This shift restored the Big Three's profitability through the 1990s—and it was this, not pressures from financial capital, that led them to close their eyes to the implications of oil price hikes for future car sales, let alone the environmental costs to society.[113]

A significant indicator of the transformation going on in the automobile industry was that US auto firms (including the Japanese transplants) through the 1990s were the leading purchasers of high-tech equipment. In steel, where US firms had lost their technological leadership, they carved out new market niches in high-quality steel while a series of mergers (especially with Japanese companies trying to escape quotas on steel imports) narrowed the technology gap with US competitors.[114] And the machinery sector responded to the increasing competition it faced from abroad, including increasingly from Asia, as it led the world in the move to computerized equipment and software.

All this brings us to the third transformation—the shift to high-tech manufacturing production. This new industrial revolution—which soon spread globally and encompassed computer and telecommunications equipment, pharmaceuticals, aerospace, and scientific instruments—was largely American-led in terms of its origins and concentration, and of the mechanisms of its subsequent diffusion abroad. The new computer and information technologies that had emerged in the 1960s really proved their worth to industrial and service corporations in the 1980s, and especially in the 1990s. Now that labor resistance was greatly diminished, corporations were more willing to undertake the additional investments in plant and equipment that were needed to integrate the new technologies with restructuring of management systems, labor processes, and relations with component suppliers. And US financial markets, as we have seen, stood uniquely ready to finance budding high-tech commercial ventures. Financial institutions were, of course, themselves early and crucial players in the information revolution, providing the major market for computers and software, and developing key information technologies and systems for themselves and others.[115]

US high-tech firms also benefited from public subsidies—sometimes indirectly, as in the case of military procurement, but often directly in the form of government laboratories linked to particular departments (defense, energy, health, agriculture); and increasingly through the growing commercial role of American universities, aided by legislation designed to expand the assertion of property rights in relation to research conducted within them. Indeed, Congress's general bias in favor of corporate interests was reinforced by its concern for US security interests in the high-tech arena. Congress also showed great flexibility in lowering standards geared to public protection, especially in pharmaceuticals, as its interest moved "from the safety issues of the 1970s to the upcoming 'bonanza' of biotechnology."[116]

With these supports, American capital proved capable of expanding even further into new research-intensive sectors, often inventing entirely new sectors for accumulation. At the turn of the century, even not counting the extensive high-tech production by US MNCs abroad, some 35 percent of global high-tech production took place within the US—the same as the share of all global manufacturing held by the US in the early 1950s. Japan and Germany ranked second and third, with shares of 21 percent and 6 percent respectively; the EU as a whole had a share of 24 percent, and China accounted for 3 percent.[117] This also helps explain why "large American companies maintained or increased their world market shares in 12 of the 18 most important global industries" right through the 1990s.[118] By the end of the century, of the top dozen global firms by sector, the US accounted for 77 percent of the world's aerospace sales, 75 percent of all sales of computers and office equipment, 91 percent of computer software sales, and 62 percent of pharmaceuticals.[119]

Shored up by its high-tech sectors, during 1983–99 US manufacturing output grew faster (4.2 percent annually) than overall GDP (3.7 percent).[120] The restructuring led to manufacturing productivity actually growing faster in these years (3.3 percent annually) than it had in the "golden" 1950s and 1960s (when it had averaged 2.4 percent).[121] This enormous productivity growth was reflected in an increase in overall manufacturing volume of 90 percent over the same period, while manufacturing employment showed virtually no increase at all (of the 34.4 million private sector jobs created in the US in these years, 99.2 percent were outside manufacturing).[122] The trajectory of the computer and peripheral equipment sector captures this well: it achieved an astonishing annual increase in real output of 29 percent throughout the 1990s; but with productivity growing at the even more extraordinary rate of 31 percent, there was no net job growth.[123]

The fourth structural transformation in the economy involved the growth of a diverse range of "professional and business services" that ranged across consulting, law, accounting, market research, engineering, computer software, and systems analysis. Here, the number of jobs increased dramatically. In 1983 employment in this broad sector was less than half that in manufacturing, but by the turn of the century employment—growing even faster than in financial services—had doubled, and matched total manufacturing employment. Not all of these jobs were "knowledge-intensive," nor were they all new—many were clerical, and had previously been done by corporations in-house. Nevertheless, they brought a new set of strategic economic relations into play. Specialization in such activities by American firms spanned many countries. Their services were sought out by foreign companies and governments looking for the "efficiencies" that would promote "competitiveness," as well as to help them navigate the new currents of international trade treaties and commercial law. At the end of the century, the US's global share of professional and business services, measured by revenue generated, was close to 40 percent.[124]

The development of this sector was closely related to the accelerating expansion of finance from the 1960s onwards. Major changes occurred in the nature of what financial institutions did, taking them beyond credit provision and directly into the heart of the accumulation process through new business services, whereby the banks also took over many of the accounting, payroll, and information systems that were previously managed by their corporate clients themselves. And the banks vastly expanded their consumer services in ways that, as with Fed-Ex or fast-food outlets, completed the delivery or saved time in acquiring a product or service (ATM machines, internet payments). This was a central element in the "expansion in both the scale and scope of credit relations" throughout society.[125] These new forms of credit, through which workers gained access to higher levels of consumption, had a profoundly negative impact on working-class organization and culture in the final two decades of the twentieth century, and underpinned all the other transformations discussed above. The generally weak resistance to the restructuring of social life can only be understood if we appreciate the extent to which American workers were not only attacked, but also materially integrated into the making of global capitalism.

The American Dream has always entailed promoting popular integration into the circuits of financial capital, whether as independent commodity farmers, as workers whose paychecks were deposited with banks and whose pension savings were invested in the stock market, or as consumers reliant on credit—and not least as home-owners subsidized by the tax deductions allowed on mortgage payments. But in the context of intensified competition, stagnant wage income, and more sophisticated financial markets, this incorporation of the mass of the American population now took on a more comprehensive quality. Gains through collective action gave way to individual adjustments in lifestyles, from young couples moving in with parents to save for a down payment on a house, to a family decision to cancel a vacation and use the money to buy a "home entertainment system"—while longer hours of work stole from workers even such time as they had once had for self-education and social and political activity. Workers reduced their savings, increased their debt, and looked to tax cuts to make up for stagnant wages; they cheered rises in the stock markets on which their pensions depended, and counted on the inflation of house prices to serve as collateral for new loans, provide some added retirement security, and leave a legacy for their children. All this, along with increasing inequalities among workers themselves, left a working class more individualized and fragmented, its collective capacity for resistance severely atrophied.

These transformations—the new age of finance, the restructuring of manufacturing, the explosion of high-tech, the ubiquity of business services, and the profound weakening of working-class organization and labor identity—reconstituted the material base of the American empire. This was crucial for the way global capitalism was "made" in the final decades of the twentieth century. A truly global financial system based on the internationalization of the US financial system became "neither a myth nor even an alarming tendency, but a reality."[126] American MNCs—expanding much faster globally than at home—transferred technology abroad (yet maintained their home research and development base), while high-tech manufacturing came to both encourage and depend on global networks of competitive production that drew on expanding pools of newly proletarianized labor. American legal, accounting, and consulting firms provided the services to foreign firms and states that they needed in order to compete in the global capitalist economy. Any adequate measure of success in this context went beyond the share of global GDP produced within the US itself. As we shall now see, capitalists, literally almost everywhere, generally acknowledged a dependence on the US for establishing, guaranteeing, and managing the global framework within which they could all accumulate.

8

Integrating Global Capitalism

Among the definitions offered by the Oxford English Dictionary for the verb "to realize" are: to bring an ambition to fruition and thus actuality; to complete and orchestrate something and thereby enrich its texture; to become clearly aware of a fact or situation; and, especially with regard to property and capital, to make a profit. It is in all of these senses that the ambitious project for the making of global capitalism, imbricated in the American empire and first articulated during World War II, was realized in the last two decades of the twentieth century.

This historic development was ideologically celebrated under the rubric of neoliberalism—a set of ideas explicitly designed to make people clearly aware of their own and their states' structural dependence on capitalist markets. In practice this involved states actively engaged in broadening the reach and deepening the meaning of "free trade," so that ever more facets of life became subject to market relations, and more and more subject to the discipline of the free movement of capital across national borders. As we shall see, with the defeat of the Left across Europe, European Economic and Monetary Union took on the neoliberal cast that was in fact crucial to the realization of globalization under continuing US leadership. We shall also see that the distinct way Japan was integrated into the informal American empire in the postwar era determined that the great successes of Japanese capitalism likewise ultimately reinforced the realization of global capitalism under the American aegis.

Moreover, amid the defeat of radical nationalist and socialist forces, the ever-deepening sclerosis of Communist regimes, and the widespread debt crisis of the 1980s, so many states in the "rest of the world" were led to adopt strategies compatible with their integration into global capitalism. Import-substitution strategies were abandoned, export-oriented strategies in East Asia succeeded in breaking with capitalist underdevelopment, and the regions of the globe that had been closed to capital accumulation under Communist regimes were added to the global capitalist economy.

The pattern of MNC expansion that was at the heart of the shift from the old imperialism to the new had meant, as we have seen, that the densest economic linkages among states in the new informal US empire were forged with the other developed capitalist countries. The global division of labor coming out of World War II was rigid and clear: manufacturing was largely concentrated in the former imperial countries and resource extraction in their dependencies. The breaking down of the old imperial order and the emergence of new nation-states did not in itself overcome but rather continued to reproduce the old global division of labor through informal means, but the dynamics of capital accumulation were not centered on North–South flows as much as on the linkages between the advanced capitalist countries of the North. This pattern did not change all that much until the 1980s, when the political conditions were established—in the North as well as increasingly in the South—that laid the grounds for a truly global capitalism.

Integrating Europe

The accelerated push towards economic and monetary union in the 1980s, emerging at a time when Europe was mired in internal stagnation, needs to be understood in the context of the continuing integration of European and American capitalism. The abandonment of the Bretton Woods framework, wherein all European currencies had been fixed in a hub-and-spokes relationship to the dollar, was initially compensated for by the European states adopting a "currency snake" designed to prevent competitive devaluations; but "the instability of the snake reflected the fact that the 1970s was a low point for European cooperation."[1] The formation of the European Monetary System in 1979—"the most significant development in the EC arising out of the long crisis from 1969 to 1983"—was the first major step towards the common currency, a development that the US did not oppose.[2] What it was much more concerned about, even in the wake of the election that brought Mrs. Thatcher to office clearly representing a powerful neoliberal response to the crisis of the 1970s, was the apparent persistence on the Western European Left of radical socialist political alternatives. This was expressed in the strength of the Bennite call for economic democracy inside the Labour Party in the early 1980s, the Swedish unions' proposals for wage-earners' funds to socialize capital, and especially by the electoral victory of the French Socialist Party in May 1981, on a program developed in concert with the Communist Party, that was unquestionably the most radical of any offered in the West by a prospective government in at least thirty years.[3]

The Mitterand government's attempt to buck the global policy trend towards budgetary austerity amid the deepest economic downturn since the 1930s involved the immediate creation of over 60,000 public-sector jobs, with the promise of another 150,000 to come, and the nationalization of the country's two largest merchant banks and five industrial groups. Although the limits of this program were clear in light of the absence of capital controls and the substantive reorientation of finance and production, Mitterand's policies produced enormous hostility from the other G7 states. As the minister of economy and finance in the new government, Jacques Delors, said later: "When they took part in international meetings, Socialist ministers were looked upon as if they had arrived from another planet, a red flag flying in their hands." This hostility was hard to bear for a French president who was cast as "Reagan's best ally" against the USSR in the Euromissile controversy (the main front of the New Cold War of the early 1980s), and who wanted to be seen as "a man beyond suspicion of betraying the 'Atlantic cause.'"[4]

But what above all determined the French Socialist government's U-turn on economic policy was the severe market pressure on the franc in the context of the high-interest-rate and austerity policies being pursued by the US, the UK, and particularly Germany. In the face of the difficulties involved in attempting even "Keynesianism in one country" (never mind socialism), the Mitterand government proposed a "European social space" in which the ten countries of the Common Market could collectively take their distance from the Volcker turn and Reaganism. This would allow for the coordination of exchange rates in line with common policies to reduce unemployment, improve labor relations, and harmonize welfare systems. But this was soundly rejected, including by Helmut Schmidt's Social Democratic government, which cleaved closely to the monetarist ortho-doxy of the Bundesbank.[5]

Significantly enough, it was not at an intra-European meeting but at the G7 Summit held at Versailles in June 1982 that France agreed to a policy of austerity, and to aid the IMF in "a more comprehensive multilateral surveil-lance exercise to promote policy convergence and exchange rate stability."[6] Within a week, the franc was devalued alongside the revaluation of the mark, in an agreement with the Germans that was conditional on the French Socialist government's promise, announced the next day, to bring its fiscal deficit below 3 percent of GDP. Over the next quarter-century this would become the most durable measure of fiscal discipline in Europe—being included in the formation of Economic and Monetary Union through the Maastricht Treaty, the Stability Pact, and the creation of the euro. For Mitterand, European integration "replaced socialism as the grand project that justified his turnaround."[7] It did not take long before French Socialist Party leaders even supported the privatization of the firms they had earlier nationalized, while the "concepts of class and capitalism, even the very word socialism, disappeared from their vocabulary."[8]

They were certainly not alone in this respect, as social democracy followed a similar trajectory throughout Europe. In the British Labour

Party the defeat of the Bennite left opened the way for "New Labour" in the 1990s.[9] And even in Sweden the wage-earners' fund proposal was converted by the early 1980s into little more than a forced savings scheme to provide employers with a new source of capital.[10] Although Sweden did not join the EU until 1995, this paragon of the European welfare state was already overseeing the liberalization of financial markets through the 1980s, largely because its "Central Bank no longer had the capacity to sustain the old regulations" in light of the enormous growth of those markets.[11] It was already clear by the mid 1980s that, as Daniel Singer put it, "the Europe of states and of big business had made infinitely more progress than the Europe of labour unions."[12] This was seen when the European Round Table of major corporations (established in 1983 in direct emulation of the Business Roundtable in the US) joined with US MNCs in Europe in expressing "unprecedented hostility" to the EC's Vredeling directive to extend workers' consultation rights, while unions turned to giving priority to work-time reduction rather than the investment planning they had proposed in the 1970s.[13] Although it took a seven-week strike in the German auto industry in 1984 to win work-time reduction, the companies increasingly used reductions in hours of work as a lever to win greater flexibility in the distribution of work-time, and works councils "lost their ability to force bargaining around overtime as a way of winning other things," as Erich Klemm, chairman of the General Works Council at Daimler, put it in a subsequent interview.[14] Thus even the primary progressive labor reform of the neoliberal era—the European reduction of work-time—proved quite limited and contradictory.[15]

Social democrats like Delors who took the lead in establishing the Single European Act of 1986 pinned their hopes on the "Social Charter" in return for facilitating "a Europe of traders and capital." What they failed to understand was that they had already "thrown away their trump cards . . . A single market for capital and goods without common fiscal, social and ecological policies could not fail to set off a downward competition between member states, each needing to bring its trade into balance."[16] To be sure, the move towards a single European market accelerated the push for a single currency, which would eliminate the internal balance-of-trade and exchange-rate constraints. But this only further reinforced the case for the complete removal of capital controls. When the governors of Europe's central banks came together in 1988 under the aegis of the Delors Commission to establish the goal of achieving monetary union within a decade, this was made conditional on the centralization of monetary authority in a European Central Bank patterned on the Bundesbank, and on the adoption of a fiscal "stability pact" involving the same rules for imposing ceilings on budgetary deficits that had forced France to effect its U-turn.[17]

Most significant in the short run, however, was the Commission's recommendation that the removal of capital controls should come at the beginning of the process of monetary integration rather than at its end. It was on this basis that the EC's Council of Ministers issued a directive requiring the removal by July 1990 of all restrictions on the movement of capital between both member- and non-member-states, in advance of the adoption of the Maastricht Treaty. In the short term, this unleashed an orgy of speculation against European currencies that were no longer protected by capital controls, inducing broader financial crises (such as the Swedish bank collapse), and reinforced financial market pressures for public sector austerity. While the currency crisis destabilized the EMS and forced the adoption of a much looser Exchange Rate Mechanism, the embrace of these measures by Europe's states meant that the march towards the single currency could be resumed with the assurance that "discipline" would prevail.

Especially significant in this respect, and indeed for the overall shift in the balance of class forces in Europe, was the transformation of European financial markets along US lines.[18] The City of London, which had since the 1960s served US banks "as a laboratory for financial innovation" at the center of the Euromarkets, was the leading site of this Americanization.[19] The removal of UK capital controls in 1979, the City of London's own "big bang" in 1987, and the new stock exchange system modeled on the automated NASDAQ in the US, were all about trying to compete with New York on a level playing field, reinforced by direct pressures from the Wall Street investment banks operating in London. It was, ironically, US regulatory changes in the 1970s requiring prudent investment on the part of US pension funds that led to the diversification of these funds into equity and bond investments abroad, and US banks in London were especially well positioned to attract such funds to the London equity market.[20] The 1987 Financial Services Act, the most "crucial piece of regulatory reform introduced in Britain," was only adopted after the US model had been closely examined by "a stream of British visitors";[21] and the first chairman of the new Securities and Investment Board explicitly acknowledged: "[W]e shall, to all intents and purposes, be exercising the power of an SEC in this country."[22]

As one experienced City insider put it:

> The triumph of American values and American ways provided an ideal background for the Wall Street investment banks. What more powerful message can there be than: "If you want to compete in an American-style market place and secure access to the vast pool of American capital who better to service you than an organization that is imbued with these practices and epitomizes these values?"[23]

Wall Street banks were even more successful on the Continent in under-writing equity offerings, arranging mergers and acquisitions, and creating and trading in derivatives. Goldman Sachs epitomized this success, initially by pouring enormous resources into a London office that until the 1980s had been regarded in New York as having "no overall vision beyond simply selling American stocks, US Government bonds, and some Eurobonds for US corporations like Ford." Gene Fife, who was sent in from the US in 1985, explained the challenge as being "to replicate Goldman Sachs in London and across Europe so the firm looked, felt, and tasted like Goldman Sachs as much as McDonald's is McDonald's in Frankfurt, Germany, or Toowoomba, Australia."[24]

Establishing this "global branding" first involved sending top traders and researchers from Goldman Sachs's US operations to develop a comprehensive pan-European strategy. Goldman's started paying very high salaries to attract the most talented local analysts to fill key positions (and in the process imported from New York an explosion in financial sector salaries and bonuses). Attention was especially given to hiring as "international advisors" prominent people in each country with extensive corporate and government connections, who met regularly to act as a "sounding board on business-development strategies and political environments in an integrating Europe."[25] They included the future prime minister of Italy, Romano Prodi, and the venerable Jacques Mayoux, the former CEO of France's leading corporate bank, Société Générale, who during the 1992 privatization of Total, France's second-largest oil company, directly and successfully intervened with its CEO to make Goldman Sachs rather than Morgan Stanley the underwriter of the stock offering. In Germany, one of Helmut Schmidt's key advisors and the former minister of economics, Hans Frederichs, became Goldman's international advisor. He played a key role in getting Daimler-Benz to use Goldman Sachs exclusively for its American-related business, including its listing on the New York Stock Exchange. Goldman's also became the co-equal underwriter with Deutsche Bank of the 1995 privatization of Deutsche Telekom, after Frederichs met privately on this with Helmut Kohl and arranged for Goldman Sachs to give the Bundestag a detailed briefing on the complexities involved in what was the largest-ever initial public offering of shares in the world at the time.[26]

As the leading German banks tried to compete with US investment banks on their home turf, they found that their "ties with specific industrial firms might then easily cause conflicts of interest between the banks' roles as consultant and owner" when it came to arranging mergers and acquisitions.[27] This led to the attenuation of the old links between finance and industry: Deutsche Bank's presence on the supervisory boards of the hundred largest German firms fell from forty in 1980 to seventeen in 1998; the share of industrial company board chairmanships held by bankers fell from 44 to 23 percent over the 1990s. For their part, German corporations looked to global capital markets for equity investment. By the mid 1990s the share of mutual funds, insurance companies, and foreign investors in the ownership of the biggest German firms had reached 21 percent; by 2005 it was no less than 46 percent, with the largest increases coming from foreign investors.[28]

The most influential European MNCs emulated American practices, while at the same time substantially increasing their investments in the US. The Daimler takeover of Chrysler—motivated by Daimler executives' "prior decision to concentrate on auto rather than diversification" and a determination "to survive as one of the 5 or 6 world auto companies"—made more waves than any similar acquisition within Europe. It was widely seen as evidence of US decline. Yet the Daimler executives themselves explicitly saw it in terms of embracing "American spirit, attitude and drive" as well as flexible production methods, venture capital markets, broad distribution networks—and lower taxes.[29] Since Daimler's CEO Jurgen Schrempp had already famously "taken on board the American management values of the 1990s" by the time Daimler-Benz (whose main shareholder was Deutsche Bank) acquired Chrysler in 1998, this "confirmed the survival of German industrial muscle but it was the very reverse of European over American managerialism."[30] Schrempp's popularization of "shareholder value" was explained by his successor, Dieter Zetsche, as being "one of the mechanisms for putting pressure" on Daimler managers and workers to stay competitive, while its "short-termist" drawbacks were seen as inevitable in light of the fact that "the American system is now more or less a world-wide system."[31]

US banks and MNCs were themselves major players in the corporate mergers and acquisitions in Europe that were so important to regional integration. By the end of the 1990s, the top five financial advisors on M&A deals of over half a billion dollars were all US investment banks (of 693 such deals in Western Europe in 1999, 53 percent were handled by US financial advisors, including 51 percent of those in the UK, 46 percent in France, and no less than 65 percent in Germany).[32] US investment banks like Morgan Stanley, Citigroup, and Merrill Lynch, as well as Goldman Sachs, also increasingly took market share from the European banks in underwriting IPOs: this was primarily based on "the power and reach of their distribution machines," particularly their access to "the 50 or so largest (predominantly American) global institutional investors who effectively decide whether an offering succeeds or fails."[33] The capital expenditures of US MNCs in Europe more than doubled in value within the first five years following the passage of the 1986 Single European Act, and continued to rise through the 1990s. And just as American capital had originally encouraged the development of the Common Market, seeing it as serving their goal of integrated production and marketing across Europe, they now continued to be corporate leaders in cross-border production inside Europe. While Opel (GM) or Ford were by no means as politically influential in Germany (or even in Brussels) as Volkswagen or Daimler, their operations were more widely dispersed across the countries that made up "Single Europe," coming closer than their competitors to realizing the ideal of a pan-European enterprise.[34]

At the same time, the two-way flow of FDI, incorporating as it did networks of production (components flowing in both directions before being assembled into final products for diverse markets), made the economies on both sides of the Atlantic more and more interdependent, and pushed the free-trade agenda well beyond European regional integration. The training of European managers was strongly linked to the leading US business schools, ensuring that the management practices that made the most impact were first "validated" in the US.[35] Even Japanese methods like Just In Time and Total Quality Management were only adopted in Europe after American corporations had embraced them. By the 1990s American IT corporations such as Apple, Hewlett-Packard, IBM, and Microsoft were supplying over 80 percent of Europe's software and computer market, and Europeans were "increasingly working with technologies and tools originally designed for the American marketplace."[36] While this certainly demonstrated the importance of European markets for leading US corporations, it also showed Europe becoming more rather than less integrated with the US as the information technology revolution proceeded. None of this is to deny the specificities of European production, but it does indicate that widespread notions of alternate production regimes and "varieties of capitalism" were misconceived: by sharply contrasting European with Anglo-American "models," they failed to recognize the degree of integration noted here.[37]

Economic and productivity growth in the major European countries, which had already slowed considerably relative to the US in the 1970s, lagged behind the US in the 1980s and 1990s, and European unemployment rates were persistently higher (see Table. 8.1). The unemployment was in large part due to the deflationary bias embedded in the form that European economic and monetary union took, but it was increasingly attributed by employers and policmakers to unit labor costs outpacing those in the US (even though wages in Europe did not keep up with productivity growth). The solution proposed was the "flexibilization" of labor markets and reductions in the social wage.

This did not write *finis* to the European variety of capitalism, embedded as it was in the deeply entrenched corporatist arrangements of "coordinated capitalism" throughout the postwar era. But these arrangements were now ever more attuned to competitiveness as the overriding goal.[38] Motivated by a concern that "business and citizens in the European Union have been slower in embracing [the] new economy than in the United States," the European Commission wanted Europe to "become the cheapest and easiest place to do business in the world."[39] Thus, having started with the seductive promise in the mid 1980s of a European and Monetary Union based on a "social charter," by the time the euro was launched in 1999 it was clear that regional economic integration was, in effect, "the antechamber to broader liberalization." As John Grahl goes on to say: "Not only financial reforms, but also labour market and social protection policies, liberalisation and privatisation of public services, the promotion of venture capital and other such measures were all put forward in a completely uncritical attempt to mimic the growth process of the US in the late '90s."[40]

Table 8.1: Economic Comparisons, US-Europe, 1983–99

Annual average growth (%)	US	France	Germany	Italy	UK
GDP	3.5	2.0	2.3	2.0	2.7
Manufacturing output per hour	3.8	3.6	2.9	3.1	3.3
Real hourly compensation	0.7	1.7	2.6	1.6	1.8
Average unemployment rate	6.3	10.8	7.5	9.0	9.3

Source: Growth data from the *Economic Report of the President* 2000, Table B110; other data from the US Bureau of Labor Statistics, available at bls.gov/bls/international.htm. The data for Germany is for West Germany alone up to 1991.

While exports among Western European countries increased by 255 percent from 1983 to 2000, their exports to North America increased by 340 percent. By the end of the century, over half of all US FDI was located in Western Europe (up from 45 percent in 1983), while Western Europe accounted for two-thirds of FDI in the US.[41] It became increasingly clear that the project of European integration had little or nothing to do with a more progressive variety of capitalism that would challenge the American empire, but was rather part and parcel of the ongoing integration of Europe itself into global capitalism under the aegis of the American empire.[42]

Japan's Contradictions of Success

Japan showed even more than Europe that the different varieties of capitalism in the second half of the twentieth century were really different varieties of integration into a US-led global capitalism. However distinctive was Japan's brand of "network capitalism,"[43] it was dependent for its success on US support. Japan's form of cartelized capitalist development relied on an undervalued yen in relation to the dollar and open access for Japanese goods to US markets, even as Japan kept its own markets largely closed. In contrast to Europe, the US tolerated this asymmetry right through the 1970s and did not insist that Japan loosen the Foreign Exchange and Foreign Trade Control law of 1949, which prohibited all cross-border capital flows except those permitted by administrative decree.[44] The toleration of this for so long partly reflected a relative lack of interest in Japanese markets on the part of US banks and MNCs, but it had more to do with the American state's accommodation to Japan's traditional political and economic elites in the context of US strategic calculations in Asia.

The interests of the most powerful units of Japanese industrial and financial capital were bound together through their horizontal *kereitsu* relations—once aptly dubbed "corporatism without labour."[45] This was reinforced by the state's powerful finance and industry ministries and the Bank of Japan, not least in requiring and underwriting the banks' provision of cheap credit to industry. Japan's "developmental state" was able to become the incubator of capital accumulation in the economic transition from light industry (textiles) through heavy industry (steel and chemicals) to manufacturing industry (autos, televisions), in good part because of the way it adopted the US Glass-Steagall Act's compartmentalization of finance and ceilings on interest rates paid on deposits.[46] The result was that the savings made by workers to compensate for their inadequate pensions, and the high cost of housing and education, became the basis for Japanese industry's low cost of capital.

The revaluation of the yen vis-à-vis the dollar in the early 1970s started the process of undoing the special advantage the US had afforded Japan in the postwar era. Japanese capitalists experienced the crisis of the 1970s very differently from capitalists in Western Europe and North America. The country certainly faced inflationary pressures and a fiscal crisis amid rapidly rising wages and social expenditures and increased commodity prices. Nevertheless Japan's rate of inflation was brought down earlier and faster. At the end of the 1970s, when the US and most of Europe were facing double-digit inflation, Japan's inflation rate was 3.6 percent.[47] Its levels of unemployment remained low (just above 2 percent), and its per capita rate of growth—while a far cry from what it had been in the 1950s and 1960s—stayed above that of the other G7 economies.

Japan was immediately able to compensate for the upward revaluation of its currency (and for the oil shock of 1973) by establishing a dramatic gap between productivity and wage increases (which had run in tandem from 1968 to 1973) that averaged over 3 percent a year from 1975 to 1985. This sustained manufacturing profit rates, after their fall in the early 1970s from the stratospheric levels of the previous two decades, at a higher level than those prevailing in the rest of the G7 until the mid 1980s.[48] A key reason for this was that increased capital investment in the leading Japanese

manufacturing sectors did not confront, as it had in the US, militant shop-
floor resistance to the organizational changes necessary to yield high
productivity increases. Even though the annual *shunto* pay round obscured
this, the consistent weakness of Japanese unions allowed for absolute
managerial control over the labor process, and for the flexibility and cost
savings afforded by extensive overtime work. This high rate of exploitation, together with the low cost of capital, was the basis for the extension
of the so-called "Japanese miracle" into the 1980s.

By the 1970s Japan's leading corporations and banks were already revealing clear signs of straining against their confinement within the incubator of
network capitalism—in rather the same way that US finance had outgrown
the banking regulations of the New Deal. They increasingly began to both
export and import capital across Japan's borders. This was readily accommodated by the state so long as it involved Japanese capital's investments in
Taiwan or South Korea, which served to sustain accumulation in the course
of the transition from light to heavy industry. But in the world of fluctuating currencies of the 1970s, Japanese firms also began to push for more
access to international capital markets, not least "since capital controls
limit[ed] opportunities . . . to hedge against foreign exchange risks."[49]
Moreover, the large manufacturing companies were not only making such
high profits in the 1970s and early 1980s that they no longer needed to
borrow as much as before from Japanese banks, but were also confident
they could raise money in international capital markets. In other words, as
Gillian Tett has noted, "they no longer needed the financial bottle-feeding
of the old self-enclosed Ikeda system."[50] Given this, the large banks were in
turn more and more attracted to breaking into the securities business and
other arenas of investment banking from which they had been excluded by
the compartmentalization of Japanese finance under network capitalism.

The Ministry of Finance only moved very slowly and inconsistently
through the 1970s to change the old framework. All along, its importance
in the developmental state was "due as much to the way it is a cockpit
within which conflicting interests battle, as to any capacity to act as the
authoritative controller of Japanese financial markets."[51] The secondary
market on its own bonds that it had established in 1975 as a way of coping
with growing public deficits after the 1973 oil crisis came to play "a critical
part in the history of financial liberalization" precisely because this rendered
problematic the maintenance of controls on the interest that banks paid on
savings accounts (similar to what happened with "Regulation Q" in the
US).[52] Corporations, institutional investors, individual savers, and the banks
themselves were drawn not only to real estate but also to the stock market,
which they had previously shunned as "an arena for speculators."[53] To allow
the large Japanese banks to compete with this trend, they were permitted
from 1979 onwards to copy what the US banks had been doing for two

decades: that is, to issue Certificates of Deposit to attract funds. But the "most prominent turning point in the history of Japanese finance" came in 1980 with the loosening of capital controls in the major amendments to the Foreign Exchange and Foreign Trade Control Law.[54]

In the ten years following the end of Bretton Woods, the pace of Japan's financial internationalization, measured in terms of the ratio of total cross-border capital flows, had already overtaken that of the US and Germany, and through the 1980s it accelerated even more. The growth in Japanese cross-border interbank assets and liabilities was averaging no less than 60 percent annually by the mid 1980s, while long-term capital movements from Japan grew from $3 billion in 1977 and $12 billion in 1978 (1.5 percent of GDP) to no less than $132 billion (6.7 percent of GDP) by 1986.[55] Japan's financial liberalization of 1980 coincided with the very high US interest rates that came with the Volcker shock. Together with the Thatcher government's elimination of capital controls in Britain, this opened the floodgates to the massive foreign purchase of Treasury bonds; the strengthening of the dollar, alongside the defeat of US domestic inflation, was the measure of Volcker's success. "The Japanese, in particular, seemed eager to lend," Volcker later wrote. "They plainly did not feel there were equally attractive alternatives in Tokyo."[56] The status of US Treasuries as "the linchpin of the global financial order" was graphically captured in R. Taggart Murphy's description of what made them so "irresistible" to large Japanese investors:

> [I]n all the blizzards of financial paper that blew through Tokyo during the 1980s—the Canadian and Australian dollar twofers, the reverse dual currency bonds, the Samurai bonds, the Sushi bonds, the instantly repackaged perpetuals, the zero-coupon bonds, the square trips and double-dip leveraged leases—US Treasury notes bills and bonds held pride of place. These securities . . . backed by the full faith and credit of the US government . . . formed a liquid market of great depth: the securities were traded around the world, and buyers and sellers were thus available twenty-four hours a day. Most other dollar debt securities were priced off Treasuries. The yields in nondollar markets were systematically compared with Treasuries, and with the development of interest and currency swaps, nondollar markets would be linked directly to Treasuries.[57]

The Japanese banks' insatiable appetite for US securities in general provided a good deal of the fodder for the fattening of Wall Street in the 1980s. Murphy, a junior Wall Street banker at the time, observed that "Japanese banks became critical subscribers to big-ticket syndicated loans . . . American lead managers often turned around and sold most of their participation in the loan to a Japanese institution."[58] This facilitated the explosion of financial securitization in the US, just as at the same time Japanese banks started copying Wall Street's innovations in currency trading and hedging. They presumed that if manufacturers like Toyota could "challenge the Americans at their own game," they could "perform the same trick with financial techniques the Americans had pioneered."[59] But they were not so much bent on challenging the American bankers as desperate to get into their game. The increasing scale of Japan's dependence on US securities and Treasury bonds not only contributed to the dramatic rise in the value of the dollar in the early 1980s, but also was crucial to the resumption of US economic growth after 1982, while growth rates elsewhere remained low. And the US remained by far the most important export market for Japanese goods through the 1980s.[60]

This is not to say that Japan's mode of integration into global capitalism in the 1980s did not produce contradictions for either the US or Japan. The cost to the US economy of the Volcker shock's renewal of confidence in the dollar was not only that the strong dollar pulled in imports, but also that it made US exports—which had grown at 8 percent annually in the 1970s (almost as fast as Japan's)—more expensive. The growth of US exports fell to 2 percent annually from 1980 to 1985, and in conjunction with the impact of Japan's export success on US manufacturing jobs this produced a protectionist backlash that threatened the trajectory towards trade liberalization that had been so central to the making of global capitalism since World War II. The growth of Japanese small car exports to the US, while 200,000 workers were laid off by GM, Ford, and Chrysler, produced the Congressional pressures that led the Reagan administration in 1981 to negotiate "voluntary export restraints" that effectively set quotas on the number of cars Japan could export to the US each year. But the US MNCs that also dominated the domestic manufacturing industry were not generally keen on protectionism, because it risked retaliatory measures that might lead to the unmaking of global capitalism. They much preferred the problem to be addressed by a realignment of the yen–dollar exchange rate.

As the recession ended in the fall of 1982, the revival of demand—and a yen that was 35 percent lower in relation to the dollar than it had been before the dollar was strengthened by the Volcker shock—pulled in Japanese exports, accentuating the Congressional appetite for protectionist legislation. It was notable, however, that the top US corporations, led by Lee Morgan, the Caterpillar board chairman who also chaired the Business Roundtable Task Force on International Trade and Investment, did not call for protection but focused instead on the exchange rate as "the single most important trade issue facing the US."[61] The MNCs' long-standing interest in the further opening of foreign markets to both imports and foreign direct investment prompted the US Treasury to address the problem of exchange

rates by calling for the strengthening of the yen through the further liberalization of Japanese capital markets, which would at the same time alleviate
the US trade deficit by opening up these markets to US financial service
providers.[62]

Reagan's first Treasury secretary, Don Regan (previously CEO of Merrill
Lynch), was reluctant to revive the previous sporadic interventions in
currency markets. The Treasury was already engaged with the Federal
Reserve in coordinating the G7 response to the Latin American debt crisis,
and taking the initial steps towards the development of international bank
capital adequacy rules.[63] Moreover, the Treasury's push for deeper and
broader capital markets in Japan resembled what it had also wanted from the
Europeans in the early 1960s, but the pressure applied now was much
greater: "[N]ever before has one country so pressed another to integrate its
financial markets with the rest of the world and to internationalize its
currency."[64] The Yen–Dollar Agreement negotiated between Japan's
Ministry of Finance and the US Treasury in 1983–84, followed by major
steps further to liberalize Japan's financial markets, reflected what Moran
termed "the alliance for change between core institutions of the American
state, notably the Treasury department, and the domestic Japanese interests
favouring reform." The latter were able to tip the balance of forces inside
the Ministry of Finance by arguing that acceding to the US Treasury's pressure for liberalization was better than suffering from protectionist legislation
by Congress. Moran's stark conclusion is apt: "There is indeed a key state
actor in the Japanese financial services revolution, but it is the American
rather than the Japanese state."[65]

The notion that the liberalization of Japan's financial markets would
relieve the upward pressure on the dollar by suddenly turning the yen into
an alternative world currency was always chimerical. While the penetration
of US banks into Japan did indeed increase, the main effect of Japan's further
financial liberalization after the Yen–Dollar Agreement was signed in May
1984 was to end the limits on currency swap transactions and to encourage
Japanese banks to issue more bonds overseas (initially mainly in the
Eurobond market). As a result, there was no marked effect on exchange
rates, and the US trade deficit continued to grow (from $31 billion in 1983
to $56 billion in 1985).[66] It was in this context, with the National Association
of Manufacturers nipping at the administration's heels to bring down the
value of the dollar, that the Treasury (where James Baker had replaced
Donald Regan as secretary after the 1984 election) initially revived the old
WP3 committee of the OECD, through which the G10 finance ministries
had done so much business in the 1960s.

Exhibiting the same impatience with regard to accommodating the
interests of the smaller members states of the G10 as they had manifested in
the late 1960s, the finance ministers and central bank governors of the US,

the UK, Japan, France, and Germany came together on their own in September 1985 to strike the famous agreement at New York's Plaza Hotel to bring down the value of the dollar by concerted interventions in the currency markets. Armed with an $18 billion dollar war-chest, split evenly between the US, Japan, and the Europeans, the interventions led to a 20 percent fall in the dollar–yen exchange rate by the end of 1985. However important their cooperation was to ensure that the dollar devaluation would be "orderly," the most pressing concern was to unite behind "the US Treasury's desire to quell protectionist pressures in Congress."[67]

This "most impressive coordinated multinational attack on currency markets by governments in history"[68] was not accompanied, however, by the coordination of domestic economic policies. Germany and Japan reneged on promises to stimulate their economies alongside the fiscal discipline promised by the US and, "unwilling to accept automatic interference in their own policies,"[69] rejected the US Treasury's proposal for an IMF surveillance scheme that would trigger such adjustments. Under these conditions, the dollar continued to fall despite halfhearted attempts to reverse this after another famous meeting of officials at the Louvre in Paris in early 1987. By September, there had been a 60 percent decline of the dollar relative to the yen in the two full years since Plaza had started. This was widely perceived as the "greatest symbolic reversal of wealth and economic power in the history of the world."[70] But in reality Plaza's significance was not what it seemed.

Far from the Louvre and Plaza negotiations being part of Japan's supplanting the US as the main actor in capitalist globalization, it was actually becoming more integrated into the US-led international financial system, more sensitive to the behavior of US financial institutions in both London and New York, and more subject to the volatility of US financial markets. The Plaza Accord only finally ended what Japan's own finance minister admitted was the American state's long-standing toleration of an exchange rate that had amounted to a "subsidy to Japan's exports to the United States and an import surcharge on US exports to Japan."[71]

Japanese banks briefly came to dominate the standard rankings of the world's largest financial institutions as they provided easy credit for Japan's historically unprecedented purchase of assets abroad, and became conduits for a real estate and stock-market bubble inside Japan. But their vastly expanded assets concealed highly questionable lending and corporate reporting practices, as well as a technological backwardness that belied their size and prominence (in the late 1980s check-clearing in Tokyo was still done by hand rather than computer, and there were as yet no twenty-four-hour ATMs).[72] Even before Plaza, Japanese banks were already implicated in the collapse of Continental Illinois, and after Plaza they were even more implicated in the US stock market crash of 1987.[73] At the same time, the

Ministry of Finance and the Bank of Japan not only had increasingly less effective control over what was happening in their domestic financial system, but also demonstrated little interest in seeing the yen displace the dollar as the world's reserve currency—much less in assuming the responsibilities of global financial leadership.

Japan was content to act as what Murphy calls "a loyal retainer," as seen in its support for the Treasury and the Federal Reserve after the 1987 crash, when the Ministry of Finance arm-twisted Japanese fund managers to renew their dollar investments and the Bank of Japan actively cooperated with the Fed to provide both domestic and global liquidity to help restore financial stability.[74] The significance of this kind of cooperation in combating financial volatility—especially coming as it did in the wake of the G7's failure to coordinate fiscal policies or establish a surveillance system to end imbalances between surplus and deficit countries—was clearly articulated by Gerald Corrigan, the head of the New York Federal Reserve. The measure of success, he argued, was

> not whether there is some major policy change or communiqué . . . Rather the measure of success is the ability of the participants to grasp more fully all the dimensions of their own situation and the situation of others and their ability to frame their own policies in a manner in which the sensitivities to the problems and perspectives of others loom larger rather than smaller.[75]

But the most fundamental role of Japan at the time, as soberly expressed by the chief economist of one of its most venerable banks, was "to assist the United States by exporting our money to rebuild your economy. This is the evidence that our economy is fundamentally weak. The money goes to America because you are fundamentally strong."[76] Between 1985 and 1989 alone, Japanese foreign direct investment in the US exploded from $2.6 billion to $21.2 billion, and the proportion of Japanese FDI going to the US increased from 40 to almost 50 percent.[77] The effect of all of this was especially clear in the auto sector. The major Japanese car firms not only absorbed the effect of the higher yen by accepting lower profits, but greatly accelerated the strategy they had begun to adopt, before Plaza, of circumventing protectionist measures by building their own plants in the US, largely in the US south, and almost all non-union. This had the effect of reinforcing the defeat of US labor while creating a strong congressional constituency favorable to these Japanese firms. Above all, it contributed not just to the geographical but also to the technological and organizational restructuring of US industry discussed in the previous chapter. Meanwhile, US exports resumed a rate of growth even more impressive than in the 1970s: in the decade after 1985 they grew at an average of over 10 percent a year. The fact that US trade deficits persisted after Plaza only showed the futility of trying to correct them through currency manipulations, and this reinforced the case for instead promoting US exports through a "free trade" offensive (see Chapter 9), which was consistent with the making of global capitalism.

During the 1980s, urban land prices in Japan almost tripled, while the value of the stock market quadrupled. The bubble that developed was further inflated with the aid of US derivatives traders who had been welcomed to Japan throughout the decade. When, in 1987, the Bank of Japan lowered interest rates (not only to offset the damage to exports caused by the raised value of the yen, but also to stimulate its economy in response to long-standing pressure from the US to do so as well as to support the global economy after the US stock market crash), this only further inflated the financial bubble, "which, by the late 1980s, had begun to look like one of the great manias in global financial history."[78] When the Ministry of Finance and Bank of Japan then tried to rein this in by raising interest rates, this triggered an economic collapse from which there was no easy exit. Through the 1990s it was Japan among the G7 that suffered the worst of the contradictions associated with the realization of global capitalism.[79]

The notion that Japan would displace the US as the hegemonic power quickly faded. As adept as Japan had been in moving from light to heavy industry, and then to motor vehicles and consumer electronics, it proved incapable of matching the US in the transition to the highest of high-tech sectors. Nevertheless, Japan remained a major exporter with large trade surpluses, while its banks were major global investors. Japan's great manufacturing firms were by no means decimated and, driven by the pressures of a realigned yen and limited markets at home, they greatly expanded their production abroad. The "overarching strategy" of Japanese capital throughout the 1990s was "to create regional operating zones in North America, Europe and Asia—with production, finance and trade increasingly integrated over the core and periphery within these zones."[80] Japanese capital consequently came to play an important role not only in sustaining the dollar, reproducing the material domestic base of the American empire, and lending support to the Treasury and the Federal Reserve in managing crises, but also in the making of global capitalism in the rest of the world.

The Rest of the World (Literally)

At the end of the twentieth century the advanced capitalist countries accounted for 90 percent of all financial assets, 65 percent of world GDP, and almost 70 percent of global exports of manufactured goods; not only did 85 percent of global FDI emanate from these countries, they were also the recipients of over two-thirds of it.[81] But these statistics mask what was going on in the rest of the world. The major shift across so many developing countries to export-led manufacturing production meant that their

place in global capitalism was no longer that of mere suppliers of raw materials to the advanced capitalist states. In fact, this transformation in the
international division of labor involved a reconfiguration of social relations
in one country after another, yielding not only new capitalist classes which
became ever more linked to international capital accumulation, but also a
massive expansion of the global proletariat. This in turn had a profound
impact on the restructuring of production, and on class relations in the
advanced capitalist countries.[82]

The integration of these regions of the world into global capitalism was
of course extremely uneven, taking very different forms according to the
nature of the state and class alignments in individual countries, and the
extent to which the integration was sponsored (or occasionally blocked) by
the advanced capitalist states. This could especially be seen in the case of
South Korea, whose export-led industrialization led it to become the
beacon of capitalist developmental success in the 1980s. Crucial to this
success, however, as Vivek Chibber has shown by contrasting it with the
Indian case, was the unique role of Japanese companies. As they vacated
light for heavy industry at home, they provided Korean firms with their
sales and marketing networks, and thus positioned themselves "as middlemen in the US markets and as suppliers of capital goods to Korean exporting
firms."[83] It was on this foundation, along with the repression of labor in the
1960s, that support from the powerful capitalist *chaebol* networks was
sustained for the transformation of the Korean state, so that it could provide
cheap finance and technological support, as well as coordination, planning,
and regulation, which considerably reduced capital's investment costs. A
"developmental state" was thus a key factor in enabling South Korea, which
was already sending half its exports to the US by 1968, to reach a level of
capitalist development that led to its admission to the OECD in the 1990s.
As in the Japanese case, in terms of the importance of securing currency
undervaluation and asymmetric access to western markets, "the role of the
US was critical."[84]

It was indeed indicative of the continuing central role of the US in the
making of global capitalism that it allowed South Korea to more or less
follow "the same periphery strategy as immediate post-war Europe and
Japan, undervaluing the exchange rate, managing sizable foreign exchange
interventions, imposing controls, accumulating reserves, and encouraging
export-led growth by sending goods to the competitive centre countries."[85]
With the share of Korea's exports coming from manufacturing exploding
from 18 percent in 1962 to 77 percent in 1970, and increasing further
through the 1970s even in the face of the devaluation of the dollar after the
breakdown of Bretton Woods, it was hardly surprising that Korea's success
was increasingly emulated by other Asian states, including at the end of the
decade by the new Chinese Communist leadership (see Table 2).[86]

Table 8.2: Manufacturing Share Of Total Exports, Asia

	1970	1980	1990	1999
South Korea	77%	90%	94%	91%
Malaysia	7%	19%	54%	80%
Thailand	5%	25%	63%	74%
Philippines	7%	21%	38%	92%
Singapore	28%	47%	72%	86%
India	1%	2%	35%	54%
China	na	26%	72%	88%

Source: World Bank, databank.worldbank.org/ddp/home.do; WTO, International Trade Statistics, wto.org/english/res_e/statis_e/tradebysector_e.htm, Table IV.30. China's 1980 data is for 1985.

Many states in other regions of the third world had also, albeit usually more tentatively, tried to move from import-substitution to export-led industrialization. Long before they were finally impelled to do so by the impact of the 1980s debt crisis, they often experienced external pressures in this direction, including from the World Bank, especially after the US shifted from tepid support for ISI in the 1950s to requiring tariff-reduction and foreign investment liberalization as conditions for its foreign aid.[87] But few states were readily able to replicate South Korea's successes. To the extent that the push for this was primarily external, the changes were limited. As Chibber showed, in the case of India the most powerful capitalist groups had emasculated the planning agencies by the late 1950s, while "the response of most firms to export promotion programs during the 1960s and 1970s was rarely more than lukewarm."[88] Moreover, unlike the Japanese in Korea, those MNCs that undertook FDI in manufacturing activities in former Third World countries were overwhelmingly oriented to supplying the domestic markets of these countries, and quite uninterested in opening the way to export markets.[89]

This was certainly true of US MNCs in Latin America, where it was only after the economic and political restructuring forced by the 1980s debt crisis that FDI increased rapidly alongside new export-oriented production. Latin American states had been drawn into the massive growth of international finance in the 1960s and 1970s, with large US banks (often operating through the Eurodollar market) taking the lead in lending to governments eager to borrow in order to cope with the increasing politicization of class conflict amid growing trade deficits and inflation.[90] But the heady comparisons sometimes made with South Korea at the time were inapt. The so-called Brazilian miracle remained in many ways "a clear descendent of

the earlier era of import substitution" in which the home market still dominated, even as many of the old ISI price and tariff regulations were loosened
and external bank financing allowed for large fiscal and trade deficits.[91] For
its part, the establishment of maquiladoras at the US–Mexican border
proved at best a partial outlet for ISI's contradictions.[92] Such industrial
development as occurred depended on a nine-fold rise in capital goods
imports, which contributed heavily to a more than six-fold increase in
public-sector foreign debt, mostly borrowed from US banks.[93]

The recycling of petrodollars through New York and London after the
1973 oil shock further fueled international bank lending to Latin American
governments. This was only partly because large US banks were encouraged to do their "patriotic duty" (as one Ford administration economic
advisor put it) by thus recycling dollars to Latin American dictatorships;[94]
the main reason was that the profits were so tempting, hitting a peak of 233
percent of their total capital and reserves in 1981.[95] This left Latin America
more subject than ever to crises generated in the North American imperial
heartland, as was fully revealed when it became the unintended casualty of
the Volcker shock. The Latin American debtors' net interest payments
skyrocketed from 33 to 59 percent of total export income between 1979 and
1981.[96] The debt crisis began with a run on the Mexican peso in February
1982, and came to a head six months later, on the eve of a presidential election, when the Portillo government first defaulted on its debt-service
payments and then nationalized Mexico's private banks, declaring that they
had "looted the nation far more than had any colonialist power."[97] This was
Latin America's equivalent of Europe's Mitterand moment, and its outcome
proved as frustrating to those looking for alternatives to integration into
global capitalism, as would be seen by the re-privatization of Mexico's
banks within the decade.

Attention, both then and later, focused on the IMF's imposition on Mexico
of a severe structural-adjustment program, which was then used as a template
for all the others to follow. But it was, in fact, the US Federal Reserve that
played the main role in managing the debt crisis, beginning with surrepti-
tiously providing overnight swaps to bolster the Bank of Mexico's accounts.
It was "with considerable unease," Volcker later admitted, that the Fed
"would transfer the money each month on the day before the reserves were
added up, and take it back the next day."[98] The Treasury and Fed also went
so far as to arrange secretly for the Department of Energy and the Bureau of
the Budget to approve a billion-dollar advance payment to Mexico for future
petroleum sales, and supplemented this by organizing bridging credit from
European and Japanese central bankers. They "instinctively understood what
was at stake," as Volcker's account makes clear, since the Mexican crisis
"brought the complex and automated international clearing machinery to the
edge of breakdown, threatening confidence in the entire system."[99]

The Fed "spoon-fed" Mexican banks until the presidential election, after which negotiations with the new De La Madrid government yielded the structural-adjustment agreement with the IMF that became the model for the rest of Latin America and beyond. This included the "thousands and thousands of high-priced negotiating hours in the 1980s," in which the most senior officials of the Fed and Treasury, as well as the IMF and World Bank, met with finance officials from other states who "by virtue of experience, tenure, and training [were] almost uniquely able to deal with each other on the basis of close understanding and frankness," as Volcker puts it. It also included the many parallel meetings that took place with the chairmen of the dozen or so largest banks in the world, trying to convince them of their "common interest" in resolving the crisis—given that if Mexico, Brazil, Venezuela, and Argentina failed to meet their payment schedules, commercial banks faced possible loan defaults totaling more than $175 billion. Volcker candidly describes these meetings:

> It was all very frustrating. The logic of the situation seemed to require that the banks at least volunteer some significant concessions on interest rates while building their reserves. But as regulators, we did not feel that we could in effect impose losses on the banks by forcing below-market interest rates or large reserves without jeopardizing their willingness to lend. As time passed, the banks did reduce their interest rate margins but it seemed to me then, as now, that the success of the whole would have been enhanced if, at an earlier stage, the banks had volunteered greater concessions. Instead, the negotiations always seemed to turn into a game of hardball in an attempt to squeeze out the last eighth of a percent or a year or two of shorter maturity on restructured loans, at the risk of undermining the cooperation of borrowers.[100]

About forty additional countries were already in arrears on their debt payments when the Mexican negotiations started in the fall of 1982. This meant that many of the world's largest banks faced insolvency, and not only led to a virtual halt in bank lending to developing countries but, by virtue of such high repayment risk in the interbank market, also threatened an imminent bank crisis in the advanced capitalist countries. The Fed developed a comprehensive strategy that radically expanded the superintendence of interbank repayment risk, focusing on how to inject liquidity into the payment system to "strengthen the international banks that had been severely weakened by the crisis."[101] The Fed took on the added short-term task of managing repayment and default risk by lending to commercial banks and restructuring bank debt at home, while the Treasury provided bridging assistance to the states negotiating with the IMF.

Throughout the 1980s the Fed and Treasury focused on ensuring that the strict conditionality the IMF attached to its loans required not just immediate measures of fiscal austerity, but long-term structural-adjustment programs designed to protect and guarantee financial assets alongside the neoiberalization of each recipient state. But even more significant for the way developing countries would over time come to manage their social and economic priorities was that the debt crisis changed the dynamics of international financing. Developing state borrowers were increasingly forced to turn to international securities markets, where risks could be more fully diversified and absorbed. They could no longer rely on their relationships with foreign and domestic banking syndicates, and could now only attract capital if they submitted fully to the discipline of impersonal global financial markets. It was this submission that made the US Treasury's Brady Plan successful, as the banks agreed to convert their debt claims into equity ownership of productive Latin American assets, as well as securities that could be sold on secondary markets.[102]

This was all taking place just as the CIA was conducting its massive counterinsurgency effort in Central America, while at the same time the State Department was engaged in "democracy promotion" to ensure that the overthrow of the dictatorships in the southern cone in particular did not lead to a break with neoliberal globalization.[103] Latin America's notorious "lost decade" of the 1980s involved a 9 percent fall in GDP per capita alongside unprecedented increases in class inequality.[104] Part and parcel of this was the change that domestic capitalist classes were undergoing. The earliest exemplar of that change was Chile, but it was not primarily the advice that Milton Freidman's "Chicago Boys" proffered to Pinochet that determined Chile's subsequent neoliberal path. Rather, the Pinochet government used the political space provided after its murderous counterrevolutionary coup to take advantage of Allende's land reforms and nationalizations to ensure that the traditional networks of landlords and capitalists did not reconstitute themselves in the ways that had previously impeded the development of Chilean capitalism. Trade liberalization and privatizations were combined with state support to transcend the economy's dependence on mining and heavy industry and expand export-oriented production in non-traditional agriculture, fisheries, and related manufacturing. The antiquated banking sector was also transformed, privatized pension funds were mobilized to increase the availability of capital and credit, and financial discipline was adopted in order to achieve greater international competitiveness.[105]

For its part, the transformation that Mexican capital went through in the 1980s was brought about less through the expansion of the maquilas than through the "apertura" involved in entering the GATT in 1986 and signing on to NAFTA in 1992. They accepted the loss of the old tariff protections and price supports as the "dose of bitter medicine . . . necessary to bring

Mexican industry into a competitive position," and as they shifted away from reliance on domestic markets and turned to foreign contracts, capital, and outsourcing, they embraced the notion, as one of them put it, that "business has no nationality."[106] In this they were at one with new techno-cratic elites "with degrees from Harvard Business School and other elite universities" who came to the fore not only in Mexico but more generally in Latin America; the old ruling-class families "underwent a qualitative transformation in the 1980s and 1990s, experiencing an unprecedented windfall in the amassing of private wealth and power, propelled by privati-zations and other opportunities opened up by neoliberal globalization, including new types of access to the world market and forms of association with extra-regional transnational capital."[107]

Powerful domestic actors—from the bankers in Mexico who secured the re-privatization of the banks to the South Korean leading industrialists who, having already turned to the burgeoning domestic securities and stock markets as important sources of financing—became leading advocates for financial sector autonomy from the state, demanding they be allowed to take advantage of competitive sources of international finance.[108] Similar trends were clearly visible in other former stalwarts of ISI, such as India, where new business groups "which gathered strength as industrialization progressed . . . came to see the system of internal controls and artificial monopolies as an obstacle to their own expansion."[109] They insisted that the liberalization process could not remain halting and uneven, on the grounds that "unless free of interruptions the logic of capital is unable to deliver the promised goods."[110] In Turkey as well, by the late 1970s, large groups of capitalists felt constrained by the existing cartelized and protected domestic markets, not to mention their problems with an increasingly militant labor movement.[111] This was a critical factor in the military takeover of 1980, after which, with the spur of an IMF agreement, Turkey became among the first countries to adopt neoliberal reforms. Even though privatization was "a rather slow process, due to the presence of strong regulatory authorities and state-owned industries, the market orientation of the economy was gradu-ally consolidated over the following two decades."[112] All this was reflected in Turkish capital's growing interest in accession to a neoliberalizing European Union.

Even more dramatic than the collapse of ISI was the grand opening to capital accumulation that "1989" represented in the USSR and Eastern Europe. The "pioneering" lending strategies of Western banks had already combined with the sclerosis of "actually existing socialism" to turn Poland, Yugoslavia, and Hungary, among other Communist states, into sizable debtor states during the 1970s, thereby initiating "the renewal of East-West economic integration" through a new relationship between "global capital markets and command economies."[113] The Eastern European states were mostly cut off from new bank loans along with the Third World states that were so severely impacted by the debt crisis in 1980s. But just at this time the new Chinese Communist leadership, having decided to adopt a strategy that might most appropriately be termed "capitalist gradualism," was able to draw in sizable flows of both bank loans and foreign direct investment. Meanwhile, in Russia, Gorbachev's "revolution from above" naively emulated a European social democracy that was itself being rapidly drawn into neoliberalism's embrace. Since *perestroika* was based on a "vague idea that some kind of socialism could be rebuilt in the context of market forces," it was hardly surprising that it soon "got out of control and spun into entropy," as Robert Cox graphically put it. "Those who gained from the "market" were pre-eminently well-placed members of the former *nomen-klatura*, speculators, and gangsters."[114]

Yet the stampede to capitalism in Russia and Eastern Europe generally produced nothing like the flow of foreign direct investment that was going to Latin America and to China by the early 1990s.[115] The interest of inter-national investors depended much less on the adoption of ersatz democracy than on a stable legal framework to guarantee contracts and secure property claims. It was estimated that in Russia, by the mid 1990s, "some 40 percent of output was being generated in the shadow economy compared to 12 percent in 1989."[116] The neoliberal "shock therapy" of privatizations and plant closures, which the US and Western European states quickly made a condition for extending loans and opening access to their markets, produced "the fragmentation of the Comecon region and its replacement by hub and spoke relations between isolated eastern states and the West." As Peter Gowan went on to observe: "The death of Communism had led the West to try to stamp out economic nationalism in favour of its own national and collective interests in the region. But this does not so much suggest a new era on the globe as something rather old fashioned which, in the days of Communism, used to be called imperialism."[117] That said, a recrudescence of inter-imperial rivalry, which so many observers expected, was not what the Europe Union's eastward expansion portended. Taking place as it did under the rubric of neoliberal European integration, and alongside the expansion of NATO, the US encouraged the EU's eastern expansion just as it had strongly encouraged the original moves towards European economic and political union in the postwar era.

Of course the whole rest of the world cannot really be fitted into the three general patterns of integration into global capitalism followed by East Asia, Latin America, and the ex-Communist countries. The Middle East and Africa conformed least in this respect, as was seen in the 1980s in the American empire's humiliation in the face of the Iranian Revolution, its loss of control over Saddam Hussein before Iraq's invasion of Kuwait, and its palpable fears that the boycott of apartheid South Africa might help bring

Communists into government there. But even in those regions where the political relationship with the American empire was to become ever more fraught, there was still nothing like an economic rupture. This was all the more remarkable given that it was states in these regions that figured so prominently in the passage of the UN General Assembly's Charter of Economic Rights and Duties of States in 1974, which asserted the right to "nationalize, expropriate or transfer ownership of foreign property." Even if, as we have seen, the US Treasury was well aware as early as 1975 of the need to "discount the rhetoric," few in Washington would have been so bold as to predict that by the 1980s the expropriations would largely have become a thing of the past. Having already declined from eighty-three in 1975 to seventeen in 1979, they fell to five in 1980, four in 1981, one in 1982, three in 1983, one each year from 1984 to 1986—and zero for the rest of the decade.[118]

Even where earlier nationalizations were not reversed, such as in the oil industry, the international oil companies were quite content not to own the oil reserves or production facilities so long as the new national oil companies were dependent on them for exploration, development, and extraction. New York and London remained the nodes of the spot and futures markets where the price of oil was set, and also of the distribution networks through which "essentially all oil exports are circulated to consumers."[119] Apart from the strategic reserves of the OECD countries that could be called into play at times of emergency to stabilize these markets, Saudi Arabia could generally be counted on to increase supply, while continuing to channel a large part of the funds accumulated via oil production "into the international organization of credit without transforming its foundations."[120]

At the other extreme, the African states that had become so heavily indebted through London and New York's recycling of petrodollars were among the most serious casualties of the 1980s debt crisis. And in the 1990s they experienced nothing like the integration into global capitalism that occurred in Latin America, in terms of either trade or FDI. In terms of debt, however, the integration grew ever more onerous, as Africa's total debt-to-GDP ratio rose from 20 percent in 1980 to 60 percent in 1990, and continued to rise through the 1990s to approach 70 percent.[121] Thus, as the World Bank admitted, "despite spreading trade liberalization, the share of trade in GDP fell in forty-four of ninety-three developing countries between the mid 1980s and mid 1990s," and it especially pointed to the tragedy of sub-Saharan Africa (which, notably, it saw in terms of "states collapsing from within").[122]

As we shall see in the following chapter, the question of how to fashion political and legal frameworks through which such a diverse array of states could be integrated into international capital accumulation, while sustaining order and containing economic crises in the face of the contradictions to which the realization of global capitalism simultaneously gave rise, was an immense challenge. The recognition of this was seen in the World Bank's call by 1997 for transcending "the sterile debate of state and market" and addressing the issue of "state effectiveness" in developing the kind of public rules and institutions that "allow markets to flourish."[123] The constitutional-izing of free trade under the rubric of the WTO, alongside the restructuring of states in the South under IMF and World Bank conditionalities, as well as a host of bilateral treaties wherein states guaranteed investor rights, provided the political carapace for a fundamental change in MNC relation-ships with the South.

The administrative and technological capacity of the MNCs to centralize the crucial functions related to control (planning, research and development, allocation of investment), while decentralizing the use of technology and selected manufacturing operations, allowed them to take advantage of local conditions like cheaper and abundant labor supplies. This finally opened the door to significant manufacturing taking place within the developing coun-tries, with a high proportion of them being in such technologically advanced sectors as electronics, transportation, and machinery. This did not mean, however, that global hierarchies in the division of labor did not persist. Most strategic activities (research, development, engineering, and capital-intensive high-valued-added production) were concentrated in the First World, as were newly emerging products and processes. Moreover, as MNCs picked and chose where to go, the distribution of FDI was very highly concentrated in a few countries of the South, with some regions, especially large parts of Africa, largely left out. Both foreign investment in these countries and their extensive dependence on global markets often came at the expense of the dense local linkages, class formations, state capacities—and synergies among all of these—that were so crucial to the development of the advanced capital-ist countries in their own formative years. Nor did the increase in global production taking place in the Third World lead to anything near a corre-sponding convergence in income relative to the advanced capitalist countries, as evidenced not only by the conditions in the factories but especially in the slums of most Third World cities. [124]

V

THE RULE OF GLOBAL CAPITALISM

9

Rules of Law: Governing Globalization

What became commonly known as globalization by the 1990s seemingly brought the whole world to a point where markets were taking on a life of their own. But, far from the globalization of production and finance "disembedding" markets from society, it was the ways in which capitalist "laws of value" were embodied in "rules of law" that made possible the further proliferation and spatial expansion of markets. Globalization was in fact intimately connected with legislative and administrative changes to deepen and extend market competition, including extensive treaties and coordination among states to this end. The accompanying new codifications of rules for the operation of "free markets" bespoke not state retreat but the restructuring and expansion of linkages between states and markets. The more capital became internationalized, the more states became concerned to fashion regulatory regimes oriented to facilitating the rapid growth of international trade and foreign investment.

It was one of the hallmarks of the centrality of the American empire in the making of global capitalism that the multilateral and bilateral treaties that established the regime of free trade and investment in the final two decades of the twentieth century were deeply inscribed with long-standing US legal and juridical rules and practices. The wide international range of US firms, as well as the relative size and importance of US markets, gave American state authorities "tremendous leverage in pressuring foreign firms and regulatory authorities" to adopt these rules and practices.[1] But the inherent limits on the extraterritorial application of US law in a world of formally sovereign states also gave rise to extensive coordination of national regulations through international institutions like the newly created WTO, the World Bank, the Bank of International Settlements, and the IMF.

The embrace of "structural adjustment" by so many states often depended on their desperation for emergency funds on the conditional terms of the "Washington Consensus." Yet it was not amiss of James Boughton to point out that what was "included in that rubric was similar to the indigenous revolution or evolution in thinking in developed and developing countries" on the part of state elites as well as capitalist classes around the world.[2] As we shall see, the interplay between "global norm making and national lawmak-ing" at the end of the twentieth century confirmed the extent to which the "spread of an international legal order with capitalism" still meant that "the power dynamics of political imperialism are embedded within the very juridical equality of sovereignty."[3]

The Laws of Free Trade

A key determinant of the realization of global capitalism at the end of the twentieth century was the capacity of the American state to maintain the postwar trajectory towards the liberalization of trade laws. We have seen in earlier chapters that, from as early as the 1890s, the US had begun to move away from the general protection of industry towards using *selective* protec-tion as a lever for opening up markets abroad; the brief reversion to general protectionism immediately after the onset of the Great Depression (when Congress pushed tariff duties to an all-time high of over 50 percent) was negated in 1934 by the Reciprocal Trade Agreement Act. This laid the foundation for the American state's leading role in trade liberalization after World War II, through the GATT system, which was "fundamentally US designed."[4] It was only with the full recovery of Western Europe and Japan—which, as we have seen, this system was explicitly intended to foster—that the leadership of the GATT process began to shift towards the "Quad group," which centered on bilateral consultations between Brussels and Washington, supplemented by "an expanded conversation" with Canada and Japan. Although the US was selective in implementing those portions of GATT treaties that most suited it, while exerting strong pres-sures on other states to meet their commitments to tariff reductions fully, by the late 1960s US tariff duties had nevertheless been reduced to 10 percent overall.[5] Their further reduction to 5 percent by the early 1980s, through the depths of a decade-long economic crisis at home, and in the face of increased competition and balance-of-payments problems, was the essential precondition for the globalization of "free trade" that followed.

The fact that the "major trade laws passed by Congress in the 1970s and 1980s were liberal in their orientation" was a very significant element in the further internationalization of the American state.[6] With the help of the Treasury's direct engagement in mobilizing US business behind it, the Trade Act of 1974 centralized trade policy in the hands of a Special Trade Representative (after 1980 called the "Office of the USTR"). In addition to becoming "the primary coordinator of US trade liberalization efforts" inside the American state, the USTR became—especially through thirty-one advisory committees with over 700 members from every industrial and agri-cultural sector, serving two-year terms—"the principle vehicle for translating capitalist interests into coherent trade policy positions."[7]

But no less crucial for the "fast track" passage of trade legislation, and for anticipating and deflecting Congressional opposition despite considerable economic dislocation and rising unemployment, was the increasing juridification of the way domestic political problems arising from trade liberalization were handled. As Chorev has shown, the changes made under the 1974 Trade Act to expedite appeals for "adjustment assistance" for workers and firms affected by increased imports was indicative of "the willingness of the American government to take on itself the cost of trade liberalization rather than imposing it on others"—while the new quasi-judicial procedures established for anti-dumping measures and countervailing duties were designed to "restructure protectionist measures in a way that would limit their negative effects." These changes allowed for tactical concessions to protectionist forces by making it easier to secure remedies for the costs of free trade. Although this was widely misperceived as a retreat from liberalization, its deliberate aim was in fact to *contain* protectionism by shifting the focus of political struggles away from trade liberalization itself. As Chorev concluded, "the *legalization* of the decision-making process would render the political influence of protectionists less determinant of the final outcome. Rules, not political considerations as such, were to govern the decision of whether a specific industry was eligible for protection."[8]

What globalization in good part entailed in the 1980s and 1990s was the extension of this process of juridification to other states, above all through the US drive to overcome "non-tariff barriers." The issue was clearly defined as early as 1971, in the Report to the President by the Commission on International Trade and Investment Policy (chaired by the CEO of IBM), which contended that the US had "not received full value for the tariff concessions made over the years because foreign countries have found other ways, besides tariffs, of impeding access to their markets."[9] By the late 1960s, in good part because of the significant flow of US manufacturing trade that already occurred within American MNCs' global operations, they were already pushing strongly for the adoption of a "non-tariff barriers" strategy. But such barriers were seen as especially affecting the export of financial services (as well as communications, accounting, management, consultancy, and other such services) which, as we have seen, had already been identified inside the American state by the early 1970s as a key to solving balance-of-trade deficits.

What was being targeted here was nothing less than a myriad of domestic laws and policies of other states—including the procurement practices, regulatory regimes, price controls, subsidies, and even general industrial policies—all of which could be designated as "unfair trade practices."[10] Unlike changes to tariff levels, agreements covering services, foreign investment, and intellectual property rights "required signatory governments to make substantive, and politically sensitive, changes to their domestic legislation and economic practices."[11] This focus on changing the domestic laws of other states to eliminate non-tariff barriers also contributed to containing protectionist pressures within the US by channeling them into much broader demands for liberalizing foreign markets, while at the same time complicating the conditions under which those affected at home could demonstrate unfair trade practices under the new juridified procedures.

But trade liberalization beyond tariffs also meant that the weakness of the GATT in ensuring effective implementation of international trade agreements now needed to be addressed. As we saw in Chapter 4, the US had aborted the creation of an International Trade Organization in the late 1940s on the grounds that the proposed provisions of its Charter for fostering economic development and full employment, and especially the scope it gave for restricting foreign direct investment, were antithetical to what Harry Truman at the time had called the American "devotion to freedom of enterprise." The shift to a focus on non-tariff barriers within states now set the stage for overcoming these problems. Although the stronger dispute-settlement procedures on non-tariff items negotiated in the GATT Tokyo Round in the 1970s had proved ineffective, especially in the face of EC and Japanese resistance, that resistance was overcome in the 1980s due to fears abroad induced by the ever more heated protectionist rhetoric in Congress, alongside its sporadic use of antidumping and countervailing laws and the USTR's "unfair trade practice" designations. The Reagan administration exploited these fears to obtain the Japanese "voluntary" auto quotas (see Chapter 8) and to induce Japanese car companies to produce in the US, as well as to advance its strong commitment to free trade in the GATT Uruguay Round.

The road to the eventual success of the Uruguay Round was paved by the 1989 Canada-US Free Trade Agreement (CUFTA). Whereas in 1911 Canadian voters' fears of annexation led them to reject a free trade agreement with the US, the process leading to CUFTA, while contested, was ultimately successful and showed what integration into the informal US empire had already meant in terms of structural dependency.[12] The CUFTA did not inaugurate, but rather extended and formalized Canada's dependence on the US, as Canadian capitalists sought to minimize the risk that their exports and investments might be treated as "foreign" by a US Congress that was in a protectionist mood. Not only was fear at play here: some elements of Canadian business had already become full players on a continental plane, and others harbored ambitions that they too might reap substantial profits if Canada embraced its "continental destiny." Notably, it was Canadian not US business that took the initiative in proposing the agreement—and it did so, moreover, with the expectation that it could be used to block both the National Energy Program and the strengthened

Foreign Investment Review Agency introduced during the crisis of the early 1980s. A strong "anti–free trade" coalition of labor, environmental, women's, and native movements emerged, and deployed the small badge of civility that a welfare state lent to Canadian social life in comparison with its US counterpart, presenting a mythologized portrait of the Canadian state as if it had always been a staunch defender of economic independence and social justice. This set the terms of debate in the 1988 election, during which Canadian business groups pledged their allegiance to the Canadian welfare state. Despite the narrowness of the victory won by the Conservatives (thanks to the anti–free trade vote being split between the Liberal and New Democratic parties), the signing of the CUFTA set the stage for two decades of neoliberal practice by Canadian governments of all political stripes.[13]

It also proved to be a staging-post for the 1994 North American Free Trade Agreement (NAFTA), encompassing Mexico and going even further in underwriting, as two of Canada's NAFTA negotiators later put it, "the new model of international exchange . . . characterized by intra-industry transactions, the increasing importance of trade in intermediate inputs, and the growing share of global business taking place on an inter-firm, intra-network, or other interrelated corporate basis." In this new world, "trade agreements address not only the relationship between nation states but also the investment interests of MNCs as well as the governance of related domestic economic policies."[14] Indeed, far more important than the reduction in tariffs were NAFTA's provisions prohibiting discrimination between national- and foreign-owned corporations, and generally creating new property rights for both national and foreign investors. These went "well beyond those recognised in Canadian and Mexican law, if not that of the United States," as Ian Robinson was one of the first to observe, when he described NAFTA as a new type of "economic constitution."[15]

The chapter on monopolies and state enterprises required public enterprises to operate "solely in accordance with commercial considerations," and to refrain from using "anticompetitive" practices that might impair benefits that investors might reasonably expect to receive under NAFTA. The chapter on intellectual property rights, which granted up to twenty years' copyright protection to a vast array of trademarks, patents, semiconductor and industrial designs, trade secrets, satellite signals, and so on, went furthest of all to "extend existing property rights by quasi-constitutionally protecting them against future democratic governments with the threat of trade sanctions . . . even though the effect of these rights is to restrict rather than enhance the free flow of ideas across national boundaries."[16] And the famous Chapter 11, on investor rights, not only proscribed attempts by governments to impose performance requirements on MNCs but also applied an expanded version of the controversial "regulatory takings" doctrine that existed in US jurisprudence and extended it to the whole of North America.

Even though the US Supreme Court did not treat the regulatory takings doctrine as a settled rule of US domestic law, it became the key device in the legal arsenal deployed in the American state's increasingly muscular defense of investments and private property in public international law. What was still seen as a tendentious legal argument in US domestic law was written into international trade law as though it were somehow a settled principle just at the time that the regime of investment arbitration became constituted as "an exceptionally important and powerful manifestation of global administrative law."[17] In the context of the Great Depression, the New Deal and World War II, the impact of the regulatory takings doctrine in domestic US law was limited, until its revival in the 1970s as a common legal argument advanced by corporate law firms. Now, however, it was given very wide application indeed in US trade policy, initially in relation to Canada and Mexico and then much more broadly.[18] The international-ization of the "takings" doctrine afforded corporations protection through arbitration mechanisms like those established under NAFTA from "indirect expropriation" and "measures tantamount to expropriation."

What is particularly important to stress, however, is that this was not something imposed on the Canadian and Mexican states by the American state. Rather, it reflected the role adopted by the Mexican and Canadian states in representing the interests of their bourgeoisies and bureaucracies, with their own myriad links to the American state and capital. President Bush and Secretary of State Baker seized President Salinas's offer to negoti-ate a free-trade pact as "a grand chance to stabilize Mexico as a free-market, democratic nation, while providing trade expansion for American export-ers."[19] As John H. Bryan, Jr., president of Sara Lee Corporation, put it, the "most important reason to vote for NAFTA is to lock in [Mexico's] reforms."[20] It was these neoliberal reforms in the 1980s that the Mexico City newspaper, La Journada, saw as producing the "booty of privatisation [that] has made multimillionaires of 13 families, while the rest of the population—about 80 million Mexicans—has been subjected to the same gradual impoverishment as though they had suffered through a war."[21]

The greatest obstacle to NAFTA's adoption actually came from the anti–free trade coalition within the United States.[22] The CEO of Salomon Brothers made the stakes abundantly clear when he said that the defeat of NAFTA "would be a slap in the face to all leaders in the Western Hemisphere who have chosen the capitalist road over government-controlled econo-mies."[23] In response, business organizations spent up to $50 million lobbying Congress to approve it, making it "one of the most expensive foreign policy campaigns in US history," while the pro-NAFTA campaign in Mexico was "the most ambitious private-public lobbying network ever assembled in Mexican history."[24] The "side deals" which the Clinton administration made on the environment and labor were crucial in order to secure

NAFTA's passage by Congress in 1993. Not surprisingly, the labor side deal did not go as far as the environmental one, and did not allow Canadian or American groups affected by NAFTA to challenge the non-enforcement of Mexican labor laws.[25] On the other hand, since the core elements of the agreement concerning property rights could not be challenged in domestic courts and could override domestic laws, the idea that it amounted to a "supraconstitution" captured well the powerful sense of NAFTA as some-thing irreversible.[26] Larry Summers, the Treasury undersecretary for international affairs at the time, later claimed that NAFTA "resulted in a profound change in the internal political dynamics in Mexico in favor of the progressive forces that believed in the market and friendship with the United States as opposed to the forces that believed more in socialism and opposition to the United States."[27]

The dispute-settlement mechanisms worked out for NAFTA were in many respects models for the successful conclusion of the Uruguay Round of trade negotiations, which began in 1986 (the planning went back to 1982). Its crowning achievement was the replacement of GATT in 1995 by the World Trade Organization, which finally came about as the direct result of what was called "the power play" by US and EC negotiators who "threatened closure of the world's two largest markets . . . to any country that did not accept all of the WTO multilateral agreements," including on intellectual property and trade in services.[28] The significance of the WTO was that it finally created an effective mechanism to adjudicate trade disputes. This made it more difficult for the US itself to practice the kind of selective implementation it had practiced under the GATT, but the US acceptance of the WTO's authority was bolstered by the doubling of the total value of US trade (exports plus imports) from 11 percent of GDP in 1970 to 23 percent by the mid 1990s.[29] Seen from the perspective of the aborted International Trade Organization almost five decades earlier, this was one of the most significant milestones in the realization of global capitalism. But what accounted for the creation at this time of the long-postponed interna-tional trade organization was not so much the sudden appearance of neoliberal ideology as the rich soil from which it could now sprout given the spread and penetration of capitalism in the intervening half-century (subtly reflected by the replacement of "international" by "world" in the new organization's title).

Virtually all of US business (including old bastions of protectionism in the textile and steel industries) had already supported the bill to endorse the very broad scope of the Uruguay Round in 1994, thereby disrupting the uneasy alliance between far-right conservative groups and the labor, consumer, and environmentalist opposition that had almost defeated NAFTA. The new adjudication mechanisms, legitimated by being embodied in juridical technicalities seen as reflecting an unassailable "international law," not only seemed to further depoliticize trade policy, but even to infringe the sovereignty of the American state. Yet they actually strengthened rather than diminished that state's capacity to promote the realization of global capitalism. Economists at the American Enterprise Institute "applauded the agreement for bringing 'the rule of law' to international trade"—while a Heritage Foundation paper declared that the WTO would "expand the sovereignty of American citizens."[30] Chorev was correct to conclude that the liberal orientation of the WTO made it no longer "an imposition by the United States" as much as "a carrier of the globalization project in its own right."[31] But insofar as this was so, it was precisely because the WTO now did fully embody the American "devotion to freedom of enterprise."

Global Investment, American Rules

"Although trade and investment issues converged in the WTO, the complexities of international rule-making in relation to property rights limited the possibility of reaching investment agreements through multilateral trade negotiations, even though it was clear to all involved that foreign investor rights to securing "market presence—a firm foothold within states—is a constituent element of real freedom of trade."[32] The development of the rule of law in relation to investor rights instead proceeded through Bilateral Investment Treaties (BITs). Although these were more limited, they did cumulatively establish a new international legal framework.

Especially important in this respect was the initiation by the US in 1977 of a bilateral investment treaty program, the central goal of which was firmly to establish in international law "the principle that the expropriation of foreign investment was unlawful unless accompanied by prompt, adequate and effective compensation."[33] This program was carefully designed to establish codified state commitments to specific standards of investment protection, and binding "depoliticized" quasi-juridical dispute-resolution procedures. These negotiations were to go beyond the non-binding conciliation and arbitration of international investment disputes established under World Bank auspices in the mid 1960s. They also went beyond the type of BITs Germany had induced Third World states to sign in that decade by offering foreign aid concessions; the US designers of the BIT program saw such inducements as "needless distractions."[34] The US State Department in particular was dubious about tying foreign aid to protection against expropriation (along the lines of the Hickenlooper Amendment advanced in Congress in the early 1960s). The argument was that American capital—and by extension American capitalism—would be better protected in the long run if the need to deter expropriation could be balanced with careful support for structural reforms in other states.

The core provision of the USTR's model BIT agreement was the protection it had been designed to afford against "expropriations." This incorporated the "Hull Formula" articulated (but not applied) at the time of the Mexican nationalizations in the oil industry in the 1930s on "prompt, adequate, and effective" compensation, adding that compensation had to reflect the investment's "fair market value" as a "going concern" and be paid in a form that was "effectively realizable [and] freely transferable at the prevailing market rate of exchange on the date of expropriation." It was the expansive definition of the "regulatory takings" doctrine in US jurisprudence, as discussed above in relation to NAFTA, that was now promoted and defended as though it were already an uncontroversial rule in customary international law.[35] There was thus no little irony in the regulatory takings doctrine, so distinctive to US legal culture, being written into BITs over the course of the 1980s and 1990s—and not exclusively into those to which the United States was a party. From the mid 1970s onwards, the growth of international commercial arbitration was closely associated with the consolidation of US power in the global legal system. The US model BIT was the institutional innovation that made it possible to transplant the "regulatory takings" doctrine from the domestic US legal system into public international law.

In 1982, the USTR presented its prototype model BIT agreement, which became the basis for BITs with ten developing states (Egypt, Panama, Cameroon, Morocco, Zaire, Bangladesh, Haiti, Senegal, Turkey, and Grenada) already strongly tied to the US.[36] This first wave of BITs, as Reagan's secretary of state, George Shultz, put it in a letter to the Egyptian government, was oriented to ensuring that capital-importing states embraced "stable and predictable" legal frameworks for foreign investment in four particular respects: a general consent to arbitration in investor-state disputes involving US nationals; free movement of US capital into and out of the capital-importing country; "national" or "most-favored-nation" treatment for US investors, along with a commitment to a minimum standard of treatment in line with the US understanding of international law; and the application of international law, as understood by the US government, to any expropriation of American-owned investment, and to determining the manner and timing of the resulting payment of compensation.[37]

It was only after the central elements of this model had been incorporated in the Canada–US Free Trade Agreement that the US BIT program really took off. Apart from its incorporation into NAFTA in 1994, the US concluded no less than twenty-seven BITs from 1990 to 1995 (ten more were signed by 2005); "suddenly nations that had for decades denounced US investment policy were rushing to embrace the pro-market principles of the BIT."[38] By the 1990s it could be truly said that "international law regarding investment is now free to grease the wheels of capitalism . . .

those looking for the text that has replaced the General Assembly's 1974 Charter of Economic Rights and Duties of States need look no further than today's bilateral investment treaties (BITs), especially the current US model draft."[39]

The spread of Americanized international law also relied on the growing prestige of the so-called "arbitration community"—a circle of technical legal experts closely associated with the leading Anglo-American international law firms, who gradually came to displace the retired Parisian jurists (many of them of Hayekian persuasion) who had earlier presided over international commercial arbitration.[40] Although the authority to interpret the rules was ceded to private arbitrators, investment treaty arbitration was basically an institution of public international law: the consent to arbitration is pursuant to a treaty ratified by states. This transported international arbitration from the domain of contract into "a governing arrangement" in the domain of public law and policy. The state's general consent to arbitration, as Gus Van Harten has explained, "incorporates within the system a broad class of potential claimants whose identity is unknown to the state at the time of the state's consent and a wide range of potential disputes arising from any exercise of sovereign authority that affects the assets of a foreign investor." To the extent that the state's participation in arbitration is compulsory and arbitration awards are binding on the parties, the general consent turns arbitration "from a form of reciprocally consensual adjudication into a governing arrangement."[41]

The establishment and spread of Americanized international rules of law not only relied on lawyers directly attached to the State Department and the office of the USTR, but also to a considerable extent on academic experts on international law. US legal scholars who produced the multiple "Harvard Drafts" on the international responsibilities of states between 1961 and 1974 had put international law and arbitration at the center of the American state's efforts to promote private investment in the developing world.[42] As a small number of large North American law firms developed an "American style" of business justice in the international legal field, it became clear that "the autonomy of the law, which is necessary to its legitimacy, is not inconsistent with serving the needs of political and economic power."[43]

The growing role of US lawyers abroad was directly related to the international spread of US MNCs and investment banks. But insofar as the *American Lawyer*'s annual list of the top fifty global law firms in terms of gross revenue and numbers of lawyers always consisted entirely of US and UK firms, it was clear that this was another version of "imperialism by invitation"; both capitalists and officials in other states increasingly wanted to buy the services of these law firms. One reason for this was that their own economic liberalization policies generated "functional pressures" that induced a shift towards legal styles and expertise already developed in the

US.[44] Another was that foreign investment was underpinned by the use that both states and MNCs made of the US and UK legal professions' expertise in international commercial law and arbitration to change and even override domestic juridical structures.[45] All this was reflected in the growing practice of US law firms in many other countries (see Table 9.1).

Table 9.1: US Law Firm Offices Overseas

	1985		1999	
	Lawyers	**Offices**	**Lawyers**	**Offices**
Western Europe	394	**43**	2,236	**99**
London	135	21	988	38
Brussels	45	2	198	12
Paris	101	12	447	18
Frankfurt	20	1	180	10
Other West Europe	93	7	423	21
Asia	**168**	**19**	**1,008**	**86**
Tokyo	20	2	170	19
Hong Kong	86	8	344	22
Other Asia	62	9	494	45
Other regions	**241**	**18**	**1,075**	**60**
East Europe	0	0	418	32
Latin America	104	7	347	12
Other	137	11	310	16
Total overseas	**803**	**80**	**4,319**	**245**

Source: R. Daniel Keleman and Eric C. Sibbit, "The Globalization of American Law," *International Organization* 58 (Winter 2004), Table 1, p. 114, from data in the *National Law Journal* and *American Lawyer*.

The cumulative effect of arbitration rulings established new standards in international law, increased the confidence of MNCs in the arbitration process, and escalated the growth in the number of cases, including before the WTO (269 dispute settlement complaints were filed in the first eight years alone of the WTO, compared with 535 in GATT's forty-seven-year history). Given the "de facto veto" that the US and EC had on the WTO's appellate bodies, "lawmaking through judicial liberalization" became especially significant as multilateral negotiations in subsequent trade rounds became stalemated, largely as an intended consequence of the offsetting impact of bilateral trade treaties.[46]

Yet it is also notable that after a slew of adventurous claims for compensation, and a construal of the regulatory takings doctrine so broad as to threaten to cripple states' tax and regulatory powers, some of the misgivings that US courts had always expressed over too broad an interpretation of the "regulatory takings" doctrine began to appear in international commercial arbitration. By 2004 an annex had been attached to the US model BIT text that asserted the parties' "shared understanding" that an "action or series of actions cannot constitute an expropriation unless it interferes with a tangible or intangible property right or property interest in an investment," and their recognition that regulatory action "designed and applied to protect legitimate public welfare objectives, such as public health, safety, and the environment, do not constitute indirect expropriation."[47] One of the principal US negotiators of NAFTA summed up the experience with a form of legal globalization that rested on the wording of the US constitution to protect property rights: "If the United States Supreme Court and arbitral tribunals could not do it in over 200 years, it was unlikely that the negotiators were going to do it in a matter of weeks with one line in a treaty."[48]

Disciplinary Internationalism

In the context of escalating global trade and especially investment, and with the rule-making regimes of NAFTA, the WTO, and so many BITs in place, it might have seemed that the era of global capitalism had been "completed." But even apart from the complications involved in applying the new laws of free trade and investment, a deeper restructuring of states was required: to ensure that the defeat of inflation would spread from the advanced capitalist states to the rest of the world; to forestall or contain economic crises as more and more states conformed with both international and domestic pressures to remove capital controls while cross-border capital flows greatly increased; and to contain the social conflicts that so often accompanied this exposure to liberalized financial markets, as well as the vast changes in social relations that attended the globalization of production. The Bank of International Settlements, the International Monetary Fund, and the World Bank were invested with new responsibilities for the orchestration of changes in domestic modes of regulation and administration designed to facilitate specific reforms and enhance the economic management capacities of government officials. This usually involved, as the reports by these international organizations have often made very clear, "increasing regulation with continued liberalization."[49]

The US was very much in the driver's seat in this respect, less due to the crucial proportion of the votes it controlled (as on the IMF Executive Board) than to its close quotidian relationship with the leadership and staff of these international financial institutions. This was not unrelated to the fact that the approval of the United States was "de facto necessary" for all senior appointments in these institutions.[50] Indeed, policy debates within and between these institutions usually mirrored those within the American state itself. But this was by no means a matter of shifting the site of regulation from national to supranational bodies, contrary to widespread but superficial expectations in so much of the globalization literature that this would be the inevitable result of economic globalization. There was no real shift of regulatory authority or autonomous power to the international financial institutions, which instead became the sites for discussing, negotiating and coordinating market-based national systems of regulation among the advanced capitalist states, and the conduits for inducing developing states to adopt them as well.

Even when the IMF was not merely the "convenient conduit for US influence" (in the words of the assistant secretary of the US Treasury, Marc Leland, in 1984),[51] it was the G7 states' network of finance ministers, in which the US retained a pre-eminent position, that largely determined what the IMF did. What Andrew Baker calls the "discourse construction" emanating from the summit meetings of the G7 states was especially important in this respect. Reflecting the G7's character as what UK Chancellor of the Exchequer Nigel Lawson termed an "anti-inflationary club," its communiqués set the general tone internationally for the 1980s by their insistence on the need for vigilance against inflation.[52] And as the global defeat of inflation was more or less accomplished in the 1990s, the emphasis in both G7 and IFI discourse increasingly stressed the importance of financial liberalization and its management.

New sets of supervisory frameworks for liberalized finance were initially developed by private-sector organizations themselves, such as the International Securities Market Association, the Federation of European Stock Exchanges, and the International Swaps and Derivatives Association, all of which established formal rules and industry standards. A prime example of this was the International Organization of Securities Commissions, which was formed in 1974 as an inter-American association, transformed into a global organization in 1984, and led the way in creating new international rules for securities markets, ratings agencies, and hedge funds. It was particularly important in spreading the practices of the US Securities and Exchange Commission abroad and creating a network of regulators eager to uphold US-style regulations on securities transactions and fraud.[53] But as much as these private institutions played a key role in governing global finance, the American state was especially active as the "dominant regulatory innovator"—as was the UK (and, to a lesser extent, the EC)—in providing the "back-up authority" for these private-sector regulatory organizations by trying to ensure that their own and other states' respective national legal environments and public regulatory landscapes were reconstructed so as to facilitate relationships of trust among financial counterparties—which was indeed an essential condition for the continuing growth of capital markets.[54]

A particularly important site for this was the Bank of International Settlements. We have already seen how this old interwar "club of central bankers" was put to work in the 1950s as the institutional locus for the European Payments Union, and then used in the 1960s as part of the G10 efforts to preserve the dollar's link to gold, before becoming in the 1970s the place where the advanced capitalist states' bank regulators came together to discuss such national regulatory changes as might be needed to enhance "the likelihood of overall stability in the international banking system."[55] Although kept from public view, the main site for this was the BIS's Committee on Banking Supervision (the Basel Committee on which Federal Reserve representatives sat as full participants even though the US did not formally become a member of the BIS executive board until 1994). The Concordat of 1975 was elaborated in 1983 so as to expand the scope of national bank supervisors by requiring banks to supply data on their international operations to them, while setting out new rules for overseeing as well as supporting cross-border liquidity flows and creating new channels for increased information-sharing between central banks.

The cornerstone of the new policy regime promulgated by the BIS was the introduction of risk-based capital standards for international banking institutions. From the mid 1970s, Federal Reserve and Bank of England officials in particular expressed concern that the vulnerabilities created by low levels of tangible bank liquidity could erode public confidence in the payments system, and they used the Basel negotiations to explore ways to create a cushion against institutional risk. In December 1981, shortly after Britain introduced a capital-rating system for its banks, the US bank regulators, led by the Fed, established minimum capital adequacy ratios for banks and bank holding companies on the basis of size (such ratios had formerly applied only when new banks were opened).[56] The seventeen largest bank organizations were initially given more leeway than other banks in adopting these ratios because of their very low existing capital-to-asset ratios and their fear of losing international competitiveness; but a 5 percent rule had been applied to the big banks even before the failure of Continental Illinois in 1984. Paul Volcker in particular was concerned to improve bank supervision, and in this context regarded international regulatory coordination as "preferable to the alternative of competitive deregulation," which in his view had "gone too far."[57] This led the Fed to place still greater emphasis on the need to strengthen bank balance sheets, and to coordinate these with

London in particular so as to overcome European and Japanese resistance and prevent large international banks from circumventing the rules.

In January 1987, the Federal Reserve and Bank of England presented a joint regulatory agreement on assessing adequate bank liquidity. The Basel Committee at this point convened intense negotiations among the G10, and by the end of 1988 unveiled the Basel I Accord—the first of a series of agreements whereby states agreed to implement tightened capital adequacy standards.[58] With other central banks facing the severe implications of new regulatory standards simultaneously coming into effect in the world's two major financial centers, this set the pattern for their acquiescence to a regulatory harmonization that, even while cooperative, was always a matter of adjusting to the "dominant regulatory innovator."[59] By requiring banks to hold more capital against riskier assets (thereby lowering the overall investment return according to the weight of such assets), the goal was to push international banks towards safer investment portfolios. It was a mark of the reinforced centrality of the American state and its dollar in the whole process that the provisions of the final agreement were strongly skewed to bank holdings of US Treasury debt—by far the most globally marketable of the zero-risk assets.

By the time the Basel I Accord had been implemented by the G10 states in the early 1990s (proving particularly onerous for Japan, with its lower capital ratios), the Federal Reserve was already moving towards a supervisory form of regulation of big banks that involved reviewing these banks' own internal risk-management procedures (thereby replacing general capital adequacy requirements on the grounds that this would allow risks to be more complexly assessed). It was this that led the Basel Accord to be subsequently amended in 1996 so that other states would also allow the large international banks to develop their own Internal Ratings Based (IRB) systems of capital adequacy. The era of international capital mobility and the coordinated state sponsorship of it through the BIS's risk-based bank regulation had the effect of reinforcing the rapidly growing role and reach of bond-rating agencies. The risk-based mode of bank supervision adopted by the Fed greatly enhanced their role in the US, and since this mandated "ratings for less sophisticated banks as a means of specifying these institutions' risk exposure," the BIS also came to play an important role in the process by which ratings agencies, including especially the American ones, were "increasingly becoming a key regulatory tool outside the United States."[60]

This was "buttressed by the transformation of the Fed into a 'cutting edge' research institution—one whose staff economists were increasingly pushed to develop in-house econometric and risk-management methodologies," a development of research capacities that was "augmented through unprecedented amounts of international participation."[61] From 1993 onwards the chairmanship of the Basel Committee on Banking Supervision was occupied by the president of the Federal Reserve Bank of New York, with the 120 economists employed there doing much of the research for the BIS and sharing data with the other central banks. This took place just as the BIS was turning its attention from the G10 to the rest of the world's banking systems, beginning with an international conference attended by representatives of 140 countries to address the risks international banks assumed by participating in foreign exchange, commodities, derivatives, and securities markets. Even though its membership was not expanded beyond the G10's representatives until the end of the 1990s, the original Basel Committee engaged throughout the decade with carefully selected supervisory authorities from fifteen non-G10 countries (some of the roots of the G20 also lie here) with the goal of establishing "the foundations for building a truly worldwide network of banking supervisors and promoting the dissemination of Basel Committee documents, recommendations, guidelines and standards."[62] In all this, the Fed and BIS worked in tandem in hosting foreign central bankers at training seminars, and developing a school for central bank staff.

As Christopher Rude has shown, the amendment and extension of the Basel capital adequacy rules in the 1990s created "a two-tiered system of banks": the large multinational ones, headquartered in the advanced capitalist states, with the resources to operate their own complex risk assessments for self-regulation, and "smaller and less sophisticated banks," largely based in the developing world, whose market risks were to be determined by the BIS's "standard measurement method."[63] In neither case was this actually a matter of less regulation. The G10 states were still required to ensure that the big international banks' independent rating systems were monitored by national financial supervisors, leading these banks to set up large special divisions to show their capital measurements were meeting regulators' standards. Developing states, for their part, would be required to make "substantive changes in the legislative framework and in the practical powers of supervisors," while the BIS committed itself to "a significant increase" in the resources it devoted to the training programs it offered, often in conjunction with the IMF and World Bank, for developing states' banking supervisors.[64]

The concern with increasing states' regulatory yardsticks, and even their capacities, went hand in hand with the push for central bank independence. Whether this was seen as countering the tendency of elected governments to bow to democratic pressures, or of authoritarian ones to serve their own self-interest, or both, the goal was to establish a regime of monetary credibility by institutionally embedding within states at least some of the discipline that had once been imposed by the gold standard.[65] Central bank independence in the making of monetary policy was designed primarily to insulate them from domestic pressures, but at the same time it meant *less* independence from the concerns of other central banks in the coordination of monetary policies oriented towards stabilizing global financial markets and promoting capital flows. This needs to be understood above all in terms of their collective responsibilities for ensuring that priority would be given to the anti-inflation parameter established in 1979 by the Federal Reserve, which increasingly played the role of the world's central bank. As Paul Volcker observed of "our counterparts abroad in central banks and finance ministries . . . I sensed they saw the Federal Reserve fighting a battle for all central banks, even though some of the side effects were troublesome."[66]

What this involved in institutional terms was reinforcing or increasing the power of those apparatuses inside each state that were responsible for managing the national debt, the money supply and foreign currency reserves, and at the same time ensuring that what the Fed–Treasury Accord had accomplished in 1951 would be internationalized, so that the policies of finance ministries would be constrained by central banks. These two state apparatuses were precisely the ones with the closest links—facilitated by "conversations, mutual learning, the sharing of ideas, expertise and personnel"[67]—not only to the international financial institutions, but also to bond markets and the powerful financial actors within them, both domestic and foreign. This certainly did not mean that demands emanating from elsewhere in society, such as those traditionally represented by ministries of industry, labor or welfare, were to be excluded from the state. What it did mean was that the latter were increasingly likely to restructure themselves so that their representation of non-financial interests would be more attuned to making demands and policy proposals that conformed to the exigencies of fiscal and monetary discipline.[68]

This sort of discipline figured at the very top of the set of policies that John Williamson was referring to when he famously coined the term "Washington Consensus" in 1989 to capture the neoliberal interface between the US Treasury and Federal Reserve, on the one hand, and the IMF and World Bank on the other.[69] And central bank independence became the institutional change that, more than any other, signaled a state's readiness to embrace the "structural adjustment" required to ensure that this discipline was enforced against democratic pressures for social expenditure. In fact, the term "structural adjustment" was first coined by Robert McNamara in 1979 to mark a shift in World Bank lending away from projects to lending for broader policy purposes. With the onset of the debt crisis, a World Bank structural adjustment lending facility was launched whose "distinguishing function would be to promote dialogue with the borrowing country about various aspects of development policy and policy reform."[70] Initially used by the Bank to promote the shift from ISI to export-orientation, the term "structural adjustment" was soon taken up by the IMF in its application of "conditionality."

As we have seen, the fears that Wall Street had about the IMF as Keynes and White conceived it in the run-up to Bretton Woods—that it would weaken the discipline of the market on borrowing countries—had been quickly allayed in the postwar era. Although it was nowhere to be found in its Charter, the IMF had used conditionality (the policy requirements placed on a member government that requested funds from the IMF) in the relatively few loans it provided to developing states right through the postwar period. The global significance of this was on the whole minor until the IMF, working in very close concert with the US Treasury and New York Federal Reserve, applied stringent conditionality to its 1976 standby loan to the UK. The emphasis the Treasury's Bill Simon at the same time placed on IMF "surveillance" to ensure against the provision of "unconditional finance" to developing countries was codified in its 1979 Guidelines on Conditionality.

In effect, the IMF moved from its formal role of advising countries on how to overcome temporary imbalances to providing a seal of approval for policies that offered guarantees to private investors and monitoring countries on a permanent basis on the behalf of lenders. The developing world's increased dependence on trade, which outpaced by far the increased size of the quotas governments could automatically draw on from the IMF, had the effect of increasing the IMF's use of conditionality even apart from the debt crisis. Notably, the IMF's imprinting of market discipline on so many states took place under Michael Camdessus, as IMF director general from 1987 to 2000. The French civil servant who had engineered the Mitterand Socialist government's momentous U-turn in the early 1980s was now in charge of making it very clear around the world that "the IMF did not circumvent the discipline of the financial market, but came to reinforce it."[71]

The global expansion of financial markets—at a rate that would have seemed inconceivable when the IMF was established—provided an alternative source of funds for borrowing countries. But the imprimatur of the IMF was increasingly looked to by private investors as they made decisions on whether and when they moved their money into any given country, and especially on whether and when they took it out. As outlined in formal agreements reached through intensive discussions between IMF and state officials—who, depending on the occasion and the context, were often prepared to use "an argument about external pressure as a way to shelter programs from criticism or domestic political debate"[72]—conditionality was increasingly applied not just to managing financial crises and guaranteeing the repayment of loans, the restoration of external balances, and the effectiveness of development projects, but also to signal the predictability of developing states' policies to private creditors. By the 1990s this went so far as to cover "bankruptcy law, privatization, deregulation, the independence of national judiciaries, and the rule of law."[73] And there was indeed a clear upward trend in such conditionality from the mid 1980s onward, growing steeper through the 1990s, with about two-thirds of the conditions falling in the areas of fiscal policy, financial-sector restructuring, and privatization.[74]

But once again it is important to stress that the policymakers in the states subject to conditionality were often as keen to sign on to "structural adjustment" as IMF officials were to impose it. Benjamin Cohen has pointed out that the powerful domestic constituencies who "benefited measurably" from financial liberalization

> included, in particular, big global tradable-goods producers, banks and other financial service firms, and large private asset holders. Exporters and importers, as well as domestic banks, gained improved access to loanable funds and lower borrowing costs; the owners and managers of financial wealth were free to seek out more profitable investments, or to develop new strategies for portfolio diversification . . . External pressure from the United States is amplified internally by the natural desire of influential societal actors to defend acquired privileges . . . No conspiracy is needed to explain a pattern of co-operation when there is so evident a confluence of interests.[75]

As the policies that had come to define structural adjustment in the 1980s became ever more elaborated in the 1990s, and as it became more difficult to differentiate between their economic and their social, political, and even cultural dimensions, the term "good governance" was increasingly adopted to cover states' institutional, administrative, and legal capacities as well as their relations to "civil society." The World Bank tentatively began to rearticulate structural adjustment in these terms as early as 1989, partly in response to anti-IMF riots (such as the one that erupted in Caracas that year); but it was only with its 1997 report *The State in a Changing World* that the Bank came out clearly as bidding to displace the "free market fundamentalism" of the Washington Consensus, which the report suggested had led many countries to "overshoot the mark."[76] Echoing the kind of "third way" arguments that had been current in social-democratic intellectual circles for the better part of a decade, the Bank now explicitly advocated a large role for the state in protecting and correcting markets. The main message was that "globalization begins at home," and the main goal was to shift "attention from the sterile debate of state and market to the more fundamental crisis of state effectiveness." Effectiveness was defined primarily in terms of recognizing that "maintaining *liberal trade, capital markets and investment regimes* is essential for economic growth," but this was understood to imply developing the kind of public rules and institutions that "allow markets to flourish."[77]

Thus, while still praising "the near-universal . . . move away from controls over financial markets and their allocation of finance," and endorsing the selection of conservative central bank governors "more opposed to inflation than society in general," the report also insisted that "liberalization [was] not the same as deregulation. The case for the regulation of banking is as compelling as ever. Only the purpose has changed, from channelling credit in preferred directions to safeguarding the health of the financial system." But this was seen as only one precondition among many for active global integration for most countries. To this end, the report insisted that states must bring themselves closer to the people, make themselves more accountable to civil society, and reflect "the full panoply of a society's interests." While it was important that "first generation reforms" should begin restructuring the state in "a few critical enclaves [that] typically include the ministry of finance, the central bank, and the tax collection agency," it would be necessary eventually to move on to reforming the legislature and judiciary, the civil service, unions, political parties, media, state and local government, and even the private sector—all to the end of "upgrading regulatory capacity."

The report was in favor of privatization in general, and especially the "hiving off" of utilities and social insurance to the private sector, but "successful" privatization depended on "winning the acquiescence of employees" through generous severance pay; winning the acquiescence of citizens through share vouchers or public offerings of shares at "attractive prices"; and developing "a regulatory system that credibly restrains the abuse of power in non-competitive markets." Even in the areas of urban hospitals, clinics, universities, and transport, where governments concentrate their spending on infrastructure and social services, the report took the view that markets and private spending could meet most people's needs, except the very poor. A major concern of the report—arguably its central concern—was the endemic corruption that attended the state–capital interface in so much of the world. Strengthening mechanisms for juridical monitoring and punishment, making rules more transparent, reducing the scope for official discretion, introducing competitive bidding processes into government—all these were advanced as administrative reforms that would help to contain the problem, albeit always in conjunction with "policies that lower controls on foreign trade, remove entry barriers for private industry, and privatize state firms in a way that ensures competition."

The report still repeatedly stressed that the role of international agencies was to provide "a mechanism for countries to make external commitments, making it more difficult to back-track on reforms," including on the international treaties through which states committed themselves to "self-restricting rules, which precisely specify the content of policy and lock it into mechanisms that are costly to reverse."[78] This was what the IMF especially had done, although by the mid 1990s it had also started to take up the governance theme and apply it broadly to the institutional "reform" of states, albeit in terms that hewed closely to the language of neoclassical economics, designed to "enhance market confidence in a context of increasingly liberalized capital accounts."[79] Notably, however, while the G7 countries wanted the IMF to be given a larger surveillance role in ensuring that emerging markets adopted legal and institutional changes to facilitate not only capital flows but also market discipline, little progress was made on the European states' proposal to amend the IMF articles of agreement so as to prohibit all restrictions on capital mobility. The US Treasury had supported the codification of these rules in the OECD's Code of Liberalization in 1989, but when it came to applying this across the globe through the IMF, it displayed a distinct lack of enthusiasm. Given the priority it attached at the time to securing the multilateral and bilateral trade agreements that would open up emerging markets to international competition in financial services, the US Treasury was reluctant to use up much political capital on changing the IMF articles.[80]

Both the US Treasury and IMF were in fact more concerned with other changes to the states of "emerging markets." In a series of high-profile decisions that marked a departure clearly associated with the collapse of Communism, the IMF even applied conditionality to the reduction of military spending as well as of corruption. And it also started making "democracy" a condition of its loans through the 1990s, alongside its new sister agency, the European Bank for Reconstruction and Development. Yet the means by which the restructuring of the old Communist states into capitalist ones was accomplished—from the stick of the economic slump created by shock therapy to the carrot of canceling no less than a half of Poland's private and public debt—essentially amounted to "rapid social engineering at a micro level to create the desired goal of a state open to FDI."[81] The loans of over $16 billion that the IMF provided to Russia in 1995 and 1996 gave Yeltsin ample resources to spend liberally for his re-election in exchange for exactly this, as well as limiting inflation and privatizing public assets. The IMF "kept lowering the hurdles" in areas where the Russian government was obviously only "pretending to conduct reforms."[82]

Of course, it was hardly only in the post-Communist societies that the reality was so far from how it was depicted in the idealized conceptions of "structural reform" and "good governance." As Dezalay and Garth observed generally of IFIs in relation to the developing world: "The grand principles associated with the cosmopolitan elite, including the rule of law, were far from being fully implemented in the local contexts of power. But both the grand principles and the local clientelism and patronage were totally embedded in local notables and balances of power."[83] This was the "crony capitalism" that the IMF would demand be extirpated in exchange for its emergency loan packages after the Asian financial crisis erupted in 1997. And when the contagion from that crisis spread to Russia the following year, it was the IMF's very public despair at not being able to do anything about this "crony capitalism" in the Russian case that led it to pull back from its emergency lending, sparking the Russian government's default in August 1998 on its foreign debt (which at $61 billion represented 17 percent of Russian GDP). Yet until then the pretence had been maintained. In August 1997, just as the Asian financial crisis reared its head and exactly a year before the Russian default, the IMF executive board proudly affirmed that its staff had "assisted its member countries in creating systems that limit the scope . . . for undesirable preferential treatment of individuals and organizations."[84]

However hard this was to credit, what was true was that, in terms of the making of global capitalism—the main objective that structural adjustment was actually designed to foster—there had been real success. Not only had inflation been reduced to 5 percent globally, but over 6,000 privatizations had been carried out in 120 developing countries since the beginning of the decade. Moreover, no less than seventeen countries in Eastern Europe and the former USSR, thirteen in Western Europe, eleven in Latin America, nine in Africa, and four in Asia had made statutory changes towards greater central bank independence, while the number of bilateral investment treaties in force, which had stood at 165 at the end of the 1970s and 385 at the end of the 1980s, had surged to over 1,850 by 1997; 153 were signed that year alone—one every two-and-a-half days. Above all, success could be measured by the 700 changes states had made to foreign direct investment regulations since the beginning of the decade; of the 151 changes made by seventy-six states in 1997, 89 percent of them were favorable to FDI.[85] The share of FDI in the GDP of developing countries and the sales of MNCs' foreign affiliates abroad exploded: with cross-border mergers and acquisitions leading the way, inflows of FDI by the mid 1990s reached an annual average of 4.4 percent of global gross fixed capital formation, almost double the 1980 level. The sales of foreign affiliates accounted for a rapidly increasing share of world exports; trading in foreign securities became commonplace in stock and bond markets around the world; the amount of foreign currency in bank deposits globally, which had stood at $1 billion in 1961, reached almost $1.5 trillion by 1998; and foreign-exchange markets processed over $1 trillion *daily*—twenty times the amount of the early 1980s.

Over the course of a half-century, the "ultimate goal" of universal free trade, which the authors of "An American Proposal" had advanced in 1942 for a new type of empire—including "to organize the economic resources of the world so as to make possible a return to the system of free enterprise in every country"—was largely realized. But just as the American state's proponents of the global flow of capital beyond all barriers in the 1990s sometimes likened it to the way jet travel has "let us go where we want more quickly, more comfortably and most of the time more safely than was possible before," so did they recognize that "the crashes, when they occur, are that much more spectacular."[86] How to cope with such crashes without allowing them to derail the ongoing maintenance and extension of global capitalism now became the new imperial challenge.

10

The New Imperial Challenge: Managing Crises

There is nothing like a crisis to clarify things. Even if the discourse of neoliberalism obscured how much states were playing a crucial role in making globalization happen, it could not obscure the extent to which states were encumbered with the responsibility for keeping it going in the face of the financial volatility to which their economies were increasingly exposed. The American state's fight against inflation in the 1980s had confirmed other states' view of it as "responsible for managing the international financial system."[1] This was reinforced in the 1990s by the pivotal role it played in containing the financial crises that attended the growing international mobility of finance. Indeed, as it increasingly became clear that the US itself was not immune to such crises, the extent to which markets *anywhere* could be expected to be "efficient" in capitalist terms was largely determined by how *effective* were the interventions of the state most central to the realization of global capitalism.

In fact, just as the Treasury, together with the Federal Reserve, was in the forefront of advancing the rules of law for allowing global financial markets to flourish, so did the constantly chaotic and intermittently crisis-prone nature of these markets increase the scope, and the demand, for global discretionary intervention on its part. The Treasury's structural position in global capitalism was largely based on the unique capability it demonstrated not only to intervene directly itself so as to limit the contagion of financial crisis, but also to orchestrate supplemental interventions by the international financial institutions and other states—and, as we shall see, by private bankers as well, at particularly crucial moments. What has been far too little appreciated in this respect is how pragmatic about this were the key figures at the head of the Treasury and Federal Reserve.[2]

They were under no illusions, in contrast to neoclassical economists, that globalization's "extension of capitalism to world markets" only involved a movement from "one state of equilibrium to another"; thus, even the ideologically libertarian Alan Greenspan was quick to add to this formulation that "systemic breakdowns occur, of course." He consistently justified the Fed's indispensability as the main regulator and overseer of America's

payments system in terms of its being able to act quickly in the face of inevitable financial crises: the key thing was to have "flexible institutions that can
adapt to the unforeseeable needs of the next crisis."[3] Treasury Secretary
Robert Rubin sounded like he had been schooled by Hyman Minsky's
Stabilizing an Unstable Economy rather than Milton Friedman's *Capitalism and
Freedom.* Rubin's "whole adult life experience" at Goldman Sachs taught
him that capitalist finance could be understood as moving from one state of
crisis to another: "[W]hen you have good times, there is an inherent
tendency in markets, grounded in human nature and the pull of fear and
greed, to go to excess."[4]

The central theme of the main study the Treasury sponsored in the 1990s
on the strengths and weaknesses of the US financial system was that the key
role of the state needed to be one of "failure containment" rather than "failure prevention."[5] Together with the Federal Reserve, it also increasingly
assumed the global lender-of-last-resort role when competitive capitalist
actors revealed their lack of collective class discipline by running for the
exits in the major financial crises of the 1990s. This occasionally strained the
Treasury and Fed's relations with the US Congress, reflecting the tensions
that exist inside the American state by virtue of its being simultaneously the
state of its own social formation *and* the state most responsible for the reproduction of global capitalism. It was indeed striking that a favorite analogy
inside the Treasury for the opposition it encountered to its global lender-of-
last-resort role was that of Congress "cutting off the water to the fire
department when the city is burning down."[6] It was no less striking that this
Congressional opposition was in every instance overcome.

Firefighter in Chief

No less than seventy-two financial crises broke out in the 1990s among
low- and middle-income countries as a direct outcome of "global capital
mobility."[7] These were very different than the 1980s debt crises, which had
centered on the issue of rescheduling the big commercial banks' long-term
bank loans to developing states. The key US policy goal in dealing with
these debt crises, which was central to what IMF structural adjustment
programs were all about, was to ensure that debtor countries "avoided lasting expulsion from international capital markets."[8] But, more than that, the
goal was also to ensure that these countries were able to access the ever
more liquid instruments that increasingly predominated in these markets,
and it was indeed the resultant surge of capital in the 1990s that exposed
more and more developing countries to the financial volatility that triggered new types of crises. As Robert Rubin would himself put it in
explaining the role the US Treasury came to play in managing these crises,
even sovereign debt was now diffused in the "vast variety of debt

instruments and derivatives [that] had been devised in the intervening years . . . held privately by various institutional and individual investors all over the world."[9]

It was precisely the liquidity of these securitized flows to "emerging markets" that made them so attractive to both foreign investors (from Japan and Europe as well as the US) and domestic investors (including the wealthy in Latin America, who now repatriated the capital that they had sent previously to foreign havens).[10] Initially spurred by lower interest rates in the US during its recession in the early 1990s, nearly $1.3 trillion in private capital moved to the private sectors of developing countries in the 1990s (compared with $170 billion in the previous decade). It was a measure of how far the project for a global capitalism had been realized by 1995 that these private flows now dwarfed the bilateral and multilateral state loans that had provided most of the capital flows to developing countries in earlier decades.

These private flows partly took the form of interbank lending, or short-term or securitized loans, which passed on much of the risk to the bondholders (bond debt rose from 20 percent of total private credit to "emerging market" countries in 1990 to 70 percent in 1997).[11] They also took the form of foreign direct investment, the proportion of which going to developing countries increased from 15 percent in 1990 to 40 percent by 1996. The vast increase of new portfolio investment in "emerging market" corporate stocks and bonds reflected the way institutional funds (whose assets multiplied from $7 trillion to $20 trillion between 1988 and 1995 alone) diversified their investments around the globe as they tried to match the very high returns they had secured in North America and Europe after the Volcker shock had pushed up interest rates to stratospheric levels. But since the composition of their portfolios was highly sensitive to interest–rate fluctuations, even marginal changes which might be hardly registered in the US could have very large effects elsewhere. As the BIS put it: "This asymmetry, coupled with the ebbs and flows that have historically characterized portfolio investment in emerging countries, highlights the potential for instability as a marginal portfolio adjustment by the investor can easily amount to a first-order event for the recipient."[12]

Even as developing states removed capital controls, liberalized their financial systems, maintained relatively high interest rates and pegged their currencies to the dollar not only to sustain their export competitiveness in US markets but also to advertise their anti–inflationary credentials in international financial markets, they also often increased their foreign–exchange reserves (which doubled for these states overall between 1990 and 2000) to provide a cushion against capital outflows.[13] But given the size of the capital flows now involved, the insufficiency of this was evident in the sheer number of financial crises during the decade, and their contagious effects due to the increasingly integrated nature of international financial markets, the convertibility of currencies, the extent of short-term private borrowing by local banks and corporations, and the ease with which currency traders could raise local credit to speculate on a national currency.[14]

The massive inflows to the US itself still dwarfed all others, of course, and in thereby reinforcing New York's place at the center of an increasingly global financial system, they also increasingly required the American state to act as global lender of last resort. But it was now the Treasury rather than the Federal Reserve that played the pivotal role in this respect. The Fed had stood in the forefront of the American state's crisis-management efforts ever since the debt crisis had begun in Mexico in 1980, not only because of its supervisory responsibilities for the big commercial banks and its swaps with other central banks, but also because not being formally part of the government provided a political shield against Congressional fears that the US taxpayer would be left holding the bag. The Treasury was, of course, quietly involved throughout, and in fact provided bridge financing in the 1980s to no less than thirty-seven countries until IMF loans could be arranged. Its discretionary Exchange Stabilization Fund (ESF), established in 1934, had not only been extensively used for this purpose after the breakdown of the Bretton Woods system in the 1970s; it was also used to pay for the expansion of the Treasury's responsibilities in the broader management of global capitalism, including to expand considerably the number of employees in the international division of the Treasury.[15] When it came to providing developing states with loans in the midst of a crisis, it of course suited the Treasury that the IMF's "role as the 'heavy' further depoliticized the process" (as a senior Fed official put it) vis-à-vis both Congress and the country in question.[16]

However, by the 1990s the US Treasury could no longer avoid taking the spotlight. This was partly due to the fact that the sheer scale of what was required to act as lender of last resort in the financial crises that struck Mexico in 1994 and Asia in 1997 overwhelmed not only the Exchange Stabilization Fund but even the IMF's resources. But it also had deeper causes—above all the fact that the Treasury's voice inside the state was amplified by the financialization of the economy (to which the Treasury's own staff and policies had mightily contributed over the previous decades, of course). DeLong and Eichengreen's pithy observation that "in any administration the Treasury Department is the listening post for Wall Street" seemingly directs attention to the Treasury's important role in conveying to private financial market actors, and indeed to the New York Federal Reserve, what is going on inside the government. But what it captured as well was the Treasury's "disproportionate influence" in conveying to the government "the growing importance of market sentiment in an era of financial liberalization."[17] Although the new National Economic Council, located in the White House itself, had been explicitly conceived as a counterweight to the Treasury, the NEC was "grossly understaffed, especially on the international financial side," in comparison with the analytic capacity concentrated at the Treasury. White House agencies and other departments "lacked the expertise to develop ideas sufficiently to argue them persuasively. The Treasury could thus exercise its veto simply by demanding a full-blown, coherent proposal, knowing that one would not be forthcoming."[18]

Rubin's promotion from the NEC to the Treasury at the start of 1995 confirmed it would act as the "listening post for Wall Street"—in both directions. And the Treasury's agenda-setting and veto power was immediately evident in the face of the Mexican financial crisis that had reached its climax at just this time. The crisis surprised most observers, since Mexico was "almost universally viewed as a model for economic recovery in the developing world."[19] But it was in fact *because* Mexico was such a model for capital mobility and free trade that it now exemplified how, in Rubin's very words, "irrespective of past efforts or achievements," any retreat from "economic discipline" could have "a severe impact on market confidence." Mexico's "past efforts or achievements" as the IMF's poster boy for structural adjustment (including fixing its exchange rate to the dollar and re-privatizing the banking system) had been capped by its being made the first new member of the OECD in twenty years and by the coming into effect of NAFTA in early 1994. Mexico had experienced 4 percent economic growth over the previous five years (in contrast with a recession in the US), while bringing inflation down from over 100 percent to under 7 percent and attracting over $30 billion of foreign capital per year, including doubling its FDI stock.[20] There were of course underlying economic weaknesses, signaled by an increasing trade deficit, which would have made the peso look overvalued in terms of its fixed link to the dollar, if not for the capital that continued to flow in.

But when the US Federal Reserve increased interest rates in 1994, this not only temporarily upset bond and derivatives markets in the US, but had a particularly deleterious effect on Mexico.[21] Even as the central bank spent $15 billion of its foreign-exchange reserves in an attempt to shore up the currency against complete collapse, Mexico's newly liberalized but under-capitalized banking system became the conduit for a massive outflow of capital (much of it from the same wealthy Mexicans who had been at the center of bank re-privatization in the 1980s). With less than $6 billion left in reserves, the Mexican state could hardly begin to cover the almost $30 billion in *tesobono* liabilities alone coming due in 1995. Absent immediate substantive guarantees against Mexican default, financial markets all the way to São Paulo and Buenos Aires—and even more ominously New York, London, and Tokyo—threatened to be engulfed by the "Tequila effect" of investor panic.

It was the securitization and integration of financial markets that led Newt Gingrich, the Republicans' populist leader in the US Congress, as well as Michel Camdessus, the sophisticated French managing director of the IMF, to identify this as "the first crisis of the twenty-first century."[22] And managing it became Robert Rubin's first task upon being sworn in as the new secretary of the US Treasury in January 1995. The historically unprecedented $40 billion rescue plan the Treasury quickly put together (six times the amount mobilized for Mexico in 1982, even after adjusting for inflation) was premised on the idea that only a "financial Powell doctrine" (that is, an intervention on the scale of the overwhelming show of military force against Iraq in the 1990 Gulf War) would convince "the markets" there would be no default on Mexican debts. Although Latin American finance ministers secretly told the Fed that their own domestic markets were "being very badly contaminated by the spill over from Mexico," and even while these same officials were "very anxious that this US government effort to help Mexico be successful,"[23] the scale of the funds required to deal with this dwarfed the Fed's capacities for swap arrangements, as well as the Treasury's Exchange Stabilization Fund. Nor did the IMF have sufficient resources, let alone the capacity for swift action, to cope with such an imminent and massive sovereign default.

The Treasury thus turned to Congress, where both the Republican and Democratic leaderships initially signaled their support. For its part, the Treasury quickly mobilized not only the Federal Reserve and the Departments of State and Commerce behind its plan, but also three former presidents and seventeen former secretaries of the departments of State, Commerce and the Treasury, as well as leading Republican governors like George W. Bush of Texas.[24] This reflected the extent to which so many sectors of the US economy, and not only Wall Street, were intertwined with developments in Mexico.

But once opinion polls suggested that public opposition was running over four-to-one against the Treasury plan (whether due to hostility to bailing out foreigners or to bailing out financial speculators was unclear), less than fifty out of 205 House Democrats were prepared to indicate they would vote for the plan. It was clear that, even with a majority of Republican House Representatives (130 of 230) indicating they were in favor, the size of this Democratic Party revolt would prevent quick passage of the plan. Rubin inferred that "many members of Congress probably meant to oppose us without actually stopping us . . . Gingrich was quoted [as saying] that if the president took responsibility for the rescue plan, he would hear a 'huge sigh of relief' from Congress. The legislators understood what needed to be done but didn't want to vote for it."[25] This would become a familiar Congressional maneuver in subsequent crises, but it effectively gave the Treasury license to do "what needed to be done" in the short run so as to "restore market confidence," especially since the growing Congressional opposition roiled markets even further.

The Treasury put together the largest nonmilitary commitment since the Marshall Plan, and the largest bailout of a sovereign in history to that point, by supplementing an unprecedented $20 billion from its Exchange Stabilization Fund with $10 billion from the Bank of International Settlements, and $18 billion from the IMF (a fifth of its total liquid resources), while getting the World Bank to target a few billion more to Mexico's banking system.[26] The rapidity, let alone the scale, of this mobilization of the IFIs was unprecedented—a testament to the importance of the imperial network of financial coordination that had been built up since the 1960s. Japan displayed its usual "follow-the-leader mentality" in a case where "neither transnational institutional linkages nor interest in the Mexican rescue were strong."[27] On the other hand, the IMF directors from Germany, the UK, the Netherlands, Belgium, Switzerland, and Norway registered their discomfort with the Treasury's ultimatum (the Executive Board was given only twenty-four hours to look at the plan) by abstaining on the vote. But this was "as strong a diplomatic sign of disapproval as they felt they could send without undermining the rescue"; they recognized that more than their aversion to "moral hazard" would be at stake if "one of the shining stars of market-oriented reform in the developing world . . . became an international financial pariah."[28] In response to Germany's continued harping about moral hazard, the IMF's chief economist, Michael Mussa, commented tersely: "And if we hadn't rescued 800 people from the *Titanic*, we would have taught everyone an even more valuable lesson about the dangers of ocean travel."[29]

If this crisis was indeed the harbinger of a new level of global financial instability, what was just as significant was that the Mexican crisis was, to a remarkable degree, effectively contained. Whereas the debt crisis that began in Mexico fifteen years earlier had spread to the rest of Latin America, the contagion from the 1994 Mexican crisis was quite limited; and in contrast to the 1980s, when it took seven years before the Mexico state could regain much access to private capital markets, it was now able to do so within seven months.[30] Mexico's total drawing on the Treasury's Exchange Stability Fund reached a peak of $11.5 billion by July 1995, after which repayments began; by early 1997 the Treasury could announce that it made a profit of almost $600 million. This partly reflected the higher rate of interest it charged than the IMF, while insisting behind the scenes on the onerous conditions which the IMF staff had negotiated with the Mexican authorities. These were seen by the Treasury as being "the crucial thing," because they would engender confidence in financial markets "that the Mexicans were serious about getting their act together."[31]

Indeed, the Mexican government showed itself to be quite anxious to return to, and even accelerate, its neoliberal reforms, including opening the banking sector to foreign suitors, balancing the fiscal budget, and restraining wages and consumption in order to promote export-led growth while introducing flexible exchange rates. Of course, all this "caused real suffering on the part of the Mexican poor and middle class— and wages were very slow to recover," as Rubin admitted.[32] But he could point with satisfaction to a recovery in Mexico's rate of growth from a fall of over 6 percent in 1995 to an increase of over 5 percent per year from 1996 to 1998, while Mexico's exports doubled from 16 to 31 percent of GDP over the 1990s. Concerns the Mexican crisis would lead other states to abandon market reforms were "proven groundless," a World Bank Report exulted. Rather, the crisis had proved to be a "wake up call" for all of South America by making it clear that "deepening reforms—and doing so more rapidly—is the only way to counter the skepticism that emerged among international financial analysts" about Mexico's commitment to neoliberalism.[33]

The Asian Contagion

The way the Mexican crisis was resolved had the effect of furthering the making of global capitalism. Having averaged $120 billion from 1990 to 1994, total capital flows to emerging markets increased to over $190 billion in 1995, and reached $240 billion by 1996. Capital flows to Latin America and the Caribbean, after falling by $5 billion in 1995 from the earlier four-year average of $40 billion, doubled to $80 billion in 1996. But it was Asia that experienced the greatest increase—from $40 billion to over $110 billion. This massive flow to "emerging markets" took place even while private investment in the US also grew very rapidly. Investors competed to get "a piece of the action . . . confident that they could get out in time if, in Thailand or elsewhere, something finally went wrong."[34]

Interbank loans were more common than equity investment in Asia compared to Latin America, and European banks (German and French more than British) were far more involved in this than American ones, as financial liberalization in Europe squeezed banks' domestic margins and set them off in search of higher returns around the world. For their part, Japanese banks' total loans in the Asian region grew six-fold (to $265 billion) between 1994 and 1996—four times as much as those of US banks. In Thailand, where the crisis was triggered in the spring of 1997, Japanese banks held over 54 percent of Thai external commercial bank debt.[35] What was known as the "yen carry trade" (borrowing cheaply in Japan to lend at higher rates elsewhere) was spurred on by Japan's very low interest rates amid its long-drawn out domestic recession. These low rates were further encouraged when the US Treasury, having proved its commitment to a strong dollar, coordinated with the Ministry of Finance a depreciation of the yen to help support the staggering Japanese economy.

But, as Mitchell Bernard insightfully demonstrated, "while various fractions of global capital were indeed central agents in the bursting of the Thai speculative bubble, the origins of the crisis lay in the way these forces of globalization were intertwined with the Thai power structure." Thai state initiatives to liberalize and expand its financial sector (underwritten by high interest rates and the pegging of the baht to the US dollar) induced ever more foreign lending, which "served the interest of various fractions of local and transnational financial capital in different ways."[36] Growth rates averaging almost 9 percent in the decade before the onset of the crisis were also fueled by the domestic real-estate bubble produced by the alliance of Japanese developers with the Thai capitalists and army generals who controlled the construction industry. China's devaluation of the renminbi in 1994 and the devaluation of the yen in 1995 particularly affected Thailand's pattern of cheap exports. The Bank of Thailand responded by using its reserves to defend the currency peg with the dollar, making it especially vulnerable to any outflow of capital. All it took to produce a massive run on the baht and a collapse in Thai asset prices was a suggestion from the Japanese Finance Ministry in early 1997 that it might hike interest rates to halt the yen's fall. In short order, the massive capital flows that had earlier poured in were suddenly a dangerous liability. In 1996, the net inflows of private capital to Thailand were 9.3 percent of GDP; in 1997 the net *outflows* were 10.9 percent of GDP—a stunning turnaround of over 20 percent in one year.[37]

Notably, while the World Bank was praising Thailand for its "outward looking orientation, receptivity to foreign investment and a market-friendly philosophy backed up by conservative macroeconomic management," the IMF grew concerned at the way the Thai central bank was propping up the baht while concealing the extent of its interventions.[38] The IMF itself soon provided a secret infusion of funds, even though the US Treasury, while insisting on tough conditionality, didn't rate the probability of financial contagion very high given how relatively small the Thai economy was in a region "still so widely viewed as economically strong and attractive to investors."[39] It expected that Japan would be able to carry the main burden in backing up the IMF as lender of last resort, although Japan had put Thailand into the IMF's hands by refusing a request for a bilateral loan. When Japan agreed at US urging to supplement the IMF package, Tim Geithner (at the time the Treasury's assistant secretary for international affairs) quipped to the Japanese vice minister of finance at the meeting where this was arranged in Tokyo in August 1997: "How does it feel to be a superpower?"[40] What became clear as soon as the Thai fire quickly spread into a regional conflagration was not only the responsibility this implied, but the inability of the Japanese state to carry it. With Japanese banks leading the run for the exits, "every large G-10 bank and security house in the region was issuing weekly reports on the rising share of non-performing loans in Asian financial systems."[41] The US Treasury now recognized that, by not openly putting its own money behind the IMF rescue package, it had "spooked the markets even further."[42]

Yet even if it was not unreasonable to expect that Japan should bear the main burden of regional lender of last resort, the truth of the matter was that the Treasury also expected it to do so under US stage direction. This was especially seen when, not long after, the Japanese Ministry of Finance advanced a hastily conceived proposal for a $100 billion Asian Monetary Fund, which might have given countries with small IMF quotas more access to funding and more flexibility on loan conditionality. When it sent details of the proposal to South Korea, Malaysia, Hong Kong, Singapore, and Indonesia without informing the US, this was treated by the Treasury as a "rude departure from the normal conduct of the US-Japanese alliance," as well as a breach of solidarity among the G7 finance ministry deputies ("I thought you were my friend!" Summers yelled over the phone to his Japanese counterpart).[43] With Geithner playing up the opposition of the region's smaller countries which, like China, "dreaded the idea of Japan controlling such a potentially powerful institution," the US was able to deny "any charge that the imperial Americans were blocking an Asian solution."[44] But, as Katada has shown, it was as much the opposition by the Japanese banks themselves— their refusal to write down bad interbank debt was related to the concern to meet BIS capital adequacy requirements, and they also feared that the Finance Ministry's Asian Monetary Fund proposal might damage their relations with US and European banks—that ensured that the proposal was quickly shelved in favor of "crisis management in collaboration with the US actors."[45]

As the crisis spread to engulf not only Indonesia but even South Korea through the fall of 1997, this collaboration increasingly took place on the Treasury's terms. Notably, this was the case inside the American state as well as internationally, as the Treasury recognized that, to cope with the "seemingly inevitable tendency" in modern capital markets "towards periodic destabilization that is difficult to anticipate and prevent," it would "need to push beyond where others wanted to go," especially including the old hands at the Asian desks of the State Department.[46] A new Treasury secretary for international affairs, David Lipton, was installed (he had earlier played a major role in setting the terms for the "shock therapy" applied to Eastern Europe, and would later play a large role with the IMF during the 2011 Euro crisis). And brought in from Goldman Sachs to deepen the Treasury's capacities in dealing with the newest developments in international financial markets was Gary Gensler (who would soon go on to become undersecretary to Summers and later head of the CFTC under Obama).

It was no accident that a legislative hurdle (the D'Amato Amendment), adopted after the Mexican crisis to prevent the Treasury from making large-scale use of the Exchange Stabilization Fund without Congressional authorization, was quietly not renewed when it expired in September 1997. When the IMF came up with an $18 billion rescue package for Indonesia at the end of October, the Treasury now directly committed a further $3 billion from the ESF as a "second line of defense," while insisting (over the misgivings of the State and Defense departments not to undermine such an old anti-Communist ally in the region) that the usual IMF conditionality of severe austerity be supplemented with a host of micro–structural adjustment requirements, including the closure of the banks closely linked to Suharto's inner circle.

The contagion had by then already spread to South Korea, as European as well as Japanese banks stopped turning over the massive short-term loans they had provided to Korean banks—and through them to the heavily indebted Korean *chaebols*. Coping with "the Asian crisis" became a round-the-clock activity at the US Treasury, where Korea was "regarded as a firewall that could not be breached."[47] As Rubin explained, since this was a "mainstream economy"—the most recent recruit to the OECD (the first since Mexico) and the eleventh-largest industrial economy in the world— "the entire financial system could be threatened, with the health of the world's largest banking institutions at risk." Moreover, as he put it, "in today's world the United States is really the only country that is in a position to provide the kind of leadership that is needed to deal with issues of this magnitude and importance to our country."[48] Once again, the IMF was formally called in after the Japanese Finance Ministry refused a Korean request to provide a bilateral emergency loan, but the Treasury now also immediately sent Lipton to Seoul to monitor the negotiations secretly.

When the IMF staff began their talks with the Korean government, they initially concentrated on severe austerity measures and the closure of a number of merchant banks as the main conditions for a rescue package of some $30 billion. But the Treasury once again invoked the "financial Powell doctrine" to insist on the need for a much larger rescue package (in the end it would be almost twice as large, the biggest in history to that point). And it also used the IMF negotiations to "crack open all these things that for years have bothered them" (as one of the IMF staff put it) about the "extremely gradual" steps South Korea had taken since the launching of its "Financial Policy Talks" with the US in 1990. The US Treasury now insisted, as a centerpiece of the IMF agreement, that the ceilings on foreign investment be lifted from 26 to 50 percent.[49] Notably, the negotiations took place right in the midst of the country's presidential election campaign— and all the candidates were required to assent to the conditions before the IMF would declare the rescue package was in place. Its success in this respect led the US economist Rudi Dornbusch to quip on a subsequent American television panel that "the positive side" of the Asian financial crisis was that South Korea "was now owned and operated by our Treasury."[50] The knowing chuckle he elicited from the other pundits may have had less to do with what this said about the extent of imperial power at the end of century than with what it implied about the shifting hierarchy of state apparatuses within Washington itself: after all, it used to be the State Department or Pentagon, rather than the Treasury, that could lay claim to the South Korean franchise.

Peter Gowan concluded at the time that "the US government *sought to use panic in the private markets dealing with Korean currency and debt as a political lever* to further its policy objectives within Korea."[51] But it was in fact misleading to see this episode simply in terms of the destruction by the neoliberal Wall Street–Treasury complex of the "Asian Development Model." The Treasury's agenda in fact partly coincided with the aims of domestic Korean social forces (including those led by Kim Dae Jung, the prominent dissident about to be elected president) that had come to the fore in the urban street rebellions and independent union mobilizations that led to the end of military rule in 1987, and had continued to mobilize against "the state–bank–conglomerate nexus" thereafter.[52] For their part, the *chaebol* capitalists themselves, as we have seen, increasingly looked to end the state's "micro-management of industry" while demanding more access to cheaper money abroad. This was especially needed, they claimed, to compensate for the higher wages extracted by a (still officially unrecognized) militant labor movement through the strike wave that had raised annual manufacturing wages by 11 percent in 1988, 18 percent in 1989, and 10 percent in 1990.[53] It was the Korean state's response to this, more than pressure from the US, that produced the increasingly dysfunctional halfway house of a partially liberalized Korean capitalism by the mid 1990s. The South Korean government had maintained stringent controls on FDI and made it difficult for Korean firms to borrow abroad; but in allowing Korea's privatized banks to borrow freely abroad, it rendered the *chaebols* increasingly dependent on these banks' highly leveraged international debt.

At the same time, the state ceased to monitor these borrowings and abandoned its role of coordinating industrial investments, culminating in the abolition of the famous Economic Planning Board in 1996 to accompany entry into the OECD, even as the *chaebols* were allowed to go on an "orgy of imprudent borrowing."[54] A growing trade deficit, signaling the likelihood that some of the leading *chaebols* would be unable to service their massive debt load, led the ruling New Korea Party, on December 26, 1996, to railroad a contentious bill through the National Assembly "in seven minutes of predawn action at a plenary session" in the absence of the opposition. It put off for three more years the long-awaited end to the ban on independent unions, while at the same time removing restrictions on unilateral company layoffs so as to make the Korean labor market more "flexible." It was the three-week general strike that ensued in January 1997, followed by a series of *chaebol* bankruptcies, that first clearly signaled to foreign investors that something was really amiss with this newest of OECD members. Their dismay was only increased, leading to credit downgrades even before the Thai bubble burst, when the government was forced by the successful general strike to legalize independent union representation and adopted a two-year moratorium on involuntary redundancy dismissals.[55]

There was thus considerable plausibility to the Treasury's claims that "the real problems with Korea were structural and that the financial system was the point of vulnerability," and that "nothing short of a major reform program in South Korea would bring back market confidence."[56] While social-democratic intellectuals were still extolling Korea's so-called "strong state" as a progressive model in the face of capitalist globalization (in contrast with the allegedly "weak" neoliberal Anglo-American states), what was being cruelly exposed was not only the Korean state's limited regulatory capacity, but even its inability to specify the size of its foreign exchange reserves.[57] "To say that South Korea's finances 'lacked transparency' at this time was an understatement, if not a joke," was how Bruce Cumings put it. Notably, as Cumings also pointed out, it was "Korean officials who pleaded to include anti-labour provisions in the reform package," thereby hoping to pass responsibility to the IMF for reversing the labor victory at the beginning of the year and restoring the legislation allowing companies to undertake immediate mass layoffs.[58]

The failure of the IMF package to quell the turmoil in financial markets was directly related to the highly publicized suggestion by the frontrunner in the presidential campaign, Kim Dae Jung, that he might withdraw his endorsement and renegotiate the terms. Although he was not the candidate of the independent unions (they had nominated one of the leaders of the general strike at the beginning of the year), the main question that the US Treasury knew the markets wanted answered, as Blustein's authoritative account puts it, "was whether the aging crusader for democracy was willing to accept the dislocations—including job losses—that would inevitably accompany the closure of weak banks and uncompetitive *chaebol* units."[59] Although, as soon as he won the election, Kim made it perfectly clear via an envoy to Washington that he would indeed implement the IMF package, Undersecretary Lipton was dispatched back to Seoul to meet with Kim directly and tell him the labor issue was "key to Korea's situation." Kim did not disappoint the Treasury's hopes that "a leader with a history of championing labor rights would be ideally situated politically to persuade workers of the need for sacrifice." Indeed, he publicly affirmed on television the same day that job security would need to take second place to the neoliberal economic adjustments outlined in the IMF package.

It was with these reassurances in hand that the US Treasury now roped together not only the Federal Reserve but Japan's Finance Ministry, the Bundesbank, and the Bank of England in coordinating a roll-over by the world's leading private bankers of their loans to Korean banks.[60] The very day Lipton met with Kim in Seoul, the Treasury arranged for the CEOs of the top six US commercial banks to assemble at the New York Federal Reserve's offices, where they were told by its president, William McDonough, that a Korean default was inevitable unless they rescheduled the debt. Before they would agree to do so, the US bankers delegated the vice chairman of Citicorp to meet with Japanese and European bankers to make sure they did the same, thereby reinforcing the personal calls Summers was making from the US Treasury to his fellow G7 finance ministry deputies to ensure their bankers also got the message. With the IMF designated to closely monitor and report on which banks in fact rolled over loans, the G7's top finance ministry and central bank officials, including Rubin himself, then called "the CEOs of banks that were balking to reiterate that a default could be catastrophic."[61] One managing director for global markets at an American bank in Hong Kong was quoted as saying: "We were all told, 'Thou shalt not cut.'" A City of London banker put the whole operation in broader perspective: "The sad fact is that international banks never accomplish much unless they are pushed by the US Treasury."[62]

Of course, whether this would actually work to stop the contagion was in the end conditional on whether the incoming Korean government would win the international bankers' confidence by keeping its promises to the US Treasury to restrain its own working class. It was only at the end of January 1998, after a newly established "Tripartite Committee" of government, business, and labor representatives immediately endorsed the ending of the moratorium on layoffs and the passage of new legislation allowing for immediate redundancy dismissals of workers, that the international banks agreed to reschedule Korean debt. There was no little irony in the fact that "the first time in Korean history the working class was granted a formal institutional position to participate in state management" became the occasion for sustaining "Kim Dae Jung's readiness to embrace IMF conditionalities [which] meant a sweeping neo-liberal attack on Korean labour."[63] While going on to offer unprecedented incentives for foreign investors, the Kim government implemented massive layoffs (at a time when Korea's social-welfare expenditures were the lowest in the OECD).[64] Although GDP fell by almost 4 percent in the first quarter of 1998 (while unemployment tripled), the harsh medicine seemed to work in capitalist terms: by 1999 economic growth had resumed at a rate of over 10 percent.

The economic effects of the crisis in Indonesia were deeper and lasted longer than anywhere else in the region: GNP dropped by 13 percent in 1998, and still registered almost zero growth in 1999, before recovering to 4.5 percent in 2000. The IMF—backed by the US Treasury after a "squabble among Washington-based IFIs and US government departments on what should happen in Jakarta"—took a much more direct role in overseeing the structural changes in Indonesia, all the way down to the choice of judges for the new commercial court established in 1998 to handle corporate bankruptcies and reorganizations.[65] In fact, the US Treasury's relentless pressure for compliance, and its insistence on political reform to see it through, effectively brought down the Suharto regime, which had served the imperial state so well since the slaughter of Indonesia's Communists in the mid 1960s. Officials at the State Department and National Security Council had strongly resented the memos coming from the Treasury saying that "as long as Suharto is in charge, this is going nowhere."[66]

The number of structural policy conditions attached to the IMF's emergency assistance in the Asian crisis—about seventy in Thailand, ninety in South Korea, and 140 in Indonesia—was considerably above the average for similar IMF programs. South Korea eventually complied with about 90 percent of these, a remarkably high compliance rate which was very much related to the fact, as interviews with Korean officials themselves made clear, that "most of the structural conditions included in the Fund program had been on the domestic reform agenda for a long time and thus were not viewed as 'imposed' on Korea."[67] To be sure, the letter of intent signed with the IMF had explicitly called for "outside experts" to assist with bank privatization, and in this—as well as in drafting new legislation, dealing with distressed financial assets, negotiating the sale of firms to foreigners, and advising on the wave of mergers and acquisitions that followed the crisis—"the key agents were American firms and especially leading investment banks, such as Goldman Sachs, JP Morgan, Lehman Brothers, Merrill Lynch and Morgan Stanley."[68]

Failure Containment

But while proof of labor and capitalist class discipline was required to contain the crisis in Korea and Indonesia, no one was under any illusion that this could contribute much to containing the contagion. In Rubin's own words, "no sooner did one country's problems seem to be under control than pressures would erupt somewhere else."[69] These aftershocks were especially felt in Japan, where GDP fell by 5 percent in the first quarter of 1998, and Japanese sovereign debt was downgraded. By June, the US Treasury intervened in the foreign-exchange market to stem fears of competitive devaluations caused by the falling yen. When the G7 held an emergency meeting in Tokyo that month, Summers described the scene at the meeting as being "like an occupying army coming in to yell at the locals . . . and tell the Japanese to get their act together."[70]

When the bankruptcy that summer of Japan's giant Long Term Capital Bank (LTCB) could no longer be prevented, it was clear to the Japanese that however much they disliked it, a new occupation could not be avoided. After Summers called for the LTCB to be nationalized and then re-privatized "as a wonderful sign to the outside world that Japan was embracing reform and becoming more international," senior Japanese bureaucrats stressed the importance of doing this so as "to appease the *Americans*."[71] Reflecting Japan's entanglement in what Gillian Tett called "the complex ties that linked money and politics together in Washington and Wall Street," Paul Volcker was recruited as an advisor to Ripplewood, the obscure American firm that was interested in buying the LTCB. He flew over to meet with Kichi Miyazawa, Japan's finance minister, whom he had first come to know in the "intimate settings" of the old G10 meetings, where they had 'built up a reserve of mutual trust". It now paid off in the extraction of a promise that foreign bidders would be treated in the same way as Japanese bidders in the course of LTCB's privatization.[72] Goldman Sachs was selected to manage the sale, while the capital to back Ripplewood's successful takeover of what had once been the key bank in Japan's network capitalism came from, among others, David Rockefeller. It was scarcely a decade earlier that Mitsubishi Real Estate's purchase of New York's Rockefeller Center had been treated as emblematic of the Japanese takeover of America. The justification for this new American role inside the Japanese financial system (if one was needed) was that, as Rubin claimed in an important speech in April, "when countries allow financial service providers into their markets—with all the competition, capital and expertise they bring with them—the strength of the financial system is greatly enhanced."[73]

But if this was expected to contribute much immediately to coping with the aftershocks, the expectation was rudely belied in 1998 as the Asian contagion spread to Russia. Aided by the IMF's commitment to Russia, "downtown Moscow was brimming with new offices and planned expansions for the financial titans of Wall Street, London, Frankfurt and Zurich."[74] But declining oil prices, which had resulted from the collapse of Asian demand, aggravated Russia's fiscal deficit. This endangered its ability to roll over the short-term bonds that were coming due at $1 billion a week by the spring of 1998 (these had been previously snapped up by international investors as a "moral hazard play," as the saying went in financial markets, on the assumption that Russia was "too nuclear to fail"). This occasioned yet another large IMF loan package, but the Russian Duma's rejection even of its most minimal conditions on tax-collection (which is the ultimate reason investors have confidence they will be repaid by the states they lend to) revealed that Yeltsin, unlike Kim Dae Jung in Korea, could not fulfill his side of the bargain. The Treasury's David Lipton was dispatched to Moscow as he had earlier been to Seoul, but this time reported to Rubin that no one in the Russian government "seemed to understand how precarious the situation was or to be too concerned about the loss of reserves." A default by Russia on its foreign debt was understood to be inevitable once it became clear to the US Treasury that putting in any more IMF money (or even using the Treasury's Exchange Stabilization Fund as a back-up) "would have undermined the credibility of the IMF in its efforts to apply conditionality elsewhere in the world."[75]

In a sense, Russia was *too big not to fail.* As the IMF's deputy director, Stanley Fischer, later admitted, Russia was "too big and the forces at work there too powerful for us to have been the decisive influence."[76] But, rather than the Russian default being taken as an exceptional case, a great danger was that the IMF and the US Treasury would now be perceived as being incapable of preventing defaults in other large economies. Even more foreboding was the prospect that developing states might resort to extensive exchange controls, just as Malaysia did two weeks after the Russian default. Indicative of the breadth of the contagion was that international banks, which had earlier in the year shifted capital from Asia to Latin America, now began to pull their loans, and especially demanded higher premiums on Brazil's bonds, fearing that its currency peg to the dollar would have to be abandoned.

But the depth of the contagion had already been registered on Wall Street, as a massive flight to the safety of US Treasury bonds after the Russian default precipitated a sharp upward revaluation of risk in bond and foreign-exchange markets, and in the derivative markets based on them. With the US commercial paper market in corporate debt already in turmoil, word quickly got out that the formerly remarkably profitable US hedge fund Long Term Capital Management (founded by two prestigious economists who had won Nobel prizes for their econometric contributions to the development of derivative markets) suddenly faced collapse. With the massive losses LTCM took on the $125 billion portfolio of securities it had amassed with money borrowed from many of Wall Street's biggest banks, its default on a trillion dollars in over-the-counter derivatives contracts appeared imminent.[77]

Since it could not be known who would be left holding the bag if all the counterparties tried to liquidate their positions with LTCM, "this was a classic set up for a run: losses were likely, but nobody knew who would get burned."[78] Reflecting the concern that credit markets generally might freeze up, Wall Street's leading CEOs were once again summoned to William McDonough's office at the New York Federal Reserve. McDonough's own account of this intervention in what "had the potential to be the worst financial crisis since the war" recalled that one of the reasons the Fed was

created was that the resolution of the 1907 financial crisis had depended on
J. P. Morgan's ability to summon fellow bankers to his library and insist that
"people who normally spend their lives trying to out-compete each other"
look at the broader picture. There "simply was no other substitute for the
New York Fed" in the crisis:

> The head of a securities firm or a bank is not paid to be a patriot; he or she
> is paid to serve the best interests of the shareholders, so the most that one
> could do in a position like mine is to say the public interest may well be
> served by Long Term Capital Management not failing . . . Now if some-
> body has had many years of experience like me, the people you're talking to
> at least think, well, this guy knows what he is talking about; he's been
> through some of these firefights himself, and so we're not dealing with
> somebody who doesn't understand how we think or what we can do.[79]

With the political implications of bailing out a private hedge fund ruling
out public funds being brought into play in this instance (as they very much
had been in the Korean bailout less than nine months earlier), and with the
pressure on them from the Fed by most accounts rather heavier than
McDonough suggests, fourteen of Wall Street's leading financial institutions agreed to organize a creditors' consortium to take over LCTM and the
responsibility to meet its obligations. "Suddenly," as Martin Wolf put in the
Financial Times, "investors discovered Russia was not too nuclear to fail, yet
a mere hedge fund could be too big to do so."[80] But however significant,
this would not have happened, nor would it have been enough, had the Fed
not already started pouring funds into the banking system. Once it was
decided to deny the Russians further bailout funds, US interest rates had to
come down, and investors' flight to the safety of US Treasury bonds would
accommodate this—the only questions were when and by how much.

This was clear to the Treasury and the Fed even before Paul Krugman
called for lower interest rates in the *New York Times*: "Mr Greenspan turned
a stock market crash into a real economy non-event in 1987; he can do it
again. But will he? That's where I start to worry. The real risk to the world
economy comes not from bad fundamentals but rigid ideologies."[81]
Krugman was wrong to point to ideology as the main problem. Greenspan
had in fact already decided to use the occasion of a speech on "the new
economy" (linking productivity growth to digital technology) to indicate
that the Fed had shifted its assessment of the "balance of risks": rather than
the concern with inflation, what would guide Fed interest rate policy would
be the concern with "international financial breakdown."[82] It took three
separate cuts to short-term interest rates in rapid succession over the following two months, reinforced by the low cost of capital at the discount
window, to calm financial markets, and to leverage the banks into

providing over $30 billion in loans to corporations—well over double the usual amount—at a time when they were unable to roll over their commercial paper.[83] Also important in stemming the crisis was the IMF's "unusually large front-loaded package of financial assistance to Brazil in an attempt to create a firebreak wide enough to prevent the crisis from spreading further."[84] With President Clinton speaking in terms of "the biggest financial challenge facing the world in a half century," the US Congress voted additional funding for the IMF. Also important in securing this Congressional support was a US Treasury report that detailed for each state in the Union the specific impact of the loss of exports due to the Asian crisis, and spelled out the even more severe impact if the contagion was allowed to spread beyond Russia to Latin America.

A far more significant report sponsored by the US Treasury, "American Finance for the 21st Century," was also published at this time.[85] It embraced "competition in financial services wholeheartedly," in contrast with the "Depression-era model" which relied on "the attempt to divide the financial world into discrete segments," a practice which had "already collapsed under its own weight." Sustaining this had become "hopeless" in the context of "today's quicksilver market place," where the growth of global competition had already spawned banks and nonbanks doing much the same things. In this context, to persist in trying to make "the financial system safer by tying the hands of institutions will inevitably put a damper on innovation, at considerable cost to the economy as a whole and potentially to America's world leadership in financial services."

To sustain the case that US financial policy itself had long been in transition, it was pointed out that the federal government had not only removed restrictions on brokerage fees in the mid 1970s, deposit interest rates in the mid 1980s, and interstate banking in the mid 1990s, but had "a history of pioneering important new financial instruments" from mortgage-backed securities at the beginning of the 1970s to inflation-indexed bonds in the late 1990s. It was also pointed out that the last time the Treasury Department issued a major report on the financial services industry, in 1991, it had also called for an end to the "enforced sequesterization of banks from other types of financial enterprises." This had since been further "eroded by regulatory and judicial circumventions," including by the Treasury's Office of the Comptroller of the Currency permitting national banks to broker securities, offer mutual funds, and sell insurance, and joining the Federal Reserve in allowing banks to engage in even broader activities through subsidiaries.

While governments would always need to require that financial institutions take reasonable precautions ("just as cities need fire codes"), finance was "a good example of a sector in which to oppose market forces is becoming an increasingly futile task, yet in which government's core functions remain as essential as ever . . . 'Big government, small government' rhetoric is of little help in financial services and is better checked at the door." The main point of supervision and regulation, however, was to promote and support the financial sector's expansion—and insofar as its "mercurial growth" inevitably gave rise to financial crises, the goal of financial policy should be seen as that of "failure containment" rather than "failure prevention."

The report argued that the creation of integrated mega-banks spurred competition and market discipline. It admitted that "moral hazard" had been encouraged by the full protections given to the uninsured depositors and creditors of banks considered "too big to fail," starting with Continental Illinois in the 1980s. But it insisted that the two great innovations in finance that the Treasury had encouraged—securitization and derivative markets—had been attended by a "renewed focus on responsibility and discipline in finance," which was proudly attributed to regulatory measures like capital-adequacy standards and quick interventions to close insolvent banks that "put the United States well ahead of much of the rest of the world." Although credit was thus taken for the fact that "the financial health of the banking industry has improved dramatically" after the record bank failures of the 1980s, it was also recognized that securitization and derivatives carried their own dangers, since "dynamic hedging strategies" could "behave more like a trampoline than a safety net" during a future downturn.

It could not have been said, therefore, that the Treasury was blindsided by the LTCM crisis. But, just as the success of US regulators in halting the spread of the 1994 derivatives crisis (sparked by Orange County's default on its municipal debt) had fortified the strategic focus on failure-containment rather than failure-prevention, so did the successful LTCM firefight, however scary at the time, bolster confidence that any fallout from getting Congress to finally repeal the Glass-Steagall Act could be managed. The continuing concern with "eliminating outmoded barriers to competition" had remained central to both the Treasury's and Fed's agendas throughout all the 1997–98 crises.[86] And while there was a turf fight as the new legislation was prepared over the division of regulatory responsibilities, what was never in dispute, as Greenspan would tell the House banking committee, was that regulation would be needed more than ever so as to be able to have the information at hand to act quickly and effectively when the next crisis occurred.[87] This was seen as going hand in hand with self-regulation by the big banks. The shift to securitization of loans and the increasing use of derivatives markets to manage risk had rendered state regulator's examinations of banks for capital adequacy so difficult and complicated that they could not guarantee to effectively limit risk exposure; and it was for this reason that the Fed, the Treasury and the BIS all came to rely on the big banks' own models for assessing risk in the hope these would set off timely alarms that would meet the regulators' "fire codes." As would become very clear a decade later, competition among the big banks in securities and

THE NEW IMPERIAL CHALLENGE: MANAGING CRISES

derivatives markets would also expose the contradictions of self-regulation; the pressures of competition would manifest themselves in indifference to the fire codes. But, as was pointed out in the *New York Times* in the wake of the containment of the LTCM crisis: "so far, the combination of large capital cushions, diversified loans, stress tests and prompt regulatory action has been enough to keep banks healthy. The system is not well equipped to handle what one Government official calls 'financial Armageddon' . . . but the fallout from Armageddon is exactly what the Federal Reserve is designed to solve."[88]

The increasingly enhanced role for the state as financial firefighter had evolved through the 1990s alongside regulatory changes that encouraged financial innovation, integration, and expansion. It was the goal of advancing this even further that led to the victory of the Treasury and the Fed in the very wake of the 1998 crisis in finally getting Congress to repeal the 1933 and 1935 banking rules. By this time, as we have seen, the old compartmentalization of banking hardly existed in its original form. As a result, the Gramm–Leach–Bliley Act of 1999 repealing the Glass–Steagall Act was more about completing a long regulatory process than about ushering in a completely new legal environment. The major effect of the bill was to simplify the regulatory framework governing bank acquisitions and to expand, rather than merely enable, the cross-fertilization of commercial and investment banking. Not only did the Act repealing Glass–Steagall draw on at least fifteen years of successful banking experience in this respect; it set out a host of new formal and informal financial rules. What was clearly involved here was the state walking the tightrope of encouraging mercurial financial markets to flourish while managing and containing the inevitable financial crises that they spawned. The ability to walk this tightrope for no less than two decades after the 1987 crash was, in fact, crucial to Wall Street's increasing ability to act as a vortex drawing in capital from around the world.

The repeal of Glass–Steagall at the end of the 1990s was motivated by the concern to remove barriers to financial dynamics that had already gathered decisive momentum within the old form of regulation, and which by this time had largely ceased to have much practical effect. Indeed, what had been called deregulation since the 1970s was less determined by an ideological commitment to getting the state out of markets than by state actors pragmatically trying to catch up with the globalizing markets they had earlier nurtured. US financial markets in fact remained "almost certainly the most highly regulated markets in history, if regulation is measured by volume (number of pages) of rules, probably also if measured by extent of surveillance, and possibly even by vigour of enforcement."[89] Indeed, rather than trying to understand the relationship between states and markets in the neoliberal era as being primarily about financial deregulation, it may be more useful to see it in terms of financialization developing through the agency of both old and new regulatory bodies. Indeed, the sheer density and continuing fragmentation of the regulatory landscape meant that either escaping or changing regulations became a key dimension in strategies of financial innovation and the construction of competitive advantage.

This could especially be seen in relation to the "derivatives revolution." As we saw in Chapter 6, the Commodity Futures Trading Commission was created in 1974 to regulate derivatives in such a way so as to facilitate their development, not least to meet the growing demand for the spreading and hedging of risk in the expansive currency and credit markets. This determined the "Why not?" approach it adopted in terms of the space it allowed for self-regulation and innovation in derivatives markets—an approach sealed by the Treasury's conclusion in 1978 that the exchange of derivatives on the US debt that the New York Fed brought to the bond markets would, by allowing for some hedging of risk, help stabilize and increase the holdings of US Treasury bonds. As financial markets exploded in both the US and internationally through the 1980s and 1990s, and new kinds of derivatives contracts were increasingly traded "over the counter" between financial institutions, the reluctance of the Treasury, the Fed, and the SEC, as well the CFTC, to rein this in was sealed by the 1992 Futures Trading Practices Act. Yet as derivative markets continued to evolve, creating new legal uncertainties, concern grew especially within the CFTC that "lack of consistent standards for measuring and disclosing risks associated with derivatives positions" allowed the media "to grossly overstate the true risk exposure of most derivatives portfolios . . . fuel[ing] the public perception of derivatives activity as a Godzilla-like monster posed to devour the financial system."[90]

Amid the 1997–98 financial contagion, Brooksley Born, whom Clinton had appointed as CFTC chair in 1996, issued a number of warnings "about the unknown risks that the over-the-counter derivatives market may pose to the US economy and to financial stability around the world."[91] But with the CFTC having "broken from the pack and reversed course" by calling for the type of derivatives regulation that would involve failure-prevention, not just failure-containment, the whole regulatory edifice supporting derivatives transactions was "now in jeopardy", in the words of the managing director of the Bank of America.[92] The danger was in fact very real that to start regulating over-the-counter derivates for failure-prevention would spark yet another crisis. As a result it was not only Senators in the pockets of Enron like Phil Gramm who mustered his troops against Born, but also Summers and Greenspan, who co-authored the 1999 Report of the President's Working Group on Financial Markets that rejected the CFTC proposals precisely due to the "legal uncertainty" this would create regarding trillions of dollars in derivative contracts.[93] It was this report that provided the conceptual basis for the Commodity Futures Modernization Act of 2000, which clarified that certain over-the-counter derivatives were outside the jurisdiction of the CFTC.

What could clearly be seen at work here was the complex intertwining of public and private careers and interests that informed the relationship between state and market institutions both geared to fostering global financialization.[94] This did not go uncontested within the Clinton administration. Indeed, the sharp criticisms Joseph Stiglitz made, as chief economist of the World Bank, of the Treasury's and the IMF's handling of the Asian crisis, was in many ways a public replay of conflicts *within* the Clinton administration.[95] The "progressive competitiveness" strategy advanced by Robert Reich when he was at the Department of Labor, often joined by Stiglitz after he replaced Rubin as the head of the Council for Economic Advisors in 1995, was all about using the state to develop individual and institutional capacities to compete on the world market without resorting to competitive austerity that diminished wages and social services. Long before this argument found its place in the World Bank's 1997 Report (discussed in the previous chapter), it had already been marginalized inside the Clinton administration.[96]

The balance of class forces this marginalization reflected was already registered in the defeat US labor had suffered over NAFTA at the hands of the Clinton administration, while the defeat of healthcare reform "foundered on the shoals of internal party divisions, before Republicans and mobilized conservative forces delivered the coup de grace."[97] Clinton's subsequent initiatives to balance the budget by "ending welfare as we know it" were accompanied by the disappointment of union hopes for labor law reforms that would help undo the loss of union rights and decline in union membership; union density, which had fallen by 4 percent in the 1980s, fell by another 2 percent in the 1990s.[98] While real annual income growth averaged 4 percent during what became known as "the Clinton expansion" from 1993 to 2000, the top 1 percent captured more than the bottom 80 percent of the total increase in personal income.[99]

The Clinton administration especially sought to integrate working-class black and Hispanic communities into mainstream housing markets as part of its goal of fostering wider access to financial services. These policies gave a significant boost to the mortgage market and to home-ownership rates, but they also installed an infrastructure for the dramatic growth of household debt. This built directly on the full implementation by 1991 of Reagan's Tax Reform Act of 1986, which, apart from its dramatic reduction of the top marginal tax rate, removed the tax break on consumer interest payments with the crucial exception of mortgages.[100] The immediate impact was that consumers could borrow on their mortgages at effectively cheaper rates because of the tax break, and use the cash received to pay off their debts on a regular basis, allowing them to keep buying on credit even if their income was stagnating.

This "democratization of finance"—following very much in train the policies the left of the Democratic Party had itself advanced in the 1970s—was one of the proudest accomplishments of the Clinton administration. In launching the "National Partners in Homeownership" at the 1994 annual meeting of the National Association of Realtors (bringing together public agencies with private banks, home-builders, securities firms, and community groups, involving no less than sixty-five leading national organizations and 131 smaller groups), Clinton affirmed that helping more Americans to own their own homes went "to the heart of what it means to harbor, to nourish, to expand the American Dream."[101] This included encouraging Fannie Mae's initiative to "Open Doors to Affordable Housing" by providing financing to lower-income borrowers and developing the guidelines and the mortgage securitization infrastructure that encouraged private financial institutions to do so, as well as providing grants and building alliances with black, Hispanic, and other low-income consumer and community groups which advocated this. This was a policy that the Federal Reserve strongly encouraged.[102] And it was also fully embraced by the Treasury, not least in its study for Congress on the strengths and weaknesses of the US financial system. Citing figures that showed that the growth in home-purchase loans was about 6 percent for whites, 36 percent for Hispanics, and 48 percent for blacks in Clinton's first three years in office, it proudly claimed: "Just as the government succeeded in helping markets democratize credit throughout the postwar period, so now it appears to be succeeding in helping ensure that creditworthy low-income and minority borrowers are not overlooked."[103] And it went further:

> Perhaps the most widely felt benefits of financial innovation in the past two decades, however, are those realized by anyone who has bought a home and financed it with a mortgage. The conversion of the individual mortgage into (in effect) a security has broadened the range of investors in mortgages far beyond the savings and loan industry that originally was created to finance home ownership. Today, pension funds, insurance companies, banks, and mutual funds—and not only American ones, but also many financial institutions and investors based abroad—hold mortgage-backed securities in their portfolios. Mortgage borrowers are the beneficiaries of what amounts to a global competition to lend to American home buyers.[104]

Indeed, by the mid 1990s household consumer and mortgage debt surpassed the total debt of nonfinancial corporations, and it also exceeded the debt of federal, state, and municipal governments combined. The global competition to lend to American workers combined with the global competition that free trade represented to integrate as well as weaken American labor. The main goal of the reform leadership slate elected to the AFL–CIO in 1995, committed to increasing the density of union organization, was to try to get "progressive competitiveness" back on the agenda: "We want to increase productivity," the AFL–CIO's new president declared in 1996. "We want to help American business compete in the world."[105]

Yet US labor's accommodation to the making of global capitalism by the end of the twentieth century was accompanied by the emergence of the new anti-globalization protest movement. This especially burst into public view after the grassroots activism that grew out of continuing opposition to NAFTA was followed by the massive protest at the G7 meeting in Seattle in December 1999, which attracted enormous media attention.[106] But one of the limits to this challenge to the making of global capitalism was that it tended to give the impression that the real decisions were made at G7, IMF and World Bank meetings. It was significant, in this respect, that when the anti-globalization protesters next gathered in Washington, DC, at the time of the IMF and World Bank meetings in April 2000, they walked quietly past the US Treasury building at 1500 Pennsylvania Avenue.

VI

THE GLOBAL CAPITALIST MILLENNIUM

11

A World After Its Own Image

The success of the US in creating "a world after its own image" by the beginning of the twenty-first century was seen in corporations around the world operating increasingly, as the *Financial Times*'s Gillian Tett put it, "in a milieu where the American way of capitalism is considered self-evidently right."[1] And whereas it was still possible in the 1960s and 1970s to represent the capitalist relationship between the global north and south in terms of "the development of underdevelopment," by the new millennium there was clearly a very remarkable, if still highly uneven, process of capitalist development taking place in the global south.[2] The networks of transnational production as well as finance that characterized this development more than ever linked other capitalist states and economies to American capitalism's central place in global capitalism. This was seen in the extent to which other countries' exports depended on access to the US consumer market, and in the increasingly integrated production networks that emanated from US MNCs' foreign direct investment, on the one hand, and the flow of global investment into the US itself on the other.

Of course, the extent of capitalist development in the "Third World" countries needed to be kept in perspective. Despite the enormous volume of manufacturing production taking place in those countries by the first decade of the twenty-first century, the advanced capitalist countries, with one-sixth of the global population, still accounted for over 70 percent of world manufacturing production by value, and over 60 percent of the value of manufactured exports. Most MNC production and sales still took place in the developed world, which in 2007 was still the recipient of 70 percent of FDI.[3]

What this reflected was that the *spread* of manufacturing came with a new hierarchy *within* manufacturing. While production in developing countries did often move upstream in terms of value-added higher-skilled labor, fixed capital investment, and new technology in this period, developed countries were generally not standing still, and used their advantages in new sectors of production, as well as in research and development, design, marketing, business services, and finance, to sustain their overall place in the global hierarchy. This was especially true of the US. In 1981, the US spent almost as much on research and development as Japan, Germany, the UK, Italy, and Canada combined; by the end of the millennium, because these US expenditures grew faster, it was spending *more* than the other G7 countries combined.[4] The US share of global high-tech sectors (aerospace, pharmaceuticals, computers and office machinery, communication equipment, and scientific—medical, precision, and optical—instruments) remained relatively steady, at 32 percent between 1980 and 2001, whereas that of Germany was halved (to 5 percent) and that of Japan fell by a third (to 13 percent), and China's and South Korea's shares were still only 9 percent and 7 percent respectively.[5]

Yet if one of the key features of global capitalism at the beginning of the twenty-first century was the continued centrality and even dominance of the American economy, there could be no mistaking that another hardly less important feature was the success of the huge and fast-growing Chinese economy. Certainly, in the wake of the Asian crisis, China's entry into the WTO in 2001 was the most significant development in terms of the making of global capitalism. The East Asian economic integration initiated by Japan four decades earlier was now increasingly reoriented around China. Yet this regional integration was still primarily directed to maintaining and expanding ultimate export markets in the US, and an unprecedented spate of bilateral trade agreements that were now made within the region also served this purpose. But the pace was now largely determined by the growth of China's exports and by related changes in production processes in other countries, all of which "were linked and collectively shaped by broader *transnational* capitalist dynamics, in particular by the establishment and intensification of transnational corporate-controlled cross-border production networks."[6] As the Asian Development Bank emphasized, "an open, rules-based global system of trade and investment remains a high regional priority"; and since "Asia's continued success depends on access to global markets," the main goal was to "move faster towards global integration."[7]

Moreover, the unevenness of capitalist competition and development sharpened inequalities among the developing countries themselves. For instance, the value of manufactured goods per capita in Brazil was ten times that of sub-Saharan Africa. In fact, in 2007 eight countries accounted for three-quarters of all the manufacturing output by the 140 developing countries in the World Bank's database. The number of people living in poverty globally, as measured by the number of people living below an absolute standard such as $1 per day, had been reduced by the millennium. But such averages could be misleading. Although inequality between countries seemed to decrease, this was only because the enormous size of China and India skewed the international distribution data; once these two countries are excluded from the data, there was a rising trend in inter-country inequality after 1980. This was especially significant since "the last two decades in the twentieth century saw a resumption in the upward trajectory of aggregate within-country inequality"—and this was as true for China and India, as it was for the advanced capitalist countries themselves.[8]

Chief Financial Architect

The many economic crises that attended capitalist globalization in the 1990s presented the need to establish, in the words of the US Treasury's Larry Summers, an "institutional architecture that links the industrialized and developing world and unifies them in the way the industrialized world is already unified."[9] What the G7 called for by way of such a "new international architecture"[10] was a series of institutional reforms, primarily involving changes to the states and financial systems of "emerging market" countries, which would allow investors to assess risks more adequately and help the IMF address crises more expeditiously. It was taken for granted that this would be modeled on Anglo-American "best practice" in regulation and supervision, not least because so much of the world's financial regulatory expertise was concentrated in the US and UK.[11] Robert Rubin, in particular, was determined that developing states that were attracting foreign investment should be required to adopt "a catalogue of best practices in such areas as debt management, bankruptcy, public statistics including the disclosure of levels of international reserves, and bank supervision."[12] Indeed, he personally held up the IMF agreement with Korea for ten hours by insisting on including provisions requiring the adoption of better accounting standards by its banks and corporations.[13] And as soon as the Korean conflagration was doused, Rubin in early 1998 embarked on a series of addresses to high-powered audiences arguing that "the Asian Crisis demonstrated how badly flawed financial sectors in a few developed countries, and inadequate risk assessment by international creditors and investors, can have significant impact in countries around the globe."[14]

The US Treasury's position, Summers explained to the American Economic Association, was that "it would be a tragedy if the lesson learned from recent events was that the flow of capital from rich to poor countries was something that should be prevented, rather than encouraged." The "correct assessment" to be drawn from the crisis was "the importance of pacing liberalization of domestic capital markets to the development of adequate regulatory and supervisory capacity and a strong domestic financial infrastructure." This meant emulating the US: "If one were writing a history of the American capital markets, I would suggest that the single most important innovation that has helped make it as successful as it is today was the idea of generally accepted accounting principles." The challenge was how to "reconcile economic integration, correcting market failure, and sovereignty," but there could be no doubt that meeting this challenge was "an especially important goal for the United States as the world's largest, richest and strongest economy. If leadership in managing integration is going to come, it is likely to have to come from our country."[15] As for the general perspective that would guide that leadership in the face of financial and economic crises, Summers employed an analogy with jet aircraft:

> Global financial markets let us go where we want more quickly, more comfortably and most of the time more safely than was possible before. But the crashes, when they occur, are that much more spectacular . . . No one sensible is against jets. But everyone sensible is for safety regulations . . . Countries need bankruptcy laws. And they need judiciaries to enforce them. That is the price of being part of a global capital market. We also need procedures for countries which get themselves into profound difficulties with their sovereign debt . . . We consider the American financial system to be strong, not because all of its institutions succeed, but in large part, at least, because the failure of one does not jeopardise the whole. We need systems that can handle failure because until the system is safe for failure, we will not be able to count on success.[16]

In April 1998, the US Treasury convened a meeting in Washington, DC of the finance ministers and central bank governors of the G7 plus Argentina, Australia, Brazil, China, Hong Kong, India, Korea, Malaysia, Mexico, Poland, Russia, Singapore, South Africa, and Thailand, with the heads of the BIS, IMF, OECD, and the World Bank attending as observers. The outcome of this first gathering of what was initially called the G22 was the creation of three working groups of representatives from various states—supported by US Treasury staff—which produced reports by the autumn of 1998 on what needed to be done to strengthen the international financial system by way of "enhancing transparency and accountability," "strengthening financial systems" and "managing international financial crises."[17] But by the time these reports were ready, the LTCM failure within the US itself did indeed "jeopardise the whole," and thus had shown that, even if "best practices" were adopted in all these areas (which for most countries was in any case a very long-term process), this would not itself prevent crises.

Moreover, the very public disagreements between the IMF and World Bank in the wake of the Asian crisis, and the widespread resentment at the way the US relaxed its own fiscal and monetary policies in the fall of 1998, after playing such a central role in the imposition of severe austerity on the Asian states, further undermined the Washington Consensus. To try to show it was now sensitive to the need for private creditors to share the burden, the IMF helped engineer the restructuring of the debt of Pakistan, Ukraine, and Ecuador, and began suggesting more broadly that it would rethink the severity of its conditionality if states would take "ownership" of neoliberal reforms.[18] And a new division of labor was announced whereby the IMF's macroeconomic and financial stability focus would be complemented by the World Bank's programs for social and institutional change, including new ones oriented to developing basic levels of health and education that would allow for the gainful employment of new workforces.[19] These programs were designed, Paul Cammack has argued, for "making poverty work."[20]

More ambitious goals for the "new international financial architecture"—from an international central bank to an international bankruptcy court to an international credit-rating agency—went nowhere. George Soros's proposal for an international debt-insurance agency was clearest among these in recognizing that since "free, competitive capital markets that keep private capital moving unceasingly around the globe in a search for the highest profits" were at the root of financial crises, all such proposals would require the IMF to regulate very closely the lending practices of international banks, as well as the borrowing practices of emerging markets.[21] But as Barry Eichengreen (who was working at the IMF at the time) has pointed out, it was precisely the unlikelihood of states, not least the US, ceding such power to an international agency that ensured that all such proposals had "not a snowball's chance in hell of being implemented."[22] All that was implemented under the rubric of the new international financial architecture was a system of IMF monitoring of emerging market states' observance of "best practice" standards.

By early 2002, the IMF had issued no less than 165 reports on how far fifty-nine states actually were observing such codes for data dissemination, monetary and financial policy transparency, fiscal transparency, banking supervision, securities and insurance regulation, payments systems, accounting and auditing standards, and corporate governance.[23] The only sanction attached to these advisory reports was whether they would put off international investors from a non-compliant country, although it was clearly hoped that this would work as well as it had with the BIS "goal of creating a 'level playing field' among banks," insofar as 143 countries had by this time agreed to a minimum 8 percent capital-adequacy standard.[24] The actual implementation of these codes and standards inevitably proved to be highly uneven. It was most successful where states favoring further liberalization had already, as in South Korea, "formed alliances with pro-reform social groups, partly through deliberate political outreach."[25] Without discussing the class alignments within the states in question, it only confused matters to speak of the IMF's imposition of conditionality in the wake of the Asian crisis as an outright attack on their "sovereignty."

The IMF agreements became a reference point for Asian capitalists looking to remove internal barriers that they had themselves come up against, not least as they faced increasing competition from China. And just as the restructuring in Asia should not necessarily be understood as occurring against the desires of states already keen to be integrated into a global capitalism, so should the predominant role of the American state in promoting neoliberal reforms not be seen as merely serving US banks and corporations. The restructuring that the US Treasury required of East Asian economies was not really about securing special privileges for US capital; its primary concern was to ensure that the region remained open to capital in general. During the crisis the office of the US Trade Representative had "made several attempts to say that we have commercial interests in Korea and Thailand," but the Treasury "rebuffed these issues as petty stuff."[26]

In any case, US corporations which had shifted their interest to more science-based and knowledge-intensive production were not particularly interested in taking over lower-tech Asian firms, even at bargain-basement prices. US corporations that needed low-cost inputs for their high-tech production could obtain these by farming the work out to Asian firms without having to make the investment and take the risks involved in formally taking them over. As Justin Robertson has shown, it was European and Japanese corporations more than American ones that rushed in after the crisis to buy or merge with Asian companies. US investment houses, led by Goldman Sachs, J. P. Morgan, and Morgan Stanley, played a more pivotal role by "steering asset sales and advising on legislative and regulatory reforms," as East Asian states "put their reform commitments into practice."[27]

But most important for the extension of global capitalism was what developing states did *not* do in the wake of the Asian contagion with regard to restricting capital flows. Although between 1998 and 2000 there was a slowdown in the removal of capital controls, and indeed even quiet encouragement by the IMF of limited controls of inflows (along Chilean lines), the liberalization trend continued into the twenty-first century, so that of the 1,938 rule changes covering foreign investment made in the ten years after 1997, 90 percent favored FDI.[28] In a much-cited paper looking at why other states did not follow Malaysia in introducing capital controls, Benjamin Cohen showed that governments abjured controls less because of ideological commitment to free-market principles than more pragmatic considerations. For one, they could not help but notice that Korea, without having introduced controls, recovered as quickly as Malaysia, while the Malaysian government itself soon relaxed its controls "to lure more foreign investors back into the country." But there was even "something more fundamental involved," Cohen wrote:

That more fundamental "something" would appear to be the United States, which continues as it has throughout most of the postwar period to set the agenda for international financial affairs ... Few governments today are inclined to overtly defy Washington's wishes on monetary and financial issues ... In fact, Washington has made no secret of its firm opposition to any significant reversal of financial liberalization in emerging markets.[29]

This was reinforced by the G7's creation of the G20, which was a prime example of "a group of powerful states creating a body in an effort to obtain the voluntary compliance of weaker states through an active process of consultation and discussion."[30] Announced at the G7 Cologne Summit in June 1999, the G20 was the direct offshoot of the G22, with Saudi Arabia, Turkey, and Indonesia now added as "systemically important countries," while Malaysia (clearly penalized for its capital controls) was dropped along with Hong Kong, Singapore, Thailand, and Poland.[31] As had been the case with the creation of the G8 to include Russia in 1997, it was never intended that meetings of the G7 would be folded into the G20. The US Treasury insisted from the very beginning that the G20's main focus would be "a commitment of its members to more intensive IMF examination of their national standards and practices."[32] Although the G20 was born out of the contradictions that produced the crisis at the end of the 1990s, it would take a decade of further global integration of finance and production, and another even more serious global financial crisis, before the G20 would be given much prominence—beginning with its being called to Washington by George Bush in the ominous autumn of 2008.

Meanwhile, the G7 remained a far more important site of coordination than the G20. Expectations of policy divergences among the G7 states in the wake of the Asian crisis came to nothing. Some saw the Europeans as more committed to "liberal rules for global finance" than the US; others predicted "a coming battle over capital controls" between Europe and the United States.[33] In reality, the Europeans remained strongly supportive of the US Treasury and Federal Reserve's determined leadership in promoting financial liberalization. And for all the emphasis on building the new Europe, the hub-and-spokes structure of the American empire still held in the first years of the twenty-first century. Not only did US FDI in Germany, France, and the UK still exceed that of any European country; the US also remained the largest recipient of German, French, and British foreign direct investment. Moreover, the MNCs of these other countries produced more inside the US than they exported to it.[34]

The European and Japanese states' strong support for the US role as the leading financial firefighter was especially seen in the G7 agreement in the fall of 1998 to join with the Fed in lowering interest rates. They did this much more readily than at the time of Carter's attempt to coordinate an international stimulus in the late 1970s, and although this was presented by the G7 finance ministers and central banks as being undertaken to promote growth in their economies on the grounds that "the balance of risks in the world economy" had shifted away from inflation, there could be no doubt that the main motive was to help the Fed pour as much liquidity into the banking system as necessary to stem a financial collapse. It was also significant that, after years of protracted negotiations, the US now finally prevailed over the EU on the harmonization of accounting standards.[35] A rather more dramatic measure of the acceptance of US imperial leadership was seen in the cooperation every European government gave to NATO's war on Yugoslavia.[36] That most of these governments were social-democratic was a remarkable testament at the end of the century to the informal alliance between US Democratic administrations and European social democracy, inaugurated under Woodrow Wilson during World War I.

The sobering effects of the 1997–98 crisis, coinciding with the election of Tony Blair's New Labour government in Britain, with its "third way" definition of social democracy largely emulating Clinton's policies, led in particular to a very close partnership between US and UK Treasury officials. A director for international finance under New Labour said he was "as likely to call up my counterpart in the US as call a colleague" in the UK Treasury. Nor did he see any fundamental differences with other G7 finance ministries: among the fifty or so officials who spoke two to three times a week and met every three to four weeks, he said, "the basic view of the world is common, the Washington Consensus still holds"; their solidarity had been deepened through collectively figuring out "how to cope with crises in the emerging market economies." Another senior UK Treasury official explained the utility of the G7 in the crisis this way:

> There is a trajectory to super-nationality but that trend is measured in centuries or half-centuries—partly because countries remain stingy about their sovereignty—with the US the stingiest about its sovereignty. In this context, G7 coordination is extremely important because commitments are informal there. It allows countries to deposit their sovereignty on an ad hoc basis to deal with crises, and then to pull back.[37]

This coordination among finance ministry officials overlapped with the networks that included central bankers, such as the Financial Stability Forum created in 1999. Their solidarity was strengthened by the Asian crisis. Even very senior German Bundesbank officials (who, as we have repeatedly seen, were always the most reluctant to bail out individual banks in trouble) recognized that "if everything goes down the river, you have to act. There is a lot of moral hazard involved in this so we need to practice constructive ambiguity. The question isn't the kind of crisis but whether and when money is needed." Nor did they think that the newly created European Central Bank would challenge the Federal Reserve's leading role as, in effect, the world's central bank. This was not only because "the Fed interest rate is the engine of the rest of the world," but also because "Europe is not united and nothing happens without the United States. We all play a role but the US in qualitatively different."[38] Those working on creating the ECB closely studied the Federal Reserve as the model, and especially envied its team of "over 200 economists in Washington performing academic research and the preparatory work on national monetary policy for the Board of Governors."[39]

It was clear that what was at stake for all these officials as they worked together through the 1997–98 crisis and its aftermath was much more than "fixing" the crisis. This was an opportunity to complete the opening of Asia and other regions to global capitalism. The G7's asymmetric macro-economic response—austerity in the developing world and stimulus in the developed world—was very much related to this. It was defended in terms of the structural logic of global finance: the earlier defeat of inflation in the advanced capitalist countries now permitted the provision of liquidity to their banking systems; in developing countries the restraint of potentially inflationary pressures through austerity was required to induce capital inflows and strengthen domestic banking systems. The main concern of the G7 finance ministers was that "domestic banks not be treated more favourably than foreign banks," as a UK official explained their reaction to Malaysia's imposition of capital controls in 1998.[40] This principle of equal treatment for foreign capital had, of course, governed the making of global capitalism, and it was largely through the American state's determination to uphold this principle that the crisis was converted into an opportunity.

The US and the Globalized Economy

One measure of the American stake in the making of global capitalism in the decades between the end of the crisis of the 1970s and the one that began in 2007 was that total US trade (exports plus imports) equaled 30 percent of GDP that year, whereas it had still been under 10 percent four decades earlier. Moreover, US foreign direct investment abroad in 2007 equaled 22 percent of domestic non-residential investment, as compared to just 10 percent in the early 1990s, as the profits that US corporations earned internationally now stood at over 25 percent of total US profits, up from some 10 percent in the 1970s. But perhaps the best measure of the inter-twining of US and global capital was foreign capital's increased presence inside the US. Foreign direct investment into the US, which was still under 5 percent of US non-residential investment until the mid 1980s, exploded in the following two decades; by 2007 FDI to the US was running at 20 percent of US non-residential investment.[41]

All this took place while, between 1980 and 2007, global GDP doubled; trade grew twice as fast as GDP, and FDI grew twice as fast as trade (see Table 11.1). This accelerated capitalist globalization entailed major changes everywhere. This could best be seen in three interrelated areas: a) the massive expansion of finance in global accumulation; b) the impact of networks of integrated production on the global division of labor; and c) the novel aspects of US economic centrality in global capitalism.

Table 11.1: Globalization 1980–2007

SHARE OF GDP	1980	2007
TRADE	32%	57%
FDI STOCK	6.5%	32%
AVERAGE ANNUAL GROWTH	1980–2007	
GDP	3%	
EXPORTS	6%	
FDI STOCK	12%	

Source: UNCTADSTAT, "Inward and Outward Foreign Direct Investment," and World Bank, World Development Indicators.

The scale of global financialization was especially stunning. While in the years 1990–2007 world trade grew at an impressive annual rate of 8.7 percent, cross-border financial flows grew at 14.5 percent, exploding over those years from $1.1 trillion to over $11 trillion a year. The turnover of derivatives, primarily interest-rate and foreign-exchange contracts, reached a *daily* level of some $3 trillion by 2004, and $5 trillion by 2007. Asset-backed derivative securities, more than three-quarters of which originated in the US (based primarily on mortgages, credit cards, and car and student loans), increased by 19 percent annually from 1990 to 2007. Along with the growth in equities, demand deposits, and government debt securities, this contributed to an explosion of global financial assets that reached a total value of almost $200 trillion in 2007 (see Table 11.2). Global management funds administered over $74 trillion in pension assets, mutual funds, and insurance pools (twice the 1998 level), and the so-called "new power brokers" such as hedge funds and private equity funds controlled another $12 trillion.[42]

Table 11.2: International Finance, 2007

VOLUME OF INTERNATIONAL CAPITAL FLOWS ($ trillion)		STOCK OF FINANCIAL ASSETS ($ trillion)	
DEPOSITS & LENDING	$6.0	EQUITIES	$65
DEBT	$2.3	DEPOSITS	$53
FDI	$1.9	PRIVATE DEBT SECURITIES	$51
EQUITIES	$0.9	GOVT DEBT SECURITIES	$28
TOTAL	$11.2	TOTAL	$196

Source: Mapping Global Capital Markets: Fourth Annual Report, San Francisco: McKinsey Global Institute, January 2008. Exhibit 1, p. 9 and Exhibit 4, p. 11.

While only a quarter of global financial flows went to the developing world, the impact of these investment flows was enormous. As one BIS study put it: "Cross-border flows provide an incomplete picture of the breadth and depth of links between mature and emerging financial markets . . . local operations of foreign financial institutions are playing an increasingly important, in some cases even dominant, role in the financial systems of many emerging markets."[43] This could be seen as the culmination of a quarter-century of financial flows to the developing world. Especially after the financial crises of the late 1990s, states and domestic capitalists encouraged the development of local securities and derivatives markets to provide, as the IMF put it, "an alternative source of funding for the public and corporate sectors and to facilitate the management of the financial risks associated with periods of high asset price volatility."[44] At the same time, international banks now "turned their focus from cross-border lending to local business and capital market activities," so much so that by 2002 their loans in domestic currencies constituted 40 percent of their total claims in emerging markets, compared with only 10 percent a decade earlier.[45]

By the end of 2008, the loans made by foreign banks and their affiliates inside developing countries "exceeded $1,500 billion in emerging Asia, $900 billion in emerging Europe and $800 billion in Latin America." Not only did international banks now become "major players in the domestic financial markets of most emerging economies"; domestic financial institutions also changed so that banking systems as a whole were transformed.[46] Crucial to this was the issuance of domestic government bonds by the developing states to absorb export earnings so they did not cause inflation. This led to the growth of local bond, securities, and consumer credit markets that made it possible "for domestic banks to engage in activities that resemble those of developed countries."[47] Apart from strengthening the links between domestic and foreign capitalists, this also involved bringing local middle and working classes into the financial system as never before, mainly by expanding mortgage and credit-card lending.

Financialization in the global south also facilitated the outward flow of capital from developing countries. Capital flows between the developing countries increased significantly, and this came not only from the foreign banks operating there, but also from local capitalists who were expanding their horizons beyond their home base.[48] Of course, the largest capital outflows from the developing world took the form of far larger purchases of US Treasuries as central bank reserves took on greater significance than ever before. Especially in the context of the Asian crisis and the further liberalization of capital markets, these purchases served as an insurance policy against future runs on local currencies, as well as a means of maintaining exchange rates relative to the dollar. This was not simply a costly transfer of wealth from the South to the North; it was also a necessary condition of successful export-oriented capitalist development. What the emphasis on building up their reserves to insure against another run on their currency now implied, however, was that exports should significantly surpass imports. Since the requirements of neoliberal free trade meant they could no longer protect their domestic manufacturing markets from foreign imports, the concern with restraining consumer imports while accelerating export competitiveness in turn required the limiting of working-class incomes.

This was related to the second dimension of capitalist globalization noted above—namely the global division of labor. At the beginning of the twentieth century almost 80 percent of manufactured goods and almost 90 percent of manufactured exports in the world were produced by the capitalist countries of Europe and North America. The rest of the world had provided them with natural resources and purchased their manufactured goods, while often facing imperial limits on their own industrial development. By 2000 manufacturing as a portion of GDP was higher in the developing countries (23 percent) than in the developed ones (18 percent).[49] The greatest changes in this respect occurred in the final decades of the twentieth century, with South Korea leading the way (see Table 11.3).

Table 11.3: Manufacturing Share of Exports by Country

	1980	2000
South Korea	87%	94%
Mexico	55%	90%
Malaysia	25%	87%
Turkey	29%	81%
India	56%	78%
Brazil	39%	60%

Source: Kozul-Wright and Rayment, "Globalization Reloaded," Table 1, p. 10. Excluding oil exports.

The new division of labor corresponded to something equally crucial to a globalized capitalism: the development of new networks of integrated production. Far from the shift of productive activity from the developed core leading to a fragmentation of production, it was part and parcel of a much greater global coordination of production through a broad range of subsidiaries, suppliers, and distributors.[50] The growing tendency on the part of multinational corporations to centralize their key strategic and administrative functions in their home country, while decentralizing labor-intensive production abroad, already discerned by Stephen Hymer in the early 1970s, had become pronounced by the mid 1980s.[51] It especially accelerated through the 1990s in response to the pressures and opportunities brought on by the liberalization of trade and capital flows, the application of the new information technologies, the development of infrastructures, and, above all, the growth of new proletariats in the developing world. The mutual flow of direct investment as well as trade, which had already created such dense interdependence in production between the advanced capitalist countries, increasingly characterized their economic relations with a significant number of developing countries.

Multinational corporations increasingly outsourced many operations, now purchasing from other companies much of what they had previously performed "in house" (from accounting to janitorial services, and a great deal of production itself). Although this often led to a greater concentration of corporate power on a global scale, it also intensified competition in each sector (and indeed among divisions within each firm), as well as between nominally independent suppliers and distributors across the world bidding for entry into global networks of integrated production. The result was a more interdependent global capitalism that required more than ever the consolidation of "free trade" to facilitate borderless production. In a mature industry like automobiles, these developments had only begun in the 1980s, although they increased much further through the 1990s. For a newer industry like computer electronics, integrated production was already common at a much earlier stage.

Apple's iPod illustrated well the competitive integration and international hierarchy of production in this sector. By having provided "the first legal music downloading service with a large library and its control of the underlying digital rights management system network," Apple could take advantage of global pools of labor, including skills and innovations developed elsewhere. The iPod's 451 parts were overwhelmingly made in Southeast Asia: the US produced some of the chips, Japan the hard drive, and South Korea and Taiwan most of the other components, with final assembly done in China, mainly by the Taiwanese-owned firm Foxconn (the world's largest electronics contract manufacturer). On top of a total factory cost of $145, Apple added $80 for its own design, software engineering, and marketing contributions; retailers in the US added $75 more, bringing the final price to $300. Thus less than half the revenue generated by the iPod went to all the producers in Asia (and only a tiny fraction—1.8 percent of the total factory cost—to China as the site of final assembly), while Apple received at least a quarter of the revenue, and over half when the iPod was sold online or through an Apple store.[52]

This was indicative of one of the key novel aspects of US economic centrality—the third dimension of accelerated capitalist globalization, noted above. Despite all the anxiety on the one hand, and *schadenfreude* on the other, about the productive capacity of American capital, US corporations were able to take special advantage of the open world they had been so central to creating. The measure of this success was not the proportion of global production that took place in the US (this had clearly fallen over time as a by-product of the successful promotion of capitalist social relations abroad), but rather the *strategic* importance of American capital in the global economy. This was most obvious in key new areas of economic activity such as information technology, where a "powerful research infrastructure" put the US "at the forefront of major breakthroughs . . . It remains undisputed leader in software technology. US venture spending far outstrips international spending."[53]

The US accounted for between 60 and 75 percent of all OECD research and development expenditures in such high-tech sectors as aerospace and scientific instruments, and 45 to 50 percent in electronics and pharmaceuticals. Even in office equipment and computers, where the US share had declined to under 40 percent of all R&D expenditure in the OECD, the US still spent twice as much as Japan, which ranked second.[54] Throughout the neoliberal era, US government agencies maintained their proactive role so that while some of the state's initiatives in this period "simply facilitated the privatization of publicly funded intellectual property . . . others significantly expanded the government's role in directing technological change."[55]

To a substantial degree, the "commanding heights" of global accumulation had shifted to these high-tech sectors, and to a range of business services (management, legal, accounting, engineering, consultancy, and financial) in which American corporations overwhelmingly dominated. As of 2007, the top three or four global firms in such diverse sectors as technological hardware and equipment, software and computers, aerospace/military, and oil equipment and services were American, as were fourteen of the sixteen top global firms in healthcare equipment and services. In global media, four of the top five corporations were American, as were two of the top three in each of the pharmaceuticals, industrial transportation, industrial equipment, and fixed-line telecommunications sectors. And five of the top six corporations in the general retail sector were American. These included Wal-Mart, which used its application of computerized information systems to become one of the world's most strategically important corporations.[56] It is wrong to see these US MNCs, however international, as "transnational" rather than American. Not only were their controlling shareholders and headquarters located in the US, so was two-thirds of their global employment and capital expenditures and 85 percent of their research and development expenditures. No less than 70 percent of the value of the goods and services they produced was accounted for by their activities in the US.[57] Even for the most internationalized US manufacturing MNCs—namely, those with more than 50 percent of their sales and employment outside the US, such as General Electric, Ford, IBM, and Proctor and Gamble—the most significant locale by far remained the US, their foreign activities being distributed among a wide variety of countries.[58]

To top it all off, nine of the top ten corporations in global financial services were American—a dominance that went beyond that in any other sector. By 2007, five US investment banks accounted for 35 percent of world revenue generated by underwriting bond issues, organizing IPOs, equity trading, syndicated loans, and over-the-counter derivatives. More than half the world's total of pension, insurance, and mutual funds were under the management of US financial firms, as were two-thirds of hedge funds and private equity funds.[59] The extent to which the activity of US finance was intimately linked to the integration of global production could be seen from their central role in cross-border mergers and acquisitions (which accounted for three-quarters of FDI). The dominant role that US investment banks had long played in arranging these deals internationally went so far by 2007 as to account for no less than 45 percent of all merger deals worth over $500 million (Swiss and UK banks came next, with 12 percent each, followed by German banks with 8 percent, French with 6 percent, and Italian with 5 percent).[60]

Of course, US corporations themselves were directly involved in financial markets. Although their high profit levels since the mid 1980s meant that they did not need to rely on issuing new shares for investment funds, they remained major players in stock markets via buybacks. Following a supportive SEC ruling in 1982, net stock issuance was negative in twenty-one of the twenty-four years between 1984 and 2007 (the years 1991–93 were the exceptions), with net stock buybacks over that period totaling $3.2 trillion.[61] And even while paying out high dividends, they were also major borrowers, raising some $3.1 trillion in the corporate bond markets over this period (60 percent of this in the last ten years), and meeting short-term expenses using commercial paper while simultaneously putting surplus funds into money markets. They were also increasingly engaged in capital markets via their consumer credit subsidiaries and employee pension plans. The activities of industry had become "financialized."[62] This was the case not only in the myriad ways they used financial markets, as described above, and the proportion of profits they earned from doing so, but also in terms of the proportion of executives', managers', and sometimes even other employees' compensation paid in stock options. Moreover, nonfinancial firms became especially involved in hedging foreign-exchange and interest-rate risks through the derivatives markets, treating these as necessary costs, similar to expenditures on transportation and telecommunications.

These developments blurred the old lines between financial and nonfinancial activities. Yet this should not be taken too far. For all the greater complexity of the interactions between finance and industry, they each retained their distinct characteristics. Finance preserved its special role in the global allocation of savings, reinforcing competitive processes of profit-equalization, and increasingly allowing the value of assets and commodities to be compared across countries and over time, while industry took part in financial markets to supplement rather than replace productive activities. Thus, while a large part of auto company profits were derived from financial services, this mainly had to do with the way they were subsidizing their credit arms to keep their plants operating at a higher capacity. The financialization of US corporations did not mean they were no longer engaged in manufacturing. Most of the investment abroad was about capturing *new* markets for manufactured products (the bulk of what US MNCs produced abroad was not exported back to supply the US domestic market). A great many American jobs were of course lost—in some cases, like textiles, entire sectors were wiped out—but to the extent that this was part of American capital's capacity to move on to new manufacturing sectors, it reflected not a hollowing-out of manufacturing but a restructuring.[63] And there was often outsourcing within the US (for example, auto suppliers going to the southern states or call centers established in prisons), as well as outsourcing abroad.

Most US job losses stemmed not from foreign outsourcing but from the impact of the sustained increases in manufacturing productivity at home, which in the boom of the 1990s was compensated for by job creation (usually at lower wages) in other sectors. In the context of the Asian crisis it was widely predicted that manufacturing unemployment would soar as Korean, Thai, Indonesian, and other currencies were devalued, but this lowered consumer prices in the US without any significant impact on US production, except for the steel industry.[64] China's entry into the WTO considerably changed the overall picture, but while US manufacturing job losses were indeed heavy after 2001 (especially in auto and electrical appliances, as well as the long-suffering textile and apparel sector), the US was still producing more manufactured goods and receiving more foreign investment in 2007 than all the BRICs (Brazil, Russia, India, and China) combined.[65]

Rather than taking the US trade deficit as a measure of industrial decline, it is instructive to consider US exports and imports separately. The growth in the volume of US exports in the two decades up to 2007—even as the trade deficit accumulated—averaged a very robust 6.6 percent, leaving it only marginally behind Germany and China, the world's largest exporters; it was the relative expansion of US imports that was the source of the growing deficit.[66] The deficit, in other words, primarily came from increased US consumption, which grew faster than in other advanced capitalist countries. This was partly linked to the very high income growth and conspicuous consumption of the most well-off segments of the US population, but it was also due to much faster population growth than in Europe and Japan, the longer hours worked by much of the US population, and, very significantly, their increased consumer debt. This was supported by the international flow of funds into the US despite the size of the trade deficit. It was in good part US consumer spending that maintained effective global demand into the first years of the twenty-first century. The US trade deficit was not an adequate measure of the overall productive power of American capital; rather, it indicated its place in global capitalism. The case of the Apple iPod illustrates this at a product level; since its final point of assembly was China, each iPod sold in the US represented an increase in the US trade deficit of $145, even though it involved an increase in the surplus captured by Apple from domestic and—especially—foreign labor.

The average annual real rate of growth of the American economy in the quarter-century after the resolution of the crisis of the 1970s (from 1983 to 2007) was 3.5 percent. This was higher than in any similar period from 1830 to 1950, and was only marginally less than during the so-called postwar "golden age"; and, unlike then, US GDP growth in the quarter-century after 1983 surpassed that of the other advanced capitalist countries.[67] In the years from 1950 to 1973, US manufacturing productivity growth averaged 2.5 percent, well below that of the other advanced capitalist countries; between 1983 and 2007, it increased quite dramatically to 3.5 percent, running ahead of all the other G7 economies. And in terms of attractiveness as a place for capitalists to invest the US was still, despite the wide dispersal of FDI to Europe and Asia by 2007, the largest single recipient of FDI inflows, and the rate of US manufacturing productivity growth ran considerably ahead of the growth in labor compensation at home.[68] As a result, the share of after-tax corporate profits relative to US GDP earned by American corporations in 2006 was at its highest level since 1945.

Moreover, US MNCs' operations abroad consistently contributed about 30 percent to total US profits in the new millennium, compared with less than 20 percent in the 1980s.[69] At the same time, the foreign operations of so many American banks (in 2007, Goldman Sachs had about 8,000 people in Europe, including consultants, over four-fifths of them in London) were a significant factor in the increasing share of total profit going to US finance.[70] Notably, those profits increasingly came from the fees charged for the provision of an array of services (some of them payroll and accounting outsourced from industry) rather than returns on loans (the share of the total bank income coming from services other than interest on loans rose from 15 percent to 35 percent between 1990 and 2006).[71]

It was largely the failure to take sufficient account of the dominance and integration of American production and finance that led to the misreading of what US trade deficits signaled by way of undermining the value of the dollar and its place as the world currency. It was the balance of capital flows more than the balance of trade that now determined the dollar's value. The issue of US "imbalances" that so many observers were fixated on in the first years of the new millennium failed to capture this central point. Far from the capital inflows signaling the dollar's weakness, and being significant mainly in offsetting US trade deficits, they highlighted the central role of US banks and MNCs in the global economy, and the extent to which the integration of so many Third World countries was dependent on the pull of both US consumer and financial markets.

The Integration of China

Nowhere was this clearer than with the integration of China into global capitalism. The crucial lesson the Chinese government drew from the Asian crisis was not so much the conventional one—that measures of financial liberalization needed to be sequenced, in order to allow time for appropriate institutional developments to take place—but rather that, in a world of such massive capital mobility, a run on the currency would overwhelm capital controls if the country's central bank was not holding massive dollar reserves. The impact of the 1994 devaluation of the renminbi on the trade balances of other East Asian countries—which put pressure on their exchange rates and portended the coming crisis in the region—already indicated China's growing importance. China's subsequent commitment to prevent a fall in its exchange rate in 1997–98, and thus avoid competitive devaluations, was much appreciated by the other East Asian governments; and it was seen by the US as signaling China's embracing of international responsibilities in global capitalism.

It was China's admission to the WTO in 2001 that positioned it to secure the massive export surpluses that enabled these reserves to be built up. The conditions that China agreed to in the key negotiations with the US for entry were "far more stringent than the terms under which other developing countries had acceded . . . in certain respects China's liberalization commitments exceed[ed] those of advanced industrial countries."[72] This was not simply a matter of imposition: domestic liberalizing forces used it to lever change. The leading US negotiator, Charlene Barshefsky, emphasized that, as with the former Communist states in the 1990s, the success of China's "domestic economic reform programs hinge[d] on the externality of international commitments to reform in a particular direction."[73] China's chief negotiator at the WTO, Long Yongtu, concurred: "China's economy must become a market economy in order to become part of the global economic system."[74] One of the key arguments Barshefsky made to Congress was that China's commitment to liberalize its distribution system was "broader actually than any World Trade Organization member has made."[75] And it was especially significant in terms of US priorities that China agreed "to substantially open its market in banking, insurance, securities, fund management and other financial services."[76]

Before it was admitted to the WTO, China's total trade (exports and imports) as a share of GDP was, at 43 percent, well below the average for low- and middle-income countries; by 2007, its 68 percent trade-to-GDP ratio was well above the average of those other countries.[77] By this time, too, China's average tariffs on industrial products were under 9 percent, compared with 27 percent in Brazil, 31 percent in Argentina, 32 percent in India, and 37 percent in Indonesia. China's growing role in transnational production networks was seen in the rising share of parts and components in its imports: these inputs into products that were eventually largely exported rose from 18 percent of all imports in 1993–94 to 44 percent by 2006–07.[78]

The surge of capital investment after China's entry to the WTO came from MNCs that wanted to use China as an export platform. But many were also interested in China's domestic market. By 2002, some two-thirds of the output of "foreign invested enterprises" (FIEs) was for sale within China, not only as inputs to transnational production networks but also as final products for sale to Chinese consumers.[79] For example, China's strategy of trying to get foreign auto companies to produce in China by erecting high tariff walls against vehicle imports was generally unsuccessful (fewer vehicles were being produced in China than in Canada in 2000). It was only after China's entry to the WTO—signaling the state's commitment to foreign property rights, nondiscriminatory treatment, and freedom to repatriate profits—that foreign auto companies aggressively moved in, contributing directly to the explosive growth of China's automobile industry (by over 60 percent *each year* from 2001 to 2004); by the end of the decade China was producing more vehicles than the US.[80] The impact of WTO membership was also very important in opening up service sectors, with multinationals champing at the bit to invest not only in the retail trade but also in transportation and telecommunications, as well as a variety of business services.

China's dramatic capitalist development affected economic activity everywhere, forcing industrial restructuring not only at home but also abroad and determining global commodity prices. Though still a relatively poor country, with a per capita GDP only 15 percent of that of the US, by 2007 China's total GDP had surpassed that of Germany and Japan to rank second only to the US.[81] The number of manufacturing workers in China alone was double the ten leading developed countries combined; its total labor force was larger than that of the US, Europe, Japan, and all Latin America combined; and its factories exported more goods than those of any other country. While its financial markets remained comparatively small, no country had larger international reserves, or was a larger holder of US Treasuries. Yet China was simultaneously able to maintain annual levels of domestic investment which, relative to GDP, were more than double those of both the US and Europe.

China's "open door" at the beginning of the twenty-first century was so utterly different from that of a century earlier because this time global capital entered by invitation. In the early 1980s Deng Xiaoping explained to the US secretary of state, George Shultz, the Communist Party's new principle of China's "two openings." The first was

> in China itself, and that was important, but it was not enough. China also had to open itself to the outside world, particularly to the United States. The reason, he said, was that China was backward and needed the knowledge, the technology, and the markets that the rest of the world in general and the United States in particular had to offer.[82]

Although Deng was especially impressed by the rapid development of Japan and South Korea, the initial Chinese reforms had by and large been creative variations on reforms attempted by other Communist states: allowing rural households to have their own plots of land; promoting collectively owned town and village enterprises (TVEs) while permitting the development of small-scale private enterprises; modest market-oriented reforms in state owned enterprises (SOEs); regional experimentation with "special economic zones" to promote exports and induce foreign investment.[83]

All of this led to strong growth, but came up against the same trade and fiscal contradictions that many other developing countries had experienced. By the end of the 1980s, the rapid rise in imports of machinery and consumer goods had left China with a negative balance of trade; this, together with the stagnation of the SOEs, had led to a serious decline in state revenues.[84] With the limits of the SOE reforms exposed, a broader strategic shift to the "second opening" was put in hand by the early 1990s. This involved a massive mobilization behind the market economy, and especially the far more comprehensive embrace of foreign direct investment than had been the case in either Japan or South Korea. This openness to foreign capital would pave the way for China to become, within a decade, the host to more foreign investment than any other country except the US (see Figure 11.1).

The remarkable boom in FDI to Hong Kong in 2000—after its return to China in 1997—reflected the fact that "TNCs planning to invest in mainland China [were] 'parking' funds in Hong Kong, in anticipation of China's expected entry into the WTO," as well as preparing by way of "major cross-border merger and acquisition (M&A) in telecommunications."

Figure 11.1: Foreign Direct Investment in China, 1980–2009

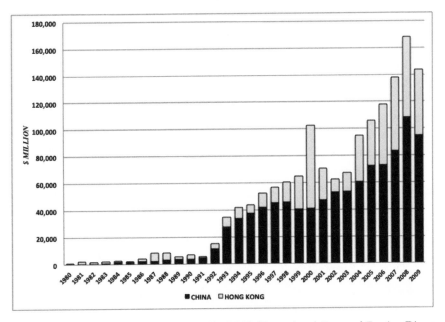

Source: This table is derived from UNCTADSTAT, "Inward and Outward Foreign Direct Investment." "FDI to Asia Booms, Fuelled by Hong Kong," UNCTAD Press Release, September 18, 2001.[85]

The first wave of foreign investors, starting in the 1980s, had come from the large Chinese business communities in Hong Kong, Taiwan, Indonesia, and elsewhere in East Asia, launching China as an assembly hub for Asian production networks and giving it access to an internationalized bourgeoisie that Russia, for example, lacked. But the subsequent waves of foreign investment in the 1990s, and particularly after the WTO admission in 2001, came increasingly from advanced capitalist countries. To some extent, the Chinese leadership seems to have treated FDI "as a substitute for the domestic private sector . . . to the extent that the Chinese government has provided a space for private capital, it has shown a revealed preference for foreign over domestic firms."[86] This preference was expressed in various ways, including the tax system, subsidies, trade regulations, and access to finance. Domestic and foreign capital effectively operated within different legal parameters, but in contrast to many other countries, the more favorable laws applied to foreign, not domestic capital.

Notably, and very much in line with what Deng had told Shultz about the US's special role in the "second opening," it was investments by US MNCs like DuPont, Ford, GE, GM, IBM, Intel, Lucent Technologies, Microsoft, and Motorola that proved especially significant. Although the US accounted for only about 10 percent of overall FDI going into China, this still put it at the top of the list of foreign investors. The significance of US FDI was less as a capital inflow (China had no shortage of capital funds) than as a source of technology and expertise.[87] The preoccupation with the latter on the part of the Chinese leadership was also apparent in the more than 50,000 Chinese students who were sent to do doctorates in science and engineering at US universities between 1987 and 2007 (exceeding by a third the total for all those doing US doctorates in these fields from Europe, Canada, and Mexico combined).[88] At the same time, US legal education became "increasingly necessary to a career in China in international trade and investment."[89]

Among the various reasons why foreign capitalists invested in China—a cheap labor force, the potentially massive domestic market, high-quality public infrastructure in transportation, communications, and education—confidence that their investments would be protected by the state was far from the least important. The host of new laws that benefited foreign investors was an element in this, but the law generally followed, rather than constructed, the realities on the ground. China's lawyers did not so much inform clients about the legal landscape as help them to establish the proper contacts with regional and state officials. In other words, it was not so much the legal system that was crucial in protecting property rights as it was "the political structure itself [that] served as an alternative to the formal legal system in providing a reasonable degree of security."[90] This was not just a matter of confidence in the central Chinese state; it also applied to regional governments, which competed to create the most favorable conditions for joint ventures.[91] Of course, as joint ventures grew in size and significance, and as Chinese firms' supplier relationships with them and with foreign MNCs expanded, the line between domestic and foreign capitalists, as well as between them and the families of Party elites and state officials at all levels, inevitably became blurred.[92] At the same time, the laws benefiting foreign investors spilled over into better protections for all private businesses, making the legal regime for Chinese capitalists "look more like the one for foreigners, not the other way around."[93]

It was still the case, however, that "the growth of mixed property forms that maintain central or local government ownership and control has far outstripped the growth of private firms."[94] State owned enterprises continued to play a very important role in the Chinese economy, even though some sectors, such as textiles, were allowed to shift into the "competitive" sector, and what remained of the state sector was significantly restructured, so that the SOE share of employment fell by 45 percent between 1995 and 2004.[95] In order to establish foreign business confidence without surrendering its control over the economy, the Chinese state clearly defined the boundaries of the state sector, promising to limit its extension into new sectors and to allow more space for foreign participation in the existing ones. To be sure, the Chinese state held on to its ability to affect the rate and direction of investment, not only in steel but also in oil, petrochemicals, auto, rail, and telecommunications—not least through state control of the largest Chinese banks (in the vast majority of cases where shares of SOEs were publicly offered, the state retained effective control). Of the top 500 companies in China in 2008, the largest forty-three were state-owned; privately-owned firms accounted for only one-fifth of the list, and for only 10 percent of total sales revenue.[96]

It was nevertheless significant that, although by the early years of the twenty-first century foreign invested enterprises (FIEs) only accounted for some 20 percent of China's industrial production, FIEs had captured 47 percent of sales in China's domestic high-tech market, while the share of SOEs had slipped to 42 percent.[97] Moreover, the FIE's share of China's industrial exports had grown to well over half (up from 17 percent in 1990). By 2003, the extraordinary reorientation of China's industrial role in the global division of labor towards electronics, telecommunications, and machinery was very clear: high-tech manufacturing already represented 27 percent of China's manufactured exports, compared to an OECD average of 18 percent.[98] But what was no less remarkable was the FIE's increasing domination in this sector: foreign firms and joint ventures accounted for almost 80 percent of China's exports of industrial machinery; 90 percent of computers, components, and peripherals; and 71 percent of electronics and telecommunications equipment.[99] Exaggerated claims about China's growing economic dominance need to be somewhat discounted in light of this. Alongside its model of rapid catch-up facing profound environmental challenges, at the time the global economic crisis began in 2007, China was still catching up technologically to Korea and Taiwan, let alone the US.[100]

Of prime importance for FIEs, and increasingly for SOEs as well, has been the restructuring and management of the immense Chinese labor force. Indeed, China's new place in the global order required nothing less than the remaking of its working class. As one group of workers tried to hang on to the remnants of the old "iron rice bowl" regime, a new generation of workers that migrated to urban centers outside their home region had no rights whatsoever.[101] In 1978, China's workforce was 70 percent agricultural and 30 percent non-agricultural; by 2004 this ratio had been exactly reversed. From 1991 to 2006, the urban workforce increased by 260 million, 85 percent of that through migration to the cities. An estimated 120 to 150 million workers, accounting for almost two-thirds of the industrial workforce and one-third of the service sector, had no formal status in the cities; they joined newly laid-off SOE workers to swell the ranks of the 270 million Chinese known as "dispatch workers"—the world's largest "precariat."[102] Notably, the commodification, deregulation, and exploitation of labor power was based, as Ching Kwan Lee has emphasized, on a "remarkable and momentous increase in law-making activity by the central authority and the professionalization of the judiciary . . ."[103] Workers were left vulnerable to local administrations competing to attract investment, and to overworked judges closely linked to the same local officials. The tens of thousands of riots and protests that took place from the late 1990s (officially called "incidents") belied the Chinese Communist Party's claims that it still provided workers with anything like a protective regulatory system. Notably, foreign capital threatened to withdraw its investments if the balance of class power was altered in the workers' favour.[104]

Ho-fung Hung has accurately summarized the relationship between the party-state and the working class that lay at the heart of China's capitalist development:

> What made the Chinese miracle possible was first, the capacity of subnational states to promote local economic growth in a single-minded manner; and, second, the capacity of the national party-state to repress labor's demands and the growth of civil society. While the autonomy and competitive pressure among local states perpetually goaded them to increase their individual attractiveness, and hence China's overall attractiveness to global capital, the authoritarian national rule kept discontent at bay without requiring large-scale income redistribution through taxation and wage increases. These two processes, when unfolding on the vast geographical and demographic scale of China, made China the most dynamic center of capital accumulation in the world system.[105]

The transformations in China lowered poverty levels, but also predict-ably and dramatically increased inequality. The official justification of "let some get rich first, so others can get rich later" oversaw China's shift from one of the world's most egalitarian societies to one of the most unequal.[106] This was reflected in Chinese household consumption: from a share of GDP in the early 1980s that, at approximately 50 percent, matched the rest of Asia and other developing countries, by 2007 the share of household consumption had fallen to 36 percent, far below that in neighboring coun-tries, or in other major developing countries such as India—never mind the over 70 percent share of GDP that household consumption took in the US (see Figure 11.2).

Figure 11.2: Consumption and Investment Shares of GDP, 2007

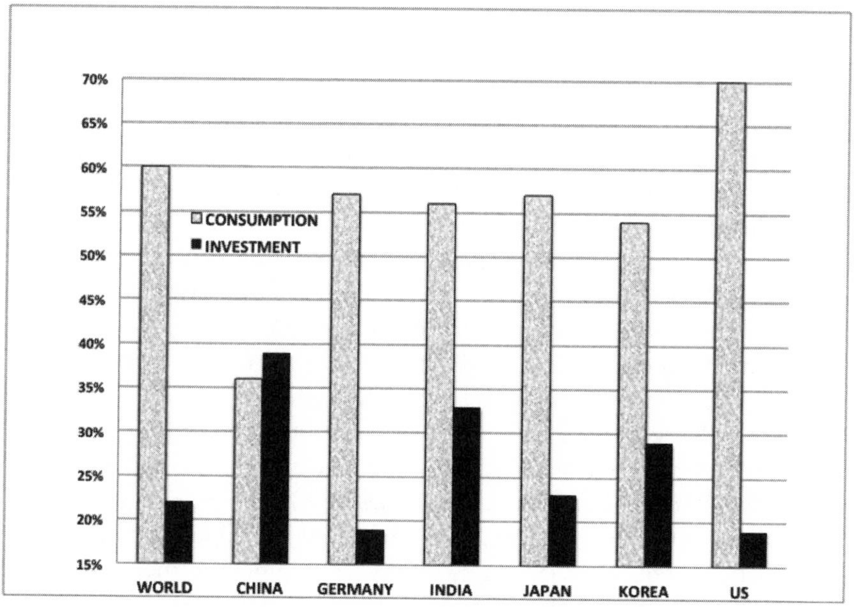

Source: Derived from World Bank, World Development Indicators.

China's low domestic consumption left it with a profound dependence on American consumer markets, sustained by the policy of keeping the renminbi low relative to the dollar despite China's ever larger trade surpluses and capital inflows. Although a managed floating exchange band was imple-mented in 2005, supported by the introduction of an over-the-counter derivatives market, and of foreign-exchange and interest-rate swaps, the renminbi's relative appreciation was small in real terms. This was only possi-ble because extensive capital controls were maintained, even as China's securities and bond markets were opened up to foreigners in line with the

WTO accession agreement. But while US institutional investors and investment banks became key players in Chinese financial markets (they were especially involved in major merger and acquisitions activity, and in purchasing the lion's share of stock offered for sale by SOEs[107]), China's capital markets, while growing fast, remained "among the smallest in the world relative to the size of the domestic economy."[108] Despite China's having consented under the WTO agreement to open its domestic banking sector to foreigners by 2007, the financial system remained dominated by five large state-owned commercial banks primarily engaged in lending to SOEs, while interest rates were administered by the central bank with the primary goal of avoiding upward pressures on the exchange rate. This system of extensive capital controls and administered interest rates, which was a crucial part of the state's arsenal for engineering and channeling its massive domestic investment, left China "considerably less integrated into the global financial system than its importance as an investment destination and major exporting country might suggest."[109]

This uneven pattern of China's integration into global capitalism reflected the party-state's development strategy. It gave it more autonomy from global financial flows, but the same development strategy also made it ever more dependent on US consumer markets and tied to US Treasury bonds. Even apart from how much China would have lost from its accumulated reserves if the dollar were devalued, and the lack of alternative assets in which to park its surpluses nearly as safely, these domestic factors were especially important for understanding why the widespread expectations that China would respond to growing US trade and fiscal deficits by pulling out its massive dollar-asset holdings were proved wrong.[110]

As we shall see in the next chapter, the first global crisis of the twenty-first century would not be caused by the build-up of external imbalances, such as the US trade deficit and indebtedness to China, triggering a collapse of the dollar. On the contrary, it was caused by the build-up of domestic contradictions rooted in US society's own envelopment in the volatility of finance. It was a crisis made in America.

12

American Crisis / Global Crisis

However much global capitalism was made in the image of American capitalism, this took place in a manner that was full of contradictions, and was also always contested. The protests in Seattle that announced the emergence of the anti-globalization movement as the twentieth century drew to a close confirmed this, and so, in a horrific manner, did the attack on the World Trade Center in New York on September 11, 2001. The turn of the century will now forever be associated with that spectacular act of symbolic violence against imperial power—and with the war unleashed by the imperial state in its aftermath.

The new Bush administration certainly appeared more interested in military interventions than economic ones, despite the millennium also opening with a stock market crash (the bursting of the "dot.com" bubble), with the scandal-ridden downfall of Enron (*Fortune* magazine's choice as "America's Most Innovative Company" for six years running), and with major financial crises in Turkey and Argentina. Bush's first secretary of the Treasury, Paul O'Neill, was publicly critical of his predecessors' repeated efforts to contain economic crises around the world, going so far as to deride Robert Rubin for playing at being "chief of the fire department." Rubin's response was that, once faced with "the messy reality of global financial crises," the new administration would soon take up its imperial economic responsibilities: "They say they won't intervene. But they will."[1]

The Treasury and Fed's dramatic interventions in 2007–08 in the face of what Ben Bernanke, in a closed-door session with the Congressional Financial Crisis Inquiry Commission in 2009, called "the worst financial crisis in global history, including the Great Depression," would prove Rubin more correct than he could have imagined.[2] Tim Geithner, President Obama's Treasury secretary (who as president of the New York Federal Reserve had also worked very closely with Henry Paulson Jr., Bush's third Treasury secretary, in trying to contain the crisis), told the Commission that "none of [the] biggest banks would have survived a situation in which we had let that fire try to burn itself out."[3] Whereas it was Volcker's experience with the moments of crisis produced by the inflationary pressures of full-employment capitalism that prepared him for his climactic role when he became Federal Reserve chair in 1979, Geithner's preparation for the job of US Treasury secretary two decades later was his experience of moments of crisis produced by the volatility of international finance.[4] When the Treasury and Fed immediately intervened in mid 2007 to try to contain the crisis, this inevitably involved acting as lender of last resort not only to domestic banks that were deemed "too big to fail," but also to foreign ones. And in the aftermath of this crisis the growing significance of the internationalization of the state in global capitalism became clearer than ever.

One indication of this was the apparent shift in the locus of strategic economic coordination from the G7 to the G20. Another was the remarkable consensus among them about strengthening rather than challenging the international regulatory regime that had fostered the development of global finance. In this respect, the crisis reinforced rather than undermined the role of the American empire. In 2011 Geithner would tell the IMF that "the rules on banks fell behind the pace of innovation in markets," and that it was especially important to develop the state capacities "necessary for the new rules to work." He concluded: "So we will do what we need to do to make the United States financial system stronger. We will do so carefully. And as we do it, we will bring the world with us."[5]

The response of the Treasury and the Fed to the first global capitalist crisis of the twenty-first century demonstrated not only the range of their interventionist capacities, but also that they had learned the lessons of the early 1930s. Their dramatic actions to save the banks and other financial institutions, followed by the largest peacetime fiscal stimulus in US history as well as the monetary policy of "quantitative easing," would have real effects in halting the economic crash. The stimulus coordination with the G20, combined with the room for maneuver provided by the international rush to hold Treasury bonds for safety in the global storm, confirmed the importance of the political infrastructure of global capitalism that had been developed over the previous decades. Nevertheless, the sangfroid that had led the Treasury by the end of the 1990s to define state intervention in the economy in terms of "failure-containment" rather than "failure-prevention," rooted in the context of asset inflation and credit consumerism, was no longer tenable. In light of the depth of the crisis a decade later, low interest rates and flooding the banks with liquidity could no longer spark sustained economic growth, nor prevent the crisis from further unraveling internationally. The empire's practice of crisis-management designed to align its own social formation with the reproduction of global capitalism, as well as to "bring the rest of the world with us," would remain beset by acute contradictions.

Smoldering Bushfires

To put the depth and scale of the crisis and the American state's responses to it in proper perspective, it is first of all necessary to examine the extent to which the US Treasury and Federal Reserve had themselves stoked the fires that led to the global financial conflagration. In contrast to what had been so common in the 1990s, it was quite remarkable that, before 2007, the Bush administration faced only two serious financial crises, both occurring in its first year.[6] Like Rubin before him with the Mexican crisis, O'Neill had barely settled into his office at the Treasury when he was confronted by the outbreak of the most severe financial crisis in modern Turkish history. With the Turkish government's attempts to maintain a currency peg undermined by financial markets' response to its rising public debt, there was no question of letting the markets decide the fate of this crucially strategic US ally. But the US Treasury was content to leave it to the IMF, which had provided conditional loans to Turkey on eighteen occasions since 1958, to contain the Turkish crisis.[7]

Nevertheless, when the Argentine crisis came to a head only six months later, in August 2001, the Treasury's behavior "encapsulated the degree to which the United States was making policy for the IMF." As Blustein's authoritative account puts it, the Treasury's initial worries that "an implosion in Argentina would spread financial turbulence worldwide" quickly led it to reassert its "primary responsibility for ensuring financial stability" at a global level. To indicate that his approach to intervention was different than Rubin's, O'Neill insisted that a large part of an $8 billion IMF loan to Argentina had to be geared towards "leveraging" bondholders into accepting a debt restructuring. This scheme was adopted by the IMF, despite being regarded by its staff as "muddle-headed," while Wall Street CEOs would soon make it clear that O'Neill's leveraging plan was "faring dismally."[8]

It would be a mistake to see this as a function of the Bush administration's unilateralism. Not only did the G7 publicly adopt a common position on Argentina, but their multilateral cooperation was also crucial a few weeks later, when Wall Street was temporarily knocked out on 9/11, and their central banks' long-standing emergency plans for keeping the international banking system going were immediately activated.[9] Thus preoccupied, the US Treasury adopted a less active stance on the Argentine crisis, backed by the view which now came to predominate in internal discussions that "pulling the plug on Argentina could not result in serious financial consequences internationally."[10]

The IMF's effective abandonment of Argentina towards the end of 2001 left its government to cope with the crisis alone. Drastic cuts in public spending, as well as restrictions on bank withdrawals and the transfer of money abroad, produced a popular revolt and a series of presidential resignations, soon followed by an inevitable default and the introduction of capital controls. Amid fierce social struggles over which classes would bear the costs of the crisis, the Kirschner government (elected in 2003 on an explicitly anti-neoliberal platform) rejected the external pressures—notably coming more from Europe and Japan than from the US—to deepen structural adjustment and prioritize debt payment. It thereby gave itself more room to intervene in the economy "in a way that would have been unthinkable in the context of traditional IMF programs."[11] Yet, despite a certain degree of *political* contagion (which contributed to derailing the Bush administration's plan for an overall Free Trade Agreement of the Americas), by the middle of the decade—once Kirschner's measures had restored financial stability without any fundamental change in class and state structures—foreign capital began to return to Argentina.[12] Strong regional growth, spurred by rising commodity prices, was a major factor in this, together with Argentina, like other states with export surpluses drawing on the lessons of the Asian crisis to build up central bank reserves.

But the main reason why there was no international financial conflagration this time was once again to be found in the global effects of US interest-rate policies. Whereas twenty years earlier a by-product of the Fed's adoption of very high interest rates to slay the dragon of inflation at home was that it triggered Latin America's "lost decade," now the region was the beneficiary of "more than five years of exceptional liquidity after the Fed, concerned to head off deflation at home, cut interest rates in 2001."[13] It is important to put this remarkable volte-face in perspective. It was no longer fears of wage-push inflation but what Greenspan called the "irrational exuberance" fueling the stock-market bubble that had motivated the Fed in determining interest-rate levels in the mid 1990s. Yet this concern was more than negated by the Fed's interest-rate cuts in the wake of the Asian crisis to contain the LTCM collapse at home and avert a Brazilian default abroad, thereby contributing to the Dow Jones index reaching a level by 2000 that was three times what it had been just six years earlier. But as unemployment came down to 4 percent in 1999 (its lowest level in three decades), the Fed's anti-inflation priority was temporarily reasserted, even in a context of price stability, and interest rates were raised six times by the first quarter of 2000. This was undertaken against opposition from a minority on the FOMC who argued that concerns a tight labor market would inevitably lead to inflation were, as the New York Federal Reserve's William McDonough put it, "a fiction of our own minds," and that it would be taken as evidence that "what we believe in is not price stability but a differentiation in income distribution that goes against the working people."[14]

With the collapse in the NASDAQ high-tech stock index in March 2000, signaling the end of the dot.com bubble and the possibility of a recession, the Fed reversed course again and adopted a very loose monetary policy that continued through 9/11 and the Argentine financial crisis, bringing interest rates down from 6 to 2 percent in the course of 2001. The short and mild recession of that year had come to an end by November 2001, just when Argentina was engulfed by economic collapse; yet interest rates were then maintained at under 2 percent for the following three years. This was partly due to the Fed's fears that the US might now replicate Japan's decade of deflation. What made it possible for the low-interest-rate policy to be sustained was, on the one hand, the weakness of non-residential domestic investment and the infamous "jobless recovery," which made it difficult for inflation hawks to call for raising the rates, and on the other, the foreign purchases of Treasury bonds and other dollar-based securities, which meant that the US did not have to cover its trade deficit by raising interest rates.

This policy was maintained in spite of the fact that investors were increasingly stretching the boundaries of financial prudence by purchasing risky securities that provided higher yields than Treasury bonds offered. This took place despite the bursting of the dot.com bubble having already unleashed a series of financial scandals, which soon brought about the demise not only of Enron and WorldCom but also of Arthur Andersen, one of the five great US global accounting firms. As Paul Volcker put it at the time, since Wall Street's "infectious greed" and Enron's "outright fraud" belied the model of "good corporate practices" which the rest of the world was being expected to follow, US laws for greater "corporate responsibility" needed to be seen as "part and parcel of an effectively operating, open, free, global financial system."[15]

It was to secure such faith in financial markets that Congress adopted the Sarbanes-Oxley Bill in 2002. Its central prescription to deal with "Enronitis" was to make CEOs, chief financial officers, and boards of directors more accountable to investors for the accuracy of financial statements, while also establishing a new public board to oversee large accounting firms. It set out to improve the quality of corporate reporting to investors, while not really limiting the bounty that financial elites could reap from their interconnections and privileged access to information. By addressing a particular aspect of the general problem, it created legitimacy for the economic and financial practices that had given rise to the problem in the first place.[16] And before the first decade of the twenty-first century was over, it would become clear that legislative measures to ensure corporate responsibility could not be expected to ensure that even the strong institutions of the US would be able to withstand the financial volatility they were still engaged in fomenting.

This was especially the case because, just at this time, American capitalism was enveloping the whole world in the enormous funding of US mortgages and consumer credit. This generated the jumble of derivative and securitized instruments which, once wrapped in the triple-A status bestowed by the rating agencies, could be spread onto the books of a wide variety of institutions both at home and abroad.[17] These included not only the great New York investment banks, but also the largest US commercial banks—as well as the European banks, which had increasingly been emulating them. And they also included the world's biggest insurance company, AIG, which aggressively sold the credit default swaps that were used to hedge the purchase of mortgage-backed securities. Much of this edifice of financial obligations was built through a "shadow banking system," whereby in order to leverage their resources and enhance their lending capacity banks created "special investment vehicles" (SIVs) which did not fall under the Fed's regulatory purview, and so were not subject to constraints such as reserve requirements.

Before the crisis hit in 2007, the financial sector's share of corporate profits reached 33 percent (more than double its share in 1980), with an increasing proportion of earnings generated by banks trading in derivatives and securities on their own account, as opposed to traditional underwriting practices. The assets of Goldman Sachs quadrupled between 1999 and 2007, growing at a rate of 21 percent a year; Bank of America's grew by 14 percent, and Citigroup's by 12 percent. The financial practices that made this growth possible involved raising debt-to-capital ratios (from 18-to-1 to 27-to-1 for Bank of America; from 18-to-1 to 32-to-1 for Citigroup; and from 17-to-1 to 32-to-1 for Goldman Sachs).[18] Wall Street was effectively engaged in a huge "carry trade" reminiscent of East Asia in the mid 1990s (i.e. borrowing at a low rate of interest to fund the purchase of assets that yield a high rate). This was facilitated by incentives in compensation schemes for financial market actors that drove "transactions that produced immediate income but exposed the financial system to massive risks."[19]

Housing finance was a particularly attractive arena for such strategies because of the collateralized nature of home loans. The acceleration of mortgage-backed securitization, taking place amid rising house prices that seemed to increase the wealth and creditworthiness of those borrowing, gave rise to the acceptance of lower standards by regulatory agencies, acting with the connivance of both parties in Congress. Securitized mortgage credit served to tie together high finance and low finance: it came to play an important role in the super-leveraging and integration of global financial markets, just as it had become a key element in consumer demand and credit. Constrained in what they could get from their labor, US workers were drawn into the logic of asset inflation not only through the investments of their pension funds, but also through the one major asset they held (or could reasonably aspire to hold) in their own hands—their family homes. As wages stagnated and the income gap widened, growing segments of the home-owning working class sustained their consumption by taking out second mortgages on the bubble-inflated values of their homes. The apparent guarantee of forever-rising housing prices led to an increase in the share of consumption financed in this way—from 1.1 percent in the 1990s to 3 percent in 2000–05 (with a similar trend occurring in the growth of investments in "home improvements").[20]

It is significant that this went so far as to include poor African-American communities, so long the Achilles heel of working-class integration into the American Dream. The roots of the subprime mortgage crisis thus lay in the way the anti-inflation commitment had since the 1970s ruled out the public expenditures that would have been required just to start addressing the crisis of inadequate housing in US cities. As we saw earlier, a key factor in the steady expansion of Americans' consumer and mortgage debt since the 1970s had been reformers' faith that private finance could be used by the state in the public interest—in other words, that financial institutions could be so regulated and reformed as to ensure their functioning in the interest of social groups that they had hitherto excluded. The rising demand for home-ownership at lower income levels had been encouraged by government support for meeting housing needs through financial markets backed by mortgage tax deductions. Of course, the desire to realize the American dream of home-ownership on the part of so many of those who had previously been excluded was one thing; actual access to residential finance markets was another. Access for such unprecedented numbers by the turn of the century was only possible because financial intermediaries were frantically creating domestic mortgage debt in order to package and resell it in the market for structured credit.

Already well underway during the 1990s, this trend was given a great fillip not only by the Fed's low interest rates but also by the Bush administration's determination to expand the scope for "entrepreneurs" in the business of selling home mortgages, although it was mainly long-established private mortgage companies like Countrywide, and new ones that specialized in subprime loans like New Century Financial, that benefited from this. How common not just lax lending practices but outright predatory lending became can be seen from the fact that between 2000 and 2007 in Florida alone, 10,500 people were licensed as mortgage brokers who had criminal records (including over 4,000 who had previously been convicted of "fraud, bank robbery, racketeering and extortion").[21] But no less responsible than those brokers, who were essentially licensed loan sharks, were the mainstream financial institutions for which the brokers were the middlemen, and which actually secured the loans for home purchases in areas they had previously redlined. With most middle-class income-earners already in the market, mortgages were structured in such a way as to capture consumers who could not otherwise have afforded home-ownership. The majority of these loans were Adjustable Rate Mortgages (ARMs) with initial two-year fixed-rate periods at lower interest rates, and many offered borrowers the option of limiting their monthly payments to the interest (or even less, so that the principal owed would increase over time). By 2004, subprime loans represented over 20 percent of total US mortgages.[22]

The whole edifice was connected to the American state itself via Fannie Mae and Freddie Mac, which, although they had been privatized three decades earlier, had remained government-sponsored enterprises (GSEs). At the beginning of the 1980s they held and guaranteed some $85 billion in mortgage assets, equivalent to 7 percent of the mortgage market; by 2002, this had grown to $3.7 trillion, equivalent to almost 45 percent of the total mortgage market; by 2007, the total had reached $5.3 trillion, although it was a slightly smaller proportion of the total mortgage market since so many others had gotten into the game. As Ralph Nader put it, referring especially to the tax deduction allowed on mortgage-interest payments, Fannie and Freddie "swiftly and skillfully managed to pick up the roughshod tactics of the private corporate world and at the same time cling tightly to the federal government's deepest and most lucrative welfare troughs."[23] Above all, given the implicit guarantee the federal government gave to GSE securities, financial markets regarded them as virtually as safe as Treasury securities while yielding a higher return—no small consideration at a time when interest rates on Treasuries were effectively negative.

Commercial banks competed to extend residential mortgages in order to bundle them and transfer them to investment banks as well as to Fannie Mae and Freddie Mac. Between 1990 and 2006, the amount of residential debt held by issuers of asset-backed securities increased from $55 billion to over $2 trillion. As house prices increased after 2000 especially (by 60 percent more than inflation—the most in over half a century), banks increasingly shifted the debt on their books to the financial marketplace. This allowed them to minimize the constraints posed by Basel capital standards, and made them more willing to increase their exposure to low-income households.

The worlds of high and low finance had never been so closely interconnected. For its part, the Fed increasingly boasted about its role in promoting, in Greenspan's words, "financial education [as] a process that should begin at an early age and last throughout life." He insisted that the increasing technological capacities of financial markets for "collecting and assimilating the data necessary to evaluate risk" ensured that "where once marginal applicants would simply have been denied credit, lenders are now able to quite efficiently judge the risk posed by individual applicants and price that risk appropriately."[24] But the promise of a mass public of informed, financially literate borrowers was already belied by how common manipulation by mortgage brokers had become, and by the readiness of the largest and most prestigious banks to securitize the debts thereby created. Securitization techniques as they had evolved over the previous decades produced tremendous pressure on, or temptation for, brokers to pursue ever more aggressive sales strategies, while the Fed joined Fannie and Freddie and the large US banks in taking all this mainstream.

It also went mainstream internationally, as foreign investors piled into mortgage-backed securities. While Middle Eastern and developing Asian states (especially China) increased their holdings of US Treasury bonds by 23 percent between 2003 and 2007 (accounting for all of the $771 billion growth in US Treasuries in those years, as purchases by US investors fell), these same states increased their purchase of Fannie and Freddie (GSE) mortgage-backed securities by no less than 231 percent to $656 billion). And while private European banks (who followed American financial institutions in expanding into off-balance-sheet SIVs) increased the holdings of these GSE securities from less than $200 billion in 2003 to over $300 billion by 2007, they also followed US investors in greatly increasing their purchases of private US mortgage-backed securities (from $100 billion in 2003 to almost $500 billion in 2007) thereby contributing to the explosive growth in these even riskier assets – from $100 billion in 2003 to almost $500 billion in 2007 (see 12.1).

Figure 12.1: Change in US Securities Holdings 2003–2007 ($ billion)

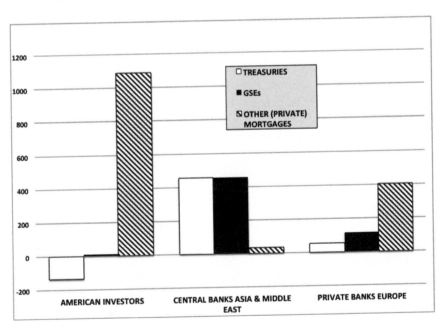

Source: This table is derived from Table 1 of Ben S. Bernanke, Carol Bertaut, Laurie Pounder DeMarco, and Steven Kamin, "International Capital Flows and the Returns to Safe Assets in the United States, 2003–2007," Board of Governors of the Federal Reserve System, International Finance Discussion Papers, Number 1014, February 2011.

The extent of the interpenetration of US and foreign financial markets was especially marked in the years leading up to the 2007 financial crisis. The infusion of foreign credit not only fueled US consumption, but also removed the constraints that a growing trade deficit would otherwise have entailed for the US economy. This did not mean that the US was merely living off its borrowings; alongside a total financial inflow of $8.3 billion from 2000 to 2006, there was an outflow of $4.4 trillion, which was indicative of the extent to which US capital had remained not only the largest source of foreign direct investment, but also "a net provider of knowledge, liquidity and insurance" to the rest of the world.[25] Yet, as foreign financial markets became intertwined with US financial markets, so did they become subject to their smoldering contradictions. European banks in particular were drawn even more heavily into the US commercial paper and inter-bank markets, and this was not discouraged by the European Central Bank, in part because it helped to lower the euro's exchange rate relative to the dollar. Since the integration of global finance meant that the stability of US financial markets now also depended on the solvency of Europe's banks, the Fed had little option as soon as the crisis hit but to supply those banks with dollars directly.

"The Worst Financial Crisis in Global History"

By 2006, the US economy had experienced three years of over 3 percent growth in real terms, with exports rising by over 8 percent, unemployment falling from 6 to 4.6 percent, and capacity-utilization returning to its long-term norm of just over 80 percent. Real non-residential investment grew by 6 percent in 2004 and 2005, and and further increased by almost 8 percent in 2006; this increase occurred even as American MNCs also quickened the pace of their investments abroad. Annual productivity growth had continued to increase right through the first six years of the new millennium: its 2.8 percent average rate of growth matched US levels during the postwar "golden age." Corporate profits were at a peak and corporate balance sheets were exceptionally strong.[26] As had happened in earlier periods of techno-logical breakthrough, the late 1990s saw very large over-investments in the computer and telecommunications sectors; although the 2001 recession was largely the result of this, it turned out to be relatively mild. Residential investment boomed and consumption continued to grow as people tapped into the inflated value of their homes via secondary mortgages.

Since non-residential investment, on the other hand, fell by over 10 percent in 2001 after the bursting of the dot.com bubble, and did not show much sign of life until well into 2003, this was sometimes taken, along with rising US trade deficits, as evidence of an unresolved crisis of overaccumula-tion going back to the 1970s.[27] But there was in fact a strong resumption of investment by 2004, accompanied by rising profits and productivity that more than matched their peaks in the 1990s. The increasingly integrated manufacturing networks of American MNCs on a global scale certainly accelerated the shift in US employment from manufacturing into consumer and business services, but this reflected the strengthening rather than weakening of American capital, while the continued inflow of foreign capital to the US, in spite of the trade deficits, also confirmed the strength of the dollar. The American crisis that started in 2007 was not caused by either domestic industrial "overaccumulation" or international trade and capital "imbalances," but rather by the volatility of capitalist finance. It was triggered in the seemingly mundane sector of mortgage credit, where finance mediated working-class access to housing, and then quickly spread into the more rarefied world of interbank lending and corporate commercial paper markets. It was because US finance had become so integral to the functioning of twenty-first century global capitalism that the ultimate impact of this crisis throughout the international economy was so profound.

As the Fed began to raise interest rates in mid 2004 (to over 5 percent by mid 2006), partly in an effort to gradually deflate the housing bubble, it faced what Greenspan called a "conundrum."[28] Housing prices peaked in 2005, accompanied by a dramatic rise in the number of mortgage defaults; yet since foreign capital was attracted all the more by the higher interest rates, there was no drying up of mortgage credit, and house-building starts only peaked at the beginning of 2006. But the end was nigh: between the last quarter of 2005 and mid 2007, residential investment fell by 22 percent, along with a sharp reduction in the number of subprime borrowers. As the rise in the default rate of non-prime borrowers started to exceed projections, the issuance of asset-backed securities slumped by almost 30 percent. Securitization everywhere quickly lost a lot of its luster, as banks ended up holding assets that they were unable to value, and rating agencies now fueled the problem by downgrading the risky securities they had previously treated as virtually equivalent to US Treasury bonds. It was now clear that once a debt had been sold on, sliced up, and mixed with a variety of other debts, there was little hope of establishing in any meaningful way the value of the resulting asset. Paul O'Neill later graphically captured the predicament facing investors: "If you had ten bottles of water and one bottle had poison in it, and you didn't know which one, you probably wouldn't drink any one."[29]

By March 2007 the newly appointed chairman of the Federal Reserve, Ben Bernanke, warned that Fannie and Freddie could be a source of "systemic risk."[30] Meanwhile, New Century Financial went bust. As late as July 2007, Tim Geithner at the New York Federal Reserve and Hank Paulson at the Treasury were still playing their appointed role of trying to calm markets with reassuring speeches about the housing slump being "at or near bottom," and financial markets outside the US being "now deeper and more liquid than they used to be."[31] But by this time an unraveling of financial positions and credit chains was already producing a liquidity crunch in the US commercial paper and money markets that had become so pivotal in global finance. It was the difficulty of raising funds on these markets that forced France's largest bank, BNS Paribas, on August 9, 2007, to suspend payments due on three of its investment funds. By September Northern Rock, the UK's fifth-largest lender, had gone to the Bank of England for emergency support, leading to a classic bank run. Within days the UK government had guaranteed Northern Rock's deposits, and the Bank of England announced that it would provide loans to keep the bank going and extend the same support to other banks.

Although President Bush declared in a major speech on the crisis at the end of August that "the government has got a role to play—but it's limited," the Treasury had by the beginning of that month already switched to full crisis-management mode, with Paulson "in hourly contact with the Fed, other officials in the administration, finance ministries and regulators overseas and people on Wall Street."[32] Meanwhile, the Fed was in contact with the European Central Bank, the Bank of Japan, and the Bank of England about the role they would all play as lenders of last resort. Bernanke, drawing on his academic work at Princeton University in the 1980s on how the Great Depression could have been prevented, had warned Paulson that massive US government loans to banks might be necessary, and Paulson had agreed. "I knew he was right theoretically," he said. "But I also had, and we both did, some hope that, with all the liquidity out there from investors, that after a certain decline that we would reach a bottom."[33] Yet what the crisis of 2007–08 proved was that without the state the private market has no secure bottom.

The really crucial point of contagion was the short-term wholesale lending market between large international financial institutions. This interbank market had become increasingly central to the operation of the global payments system, and with seven out of every ten transactions taking place in US dollars, it was the most important focus of the Fed's monetary policy; a select few Wall Street banks, operating as "market makers," were especially central in reallocating the liquidity provided by the Fed.[34] Since the benchmark for the trading of wholesale funds was the London Interbank Offer Rate (LIBOR)—effectively the internationally "traded version" of the Fed's interest rate—the increasing spread between the Federal funds rate and LIBOR (as banks feared that their loans to other banks might not be repaid) represented a near-freezing of the payment networks between the world's largest financial institutions, and endangered the capacity of the Federal Reserve to manage the global financial system. As a result, the Fed acted quickly to ensure that banks all over the world had access to an adequate amount of dollar holdings to meet their obligations. By mid August, lining up at the New York Fed's discount window for hundreds of millions were not only US banks such as J. P. Morgan Chase, Bank of America, and Wachovia, but also Germany's Commerzbank, and even the Bank of China Ltd.[35]

For all the talk over the previous decade about the need for financial transparency, these loans were concealed for fear that they would further undermine market confidence and stir up domestic populist resentments (they would only be revealed by a court order in April 2011, almost four years later). To get around this political problem, the Fed established new swap lines of credit to funnel dollars to foreign central banks so they could allocate dollars directly to their banks.[36] Unlike earlier swap arrangements between central banks, set up to compensate for balance-of-payments deficits, these arrangements were explicitly aimed at providing international liquidity, with the additional effect of getting foreign central banks to act as conduits for the application of the Fed's looser monetary policy to their own domestic economies. The US Federal Reserve was indeed acting as the world central bank in the context of the crisis, trying to ensure thereby that interbank rates would decrease and normal mechanisms for access to dollar funding would be restored.

For its part, the US Treasury organized, first, a consortium of international banks and investment funds, and then an overlapping consortium that included mortgage companies and financial securitizers, to take concrete measures to calm the markets. As they had done a decade earlier during the Long Term Capital Management (LTCM) crisis, Treasury officials convened the CEOs of the nation's ten largest commercial banks in September 2007, with the goal of determining whether there were "market-based solutions that could help reduce the possibility of a disorderly solution in the marketplace."[37] Sovereign wealth funds of other countries were also encouraged to invest directly in Wall Street banks to beef up their capital. Both the Treasury and Federal Reserve staff also continued to work through the President's Working Group on Financial Markets (established after the stock market crash of 1987) to coordinate their firefighting activities with the Securities Exchange Commission and the Commodity Futures Trading Commission.[38]

At the beginning of 2008 insurers of US municipal bonds were in deep trouble, and stock markets in Asia and Europe were shaken at the prospect of a serious American recession.[39] The Fed made a large emergency cut in interest rates, and soon followed this by supplying other central banks with even more dollars.[40] By March, just as the Treasury was about to issue a "Blueprint for a Modernized Financial Regulatory Structure" designed to enhance the Fed's regulatory authority over the whole financial system, two Bear Stearns hedge funds went bust. The Fed directed, oversaw, and guaranteed to the tune of $30 billion, J. P. Morgan's takeover of Bear Stearns, which was so highly leveraged that it was borrowing as much as $70 billion in overnight markets. (Ironically, Bear Stearns was the lone major investment bank which had refused to cooperate with the Fed-engineered bailout of Long Term Capital Management a decade before.) The Fed placed examiners inside each of Wall Street's investment banks (thereby compensating for the SEC's failure to do so). And the Fed dramatically expanded the programs through which it provided liquidity to banks, including taking mortgage-backed securities onto its own books.[41] By taking responsibility for illiquid securities that otherwise could not be sold, or even find a value, the Fed was thereby acting not only as lender of last resort but also as "market maker of last resort."[42] Indeed, what was being recognized in all this was that the key monetary policy instrument during the Greenspan era—the lowering of the federal funds rate—would not have much leverage in a situation where the interbank market had become almost fully paralyzed. Increasingly, the Trading Desk at the New York Fed now effectively functioned as a "lender of only resort."[43]

But while all this state intervention resembled similar activism that had succeeded relatively well in containing crises in the past, it could not prevent this crisis from assuming still greater proportions. In early September 2008, after a summer of considerable turbulence, uncertainty and anxious anticipation, during which major investors began selling their holdings of GSE securities and seeking refuge in Treasury bonds, the American government took direct control of Fannie Mae and Freddie Mac. Given the importance of these two giant GSEs, not only for households' spending power but also for interbank rates and foreign economic relations, the top priority was to preserve their operations and prevent any market rumors of default.[44] The GSE takeover prevented a full-scale meltdown, and had the crucial effect of converting their debt into Treasury debt, but it added little additional liquidity in the markets for mortgage-backed securities, and could not prevent the demise of two major investment banks. One catastrophe was averted when, through the Treasury's orchestration, Merrill Lynch was sold to the Bank of America (which would itself receive $45 billion in federal aid in the coming months). But another catastrophe—at Lehman Brothers, whose banking business had begun with commodities-trading and brokerage operations in the 1850s—was not.[45]

When Geithner once again convened Wall Street CEOs, now in the depths of the greatest crisis they had ever seen, and urged them to arrange a private-sector bailout of Lehman, their fear of ending up with each other's bad debts ruled out the kind of collective action they had agreed to a decade earlier with LTCM.[46] As Lehman went bankrupt, and investors immediately questioned both the government's commitment and organizational capacity to support the private institutional pillars of the financial system, Fed Chairman Bernanke came to the conclusion that twelve of the thirteen most important institutions in the United States "were at risk of failure within a period of a week or two."[47] What had to be faced most immediately was the imminent collapse of AIG, the world's largest insurance company, which had provided so much credit-default-swap protection for the investment banks.[48]

The Federal Reserve had already gone well beyond the normal boundaries of its regulatory remit by extending help to investment banks, but it now ventured into even newer territory as it took responsibility for the survival of an insurance company whose commitments constituted a key pillar of the markets for securitized products and complex derivatives. By virtue of this bailout of AIG, which involved paying 100 percent of face value to AIG's credit default swap counterparties, Goldman Sachs notoriously received almost $20 billion; but upwards of two-thirds of the payments to AIG counterparties actually went to foreign financial institutions, including some $17 billion to Société Générale, $15 billion to Deutsche Bank, $8.5 billion to Barclay's, and $5.5 billion to UBS.[49] The Fed now fast-tracked applications by both Goldman Sachs and Morgan Stanley to be regulated as bank holding companies, thereby giving them permanent access to the Fed's discount window. The importance of this only became clear when, almost three years later, the Fed released documents that showed that, in the days before this access was secured, Morgan Stanley drew $48.4 billion from the Primary Dealer's Credit Facility, while Goldman Sachs drew $12 billion; the PDCF had not been set up to sustain drawings on this scale.[50] The Fed also extended a lifeline to the huge Reserve Primary money market fund (which had been forced to write off $785 million of commercial paper following Lehman's bankruptcy). And this was soon followed by the Treasury's blanket guarantee on the $3.4 trillion in mutual fund deposits, a ban on short-selling of financial stocks, and the seizure and fire-sale of Washington Mutual to prevent the largest bank failure in US history.

At the same time, the New York branches of foreign banks were given greater access than ever to the Fed's discount window; indeed, as the crisis reached its peak they were the biggest borrowers there, "accounting for at least 70 per cent of the $110.7 billion borrowed during the week in October 2008 when use of the program surged to a record."[51] The integration of global financial markets was now such that the Belgian bank Dexia, which guaranteed bonds such as those issued by the Texas State Veterans Land Board and the Los Angeles Transportation Authority, received $37 billion from the Fed in the eighteen months after Lehman's collapse. Had this not been forthcoming, it would have led to "a catastrophe for municipal finance and money funds" in the US itself.[52] The further expansion of the Fed's swap lines to other central banks provided foreign banks with more than $560 billion by the end of 2008. The justification later offered for the Fed's acting as the world's central bank was that "foreign banks support the trade of other countries with the United States, facilitate international purchases of US financial assets and foreign direct investment in the country, and deepen global financial markets for dollar assets."[53]

With the end to the crisis still nowhere in sight, the Fed and the Treasury now faced the prospect of becoming involved in an endless series of interventions that would have entangled them in patchworks of ad hoc financial arrangements. In this situation, the government proposed a sweeping plan to try to flush sufficient toxic debt out of the system to restore its liquidity. In early October 2008, after weeks of resistance, a reluctant Congress was finally induced to pass the Economic Stabilization Act, which included a $700 billion Troubled Assets Relief Program (TARP). A particularly memorable example of US elites accommodating to—and at the same time overcoming—a populist political culture was the way Henry Paulson, who as head of Goldman Sachs had but recently been Wall Street's highest-paid CEO, structured his testimony before the House Financial Services Committee as he tried to get his TARP plan through Congress. Paulson acknowledged that Wall Street's exorbitant compensation schemes were "a serious problem," going so far as to declare that "the American people are angry about executive compensation and rightfully so." But he immediately added: "We must find a way to address this in legislation *without undermining the effectiveness of the program*."[54] What was clearly implicit in this statement was that the cooperation from bankers, which was the sine qua non for the program to work, would not be forthcoming if they were asked to bear what they considered to be too heavy a financial burden.

The Treasury was given full discretion over the allocation of the TARP funds—and it soon exploited this latitude, when Paulson announced that most of the funds would be used to purchase equity stakes in financial institutions. In buying bank shares, they were following the lead of the UK's Labour government, whose prime minister, Gordon Brown, was widely credited with having saved the financial system by initiating the provision of massive public capital to the banks in the fall of 2008; but it was quickly also made clear that the nationalized banks would still "operate on a commercial basis at arm's length" from any government direction or control.[55] With the US taking the same route, so that the federal government soon owned a third of Citigroup's shares, both the US and the UK were effectively socializing the losses of the private banks.[56] But socializing their losses did not entail socializing control. The fact that the Treasury did not ask for much in return for covering the bank's losses threw into sharp relief the accumulating political contradictions that came with this crisis. With one firm after another apparently buckling under the weight of their bad investments, the socialization of the banks' losses was increasingly seen to be both ineffective and unfair—a factor that had already played its part in the outcome of the November 2008 presidential election.

The TARP's emphasis on the recapitalization of American banks helped to reduce the spread between the rates at which the state was lending to the banks and what banks charged borrowers, but the trickle-down effects were limited because lending institutions, still unsure how to evaluate financial risk, tightened the terms on all major types of loans. This reluctance to lend was related to the fact that when a housing bubble bursts it affects not just the financial system, but the whole economic system, in a way stock market meltdowns do not. Since for most people the value of the family home accounts for most of their wealth by far, any significant decline in that value can undermine consumer confidence, with effects that go well beyond the most immediate impact on the construction industry and the purchase of furniture, appliances, and even cars.[57] In contrast with the recession of 2001, a slowdown in consumption preceded the beginning of the recession in late 2007, and turned into a massive collapse in the second half of 2008. Although non-residential investment did not immediately match the fall in residential investment, its growth had begun tailing off as soon as the financial crisis hit in mid 2007 and had turned down by the time the financial conflagration reached its climax in the fall of 2008, after which it fell dramatically (see Figure 12.2).

Figure 12.2: Real GDP, Consumption, and Investment, 2004(1)=100

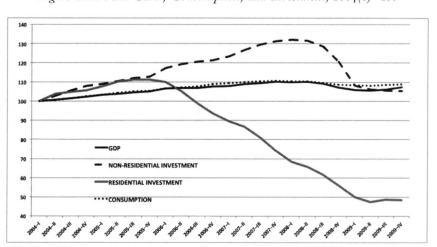

Source: US Bureau Of Economic Analysis, NIPA Table 1.1.3.

The depth of the crisis was directly related to home mortgages having become such a central component of financial markets. The rapid effect of the collapse in the mortgage market on the whole economy was seen between mid 2007 and the end of 2008, as 3.3 million jobs disappeared (over 1 million in manufacturing), as the S&P index fell by 40 percent, and as—with the market value of their homes and retirement assets rapidly declining—households lost $14 trillion (22 percent) of their net worth. From the third quarter of 2008 through the third quarter of 2009 the absolute fall in both annual US retail sales (8 percent) and capital investment (17 percent) was unprecedented since World War II.[58] Before the year was out, General Motors—the iconic American corporation of the twentieth century, which in 2000 had been ranked by Fortune as the largest corporation in the world—had lost over $30 billion, and was petitioning the Bush administration for an equivalent amount in order to stave off bankruptcy.

The Empire's Not So New Clothes

A great many commentators since the summer of 2007 had predicted widespread "delinking" from the US-centered global order. European media and policymakers in particular had expressed considerable *schadenfreude* at the damage that "Anglo-American capitalism" had inflicted on itself through its lack of responsibility and prudence, all the while proclaiming "Euroland" as the new standard for civilized capitalism.[59] In the event, the satirical newspaper *The Onion* contributed more insight: "Bush Proud US Economic Woes Can Still Depress World Markets."[60] It was not only British banks, with their long tradition of a wide variety of transatlantic linkages, which quickly succumbed to the US subprime crunch in 2007; so did German regional banks (often still seen as epitomizing the virtues of coordinated capitalism and bank-based financial systems) that had invested heavily in American mortgage-backed securities. Initial expectations that the Asian countries would be able to decouple themselves from the US amid the crisis also proved illusory. The impact of the crisis varied across regions, and the countries within them, depending on the specifics of their housing market, their degree of global integration through trade and finance, their fiscal positions, and the responses of their states. What they all had in common, however, was that they could not avoid being affected by the crisis; and, as they were forced to react to it, they inevitably looked to the US for leadership.

Most remarkably, the crisis actually had the effect of strengthening the global role of the dollar. As many investors found that their attempts to extricate themselves from unfavorable positions required dollar-denominated transactions, the vortex-like capacity of American financial markets to draw in foreign funds was once again confirmed. But it was the special value and liquidity of US Treasury bonds for both governments and private investors that was the main factor driving the international flight to the dollar. By early 2009, the market for US Treasury debt was virtually the only financial sector marked by vigorous growth and trading.[61] Investment firms that had spent most of the past decade playing the markets for corporate stock and asset-backed securities now shifted their attention and resources to government bond trading, in large part to exploit some of the bountiful opportunities offered by the mammoth expansion of Treasury debt sales (this was also a hedge against the very real threat of deflation).[62]

It was not only financial linkages that were at work here. US consumption had accounted for over a third of the growth in global consumption between 2000 and 2007.[63] Through 2007, global exports increased at more or less the same rate as in the period since 1994 (an average of 7.4 percent per year); then, in 2008, global export growth slowed to 3.4 percent; and in 2009 global exports decreased by an unprecedented 11.3 percent (the last decrease was in 1975, when, amid the twinned economic and energy crises, global exports fell by 2.9 percent). Given that world GDP growth, which had run at 3 percent annually from 2000 to 2007, also decreased in 2009 for the first time since World War II, a slowdown in trade was hardly surprising. But global trade (exports plus imports) that year in fact fell much more than GDP itself, largely reflecting the drying up of trade credit. What this fall notably did not reflect, in spite of the scale of the global crisis, was any rise in protectionism.

This was not left to chance. The leaders of the G20—of which little had been heard after the dust from the 1997–98 financial crisis had settled—were suddenly summoned to Washington in November 2008. At one of the preparatory meetings of finance ministry deputies held in São Paolo a week before, a senior US Treasury official averred that "a big proportion of what's happened has been due to some of the challenges we've had in the United States. We recognize our responsibility to take leadership."[64] The consensus that was reached on a process for adopting new global banking regulations was significant, but the real work would be done by the representatives of the advanced capitalist states on the BIS's Basel Committee, supplemented by an expanded Financial Stability Forum.[65] What was really important about the first G20 leaders' summit—at a time when the financial conflagration was triggering a deep economic collapse—was what it did to avoid a descent into protectionism, which would obviously have had even worse consequences than in the 1930s, given current global networks of integrated production. In this respect, the "Commitment to an Open Global Economy" in the final communiqué was most significant: "We underscore the critical importance of rejecting protectionism and not turning inward . . . we will refrain from raising new barriers to investment or to trade in goods and services, imposing new export restrictions, or implementing World Trade Organization inconsistent measures to stimulate exports."[66]

Meanwhile, a "Global Plan for Recovery"—jointly advanced by the UK and US in the face of more economically orthodox opposition from Germany and France[67]—was agreed at the second G20 Summit in London in April 2009. It attempted on an even grander scale the kind of coordinated G7 stimulus that the Carter administration had proposed towards the end of the 1970s, and that had been accomplished more successfully by the Clinton administration in late 1998. The much-trumpeted $5 trillion collective global stimulus pledged was not nearly as important as the guarantee given for collective action, without which there was the danger that stimulus by any one state would simply lead to more increased imports and balance-of-payments problems, as well as larger government deficits and accusations of fiscal laxity. The actual stimulus undertaken varied from country to country: in China, massive loans by state banks and even larger investments in infrastructure; in Germany, subsidized reductions in work-time; in the UK and Brazil (despite both being governed by labor parties) the stimulus was overwhelmingly through tax cuts. [68]

In the US, Obama's election had already paved the way for the American Recovery and Reinvestment Act passed in February 2009. Of the $530 billion stimulus at the federal level ($250 billion more was set aside for the states), over half came as tax cuts, compared to less than a quarter as direct public expenditures (the remainder took the form of transfer payments). The *Wall Street Journal* decried this as "one of the largest single stimulus packages in history"—and indeed it constituted 39 percent of the total global fiscal stimulus in 2009, dwarfing the 13 percent contributed to the global stimulus by China.[69] But any expectations that radical Keynesian economists would now be running the Treasury proved otherworldly. Paulson's conversations with Obama before the 2008 election, at the height of the financial crisis, had convinced him that Obama "genuinely seemed to want to do the right thing. He wanted to avoid doing anything publicly— or privately—that would damage our efforts to stabilize the markets and the economy."[70] Obama's appointment of Geithner as his secretary of the Treasury was in fact predicated on this; as head of the New York Federal Reserve Bank, Geithner was particularly seen as "onside" with Wall Street.

Ironically it was Paul Volcker, despite his central role in overcoming Keynesian-era inflation three decades earlier, who was now seen as Obama's most economically progressive advisor. Geithner's "Financial Stability Plan," introduced in March 2009, followed what had gone before. The Treasury would purchase more bank stock, while emphasizing that the long-term objective was to keep the banks in private hands. The new asset-management funds the Treasury would set up to unblock financial markets (along the lines of the Resolution Trust Corporation during the Savings and Loan crisis) were accurately described by the *Financial Times*'s Martin Wolf: "Under the scheme, the government provides virtually all the finance and bears almost all the risk, but it uses the private sector to price the assets. In return, private investors obtain rewards—perhaps generous rewards—based on their performance via equity participation, alongside the Treasury. I think of this as the 'vulture fund relief scheme.'"[71]

Amid public outrage over the millions the banks were still paying to the executives who had created the mess, President Obama justified his Treasury secretary's plan with words very similar to Paulson's six months earlier: "You've got a pretty egregious situation here that people are understandably upset about . . . So let's see if there are ways of doing this . . . that are constitutional, that uphold our basic principles of fairness, *but don't hamper us from getting the banking system back on track.*"[72] Obama's "but" spoke volumes, since it showed that the incentives that capitalists insisted on as necessary to save the economy trumped basic principles of justice. Paying bankers so astronomically much more than workers could, in the context of the crisis, hardly be justified in terms of their contribution to market efficiency. It could only be explained in terms of "failure-containment." This was also clearly seen in the role the Fed and Treasury played in preventing the "pay czar," whom Obama appointed to oversee executive salaries in the businesses that the US government now formally owned, from drastically cutting the salaries of Chrysler and General Motors managers, even though the conditions imposed under the March 2009 bailout legislation required massive concessions on wages, pensions, and working conditions from the rest of the workforce—explicitly taking non-unionized Japanese auto plants as the model.[73] All this in fact meant that the system of class power and inequality that had generated the crisis was being reproduced.

Just as unemployment was well on its way to reaching over 10 percent (from under 6 percent as late as mid 2008), the "stress tests" the Fed conducted on the nineteen largest US bank holding companies in May 2009 showed that nine of them already had adequate capital.[74] And in June 2009 the White House, declaring that financial regulatory reform would be a top priority alongside healthcare reform, released *A New Foundation: Rebuilding Financial Supervision and Regulation.* Alongside its promise of greater oversight and increased transparency in financial markets, as well as a new consumer protection agency, what was most remarkable was how little it aimed to disrupt the regulatory status quo. There was no move to place absolute limits on the size of bank holding companies or to change the nature of the private rating system, let alone to reinstate Glass-Steagall. With Goldman Sachs's net income surging to a record $13.4 billion for the year, while unemployment remained stuck at 10 percent, Obama's frustration at the political costs of this—which were hardly mitigated by Goldman's promise to reduce its annual bonus pool from $22 billion to $16 billion, and to donate $500 million to charities—led the president to propose two new measures in January 2010. One was a "Financial Crisis Responsibility Fee"

to be paid by the largest banks; the other was to prohibit "proprietary trading" by deposit-taking banks (i.e. using their own capital to speculate as
well as operate their own hedge funds)—a reform prominently associated
with Volcker.[75]

Expressing his irritation over "the activities of lobbyists on behalf of those
institutions" against such measures, Obama proclaimed that he "did not run
for office to be helping out a bunch of fat cat bankers"; and he warned them
that now the banks were "back on their feet we expect an extraordinary
commitment from them to help rebuild our economy."[76] This served to
present the minor reforms he was advancing in a way that led to misleading
headlines such as "Obama Declares War on Wall Street" and "Banks Face
Revolutionary Reform." It also obscured the fact that the Fed and the
Treasury shared a distinct lack of enthusiasm for even such modest proposals
because of what they saw as their problematic implications for a highly integrated financial system: the responsibility fee could further limit lending by
banks and complicate the conduct of monetary policy. And they recognized
that isolating banks' own proprietary trading would be very difficult, since
this practice was so closely related to the trades in stocks, bonds, and derivatives they carried out for their clients. Indeed, the integration of commercial
and investment banking on a global scale now made any return to the New
Deal type of regulation virtually impossible. Even Volcker spoke not in
terms of reviving Glass-Steagall but only of returning to its "spirit."[77]

In fact, the new regulations introduced under the Obama administration
conformed to the regulatory regime that had facilitated the immense growth
of US and global financial markets since the 1970s: "failure-containment,"
more than "failure-prevention," was still the operative doctrine, with the
goal being less to save any given financial institution than to limit the
systemic financial risk that might be caused by its insolvency, and to take
macro and micro prudential measures that would limit the scope of bank
failure and make containment possible. The Fed and Treasury's response in
the wake of the crisis was not so much to alter the direction of financial
regulation as to close off some of the more glaring loopholes and remove
some of the deficiencies of the existing system. The Wall Street Reform and
Consumer Protection Act, passed into law in July 2010, was largely based on
drafts by Federal Reserve and Treasury staff, although its proposals were
given a tremendous political fillip by the way Senators Chris Dodd and
Barney Frank arranged a merger between Senate and House versions of the
legislation.[78] Dodd-Frank (as the Act came to be known) established a new
Financial Stability Oversight Council (composed of various regulatory
agencies, including the Fed and chaired and advised by the Treasury), which
limited the Fed's ability to lend directly to financial firms in trouble by
preventing it from extending credit other than through programs with
"broad-based eligibility."[79]

While the Act narrowed the Fed's emergency lending powers that had drawn so much popular ire, the practical impact of the legislation was to give the Fed the central role in the supervision and regulation of "systemically important financial institutions" (SIFIs), including big hedge funds and insurance companies.[80] All those with assets exceeding $50 billion would be subjected to greater scrutiny by the Fed. Since the Oversight Council could also place other financial firms under the Fed's authority, its potential regulatory and firefighting range was considerably expanded. The higher capital adequacy requirements were carefully constructed so as not to undercut the competitive advantages enjoyed by large financial firms. The hype about Dodd-Frank's prohibition of proprietary trading ("the Volcker rule") was largely negated by the numerous exceptions it specified, and in effect left it to the Fed to impose greater capital requirements and some broadly defined limits on these activities. Dodd-Frank allowed the Federal Reserve to preserve its key interventionist tools, as well as the room to develop new ones. Broadening the Fed's regulatory remit over the financial system was, as we have seen, precisely the direction in which the American state had been heading for more than two decades.

Potentially more important in setting a new direction was the regulation of derivative transactions. Although towards the end of the Clinton administration the Treasury and Fed had combined to prevent this, the Obama administration made it a key aspect of its legislative agenda. By May 2009 it had set out a plan to require standardized derivatives to be centrally cleared along the lines of the Chicago Mercantile Exchange, with financial safeguards and comprehensive oversight. The leading derivative dealers, despite having resisted such a move for two decades, were now prepared to support this for reasons that were "not entirely defensive," since it was "in the long-term material interest of the derivatives industry given the economic costs experienced during the crisis"; their main concern was for "a form of regulation that was flexible and which delegated the details and implementation to the private sector."[81] Nor did the plan upset the largest Wall Street banks such as Goldman Sachs, J. P. Morgan Chase, or Morgan Stanley, which were confident that they could dominate the clearing-houses.[82]

In the event, Dodd-Frank's provisions on derivatives regulation largely left it to the regulators to work out the details. It was not long before the Treasury announced that the most commonly used derivatives, foreign-exchange swaps and "forwards"—"a vital tool of business" used to hedge against fluctuations in currency values—would be exempt from the rules because an "additional process" of regulation "could have serious negative economic consequences" on global trade and capital flows.[83] This was similar to what happened when the ratings agencies responded to Dodd-Frank's provisions by refusing to allow their evaluations of these securities to be publicly disclosed. Since this negated the government's goal of re-establishing a private mortgage market, the SEC immediately issued a "no action letter" indicating that it would not enforce this provision.[84]

It cannot, however, be said that the state was literally "captured," in the sense of being told what to do by the Wall Street banks, let alone by other derivatives dealers or the ratings agencies. In fact, the Treasury and Fed were genuinely concerned with strengthening their own capacities to manage the effects of systemic financial volatility, and to establish new measures to increase these dominant market actors' own capacities to stabilize large diversified financial firms. Offering a remarkably clear example of the relative autonomy of the state, Geithner addressed the issue head-on at a meeting of bankers from twenty-seven countries organized by the American Bankers Association in Atlanta in June 2011: "The success of the Dodd–Frank Act will depend on a sustained effort to improve the level of expertise in the regulators charged with oversight and to ensure there are enough 'cops on the street.'" He insisted that those in the US financial community who were "looking for leverage over the rules still being written" by supporting Congressional efforts to block resources and appointments would only "create the conditions again for a situation in which the weak and poorly managed risk bringing down the financial system." In making the case for "tougher rules to limit risk and leverage in individual institutions" as well as "shock absorbers that are critical to limiting catastrophic risk in modern financial systems," Geithner articulated the state's central challenge in making financial markets flourish in the wake of the crisis:

> This is a complicated endeavor. It requires judgments about the costs and benefits of too much or too little capital and the tradeoffs between innovation and stability. It requires employing the power of disclosure and market discipline to reinforce the constraints and incentives we establish through regulation. It requires better supervision, because no system of rules can anticipate all sources of risk. And it requires better ways of managing the inevitable failures that will happen in competitive markets, by adapting bankruptcy type processes to handle the unique difficulties in unwinding large, leveraged financial institutions. And because of technology and the much tighter integration of national financial systems, the challenge of reducing the risk of contagion from a financial crisis requires much more global coordination internationally than has ever been the case.[85]

The continued attention the Fed attached to monitoring Wall Street firms was seen when the Fed institutionalized the Comprehensive Capital Analysis and Review, which required the thirty-five biggest banks to prepare and submit annual plans "to ensure that institutions have robust, forward-looking capital planning processes that account for their unique risks and that permit continued operations during times of economic and financial stress."[86] Also significant was the New York Fed's new Financial Institutions Supervisory Group, in which some 150 of its staff (projected to increase to 300, and supported by many hundreds of others working inside the Fed) were directly placed inside big Wall Street firms to participate in crafting as well as monitoring their internal risk strategies. This was apart from the broader group of Fed field examiners, which climbed to 1,948 by 2011 (up 40 percent from 2006), and the 500 staff from the Treasury's comptroller of the currency, who also worked on location in big banks.[87] This meant that Fed officials would virtually become integrated with the management structure of these firms, including their boards of directors. The further development of state capacity that all this entailed was designed to address "too big to fail" in a way that strengthened large diversified financial institutions, and thereby reinforced the central role they played in integrated financial markets.

But as the Fed went through yet another phase of what it saw as "institutional learning," perhaps the most important innovations occurred in the conduct of monetary policy. In the first stages of the crisis, the Fed had sterilized the money chain—it did not increase the money supply, but rather exchanged the bad credit banks were holding (such as securitized mortgages) with good credit (particularly Treasuries); this was intended to stabilize the banks rather than stimulate the economy. But in the aftermath of the collapse of Lehman and the ensuing panic in financial markets, the Fed turned to increasing the overall liquidity in the system to levels never seen before. But as it did so, the Fed's ability to influence short-term interest rates and bank activity was severely eroded. It was in this context that the Fed moved to a very different system of monetary policy management—one based for the first time on paying interest on the reserves that banks held at the Fed. By manipulating the spread between its "interest on reserves" (IOR) rate in relation to market rates, the Fed now had greater capacity to influence the aggregate quantity of reserves, and to direct liquidity to specific sections of the banking system, with the goal in particular of reducing systemic risk in the interbank market.

The centerpiece of this new system was what came to be known as the practice of "quantitative easing."[88] At a time when interest rates were already near zero, this essentially involved flooding the financial markets with so many dollars as to prevent what economists called a "liquidity trap." The US had not objected when this had been undertaken by Japan at the beginning of the decade, and this was no doubt a factor in ensuring it did not produce a run on the yen; its application in the US was seriously explored as a matter of Treasury policy as early as 2005.[89] Previously, anyone suggesting such direct and massive pump-priming would have been judged economically illiterate. A sell-off of Treasuries by other purchasers would have been predicted, amid a massive run on the dollar. That nothing like this occurred, and that the Treasury's endorsement of quantitative easing initially elicited little critical comment, was a strong measure of the recognition on the part of global capital—and of the other capitalist states—of the central role of the American state in keeping the system going. The ultimate aim of quantitative easing was to try to get the banks to lend so as to stimulate the economy at a time when, despite continued high unemployment, the balance of Congressional forces was shifting against any further fiscal stimulus.

Quantitative easing essentially involved an audacious printing of US dollars, and thus relied on the willingness of foreign investors and central banks to continue to hold dollars; it served as the strongest reminder to date of the special ongoing attractiveness of the dollar. Although the loose monetary policy lowered the price of the American dollar, it did not undermine its status, or role, as the global currency. Other states faced a Hobson's choice. A lower dollar devalued their holdings of US assets, undermined the relative competitiveness of their economies, and—as excess dollars found their way abroad—aggravated inflationary pressures. But given these states' structural positions within global capitalism, and their economic ambitions, they saw no option but to continue to hold and even increase their dollar holdings. Although there was no little handwringing at home and abroad about the potentially inflationary effects of quantitative easing, inflation was not a problem in the US, especially given the continuing weakness of American labor, and this was reinforced by high unemployment. As for Europe, although quantitative easing did provide additional liquidity for European banks, inflation was also not a serious problem there. This was because European governments had already been forced to move so far in the direction of austerity by the toll financial markets had exacted on the bond sales that many of them needed to cover fiscal deficits following the bailouts of their banks and decline in tax revenue. It was capitalism's emerging market states that experienced significant inflation (ranging from 15 to 30 per cent in Brazil, Russia, India, and China in 2010–11); this was spurred by higher growth rates, and monetary policies that could not stray far from the objective of keeping currencies aligned with the dollar.

Indeed, whatever grumblings were evinced, and whatever fantasies of an alternative reserve currency were concocted, the US monetary policy turn did not result in a substantive challenge to the role of the dollar and the centrality of the Federal Reserve as the world's global banker.[90] As an advisor to the People's Bank of China put it: "It's ironic isn't it? The US is the epicentre of the global financial crisis, but the US dollar is the monetary safe haven."[91] Moreover, as he pointed out, the Chinese leadership's ambition eventually to establish the renminbi as an international currency involved accepting the leadership of the US in the international monetary sphere.

Even amid tensions with emerging market states over US quantitative easing, a remarkably quick consensus was reached on continuing with the same operating principles and the same regime of international regulatory coordination as before the crisis. This is precisely what the US Treasury insisted was now required more than ever for the recovery of global finance.

As we have seen, after the 1974 Herstaat crisis it had taken some fifteen years for the central bankers who made up the BIS Basel Committee on Banking Standards to come up with the so-called Basel I accord on capital adequacy.[92] As for Basel II, which was initiated soon after the US move, in the mid 1990s, to allow capital adequacy self-regulation based on the large banks' "risk models," this had only been agreed in 2004, and was still not fully implemented when the crisis began in 2007. By contrast, in September 2009, less than a year after the 2008 G20 meeting in Washington, the BIS Committee arrived at a framework for Basel III, and this was endorsed by the G20 the following year at its November 2010 meeting in Seoul. Indeed, the fact that Dodd-Frank largely left the specifics of new capital-adequacy requirements to be worked out by the Basel Committee already reflected Washington's confidence that an international consensus would quickly be reached which, like Dodd-Frank itself, would not disturb the basic pillars of the existing regulatory system. Despite the fact that more emerging market states, including China, were now involved, the Basel III framework did not depart from the basic principles of Basel I and II. The negotiations took off from rules already being developed, not only in the US but also in Germany and the United Kingdom, that were designed to tighten and improve the bank's methods of measuring risk, and increase the amount of top-quality capital that banks would eventually be required to set aside.[93]

The overall result was that, with the G20's blessing, "the dominant outcome of the crisis has been, and is likely to continue to be, a strengthening of the international standards regime and reduction in variation across jurisdictions," as Tony Porter has put it. "Alternatives such as bank taxes, breaking up banks seen as too big to fail, or the separation of deposit taking and investment banking activities, have not made it onto the agenda."[94] Basel III was deliberately constructed to produce a greater symmetry between national and international regulations than in the past, but the accord still left room for further contention and compromise as to the form in which these would actually be applied by individual states, and the schedule for full implementation was stretched out over nine years. This was much longer than the US Treasury and Fed would have preferred and, especially in light of the fact that the largest US banks had already more than reached the capital-adequacy levels specified in Basel III, it did not take long before they were exerting pressure on other states to speed up implementation along US lines.

It was notable in this respect that not only had Japan proved compliant again, but so had the Chinese leadership. Ever since the Asian Crisis, China had followed Korea, Indonesia, and Thailand in looking above all "towards US rules and practices," having concluded that "there was only one game in town as regards financial regulation."[95] This was due less to international pressure than to the fact that "key actors in China's domestic political economy continue to see advantages in continuing to import financial regulatory and managerial 'technology' from the advanced countries." They were reluctant to discredit BIS financial standards, since these provided "a powerful weapon which Chinese reformers, as elsewhere in Asia, used to sideline opponents of reform." Although the Basel Committee faced some muted criticism from Chinese officials in the wake of the crisis, it remained "the only game in town for Beijing and its membership of this body reduces the likelihood of rival standards emerging."

Indeed, the US Treasury was more anxious about Europe's implementation of Basel III (as well as the specifics of their derivatives regulation). The US concern to quickly create a level trans-Atlantic playing field was partly related to reassuring the large US banks that meeting the capital-adequacy requirements ahead of schedule (as they had done) would not leave them in an uncompetitive position.[96] But it also reflected the Treasury's own concern that insolvencies of European counterparties in the international interbank market might immediately trigger another systemic crisis on Wall Street and in global finance. For all the critical comments by politicians about lax American regulation, not only were the actual measures adopted by most European governments laxer than those in the US, but financial capital strutted its traditional orthodoxies more boldly on the European political stage than it was able to do in the US.[97] As the idea that the euro could be an alternative to the dollar as a reserve currency was exposed as an illusion, so was the myth of Europe's allegedly more progressive "variety of capitalism." The European Commission and the European Central Bank were fully in tune with the demands of Deutsche Bank (as well as French and British banks) over the application of "rescue packages" to Greece, Ireland, and Portugal, with conditionalities of austerity and privatization that were just as draconian as those that had been attached to IMF structural-adjustment programs for developing countries in the 1980s.[98]

The tensions between the US and Europe over relatively slight differences in the application of new banking and derivatives regulations amounted to very little in 2010, compared with the neoliberal solidarity all the advanced capitalist states showed in embracing fiscal austerity as the primary means of coping with the so-called "exit costs" of the crisis. The barrier to further quantitative easing and stimulus in the US did not come from the international sphere, but rather from renewed populist fixations about "big government" that were generated as much by the *Wall Street Journal* as by the Tea Party, while a capitalist crisis of historic proportions was still playing itself out in high unemployment and a stagnating economy. In spite of the widespread anger at the role of Wall Street in causing the crisis, US finance emerged not only more concentrated, but also still encompassing the general interest of capital amid a broader neoliberal consolidation of class power.

But while the bailouts and stimulus to stave off a complete collapse had done their work, they prompted no sustained upturn. As the crisis that was initially triggered in mid 2007 entered its fifth year in the summer of 2011, the level of GDP in the US stood where it had been at the end of 2007, which showed how shallow was the recovery after the deep fall in GDP in 2008–09. When the final numbers on the cost of containing the financial conflagration itself came in—the $1.2 trillion lent by the Fed (with almost half of its top borrowers being European firms) was equivalent to more than the total earnings of all US banks in the decade up to 2010—so did the news that the major restructuring in US finance had led to an 11 percent drop in the sector's workforce.[99] The loss of these jobs—no less real than the loss of those in the manufacturing sector—also needed to be counted in the doubling of US unemployment from 7 million in 2006 to 14 million by 2009, a level that remained largely unchanged two years later.

Nevertheless, the stagnant growth and employment were not due to falling profits—corporate profits had quickly recovered after the 2009 downturn, and by mid 2011 were not only 23 percent above the mid 2007 level but even 16 percent above their record peak in mid 2006. The persistence of stagnation and high unemployment was due to three other factors: the lack of investment (as firms were hoarding their profits in liquid assets); the reluctance of the banks to lend (despite the liquidity with which the state had provided them); and declining consumption (most consumers were no longer able to leverage rising house prices into credit, while a great many others had to "deleverage" in order to pay off debt).[100] With the cooperation of unions in strategies to make workers bear the brunt of private-sector restructuring, most successfully in auto, and the US labor movement in general being too weak to prevent the new assault on public-sector workers and services at the state level, this further undermined a revival of consumer demand and offset the overall effect of federal stimulus.[101]

In the context of the fiscal deficits generated by the earlier tax cuts and the impact of the crisis, state revenues fell to their lowest level, relative to GDP, in six decades. Demands for even lower taxes rather than social expenditures, highlighted in the revolt by the populist Tea Party against the Obama administration, were supported by the very bankers just saved by state intervention. Even as deflation loomed, they repeated their traditional ideological orthodoxies regarding fiscal deficits leading to inflation, while the wealthy generally refused to contemplate giving up any part of the enormous tax benefits they had previously been given. The pressures for austerity this created left the Treasury and Fed unsteadily walking a tight-rope between the need for further stimulus and the promise to cut the deficit. This came to a head with the political saga that concentrated the world's attention on Washington, DC in the summer of 2011 over the Treasury's need to secure Congressional approval (required since 1917, and secured seventy-two times since 1962) for increasing the "debt ceiling"—i.e. the total sale of Treasury bonds that investors in the US as well as the rest of the world were so eager to buy.

This confrontation between the Treasury and Congress starkly revealed the tensions the American state experienced between the governance of its own social formation and its imperial responsibilities for the reproduction of global capitalism. Although this tension was much amplified during what in fact had emerged as the first global crisis of the twenty-first century, the deal that was finally struck to raise the debt ceiling was reminiscent of the problem the Treasury had confronted during the Mexican financial crisis in early 1995 when Rubin, it will be recalled, accurately described Congress's behavior as "meant to oppose us without actually stopping us."

The continuing centrality of the American state in the global economy was in fact reinforced as the crisis unfolded, with virtually no trace of such inter-imperial conflict that a century earlier had given rise to world war. This is not to say that the problems of crisis-management became any less acute, as was especially evident in the crisis of the euro. By refashioning for themselves a system of fixed exchange rates thirty years after the American state had abandoned them for the dollar, while simultaneously advancing the policies of free trade and neoliberal finance, the European states had reproduced the disjuncture between democracy and capitalism that appeared so starkly when they attempted to resurrect the automatic discipline of the gold standard in the interwar period.

It is notable that, the conflicts that have emerged today in the wake of the greatest capitalist crisis since the 1930s are taking shape, not only in Europe but much more generally, less as conflicts *between* capitalist states and their ruling classes than as conflicts *within* capitalist states. It is to the political signifi-cance of the fault-lines of global capitalism running within states rather between states, and the implications of this for the American empire's capac-ity to sustain global capitalism, that we now turn in conclusion.

Conclusion

Although Marx discerned in the middle of the nineteenth century that a new class of capitalists was creating "a world after its own image," it actually took until the beginning of the twenty-first century before "a constantly expanding market" could be said to have fully spread capitalist social relations "over the entire surface of the globe." Moreover, it was not a generic "bourgeoisie" driven by competition to "nestle everywhere, settle everywhere, establish connections everywhere" that alone made global capitalism after its own image. It took an empire of a new kind, founded on US capitalism's great economic strength and centered on the capacities of the American state, to make global capitalism a reality. Yet no sooner did the task look to be more or less complete when the fourth great crisis of global capitalism (after those of the 1870s, the 1930s, and the 1970s) spread rapidly across the world. Marx's observation 150 years earlier that the making of capitalism on a global scale was "paving the way for more extensive and more destructive crises" while at the same time "diminishing the means whereby crises are prevented," seemed all too fully confirmed. And it was now the American empire that seemed to resemble "the sorcerer who is no longer able to control the powers of the nether world whom he has called up by his spells."[1]

Given the severity and duration of the latest crisis in a global capitalist economy that the American state had been so central to constructing, it was hardly surprising to see a resurgence of pronouncements that US hegemony was coming to an end. As pundits of every persuasion once again blur the lines between a capitalist crisis and the decline of the US empire, it is especially important to recognize the central role which the American state continues to play in reproducing global capitalism. The current crisis has amply demonstrated the many challenges and contradictions it faces in doing this; but it has also demonstrated that, while the American empire is certainly not always able to control the spirits it has called up from the deep, it nevertheless remains critical to the system's survival.

The new crisis has confirmed more generally the continuing significance of states in global capitalism. Although the institutions of the European

Union have more constitutional authority than other international organizations, their inability to intervene so as to resolve the debt crisis of their smaller member-states is largely due to the internal political dynamics within *other* member-states, above all Germany. The eurozone crisis also confirms a basic fact about the nature of both globalization and informal empire: state sovereignty is not effaced within it. This can be seen in the difficulties the American state has continually had to confront in getting the German state—from the time of the Herstaat banking crisis in the 1970s to the Mexican crisis in the 1990s to the crisis of the euro today—to overcome its obsession with inflation and "moral hazard," and to take its share of responsibility for containing crises. Yet this cannot be understood in terms of states, least of all Germany, retreating from free trade and free capital flows in favor of economic nationalism. After decades of economic integration, there are no national bourgeoisies like those that supported the fascist turn in Germany or Italy in the interwar period.

When the term "empire" was openly embraced to characterize the American state at the time of the Bush administration's response to 9/11 (including by some of its advisors), the stress was placed, in Niall Ferguson's words, on the "potential advantages of a self-conscious American imperialism" as against "the grave perils of being an 'empire in denial.'" The anxieties of a Kansas farmer that "we are trying to run the world too much . . . like the Romans used to" were taken as exemplifying not just the difficulties of mediating the American state's international and domestic roles, but the loss of imperial vigor and discipline—the main measure of which, allegedly, was that the bill for Social Security in the US was larger than the bill for national security. Notably, it was not a new world of rival imperial states that occupied the minds of such analysts of US empire. The resentments over the disloyalty of Germany and France at the time of the invasion of Iraq quickly dissolved once these states introduced the motion at the UN to have it endorse the occupation a year later; while the US integration with China was such that Ferguson himself dubbed it "Chimerica." With the typical hyperbole that was so common in the years after 9/11, he rather claimed it was now only "non-state actors" like criminal organizations and terrorist cells "who truly wield global power."[2]

The real problems of the US empire today appear in a very different light. As the global economic crisis triggered by the American financial crisis of 2007–08 persists, these problems have more to do with the difficulties of implementing adequate measures for "failure-containment," let alone "failure-prevention." Yet, unlike in the 1930s, this has not been due to a breakdown of cooperation among capitalist states. As the G20 Toronto Summit communiqué of June 2010 proclaimed: "While the global economic crisis led to the sharpest decline of trade in more than seventy years, G20 countries chose to keep markets open to the opportunities that trade and investment offer. It was the right choice." The leaders renewed their "commitment to refrain from raising barriers or imposing new barriers to investment or trade in goods and services [and] minimize any negative impact on trade and investment of our domestic policy actions, including fiscal policy and action to support the financial sector."³

But capitalist state solidarity itself could not resolve the crisis of a finance-led global economy, where the orthodoxy of insisting on austerity—both to ensure that states pay their bond-holders and to maintain vigilance against inflation—reinforces the stagnationist tendencies of underconsumption that come with the diminished consumer credit available to sustain effective demand. The liberalization and expansion of finance, as this book has shown, was essential to the making of global capitalism, yet it came with a degree of volatility that threatened economic stability. Reviving capitalist health today requires strengthening the confidence of bankers that their activities will be appreciated and their assets protected. The unresolved dilemma for all capitalist states today is how to both stimulate the economy and regulate financial markets so as to limit increasingly dangerous volatility without undermining the ability of finance to play its essential role in global capitalism.

For most states, any attempt at fiscal stimulus aggravates the fears of bond-holders that they won't be repaid, and the increased rate of interest on the bonds necessary to fund fiscal and trade deficits requires the restructuring of state expenditure to prioritize interest payments over social expenditures, infrastructure development, and public employment—thereby negating the very attempt at stimulus. This is less true for the US itself due to the "safe haven" that Treasury bonds represent, the appreciation of which is inseparable from the role of the American state as the ultimate guarantor of global capitalist interests. But the US faces its own policy dilemmas in relation to economic stimulus. The one immediate measure the US administration could take on its own to quickly revive effective demand—instructing the US housing agencies it directly controls to write off mortgage debt above the current value of existing homes—has been ruled out because it would reduce the banks' mandated capital adequacy just as they are being required to raise it, and lower their revenues as home-owners made smaller monthly payments. This once again reveals the structural relationship between Wall Street and Washington: what makes such a move so unlikely is not the state of play in Congress, but rather that it would threaten the solvency of some of the very large banks who are more than ever "too big to fail"—because their failure would trigger the failures of other financial institutions, not only in the US but around the world.⁴

To be sure, the conflict between Congress and the administration, reflecting the internal contradiction which the American state faces in acting as both the state of the United States and the "indispensable" state of global capitalism, has certainly worried leading capitalists and officials. The CEO of Caterpillar, the world's largest manufacturer of construction and mining equipment, called Washington's debt-ceiling saga in the summer of 2011 not only "ugly" but also "a red herring," which got in the way of Congress's ratification of outstanding free-trade agreements, as well as much-needed domestic infrastructure programs.[5] The Fed's Ben Bernanke, noting that Congress had "disrupted financial markets," warned that "similar events in the future could, over time, seriously jeopardize the willingness of investors around the world to hold US financial assets or to make direct investments in job-creating US businesses."[6] Yet, although it was precisely on these grounds that the credit-rating agency Standard & Poor's downgraded US Treasury bonds, what was especially remarkable was that the appetite for these bonds, even at record-low interest rates, far from abating, increased.[7] Ruminations about an alternative reserve currency went nowhere—especially as the smoldering crisis in Europe's interbank markets burst into flames, sending the widespread earlier expectations that the euro would challenge the dollar up in smoke.

Much like Germany in the crisis of the 1970s, even China today explicitly speaks in terms of the US's unique responsibilities for "the world's economic soundness," given its status as "the world's largest economy and the issuer of the dominant international reserve currency." American political leaders were reminded that "political brinkmanship in Washington is dangerously irresponsible . . . It risks, among other consequences, strangling the still fragile economic recovery of not only the United States but also the world as a whole."[8] Similarly, the concerns of many capitalists in developing states were that the US might now abandon them. The extent to which they continued to look to the American state to help them restructure their own states was seen when Obama visited India in November 2010, accompanied by the largest-ever entourage of US businessmen on such a trip, and told an assembly of Mumbai capitalists: "We don't simply welcome your rise, we ardently support it. We want to invest in it."[9] The importance of this to Indian capitalists was made very clear by the co-founder of India's National Association of Software and Service Companies, who recalled that the US "was the one who said to us . . . 'Go for free trade and open markets.'" This was crucial to his industry's success in "pushing our government to open our markets for American imports, 100 percent foreign ownership of companies and tough copyright laws when it wasn't fashionable." Stressing the continuing importance of the US in overcoming "the socialist/protectionists among India's bureaucrats," he emphasized: "We don't want America to lose self-confidence . . . there is nobody else to take that leadership. Do we want China as the world's moral leader? No. We desperately want America to succeed."[10]

There were deep structural factors at work here, reflecting the extensive networks that link the world's capitalists not only to US MNCs, but to US financial, legal, and business services more generally. The enormous demand for US Treasury bonds showed the extent to which the world remained on the dollar standard and the American state continued to be regarded as the main underwriter of value. Also confirmed was the US Treasury and Fed's central role in global crisis-management—from currency swaps to provide other states with much needed dollars, to overseeing policy cooperation among the G20 as well as G7 central banks and finance ministries. It was the formerly highly touted supranational system of European governance— exposed in the crisis for its lack of central authority over taxation, bond issuance, and budget approval—which now appeared most dysfunctional for the management of global capitalism.

The eurozone crisis was not something that cheered the American state. The Fed's provision of liquidity to US financial institutions was undertaken with one eye to their passing that liquidity to Europe through the interbank market. The Treasury was intimately involved in policy discussions, directly as well as through the IMF, with Geithner discretely "pressing Europe to take more decisive action" at the regular conference calls of the G7 finance ministers now taking place almost weekly. It was a sign of "the growing concern in Washington at Europe's handling of its debt crisis" by the fall of 2011 that Geithner flew over to attend meetings of European finance ministers.[11] Particularly frustrating was the limited extent to which the European Central Bank was prepared to act as lender of last resort. But behind this lay a frustration with the European states themselves. At a meeting in Washington an ECB official was greeted by his American host, who "brandished the Articles of Confederation, the 1781 precursor to the United States Constitution, to use as an example of why stronger unions become necessary."[12]

It was clear by this time that all the heady talk between Russia, China and other emerging market states about using "SDRs" (the IMF's "special drawing rights"), let alone the euro, to displace the dollar as the international reserve currency had amounted to little more than rhetoric. Rumors that the Middle East's oil-exporting states would abandon the dollar vanished with the 2011 "Arab Spring," just as May '68 put a stop to expectations that France might lead a return to the gold standard. The dollar's continuing central global role certainly produced problems for rapidly growing emerging market economies, which experienced high capital inflows and currency appreciation as a result of the Fed's low interest rates and quantitative easing policies. This stoked real-estate and stock-market bubbles in these countries, and threatened to undermine their competitiveness and bring back hyperinflation. But criticisms such as those repeatedly heard in 2011 from Brazil—that US policy might lead to "currency wars"— amounted to nothing like a challenge to US hegemony.

The notion that the G20 would effectively become the linchpin of crisis-management and policy-coordination appeared mere window dressing by the time of the Cannes summit in the fall of 2011, with the BRIC countries left to insist that whatever financial contributions they might make to the European bailout would be channeled through an IMF still dominated by the G7, and especially the US Treasury. The most significant change from the pattern of crisis-management in the 1980s and 1990s was that, whereas it had earlier been the developing states that were required to practice austerity, the prescription of a capitalist cure for this structural crisis was reversed: the G7 states now committed themselves to austerity, while encouraging the emerging market states to stimulate their economies. This reflected the fact that the major developing states were now much more an integral part of global capitalism, so the priority was no longer just to restructure them to facilitate free trade but also to make them more responsible for sustaining global demand. Yet the rising purchasing power of the developing countries could hardly make up for stagnation in the developed ones (US consumption expenditure alone in 2010 was still over three times that of China and India combined).[13]

The real issue was less about changing consumption patterns than whether any other state would be capable of playing the crucial role in the reproduction of global capitalism played by the American state. Claims that this would be a European supra-state now looked threadbare indeed. And amid all the talk about the impending dominance of China, the crucial question rarely posed was whether the Chinese state had the capacity to take on extensive responsibilities for managing global capitalism. No one seriously imagines Russia, even with its admission to the WTO, could readily develop such capacity; but even China is manifestly still a very long way from being able to do so. To this point, far from displacing the American empire, China rather seems to be duplicating Japan's supplemental role of providing the steady inflow of funds needed to sustain the US's primary place in global capitalism.[14]

Were this to change, it would require deeper and much more liberalized financial markets within China, which would entail dismantling the capital controls that are key pillars of Communist Party rule—at a time, moreover, when its own banking system is under severe stress. Furthermore, a major reorientation of Chinese patterns of investment and production away from exports towards domestic consumption would have incalculable implications for the social relations that have sustained China's rapid growth and global integration. It would involve a restructuring of the country's coastal industries, which would come up against powerful vested interests among Chinese capitalists and regional officials. And getting households to spend their savings on current consumption would also require the development of a welfare state, as well as ongoing increases in wages. Given the redistribution of income that this would entail, which could only happen through a substantial shift of power to the working class, all of this—while certainly possible in the long run—would meet resistance that would go well beyond just those firms involved in exporting low-wage goods.

The current conflicts in which Chinese workers are engaged—as seen in strike waves that have yielded some large wage increases but no clear organizational transformation in Chinese trade unionism—pose increasingly sharp choices for the whole of Chinese society.[15] It cannot be known in advance whether working-class struggles in China will lead to the emulation of the West's individualized consumerism, or whether they will lead to new collectivist claims. What is clear is that the outcome cannot but impinge on, and possibly even be affected by, the direction working classes elsewhere take out of the current crisis.

While the first global capitalist crisis of the twenty-first century was rooted in the volatility of finance, not in a crisis of production, an important factor in generating the conditions that led to it was what had happened with the world's working classes since the crisis of the 1970s. The massive growth of the global proletariat that has been the sine qua non of capitalist globalization produces tendencies towards a narrowing of the differences in wages and conditions between developed and developing countries, and the continuing travail of trade unionism in the developed capitalist countries has partly been a reflection of this. The very financialization through which global capitalism was realized was also the means through which workers were disciplined; and the political and organizational defeats they had suffered since the 1980s were closely linked to the recovery of corporate profitability—albeit a recovery characterized by new vulnerabilities, above all that so much consumption was dependent on credit.

The severity and extent of the current crisis has once again exposed how far the world's states are enveloped in capitalism's irrationalities. Even when states committed in 2009 to stimulate their economies, they felt impelled at the same time to lay off public-sector workers or cut back their pay, and to demand that bailed-out companies do the same. And while blaming the volatile derivatives market for causing the crisis, states promoted derivatives trading in carbon credits in the hope that green capitalism would provide a two-for-one remedy for the global climate and economic crises. In the context of such readily visible irrationalities, a strong case can be made that, if jobs and the communities that depend on them are to be saved in a way that will convert production and distribution to conform with ecologically sustainable priorities, there must be a break with the logic of capitalist markets rather than the use of state institutions to reinforce them.

When in 1942 "An American Proposal" envisaged the replacement of "a dead or dying imperialism" with an American empire of a new kind, in order to establish "universal free trade" by reorganizing "the economic resources of the world so as to make possible a return to the system of free enterprise in every country," it acknowledged that the primary barrier to this was the "uprising of the international proletariat" that had occurred over the previous twenty years.[16] Despite all the subsequent Cold War rhetoric, it was not the threat of external Soviet military expansion but the new political and economic strength of working classes in so many societies, including within the advanced capitalist countries, which was the real barrier. It was only overcome, as we have seen, once the postwar contradictions of strong working classes coexisting with increasingly strong capitalist classes had led to the crisis of the 1970s, and then to the defeats suffered by the working classes in its wake. To the extent that, in the course of the postwar years, the working classes increasingly lost interest in the idea of socialism, this had much to do with the belief that the Bretton Woods agreement and Keynesian economics would usher in a crisis-free, socially just "mixed economy." Yet not only the crisis of the 1970s, but also the economic instability and growing inequality of the neoliberal decades that followed, proved this to be an illusion.

Equally illusory is the belief that there is a way back to a supposed postwar "real economy" from the finance-led capitalism which greased the wheels of globalization. Capitalist finance is in truth no less real than capitalist production—and not just because of the way it affects the rest of the economy during both boom and bust, but because it is integral to capitalist production and accumulation as well as to the extension and deepening of global capitalism.[17] There is in fact no possibility of going back to the largely mythical "mixed economy" the New Deal and Keynesian welfare state are imagined to have represented. In the US itself, as the last chapter showed, just as democracy appeared to trump race with the election of a black president, so did he reinforce once in office, even through his timid reforms, the neoliberal system of class power and inequality. We have seen Southern and Eastern Europeans being sharply rebuked for even having aspirations to catch up with what Northern Europeans can still claim from their reduced welfare states after the neoliberal reforms of recent decades. An already marked democratic deficit in Europe was further expanded, as the crisis in Greece and Italy ushered in "national unity" governments headed by central bank technocrats, whose mettle was supposed to be tested by whether they could calm German anxieties about "moral hazard"—which would itself largely depend on whether they could "get tough enough with the unions."[18]

The real danger the eurozone crisis poses to global capitalism is that states that had sworn off capital controls forever may be forced by domestic class struggles into adopting them, not least as a way of coping with electoral outcomes that effectively narrow the democratic deficit while expanding economic contradictions. Against this, similar external pressures to those that led most developing states to abjure capital controls for pragmatic rather than ideological reasons in the wake of the Asian crisis (see Chapter 11) are being felt by states in Europe today. Whether changes in the balance of class forces as well as other pragmatic considerations—not only the concern with their own legitimacy, but the accumulating irrationalities of an orthodoxy that demands austerity without much prospect of growth through exports—will instead lead these states to opt for capital controls will be a key sign of whether the American empire is indeed unable to control the spirits it has called up by its spells.

Yet to break with the politics of austerity by defaulting on public debt and adopting capital controls is daunting for any state. This is not only due to the strength of external and internal capitalist forces that are opposed to it. It is also because the costs for most of its citizens would in fact be severe. The popular sacrifices required would be reduced in any given country were there also to be a shift in the balance of class forces in other countries that would lay the grounds for measures of international solidarity with, rather than retribution against, any state that set out to break with the logic of capitalist financial markets by introducing capital controls. This brings us back to one of the central dilemmas of the revolutionary politics earlier associated with the "uprising of the international proletariat," that is, the very uneven political landscape in the nation-states within which that uprising was politically located (as the very different trajectories of Russia and Germany after World War I made all too clear).

That said, the widespread conviction that global socialism, whether gradually achieved or otherwise, would effectively constitute the alternative to global capitalism remained one of the greatest strengths of the world's proletariat in the middle of the last century. As it turned out, the working-class political institutions that fostered the socialist idea in the twentieth century proved unsuitable for realizing it. Even so, it was only through a long and contradictory path that individualized consumerism rather than collective services and a democratized state and economy became the main legacy of working-class struggles in the twentieth century. Yet capitalism's capacity to sustain this is now in severe doubt, especially when it is put in the context of the ecological limits to capitalist growth. Whether there can be a radical redefinition of socialist politics in the context of new working-class struggles, both in the North and the South, is now on the agenda as never before.

The enormous inequalities as well as insecurities that the state's promotion of capitalist markets engenders within each country, and the protests and even revolts that this provokes, provide fertile ground for replanting the idea of an alternative to global capitalism. For well over a decade before the onset of the current crisis, there were many signs of the exhaustion of popular faith in capitalist markets, and a growing impatience with the political institutions that fostered their globalization. The lesson the World Bank claimed states needed to draw from the 1994 Mexican crisis was that neoliberal reform was "a continuing process which never stops . . . The global economy is a bit like *Alice, Through the Looking Glass*: it takes all the running you can do to keep in the same place."[19] It was as an indignant response—initially inspired by the uprising in Chiapas—to such an all-encompassing competitive capitalist logic, that the anti-globalization movement took root in the late 1990s.

A revival of progressive economic nationalism in most developing states today is ruled out by the absence of anything like a national bourgeoisie for popular classes to ally with. This is an old story within the advanced capitalist countries, which increasingly determines just how limited is the room for progressive reform within them. It is thus hardly surprising that the relentless drive to reduce living standards amid this crisis has triggered not only riots but also searches for new forms of collective action and social organization. "They call it the American Dream," read one handmade sign at Occupy Wall Street in October 2011, "because you have to be asleep to believe in it. Wake up!"

Yet the gap that exists between the stubborn realities of capitalism and the revolutionary spirit so manifest in public squares around the world which inspired the occupations in the US itself teaches a sobering lesson. It is not in fact possible to change the world without taking power.[20] It is precisely because the aspiration for a world beyond capitalism is once again so broadly extant today that it is especially useful to recall "one of the basic axioms of historical materialism: that secular struggle between classes is ultimately resolved at the *political*—not at the economic or cultural—level of society."[21] Whether called socialism or not, today's revived demands for social justice and genuine democracy could only be realized through such a fundamental shift of political power, entailing fundamental changes in state as well as class structures. This would need to begin with turning the financial institutions that are the life-blood of global capitalism into public utilities that would facilitate, within each state, the democratization of the decisions that govern investment and employment. But very different movements and parties from those that carried the socialist impulse in the previous century would be necessary to see this through.[22]

Advancing such a radical politics requires a sober perspective on what currently exists, and how we got here, so as to understand more clearly the nature and scale of the task involved in getting somewhere better. This has been our goal in writing this account of the making of global capitalism. Its unmaking will only be possible if the states that have made it are themselves transformed—and that applies, above all, to the American state.

Notes

Introduction

1 See David Held's early definition of "globalization" as a distinctively new "international order involving the emergence of a global economic system which stretches beyond the control of a single state (even of dominant states)," in his "Democracy: From City-States to a Cosmopolitan Order?" *Political Studies*, XL, Special Issue (1992), pp. 32–4; and the critique of this in Leo Panitch, "Globalization and the State," *Socialist Register 1994*, London: Merlin, 1994. Although Held would later come to speak in terms of the "transformation" of states by globalization, the substance of the argument did not really change. In this type of discourse, usually the very things that were taken as the measures of globalization—the free flow of capital, the intensification of world-wide competition, the revolution in communications technology—were simultaneously offered as the explanations of it. See Justin Rosenberg, *The Follies of Globalization Theory*, London: Verso, 2000. See also Saskia Sassen, *Losing Control? Sovereignty in a Age of Globalization*, New York: Columbia University Press, 1996.

2 The quote is from Eric Hobsbawm, *Age of Extremes*, London: Michael Joseph, 1996, p. 281. For an outstanding overview of the literature on states and globalization, as well as an analysis in good part complementary to our own of the extent to which changes in state structures, including their modes of regulation, were constitutive of globalization, see Saskia Sassen, *Territory, Authority, Rights: From Medieval to Global Assemblages*, Princeton: Princeton University Press, 2006.

3 "For globalization to work, America can't be afraid to act like the almighty superpower that it is" were the words emblazoned on the cover of the *New York Times Magazine* to feature Thomas Friedman's "Manifesto for a Fast World" in its March 28, 1999 issue (similar treatment was accorded to "The American Empire—Get Used to It," by Michael Ignatieff, on January 6, 2003, in the run-up to the invasion of Iraq). On the other hand, Hardt and Negri's best-selling book *Empire* argued that the term should be applied to the process of globalization itself—a process that ensured that the "United States does not, and indeed no nation state can today, form the centre of an imperialist project." Michael Hardt and Antonio Negri, *Empire*, Cambridge, MA: Harvard University Press, 2000. For a broader review of the use of the term "empire" as applied to the US at this time, see Niall Ferguson, *Colossus: The Rise and Fall of American Empire*, New York: Penguin, 2005, esp. pp. 3–7.

4 For our earlier work on this, see "The New Imperial State," *New Left Review* II/2 (March–April 2000); "Global Capitalism and American Empire," *Socialist Register 2004*, London: Merlin, 2003; "Finance and American Empire," *Socialist Register 2005*, London: Merlin, 2005; and "Superintending Global Capital," *New Left Review* II/35 (September–October 2005).

5 See *The Communist Manifesto*, London: Merlin, 1998, p. 4; and *Grundrisse: Foundation of the Critique of Political Economy*, Harmondsworth: Penguin, 1973, p. 410.

6 *The Great Transformation*, Boston: Beacon, 1957, p. 18.

7 Philip McMichael, "Revisiting the Question of the Transnational State: A Comment on William Robinson's 'Social theory and Globalization,'" *Theory and Society* 30 (2001), p. 202.

8 As in much of social science, there is an unfortunate tendency within Marxism to write theory in the present tense. We are sympathetic to E. P. Thompson's famous lament that Marx himself became for a period "caught into the trap" baited by classical political economy's search for "fixed and eternal laws independent of historical specificity." *The Poverty of Theory and Other Essays*, London: Merlin, 1978, esp. pp. 251–3.

9 In light of widespread misguided assumptions—and often misrepresentations—of what is entailed in such a theory, it is important to stress that we are not proceeding from an ideal-typical notion of what capitalism requires, and then asserting in a functionalist manner that states must meet such requirements. Nor do we see the relationship between policymaking and capital accumulation as a matter of capitalists telling state actors what to do. For excellent discussions of the extent to which Miliband, Poulantzas, and others who have sought to develop a theory of the capitalist state successfully avoided such problems, see especially Stanley Aronowitz and Peter Bratsis, eds., *Paradigm Lost: State Theory Reconsidered*, Minneapolis: University of Minnesota Press, 2002; Paul Wetherly, Clyde W. Barrow, and Peter Burnham, *Class Power and the State in Capitalist Society*, London: Palgrave Macmillan, 2008; and Alexander Gallas, Lars Bretthauer, John Kannankulam, and Ingo Stützle, eds., *Reading Poulantzas*, London, Merlin Press, 2011.

10 See Hannes Lacher, *Beyond Globalization: Capitalism, Territoriality and the International Relations of Modernity*, London: Routledge, 2006; as well as Perry Anderson's earlier classic, *Lineages of the Absolutist State*, London: New Left Books, 1974.

11 See Panitch, "Globalization and the State," pp. 69–71; as well as Robert Cox, *Production, Power and World Order*, New York: Columbia University Press, 1987, esp. pp. 132–3; and Nicos Poulantzas, *Classes in Contemporary Capitalism*, London: New Left Books, 1974, esp. p. 73.

12 Among the pre-capitalist absolutist states that founded Europe's mercantile empires, by the eighteenth century only England had developed a "conception of empire rooted in capitalist principles in pursuit of profit derived not simply from exchange but from the creation of value in competitive production." Ellen Meiksins Wood, *Empire of Capital*, London: Verso, 2003, p. 100. And just as a highly active British state was involved in developing the differentiation between the economic and political that went by the name of "laissez faire," so did its practice of the "imperialism of free

trade" in the nineteenth century, especially in Latin America, establish the prototype of an "informal empire." The conventional notion that free trade and imperialism did not mix was a misconception carried into the twentieth century by thinkers as diverse as Lenin and Schumpeter, but it was in fact rooted in the views of the free-trade liberals themselves. It was belied by the innumerable occupations and annexations, the addition of new colonies, and especially by the importance of India to the empire, during the heyday of free trade between the 1840s and the 1870s. John Gallagher and Ronald Robinson originally explained what this meant for the nature of British imperialism: "The type of political line between the expanding economy and its formal and informal dependencies . . . tended to vary with the economic value of the territory, the strength of its political structure, the readiness of its rulers to collaborate with British commercial and strategic purposes, the ability of the native society to undergo economic change without external control, the extent to which domestic and foreign political situations permitted British intervention, and, finally, how far European rivals allowed British policy a free hand." "The Imperialism of Free Trade," *Economic History Review* VI: 1 (1953), pp. 6–7.

13 Colin Leys, "Conflict and Convergence in Development Theory," in W. J. Mommsen and J. Osterhammel, eds., *Imperialism and After*, London: Allen & Unwin, 1986, p. 322. See also Norman Etherington, *Theories of Imperialism: War, Conquest and Capital*, London: Croom Helm, 1984. The failure to make this distinction ensured that the words that opened Kautsky's infamous essay in 1914—the one that so attracted Lenin's ire—increasingly rang true: "First of all, we need to be clear what we understand from the term imperialism. This word is used in every which way, but the more we discuss and speak about it the more communication and understanding becomes weakened." "Der Imperialismus," *Die Neue Ziet*, Year 32, XXXII/2 (September 11, 1914), p. 908.

14 The increasingly severe analytic problems with Hobson's as well as the Marxist theories of imperialism gave rise by the 1970s to complaints that their association of imperialism with "an undifferentiated global product of a certain stage of capitalism" reflected their lack of "any serious historical or sociological dimensions." Gareth Stedman Jones, "The Specificity of US Imperialism," *New Left Review* I/60 (March–April 1970), p. 60 n. 1. Giovanni Arrighi went so far as to say that "by the end of the 60s, what had once been the *pride* of Marxism—the theory of imperialism—had become a tower of Babel, in which not even Marxists knew any longer how to find their way." Giovanni Arrighi, *The Geometry of Imperialism*, London: NLB, 1978, p. 17.

15 Our argument in this respect is thus quite different from that of Niall Ferguson, who at various points adopts something close to a historical-materialist definition of the US as a *liberal empire*—"one that not only underwrites the free international exchange of commodities, labor and capital but also creates and upholds the conditions without which markets cannot function"—but insists, despite much of the evidence in his own book, that in practice the US "has been a surprisingly inept empire builder." *Colossus*, p. 2.

16 The classic study in this vein is William Appleman Williams, *The Contours of American History*, Chicago: Quadrangle, 1966. Andrew J. Bacevich embraced this interpretation

in his *American Empire: The Realities and Consequences of US Diplomacy*, Cambridge, MA: Harvard University Press, 2002, even though it fails to register the small contribution that exports made to capital accumulation relative to the domestic economy at the time, and gives vastly disproportionate weight to the significance of US capitalist expansion in Central America at a time when California was barely yet a site of US capital accumulation. Others who have recently embraced this Open Door explanation of US foreign economic policy have acknowledged that "US economic well-being did not objectively depend on trade," but still insist that "policy makers in Washington *believed* that prosperity was tied to its exports abroad." Christopher Layne, *The Peace of Illusions: American Grand Strategy from 1940 to the Present*, Ithaca: Cornell University Press, 2006, p. 72. As Gabriel Kolko long ago pointed out, this interpretation suggests a kind of "transcendental false consciousness" whereby capital and the state "failed to perceive where it was their main gains were to be made." But despite his insistence on the need for a more sophisticated explanation than "the specific needs of this or that business interest," Kolko unfortunately offered only an uncritical reference to the "general theory of the role of imperialism in resolving United States capitalism's structural contradictions." Gabriel Kolko, *Main Currents in Modern American History*, New York: Harper & Row, 1976, p. 36.

17 An insistent line of interpretation, originally advanced by radical scholars but today also embraced much more widely, has made this error in directly tracing US policy to the influence of "large capital-intensive corporations that looked to overseas markets and outward-looking investment banks" (as opposed to "labour-intensive industries that favoured economic nationalism"). And if it is admitted, on this interpretation, that it is not quite correct to speak of these capitalist "dominant elites" as "hijacking the state," it is only because they allegedly "*are the state*." See Layne, *Peace of Illusions*, esp. pp. 200–1, which explicitly draws here on Tom Ferguson's famous essay, "From Normalcy to New Deal," *International Organization* 38: 1 (Winter 1984).

18 See Charles P. Kindleberger, *The World in Depression 1929–39*, Berkeley: University of California Press, 1973, esp. pp. 28, 298.

19 We share Rhonda Levine's assessment that, while Theda Skocpol and her associates were correct in showing how much the New Deal enhanced state capacities, their attempt to counterpose this against a rather "caricatured reading" of the 1970s Marxist theory-of-the-state debate was unjustified, and itself involved a misleading conceptualization of the state "as being independent from the social relations of capitalism," including "the limits imposed by the accumulation process on class forces" as well as directly on the state itself. See Rhonda F. Levine, *Class Struggle and the New Deal*, Lawrence: Kansas University Press, 1988, pp. 9–13.

20 "Even when it did not speak first, the allies always had to figure America's response into their actions. This defining function was crucial." Geir Lundestad, *The United States and Western Europe since 1945*, Oxford: OUP, 2003, p. 64.

21 John G. Ruggie, "International Regimes, Transactions, and Change: Embedded Liberalism in the Postwar Economic Order," *International Organization* 36: 2 (Spring 1982), pp. 405, 410.

22 See especially Hannes Lacher, "The Politics of the Market: Re-Reading Karl Polanyi," *Global Society* 13: 3 (1999); and "Embedded Liberalism, Disembedded Markets: Re-Conceptualizing the *Pax Americana*," *New Political Economy* 4: 3 (1999).

23 Our argument that Bretton Woods laid the foundation for financial globalization runs counter to the influential interpretation offered in Eric Helleiner, *States and the Reemergence of International Finance*, Ithaca: Cornell University Press, 1994, as well as in Saskia Sassen, *Territory, Authority, Rights.*

24 Stefano Battilossi, "Introduction: International Banking and the American Challenge in Historical Perspective," in Stefano Battilossi and Youssef Cassis, eds., *European Banks and the American Challenge*, Oxford: OUP, 2002, p. 27.

25 See Stephen Gill, "The Emerging World Order and European Change: The Political Economy of European Union," *Socialist Register 1992*, London: Merlin, 1992; as well as his *Power and Resistance in the New World Order*, London: Palgrave Macmillan, 2003.

26 Apart from Poulantzas's penetrating theoretical critique of the notion of a "transnational capitalist class" in the 1970s in his *Classes in Contemporary Capitalism*, and the strong empirical refutation in Winfried Ruigrok and Rob van Tulder, *The Logic of International Restructuring*, London: Routledge, 1995, see the more recent analysis by Geoffery G. Jones, which demonstrates how much, in the new millennium as before, "the influence of nationality on multinational corporations is still strong today. The composition of boards of directors remains heavily biased toward home-country nationals, despite the fact that equity ownership of large corporations is now widely dispersed among countries . . . Today, technological advances may permit different parts of the value chain to operate in different places, companies may hold portfolios of brands with different national heritages, and leaders, shareholders, and customers may be dispersed. Still, the nationality of a firm is rarely ambiguous. It usually has a major influence on corporate strategy, and it seems to be growing in political importance." "The Rise of Corporate Nationality," *Harvard Business Review*, October 2006, pp. 20–2. See this argument presented more fully in his "Nationality and Multinationals in Historical Perspective," Harvard Business School Working Paper, 06-052, 2005. It is especially useful to bear all this in mind when reading Leslie Sklair, *The Transnational Capitalist Class*, Oxford: Blackwell, 2001; William I. Robinson, *A Theory of Global Capitalism*, Baltimore: Johns Hopkins University Press, 2004; Jonathan Nitzan and Shimson Bichler, *Capital as Power*, New York: Routledge 2009; and William K. Carroll, *The Making of a Transnational Capitalist Class*, Zed Books, New York, 2010.

27 Bacevich, *American Empire*, p. 4.

28 John Lewis Gaddis, "The Tragedy of Cold War History," *Diplomatic History* 17: 1 (Winter 1993), pp. 3–4.

29 For instance, Kolko (despite having criticized the Open Door interpretation as it pertained to the beginning of the century) seemed to accept the plausibility of it at mid-century, especially by giving far too much weight in his *The Politics of War* (New York: Vintage Books, 1968) to Secretary of State Hull's free-trade pronouncements during World War II. It would once again have amounted to "transcendental false consciousness" to base policy on the notion that exports rather than domestic

accumulation would save the US from another depression after the war. And Kolko was joined in this by many others who took it as a simple matter of fact that postwar policy was driven by the belief that "the US would have to be a major exporter in order to maintain full employment in the transition back to peacetime life." Michael Hudson, *Super Imperialism: The Origins and Fundamentals of US World Dominance*, second edn., London: Pluto, 2003 [1972], p. 19.

30 Peter Gowan, "The American Campaign for Global Sovereignty," *Socialist Register 2003*, London: Merlin, 2003, p. 5.

31 See David Harvey, *The New Imperialism*, New York: OUP, 2003, pp. 26–33.

32 Despite their contributions in detailing the extent of US foreign interventions and global military installations, many critics often fail to see the significance of this crucial point. See, for instance, Noam Chomsky, *Hegemony or Survival: America's Quest for Global Dominance*, New York: Henry Holt, 2004; and Chalmers Johnson, *The Sorrows of Empire: Militarism, Secrecy and the End of the Republic*, New York: Metropolitan Books, 2004.

33 Amy Myers Jaffe, "United States and the Middle East: Policies and Dilemmas," in Bipartisan Policy Center, *Ending the Energy Stalemate*, Washington, DC: National Commission on Energy Policy, 2004, pp. 1–2.

34 See Robert Keohane, *After Hegemony: Conflict and Discord in the World Political Economy*, Princeton: Princeton University Press, 1984.

35 Paul Volcker and Toyoo Gyohten, *Changing Fortunes: The World's Money and the Threat to American Leadership*, New York: Times Books, 1992, pp. xiv–xv.

36 See Ernest Mandel, *Europe vs. America: Contradictions of Imperialism*, New York: Monthly Review Press, 1970; and *Late Capitalism*, London: Verso, 1975, esp. Chapter 10.

37 *Classes in Contemporary Capitalism*, p. 87. Poulantzas understood clearly what the series of successive European "withdrawals" on capital controls, monetary policy, and the oil crisis in the early 1970s meant: "These withdrawals are generally interpreted as an 'offensive by American capital designed to restore its tottering hegemony' . . . these people simply cannot see the wood for the trees; American capital has no need to re-establish its hegemony, for it has never lost it." See also Otto Holman and Kees van der Pijl, "The capitalist class in the European Union," in George A. Kourvetaris and Andreas Moschonas, eds., *The Impact of European Integration*, Westport, CT: Praeger, 1996, esp. pp. 58–63.

38 See Strange's seminal essay, "Towards a Theory of Transnational Empire," in Ernst-Otto Czempiel and James N. Rosenau, eds., *Global Changes and Theoretical Challenges*, Lexington: Lexington Books, 1989.

39 Peter Gowan, *The Global Gamble*, London: Verso, 1999, p. 19.

40 Charles P. Kindleberger, *International Money: A Collection of Essays*, London: Allen & Unwin, 1981, p. 103.

41 E. Richard Gold, "The Legal Foundations of the US Dollar: 1933–1934 and 1971–1978," in David M. Andrews, ed., *Orderly Change: International Monetary Relations since Bretton Woods*, Ithaca: Cornell University Press, 2008, pp. 186–7.

42 As the New York Federal Reserve emphasized in its 1975 Report, whatever the "great

difficulties in coordinating policies internationally . . . stability in exchange markets cannot be sought independently of stability in domestic economies." Federal Reserve Bank of New York, 1975 Annual Report, p. 21.

43 See for instance Robert Gilpin, *The Political Economy of International Relations*, Princeton: Princeton University Press, 1987; and Paul Kennedy, *The Rise and Fall of the Great Powers*, New York: Random House, 1987.

44 See especially Robert Brenner, "The Economics of Global Turbulence", *New Left Review*, I/229 (May-June), 1998; and *The Boom and the Bubble: The US in the World Economy*, New York: Verso, 2002. See also Robert Pollin, *Contours of Descent: US Economic Failures and the Landscape of Austerity*, New York: Verso, 2003; and John Bellamy Foster and Fred Magdoff, *The Great Financial Crisis: Causes and Consequences*, New York: Monthly Review Press, 2009.

45 See Michel Albert, *Capitalism vs. Capitalism*, New York: Four Walls Eight Windows Press, 1993; Daniel Drache and Robert Boyer, eds., *States Against Markets: The Limits of Globalization*, London: Routledge, 1996; Paul Hirst and Graham Thompson, *Globalization in Question*, London: Polity, 1996; and Peter Hall and David Soskice, eds., *Varieties of Capitalism*, Oxford: OUP, 2001. For critical overviews see Panitch et al., *Globalization Decade*; and David Coates, ed., *Varieties of Capitalism, Varieties of Approaches*, London: Palgrave, 2005.

46 See Riccardo Bellofiore, Francesco Garibaldo, Joseph Halevi, "The Global Crisis and the Crisis of European Neomercantilism," *Socialist Register 2011*, London: Merlin, 2010.

47 *World Development Report 1997: The State in a Changing World*, Washington, DC: World Bank, 1997.

48 Amy Bartholomew and Jennifer Breakspear, "Human Rights as Swords of Empire," *Socialist Register 2004*. See also Amy Bartholomew, ed., *Empire's Law: The American Imperial Project and the "War to Remake the World,"* London: Pluto, 2006.

49 Joshua Cooper Ramo, "The Three Marketeers," *Time*, February 15, 1999.

50 Lawrence Summers, "Go With the Flow," *Financial Times*, March 11, 1998.

51 Paul Volcker, speech at Toronto Board of Trade, October 2, 2002, published as "International Financial Markets: The Prospects for Growth and Stability" in Peter White and Michael Wilson, eds., *At the Global Crossroads: The Sylvia Ostry Foundation Lectures*, Montreal and Kingston: McGill–Queens University Press, 2003, pp. 85–98.

52 Michael Hunt, *The Making of the Special Relationship: The United States and China to 1914*, New York: Columbia University Press, 1983, esp. Chapter 5.

53 The notion that the US was in "terminal decline" as the center of capital accumulation shifted to East Asia was the central theme of Giovanni Arrighi's *The Long Twentieth Century* (New York: Verso, 1994), and was taken up again in his *Adam Smith in Beijing: Lineages of the Twenty-First Century* (New York: Verso, 2007). See also Andre Gunder Frank, *ReORIENT: Global Economy in the Asian Age*, Berkeley and Los Angeles: University of California Press, 1998.

54 Insofar as overaccumulation can be said to have been a factor in generating the crisis, it needs to be very specifically located in the interface between the construction

industry and real-estate finance. See David Harvey, "The Urban Roots of Financial Crises: Reclaiming the City for Anti-Capitalist Struggle," *Socialist Register 2012*, London: Merlin, 2011.

1. *The DNA of American Capitalism*

1   When Washington spoke of the new state as "a rising empire," he was thinking in terms of the mercantile colonial empires of the eighteenth century. Alexander Hamilton also spoke in terms of the US becoming "a great empire" by "diffusing its force . . . through a judicious arrangement of subordinate institutions" in the image of "one great American system superior to the control of all transatlantic force or influence and able to dictate the terms of connection between the old and the new world!" See Clinton Rossiter, ed., *The Federalist Papers*, New York: Mentor, 1999, pp. 59, 66.

2   Quoted in John H. Kautsky, "J. A. Schumpeter and Karl Kautsky: Parallel Theories of Imperialism," *Midwest Journal of Political Science* 5: 2 (May 1961), p. 115.

3   Perry Anderson, "Force and Consent," *New Left Review* II/17 (September–October 2002), pp. 24–5.

4   Anderson, "Force and Consent," p. 25. See also Daniel Lazare's *The Frozen Republic* (New York: Harcourt Brace, 1996), which fails to distinguish between the democratic constraints and domestic policy gridlocks that the old elitist system of checks and balances produced and the remarkable informal imperial "carrying power" of the American constitution in the sense argued here.

5   See Hardt and Negri, *Empire*, esp. pp. 160–7. For our critique, see Panitch and Gindin, "Gems and Baubles in *Empire*," *Historical Materialism* 10: 2 (2002).

6   See especially Charles Post's compelling historical materialist analysis of the transition, starting in the last decades of the eighteenth century, of the independent family farmers from household to commodity producers in agricultural markets, and the growing divergence, in the first half of the nineteenth century, between the burgeoning agro-industrial complex of social relations in the northeast and midwest states and the plantation states of the old south. *The American Road to Capitalism: Studies in Class Structure, Economic Development and Political Conflict, 1620–1877*, Chicago: Haymarket, 2012.

7   Quoted in William Appleman Williams, *Empire as a Way of Life: An Essay on the Causes and Character of America's Present Predicament Along With a Few Thoughts About an Alternative*, New York: OUP, 1980, p. 61.

8   Brian Page and Richard Walker, "From Settlement to Fordism: The Agro-Industrial Revolution in the American Midwest," *Economic Geography* 67: 4 (October 1991). See also the seminal article by Charles Post, "The American Road to Capitalism," *New Left Review*, I/133 (May–June 1982), and the broadly similar approach to understanding the role of independent commodity production in Canada's capitalist development, and its trajectory to a "rich dependency" of the American empire, in Leo Panitch, "Dependency and Class in Canadian Political Economy," *Studies in Political Economy* 6 (1981).

9   Gabriel Kolko rightly pointed out that "no national ruling class ever passively allowed

an industrial reserve army to emerge to destroy the existing order, and they attempted to rely on imperialism, migration, or whatever to sustain their hierarchical social orders. Nor will all workers wait for socialism to find bread. However reticent they may initially be, many will migrate before starving . . . this escape valve for the human consequences of economic crises in one state by relying on the growth of others is among the central events in modern history." *Main Currents*, p. 68.

10　Alexis de Tocqueville, *Democracy in America*, New York: Vintage, 1945 [1835], Chapter 20, pp. 168–71.

11　See Michael Best, *The New Competition: Institutions of Industrial Restructuring*, Cambridge, MA: Harvard University Press, 1990.

12　Thomas K. McCraw, "American Capitalism," in Thomas K. McCraw, ed., *Creating Modern Capitalism: How Entrepreneurs, Companies, and Countries Triumphed in Three Industrial Revolutions*, Cambridge, MA: Harvard University Press, 1997, p. 319.

13　McCraw, "American Capitalism," p. 321 and Table 9.1.

14　These figures are drawn from Angus Maddison, *Phases of Capitalist Development*, Oxford: OUP, 1982, and David Gordon, "The Global Economy," *New Left Review* I/168 (March–April 1988), as well as McCraw, "American Capitalism", and Kevin H. O'Rourke and Jeffery G. Williamson, *Globalization and History: The Evolution of a Nineteenth-Century Atlantic Economy*, Cambridge, MA: MIT Press, 1999.

15　See Martijn Konings, *The Development of American Finance,* Cambridge, UK: CUP, 2011.

16　See William Cronon, *Nature's Metropolis: Chicago and the Great West*, New York: Norton, 1992, esp. Chapter 4, "Pricing the Future: Grain." The Chicago Mercantile Exchange (CME), still the world's central futures market in livestock long after the slaughterhouses were gone from Chicago, invented the futures market in currencies after the collapse of the Breton Woods system of fixed exchange rates; and the Chicago Board of Trade, the world center for wheat, corn, and soya futures long after grain was no longer stored in Chicago, soon followed by launching the futures markets in US Treasury securities. The financial futures revolution could not have been implemented, as the head of the CME who initiated the process in 1971 (with the help of Milton Friedman) put it, "without the cadre of traders who left the known risks of the cattle, hog and pork belly pits for the unknown dangers of foreign exchange." Leo Melamed, *Leo Melamed on the Markets: Twenty Years of Financial History as Seen by the Man Who Revolutionized the Markets*, New York: John Wiley, 1993, p. 43.

17　As Bruce Cumings has put it, "The transcontinental railway symbolized the completion of the national territory—by the 1860s America was a linked continental empire. But distant connections to isolated Western towns and farms, Pony Express mail service, and peripheral mudflats like Los Angeles, do not a national market make. Instead for fifty years (roughly from 1890 to 1940) Americans peopled and filled in the national territory. At the same time that the US became the leading industrial power in the world . . . the dominant tendency was expansion to the coast and exploitation of a vast and relatively new market." Bruce Cumings, "Still the American Century," *Review of International Studies* 25: 5 (1999), p. 282.

18　See Peter Cain, *Hobson and Imperialism: Radicalism, New Liberalism and Finance*

1887–1938, Oxford: OUP, 2002, pp. 111–15; and Carl P. Parrini and Martin J. Sklar, "New Thinking about the Market, 1896–1904: Some American Economists on Investment and the Theory of Surplus Capital," *Journal of Economic History* 43: 3 (September 1983).

19 "The emergence of a vast capital market to promote mergers among many firms, a phenomenon which historians and economists generalized into the future with projections which were wrong or misleading, began in 1898 and lost its steam in 1904." Kolko, *Main Currents*, p. 5. See also Martin J. Sklar, *The Corporate Reconstruction of American Capitalism, 1890–1916: The Market, the Law, and Politics*, Cambridge, UK: CUP, 1988, pp. 21ff.

20 Konings, *Development of American Finance*, p. 40.; see also William G. Roy, "The Organization of the Corporate Class Segment of the US Capitalist Class at the Turn of This Century," in Scott G. McNall, Rhonda F. Levine, and Rick Fantasia, *Bringing Class Back In: Contemporary and Historical Perspectives*, Boulder: Westview, 1991, pp. 148–9.

21 Mira Wilkins, *The Emergence of Multinational Enterprise: American Business Abroad from the Colonial Era to 1914*, Cambridge, MA: Harvard University Press, 1970, p. 35.

22 Aspects of the corporate productive form were certainly also evident within the British economy at the end of the nineteenth century, especially in its trading companies, many of which diversified from trading in resources into manufacturing and services, and large manufacturing establishments also emerged in Germany as a response to the desire to catch up with the UK. But in neither case had the modern corporate form become the *main* form of business organization. In Britain, where the primary response to relative economic decline was greater reliance on its predominance in international finance and services, rather than a radical restructuring of its manufacturing sector, family firms continued to prevail. In Germany, state-sanctioned agreements among firms to regulate their competition offered an alternative to the mergers that characterized early-twentieth-century restructuring in the US.

23 McCraw, "American Capitalism," p. 327.

24 See Sklar, *Corporate Reconstruction of American Capitalism*.

25 Quoted in ibid., pp. 215–17.

26 William Thomas Stead, *The Americanisation of the World, or the Trend of the Twentieth Century*, London; William Clowes and Sons, 1901, preface.

27 See especially Federalist Paper Number 10, in Clinton Rossiter, ed. *The Federalist Papers,* pp. 45–52. See also John F. Manley, "The Significance of Class in American History and Politics," in Lawrence C. Dodd and Calvin C. Jilson, eds., *New Perspectives on American Politics*, Washington, DC: Congressional Quarterly Press, 1994, esp. pp. 16–19.

28 "[T]he usual pattern was for territories, newly settled and organized, to fall all over themselves to join the federal union. While this was often, paradoxically, a move by local elites to consolidate their power in the territories, it nevertheless lent a voluntaristic, consensual tone to the expansion of the American state." Thus, even though the federal government was in the end the creator of most of the states, this process

"underscored the fundamental originality of the federation: the central government was the creation of its constituent units." Charles C. Bright, "The State in the United States During the Nineteenth Century," in Charles Bright and Susan Friend Harding, eds., *Statemaking and Social Movements: Essays in History and Theory*, Ann Arbor: University of Michigan Press, 1984, p. 124. See also Victor G. Kiernan, *America: The New Imperialism: From White Settlement to World Hegemony*, London: Verso, 2005, p. 7.

29 For the importance of state governments' expansive capacity to use their constitutional "police powers" to regulate myriad dimensions of social life, see Gary Gerstle, "The Resilient Power of the States across the Long Nineteenth Century: An Inquiry into a Pattern of American Governance," in Lawrence Jacobs and Desmond King, eds., *The Unsustainable American State*, Oxford: OUP, 2009.

30 Despite manifest racial and gender exclusions, even poor farmers had the right to vote from the beginning, and by the 1830s so did all white men regardless of whether or not they owned property (with 80 percent of them actually voting in national elections over the rest of the century).

31 Bright, "The State in the United States," pp. 121–2; see also Kimberley S. Johnson, "The First New Federalism and the Development of the Modern American State: Patchwork, Reconstruction, or Transition?" in Jacobs and King, *Unsustainable American State*.

32 See Stephen Skowronek, *Building a New American State: The Expansion of National Administrative Capacities, 1877–1920*, Cambridge, UK: CUP, 1982.

33 For an outstanding essay on American state development, broadly supportive of the argument here, see William J. Novak, "The Myth of the 'Weak' American State," *American Historical Review* 113: 3, June 2008.

34 McCraw, "American Capitalism," p. 316. In calling this a public "hothouse" without which "the flowers of private enterprise . . . could never have blossomed so spectacularly," McCraw uses a metaphor that may be rather inapt, since he himself had already pointed out that "cities such as Pittsburgh and Chicago grew so dirty from the burning of coal that sunlight could hardly pierce their smoky air."

35 See Morton Horwitz, *The Transformation of American Law 1780–1860*, Cambridge, MA: Harvard University Press, 1977, and "The History of the Public/Private Distinction," *University of Pennsylvania Law Review* 130 (1982). At the level of the federal courts, which had increasingly come to articulate "the general principles of commercial law," support for the instrumental jurisprudence practiced at the state level began to wane by the 1850s. Especially after the panic of 1837, many states were reluctant to undertake public works (or could not get the loans even if they wanted to) and began to use corporate charters to encourage businessmen to raise capital and undertake economic ventures. All of these charters had reserve clauses protecting the public interest— which, even though state capacities for surveillance were limited, capitalists saw as potentially threatening to their freedom of action. These fears were allayed as the courts not only protected capitalists from personal liabilities for their corporations' actions, but completely buried the traditional reserve clauses of corporate charters that defined their public responsibilities. With the New Jersey Incorporation Act of 1889,

under which most large corporations immediately registered, capitalists were able to secure incorporation of any business "for any lawful purpose whatever." See Oscar and Mary Handlin, "Origins of the American Business Corporation," *Journal of Economic History* 5: 1 (May 1945).

36 In a crucial 1871 case, *Pumpelly v. Green Bay Co.*, the US Supreme Court went beyond the commonly accepted "absolute" taking (that is, confiscation of land by the state), to require compensation in situations where there is "such serious interruption to the common and necessary use of property as will be equivalent to a taking."

37 Frederick Engels, "1891 Introduction" to Karl Marx, *The Civil War in France*, New York: International Publishers, 1968, p. 20.

38 See Skowronek, *Building a New American State*, esp. pp. 50–2.

39 David Sarai, "US Structural Power and the Internationalization of the US Treasury," in Leo Panitch and Martijn Konings, eds., *American Empire and the Political Economy of Global Finance*, London: Palgrave, 2008, p. 74.

40 Robert G. Gordon, "'The Ideal and the Actual in the Law': Fantasies and Practices of New York City Lawyers, 1870–1910," in Gerard W. Gawalt, *The New High Priests: Lawyers in Post-Civil War America*, Westport, CT: Greenwood Press, 1984, esp. pp. 53, 58, 65–6.

41 Ibid.

42 Daniel B. Fusfeld, "Government and the Suppression of Radical Labour, 1877–1902," in Bright and Harding, *Statemaking and Social Movements*, esp. pp. 349–60.

43 Williams, *Contours of American History*, p. 361. See also Roy, "Organization of the Corporate Class Segment"; Walter Dean Burnham, "The System of 1896: An Analysis," in Paul Kleppner Walter Dean Burnham, Ronald P. Formisano, and Samuel P. Hays, eds., *The Evolution of American Electoral Systems*, Westport, CT: Greenwood, 1981; and Thomas Ferguson, *Golden Rule: The Investment Theory of Party Competition and the Logic of Money-Driven Political Systems*, Chicago: University of Chicago Press, 1995, Part I.

44 See Frances Fox Piven and Richard Cloward, *Why Americans Still Don't Vote and Why Politicians Want It That Way*, Boston: Beacon, 2000, esp. Chapter 4.

45 Kolko, *Main Currents*, p. 9.

46 David A. Lake, "The State and Trade Strategy in the Pre-Hegemonic Era," in David A. Lake, G. John Ikenberry, and Michael Mastanduno, eds., *The State and American Foreign Economic Policy*, Ithaca: Cornell University Press, 1988, p. 40. See also Emily S. Rosenberg, *Spreading the American Dream: American Economic and Cultural Expansion, 1890–1945*, New York: Hill & Wang, 1982, pp. 51–2.

47 Quoted in William Appleman Williams, *The Tragedy of American Diplomacy*, New York: Norton, 1972, p. 48.

48 Rosenberg, *Spreading the American Dream*, p. 56.

49 The Platt Amendment, passed by the US Senate at the instigation of the secretary of war in 1901, and soon incorporated into Cuba's constitution, not only infamously gave the US extensive control over Cuba's fiscal, debt, and land policies, but leased Guantanamo Bay to the United States.

50 The sporadic but by no means few military interferences before 1898 were amply documented in a paper boldly called "An Indicator of Informal Empire" prepared for the US Center for Naval Analysis (cited in Williams, *Empire as a Way of Life*, p. 122): between 1869 and 1897 the US Navy, as small and under-equipped as it was, made no less than 5,980 ports of call to protect American commercial shipping in Argentina, Brazil, Chile, Nicaragua, Panama, Columbia, and elsewhere in Latin America. The temptations to this sort of practice had grown especially in Central America, as the problems of servicing the far-flung states of California and Oregon, and the issue of who would build and operate the canal through the isthmus, came increasingly into the sights of US businessmen and policymakers. But in the first decades of the new century, the "spillover" of American capital south of the border greatly increased the regularity and almost systematic use of such practices, so much so that the Office of Naval Intelligence could later produce a startlingly honest document, entitled "The United States Navy as an Industrial Asset," in which the role of its "five small second-class cruisers of little or no use in the line of battle" was defined in terms of protecting "our tremendous fruit, sugar, and hemp trades, as well as oil and mining interests." Quoted in Benjamin H. Williams, *Economic Foreign Policy of the United States*, New York: Howard Fertig, 1967 [1929], p. 155.

51 See Clyde W. Barrow, *More Than a Historian: The Political and Economic Thought of Charles A. Beard*, New Brunswick: Transaction, 2000, pp. 208–9.

52 Ibid.

53 See the very rich conceptualization of this by Hannes Lacher, *Beyond Globalization: Capitalism, Territoriality and the International Relations of Modernity*, London: Routledge, 2006.

54 Williams, *Economic Foreign Policy*, p. 307.

55 See Ted Magder, "The Origins of International Agreements and Global Media: The Post, the Telegraph, and Wireless Communication Before World War I," in Robin Mansell and Marc Raboy, eds., *The Handbook of Global Media and Communication Policy*, Oxford: Blackwell, 2011.

56 Lacher, *Beyond Globalization*, pp. 137, 141.

57 Paul S. Reinsch, *Colonial Government: An Introduction to the Study of Colonial Institutions*, New York: Macmillan, 1902, pp. 85–6.

58 Paul S. Reinsch, *World Politics at the End of the Nineteenth Century: As Influenced by the Oriental Situation*, New York: Macmillan, 1900, pp. 41–2. For the distinction between the Roman and "national imperialist" empires, see also pp. 12–13.

59 Gareth Stedman Jones, "The Specificity of US Imperialism," *New Left Review* I/60 (March–April 1970), p. 63.

60 Emily S. Rosenberg, *Financial Missionaries to the World: The Politics and Culture of Dollar Diplomacy, 1900–1930*, Cambridge, MA: Harvard University Press, 1999, pp. 9–10.

61 Ibid., pp. 2–3

62 See Eric Helleiner, "Dollarization Diplomacy: US Policy towards Latin America Coming Full Circle?" *Review of International Political Economy* 10: 3 (August 2003), p. 409.

63 See Williams, *Economic Foreign Policy*, pp. 309–10.

64 The quotation is from Elihu Root's widely cited 1910 address to the American Society of International Law: "The great accumulation of capital in the money centers of the world, far in excess of the opportunities for home investment, has led to a great increase of international investment extending over the entire surface of the earth, and these investments have naturally been followed by citizens from the investing countries prosecuting and caring for the enterprises in the other countries where there investments are made . . . Each country is bound to give to nationals of another country in its territory the benefit of the same laws, the same administration, the same protection, and the same redress for injury which it gives to its own citizens, and neither more nor less: provided the protection which the country gives to its own citizens conforms to the established standard of civilization . . . If any country's system of law and administration does not conform to that standard of justice . . . no other country can be compelled to accept it as furnishing a satisfactory measure of treatment to its citizens." "The Basis of Protection to Citizens Residing Abroad," *American Journal of International Law* 4: 3 (July 1910), pp. 518–21.

65 Theodore Roosevelt, State of the Union Address, December 6, 1904.

66 Thomas McCormick, "From Old Empire to New: The Changing Dynamics and tactics of American Empire," in Alfred W. McCoy and Francisco A. Scarano, *Colonial Crucible: Empire in the Making of the Modern American State*, Madison: University of Wisconsin Press, 2009, pp. 74–5, 78–9.

67 See James Dunkerley, *Power in the Isthmus: A Political History of Modern Central America*, London: Verso, 1988, esp. p. 61; and Kiernan, *America*, esp. p. 166.

68 See Minxin Pei and Sarah Kasper, "Lessons from the Past: The American Record on Nation Building," Policy Brief 24, Carnegie Endowment for International Peace, May 2003, Table 1, p. 4.

69 Quoted in Williams, *Empire as a Way of Life*, p. 132. See Panitch, "Dependency and Class," pp. 7–34; Wallace Clement, *Continental Corporate Power: Economic Elite Linkages between Canada and the United States*, Toronto: McLelland & Stewart, 1977; and Wilkins, *Emergence of Multinational Enterprise*.

70 Kiernan, *America*, p. 198.

71 Engels got it wrong when he wrote in a letter penned on September 10, 1888, after having traveled to Toronto, Kingston, and Montreal from his visit to Niagara: "Here you can see how essential the American's feverish spirit of speculation is to the rapid development of a new country (given capitalist production as its basis). In ten years this sleepy Canada will be ripe for annexation—by which time the farmers in Manitoba, etc., will be demanding it themselves. In any case this country has already been half annexed from the social point of view—hotels, newspapers, advertisements, etc., all conform to the American pattern. And however much they may resist, the economic need for an infusion of Yankee blood will assert itself and abolish this ludicrous boundary line." *Collected Works of Marx and Engels*, vol. 26: 1882–1889, New York: International Publishers, 1990, p. 113.

72 J. Lawrence Broz, *The International Origins of the Federal Reserve System*, Ithaca: Cornell University Press, 1997, p. 5.

73 Ibid.

74 See Elmus Wicker, *Banking Panics of the Gilded Age*, Cambridge: CUP, 2000, Chapter 5.

75 Ron Chernow, *The House of Morgan: An American Banking Dynasty and the Rise of Modern Finance*, New York: Simon & Schuster 1990, pp. 125.

76 Ibid., p. 128.

77 See Serai, "US Structural Power and the Internationalization of the US Treasury"; as well as Murray N. Rothbard, "The Origins of the Federal Reserve," *Quarterly Journal of Austrian Economics* 2:3 (Fall 1999); and James Livingston, *Origins of the Federal Reserve System: Money, Class, and Corporate Capitalism, 1890–1913*, Ithaca: Cornell University Press, 1986.

78 Quoted in Broz, *International Origins of the Federal Reserve System*, p. 150.

79 Chernow, *House of Morgan*, p. 131.

80 Quoted in André C. Drainville, *Contesting Globalization: Space and Place in the World Economy*, London: Routledge, 2004, p. 65.

81 Edwin G. Burrows and Mike Wallace, *Gotham: The History of New York City to 1898*, Oxford: OUP, 1999, p. 1,236.

2. American State Capacities: From Great War to New Deal

1 These are the words of Isaiah Bowman, who was the executive director of the think tank (known as the Peace Inquiry Bureau) that was set up to advise Wilson. See Neil Smith, *American Empire: Roosevelt's Geographer and the Prelude to Globalization*, Berkeley and Los Angeles: University of California Press, 2003, pp. 119, 131. Notably, George Kennan later noted that the State Department's diplomatic outposts were also weaker in their political capacities than in their business promotional ones, thereby reflecting the lack of "sophistication" that he spoke of in his *Memoirs (1925–1950)*, Boston: Bantam, 1967, p. 48.

2 Rosenberg, *Spreading the American Dream*, p. 145 (for the Hoover and Coolidge quotations in this paragraph, see pp. 140, 157). See also Costigliola, *Awkward Dominion*; and Jeff Frieden, "Sectoral Conflict and US Foreign Economic Policy, 1914–1940," in Lake et al., *The State and American Foreign Policy*.

3 Rosenberg, *Spreading the American Dream*, p. 64.

4 Cited in Kiernan, *America*, p. 179; and in Ferguson, *Colossus*, p. 53.

5 George Ramsey Clark, *A Short History of the United States Navy*, Philadelphia: Lippicott, 1929, p. 513.

6 Eric F. Goldman, *Rendez-vous with Destiny*, New York: Vintage, 1956, p. 196.

7 Arno J. Mayer, *Political Origins of the New Diplomacy, 1917–1918*, New Haven: Yale University Press, 1959, p. 391.

8 Quoted in Kolko, *Main Currents*, p. 54. Or, as Wilson's legal advisor, David Hunter Millert, put it: "Europe is bankrupt financially and its governments are bankrupt morally. The mere hint of withdrawal by America by reason of opposition to her views for justice, for fairness, for peace would see the fall of every government in

Europe without exception, and a revolution in every country in Europe with one possible exception." Cited in Margaret MacMillan, *Paris 1919: Six Months that Changed the World*, New York: Random House, 2003, p. 10.

9   See MacMillan, *Paris 1919*, p. 96.

10 The classic account is Michael Hudson, *Super Imperialism: The Origins and Fundamentals of US World Dominance*, second edn., London: Pluto, 2003 [1972]; but see also MacMillan, *Paris 1919*, esp. p. 184.

11 Skowronek, *Building a New American State: The Expansion of National Administrative Capacities, 1877–1920*, Cambridge, UK: CUP, 1982, p. 236. It was especially significant that Wilson—the only professional political scientist ever to occupy the White House, who had written *The Study of Administration* in 1887 and been vice president of the National Civil Service Reform League—did little to extend the merit principle in the federal civil service. More than thirty years after the Civil Service Commission and the merit principle had first been introduced, 30 percent of federal state positions still lay outside its purview.

12 Cited in John J. Broesamle, *William Gibbs McAdoo: A Passion for Change, 1863–1917*, Port Washington, NY: Kennikat Press, 1973, p. 129.

13 Arrighi, *Long Twentieth Century*, p. 272.

14 See Joan Hoff Wilson, *American Business and Foreign Policy*, Lexington: University Press of Kentucky, 1971, pp. 14–17.

15 Thomas J. McCormick has offered an arresting picture of the actual range of opinion among senators which reveals the extent to which, far from regarding the Versailles Treaty as a new departure, they all saw it as reinforcing an unacceptable status quo. Some senators saw the Treaty as "punitively anti-German, and feared that the League's role in enforcing it would trap the United States into supporting a policy of repressing an inevitable German revival rather than encouraging its integration into the collective framework." Others "feared that American membership in the League would deny the United States the freedom to encourage the break-up of those colonial systems and their integration into an American imperium or sphere of influence." There were even a few who reflected the opinion that the Versailles Treaty was "an imperialist, antirevolutionary, anti–Third World instrument whose hypocritical mandate system and rejection of racial equality vitiated Wilson's commitment to self-determination and decolonization." Thomas J. McCormick, *America's Half-Century*, Baltimore: Johns Hopkins, 1995, pp. 23–4.

16 Martin Hill, *The Economic and Financial Organization of the League of Nations: A Survey of Twenty-Five Years' Experience*, Washington: Carnegie Endowment for International Peace, 1946, p. 8. See also Wallace McClure, *World Prosperity as Sought Through the Economic Work of the League of Nations*, New York: Macmillan, 1933. The "centrist-internationalist" designation is McCormick's in *America's Half-Century*.

17 As Polanyi eloquently put it: "The 1920s saw the prestige of economic liberalism at its height. Hundreds of millions of people had been afflicted by the scourge of inflation; whole social classes, whole nations had been expropriated. Stabilization of currencies became the focal point in the political thought of peoples and governments; the

restoration of the gold standard became the supreme aim of all organized effort in the economic field. The repayment of foreign loans and the return to stable currencies were recognized as the touchstones of rationality in politics; and no private suffering, no infringement of sovereignty, was deemed too great a sacrifice for the recovery of monetary integrity. The privations of the unemployed made jobless by deflation; the destitution of public servants dismissed without a pittance; even the relinquishment of national rights and the loss of constitutional liberties were judged a fair price to pay for the fulfillment of the requirements of sound budgets and sound currencies, those a priori of economic liberalism." Polanyi, *Great Transformation*, p. 142.

18 The most detailed account is still Wilson, *American Business and Foreign Policy*.

19 Maddison, *Phases of Capitalist Development*, Tables A8 and F4, pp. 175, 251.

20 "Considerable economic aid had been extended to Europe from the US after World War I, first by the Herbert Hoover–led relief and reconstruction effort and then by private capital speculating on a restoration of monetary stability and pre–World War I exchange rates ... Post–World War I reconstruction loans had been sold as sound private investments ... American private investors were eager after World War I to make loans for European recovery. In the decade after World War I, they loaned more than $1 billion a year overseas, primarily to European nations." J. Bradford DeLong and Barry Eichengreen, "The Marshall Plan: History's Most Successful Structural Adjustment Program," paper prepared for the Conference on Post–World War II European Reconstruction, Hamburg, September 5–7, 1991, p. 12.

21 Maurice Dobb cites the US Department of Commerce for these words in his classic text, *Studies in the Development of Capitalism* (London: Routledge & Kegan Paul, 1946, p. 332).

22 Mira Wilkins, *The Maturing of Multinational Enterprise: American Business Abroad 1914–1970*, Cambridge, MA: Harvard University Press, 1974, Table III.1, p. 155; Kees van der Pijl, *The Making of an Atlantic Ruling Class*, London: Verso, 1984, p. 93.

23 Lendol Calder, *Financing the American Dream: A Cultural History of Consumer Credit*, Princeton: Princeton University Press, 1999, p. 252.

24 See Victoria de Grazia, *Irresistible Empire: America's Advance through Twentieth-Century Europe*, New York: Belknap Press, 2005.

25 Benjamin Williams, *Economic Foreign Policy of the United States*, New York: Howard Fertig, 1967 [1929], pp. 264–5.

26 The quotations are from William Appleman Williams, *Tragedy of American Diplomacy*, pp. 137–8; but see especially Ellis W. Hawley, ed., *Herbert Hoover as Secretary of Commerce*, Iowa City: Iowa State Press, 1981.

27 Quoted in Kevin Ozgercin, "The History of the Bank for International Settlements," doctoral dissertation, Graduate Center of the City University of New York, 2005, p. 21.

28 See Liaquat Ahamed, *Lords of Finance: The Bankers who Broke the World*, New York: Penguin, 2009; and Louis W. Pauly, *Who Elected the Bankers?* Ithaca: Cornell University Press, 1997.

29 See Rosenberg, *Spreading the American Dream*, pp. 154–5. It should be noted that the

Republican administrations of the 1920s were by no means loath to impose restrictions on American capital's international activities to make sure they conformed to the central foreign policy goal of reconstructing the world's states along economic liberal lines. Bankers were required to notify the State Department before making foreign loans, and approval was denied for loans to governments (such as the USSR) that were not recognized by, and/or were in default with loans from, the US government. Approval was also denied for loans to governments which were thought likely to use them to fund budget deficits or foreign monopolies or arms expenditures.

30   Rather more successfully, it was left to the major American petroleum companies to negotiate a new international oil regime. The Commerce and State Departments used the Open Door argument to insist on the US companies' being allowed to participate in the exploitation of the rich oilfields of British-mandated Mesopotamia (Iraq). The conduct of the negotiations leading to the Red Line Agreement of 1928, which recognized Britain's imperial administration but guaranteed the US a joint stake in the development and operation of the oilfields, was left to a private consortium of American oil companies. And the international baseline for the price of a barrel of oil now followed the almost half-century-old US domestic baseline of the cost of extracting Texas oil. See Daniel Yergin, *The Prize: The Epic Quest for Oil, Money, and Power*, New York: Free Press, 1992, pp. 194–206.

31   See especially Barry Eichengreen, *Golden Fetters: The Gold Standard and the Great Depression*, New York: OUP, 1995; as well as his *Globalizing Capital: A History of the International Monetary System*, Princeton: Princeton University Press, 1996.

32   Peter Temin, *Lessons from the Great Depression*, Cambridge, MA: MIT Press, 1996, pp. 1–40.

33   Michael J. Hogan, "Revival and Reform: America's Twentieth-Century Search for a New Economic Order Abroad," *Diplomatic History* 8:4 (Fall 1984), p. 299.

34   For two interesting recent National Bureau of Economic Research studies that draw parallels and contrasts between the real-estate bubbles of the 1920s and early 2000s, see Eugene N. White, "Lessons from the Great American Real Estate Boom and Bust of the 1920s," NBER Working Paper No. 15573, December 2009; and William N. Gotzmann and Frank Newman, "Securitization in the 1920s," NBER Working Paper No. 15650, January 2010. On the stock-market bubble, the classic study remains John Kenneth Galbraith, *The Great Crash: 1929* (Boston: Houghton Mifflin), especially the 1988 edition with a new introduction, "1929 and the Crash of '87."

35   David Gordon, "The Global Economy," *New Left Review* I/168 (March–April 1988), Table 1, p. 32.

36   See Michael A. Bernstein, *The Great Depression: Delayed Recovery and Economic Change in America, 1929–1939*, Cambridge: CUP, 1987; and Gerard Dumenil and Dominique Levy, *Capital Resurgent: Roots of the Neoliberal Revolution*, Cambridge, MA: Harvard University Press, 2004, esp. Chapter 19.

37   See Michael A. Bernstein, "The Great Depression as Historical Problem," *Organization of American Historians Magazine of History* 16 (Fall 2001); and Bradford DeLong, "Slouching Towards Utopia? The Economic History of the Twentieth Century," February 1997, available from DeLong's website at j-bradford-delong.net.

38 Geoffery Ingham, "States and Markets in the Production of World Money: Sterling and the Dollar," in Nigel Thrift, Stuart Corbidge, and Ron Martin, eds., *Money, Power and Space*, Oxford: Blackwell, 1994, p, 32.

39 For an excellent overview of US labor struggles in the early 1930s, see Levine, *Class Struggle and the New Deal*, pp. 52–7.

40 "The Inaugural Address," in John Major, ed., *The New Deal*, London: Longmans, 1968, pp. 64–6.

41 Alan Brinkley, *The End of Reform: New Deal Liberalism in Recession and War*, New York: Knopf, 1995, p. 63. Rhonda Levine's examination of memoranda prepared by Roosevelt's "brain trust" of Adolph Berle, Raymond Mosley, and Rex Tugwell, while also arguing that "what is evident from the personal papers of Roosevelt's advisors, as well as from government documents of the period, is that the entire New Deal program was not clearly thought out by anyone"—beyond, that is, a general commitment to being proactive in "regulating and unifying" capitalist actors. See Levine, *Class Struggle and the New Deal*, pp. 65–7. On the "overarching philosophy of political pragmatism that informed the New Deal," see also Brian Stipelman, "The New Deal's Theory of Practice," *New Political Science* 32: 2 (June 2010).

42 Quoted in Willard Rudge, *Franklin D. Roosevelt's World Order*, Athens, GA: University of Georgia Press, 1959, p. 36. Unless otherwise indicated, the subsequent quotations from FDR in this and the following two paragraphs are from this book at pp. 53, 146–7, 153.

43 Franklin D. Roosevelt, "Our Foreign Policy: A Democratic View," *Foreign Affairs* 6 (1928), esp. pp. 582–4.

44 McClure, *World Prosperity*, p. 233ff.

45 Quoted in Hudson, *Super Imperialism*, p. 106.

46 Charles A. Beard and Mary Beard, *America in Midpassage*, vol. 1, New York: Macmillan, 1939, p. 212.

47 Ron Chernow, *The House of Morgan: An American Banking Dynasty and the Rise of Modern Finance*, New York: Simon & Schuster, 1990, p. 375.

48 Thomas Ferguson, *Golden Rule: The Investment Theory of Party Competition and the Logic of Money-Driven Political Systems*, Chicago: University of Chicago Press, 1995, p. 140ff.

49 The Agricultural Adjustment Act created an administrative body that was able to rely on the Department of Agriculture's longstanding ties to the "land-grant colleges" (established in the nineteenth century to focus on the teaching of practical agriculture, science and engineering) to recruit "experts trained for entire commodity systems and even for agriculture as a whole." Kenneth Finegold and Theda Skocpol, *State and Party in America's New Deal*, Madison, WI: University of Wisconsin Press, 1995, p. 176.

50 Roosevelt had initially opposed this as "both unconstitutional and further likely to paralyze business," but finally agreed to it being inserted in the NIRA as an alternative to Senator Black's radical "30-hour week" work-sharing bill. See Finegold and Skocpol, *State and Party*, p. 171.

51 Ibid., pp. 174–5.

52 Levine, *Class Struggle and the New Deal*, p. 90.

53 Melvyn Dubofsky, "Labor Unrest in the United States," in Beverly J. Silver, Giovanni Arrighi, and Melvyn Dubofsky, eds., *Labor Unrest in the World Economy 1870–1990*, special issue of *Review* xviii: 1 (Winter 1995), p. 127.

54 See Michael Goldfield, "Worker Insurgency, Radical Organization and the New Deal Labor Legislation," *American Political Science Review* 83: 4 (December 1989); and Frances Fox Piven and Richard A. Cloward, *Why Americans Still Don't Vote*, Boston: Beacon Press, 2000, esp. Chapter 5.

55 Brinkley, *End of Reform*, p. 39.

56 Michael Moran, *The Politics of the Financial Services Revolution*, New York: Macmillan, 1991, p. 29.

57 Quoted in Bruce Minton and John Stuart, *The Fat and Lean Years*, New York: Modern Age Books, 1940, p. 313.

58 Stanley Vittoz, *New Deal Labour Policy and the American Industrial Economy*, Chapel Hill: University of North Carolina Press, 1987, p. 149.

59 See Ferguson, *Golden Rule*, esp. Ch 2; and, for its continuing influence, Christopher Layne, *The Peace of Illusions: American Grand Strategy from 1940 to the Present*, Ithaca: Cornell University Press, 2006, pp. 200–1. For a contrary view, see Michael J. Weber, "Business, the Democratic Party and the New Deal: An Empirical Critique of Thomas Ferguson's 'Investment Theory of Politics,' " *Sociological Perspectives* 34: 4 (Winter 1991).

60 See Vittoz, *New Deal Labor Policy*, pp. 147–51; Karl E. Klare, "Judicial Deradicalization of the Wagner Act, and the Origins of Modern Legal Consciousness, 1937–1941," *Minnesota Law Review* 62 (1978), pp. 285–9; and Stephen Norwood, "Ford's Brass Knuckles: Harry Bennett, the Cult of Muscularity, and Anti-Labor Terror, 1920–1945," *Labor History* 37: 3 (Summer 1996): pp 366–7.

61 Nelson Lichtenstein, *The Most Dangerous Man in Detroit*, New York: Basic Books, 1995, pp. 61–2.

62 Seymour Martin Lipset, "Roosevelt and the Protest of the 1930s," *Minnesota Law Review* 68 (1983). Nor was it fair for them just to blame FDR, as can be seen from the rhetoric employed by Harry Truman, a by no means radical Missouri haberdasher, in a Senate speech in December 1937: "One of the difficulties, as I see it, is that we worship money instead of honor . . . It makes no difference if the billionaire rode to wealth on the sweat of little children and the blood of underpaid labor. No one ever considered Carnegie libraries steeped in the blood of the Homestead steel workers, but they are. We do not remember that the Rockefeller Foundation is founded on the dead miners of the Colorado Fuel and Iron Co. and a dozen other similar performances . . . It is a pity that Wall Street, with its ability to control all the wealth of nations . . . are still employing the best brains to serve greed and selfish interest. People can only stand so much, and one of these days there will be a settlement. We shall have one receivership too many, and one unnecessary depression out of which we will not come with the power still in the same old hands." Proceeding and Debates of the second session of the Seventy-Fifth Congress, *Congressional Record*, December 20, 1937. p. 1,923.

63 Kolko, *Main Currents*, p. 154. When Roosevelt, anticipating that the Supreme Court was poised to invalidate the key legislative measures of the Second New Deal, attempted to use his massive popular mandate to reshape the Court, he ran into massive opposition in Congress. With Southern Democrats especially worried that a more liberal Court might challenge the mechanisms that sustained white racial domination, charges of dictatorship—to this point mainly heard from conservative business circles—were now much more widely echoed. But in the midst of this the Supreme Court reversed course and endorsed the Wagner Act (while, however, adopting a very limited view of the right to strike). Whether the Court's endorsement was a direct response to Roosevelt's threat, or rather reflected a gradual shift towards "legal realism" detectable in its earlier rulings, remains hotly debated. As Alan Brinkley has argued, the two positions are not incompatible once one recognizes that even a gradual shift towards legal realism cannot be thought to have occurred in a juridical vacuum, untouched by the social, economic, and political turbulence of the Great Depression. "Introduction to the Debate over the Constitutional Revolution of 1937," *AHR Forum*, October 2005.

64 See Brinkley, *End of Reform*, pp. 73, 303 n. 23.

65 Ibid., esp. pp. 31–4, 56–7; and Dean L. May, *From New Deal to New Economics: The American Liberal Response to the Recession of 1937*, New York: Garland, 1981.

66 Brinkley, *End of Reform*, p. 142.

67 See especially Klare, "Judicial Deradicalization of the Wagner Act."

68 See Barry Dean Karl, *The Uneasy State: The United States from 1915 to 1945*, Chicago: University of Chicago Press, 1983, p. 128; and Brian Waddell, *The War against the New Deal: World War II and American Democracy*, De Kalb: Northern Illinois University Press, 2001, p. 37.

69 The new agencies ranged from the Federal Deposit Insurance Corporation, the Securities and Exchange Commission, and the Federal Communications Commission to the Social Security Administration, the National Labor Relations Board, the Federal Housing Administration, and the Works Project Administration. Whereas state and local employment grew by only 27 percent from 1930 to 1940, federal employment almost doubled over the decade. It would almost double again by 1950. See Ann-Marie Burley, "Regulating the World," in John. G. Ruggie, ed., *Multilateralism Matters*, New York: Columbia University Press, 1993, p. 134; and David Plotke, *Building a Democratic Political Order*, Cambridge, MA: CUP, 1996, p. 222.

70 Michael K. Brown, "State Capacity and Political Choice," *Studies in American Political Development* 9 (Spring 1995), p. 210.

71 Moran, *The Politics of the Financial Services Revolution*, p. 29.

72 Brown, "State Capacity and Political Choice," pp. 192–3.

73 See Brinkley, *End of Reform*, pp. 89–90, 303 n. 23.

74 Ibid., p. 104. Although the Federal Reserve under Mariner Eccles had advanced Keynesian-style ideas for stimulative fiscal spending, the Treasury had to this point remained the bastion of fiscal orthodoxy. Except for an unintended stimulus provided in 1936 by a one-time payment to war veterans, overall fiscal policy in

every other year had been deflationary, once municipal and state budget cuts were taken into account.

75 Roosevelt justified his moderate Keynesian spending program in his April 1938 "Fireside Chat" in exactly these terms. See May, *From New Deal to New Economics*, pp. 132–3, 138–9.

76 Levine, *Class Struggle and the New Deal*, pp. 170–1, 176.

77 Brian Waddell, "Corporate Influence and World War Two: Resolving the New Deal Political Stalemate," *Journal of Policy History* 11: 3 (1999), p. 2.

3. Planning the New American Empire

1 "An American Proposal," *Fortune*, May 1942. This joint *Fortune, Time* and *Life* editorial introduced a series of reports on "The United States in a New World" and its potential courses of action—the first on relations with Britain, and the second later in the year on relations with the Far East. The famous *Life* magazine editorial (February 17, 1940) on "The American Century" by Henry Luce (the owner of all three magazines, who also wrote the preface to "An American Proposal") should be seen as part of this exercise. On *Fortune*'s role through the 1930s in opening up "a more cosmopolitan vision of business," see also Kevin S. Reilly, "Dilettantes at the Gate: Fortune Magazine and the Cultural Politics of Business Journalism in the 1930s," *Business and Economic History* 28: 2 (Winter 1999).

2 See especially Patrick J. Hearden, *Architects of Globalism: Building a New World Order During World War II*, Fayetteville: University of Arkansas Press, 2002.

3 Thus, in terms of domestic policy, "An American Proposal" recognized the Treasury's Keynesian turn, affirming that "no US Government can ever permit a major depression again," and recognizing that "the art of managing government fiscal policy" had become a "new weapon in the people's hands." But it endorsed this only so long as deficits were deployed "to stimulate the maximum of private investment," and this required "a far higher degree of mutual trust between the businessman and his government than was ever achieved under the New Deal," so that the government could not only "use its fiscal policy as a balance wheel" but also "use its legislative and administrative power to promote and foster private enterprise, by removing barriers to its natural expansion."

4 Indeed, *Fortune*'s assembly of corporate leaders was part of a wider set of "business conversations" in the run-up to American entry to the war which were reported back to Roosevelt as sounding "like a conference of Administration whips." See Lloyd C. Gardner, *Economic Aspects of New Deal Diplomacy*, Madison, WI: University of Wisconsin Press, 1964, p. 163. The Council on Foreign Relations (CFR)—since 1921 the link and buckle between leading elements of the capitalist class (and especially leading New York corporate lawyers and bankers), the elite universities, and the State Department—also set up the War and Peace Studies Project in 1939, with expert research groups acting as "think tanks" tasked with providing assistance to the State Department in the form of "concrete proposals designed to safeguard American

interests" and "contribute to the future organization of the world." As the CFR's President Norman Davis put it in 1939: "The British Empire as it existed in the past will never reappear and . . . the United States may have to take its place." This was, of course, said behind closed doors—in speaking so openly in terms of a new American imperialism, *Fortune* was uncommonly direct. See Neil Smith, *American Empire: Roosevelt's Geographer and the Prelude to Globalization*, Berkeley and Los Angeles: University of California Press, 2003, pp. 326, 350.

5   *Economist*, July 18, 1942.

6   Dean Acheson, *Present at the Creation: My Years in the State Department*, New York: Norton, 1969, p. 3.

7   Gaddis Smith, *Dean Acheson*, New York: Cooper Square Publishers, 1972, p. 416.

8   Thomas J. McCormick, *America's Half-Century: United States Foreign Policy in the Cold War and After*, Baltimore: Johns Hopkins University Press, 1995, p. 31. For an excellent overview of the historiography on US entry into World War II, see Justus D. Doenecke, "The United States and the European War, 1939–1941: A Historiographical Review," in Michael J. Hogan, ed., *Paths to Power: The Historiography of American Foreign Relations to 1941*, Cambridge, UK: CUP, 2000.

9   Dean Acheson included this speech and a similar one he gave the same year to the International Ladies Garment Workers Union in his *Morning and Noon*, Boston: Houghton Mifflin, 1965, pp. 218–22, 267–75. Bruce Cumings goes so far as to say that Acheson came closest "to being the singular architect of American strategy" in the postwar period. See his "Still the American Century," *Review of International Studies* 25: 5 (1999), p. 281.

10 See Gardner, *Economic Aspects*, p. 42; and Karen E. Schnietz, "The Institutional Foundation of US Trade Policy: Revisiting Explanations for the 1934 Reciprocal Trade Agreements Act," *Journal of Policy History* 12: 4 (2000), p. 425.

11 Gardner, *Economic Aspects*, p. 283; Hearden, *Architects of Globalism*, p. 16.

12 Nitsan Chorev, *Remaking US Trade Policy: From Protectionism to Globalization*, Ithaca: Cornell University Press, 2007, p. 46. See also Stephen Haggard, "The Institutional Foundations of Hegemony: Explaining the Reciprocal Trade Agreements Act of 1934," and Judith Goldstein, "Ideas, Institutions and American Trade Policy," both in Ikenberry et al., *The State and American Foreign Economic Policy*.

13 These are the words of a Committee on Trade Agreements memo (February 13, 1935) quoted in Alfred E. Eckes, Jr., "US Trade History," in William A. Lovett, Alfred E. Eckes, and Richard L. Brinkman, *US Trade Policy: History, Theory and the WTO*, London: M.E. Sharpe, 2004, p. 56.

14 Helleiner, *States and the Reemergence of International Finance*, pp. 29–31. The difference had even been apparent at the London Economic Conference where, despite the very different British, French, and American agendas, there was a common goal of keeping capital markets as open as possible—and a recognition by all three delegations that doing so especially depended on the actions of the American state. See Barry Eichengreen and Marc Uzan, "The 1933 World Economic Conference as an Instance of Failed International Cooperation," in Peter B. Evans, Harold K. Jacobson, and

Robert D. Putnam, *Double-Edged Diplomacy: International Bargaining and Domestic Politics*, Berkeley: University of California Press, 1993; and John S. Odell, "From London to Bretton Woods: Sources of Change in Bargaining Strategies and Outcomes," *Journal of Public Policy* 8: 3/4 (July–December 1988).

15 Arthur I. Bloomfield, *Capital Imports and the American Balance of Payments 1934–1939: A Study in Abnormal International Capital Transfers*, Chicago: University of Chicago Press, 1950, p. 25.

16 See David Sarai, "US Structural Power and the Internationalization of the Treasury," in Leo Panitch and Martijn Konings, eds., *American Empire and the Political Economy of Global Finance*, London: Palgrave Macmillan, 2008.

17 Helleiner, *States and the Reemergence of International Finance*, pp. 30–1.

18 Leonard Seabrooke, *US Power in International Finance: The Victory of Dividends*, New York: Palgrave, 2001.

19 Acheson, *Present at the Creation*, p. 16. Little progress in developing its own research capacity was made in the State Department until the US entered the war after Pearl Harbour, and it was only well into 1943 that a considerable research and planning staff was really developed, as the Council on Foreign Relations' policy groups were imported directly into the department, and numerous "political scientists, historians, international lawyers, and economists" were recruited from academe. See Harley A. Notter, *Postwar Foreign Policy Preparation 1939–1945*, Westport: Greenwood Press, 1975 (originally published by the Department of State in 1949), esp. pp. 18–40, 149–59; and Inderjeet Parmar, *Think Tanks and Power in Foreign Policy: A Comparative Study of the Role and Influence of the Council on Foreign Relations and the Royal Institute of International Affairs, 1939–1945*, Palgrave: New York, 2004.

20 See Sarai, "US Structural Power"; Helleiner, *States and the Reemergence of International Finance*, pp. 31–2; James M. Boughton, "New Light on Harry Dexter White," *Journal of the History of Economic Thought* 26: 2 (June 2004); and R. Bruce Craig, *Treasonable Doubt: The Harry Dexter White Spy Case*, Lawrence: University Press of Kansas, 2004, pp. 36–9.

21 Quoted in Hearden, *Architects of Globalism*, p. 13.

22 Ibid., p. 21.

23 Ibid., p. 26.

24 During the initial negotiations of Lend-Lease just before the Atlantic Charter in the summer of 1941, Keynes too had disparaged the "lunatic proposals of Mr Hull" which conjured up "all the old lumber, most-favoured nation clause and the rest which . . . made such a hash of the world . . . It is the clutch of the dead hand. If it was accepted it would be the cover behind which all the unconstructive and truly reactionary people of both countries would shelter." Robert Skidelsky, *John Maynard Keynes: Fighting for Freedom, 1937–1946*, New York: Viking, 2001, pp. 130–1.

25 See Kenneth A. Oye, "The Sterling-Dollar-Franc Triangle: Monetary Diplomacy 1929–1937," *World Politics* 38: 1 (October 1985); Michael D. Bordo, Owen Humpage, and Anna J. Schwartz, "The Historical Origins of US Exchange Market Intervention Policy," NBER Working Paper 12662 (November 2006); and C. Randall Henning,

The Exchange Stabilization Fund: Slush Money or War Chest? Washington, DC: Institute for International Economics, 1999, pp. 11–14.

26 See Robert D. Schulzinger, *The Wise Men of Foreign Affairs: The History of the Council on Foreign Relations*, New York: Columbia University Press, 1984, p. 68. On White's turn to Keynesianism, see Boughton, "New Light on Harry Dexter White."

27 The immediate purpose of this was to contribute to the Allied war effort by offering an American assurance that the end of this war would not mean "another two decades of economic uneasiness, bickering, ferment, and disruption," and promising that the United States regarded "prosperity, like peace, as indivisible." Morgenthau would adopt almost these exact words in publicly introducing White's revised plan of July 1943. See "A Preliminary Draft for a United Nations Stabilization Fund and a Bank for Reconstruction and Development of the United and Associated Nations" ("The White Plan," April 1942) in J. Keith Horsefield, *International Monetary Fund 1945–65, Volume III: Documents*, Washington, DC: IMF, 1965, pp. 38–9 (for Morgenthau's introduction to the revised plan, see pp. 83–5).

28 Anne-Marie Burley, "Regulating the World: Multilateralism, International Law, and the Projection of the New Deal Regulatory State," in J. G. Ruggie, ed., *Multilateralism Matters: The Theory and Praxis of an Institutional Form*, New York: Columbia University Press, 1993, pp. 126, 145.

29 Robert Higgs, *Depression, War, and Cold War*, New York: OUP, 2006, p. 19.

30 As early as October 1939, a report by the War Resources Board to Roosevelt stated: "Adequate powers must be given to experienced executives having the confidence of industry . . . we recommend that wartime powers be vested in specially-created war-time agencies which will be automatically demobilized when war is over. Should wartime powers be granted to existing executive or quasi-judicial agencies of the government it will be next to impossible to separate the wartime from the peace-time functions of the government." Quoted in Waddell, *The War Against the New Deal*, p. 68. See also Roland M. Stromberg, "American Business and the Approach of War, 1935–1941," *Journal of Economic History* 13: 1 (Winter 1953), pp. 58–78.

31 John Chamberlain, writing in *New Republic*, September 6, 1939, quoted in Brinkley, *End of Reform*, p. 163.

32 Notter, *Postwar Foreign Policy Preparation*, p. 151.

33 Harry Dexter White, "Postwar Currency Stabilization," *American Economic Review* 33: 1 (March 1943), p. 383.

34 Ibid., p. 386.

35 Ibid., p. 387.

36 Ibid., p. 383.

37 See Kevin M. Casey, *Saving International Capitalism During the Early Truman Presidency: The National Advisory Council on International Monetary and Financial Problems*, New York: Routledge, 2001, p. 27 for the quotations here from the Treasury's November 1943 "draft outline" for the Bank; and on the change of the Bank's mandate to include development, see Devish Kapur, John P. Lewis and Richard Webb, *The World Bank:*

Its First Half Century, Volume One: History, Washington, DC: Brookings Institution Press, 1997, Chapter 2.

38   See Horsefield, *International Monetary Fund*, esp. pp. 68, 71, 74–5.

39   Reciprocal capital controls of some kind had indeed been proposed to the French by the Americans at the time of the 1936 Tripartite Agreement (they were rejected by the former as "unrealistic"), and had also been a subject of some discussion with the British in the late 1930s. As the initial White plan put it, "after the war a number of countries could request the United States not to permit increases in the deposits or holdings of their nationals, or to do so only with a license granted by the government making the request. Or, some countries greatly in need of capital might request the United States to supplement their efforts to attract capital back to the native country by providing information, or imposing special regulations or even special taxes, on certain types of holdings of the nationals of the foreign countries." See Horsefield, *International Monetary Fund*, pp. 40–1; cf. pp. 66, 102, 128–35.

40   Skidelsky, *John Maynard Keynes*, p. 310. These were the very words which senior officials at the German Bundesbank used in an interview we conducted in October 2002 to describe the relationship between themselves and the US Treasury and Federal Reserve.

41   Once Britain went off gold, only the dollar remained convertible to gold, and this confirmed the end of sterling as an international currency. Skidelsky notes (*John Maynard Keynes*, p. 330) that although "Keynes had tried to disguise this unpalatable truth by putting the dollar behind sterling in the form of 'bancor' or 'unitas,' America's rejection of [both] removed the fig-leaf: any post-war monetary order which allowed for multilateral clearing was bound to be based on the dollar." For his part, White would remind the delegates and experts from the forty-four countries involved in striking the final agreement at Bretton Woods that the United States could "dominate . . . the financial world because we have the where-with-all to buy any currency we want." Quoted in Alfred E. Eckes, Jr., *A Search for Solvency: Bretton Woods and the International Monetary System, 1941–1971*, Austin: University of Texas Press, 1975, p. 126.

42   Fred Block, *The Origins of International Economic Disorder: A Study of United States International Monetary Policy from World War II to the Present*, Berkeley: University of California Press, 1978, p. 59. Of course, bringing Britain into the fold was especially critical, given that the sterling area accounted for one-third of world trade, and given the continuing importance of London as a financial center. But while the State Department looked to end Britain's imperial trade preferences through the direct pressures of renewing Lend-Lease, the Treasury's strategy of concentrating on bringing Britain into a dollar-based multilateral payments system was designed to undo the sterling area on which the imperial trading system was based.

43   These are the words of Edward Bernstein, a key Treasury official at the time. See Stanley W. Black, *A Levite Among the Priests: Edward M. Bernstein and the Origins of the Bretton Woods System*, Boulder: Westview Press, 1991, p. 38. Sufficient compromises— however vaguely worded—were agreed that softened the conditions for adjusting

exchange rates, accessing the Fund's resources, permitting protective policies in the face of persistent balance-of-payments surpluses by countries with "scarce currencies" (read: the US), and extending to five years the time limit for "the general abandonment of restrictions" on currency exchange so as to win the UK Treasury's endorsement of White's revised plan rather than Keynes's plan as the basis for Bretton Woods.

44 Quoted in Skidelsky, *John Maynard Keynes*, p. 324, and Casey, *Saving International Capitalism*, p. 32. Casey also quotes Richard Law, head of the British negotiating team that came to Washington in 1943, who described the process that brought technicians from the two Treasuries together as "probably the first time in history that officials of different countries met on such a basis."

45 See Skidelsky, *John Maynard Keynes*, pp. 331, 336.

46 See especially Brinkley, *End of Reform*, pp. 140–54.

47 Quoted in Black, *A Levite Among the Priests*, p. 39.

48 There was resentment on Wall Street to Morgenthau and White's occasional bravado that they had "shifted the center of financial power from London and Wall Street to Washington" (even though at the same time they argued that both the Fund and Bank headquarters should be located in Washington because "New York had become the financial capital of the world"). See Skidelsky, *John Maynard Keynes*, p. 352.

49 See Casey, *Saving International Capitalism*, esp. pp. 45–7; and Eckes, *Search for Solvency*, pp. 174–6.

50 As the Congressional vote approached, the Treasury "orchestrated the presentation of written and oral testimony supporting the Bretton Woods agreement from all sectors of American society," and supplemented this with radio and film spots, pamphlets, and newspaper, magazine and scholarly articles, as well as major speeches by Morgenthau in Detroit and Minneapolis, to win the support of industrial and farm elites. See Eckes, *Search for Solvency*, p. 168; Casey, *Saving International Capitalism*, p. 48.

51 Horsefield, *International Monetary Fund*, p. 176.

52 As IMF historian James Boughton points out, although the Fund was empowered to require countries to impose controls on capital as a precondition for borrowing in the midst of a flight of capital, "[i]n practice, this provision has never been invoked." He further notes, with reference to White, that though his view of capital controls evolved over time, "his considered opinion was that controls were a necessary evil that should be used with discretion so as to avoid discouraging useful flows." See James M. Boughton, "Harry Dexter White and the International Monetary Fund," *Finance and Development* (quarterly journal of the IMF) 35:3 (September 1998), p. 14.

53 Sarah L. Babb and Bruce G. Carruthers, "Conditionality: Forms, Function and History," *Annual Review of Law and Social Science* 4 (2008), pp. 16–17.

54 Acheson, *Present at the Creation*, p. 107.

55 The quotations in this paragraph are from the superb account of the Bretton Woods meeting in Skidelsky, *John Maynard Keynes*, esp. pp. 348, 350–1, 355.

56 Henry L. Stimson, "The Challenge to Americans," *Foreign Affairs*, October 1947, p. 12.

57 Michael Hogan, "Revival and Reform," *Diplomatic History* 8: 4 (October 1984), pp. 300–1.

58 Calvin B. Hoover, *International Trade and Domestic Employment*, Committee for
    Economic Development Research Study, New York: McGraw-Hill, 1945, pp. 6–7.
    In this, the Report was only echoing a 1943 Commerce Department study that had
    turned on its head the old Open Door "export or stagnate" argument. The key to "a
    more successful conduct of our economic and financial relations in the future" was
    "not in the field of foreign economic policy as such but in the attainment of a more
    smoothly operating domestic economy." Hal B. Lary, *The United States in the World
    Economy: The International Transactions of the United States During the Interwar Period*, US
    Department of Commerce, 1943, pp. 19, 24. For its part, the National Planning
    Association, itself a business lobby group supporting export expansion, bluntly
    acknowledged in testimony before Congress that exports were not a panacea for post-
    war economic stability: "foreign trade will not make or break full employment in the
    United States." See Alfred E. Eckes, Jr., "Open Door Expansionism Reconsidered:
    The World War II Experience," *Journal of American History* 59: 4 (March 1973), p. 915.

59 The European demand for basic foodstuffs and energy during the harsh winter in
    Europe was responsible for a spike in US exports in 1947, after which exports settled
    at the 5 percent level they had stood at in 1929. See the US Department of Commerce,
    Series U 201–206, "Foreign Trade Related to Various Measures of Production:
    1869–1970."

60 An influential report in 1948 for the Organization of European Economic Cooperation
    showed that European imports from the US would in fact have to *decrease* until at least
    the early 1950s. John Williams, "Report to Robert Marjolin, Secretary-General
    OEEC," November 23, 1948, p. 13 (Truman Library files, accessed online). In fact, a
    key condition of Marshall Plan aid was that Europe's "per capita consumption should
    not rise above 1938 levels before the end of the aid program in 1952." Anthony Carew,
    "Labour and the Marshall Plan," in Charles S. Maier, ed., *The Cold War in Europe: Era
    of a Divided Continent*, New York: Markus Weiner, 1996, p. 326.

61 "Economists knew," Martin Bronfenbrenner wrote, looking back from 1948 to the
    prevailing opinion at war's end, "that V-J Day meant major depression and mass
    unemployment. Econometricians knew . . . how major would be the depression and
    how massive the mess." Martin Bronfenbrenner, "Postwar Political Economy: The
    President's Reports," *Journal of Political Economy* 41: 5 (October 1948), p. 373.
    Bronfenbrenner might have been exaggerating—others were at the time concerned
    that the main issue would be inflation—but this does speak to the uncertainty that
    prevailed at the time over the restoration of a stable domestic economy. A sense of the
    size of the challenge is provided by the contrast between the 20 percent of the work-
    force involved in the military demobilization in 1945 against less than 1 percent after
    Korea and less than 2 percent after Vietnam. See J. Davidson Alexander, "Military
    Conversion Policies in the USA: 1940s and 1990s," *Journal of Peace Research* 31: 1
    (1994). See also Gregory Hooks, "The Legacy of World War II in Regional Growth
    and Decline," *Social Forces* 71: 2 (December 1992), esp. pp. 305–6.

62 See Alexander J. Field, "The Most Technologically Progressive Decade of the
    Century," *American Economic Review* 93: 4 (November 2003). See also Michael

Bernstein, *The Great Depression: Delayed Recovery and Economic Change in America, 1929–1939*, New York: CUP, 1987.

63 *The Economic Report of the President*, Washington, DC: US Government Printing Office, January 1947, pp. 16, 46. Available at fraser.stlouisfed.org.

64 Kim McQuaid, *Big Business and Presidential Power: From FDR to Reagan*, New York: Morrow, 1982, pp. 123–31.

65 Nelson Lichtenstein, "Class Politics and the State During World War Two," *International Labor and Working Class History* 58 (Fall 2000), p. 264. See also Matthew Baum and Samuel Kernell, "Economic Class and Popular Support for Franklin Roosevelt in War and Peace," *Public Opinion Quarterly* 65 (2001), pp. 198–229.

66 For two graphic accounts, see Mike Davis, *Prisoners of the American Dream*, London: Verso, 1986, pp. 86–7; and Michael Goldfield, *The Color of Politics*, New York: New Press, 1997, pp. 235–8.

67 See National Income and Product Accounts, National Income by Type of Income, Table 1.12; Office of Management and Budget, Historical Tables, Outlays by Superfunction and Function, Table 3.1.

68 Quoted in *Business Week*, May 31, 2004.

69 Quoted in Frederick H. Harbison, "The General Motors–United Auto Workers Agreement of 1950," *Journal of Political Economy* 58: 5 (October 1950), p. 402.

70 Alfred P. Sloan, Jr., *My Years with General Motors*, New York: Doubleday, 1990.

71 Peter Dicken, *Global Shift*, New York: Guilford Press, 2003, p. 355.

72 See Alfred D. Chandler, Jr., "The United States: Engines of Economic Growth in the Capital-Intensive and Knowledge-Intensive Industries," in Alfred D. Chandler, Franco Amatori, and Takashi Hikino, eds., *Big Business and the Wealth of Nations*, Cambridge, UK: CUP, 1997, pp. 83–98.

73 Tony Golding, *The City: Inside the Great Expectations Machine*, London: Pearson Education, 2001, pp. 25–6.

74 See R. C. Smith and I. Walter, *Global Banking*, New York: OUP, 1997.

75 U.S. Department of Commerce, Bureau of Economic Analysis, Corporate Profits After Tax by Industry, Table 6.19B, lines 12 and 52, available at bea.gov.

76 This was marked by Morgenthau's resignation in 1945 and the shunting off to the IMF of White (who soon became one of the first prominent victims of the anti-Communist crusade), and the appointment, as secretary of the Treasury, first of "the cautious Fred Vinson" and then of the St. Louis banker John W. Snyder, who had been particularly outspoken in his opposition to federal deficit spending. See McQuaid, *Big Business and Presidential Power*, esp. p. 130, and Helleiner, *States and the Reemergence of International Finance*, esp. p. 60.

77 Ron Chernow, *The House of Morgan: An American Banking Dynasty and the Rise of Modern Finance*, New York: Simon & Schuster, 1990, p. 402; Charles R. Geisst, *Wall Street: A History*, New York: OUP, 1997, p. 272.

78 The quotations in this paragraph are from Robert Hetzel and Ralph F. Leach, "After the Accord: Reminiscences on the Birth of the Modern Fed," in Federal Reserve Bank of Richmond, *Economic Quarterly* 87: 1 (Winter 2001), pp. 57–63. See also their

"The Treasury-Fed Accord: A New Narrative Account," in the same volume. Leach, who later became a leading J.P. Morgan executive, was at the time of the Accord the chief of the Government Planning Section at the Board of Governors of the Federal Reserve System.

79 Gerald A. Epstein and Juliet B. Schor, "The Federal Reserve–Treasury Accord and the Construction of the Postwar Monetary Regime in the United States," *Social Concept*, 1995, p. 27. See also Edwin Dickens, "US Monetary Policy in the 1950s: A Radical Political Economy Approach," *Review of Radical Political Economics* 27: 4 (1995); and "Bank Influence and the Failure of US Monetary Policy during the 1953–54 Recession," *International Review of Applied Economics* 12: 2 (1998).

80 Robert J. Hetzel, *The Monetary Policy of the Federal Reserve: A History*, New York: CUP, 2008, pp. 49, 58.

81 The Kolkos' understanding that the US "emerged from the war self-conscious of its new strength and confident of its ability to direct world reconstruction along lines compatible with its goals" nevertheless linked the State Department's strategic role far too closely to a continuation of the old Open Door policy. In classically under-consumptionist fashion, moreover, they vastly exaggerated the extent to which the continued strength and expansion of the US economy depended on the increase in defense expenditures occasioned by the Korean War. See Joyce and Gabriel Kolko, *The Limits of Power*, New York: Harper & Row, 1972, esp. pp. 2–3, 11.

4. Launching Global Capitalism

1 Alan S. Milward, *The European Rescue of the Nation-State*, London: Routledge, 2000.

2 J. Bradford DeLong and Barry Eichengreen, "The Marshall Plan: History's Most Successful Structural Adjustment Program," paper prepared for the Center for Economic Performance and Landeszentralbank Hamburg conference on Post–World War II European Reconstruction, Hamburg, September 5–7, 1991, subsequently published as Working Paper 3899, National Bureau of Economic Research, November 1991.

3 Quoted in Tony Judt, *Postwar: A History of Europe since 1945*, London: Penguin, 2005, p. 94. Averell Harriman put it this way in his testimony to Congress supporting the Marshall Plan: "We seek recovery of Europe's industrial productivity so that she may be able to sell abroad in payment for what she needs to buy abroad. To be sure there will be more competition for certain of our products. There will, however, be bigger and sounder markets in Europe and elsewhere." Quoted in Lynn Eden, "Capitalist Conflict and the State: The Making of United States Military Policy in 1948," in C. Bright and S. Harding, eds., *Statemaking and Social Movements*, Ann Arbor: University of Michigan Press, 1984, p. 240.

4 The US Department of Commerce's *Survey of Current Business* of August 1956 and August 1957 showed that between 1945 and 1956 the share of US FDI going to Canada was 37 percent, and to Latin America was 30 percent. Even if we limit the comparison to FDI in manufacturing, Canada alone received half of new US FDI and Europe only

a quarter. Latin America, where US FDI was overwhelmingly directed at natural resources (and primarily at petroleum in Venezuela in this period), received just over 15 percent of new US FDI in manufacturing.

5 Council of Economic Advisors, *Economic Report to the President*, Washington, DC, 1947, p. 91.

6 See Strange, "Towards a Theory of Transnational Empire." For his part, Nicos Poulantzas never explained why it took until the 1960s for major new inroads by US MNCs to be made in Europe. See Nicos Poulantzas, *Classes in Contemporary Capitalism*, London: New Left Books, 1976, esp. pp. 42–7.

7 See especially Geir Lundestad, "Empire by Invitation? The United States and Western Europe, 1945–52," *Journal of Peace Research* 23: 3 (September 1986).

8 As one of Jean Monnet's associates, Pierre Uri, put it: "We used the Americans to impose on the French government what we deemed necessary." Quoted in Judt, *Postwar*, p. 96. At the same time, as Kees van der Pijl has noted, "the concept guiding class formation of the European bourgeoisie henceforward would tend toward the corporate liberalism dominant in the US." Van der Pijl, *Making of an Atlantic Ruling Class*, p. 161.

9 Henry L. Stimson, "The Challenge to Americans," *Foreign Affairs* 26: 5 (1947), p. 11. Will Clayton, while negotiating the Lend-Lease loan to Britain for the State Department, affirmed that "we loaded the British loan negotiations with all the conditions the traffic would bear"; he added at the same time that "I don't know of anything that we could or should do to prevent England or other countries from socializing certain of their industries." Quoted in Lundestad, *United States and Western Europe Since 1945*, p. 103. See also, Gregory A. Fossedal, *Our Finest Hour: Will Clayton, the Marshall Plan and the Triumph of Democracy*, Stanford: Hoover Institution Press, 1993, Chapter 11.

10 Samuel Hutchison Beer, *Modern British Politics: Parties and Pressure Groups in the Collectivist Age*, London: Faber, 1965, pp. 200–1. For the Labour government's articulation of the philosophy of democratic planning, see its *Economic Survey for 1947*, Cmd. 7046, pp. 5–9, and the 1948 White Paper on European Cooperation, Cmd. 7572, Preface and Chapter 1. See generally on this, Leo Panitch, *Social Democracy and Industrial Militancy: The Labour Party, the Trade Unions and Incomes Policies, 1945–1974*, Cambridge: CUP, 1976, esp. Chapter 1.

11 For the quotations in this paragraph, see Kevin M. Casey, *Saving International Capitalism During the Early Truman Presidency: The National Advisory Council on International Monetary and Financial Problems*, New York: Routledge, 2001, pp. 63, 145, 193. The NAC consisted of the secretaries of the Treasury, State and Commerce Departments and the chairmen of the Federal Reserve and Export-Import Bank.

12 On the overwhelming US influence in the constitution of the IMF, and the establishment of its loan conditionalities, see Sarah Babb, "The IMF in Sociological Perspective: A Tale of Organizational Slippage," *Studies in Comparative International Development* 38: 2 (2003); Mark D. Harmon, *The British Labour Government and the 1976 IMF Crisis*, New York: St. Martin's Press, 1997, esp. Chapter 1; and Fred Block's classic study, *The*

Origins of International Economic Disorder: A Study of United States International Monetary Policy from World War II to the Present, Berkeley: University of California Press, 1977.

13 William Y. Elliott, National Planning Association, and Woodrow Wilson Foundation, *The Political Economy of American Foreign Policy: Its Concepts, Strategy, and Limits*, Report of a Study Group sponsored by the Woodrow Wilson Foundation and the National Planning Association, New York: Holt & Co., 1955, p. 213.

14 A report presented to the Federal Reserve's Board of Governors at the beginning of 1950 clearly outlined the phases through which American international economic policy passed in the early postwar years. The first, overseen by the NAC, was the "relief and rehabilitation" phase of the immediate postwar years. The second, more developmental phase was inaugurated in 1947 by the State Department, and administered by the Marshall Plan's Economic Cooperation Administration, oriented to enabling "the Western European countries to maintain a progressive rise in production . . . and to expand exports" while at the same time "arresting inflationary trends." A third phase was opened with the American acceptance of the coordinated devaluation of European currencies relative to the dollar in the fall of 1949, in which the central bankers now played an "increasingly important role" in setting the stage for "the elimination of controls that impede the broad convertibility of currencies, and liberalization of trade and payments," while also fostering "private activities in the field of foreign trade and credit . . . and encouraging private investments in foreign ventures." "The International Role of The Federal Reserve," presented by M. S. Szymczak to a joint meeting of the chairmen and directors of the Federal Reserve Banks, Washington, January 16, 1950, pp. 1, 12.

15 "Statement by the President Upon Appointing the Committee for Financing Foreign Trade," June 26, 1946, Public Papers of the Presidents, Harry S. Truman Library, available at trumanlibrary.org. This committee was composed of the chief executives of the leading corporations and banks as to advise the NAC and to facilitate, as Truman put it, "the fullest cooperation between the governmental agencies and private industry and finance." The Aldrich Committee, as it was known, worked closely with the NAC to establish an initial market for World Bank bonds, lobbying for the removal of currency controls on US foreign investments and foreign investment protection agreements in economic treaties. It was the failure to secure the latter to its satisfaction that was the key reason for the American business opposition that scuttled the International Trade Organization and the American state's subsequent pursuit of it through bilateral treaties. See Casey, *Saving International Capitalism*.

16 Helleiner, *States and the Reemergence of International Finance*, p. 52.

17 Truman's speech of 6 March, 1947 is available at Public Papers of the Presidents, The American Presidency Project, at presidency.ucsb.edu.

18 Quoted in Nitsan Chorev, *Remaking US Trade Policy: From Protectionism to Globalization*, Ithaca: Cornell University Press, 2007, p. 52. See also Thomas W. Zeiler, "Managing Protectionism: American Trade Policy in the Early Cold War," *Diplomatic History* 22: 3 (Summer 1998), esp. p. 341; and Thomas L. Brewer and Stephen Young, *The Multilateral Investment System and Multinational Enterprises*, Oxford: OUP, 1998, esp. p. 68.

19 Fossedal, *Our Finest Hour*, p. 254.

20 Chorev, *Remaking US Trade Policy*, p. 67.

21 This especially allowed Britain to escape the non-discrimination clauses that the US had insisted on as the centerpiece of Lend-Lease and the postwar loan accords to end the imperial trade preference system that had so fixated the State Department since the early 1930s.

22 See Chorev's excellent critique of Ruggie in *Remaking US Trade Policy*, p. 66.

23 Ibid., p. 57.

24 The perception that this was now a critical issue was triggered by the British request at the beginning of 1947—in the context of severe economic problems that winter which led it to rescind the currency convertibility the US loan had prematurely forced it into—that the US should take over the UK's "responsibilities" in Greece. Although the Soviet Union had made it clear that it would not intervene in the Greek civil war, the concern was that a Communist victory there would set a dangerous example. As Acheson put it at a meeting in the White House with the president and the newly appointed secretary of state, General Marshall: "Like apples in a barrel infected by one rotten one, the corruption of Greece would infect Iran and all to the east. It would also carry the infection to Africa through Asia Minor and Egypt, and to Europe through Italy and France, already threatened by the strongest Communist parties in Western Europe." Acheson, *Present at the Creation*, p. 219.

25 Ibid., pp. 232–3, emphasis in original.

26 Acheson himself makes this perfectly clear; see *Present at the Creation*, esp. pp. 227, 232.

27 Quoted in Layne, *Peace of Illusions*, p. 74. Henry Stimson put it this way publicly in his 1947 "Challenge to Americans" *Foreign Affairs* article: "No private program and no public policy, in any sector of our national life, can now escape from the compelling fact that if it is not framed with reference to the world, it is framed with perfect futility. This would be true . . . if all the land eastward from Poland to the Pacific were under water." The only question was whether the US could make democracy, freedom and prosperity "as we understand these words" a reality "in the present world."

28 *United States Objectives and Programmes for National Security*, NSC-68, Part VI, Section A.

29 Alan Milward, *The Reconstruction of Western Europe, 1945–51*, London: Methuen, 1984, esp. Chapter 3.

30 On "offsetting financing," see Helleiner, *States and the Reemergence of International Finance*, p. 61.

31 Charles S. Maier, "The Two Postwar Eras and the Conditions for Stability in Twentieth-Century Europe," *American Historical Review* 86: 2 (April 1981), p. 342 n. 36.

32 DeLong and Eichengreen, "Marshall Plan," pp. 46–8, 51–3.

33 Speech at dinner held by the president of the Netherlands Bank and the Bank for International Settlements, Washington, DC, May 15, 1997.

34 Quoted in Eden, "Capitalist Conflict and the State', p. 241. On McCloy, see Jochen Kraske, William H. Becker, William Diamond, and Louis Galambos, *Bankers with a Mission: The Presidents of the World Bank, 1946–91*, Oxford: OUP, 1996, Chapter 2.

35 James C. Van Hook, *Rebuilding Germany: The Creation of the Social Market Economy, 1945–1957*, Cambridge: CUP, 2004, p. 3.

36 David J. Gerber, "Constitutionalizing the Economy: German Neo-liberalism, Competition Law and the 'New' Europe," *American Journal of Comparative Law* 42: 1 (January 1994), p. 59. The influential Freiburg School defined its "ordoliberalism" in terms of a commitment to embedding free markets in a constitutional order.

37 See Bob Jessop, "The Transformation of the State in Post-War Britain," in Richard Scase, ed., *The State in Western Europe*, London: Croom Helm, 1980.

38 With the help of Keynes's intervention at Bretton Woods, the BIS had earlier survived the US Treasury's attempt to extinguish it at the end of World War II in the face of strong opposition from both European and American private and central bankers. The BIS operated the monthly adjustments in the European Payments Union clearing house, while the central bank governors met every month at BIS headquarters in Basel. See Jacob Kaplan and Günter Schleiminger, *The European Payments Union: Financial Diplomacy in the 1950s*, Oxford: Clarendon Press, 1989; as well as Kevin Ozgercin, "The History of the Bank for International Settlements," PhD dissertation, Graduate Center of the City University of New York, 2005.

39 Jacobsson also pointed out that on a recent visit to the US he had emphasized to his listeners (mainly branch groups of the Council on Foreign Relations) "that Europe would have had to be reconstructed even if there had been no strong Soviet Union." Indeed, he had endorsed the observation made in the *New Statesman and Nation* which warned that "[i]n 1946 there could have been an Anglo-French Socialist policy, since the left was still united and in the ascendant all over Europe." We are indebted to Kevin Ozgercin for making available to us this letter of April 19, 1948 from Jacobsson to Allen Dulles, in the BIS Files 48 185.

40 Kees van der Pijl aptly summarized the outcome as "welding together the reformist unions in the North Atlantic area, and isolating the Communist or class-conscious Socialist elements." These developments, he argued, "were the most conspicuous achievements of the Marshall Plan with respect to the Western European working class." Van der Pijl, *Making of an Atlantic Ruling Class*, p. 155.

41 Charles S. Maier, "The Politics of Productivity: Foundations of American International Economic Policy After World War II," in Peter J. Katzenstein, ed., *Between Power and Plenty: Foreign Economic Policies of Advanced Industrial States*, Madison: University of Wisconsin Press, 1978.

42 These leaders had internalized the argument that a "managerial revolution" had made ownership irrelevant and "undervalued mass activity in industry, while elevating to a lofty plane technicism and the logic of management science"—so much so that "organized labour in Britain and elsewhere in Europe had been steered away from some of the more radical objectives it had briefly and vaguely harboured in 1945." Anthony Carew, "Labour and the Marshall Plan," in Maier, ed., *Cold War in Europe*, pp. 332–4.

43 Paul Hoffman, the head of the Economic Cooperation Administration (ECA) and perhaps the most important American official in Europe, made this clear in a later interview that returned to internal debates within the American state over fighting

Communism versus focusing on growth. "We were," Hoffman admitted, "in fact under continuing attack because we did not devote our energies to directly fighting communism." He then went on to say: "It was our feeling that such an effort would be diversive [sic] and would slow down recovery. Contrariwise, we felt that if speeding recovery did take place as a result of concentrating solely on that goal, the peoples of Europe would realize that they did not have to give up their freedoms to assure lives of decency and dignity." Interview, October 25, 1964, by Dr Phillip Brooks, Truman Library Archives.

44 Angus Maddison, studying the relative productivity gap in the mid fifties, concluded that "on the basis of these observations, it would seem that the future holds a prospect of growing inequality between American and European productivity and living standards." "Industrial Productivity Growth in Europe and the US," *Economica* (new series) 21: 84 (November 1954), p. 313.

45 Maier, "Politics of Productivity," p. 45.

46 For a good account of this, see Frank Southard, Jr., *The Evolution of the International Monetary Fund*, Essays in International Finance No. 135, Department of Economics, Princeton University, December 1979, pp. 25–6.

47 ECA Administrator Paul Hoffman, quoted in Kaplan and Schleiminger, *European Payments Union*, p. 30.

48 The EPU was thus "a more detailed if geographically limited version of the commitment of the Bretton Woods Agreement to remove all restrictions on current account transactions [but it] admitted what had gone unsaid at Bretton Woods: that the postwar international monetary regime was an asymmetric system in which the United States and the dollar played exceptional roles." Eichengreen, *Globalizing Capital*, p. 107.

49 Michael Kreile, "West Germany: The Dynamics of Expansion," in Katzenstein, *Between Power and Plenty*, p. 194.

50 Perry Anderson, "Under the Sign of the Interim," *London Review of Books* 18: 1 (January 4, 1996), pp. 14–15. Anderson argues that Monnet's "decisive advantage, as a political operator across national boundaries, was the closeness of the association he formed with the US political elite . . . during his years in New York and Washington" as a successful international financier in the 1930s and as a consummate French diplomat in exile during the war. Anderson further suggests that it is "possible that Monnet was first set thinking about post-war integration by discussions in the US, and certain that his subsequent achievements depended critically on US support." For a similar assessment of the depth of US policy commitment to European integration and the significance of US influence, contra Milward, see Lundestad, *United States and Western Europe since 1945*. See also Acheson, *Present at the Creation*, p. 384.

51 Though much of Europe's public infrastructure was devastated by the war, this was less true of industry; in Germany, for example, "only" 20 percent of industry was apparently destroyed. See Judt, *Postwar*, p. 83.

52 The Anglo-American Productivity Council was put in place in 1948, and by the time it was disbanded it had sponsored sixty-six visits to the US (the inclusion of British trade unionists was an important dimension of such visits) and distributed over 500,000

copies of their reports and studies on standardization and simplification in industry. See Michael J. Hogan, "American Marshall Planners and the Search for a European Neocapitalism," *American Historical Review* 90: 1 (February 1985), p. 62.

53 C. Kleinschmidt, "Driving the West German Consumer Society: The Introduction of US Style Production and Marketing at Volkswagen, 1945–70," in Volker R. Berghahn, *The Americanization of West German Industry, 1945–73*, London: CUP, 1986, esp. p. 81.

54 Marie-Laure Djelic, *Exporting the American Model: The Postwar Transformation of European Business*, Oxford: OUP, 2001, p. 3. As another study shows, "Even German scientists, engineers and managers, insistent on tradition and confident of their own technology and management, became desperate to absorb technology and management skills from the US." Akira Kud, Matthias Kipping and Harm Schröter, "Americanization: Historical and Conceptual Issues," in Kud, Kipping and Schröter, eds., *German and Japanese Business in the Boom Years: Transforming American Management and Technology Models*, London: Routledge, 2004, p. 10.

55 Paul Hoffman, testimony before the US Senate's Appropriations Committee, cited in Berghahn, *Americanization of West German Industry*, p. 137.

56 Berghahn, *Americanization of West German Industry*, p. 143.

57 See Milward, *European Rescue of the Nation-State*, p. 136, Table 4.3.

58 The most trenchant argument on Britain's resistance to American pressures is Peter Burnham, *The Political Economy of Postwar Reconstruction*, London: Macmillan, 1990. On the trend in the City, see P. L. Cottrell, "Established Connections and New Opportunities: London as an International Financial Centre, 1914–1918," in Yousseff Cassis and Éric Bussiére, *London and Paris as International Financial Centres in the Twentieth Century*, Oxford: OUP, 2005, esp. pp. 173ff.

59 See Kolko and Kolko, *Limits of Power*, p. 14.

60 *Economic Report to the President*, Council of Economic Advisors, Washington, DC, 1947, pp. 91, 122. Although the US was already dependent on key raw material imports by the end of the 1930s, its own production matched or exceeded its consumption of iron ore, lead, aluminum, copper, and most importantly petroleum. But postwar projections showed that the US would become much more reliant on importing these resources through the 1950s. See the *US Economic Report of the President*, Washington, 1951, and the *President's Materials Policy Commission* (known as the Paley Commission), Washington, 1952.

61 Yergin, *The Prize*, pp. 829–30.

62 These were the words of an American official cited in ibid., p. 427.

63 Simon Bromley, "The United States and the Control of World Oil," *Government and Opposition* 40: 2 (Spring 2005), p. 231.

64 David S. Painter, "Oil and the Marshall Plan," *Business History Review* 58: 3 (Autumn 1984), p. 361. At the time this article was written, Painter was an historian at the State Department.

65 Jaffe, "United States and the Middle East."

66 Painter, "Oil and the Marshall Plan," pp. 362, 383.

67 Similar reports came out of the Council of Foreign Relations, the Council on

Economic Development, the National Free Trade Council, and the US Chamber of Commerce. See Sylvia Maxfield and James H. Nolt, "Protectionism and the Internationalization of Capital: US Sponsorship of Import Substitution Industrialization in the Philippines, Turkey and Argentina," *International Studies Quarterly* 34: 1 (March 1990), pp. 49–81.

68 Gerald K. Haines, *The Americanization of Brazil: A Study of US Cold War Diplomacy in the Third World, 1945–1954*, Wilmington, DE: Scholarly Resources Inc., 1989, p. ix.

69 See Stephen G. Rabe, "The Elusive Conference: United States Economic Relations With Latin America, 1945–52," *Diplomatic History* 2: 3 (1978), p. 292.

70 See Maxfield and Nolt, "Protectionism and Internationalization," p. 54, Table 1.

71 On the US shift from "dollar diplomacy" to support for national control over monetary policy, see Helleiner, "Dollarization Diplomacy."

72 Maxfield and Nolt, "Protectionism and Internationalization," p. 77. For an exhaustive account of the fraught relationship between the US and ECLA, see Edgar J. Dosman's definitive biography, *The Life and Times of Raul Prebisch, 1901–1986*, Montreal: McGill-Queen's University Press, 2008, esp. Chapters 12 and 13.

73 Maxfield and Nolt, "Protectionism and Internationalization," pp. 67–8.

74 *Fortune*, March 1949, p. 76.

75 Benedict Anderson, "From Miracle to Crash," *London Review of Books* 20: 8 (April 16, 1998).

76 Bruce Cumings, "The Origins and Development of the Northeast Asian Economies: Industrial Sectors, Product Cycles and Political Consequences," *International Organization* 38: 1 (Winter 1984), pp. 16–17. Robert Solomon defensively notes that his "relative neglect of Japan" in his *The International Monetary System, 1945–1979: An Insider's View*, "corresponds somewhat to the prevailing attitude to Japan in the 1950s . . . as a ward of the United States."

77 US Bureau of Labor, "International Comparisons of GDP Per Capita and Per Hour, 1960–2010," Table 2a, at bls.gov.

78 Gary Dean Allinson, "The Moderation of Organized Labor in Postwar Japan," *Journal of Japanese Studies* 1: 2 (Spring 1975). See also Michael A. Cusumano, *The Japanese Automobile Industry: Technology and Management at Nissan and Toyota,* Cambridge, MA: Harvard University Press, 1985.

79 Elliott et al., *Political Economy of American Foreign Policy*, p. 133. The report went on to say: "[T]hough Japan has the internal elements of reasonably good economic health, its problem of finding export markets and for paying for necessary imports is considerably worse than that of industrial Europe" (p. 135).

80 This was most clearly set out in the Dodge report in 1949. See also Kolko and Kolko, *Limits of Power*, pp. 521–4, as well as Shigeto Tsuru, *Japan's Capitalism: Creative Defeat and Beyond*, Cambridge, UK: CUP, 1993; Takatoshi Itoh *The Japanese Economy*, Cambridge, MA: MIT Press, 1991; and Dennis B. Smith, *Japan since 1945: The Rise of an Economic Superpower*, New York: St. Martin's Press, 1995.

81 Elliott et al., *Political Economy of American Foreign Policy*, p. 314. Moreover, after the Korean War, US foreign aid funds were massive, paying for 70 percent of South

Korean imports between 1955 and 1958. See Barry Gills, "The International Origins of South Korea's Export Orientation," in Ronen P. Palan, *Transcending the State-Global Divide: A Neostructuralist Agenda in International Relations*, Boulder: Lynne Reiner, 1994, p. 211.

82 Hugh Parker, "Dollar, Dollar, Who Has the Dollar? Relationship between the Japanese and American Balance of Payments," *Asian Survey* 6: 8 (August 1966), p. 439.

5. The Contradictions of Success

1 Marcello de Cecco, "International Financial Markets and US Domestic Policy Since 1945," *International Affairs* 52: 3 (1976), p. 388.

2 Stephen Hymer, "The Multinational Firm and the Law of Uneven Development," in Jagdish Bhawgwati, ed., *Economics and World Order from the 1970s to the 1990s*, New York: Free Press, 1972.

3 Quoted in Paolo N. Rogers, "Multinational Corporations: A European View," *Annals of the American Academy of Political and Social Science* 403 (September 1972), p. 61.

4 Jean-Jacques Servan-Schreiber, "The American Challenge," *Harper's Magazine*, July 1968, p. 32. In the context of European discussions on unifying European markets, Servan-Schreiber added that the establishment by US firms of European headquarters to coordinate Europe-wide activities was "true federalism—the only kind that exists in Europe on an industrial level" (p. 33).

5 France was a partial exception to this in the late 1960s since, as Nicos Poulantzas pointed out, its Fourth Economic Plan emphasized the need for a "restriction of direct investment from abroad, in order to safeguard the basic long-term interests of the French economy"; but the Fifth Plan, in the first half of the 1970s, assumed "a very open attitude on the part of the authorities in relation to foreign investment, if not a still more open attitude" which looked to a doubling of US direct investment by 1975 relative to a decade earlier. Poulantzas, *Classes in Contemporary Capitalism*, p. 68.

6 See Peter Dicken, *Global Shift: Reshaping the Global Economic Map in the 21st Century*, New York: Guilford Press, 2003, p. 52.

7 See the time series data in "Historical Measures," *Survey of Current Business*, US Department of Commerce, July 2005, and the monthly data for November 1965 and January 1966. In the early 1960s, US firms were mainly self-financing, in contrast with German, French, and Japanese corporations, whose profits were insufficient to sustain their great expansion, leading them to rely on their close ties with banks for between 30 and 40 percent of their investments. By the end of the decade US firms would increasingly also come to rely on external financing at home. See Andrew Glyn, Alan Hughes, Alan Lipietz, and Ajit Singh, "The Rise and Fall of the Golden Age," in Stephen A. Marglin and Juliet B. Schor, eds., *The Golden Age of Capitalism: Reinterpreting the Postwar Experience*, New York: OUP, 1991, p. 99; and Philip Armstrong, Andrew Glyn, and John Harrison, *Capitalism since World War Two*, London: Fontana, 1991, p. 189, Table 11.11.

8 As Servan-Schreiber put it: "Recent efforts by European firms to centralize and merge are inspired largely by the need to compete with American giants." See his "American Challenge," p. 32. Marie-Laure Djelic, on the basis on her examination of firms in Germany, France, and Italy, shows that in 1950 the size gap between European and US firms was profound; measured in terms the percentage of workers in establishments with over 500 workers, the relative size of European manufacturing firms was roughly half that of those in the US. The transformations in European industry over the next two decades brought them, by the end of the 1960s, to where the US had been a quarter-century earlier. See Marie-Laure Djelic, *Exporting the American Model: The Postwar Transformation of European Business*, Oxford: OUP, 2001, esp. pp. 6–7, 271.

9 Christopher D. McKenna, *The World's Newest Profession: Management Consulting in the Twentieth Century*, New York: CUP, 2006, esp. pp. 81, 175.

10 Mick Carpenter and Steve Jefferys, *Management, Work and Welfare in Western Europe: A Historical and Comparative Analysis*, Cheltenham, UK: Edward Elgar, 2000, pp. 78–80.

11 Randall D. Germain, *The International Organization of Credit: States and Global Finance in the World-Economy*, Cambridge, MA: CUP, 1997, p. 82.

12 Djelic, *Exporting the American Model*, p. 3.

13 See Raymond Aron, *The Imperial Republic: The United States and the World 1945–1973*, Cambridge, MA: Winthrop, 1974, esp. pp. 168, 217; and Poulantzas, *Classes in Contemporary Capitalism*, esp. pp. 39, 57.

14 John Humphrey and Olga Memedovic, "The Global Automotive Industry Value Chain: What Prospects for Upgrading by Developing Countries?" Vienna: UNIDO, 2003, p. 10.

15 Henry Fowler, "Remarks by Secretary of the Treasury Fowler, Dec. 8, 1965 before US Council of the US International Chamber of Commerce," *1966 Report of the Secretary of the Treasury*.

16 Ibrahim Shihata, "Toward a Greater Depoliticization of Investment Disputes: The Roles of ICSID and MIGA," *ICSID Review: Foreign Investment Law Journal* I (1986), pp. 1–45. See also Andrew Guzman, "Why LDCs Sign Treaties that Hurt Them: Explaining the Popularity of Bilateral Investment Treaties," *Virginia Journal of International Law* 38 (1997–98), pp. 639–51. The League of Nations' *Protocol on Arbitration Clauses* (Geneva Protocol 1923) and *Convention on the Execution of Foreign Arbitral Awards* (Geneva Convention 1927) had already recognized the right of private parties to settle cross-jurisdictional contractual disputes in arbitration, and established some conditions for court enforcement within states. The UN *Convention on the Recognition and Enforcement of Foreign Arbitral Awards* (known as the New York Convention of 1958) made recognition and enforcement of foreign arbitral awards a treaty obligation for a much larger number of countries. The proposal to found the ICSID in the World Bank grew out of a perceived need to formalize the ad hoc role it had already acquired as a mediator in disputes pitting developed and developing countries against one another. See Andreas F. Lowenfeld, *International Economic Law*, Oxford: OUP, 2002, pp. 456–70. For the perspective of the first director of the ICSID,

see Aron Broches, *Selected Essays: World Bank, ICSID and Other Subjects of Private and International Law*, The Hague: Martinus Nijhoff, 1995.

17 Gary Burn, "The State, the City and the Euromarkets," *Review of International Political Economy* 6: 2 (Summer 1999), pp. 247–8.

18 The loophole in exchange controls was initially used to set up Soviet and Chinese dollar accounts in London after the US seizure of Yugoslavia's assets made these states wary of banking in New York. The key move to create an open dollar market in London was made by Sir George Bolton, Britain's foremost expert on foreign exchange, who "regarded the collapse of sterling as a reserve currency as a disaster." While still in the midst of moving from his position as deputy director of the Bank of England to his new position as head of the private Bank of London and South America (BOLSA), Bolton evolved a strategy for withdrawing from sterling and buying up dollar deposits in London to finance international trade. In a memorandum written for BOLSA in 1956, while still serving as a Bank of England official, Bolton wrote that London "has barely succeeded in maintaining its international banking system following the loss of political influence by the UK, the weakened position of sterling and the incapacity of the London market to increase its foreign investment net . . . Whatever may be the future of banks engaged in exclusively domestic banking, those whose main business is to maintain and develop a position in the foreign field will have to adapt their structure to meet the needs of our time." As Burn ("The State, the City and the Euromarkets," p. 234) aptly commented, this read "like a Declaration of Intent, a manifesto for the Eurodollar."

19 Niall Ferguson's *High Financier: The Lives and Times of Siegmund Warburg* (New York: Penguin, 2010) traces Warburg's early recognition of the need for this, and his subsequent central role in creating the Eurobond market, to his partnership for many years in the American investment bank, Kuhn, Loeb & Co.

20 Catherine R. Schenk, "The Origin of the Eurodollar Market in London: 1955–1963," *Explorations in Economic History* 35 (1998), pp. 230–2. See also Richard Roberts, "The London Financial Services Cluster since the 1970s: Expansion, Development and Internationalization," paper presented to the Paris Congress, Paris School of Economics, January 30, 2008, pp. 10–11, available at pse.ens.fr.

21 Youssef Cassis, "Before the Storm: European Banking in the 1950s," in Stefano Battilossi and Youssef Cassis, eds., *European Banks and the American Challenge: Competition and Cooperation in International Banking under Bretton Woods*, New York: OUP, 2002, p. 42.

22 Marcello de Cecco, "The Lender of Last Resort," CIDEI Working Paper no. 49 (October 1998), p. 4. See also Sarai, "US Structural Power," esp. pp. 74–6.

23 See Scott Aquanno, "US Power and the International Bond Market: Financial Flows and the Construction of Risk Value," in Panitch and Konings, *American Empire*, pp. 122–6.

24 Martijn Konings, "American Finance and Empire in Historical Perspective," in Panitch and Konings, *American Empire*, p. 60. It is quite remarkable how little attention even radical economists—from Baran and Sweezy to Galbraith—paid to this at the

time, reflecting their preoccupation with the self-financing of investment by industrial corporations.

25 Eugene N. White, *The Comptroller and the Transformation of American Banking 1960–1990*, Washington, DC: Comptroller of the Currency, 1992, pp 11–14.

26 Ibid., p. 20.

27 See Gordon L. Clark, *Pension Fund Capitalism*, Oxford: OUP, 2000, esp. pp. 51–2. More generally, see Randy Martin, *The Financialization of Daily Life*, Philadelphia: Temple University Press, 2002, esp. pp. 133–4.

28 Peter Drucker, *The Unseen Revolution: How Pension Fund Socialism Came to America*, New York: Harper & Row, 1976.

29 White, *The Comptroller and the Transformation of American Banking*, p. 10.

30 Richard Sylla, "United States Banks and Europe: Strategy and Attitudes," in Battilossi and Cassis, *European Banks and the American Challenge*, p. 62.

31 This and the following two quotations are from Michael Moran, *The Politics of the Financial Services Revolution*, London: Macmillan, 1991, pp. 39, 46.

32 "[R]egulation of interest rates on time and savings deposits is in conflict with the principle that money rates and bond yields should be permitted to fluctuate to changing market conditions, and that commercial banks should be free to adjust rates (paid and charged) to those conditions." Comptroller of the Currency, *National Banks and the Future* (1962) quoted in White, *The Comptroller and the Transformation of American Banking*, p. 9.

33 Moran, *Politics of the Financial Services Revolution*, p. 43.

34 Stephen H. Axelrod, *Inside the Fed: Monetary Policy and Its Management, Martin Through Greenspan to Bernanke*, Cambridge, MA: MIT Press, 2009, p. 26. Axelrod was "the ultimate Federal Reserve insider," having begun his three-decade career in 1952 working in what was then seen as the Fed's "backwater" Division of International Finance.

35 David M. Andrews, "Kennedy's Gold Pledge and the Return of Central Bank Collaboration," in David M. Andrews, ed., *Orderly Change: International Monetary Relations since Bretton Woods*, Ithaca: Cornell University Press, 2008, p. 101.

36 Andrews continues: "On the one hand, as the central banking foxes took increasing charge of the financial hen house, the difficulties of managing a fixed exchange-rate system mounted. On the other hand, those foxes were a wily bunch and helped develop a sufficiently resilient set of policy instruments that the demise of the system was forestalled for over a decade." Andrews, "Kennedy's Gold Pledge," p. 119.

37 During the 1960s and 1970s, as Volcker later put it, "The undersecretary for monetary affairs was the one official in the United States government . . . who had substantial direct operating responsibility for both domestic and international policy. Most governments divide up these responsibilities. But, so long as the position existed, no budget or tax proposal, no debt flotation, no comment on monetary policy—essentially, nothing important concerning domestic economic policy—would clear the Treasury without at least some consideration of the implications for the dollar and the impact abroad. Nor, conversely, could international financial policy be isolated from

its domestic implications." Paul A. Volcker and Toyoo Gyohten, *Changing Fortunes: The World's Money and the Threat to American Leadership*, New York: Times Books, 1992, p. 23.

38 See John T. Woolley, *Monetary Politics: The Federal Reserve and the Politics of Monetary Policy*, Cambridge, UK: CUP, 1984, p. 112.

39 US National Archives, General Records of the Treasury, Record Group 56: Office of the Deputy to the Assistant Secretary for International Affairs, Chronological Files, 1977–81. See also James P. Hawley, *Dollars and Borders: US Government Attempts to Restrict Capital Flows, 1960–1980*, New York: M.E. Sharpe, 1987, esp. p. 23.

40 Volcker and Gyohten, *Changing Fortunes*, pp. 29–30.

41 Ibid., p. 32.

42 See Harriet Friedmann, "The Political Economy of Food: The Rise and Fall of the International Food Order," in Michael Buroway and Theda Skocpol, *Marxist Inquiries: Studies of Labor, Class and States*, special supplement of *American Journal of Sociology*, 88(1982), p. S276.

43 The Brookings Institution study, *The United States Balance of Payments in 1968*, published in 1963, was "the most influential expression of this view," and it had considerable impact "on all sectors of opinion at least through 1965. The study's assumptions were Keynesian and trade-based to the core. Direct investment was dismissed as relatively unimportant." Hawley, *Dollars and Borders*, p. 14.

44 Their argument was that FDI was determined "by basic considerations of markets, costs and sources of supply and will not be affected by marginal incentives," especially at a time when the new pattern of trade and investment under European Common Market left American businesses with "no effective alternative" to its FDI there. Hawley, *Dollars and Borders*, p. 30.

45 Volcker and Gyohten, *Changing Fortunes*, pp. 33–4.

46 To this end, the Treasury published a comparative study of European capital markets in 1963 that documented the segmentation of credit and capital structures, and argued against state practices that insulated domestic capital markets from external influences and limited the availability of credit to the private sector. US Department of the Treasury, *A Description and Analysis of Certain European Capital Markets*, Washington, DC: GPO, 1964. See also Robert Solomon, *The International Monetary System, 1945–1976: An Insiders View*, New York: Harper & Row, 1977, esp. pp. 42ff; and Rawi Abdelal, *Capital Rules: The Construction of Global Finance*, Cambridge, MA: Harvard University Press, 2007, esp. Chapter 3.

47 Emil Despres, Charles P. Kindleberger, and Walter S. Salant, "The Dollar and World Liquidity," *Economist*, 5 February 1966. A version of this famous essay that added "a few points that the authors considered important" later appeared in Lawrence H. Officer and Thomas D. Willett, eds., *The International Monetary System: Problems and Proposals*, Englewood, NJ: Prentice-Hall, 1969.

48 Robert V. Roosa, "The American Share in the Stream of International Payments," *Annals of the American Academy of Political and Social Science* 384 (July 1969), pp. 22, 26.

49 Despres, Kindleberger, and Salant, "The Dollar and World Liquidity."

50 Secretary of the Treasury Dillon noted in a 1963 briefing to President Kennedy that "the possibilities of the continued squeezing of European business profits between rising costs and less rapidly rising prices were about exhausted, and this and other forces would continue to drive European prices up." See US Foreign Relations Series, April 18, 1963. Available at dosfan.lib.uic.edu.

51 See Leo Panitch, "The Development of Corporatism in Liberal Democracies," *Comparative Political Studies* 10: 1 (April 1977), and *Working Class Politics in Crisis: Essays on Labour and the State*, London: Verso, 1986.

52 See Leo Panitch, *Social Democracy and Industrial Militancy: The Labour Party, The Trade Unions and Incomes Policy, 1945–1974*, Cambridge, UK: CUP, 1976, Chapters 3–6. See also Barry Eichengreen, *The European Economy since 1945: Coordinated Capitalism and Beyond*, Princeton: Princeton University Press, 2008, Chapter 8.

53 Quoted in Robert Flanagan, David Soskice, and Lloyd Ulman, *Unionism, Economic Stabilization and Incomes Policies*, Washington, DC: Brookings Institution, 1983, pp. 141–2.

54 Eichengreen, *Globalizing Capital*, p. 128.

55 Giovanni Arrighi, "The Social and Political Economy of Global Turbulence," *New Left Review* I/20 (March–April 2003), pp. 35–6.

56 Department of Commerce, Bureau of Economic Analysis, National Income and Product Accounts, Table 3.1. Available at bea.gov.

57 Edwin Dickens, "A Political-Economic Critique of Minsky's Financial Instability Hypothesis: The Case of the 1966 Financial Crisis," *Review of Political Economy* 11: 4 (1999), pp. 392–3.

58 "In addition to limiting the buildup of dollar assets in foreign official hands, these goals included easing Treasury financing operations, limiting financial disintermediation, promoting the growth of bank credit, especially mortgage loans, discouraging inflation, and clearly the top priority, encouraging a more complete utilization of the nation's [resources]." Richard N. Cooper and Jane Sneddon Little, "US Monetary Policy in an Integrating World: 1960 to 2000," *New England Economic Review* 3 (2001), p. 86.

59 Quoted in Hawley, *Dollars and Borders*, p. 97.

60 See Aaron Major, "The Fall and Rise of Financial Capital," *Review of International Political Economy* 15: 5 (December 2008).

61 Hawley, *Dollars and Borders*, pp. 112, 119–20.

62 Joanne Gowa, *Closing the Gold Window: Domestic Politics and the End of Bretton Woods*, Ithaca: Cornell University Press, 1983, p. 99.

63 These are the words of a Federal Reserve official interviewed in Gowa, *Closing the Gold Window*, p. 145.

64 Ibid., pp. 63, 129. See also Volcker and Gyohten, *Changing Fortunes*, pp. 61–8.

6. Structural Power through Crisis

1 Friedman actually said, "In one sense, we are all Keynesians now; in another, nobody is any longer a Keynesian." In a letter correcting the misquote, Friedman added that "the second part is at least as important as the first." *Time*, February 4, 1966.

2 See especially James O'Connor, *The Fiscal Crisis of the State*, New York: St. Martin's Press, 1973.

3 Robert Skidelsky, "Keynes," in D. D. Raphael, Donald Winch, and Robert Skidelsky, *Three Great Economists: Smith, Malthus, Keynes*, Oxford: OUP, 1997, p. 350.

4 See Stephen J. Kobrin, "Expropriation as an Attempt to Control Foreign Firms in LDCs: Trends from 1960 to 1979," *International Studies Quarterly* 28: 3 (September 1984), p. 333, Table 1.

5 The newly emerging academic field of international political economy was almost entirely focused on the threat to liberal multilateralism posed by a declining US hegemony, but see also H. L. Robinson, "The Downfall of the Dollar," in R. Miliband and J. Saville, eds., *Socialist Register 1973*, London: Merlin, 1973; Paul Sweezy and Harry Magdoff, "The Doccar Crisis," *Monthly Review* 28:1 (May 1973); and Ernest Mandel, *Late Capitalism*, London: Verso, 1975, esp. Chapter 10.

6 Eric Helleiner in particular has presented the outcome of the Bretton Woods crisis in terms of the American state—well-armed with neoliberal Friedmanite ideas under Nixon and his successors—imposing its free-market will against European and Japanese states who were more prepared to use multilateral capital controls. See his *States and the Reemergence of Global Finance*, esp. Chapter 5.

7 "The postwar growth of our trading partners was in fact encouraged as a deliberate act of American policy": Volcker and Gyohten, *Changing Fortunes*, pp. xv.

8 Andrew Baker, *The Group of Seven: Finance Ministries, Central Banks and Global Financial Governance*, London: Routledge, 2006, pp. 11, 27.

9 Philip Armstrong, Andrew Glyn and John Harrison, *Capitalism Since 1945*, Cambridge, MA: Blackwell, 1991, Data Appendix, Table A2.

10 US Bureau of Economic Analysis, Fixed Assets Accounts, Table 4.2. Available at bea.gov.

12 The classic "profit squeeze" thesis is to be found in Andrew Glynn and Bob Sutcliffe, *British Capitalism, Workers and the Profit Squeeze*, London: Penguin 1972. For the debate it generated at the time, see Leo Panitch, "Profits and Politics: Labour and the Crisis of British Capitalism," *Politics and Society* 7: 4 (1977). For American versions, see Raford Boddy and James R. Crotty, "Wages, Prices and the Profits Squeeze," *Review of Radical Political Economics* 8: 2 (July 1976); and Samuel Bowles, David M. Gordon, and Thomas E. Weisskopf, *Beyond the Waste Land*, New York: Anchor Books, 1984. Robert Brenner's challenge to this explanation of declining profits was issued in "The Economics of Global Turbulence," *New Left Review*, I/229 (May–June 1998).

13 See Gerard Dumenil and Dominique Levy, *Capital Resurgent: Roots of the Neoliberal*

Revolution, Cambridge, MA: Harvard University Press, 2004; and Anwar Shaikh, "Explaining the Global Economic Crisis," *Historical Materialism*, 5 (1999). Each of these texts provides a careful consideration of the role of the rising cost of productivity improvements, but they both see this as determined by the inherent tendency of capitalists in the face of class and competitive pressures to displace labor by fixed capital. This does not capture the extent to which worker resistance within the workplace in the 1960s provided a conjunctural barrier to the optimal application of capital, technology and work reorganization.

14 Walter Reuther, quoted in *Wall Street Journal*, April 20, 1970. The phrase "gold-plated sweatshops" is also Reuther's, as quoted in Nelson Lichtenstein, *State of the Union: A Century of American Labor*, Princeton University Press, 2002, p. 189.

15 For the US, see Kim Moody, *An Injury to All: The Decline of American Unionism*, New York: Verso, 1988, pp. 84–94. And for Europe, see Pierre Dubois, "New forms of Industrial Conflict," in Colin Crouch and Alessandro Pizzorno, *The Resurgence of Class Conflict in Western Europe Since 1968*, New York: Holmes & Meier, 1978; and Mick Carpenter and Steve Jefferys, *Management, Work and Welfare: A Historical and Contemporary Analysis*, Cheltenham, UK: Edward Elgar, 2000, esp. p. 94ff.

16 In the auto industry, for example, GM sometimes even maintained extra facilities partly in order to be ready to beat out competitors for unanticipated increases in market demand, but also a safety valve against wildcats in one plant, allowing the corporation to step up production in other plants.

17 Robert Brenner, who has advanced the foremost argument against the thesis of a profit squeeze determined by wage militancy, relies on data indicating that real wages (money wages adjusted for consumer price inflation) lagged behind productivity growth from 1965 to 1973. But this is misleading for two reasons. First of all, since benefits rose faster than wages in this period, US industry's *total* compensation costs kept up with productivity growth. Moreover, the relevant measure of real compensation from the perspective of industrial profits is not wages plus benefits adjusted by the consumer price index (CPI) but the producer price index (PPI)—the price corporations get for their product. Measured this way, real compensation grew *faster* than productivity in this period, and workers received a growing share relative to capital of the value added in industrial production.

18 Quoted in Robert J. Hetzel, *The Monetary Policy of the Federal Reserve: A History*, New York: CUP, 2008, p. 75.

19 Frederick Schadrack and Frederick Breimyer, "Recent Developments in the Commercial Paper Market," Federal Reserve Bank of New York *Monthly Review*, December 1970, p. 289. The impending crisis had been well in train since the beginning of 1970, as was shown by subsequent SEC reports and successful lawsuits against Goldman Sachs. See Martin H. Wolfson, *Financial Crises: Understanding the Postwar Experience*, Armonk, NY: M.E. Sharpe, 1986, pp. 192–4, esp. Figures 13.1 and 13.2. It is notable that the Final Report of the National Commission on the Causes of the Financial and Economic Crisis of 2007–08 traces that later crisis all the way back to this crisis in 1970. See *The Financial Crisis Inquiry Report*, New York: Public Affairs, 2011, pp. 29–31.

20 See Charles D. Ellis, *The Partnership: The Making of Goldman Sachs*, New York: Penguin, 2009, Chapter 7; and William D. Cohan, *Money and Power: How Goldman Sachs Came to Rule the World*, New York: Doubleday, 2011, Chapter 7.

21 See Wolfson, *Financial Crises*, p. 194, Figure 13.3.

22 Richard F. Janssen and Charles N. Stabler, "Empty Coffers," *Wall Street Journal*, June 12, 1970.

23 See Charles W. Calomiris, "Is the Discount Window Necessary? A Penn Central Perspective," Federal Reserve Bank of St. Louis *Review*, May 1994.

24 The most intensive study of the Fed in this period sustains this view. See Woolley, *Monetary Politics*, esp. Chapter 8. Woolley makes it clear (pp. 170–5) that the Fed's caution about subsequently returning to a tight monetary policy reflected more than an accommodation to getting Nixon re-elected; rather, in the context of Nixon's control program, the Fed was mainly concerned not to aggravate pressure from Congress to extend mandatory controls to the interest rates banks charged, which Burns saw as representing the gravest danger to central bank independence.

25 Arthur F. Burns, *Reflections of an Economic Policy Maker: Speeches and Congressional Statements, 1969–1978*, Washington, DC: American Enterprise Institute for Public Policy Research, 1978, p. 111.

26 See White, *Comptroller*, p. 21; Jane W. D'Arista, *The Evolution of US Finance, Volume II: Restructuring Institutions and Markets*, New York: M.E. Sharpe, 1994, esp. pp. 129–35; and Edward M. Gramlich, *Subprime Mortgages: America's Latest Boom and Bust*, Washington, DC: Urban Institute Press, 2007, esp. pp. 14–15.

27 Quoted in Louis Hyman, *Debtor Nation: The History of America in Red Ink*, Princeton, NJ: Princeton University Press, 2011, p. 226. Well over a hundred cities were aflame in the US in the mid sixties. In Watts, a section of Los Angeles, thirty-four people died in the 1965 riots, and 1,100 were injured; in Newark, New Jersey, twenty-six people died in the 1967 explosion and 1,100 were injured; in Detroit the same year, forty people died and 2,000 were injured. See *Report of the National Advisory Commission on Civil Disorders (Kerner Commission)*, Washington, DC: US Printing Office, 1968.

28 Hyman, *Debtor Nation*, pp. 224–5.

29 Woolley, *Monetary Politics*, p. 61. In 1961, 4 percent of housing starts were subsidized by the state, but by 1971 this had increased to 30 percent. See Hyman, *Debtor Nation*, p. 226.

30 See Aaron Brenner, *Rank-and-File Rebellion, 1966–1975*, PhD thesis, Columbia University, 1996, p. 41.

31 These quotes from the FMOC Minutes are in Edwin Dickens, "The Federal Reserve's Low Interest Rate Policy of 1970–72: Determinants and Constraints," *Review of Radical Political Economics* 28: 3 (1996), pp. 121, 123. Burns expressed much the same views in his speech to the American Bankers Association in May 1970, reprinted in his *Reflections of an Economic Policy Maker*, pp. 91–102.

32 See FRBNY Annual Reports 1970 (p. 35) and 1971 (p. 11).

33 Although inflationary pressures had cooled somewhat by early that year, a

threatened steelworkers' strike over wages lagging behind inflation resulted in a 31 percent wage increase over three years, and was immediately followed by an 8 percent price hike by US Steel. This was the crucial backdrop to the decision to impose wage and price controls.

34 David Vogel, "The Power of Business in America: A Reappraisal," *British Journal of Political Science* 13: 1 (January 1983), p. 24. See also White, *Comptroller*, p. 21.

35 Quoted in White, *Comptroller*, p. 21.

36 Ibid., p. 29

37 Cited in Leonard Silk and David Vogel, *Ethics and Profits: The Crisis of Confidence in American Business*, New York: Simon & Schuster, 1976, p. 21.

38 Robert Rubin, with Jacob Weisberg, *In an Uncertain World: Tough Choices from Wall Street to Washington*, New York: Random House, 2003, p. 81.

39 Cited in Dan Clawson, *The Next Upsurge: Labor and the New Social Movements*, Ithaca: Cornell University Press, 2003, p. 38.

40 Cited in Richard Peet, *Geography of Power*, New York: Zed Books, 2007, pp. 86–7.

41 The chief protagonist in the battles over this inside the British Labour Party, Tony Benn, presciently outlined what was in store if such an alternative strategy was not implemented: "[the] philosophy of government, now emerging everywhere on the right, [takes] as the starting point of its analysis that modern society depends on good management and that the cost of breakdowns in the system is so great that they really cannot be tolerated and that legislation to enforce greater and more effective discipline must now take priority over other issues. The new citizen is to be won over to an acceptance of this by promising him greater freedom from government, just as big business is to be promised lower taxes and less intervention and thus to be retained as a rich and powerful ally." Tony Benn, *The New Politics: A Socialist Reconnaissance*, Fabian Tract 402, September 1970, p. 12.

42 Robin C. A. White, "A New International Economic Order," *International and Comparative Law Quarterly*, July 1975, pp. 546–7.

43 Daniel Patrick Moynihan, with Suzanne Weaver, *A Dangerous Place*, Boston: Little, Brown, 1978, p. 32.

44 "Suggested Talking Points for Use with Republican Study Group," June 30, 1976, William Simon Papers, IIIB, 23: 29, pp. 3–4. We are grateful to Jeffrey Sommers for his help with the documents in this collection.

45 It is often now forgotten that, while the impeachment proceedings against Nixon were going on, Vice President Spiro Agnew pleaded no contest to taking bribes, while the next man in line under the Constitution, House Speaker Carl Albert, was being treated for alcoholism.

46 Volcker and Gyohten, *Changing Fortunes: The World's Money and the Threat to American Leadership*, New York: Times Books, 1992, p. 125.

47 Notably, the cost to firms of insuring against risk through forward contracts in the new derivatives markets was only "a small fraction of one percent for major foreign exchange markets." Thomas D. Willett, "Material on Exchange Rate Flexibility and US Trade," Memorandum for Deputy Secretary Dixon, US Treasury Department, July 22, 1976, William Simon Papers, III B, 11: 19, pp. 1, 6.

48 Yoishi Funabashi, *Managing the Dollar: From the Plaza to the Louvre*, Washington, DC: Institute for International Economics, 1988, p. 131.

49 Volcker and Gyohten, *Changing Fortunes*, p. 124. Before the US moved to float its currency, Germany had already done so twice. Volcker had taken this as clearly demonstrating that Germany "was willing to depart from a fixed exchange rate if that conflicted seriously with its domestic priority of fighting inflation" (p. 104). For detailed accounts of the 1971–74 negotiations, see John Williamson, *The Failure of World Monetary Reform*, New York: New York University Press, 1977; and Robert Solomon, *The International Monetary System 1945–1976*, New York: Harper & Row, 1977.

50 That the American state was not trying to limit free trade but support and expand it as part of the larger American role in the world was made clear by Nixon in 1972, shortly after the 1971 increase in tariffs: "Trade is part of a bigger package . . . we may have to give more than our trade interest, strictly construed, would require." President Carter was even more adamant about the centrality of the US not moving to protectionism: "free access to US markets is a matter of ranking importance for our allies and almost all the developing countries of the world." Internal Treasury memorandum cited in Judith Stein, "The 1970s Crisis: Prelude to the Present," Workers and World Crises Conference, Georgetown University, September 22–4, 2011, p. 8.

51 Personal interview with Paul Volcker, New York, March 2003.

52 See William Glenn Gray, "Floating the System: Germany, the United States, and the Breakdown of Bretton Woods, 1969–73," *Diplomatic History* 31: 2, April 2007; and Hubert Zimmerman, "West German Monetary Policy and the Transition to Flexible Exchange Rates, 1969–1973," in David M. Andrews, ed., *Orderly Change: International Monetary Relations since Bretton Woods*, Ithaca: Cornell University Press, 2008.

53 See John Williamson and Molly Mahar, *A Survey of Financial Liberalization*, Essays in International Finance, No. 211, Department of Economics, Princeton University, Princeton, New Jersey, November 1998. The measures for this were how far each country had gone by this time towards the elimination of capital controls, the deregulation of interest rates, free entry into the financial services industry, bank autonomy, private ownership, and liberalization of international capital flows. The US limits on deposit interest rates, the types of assets S&Ls could acquire, and prohibitions on interstate banking placed the US behind Germany on the liberalization scale.

54 Helleiner, *States and the Reemergence of International Finance*, pp. 104, 110, 113–4.

55 See the insightful portrayal of Simon as the leading trader of government bonds at Salomon's in Martin Mayer, *Nightmare on Wall Street*, New York: Simon & Schuster, 1993, pp. 50–4. Mayer notes that, every Thursday morning, a senior trader in Treasury bonds from Salomon's would go to the New York Fed's headquarters to meet with his counterpart. "On an informal basis the Salomon trader would lay bare for the Fed his firm's position and his views of what others in the market were doing." For how Simon combined this acute awareness of financial capital's umbilical link to the state with his "free market" ideology, see his autobiography, *A Time for Reflection*, Washington, DC: Regnery Publishing, 2004.

56 "Address of the Honorable William E. Simon, Secretary of the Treasury of the United States before the 1974 Annual Meetings," Department of the Treasury News, October 1, 1974, p. 5, in William Simon Papers, V, 38: 56.

57 Quoted in Hudson, *Super Imperialism*, p. 327.

58 Jeremy Seabrooke, *US Power in International Finance: The Victory of Dividends*, London: Palgrave, 2001, p. 68.

59 See Charles P. Kindleberger, *The International Corporation: A Symposium*, Cambridge, MA: MIT Press, 1970, p. 155. As of 1967, the US had well over twice as many qualified engineers and scientists as the nine leading capitalist European countries combined. See Eichengreen, *European Economy Since 1945*, p. 26.

60 By 1975, two-thirds of the world's semiconductors and three-quarters of integrated circuits were made by US corporations. See Jeffrey Hart, *Rival Capitalists: International Competitiveness in the United States, Japan, and Western Europe*, Ithaca: Cornell University Press, 1992, p. 14; Rowena Olegrio, "IBM and the Two Thomas J. Watsons," in Thomas K. McCraw, *Creating Modern Capitalism: How Entrepreneurs, Companies, and Countries Triumphed in Three Industrial Revolutions*, Cambridge, MA: Harvard University Press, 1997, pp 354–5; and Christophe Lecuyer, *Making Silicon Valley: Innovation and the Growth of High Tech, 1930–1970*, Cambridge, MA: MIT Press, 2006, p. 25.

61 On the increased proportion of US agricultural production going to export in the 1970s, see Kenneth C. Clayton, "US Agriculture in the 1980s: Economic Perceptions," Economic Research Service, US Department of Agriculture, n.d., available at agecon-search.umn.edu.

62 Fred Block, "Swimming Against the Current: The Rise of a Hidden Developmental State in the United States," *Politics and Society* 36: 2 (2008), pp. 174–5. Especially important for the development of computers was the Advanced Projects Research Agency (APRA), an office of the Department of Defense, whereas the National Institutes of Health were key for biotechnology, where commercial applications began to accelerate by the late 1970s after research breakthroughs in the splitting of genes between 1967 and 1971.

63 See R. McCulloch, "Why Corporations Are Buying into US Business," *Annals of the American Political Science Association* 516 (July 1991).

64 "Memo for George Shultz from Wm. J. Casey, Under Secretary of State for Economic Affairs," dated April 19, 1973, in William Simon Papers, I, 14: 46, May 9, 1993. The memorandum included a speech Casey gave in March 1973 on "The Internationalization of the Capital Markets."

65 "Memo for George Shultz," Simon Papers, I, 14: 46.

66 Casey's brief was designed to enhance the position of Wall Street, but it did not for all that indicate a lack of "relative autonomy," since it also drew Shultz's attention to the problematic situation whereby "20 banks control 100 companies which can get all the money they want . . . while the banks command a large enough slice of brokerage commissions to determine which brokers stay in business." Notably, this point was made in Casey's covering letter to Secretary of State Shultz when he submitted his memorandum.

67 *The Report of the President's Commission on Financial Structures and Regulation,* December 1971, p. 9.

68 "Recommendations of Change in the US Financial System," Department of the Treasury, August 3, 1973.

69 Moran, *Politics of the Financial Services Revolution,* p. 46. As Moran argued, moreover, it was not so much neoliberal ideology that broke the old system of financial regulations as it was the increasingly dysfunctional effects of the New Deal's corporatist financial controls, precisely because of the growth in the complexity and scale of the financial sector that had already taken place. There were ample profitable options open to investment bankers in the commercial paper and mutual fund money markets when they lost their fixed margins on brokerage services.

70 Melamed, *Leo Melamed on the Markets,* p. 43

71 Ibid., p. 108. See also Bob Tamarkin, *The Merc: The Emergence of a Global Financial Powerhouse,* New York: HarperCollins, 1993, p. 217.

72 See C. M. Seeger, "The Development of Congressional Concern about Financial Futures Markets," in Anne Peck, ed., *Futures Markets: Their Economic Role,* Washington, DC: American Enterprise Institute for Public Policy Research, 1985, pp. 12–14.

73 Melamed, *Melamed on the Markets,* p. 70.

74 See Donald Mackenzie, *An Engine, Not a Camera: How Financial Models Shape Markets,* Cambridge, MA: MIT Press, 2006.

75 Scott Aquanno, "US Power in the International Bond Market: Financial Flows and the Construction of Risk Value," in Leo Panitch and Martijn Konings, eds., *American Empire and the Political Economy of Global Finance,* second edn., London: Palgrave, 2009, pp. 124–5.

76 "Statement of Secretary Shultz to the Commission on the Organization of the Government for the Conduct of Foreign Policy," February 20, 1974, William Simon Papers, IV, 32: 22, pp. 7–8.

77 "Statement of the Honorable William E. Simon, Secretary of the Treasury before the Commission on the Organization of the Government for the Conduct of Foreign Policy," March 31, 1975, William Simon Papers, IV, 32: 22.

78 See Nitsan Chorev, *Remaking US Trade Policy: From Protectionism to Globalization,* Ithaca: Cornell University Press, 2007, esp. Chapters 5 and 6; Steve Dryden, *Trade Warriors: USTR and the American Crusade for Free Trade,* New York: OUP, 1995, esp. Chapter 10; and Jamey Essex, "Getting What You Pay For: Authoritarian Statism and the Geographies of US Trade Liberalization Strategies," *Studies in Political Economy* 80 (Autumn 2007).

79 "Rationale for a Dynamic Export Policy," internal Treasury Department memorandum on export policy and exchange rates, William Simon Papers, III B, 21: 4, April 1975, p. 4.

80 "The Financial Conference on Inflation: Narrative Summary," September 20, 1974, William Simon Papers, III B, 22: 46. The quotation is from the FMOC Minutes, January 22, 1974, as cited in Robert L. Hetzel, *The Monetary Policy of the Federal Reserve: A History,* New York: CUP, 2008, p. 93.

81 Hetzel, *Monetary Policy of the Federal Reserve*, p. 92.

82 Volcker and Gyohten, *Changing Fortunes*, p. 103.

83 White, *Comptroller*, p.25.

84 Ibid., p. 29.

85 Joan Edelman Spero, *The Failure of the Franklin National Bank: Challenge to the International Banking System*, Washington, DC: Beard Books, 1999, p. 132. See also Ethan B. Kapstein, *Governing the Global Economy: International Finance and the State*, Cambridge, MA: Harvard University Press, 1994, esp. pp. 41–2.

86 Richard Lambert, "A Tale of Two Banking Crises," *Financial Times*, December 2, 2008; see also Margaret Reid, *The Secondary Banking Crisis: Its Causes and Course*, London: Macmillan, 1982.

87 Quoted in Kapstein, *Governing the Global Economy*, p. 40.

88 Robert E. Litan, with Jonathan Rauch, *American Finance for the 21st Century*, Washington, DC: Brookings Institution Press, 1998, pp. 122–3, 156–7.

89 Kapstein, *Governing the Global Economy*, p. 42

90 This was confirmed by our interviews with senior Bundesbank officials in Frankfurt in 2002.

91 Ethan B. Kapstein, "Architects of Stability? International Cooperation among Financial Supervisors," BIS Working Paper 199, Basel: Bank of International Settlements, 2006, p. 6.

92 See Catherine Schenk, "Crisis and Opportunity: The Policy Environment of International Banking in the City of London, 1958–1980," in Cassis and Bussière, *London and Paris*, Oxford: OUP, 2005, p. 222; White, *Comptroller*, pp. 35–6; and Kapstein, *Governing the Global Economy*, p. 43.

93 This was made explicit in the *The Strategic Plan of the Office of the Comptroller of the Currency*, October 1981, pp. 22–3.

94 Volcker and Gyohten, *Changing Fortunes*, pp. 29–31, 116, 126–7.

95 Baker, *Group of Seven*, p. 28.

96 A National Advisory Council working paper in June 1973 called the World Bank "essentially an American-run institution," and expressed general confidence regarding "the extent to which the US can prevent the IFIs from pursuing policies contrary to US policy objectives." "Task 1: Provisional Treasury Decision on Funding IFIs," internal Treasury memorandum draft, May 19, 1973; and "Task 2: US Executive Branch Decision," NAC Working Group Paper, draft, June 7, 1973, William Simon Papers, IV, 31: 14, pp. 5, 25, 39. These assessments were reflected in various statements by Simon and Shultz before Congress. See William Simon Papers, IIIB 23: 28.

97 Volcker and Gyohten, *Changing Fortunes*, p. 116. At the same time, the Treasury's position was that "the degree of inflationary problems in domestic economies" made the time not "ripe for introducing a highly organized monetary reform" through the C-20. Press Conference held by Paul A. Volcker, Department of Treasury, May 30, 1974, William Simon Papers, IIIB, 23: 27, pp. 2–3.

98 "Suggested Talking Points For Use With Republican Study Group," June 30, 1976, William Simon Papers, IIIB, 23: 29, p. 3. See also Herbert Rowan, "US Is Big Winner at IMF Talks," *Washington Post*, January 18, 1976.

99 See especially David E. Spiro, *The Hidden Hand of American Hegemony: Petrodollar Recycling and International Markets*, Ithaca: Cornell University Press, 1999. Although Simon was indeed meeting with the Saudis on "luring oil dollars back home" (as was reported by Bruce Agnew in *Washington Outlook* as early as October 6, 1973), there is no evidence in the Simon papers that he was pushing for the OPEC price increase, as Peter Gowan suggested (*The Global Gamble: Washington's Faustian Bid for World Dominance*, London: Verso, 1999, p. 21). Indeed, in a number of confidential memoranda Simon wrote to the White House, he insisted "we must do all we can to get down the international price of oil," and that it was essential that the oil-producing states come to recognize the need for lower oil prices, "both in terms of their narrow self-interest in maintaining their market for future oil sales and because of their stake in the operation of the international economic system." William Simon Papers, Memorandum to the President, "Current Situation in the International Financial Markets," June 27, 1974, IIIB 22: 57; and Memorandum for Members of the Executive Committee of the Economic Policy Board, October 29, 1974. William Simon Papers, IIIB 25: 28.

100 Address to IMF, Department of Treasury News, October 1, 1974, William Simon Papers, V, 38: 56.

101 "Summary of Panel Discussion on outlook for Current Account Financing via Private Capital Markets," William Simon Papers, IIIB, 23: 23. pp. 2–3. It was also noted that "Wall Street bankers took the view that Kuwait, Saudi Arabia and the United Arab Emirates" (which accounted for most of the financial accumulations in New York) were "all very conservative governments, not interested in takeovers but in portfolio and real estate investments . . . OPEC is only starting to learn of the size and diversity of the U.S. capital market. Compared to these, OPEC funds are small, and they will diversify over time."

102 Germain, *International Organization of Credit*, pp. 97, 119.

103 World fertilizer consumption doubled and Latin American fertilizer consumption more than tripled between 1965 and 1975, while the number of tractors used in agriculture increased globally by 80 percent and in Latin American by 75 percent. In Brazil, Chase Manhattan invested over $100 million into soybean production (which increased by between 8 and 12 percent per year there in the 1970s). See Roger Burbach and Patricia Flynn, *Agribusiness in the Americas*, New York: Monthly Review Press, 1980; Dan Morgan, *Merchants of Grain*, New York: Viking, 1979; and Farshad Araghi, "The Great Global Enclosure of Our Time: Peasants and the Agrarian Question at the End of the Twentieth Century," in Fred Magdoff, John Bellamy Foster and Fredrick H. Buttel, eds., *Hungry For Profit: The Agribusiness Threat to Farmers and the Environment*, New York: Monthly Review Press, 2000.

104 Philip McMichael, *Development and Social Change: A Global Perspective*, Thousand Oaks, CA: Pine Forge Press, 2004, p. 51.

105 Kapstein, *Governing the Global Economy*, p. 66.

106 "LDCs and the Financing Problem," William Simon Papers, IIIB, 23: 29, pp. 3–4.

107 Ibid., pp. 3–4.

108 Statement by the Honorable William E. Simon at the Annual Meetings of the Board of Governors, International Finance Corporation, International Development Association, Manila, The Philippines, October 5, 1976, William Simon Papers, V, 40: 82.

109 The following paragraphs draw on Leo Panitch and Colin Leys, *The End of Parliamentary Socialism: From New Left to New Labour*, second edn., London: Verso, 2001, pp. 107–26.

110 James Callaghan, *Time and Change*, London: Fontana, 1988, pp. 425–7.

111 The clandestine meeting took place at an exclusive London tailor's, and cost Simon the price of three suits. It was, he later said, well worth it. See Mark D. Harmon, *The British Labour Government and the 1976 IMF Crisis*, London: Palgrave Macmillan, 1997, pp. 193–5.

112 As Simon Clarke has aptly put it, "Monetarism triumphed not because of its own merits, whether as an economic theory or political ideology, but because of the failures of Keynesianism. The ideological power of monetarism derived from the fact that it could explain and legitimate policies that had been forced on Keynesian governments." "Capitalist Crises and the Rise of Monetarism," *Socialist Register 1987*, London: Merlin, 1987, p. 396.

113 Quoted in Stephen Fay and Hugo Young, *The Day the Pound Nearly Died*, London: Sunday Times, 1978, p. 30.

114 Kathleen Burk and Alec Cairncross, *Goodbye, Great Britain: The 1976 IMF Crisis*, Princeton: Yale University Press, 1992, pp. 8, 42.

115 See Colin Leys, "Thatcherism and British Manufacturing: A Question of Hegemony," *New Left Review* I/151 (May–June 1985).

116 See Panitch and Leys, *End of Parliamentary Socialism*, esp. p. 148.

7. *Renewing Imperial Capacity*

1 *Fortune*, vol. 93 (March 1976).

2 Thomas Edsall, *The New Politics of Inequality*, New York: W.W. Norton, 1985, p. 128. See also Joseph G. Peschek, *Policy-Planning Organization: Elite Agendas and America's Rightward Turn*, Philadelphia: Temple University Press, 1987.

3 See Stephen Gill, *American Hegemony and the Trilateral Commission*, New York: CUP, 1990.

4 Volcker and Gyohten, *Changing Fortunes*, p. 167.

5 US Treasury Secretary Donald Regan thought it to be a "fraud" that the US was offering bonds paying 5 percent interest while inflation was up around 13 percent. He corrected this by offering "savings bonds that yielded as much as 8 percent. By then the rate of inflation was down to 4 percent and I had no trouble in recommending the bonds as a good investment to anyone." See Donald Regan, *For the Record: From Wall Street to Washington*, New York: Random House, 1988, esp. pp. 161–2.

6 See John Grahl, "Notes on Financial Integration and European Society," paper presented to "The Emergence of a New Euro-Capitalism?" conference, Marburg, October 11–12, 2002, published in M. Beckmann, H.-J. Bieling, and F. Deppe,

394 NOTES TO PAGES 164 TO 166

Euro-Kapitalismus und globale politische Okonomie, Hamburg: VSA Verlag, 2003, p. 1. By

the end of the 1970s, foreign exchange transactions were already ten times higher than those of trade, although this represented only a taste of the explosive growth to come.

7 Patrick J. Akard, "Corporate Mobilization and Political Power: The Transformation of US Economic Policy in the 1970s," *American Sociological Review* 57: 5 (October 1992), pp. 601–2.

8 Jamey Essex, "Getting What You Pay For: Authoritarian Statism and the Geographies of US Trade Liberalization Strategies," *Studies in Political Economy* 80 (Autumn 2007), p. 84.

9 Quoted in Nitsan Chorev, *Remaking US Trade Policy: From Protectionism to Globalization*, Ithaca, NY: Cornell University Press, 2007, pp. 73–4.

10 William E. Simon, with John M. Caher, *A Time for Reflection: An Autobiography*, Washington, DC: Regnery, 2004, p. 150. Notably, before he came to the Treasury, Simon had been a senior partner in Salomon Brothers in charge of municipal bond sales, and a member of the New York City comptroller's Technical Debt Advisory Committee at the beginning of the 1970s.

11 Doug Henwood, who describes the municipal unions as "weak, divided, self-protective, [and] unimaginative," quotes Jack Friedgut of Citibank as follows on the advantages that the banks had over the unions: "One is that since we were dealing on our home turf in terms of finances, we knew basically what we were talking about and . . . had a better idea of what it takes to reopen the market and sell this bond or that bond . . . The second advantage is that we do have a certain noblesse oblige or tight and firm discipline . . . when we spoke to the city or the unions we could speak as one voice." *Wall Street: How it Works and for Whom*, New York: Verso, 1997, pp. 296–7. See also Kim Moody, *From Welfare State to Real Estate: Regime Change in New York City, 1974 to the Present*, New York: New Press, 2007, p. 41; and David Harvey, *A Brief History of Neoliberalism*, Oxford: OUP, 2005, esp. pp. 44–8.

12 Alan Greenspan, *The Age of Turbulence*, New York: Penguin, 2007, p. 72.

13 W. Carl Biven, *Jimmy Carter's Economy: Policy in an Age of Limits*, Chapel Hill: University of North Carolina Press, 2002, pp. 36–7.

14 David Vogel and Leonard Silk, *Ethics and Profits: The Crisis of Confidence in American Business*, New York: Simon & Schuster, 1976, pp. 39–42.

15 Akard, "Corporate Mobilization and Political Power," pp. 603–4.

16 Harvey L. Schantz, "The Evolution of Humphrey-Hawkins," *Policy Studies Journal* 8: 3 (Winter 1979), p. 371. This bill was originally introduced in the House by labor-oriented black Congressmen in 1974, and reintroduced in the Senate to coincide with the thirtieth anniversary of the Employment Act of 1946. The Bill sought finally to go beyond the limited postwar commitment to full employment by making the achievement of a 3 percent unemployment rate a national priority, including by means of a clause requiring the federal government to act as employer of last resort at fair rates of compensation.

17 Jefferson Cowie, *Stayin' Alive: The 1970s and the Last Days of the Working Class*, New York: New Press, pp. 270–271.

18 The centerpiece of Carter's initial stimulus package in January 1977—a modest across-the-board $50 income tax rebate—was withdrawn three months later. In any case, "the package was not large by historical standards . . . less than 1 percent of the GNP for 1977, whereas the Kennedy package was 1.7 percent and the Ford package 1.5 percent of GNP." Biven, *Jimmy Carter's Economy*, p. 71.

19 The Fed established and expanded swap lines of credit with major foreign central banks, while the Treasury used the Exchange Stabilization Funds, drew on its reserve position at the IMF, resumed public auctions of gold, and sold special drawing rights to the Bundesbank for marks. It also attempted to navigate the growing financial market revolt by issuing US bonds denominated in foreign currencies in the German and Swiss capital markets. The sale of these so-called Carter bonds rested on a conceptual distinction between the credibility of the US state and the forward value of the US dollar. This was supported by the European central banks, who nevertheless rejected a proposal the Fed floated for an international agreement to have reserve requirements on Eurodollar accounts, once again demonstrating that the European states were unwilling to embrace cooperative capital controls, even to prevent the demise of Keynesianism. See J. Hawley, "Protecting Capital From Itself: US Attempts to Regulate the Eurocurrency System," *International Organization* 38: 1 (Winter 1984); Andrew Baker, *The Group of Seven: Finance Ministries, Central Banks and Global Financial Governance*, London: Routledge, 2006, pp. 29–30; and I. M. Destler and C. Randall Henning, *Dollar Politics: Exchange Rate Policymaking in the United States*, Institute for International Economics: Washington, DC, 1989.

20 Carter's speech can be accessed at millercenter.org.

21 Stephen H. Axelrod, *Inside the Fed*, Cambridge, MA: MIT Press, 2009, p. 89.

22 Paul Volcker, "The Role of Monetary Targets in the Age of Inflation," *Journal of Monetary Economics* 4 (1978), p. 334. See also his "The Political Economy of the Dollar," Fred Hirsch Lecture, Warwick University, November 9, 1978.

23 See Woolley, *Monetary Politics: The Federal Reserve and the Politics of Monetary Policy*, Cambridge: CUP, 1984, esp. pp. 102–5, 124, 140–5. See also P. Johnson, *The Government of Money: Monetarism in Germany and the United States*, Ithaca: Cornell University Press, 1998, esp. pp. 178–9.

24 On the Fed under Miller's brief "interlude," see especially Stephen H. Axelrod, *Inside the Fed: Monetary Policy and its Management, From Martin through Greenspan to Bernanke*, Cambridge, MA: MIT Press, 2009, Chapter 4.

25 Paul Volcker, "The Triumph of Central Banking," Per Jacobsson Lecture, Per Jacobsson Foundation, Washington, DC, September 23, 1990, p. 5.

26 Greta R. Krippner, "The Making of US Monetary Policy: Central Bank Transparency and the Neoliberal Dilemma," *Theory and Society* 36 (2007), p. 488.

27 Chris Rude, "The Volcker Monetary Policy Shocks: A Political-Economic Analysis," unpublished paper, Department of Economics, New School University, January 2004, p. 13.

28 Allan H. Meltzer, *A History of the Federal Reserve, Volume 2, Book 2, 1970–1986*, Chicago: University of Chicago Press, 2009, p. 1,034.

29 Paul Volcker, "A Time of Testing," Remarks to the American Bankers Association, New Orleans, Louisiana, October 9, 1979, p. 4. Available at fraser.stlouisfed.org.

30 The federal funds rate had averaged 10.4 percent over the first nine months of 1979. After its peak in April 1980 it was temporarily reduced for a few months when Carter's insistence on supplementing the anti-inflation policy with credit controls led to a sudden and unanticipated collapse of consumer demand. In the face of continuing double-digit inflation and only slowly rising unemployment, the Fed quickly returned to pushing interest rates back to stratospheric levels.

31 On the exact, carefully chosen words, and Greenspan's interpretation of them at the time ("They have eased"), see Joseph B. Treaster, *Paul Volcker: The Making of a Financial Legend*, New York: Wiley, 2004, pp. 162–3.

32 "Memo for Mr Simon from Alan Greenspan," April 30, 1974, in William Simon Papers, III B, 20: 2.

33 Volcker, "Triumph of Central Banking," p. 5.

34 See especially Andrew C. Sobel, *State Institutions, Private Incentives, Global Capital*, Ann Arbor: University of Michigan Press, 1999, esp. pp. 56–69.

35 As the 1979 Economic Report of the President put it: "The reduced sensitivity of mortgage credit availability to rising market interest rates smoothes the adjustment of the economy to credit restraint. It also implies, however, that interest rates must move through somewhat larger cyclical swings to achieve the effect on aggregate demand that would formerly have resulted from variations in both credit availability and interest rates" (p. 52).

36 See especially White, *The Comptroller and the Transformation of American Banking*, pp. 51–2; and Meltzer, *History of the Federal Reserve*, pp. 994–8, 1,066–9.

37 Ross M. Robertson, *The Comptroller and Bank Supervision: A Historical Appraisal*, Washington, DC: Office of the Comptroller of the Currency, 1995, p. 217.

38 The quotation is from the Treasury OCC Comptroller Heimann. See Robertson, *The Comptroller and Bank Supervision*, p. 216. The earlier Financial Institutions Regulatory and Interest Rate Control Act of 1978 established the Federal Financial Institutions Examination Council (FFIEC) to promote uniformity in the supervision and examination of financial institutions, including a "Uniform Interagency Bank Rating System," and secure a more efficient division of labor between the OCC and the Federal Reserve in regulating bank holding companies. Although the OCC was the principal regulator of national banks, oversight for holding companies owning national banks fell to the Federal Reserve. To remedy this problem, the FFIEC recommended coordinated inspections and examinations of holding companies and their lead banks. See White, *The Comptroller and the Transformation of American Banking*, esp. p. 44.

39 White, *The Comptroller and the Transformation of American Banking*, p. 57. See also FDIC, "The First Fifty Years: A History of the FDIC 1933–1983." Available at fdic. gov. In another unprecedented intervention, the Fed even went so far as to loan $1.1 billion dollars to the notorious Texas oil baron H. L. Hunt and his brother to cover what they owed to no fewer than twelve domestic banks, four foreign banks, and five brokerage houses. After initially having made billions in speculating against the dollar

in the silver market, the value of their silver holdings collapsed as the rising interest rates lifted the value of the dollar. The Fed subsequently organized an additional billion-dollar loan to the Hunts from a consortium of private banks. Meltzer, *History of the Federal Reserve*, pp. 1,051–2.

40　Rude, "The Volcker Monetary Policy Shocks," p. 16.

41　Personal interview with Paul Volcker, March 2003.

42　See Hetzel, *Monetary Policy of the Federal Reserve*, pp. 135–6.

43　See Volcker, "A Time of Testing," p. 6. The fact that "industrialists were not a problem," as Volcker put it in our interview with him, was also confirmed by our interviews with senior executives of the American auto corporations.

44　Even the construction industry—which screamed bloody murder at the unprecedented level of interest rates—came around in the end: when Volcker addressed the 1982 convention of the National Association of Home Builders, "although they had been especially badly hurt they gave him a standing ovation." See Allan Meltzer, "Inflation Nation', *New York Times*, May 3, 2009, as well as his *History of the Federal Reserve*, p. 1,128. See also the 1979 *Economic Report of the President*, p. 51.

45　See Meltzer, *History of the Federal Reserve*, pp. 989–90, 1,086–7.

46　Kim Moody, *An Injury to All: The Decline of American Unionism*, New York: Verso, 1988, p. 152. While rank-and-file militancy had already been somewhat dissipated by the sharp rise in unemployment in 1973–75, and further worn down by the union leadership even before the strategic turn, concessions were resisted in many plants. This was finally overcome only by the active collaboration of the UAW national office with management in threats to close such plants unless the local leadership was repudiated by the workers, as well as by cancelling the opportunity the 1982 collective bargaining conference might have created for a rebellion from below. (This conference had, since the foundation of the union, brought together elected delegates from every local in advance of each round of bargaining.)

47　Moody, *An Injury to All*, pp. 168–9.

48　Alan Greenspan, "The Reagan Legacy," Speech at the Ronald Reagan Library, Simi Valley, California, April 9, 2003. Available at federalreserve.gov.

49　For the fullest account see Joseph A. McCartin, *Collision Course: Ronald Reagan, the Air Traffic Controllers, and the Strike That Changed America,* New York, OUP, 2011.

50　Personal interview with Paul Volcker, March 2003.

51　Allen N. Berger, Anil Kashyap, and Joseph M. Scalise, "The Transformation of the US Banking Industry," Brookings Papers on Economic Activity, No. 2, 1995, p. 57.

52　Steven K. Vogel, *Freer Markets, More Rules: Regulatory Reform in Advanced Industrial Countries*, Ithaca: Cornell University Press, 1996, p. 3.

53　See Gary H. Stern and Ron J. Feldman, *Too Big to Fail: The Hazards of Bank Bailouts,* Washington, DC: Brooking Institute Press, 2009, p. 154.

54　The Federal Home Loan Bank Board and the Federal Savings and Loan Insurance Corporation were simply "not designed to function in the complex new environment of the 1980s." These agencies' examination, supervision and enforcement powers were always weaker than those of federal banking regulators like the Fed and OCC, since they were supposed to be regulating an industry with limited financial scope and relatively few failures that "performed a type of public service." Now that they found themselves so "understaffed, [and] poorly trained for the new environment," they came to be called "the doormats of financial regulation." See FDIC, *History of the 1980s: Lessons for the Future*, vol. 1, Chapter 4: "The Savings and Loan Crisis and Its Relationship to Banking," Washington, DC: FDIC, Division of Research and Statistics, 1992, esp. pp. 171–5.

55 Alan Greenspan, "Remarks Before a Conference on Mortgage Markets and Economic Activity Sponsored by America's Community Bankers," Washington, DC, 1999, pp. 1–2. Available at federalreserve.gov.

56 Berger et al., *Transformation*, pp. 66–7.

57 See White, *The Comptroller and the Transformation of American Banking*, pp. 54, 61; and Meltzer, *History of the Federal Reserve*, p. 1,200; as well as Dean F. Amel and Michael J. Jacowski, "Trends in Banking Structure since the Mid-1970s," *Federal Reserve Bulletin*, March 1989; A. Berger, "The Economic Effects of Technological Progress: Evidence From the Banking Industry," *Journal of Money, Credit, and Banking*, April 2003; and Stephen A. Rhoades, "Bank Mergers and Banking Structure in the United States, 1980–1998," FRB Staff Study 174, August 2000.

58 Michael Lewis, *Liar's Poker*, New York: Penguin 1989, pp. 35–6. See also John Lanchester, *I.O.U.: Why Everyone Owes Everyone and No One Can Pay*, Toronto: McLelland & Stewart, 2010, p. 20.

59 Philip Augar, *The Greed Merchants: How the Investment Banks Played the Free Market Game*, London: Penguin, 2005, p. 56. See Alan Greenspan's comments at the time, "Testimony Before the Subcommittee on Financial Institutions Supervision, Regulation and Insurance," Committee on Banking, Finance and Urban Affairs, US House of Representatives, November 18, 1987, p. 5.

60 Charles D. Ellis, *The Partnership: The Making of Goldman Sachs*, New York: Penguin, 2008, p. 403. See generally Donald Mackenzie, *An Engine, Not a Camera: How Financial Models Shape Markets*, Cambridge, MA: MIT Press, 2006.

61 Gillian Tett, *Fool's Gold*, London: Little Brown, 2009, pp. 4, 17–19. See especially Karen Ho, *Liquidated: An Ethnography of Wall Street*, Durham: Duke University Press, 2009.

62 This data comes from the important report by the US General Accounting Office (GAO), *Financial Derivatives: Action Needed to Protect the Financial System*, May 1994, esp. pp. 36–7.

63 Dick Bryan and Michael Rafferty, *Capitalism with Derivatives*, London: Palgrave, 2006, p. 49.

64 See Tett, *Fool's Gold*, pp. 57–63.

65 Laurence D. Fink, "The Role of Pension Funds and Other Investors in Securitized Debt Markets," in L. T. Kendall and M. J. Fishman, eds., *A Primer on Securitization*, Cambridge, MA: MIT Press, 1976, pp. 121–2.

66 See GAO, *Financial Derivatives*, Appendix I. Pension funds had become a key component of the union-negotiated, highly tax-subsidized "private welfare state": no less than 80 percent of union members had a pension plan by 1979, and this accounted for half the total workforce with employer pension plans. Total private-sector pension

fund assets had doubled between 1970 and 1975, and doubled again between 1975 and 1980 to over $500 billion, spurred by the tax advantages under the Employee Retirement Income Security Act (ERISA) of 1974. See Steven Sass, *The Promise of Private Pensions: The First One Hundred Years*, Cambridge, MA.: Harvard University Press, 1997, p. 139; and Philip E. Davis and Benn Steil, *Institutional Investors*, London: MIT Press, 2001, esp. pp. 247–50.

67 M. Goodfriend, "Monetary Policy Comes of Age: A Twentieth Century Odyssey," FRB of Richmond, *Economic Quarterly* 83: 1 (Winter 1997), p. 1.

68 This was effectively admitted in the 1981 Fed Report, which said that money supply targeting had become virtually impossible with current definitions of money aggregates. See the account by the New York Fed's chief expert on the subject, J. Wenninger, "Money Aggregates and Intermediate Targets," in *Intermediate Targets and Indicators for Monetary Policy: A Critical Survey*, New York: FRBNY, 1990. See also Greenspan's famous speech at Stanford University, "Rules vs. Discretionary Monetary Policy," September 5, 1997. Available at federalreserve.gov.

69 Krippner, "Making of US Monetary Policy," p. 488.

70 See Meltzer, *History of the Federal Reserve*, pp. 1,107, 1,196–7, 1,207.

71 Eric Newstadt, "Neoliberalism and the Federal Reserve," in Panitch and Konings, eds., *American Empire and the Political Economy of Global Finance*, p. 101.

72 Meltzer, *History of the Federal Reserve*, pp. 1,179, 1,205–6.

73 Federal Reserve Bank of New York, 1986 Annual Report, p. 22.

74 Ibid., p. 4.

75 This initially emanated less from the Fed than it did from the Treasury, where Donald T. Regan moved from Merrill Lynch to Treasury secretary loudly promising to put a stop to state intervention in international exchange markets. He secured "a kindred spirit" in the comptroller of the currency, C. T. Conover, who was described by the *American Banker* as "a capitalist to the hilt" determined to "aggressively promote" deregulation. But, as the official history of the OCC points out, the "heyday of deregulation under Conover was actually over soon after it began." Robertson, *The Comptroller and Bank Supervision*, pp. 218–23.

76 Vogel, *Freer Markets*, p. 3. See also F. S. Mishkin, *The Economics of Money*, p. 41.

77 White, *The Comptroller and the Transformation of American Banking*, pp. 61–2.

78 Quoted in Meltzer, *History of the Federal Reserve*, p. 1,105 (emphasis added).

79 White, *The Comptroller and the Transformation of American Banking*, pp. 58–60.

80 This phrase appears to have been used originally by *Business Week* in 1975 to refer to government interventions, notably beginning with Penn Central in 1970, to save corporations that "have become so important to the US economy that government does not dare let one go under." See Gary H. Stern and Ron J. Feldman, *Too Big to Fail: The Hazards of Bank Bailouts*, Washington, DC: Brooking Institution Press, 2009, pp. 14–15, 31–2.

81 Meltzer, *History of the Federal Reserve*, pp. 1,195.

82 Mackenzie, *An Engine, Not a Camera*, p. 184.

83 The Presidential Task Force on Market Mechanisms (the Brady Commission)

appointed to investigate the causes of the crash concluded that the major factor was the failure of stock markets and derivatives markets to operate in sync. For an especially incisive analysis, see Botis Holzer and Yuval Millo, "From Risk to Second-Order Dangers in Financial Markets: Unintended Consequences of Risk Management Systems," *New Political Economy* 10: 2, June 2005.

84 US General Accounting Office, *Financial Crisis Management: Four Financial Crises in 1980s*, May 1997, p. 61.

85 Ibid., p. 62.

86 The quotations here draw on the historical account prepared twenty years later by the Fed's Divisions of Research and Statistics and Monetary Affairs. Mark Carlson, "A Brief History of the 1987 Market Crash with a Discussion of the Federal Reserve Response," Washington, DC: Federal Reserve Board, 2007.

87 J. Stewart and D. Hertzberg, "How the Stock Market Almost Disintegrated a Day After the Crash," *Wall Street Journal*, November 20, 1987.

88 Carlson, "A Brief History," pp. 17–20.

89 See especially the discussion of this in the 1991 Report of the Federal Reserve Bank of New York.

90 See "Ten Years since the Crash of 1987," a special issue of the *Journal of Financial Services Research* 13: 3 (June 1998).

91 See John Embry and Andrew Hepburn, "Move Over, Adam Smith: The Visible Hand of Uncle Sam," Toronto: Sprott Asset Management Inc., 2005, esp. p. 31.

92 1992 Report of the Federal Reserve Bank of New York, p. 9.

93 Suzanne McGee, *Chasing Goldman Sachs*, New York: Crown Business, 2010, p. 278.

94 One prominent example of this was the essay that went on to win the National Magazine Award as the "best public interest article of the year" by Peter G. Peterson— "The Morning After," *Atlantic Monthly*, October 1987. Peterson had been secretary of commerce under Nixon, and subsequently the CEO of Lehman Brothers, before succeeding David Rockefeller at the Council on Foreign Relations in 1984. But this anxiety was equally, or perhaps even more, pronounced on the Left—from Samuel Bowles, David M. Gordon and Thomas E. Weisskopf, *Beyond the Waste Land*, New York: Anchor Books, 1984, to Robert B. Reich, *The Work of Nations*, New York: Vintage, 1992.

95 Michael Ignatieff, "The American Empire: (Get Used To It)," *New York Times Magazine*, January 5, 2003; James H. Stock and Mark W. Watson, "Has the Business Cycle Changed and Why?" NBER Working Paper 9127, September 2002.

96 As Fine et al. put it: "Obsessive preoccupation with the level of the rate of profit is entirely inappropriate, and Marx himself placed much more emphasis on the capacity to continue to accumulate the mass of surplus value produced (as opposed to the rate of profit at which it is realised)." Ben Fine, Aristeidis Petropoulos, and Hajime Sato, "Beyond Brenner's Investment Overhang Thesis: The Case of the Steel Industry," *New Political Economy* 10: 3 (March 2005), p. 61. The overriding importance of the mass of profit was noted even by the most orthodox of Marxist theorists of overaccumulation, Heinrich Grossman, in his 1929 book *The Law of Accumulation and Collapse*

of the Capitalist System: "Why does the capitalist class need to worry if the mass of profit grows? The falling rate of profit is only an index signifying the relative fall of the mass of profits . . . Only in this sense can it also be said that with the fall in the rate of profit the system collapses, since the profit rate falls because the mass of profit relatively decreases." Quoted in Russell Jacoby, "Politics of the Crisis Theory," *Telos*, Spring 1975, p. 35.

97   See Simon Mohun, "Distributive Shares in the US Economy 1964–2001," *Cambridge Journal of Economics* 30: 3 (2006).

98   For wages and labor compensation, see *Economic Report of the President*, Washington, DC, 2002, Tables, B-47, B-48, and B-60. For CEO compensation, see Emmanuel Saez and Thomas Piketty, "Income Inequality in the United States, 1913–1998," *Quarterly Journal of Economics* 118: 1 (2003), Table b4, column 6, updated at elsa.berkeley.edu.

99   US Bureau of Labor Statistics, International Labor Comparisons: Productivity and unit labor costs in manufacturing, Table 1, available at bls.gov. Note as well that productivity measures in manufacturing are much more reliable than in the service sector, where difficulties in measuring output understate the numbers.

100   For a convincing empirical link between the recovery in the rate of profit after the early 1980s and trends in the output per unit of capital stock (capital productivity), see Gerard Duménil and Dominique Lévy, "The Profit Rate: Where and How Much Did It Fall? Did It Recover? (USA 1948–2000)," *Review of Radical Political Economy* 34 (2002). See also Dumenil and Levy, *The Crisis of Neoliberalism*, Cambridge, MA: Harvard University Press, 2011, esp. 267–71 ; and M. J. Webber and D. L. Rigby, *The Golden Age Illusion*, New York: Guilford Press, 1996.

101   See Stacey Tevlin and Karl Whelan, *Explaining the Investment Boom of the 1990s*, Federal Reserve Board Finance and Economics Discussion Series, Working Paper 2000–11, 2000.

102   "[N]et investment, independent of other measurement problems, understates capital formation. When scrapped old equipment is replaced by new equipment of equal market value, no net investment occurs. Nevertheless, the newer vintage plant or equipment embodies a newer technology and is more productive than the older, discarded plant or equipment so that output rises despite the absence of net investment." John A. Tatom, "US Investment in the 1980s: The Real Story," Federal Reserve Bank of St. Louis *Review*, March–April, 1989, p. 12.

103   Richard C. Edwards, "Stages in Corporate Stability and the Risks of Corporate Failure," *Journal of Economic History*, June 1975.

104   *2003 Economic Report of the President*, Washington, DC: US Government Printing Office, 2003, Table B-96.

105   The data here comes from the Regional Economic Accounts of the Bureau of Economic Analysis, US Department of Commerce.

106   *Economic Report of the President 2008*, Washington, DC, 2008, Table B-91.

107   Federal Reserve Board, Flow of Funds, available at federalreserve.gov.

108   For a useful overview of such arguments, see Ozgur Orhangazi, *Financialization and the US Economy*, Northampton, MA: Edward Elgar, 2008.

109 See Greta R. Krippner, "The Financialization of the American Economy," *Socio-Economic Review* 3: 2 (May 2005) for useful data on this, although she does not address the extent to which these activities were connected to accumulation in the sphere of production, along the lines discussed here.

110 See Julie Froud, Colin Haslam, Sukhev Johal, and Karel Williams, "Shareholder Value and Financialization: Consultancy Promises, Management Moves," *Economy and Society* 29: 1 (February 2000).

111 Paul Gompers and Josh Lerner, *The Venture Capital Cycle*, Cambridge, MA: MIT Press, 1999, p. 13. McGee's *Chasing Goldman Sachs* provides an excellent window on Wall Street's role in supplying venture capital for Silicon Valley from the early 1980s onwards; see esp. pp. 34–44.

112 See Nicole Aschoff, *Globalization and Capital Mobility in the Automobile Industry*, PhD thesis, Johns Hopkins University, 2009, as well as her "A Tale of Two Crises: Labor, Capital and Restructuring in the US Auto Industry," *Socialist Register 2012*, London: Merlin, 2011. See also Christopher J. Singleton, "Auto Industry Jobs in the 1980s: A Decade of Transition," *Monthly Labor Review*, February 1992; and Benjamin Collins, Thomas McDonald, and Jay A. Mousa, "The Rise and Decline of Auto Parts Manufacturing in the Midwest," *Monthly Labor Review*, October 2007.

113 GM's nemesis, Toyota, was long used as the counterexample—a corporation that did not suffer from short-termism because of, among other things, the link between finance and industry in Japan. When Toyota's reputation for quality faltered in 2010 with the "spontaneous acceleration" brake scandal, and Toyota was itself accused of sacrificing its long-term reputation for short-term growth, the distinctiveness of Japanese corporate-financial relations suddenly seemed less relevant.

114 See Fine et al., "Beyond Brenner's Investment Overhang Thesis."

115 L. Klein, C. Saltzman and V. Duggal, "Information, Technology and Productivity: The Case of the Financial Sector," *Survey of Current Business*, August 2003; Berger, et al., "Transformation."

116 Rodney Loeppky, "International Restructuring, Health and the Advanced Industrial State," *New Political Economy* 9: 4 (2004), p. 503.

117 National Science Foundation, *Science and Engineering Indicators 2010*, Appendix to chapter 6, Table 6-5. Available at nsf.gov.

118 Lawrence G. Franco, "Global Competition in the 1990s: American Renewal, Japanese Resilience, European Cross-Currents," *Business Horizons*, May–June 2002, p. 25.

119 Ibid., Tables 1, 2.

120 *Economic Report of the President 2002*, Tables B-2 and B-51.

121 This data was supplied on request by the US Bureau of Labor Statistics.

122 The peak of US manufacturing employment had occurred in 1979; by 1999 the number of workers in US manufacturing was 2.5 million lower than in 1979, and below where it had been in 1966, even though overall US employment had doubled since then. *Economic Report*, Tables B-46 and B-51. The decline in manufacturing jobs affected virtually every advanced capitalist country. See André Bernard, "Trends in Manufacturing Employment', *Perspectives*, February 2009, Statistics Canada. Available at statcan.gc.ca.

123 US Bureau of Labor Statistics. Available at ftp.bls.gov.

124 *Science and Engineering Indicators 2010,* Table 6-3.

125 Paul Langley, *The Everyday Life of Global Finance: Saving and Borrowing in Anglo-America,* Oxford: OUP, 2008, p. 164.

126 John Grahl, "Globalized Finance: The Challenge to the Euro," *New Left Review* II/8 (March–April 2001), p. 44.

8. Integrating Global Capitalism

1   Eichengreen, *European Economy since 1945,* p. 250.

2   Andrew Moravcsik, *The Choice for Europe,* Ithaca: Cornell University Press, 1998, p. 238. Although the EMS was created at a time of considerable friction between the Schmidt and Carter administrations, and was viewed with some suspicion as another instance of Germany trying to get the US to bear the brunt of currency adjustment, the US Treasury explicitly decided to adopt a neutral stance towards it. See Yoishi Funabashi, *Managing the Dollar: From the Plaza to the Louvre,* Washington, DC: Institute for International Economics, 1988, p. 31.

3   See R. W. Johnson, *The Long March of the French Left,* New York: St. Martin Press, 1981; and Donald Sassoon, *One Hundred Years of Socialism: The West European Left in the Twentieth Century,* London: I.B. Taurus, 1996.

4   Daniel Singer, *Is Socialism Doomed? The Meaning of Mitterrand,* New York: OUP, 1988, esp. pp. 103, 223, 226.

5   Moravcsik, *Choice for Europe,* p. 247.

6   Baker, *Group of Seven,* p. 25. See also Singer, *Is Socialism Doomed?* pp. 132–3, 245–7. The U-turn was completed in 1983 when the French completely gave up the option of floating the franc by detaching from the EMS. Michel Camdessus, the most senior official in the French Treasury at the time, and subsequently head of the IMF, advised that "withdrawal from the EMS might lead to a 20 percent devaluation and require 20 percent interest rates to stabilize the currency—a point apparently decisive for Miterand." Moravcsik, *Choice for Europe,* p. 271.

7   Bernard H. Moss, *Monetary Union in Crisis: The European Union as a Neo-Liberal Construction,* New York: Palgrave Macmillan, 2005, p. 19.

8   Singer, *Is Socialism Doomed?* p. 267.

9   See Panitch and Leys, *End of Parliamentary Socialism,* esp. Chapter 9.

10 See Jonas Pontusson, *The Limits of Social Democracy: Investment Politics in Sweden,* Ithaca: Cornell University Press, 1992, esp. Chapter 7.

11 As Ryner explained: "The rise of a grey capital market in the wake of sustained inflation, and currency swaps by Swedish multinationals, made it impossible to maintain regulations." J. Magnus Ryner, *Capitalist Restructuring, Globalization and the Third Way: Lessons from the Swedish Model,* New York: Routledge, 2002, p. 161. See also Peter Englund, "The Swedish Banking Crisis: Roots and Consequences," *Oxford Review of Economic Policy,* 15: 3 (1999), pp. 80–97. This is not to say the Swedish state suddenly became "weak"; in fact, its quick response to Sweden's

massive banking crisis of the early 1990s—including socializing the banks' bad debts, and then developing a new pension system to provide them with a steady flow of workers' savings—showed how a "strong state" was able to harness both social benefits and strong unions to the liberalization project in the course of coping with its inherent economic instabilities.

12 Singer, *Is Socialism Doomed?* p. 246.

13 Wolfgang Streek and Sigurd Vitols, "Europe: Between Mandatory Consultation and Voluntary Information," in Joel Rodgers and Wolfgang Streek, eds., *Works Councils: Consultation, Representation and Cooperation in Industrial Relations*, Chicago: University of Chicago Press, 1995, pp. 250–1.

14 Personal interview with the authors, Stuttgart, October 16, 2002. Klemm continued: "This hasn't necessarily reduced the power of the works councils—they get more power in interacting with and educating the local groups. Workers are consequently less stubborn and negative and more open to negotiating change—but they are working harder." For a perceptive look at the complex union politics behind work-time reduction in Germany, see Stephen J. Silva, "Every Which Way But Loose: German Industrial Relations Since 1980," in Andrew Martin and George Ross, eds., *The Brave New World of European Labour*, New York: Berghahn Books, 1999, pp. 99–100.

15 By the time the legislation implementing a thirty-five-hour working week was finally passed in France in 1998, French employers were ready with the type of agreement that was immediately struck with the unions in the engineering sector, whereby the legislation's goal of job-creation was frustrated by annual increases in the ceiling on regular and overtime work. This accommodation of employer demands for "flexibility" was quickly incorporated into the legislation, long before this reform was effectively rescinded in 2005. See Robert Graham, "Unions Split over 35-Hour Week," *Financial Times*, October 14, 1998; and "Turning Back the Clock," *Financial Times*, July 29, 1999.

16 Alain Lipietz, *Towards a New Economic Order*, Oxford: OUP, 1992, pp. 156–9.

17 In the run-up to Maastricht, it was already determined that price stability would become the primary objective of the European Central Bank—so much so that the definition of its responsibilities "in terms of monetary stability is stronger even in comparison to the responsibilities of the Bundesbank as defined in the Bundesbank Act of 1957." Kenneth Dyson, Kevin Featherstone and George Michalopoulos, "Strapped to the Mast: EU Central Bankers Between Global Financial Markets and Regional Integration," in William D. Coleman and Geoffrey R. D. Underhill, eds., *Regionalism and Global Economic Integration: Europe, Asia and the Americas*, London: Routledge, 2002, p. 176.

18 For an excellent recent overview, see John Grahl, ed., *Global Finance and Social Europe*, Cheltenham: Edward Elgar, 2009.

19 Michael Moran, "The State and the Financial Services Revolution: A Comparative Analysis," *West European Politics* 17: 3 (July 1994), p. 169.

20 Tony Golding, *The City: Inside the Great Expectations Machine*, London: Pearson Education, 2001, p. 108.

21 Steven K. Vogel, *Freer Markets, More Rules: Regulatory Reform in Advanced Industrial Countries*, Ithaca: Cornell University Press, 1996, pp. 109, 114.

22 Quoted in Michael Moran, *The Politics of the Financial Services Revolution: The USA, UK and Japan*, New York: Macmillan, 1991, p. 58. This British emulation under Thatcher of a US state agency created during the New Deal is yet another illustration of how little the liberalization of finance was really about freeing markets from states as opposed to making state agencies the enablers of markets.

23 Golding, *The City*, p. 26.

24 Charles D. Ellis, *The Partnership: The Making of Goldman Sachs*, New York: Penguin, 2008, p. 514.

25 Ibid., pp. 520–1.

26 Ibid., p. 531.

27 Thomas Sablowski, "Towards the Americanization of European Finance? The Case of Finance-Led Accumulation in Germany," in Panitch and Konings, eds., *The American Empire and the Political Economy of Global Finance*, p. 146–7.

28 Ibid., Table 7.1, p. 148. Foreign investors also came to control over 40 percent of the capital of the forty largest French companies. See Golding, *The City*, p. 121.

29 Personal interview by the authors with Matthias Kleinert, the senior vice president, and Norbet Orben, the director of policy issues, in Daimler's External Affairs and Public Policy Division, Stuttgart, October 16, 2002. For details on the takeover, see Sydney Finkelstein, "The Daimler-Chrysler Merger," Tuck School of Business case study 1–0071, 2002.

30 Mick Carpenter and Steve Jefferys, *Management, Work and Welfare in Western Europe: A Historical and Contemporary Analysis*, Northampton, MA: Edward Elgar, 2000, p. 154. On the general effect of "share-holder value," see also Photis Lysandrou, "The Transformation of Corporate Europe," in Grahl, *Global Finance and Social Europe*.

31 Personal interview with the authors, Auburn Hills, Michigan, April 25, 2003. Zetsche was at the time the head of Daimler-Chrysler.

32 We are indebted to Sean Starrs, our research assistant at York University, for deriving this data from the reports issued by Thompson Financial Services and UNCTAD's annual *World Investment Report*.

33 Golding, *The City*, p. 89. For the ownership data on France, see *idem*, p. 121; on Germany, see Sablowski, "Towards the Americanization of European Finance?" p. 148.

34 This was confirmed in our personal interviews with various executives of these firms—in particular Martin Leach, president and chief operating officer of Ford of Europe, October 14, 2002.

35 Carpenter and Jefferys, *Management, Work and Welfare in Western Europe*, p. 166.

36 Ibid., p. 119.

37 See Leo Panitch and Sam Gindin, "Euro-Capitalism and American Empire," in D. Coates, ed., *Varieties of Capitalism, Varieties of Approaches*, Basingstoke and New York: Palgrave Macmillan, 2005.

38 For a useful analysis of the dialectic between "path dependency" and "model change"

in this respect, see Stefan Beck, Frank Klobes, and Christoph Sherrer, eds., *Surviving Globalization: Perspectives for the German Economic Model*, Norwell, MA: Springer, 2005.

39 This was how the Commission articulated its objective in its report to the European Council meeting in Stockholm in March 2001. Available at eur-lex.europa.eu.

40 John Grahl, "The European Union and American Power," in Panitch and Leys, *Socialist Register 2005*, London: Merlin, 2004, p. 293.

41 The sources for the data here are WTO (wto.org), UNCTAD (the 2001 *World Investment Report* and stats.unctad.org), and US Survey of Current Business (bea.gov).

42 For relatively recent misleading proclamations of EU ascendance, see Jeremy Rifkin, *The European Dream: How Europe's Vision of the Future is Quietly Eclipsing the American Dream*, Cambridge: Polity Press, 2004; T. R. Reid, *The United States of Europe: The New Superpower and the End of American Supremacy*, New York: Penguin, 2004; Mark Leonard, *Why Europe Will Run the 21st Century*, New York: HarperCollins, 2005; Charles A. Kupchan, "The End of the West," *Atlantic Monthly*, November 2002.

43 See I. Nakatani, "The Economic Role of Financial Corporate Groupings," in M. Aoki, ed., *The Economic Analysis of the Japanese Firm*, Amsterdam: North Holland, 1984; Chalmers R. Johnson, *MITI and the Japanese Economic Miracle*, Palo Alto, CA: Stanford University Press, 1982; and Rob Steven, *Classes in Contemporary Japan*, Cambridge: CUP, 1983.

44 Limited changes introduced which allowed certain flows closely related to trade were deemed enough for Japan to be admitted in 1964 to the IMF and OECD. See J. B. Goodman and L. W. Pauly, "The Obsolescence of Capital Controls?" *World Politics* 1 (1993), esp. p. 308.

45 T. J. Pempel and K. Tsunekawa, "Corporatism without Labor? The Japanese Anomaly," in P. Schmitter and G. Lehmbruch, eds., *Trends Toward Corporatist Intermediation*, London: Sage, 1979, pp. 119–46.

46 On the Japanese adaptation of Glass-Steagall, see Richard Dale, *International Banking Deregulation*, Oxford: Blackwell, 1994, pp. 86–9.

47 The one exception in Europe was Germany, with an inflation rate of 4 percent by 1979.

48 See Armstrong, Glyn, and Harrison, *Capitalism Since 1945*, Appendix Table A1 and Table A3; OECD Historical Statistics, National Accounts 1970–2000 (oecd.org); and US Bureau of Labor, International Statistics (bls.gov).

49 Toru Iwami, "Removing Capital Controls: Japanese Case," Discussion Paper, University of Tokyo, February 1994, pp. 24–5. See also his *Japan in the International Financial System*, London: Macmillan, 1995.

50 Gillian Tett, *Saving the Sun*, New York: HarperCollins, 2003, p. 19. The Ikeda system for providing cheap credit to industry was named after the finance minister during the crucial transition years of the late 1950s.

51 Moran, *Politics of the Financial Services Revolution*, p. 93.

52 Vogel, *Freer Markets*, p. 173.

53 In contrast to Susan Strange's lament that Japan was opened up to the Western-style "casino capitalism," Michael Moran points out that Japanese stock markets "have

historically been, precisely, casinos—and, in British and American terms, casinos where trading took place in remarkably dishonest ways . . . The exchanges were privately controlled bodies whose purpose was to organize arenas for particular sorts of gambling, not to provide funds for industrial investment." *Politics of the Financial Services Revolution*, pp. 112–13.

54 Iwami, "Removing Capital Controls," p. 23.

55 See K. Osugi, "Japan's Experience of Financial Deregulation since 1984 in an International Perspective," *BIS Economic Papers*, no. 26 (January 1990); Iwami, "Removing Capital Controls," p. 5; Goodman and Pauly, "The Obsolescence of Capital Controls?" p. 309.

56 Paul Volcker and Toyoo Gyohten, *Changing Fortunes*, New York: Times Books, 1992, p. 239.

57 R. Taggart Murphy, *The Weight of the Yen*, New York: Norton, 1996, pp. 144–5.

58 Ibid., p. 64.

59 Tett, *Saving the Sun*, p. 22.

60 In 1980 the US and Southeast Asia each accounted for 24 percent of Japanese exports, and Western Europe accounted for 17 percent; by 1984 Southeast Asia's portion had fallen to 22 percent and Western Europe's to 14 percent, while the US portion had risen to 35 percent. Osugi, "Japan's Experience," p. 49, Table 19.

61 Quoted in I. M. Destler and C. Randall Henning, *Dollar Politics: Exchange Rate Policymaking in the United States*, Washington, DC: Institute for International Economics, 1984, p. 33. On the especially important role of Congress banking committees in the mid 1980s, see pp. 99ff.

62 See especially Murphy, *Weight of the Yen*, pp. 153.

63 Ethan B. Kapstein, "Resolving the Regulator's Dilemma: International Coordination of Banking Regulations," *International Organization* 43: 3 (Spring 1989).

64 Fred Bergsten, Preface to Jeffrey A. Frankel, *The Yen-Dollar Agreeement: Liberalizing Japanese Capital Markets*, Washington, DC: Institute for International Economics, 1984, p. ix. In the 1960s this was put forward as obviating the outflow of dollars to Europe; in the 1980s it was put forward as obviating the inflow of Yen to the US. But in both cases the issue for the Treasury was to share the burden that went with being a center of financial capital.

65 Moran, *Politics of the Financial Services Revolution*, pp. 92, 108.

66 Murphy, *Weight of the Yen*, pp. 153.

67 Baker, *Group of Seven*, p. 33. While the discussions focused primarily on the yen–dollar relationship, Funabashi's study of the Plaza Accord shows that they also had to address Germany's concerns that a depreciation of the dollar would increase speculation on the mark and destabilize the EMS. Notably, "orderly" was the word that both Volcker and Karl Otto Pohl, the Bundesbank president, insisted on inserting in the final communiqué, while "at the behest of the US Treasury, each country declared its determination to resist protectionism at home." Funabashi, *Managing the Dollar*, p. 16.

68 Murphy, *The Weight of the Yen*, p. 182.

69 Funabashi, *Managing the Dollar*, p. 131.

70   Murphy, *The Weight of the Yen*, p. 181.

71   Funabashi, *Managing the Dollar*, p. 40.

72   See Tett, *Saving the Sun*, p. 49, as well as R. Taggart Murphy, "Power Without Purpose: The Crisis of Japan's Global Financial Dominance," *Harvard Business Review*, March–April 1989, p. 77.

73   Murphy, *Power Without Purpose*, pp. 72–3.

74   R. Taggart Murphy, "A Loyal Retainer? Japan, Capitalism and the Perpetuation of American Hegemony," in Leo Panitch, Greg Also, and Vivek Chibber, eds., *The Crisis This Time: Socialist Register 2011*, London: Merlin 2010. See also US General Accounting Office, *Financial Crisis Management: Four Financial Crises in the 1980s*, May 1997, pp. 60–3; and Helleiner, *States and the Reemergence of Global Finance*, pp. 184–6.

75   Federal Reserve Bank of New York, 1992 Annual Report, p. 14.

76   Quoted in Arrighi, *Long Twentieth Century*, p. 15, from Joel Kotkin and Euroko Kishimoto, *The Third Century: America's Resurgence in the Asian Era*, 1988, pp. 122–3. Although Arrighi derided the statement, it was proved far more right than wrong.

77   See Japanese External Trade Organization (jetro.go.jp.en.reports).

78   Murphy, "A Loyal Retainer?" and *Weight of the Yen*, pp. 236, 263.

79   See especially Richard Katz, *Japan: The System that Soured*, New York: M.E. Sharpe, 1998.

80   Paul Burkett and Martin Hart-Landsberg, *Development, Crisis and Class Struggle*, New York: St. Martin's, 2000, p. 127.

81   M. Ayhan Kose, Eswar Prasad, Kenneth Rogoff, and Shang-Jin Wei, "Financial Globalization: A Reappraisal," National Bureau of Economic Research, Working Paper 12484, August 2006, Table I; Peter Dicken, *Global Shift: Reshaping the Global Economic Map in the 21st Century*, New York: Guilford, 2003, pp. 34–42. See generally IMF (imf.org), UNCTAD (stats.unctad.org) and WTO (stat.wto.org).

82   For the classic early recognition of this, see Folker Fröbel, Jürgen Heinrichs, and Otto Kreye, *The New International Division of Labour: Structural Unemployment in Industrialised Countries and Industrialisation in Developing Countries*, Cambridge: CUP, 1980.

83   Vivek Chibber, *Locked in Place: State-Building and Late Industrialization in India*, Princeton: Princeton University Press, 2003, pp. 234–5.

84   Ibid., p. 238. See also Martin Hart-Landsberg, *The Rush to Development*, New York: Monthly Review, 1993, p. 158.

85   Michael P. Dooley, David Folkerts-Landau and Peter Garber, "An Essay on the Revived Bretton Woods System," National Bureau of Economic Research, Working Paper 9971, September 2003, p. 2.

86   See Sylvia Maxfield and Ben Ross Schneider, eds., *Business and the State in Developing Countries*, Ithaca: Cornell University Press, 1997; Kevin Hewison, Richard Robinson, and Garry Rodan, *Southeast Asia in the 1990s: Authoritarian Democracy and Capitalism*, London: Allen & Unwin, 1993.

87   As the US Department of Agriculture put it in an important 1967 document surveying its food aid policy, "an important measure of the success of foreign policy goals is the transition of countries from food aid to commercial trade." Cited in Harry Magdoff,

The Age of Imperialism: The Economics of US Foreign Policy, New York: Monthly Review, 1969, p. 135. See also Susan George, *How the Other Half Dies: The Real Reason for World Hunger*, New York: Penguin Books, 1997.

88 Chibber, *Locked in Place*, pp. 234; see also pp. 218–19.

89 See the broad comparative analysis in Ha-Joon Chang, *Globalisation, Economic Development and the Role of the State*, London: Zed Books, 2003, esp. Chapter 7.

90 Robert Pringle, the director of the prestigious "Group of 30" financial leaders, described the "pioneering" role of US banks in this respect, including teaching Latin American central bankers "what a syndicated loan was and how they could benefit from it." Quoted in Jeffrey A. Frieden, *Banking on the World: the Politics of American International Finance*, New York, Harper & Row, 1987, p. 129.

91 Barry Eichengreen and Albert Fishlow, "Contending with Capital Flows: What is Different about the 1990s," in Miles Kahler, ed., *Capital Flows and Financial Crises*, Ithaca: Cornell University Press, 1998, p. 39. See also Jessica Gordon Nembrand, *Capital Controls, Financial Regulation, and Industrial Policy in South Korea and Brazil*, London: Praeger, 1996; and Peter Evans, *Embedded Autonomy: States and Industrial Transformation*, Princeton: Princeton University Press, 1995.

92 Even by 1980, the 120,000 jobs in the maquiladoras corresponded to less than a quarter of the half-million Mexicans that had been repatriated from the US in 1965 when it terminated its guest-worker program and began encouraging cross-border production instead. See William I. Robinson, *Latin America and Global Capitalism: A Critical Globalization Perspective*, Baltimore: Johns Hopkins University Press, 2008, pp. 96–101, esp. Table 2.9. Indeed, by the late 1970s the core of Mexico's export-oriented auto industry had shifted to new assembly and engine plants built outside the maquila zones. These plants were the Mexican nodes of regionally integrated auto production under NAFTA. See R. Constantino and A. Lara, "The Automobile Sector," in Mario Cimoli, ed., *Developing Innovation Systems: Mexico in a Global Context*, New York: Continuum, 2000, pp. 245–6; and Kevin J. Middlebrook, "The Politics of Restructuring: Transnational Firms' Search for Flexible Production in the Mexican Automobile Industry," *Comparative Politics*, April 1991, pp. 275–6.

93 James D. Cockcroft, *Mexico: Class Formation, Capital Accumulation, and the State*, New York: Monthly Review Press, 1983, p. 256.

94 L. William Seidman, *Full Faith and Credit: The Great S&L Debacle and Other Washington Sagas*, New York: Random House, 1993, p. 38. Even though lending to developing countries was initially encouraged, by 1979 both the Treasury's Office of the Comptroller of the Currency and the Federal Reserve Board began to push US banks to undertake "voluntary restraint in new lending." FDIC, *History of the 1980s*, p. 203.

95 Federal Deposit Insurance Corporation, *History of the 1980s: Lessons for the Future*, Washington, DC: FDIC, 1997, Table 5.1a., p. 196.

96 See Frieden, *Banking on the World*, pp. 142–3.

97 Cockcroft, *Mexico*, p. 308. Cockcroft's observation that "more thoroughgoing Cardenas-style reforms, whether in the areas of oil, technology, or heavy industry, or against the TNCs altogether, would have forced Mexico into an anti-imperialist

posture in practice as well as rhetoric" clearly indicates the limits of Portillo's bank nationalization.

98   Volcker and Gyohten, *Changing Fortunes*, pp. 198–9.

99   Ibid., pp. 201, 217

100 Ibid., pp. 210, 213.

101 Ethan Kapstein, "Between Power and Purpose: Central Bankers and the Politics of Regulatory Convergence," *International Organization* 46: 1 (Winter 1991/92), p. 271.

102 Joan E. Spero "Guiding Global Finance," *Foreign Policy* 73 (Winter 1988/89), p. 115. Notably, the largest expansion of the Eurobond market "came after 1982 when the debt crisis shut down the growth of the syndicated Euroloan." See Ephraim Clark, *International Finance*, London: Thomson, 2002, p. 453.

103 See William I. Robinson, *Promoting Polyarchy: Globalization, US Intervention, and Hegemony*, New York: CUP, 1996; and Greg Grandin, *Empire's Workshop: Latin America and the Roots of US Imperialism*, New York: Holt, 2006.

104 See Victor Bulmer-Thomas, *The Economic History of Latin America Since Independence*, Cambridge, UK: CUP, 2003, Table 11.4, p. 383. See also Sebastian Edwards, *Crisis and Reform in Latin America*, Oxford: OUP, 1995.

105 We draw especially here on T. D. Clark's forthcoming York University PhD dissertation, "The State and the Making of Capitalist Modernity in Chile"; see also Javier Martínez and Álvaro Díaz, *Chile: The Great Transformation*, Washington, DC: Brookings, 1996; Eduardo Silva, "Business Elites, the State and Economic Change in Chile," in Maxfield and Schneider, *Business and the State in Developing Countries*; and Marcus Taylor, "From National Development to 'Growth with Equity': Nation-Building in Chile, 1950–2000," *Third World Quarterly* 27: 1 (2006).

106 Judith Adler Hellman, *Mexican Lives*, New York: New Press, 1994, pp. 91–2, 110–11.

107 Robinson, *Latin America and Global Capitalism*, pp. 5, 15.

108 See especially the essays by Sylvia Maxfield on Mexico and Meredith Woo-Cuming on South Korea, in Michael Loriaux, *Capital Ungoverned: Liberalizing Finance in Interventionist States*, Ithaca: Cornell University Press, 1997.

109 Chibber, *Locked in Place*, p. 253. See also Atul Kohli, "The Politics of Economic Growth in India, 1980–2005" *Economic and Political Weekly*, April 1 and April 8, 2006.

110 Ananya Mukherjee Reed, *Perspectives on the Indian Corporate Economy*, New York: Palgrave, 2001, p. 175.

111 See Fuat Ercan and Sebnem Oguz, "Rethinking Anti-Neoliberal Strategies Through the Perspective of Value Theory: Insights from the Turkish Case," in *Science and Society* 71: 2 (2007). See also Nilgun Onder, "The Political Economy of the State and Social Forces: Changing Forms of State-Labour Relations in Turkey," PhD dissertation, York University, 2000.

112 Yildiz Atasoy, "The Islamic Ethic and the Spirit of Turkish Capitalism Today," in L. Panitch and C. Leys, eds., *Socialist Register 2008*, London: Merlin 2007, p. 121.

113 See Andrew Sobel, *State Institutions, Private Incentives, Global Capital*, Ann Arbour: University of Michigan Press, 1999, pp. 89–105.

114 Robert W. Cox, "Global Perestroika," R. Miliband and L. Panitch, eds., *Socialist Register 1992*, London: Merlin, 1992, p. 26.

115 The FDI that went to Eastern Europe was generally concentrated in a small number of countries and in specific sectors. Auto in particular was a site of great interest, and the investments here were not in green-field sites but in the takeover of the existing producers. By 1998, seven of the nine producers were majority owned by Western car companies. See Rob van Tulder and Winfried Ruigrok, "European Cross-National Production Networks in the Auto Industry: Eastern Europe as the Low End of European Car Complex," Berkeley Roundtable on the International Economy, Working Paper 121, 1998, p. 3.

116 Michael J. Haynes, "Labour, Exploitation and Capitalism in Russia Before and After 1991," *Critical Sociology* 34: 4 (2008), p. 571. See also Branko Milanovic, *Income Inequality and Poverty during the Transition from Planned Economy to Market Economy*, Washington, DC: World Bank, 1998.

117 Gowan, *Global Gamble*, pp. 191, 241.

118 See Michael S. Minor, "The Demise of Expropriation as an Instrument of LDC Policy, 1980–1992," *Journal of International Business Studies* 25: 1 (1994), Table 1, p. 180.

119 Thomas W. O'Donnell, "The Political Economy of Oil in the US-Iran Crisis: US Globalized Oil Interests vs. Iranian Regional Interests," International Affairs Working Paper, New School University, October 2009, Available at gpia.info.

120 Randall Germain, *The International Organization of Credit*, Cambridge, MA: CUP, 1997, pp. 114–15. For an up-to-date analysis of the development of financial capital in the Gulf, see Adam Hanieh, *Capitalism and Class in the Gulf Arab States*, New York: Palgrave Macmillan, 2011.

121 See Patrick Bond, *Talk Left, Walk Right: South Africa's Frustrated Global Reforms*, Scottsville, SA: University of KwaZulu-Natal Press, 2004, Figure 5, p. 7.

122 *World Development Report 1997: The State in a Changing World*, Washington, DC: World Bank, 1997, p. 134.

123 World Bank, *The State in a Changing World*, pp. 1, 25.

123 Mike Davis, *Planet of Slums*, New York, Verso, 2006.

124 Ibid.

9. Rules of Law: Governing Globalization

1 See Tony Porter, *Globalization and Finance*, Cambridge: Polity Press, 2005, pp. 60, 80.

2 James M. Boughton, "The IMF and the Force of History," IMF Working Paper, May 2004, p. 18.

3 See China Miéville, "The Commodity-Form Theory of International Law: An Introduction," *Leiden Journal of International Law* 17 (2004), p. 297. For a powerful analysis of the co-evolution of imperialism, capitalist classes, nation states and legal orders, see Saskia Sassen, *Territory, Authority, Rights: From Medieval to Global Assemblages*, Princeton: Princeton University Press, 2006.

4 Judith Goldstein and Richard Steinberg, "Regulatory Shift: The Rise of Judicial

Liberalization at the WTO," in Walter Mattli and Ngaire Woods, *The Politics of Global Regulation*, Princeton: Princeton University Press, 2009, pp. 217–18.

5   See Robert Hudec, *Enforcing International Trade Law*, Salem, NH: Butterworth, 1993, esp. p. 303.

6   Nitsan Chorev, *Remaking US Trade Policy*, Ithaca: Cornell University Press, 2007, p. 139.

7   Jamey Essex, "Getting What You Pay For: Authoritarian Statism and the Geographies of US Trade Liberalization Strategies," *Studies in Political Economy* 80 (Autumn 2007), pp. 84–6.

8   Chorev, *Remaking US Trade Policy*, pp. 32, 87–8, 92.

9   Commission on International Trade and Investment Policy Report to the President, *United States International Economic Policy in an Interdependent World* (the Williams Report), Washington, DC, 1971, p. ix.

10   Steve Dryden, *Trade Warriors: USTR and the American Crusade for Free Trade*, New York: OUP, 1995, esp. p. 165.

11   Chorev, *Remaking US Trade Policy*, pp. 150, 157.

12   As Canadian exports were increasingly directed towards US markets, and as US MNCs were welcomed with open arms as "good corporate citizens" and funded by Canadian banks, Canada had completed its move from formal colonial status as a privileged white Dominion in the old British Empire to a formally independent, but in reality more and more dependent status in the US empire. Yet this "rich dependency" status was still a privileged one, and Canadians shared in the spoils that went with American hegemony in the postwar order. See Leo Panitch, "Dependency and Class in Canadian Political Economy," *Studies in Political Economy* 6 (Autumn 1981).

13   See Stephen Clarkson, *Uncle Sam and Us: Globalization, Neoconservatism and the Canadian State*, Toronto: University of Toronto Press, 2002.

14   Michael Hart and Bill Dymond, cited in Alan S. Alexandroff, ed., *Investor Protection in the NAFTA and Beyond*, C. D. Howe Institute Policy Study 44, Ottawa: Renouf, 2006. p. 10.

15   Ian Robinson, *North American Free Trade as if Democracy Mattered*, Ottawa: Canadian Centre for Policy Alternatives, 1993, p. 2. Stephen Clarkson and Stepan Wood would later put the point this way: "NAFTA provides by far the most extensive protection of private property rights in Canada. Its rights for foreign investors are unprecedented in Canadian law and inconsistent with the treatment of private property in the Canadian constitution, which gives no protection against the taking of private property." *A Perilous Imbalance: The Globalization of Canadian Law and Governance*, Vancouver: UBC Press: 2010, p. 77.

16   Robinson, *North American Free Trade*, p. 20.

17   Gus Van Harten and Martin Loughlin, "Investment Treaty Arbitration as a Species of Global Administrative Law," *European Journal of International Law* 17: 1 (2006), p. 149.

18   As we saw in Chapter 1, after the Civil War the US Supreme Court went beyond the commonly accepted "takings" rule in the Fifth Amendment of the Constitution (which dealt with the confiscation of land for public use purposes) to require compensation in situations where the use of taxation or regulatory powers might lower expected profits or the market value of private property and corporate assets. This interpretation was further expanded in the early 1920s in a majority opinion by Oliver

Wendell Holmes that articulated the modern regulatory takings doctrine: "while property may be regulated to a certain extent, if it goes too far, it will be recognized as a taking." This shifted the judicial principle from the government's *intent* to expropriate, and the specific state power exercised, to the *effect* of state action on the use and enjoyment of private property. See Morton Horwitz, *The Transformation of American Law 1780–1860*, Cambridge, MA: Harvard University Press, 1977.

19 Dryden, *Trade Warriors*, p. 369.

20 *Business Week*, November 22, 1993, p. 34.

21 Quoted in *Globe and Mail Report on Business*, Toronto, November 1, 1993.

22 See Frederick, W. Mayer, *Interpreting NAFTA: The Science and Art of Political Analysis*, New York: Columbia University Press, 1998, esp. Chapter 7.

23 *Business Week*, November 22, 1993, p. 35.

24 Ronald W. Cox, "Transnational Capital, the US State and Latin American Trade Agreements," *Third World Quarterly* 29: 8 (2008), pp. 1,530, 1,532.

25 See Maxwell A. Cameron and Brian W. Tomlin, *The Making of NAFTA: How the Deal was Done*, Ithaca: Cornell University Press, 2000, pp. 185–200.

26 This is the term Clarkson and Wood deploy in *A Perilous Imbalance* in indentifying NAFTA as part of the "emerging supraconstitution" which contributes to "making the world safe for transnational capital." See also their "NAFTA Chapter 11 as Supraconstitution," Comparative Research in Law and Political Economy (CLPE) Research Paper 43, Osgoode Hall Law School, Toronto 2009, pp. 5–7.

27 Transcript of interview with Lawrence Summers for the Public Broadcasting Service documentary in 2002, *The Commanding Heights* (pbs.org).

28 Goldstein and Steinberg, "Regulatory Shift," p. 218.

29 World Bank, "World Development Indicators, United States: Trade as Percentage of GDP." Available at databank.worldbank.org.

30 Cited in Chorev, *Remaking US Trade Policy*, p. 161.

31 Ibid., p. 208.

32 David Schneiderman, *Constitutionalizing Economic Globalization: Investment Rules and Democracy's Promise*, Cambridge: CUP, 2008, pp. 25–6.

33 Kenneth J. Vandervelde, "The BIT Program: A Fifteen Year Appraisal," panel on "The Development and Expansion of Bilateral Investment Treaties," *Proceedings of the 86th Annual Meeting of the American Society of International Law*, April 1–4, 1992, pp. 534.

34 Vandervelde, "The BIT Program," p. 536. See Robert A. Pastor, *Congress and the Politics of US Foreign Policy*, Berkeley: University of California Press, 1980, esp. p. 292.

35 Vicky Been and Joel C. Beauvais, "The Global Fifth Amendment: NAFTA's Investment Protections and the Misguided Quest for an International 'Regulatory Takings' Doctrine," *New York University Legal Review* 78 (2003).

36 See Kenneth Vandervelde, *US International Investment Agreements*, Oxford: OUP, 2009, p. 470.

37 Vandervelde, *US International Investment Agreements*, p. 34.

38 See International Center for the Settlement of Investment Disputes (ICSID), available at icsid.worldbank.org; Vandervelde, "The BIT Program," p. 539.

39   José E. Alvarez, introductory remarks to panel on "The Development and Expansion of Bilateral Investment Treaties," *Proceedings of the 86th Annual Meeting of the American Society of International Law*, April 1–4, 1992, p. 532.

40   Yves Dezalay and Bryant G. Garth, *Dealing in Virtue: International Commercial Arbitration and the Construction of a Transnational Legal Order*, Chicago: University of Chicago Press, 1997.

41   Gus Van Harten, *Investment Treaty Arbitration and Public Law*, Oxford: OUP, 2007, pp. 63–4.

42   The Harvard Draft came to be regularly cited as an authoritative source in ICSID arbitration awards even though it has never been signed into law by a state or a multilateral organization, and is still seen as a distillation of the distinctive American perspective on the law of investor protection and investment treaty interpretation. One arbitrator has referred to it as "something of a high water mark in the statement of the law for the protection of aliens." Andrew Newcombe and Lluis Paradell, *Law and Practice of Investment Treaties*, The Hague: Kluwer Law International, 2009: 22–3.

43   Dezalay and Garth, *Dealing in Virtue*, p. 98. See also their "Law, Lawyers and Social Capital: 'Rule of Law' versus Relational Capitalism," *Social and Legal Studies* 6: 1 (1997); and "Law, Lawyers, and Empire" in *The Cambridge History of Law in America*, Volume III, Cambridge: CUP, 2008.

44   R. Daniel Keleman and Eric C. Sibbit, "The Globalization of American Law," *International Organization* 58, Winter 2004, p. 104.

45   The *American Lawyer* recounted one graphic example of this in the "intense, complex, and protracted" negotiations in the late 1990s between the BP-led consortium of companies and states involved in building the $3.5 billion, 1,000-plus-mile pipeline designed to carry oil from under the Caspian across Azerbaijan, Georgia, and Turkey to western markets. The US law firms involved in drafting the commercial contracts also drafted a binding intergovernmental treaty between the three host countries that did not "trump only current domestic laws, *but also all future laws*—for up to 60 years." The juridical enforcement of this was placed in the hands not of local courts but of private arbitration under United Kingdom law. George Goolsby, the lead lawyer for the US Baker Botts law firm working for all three host governments, put it this way: "The foreign companies want confidence . . . Without having to amend local laws, we went above or around them by using a treaty." See Daphne Eviatar, "Wildcat Lawyering," *American Lawyer*, November 24, *2002*, p. 80.

46   Goldstein and Steinberg, "Regulatory Shift", pp. 221–37.

47   See "Bilateral Investment Treaties 1995–2006, Trends in Investment Rulemaking," UNCTAD, Geneva, 2007, esp. p. xi.

48   Daniel Price, cited in Been and Beauvais, "The Global Fifth Amendment," p. 55. See also Vicky Been, "Does an International 'Regulatory Takings' Doctrine Make Sense?" *NYU Environmental Law Journal* 11, pp. 49–63.

49   See *World Investment Report 2010: Investing in a Low-Carbon Economy*, UNCTAD: Geneva, 2010, p. 16; and Jiro Honda, *Do IMF Programs Improve Economic Governance?* Washington, DC: International Monetary Fund, 2008, esp. p. 4.

50 See Ngaire Woods, "The United States and the International Financial Institutions: Power and Influence within the World Bank and the IMF," in R. Foot, S. N. MacFarlane and M. Mastanduno, eds., *US hegemony and International Organizations: The United States and Multilateral Institutions*, Oxford and New York: OUP, 2003; and Ruth Felder, "From Bretton Woods to Neoliberal Reforms: The International Financial Institutions and American Power," in Panitch and Konings, *American Empire and the Political Economy of Global Finance*.

51 Quoted in Benjamin Cohen, *In Whose Interest? International Banking and American Foreign Policy*, New Haven: Yale University Press, 1986, p. 229.

52 See Baker, *Group of Seven*, pp. 109–10.

53 Porter, *Globalization and Finance*, esp. pp. 79–81. See also Walter Mattli, "Public and Private Governance in International Standard Setting," in Miles Kahler and David Lake, eds., *Governance in a Global Economy*, Princeton: Princeton University Press, 2003.

54 For a useful elaboration of the concept of the "dominant regulatory innovator," see especially Beth A. Simmons, "The International Politics of Harmonization: The Case of Capital Market Regulation," *International Organization* 55: 3 (Summer 2001).

55 Kapstein, "Architects of Stability?" p. 6. See also Chapter 6, above.

56 White, *The Comptroller and the Transformation of American Banking*, p. 56. Community banks were required to keep a minimum primary capital-to-asset ratio of 6 percent, while a 5 percent ratio was set for large regional. The other regulatory agencies were initially less enthusiastic than the Fed in adopting these new standards, for both political and technical reasons.

57 See Ethan Kapstein, "Resolving the Regulator's Dilemma: International Coordination of Banking Regulations," *International Organization* 43: 2 (Spring 1989), esp. p. 336, as well as his *Governing the Global Economy*, Cambridge: Harvard University Press, 1994.

58 Banks were required to maintain a base of 8 percent of their balance-sheet and off-balance-sheet assets in core capital (defined as Tier 1 capital plus Tier 2 capital), and were required to keep at least half of these core liabilities in Tier 1 capital. Prior to the accord, not only were the reserves held by most international banks very low, standing generally between 2 and 5.5 percent, but capital was only required to be held against on-balance-sheet assets, and the quality and liquidity of bank liabilities was not subject to any form of supervision. By weighing the credit risk of the assets held by banks in calculating core capital requirements, the Basel Accord focused attention on the quality of loans and opened up the asset side of bank balance sheets to regulatory scrutiny. As against the standardized approach, which required capital to be set against each asset equally, Basel I divided assets into five basic tranches (OECD government debt, public sector debt, development bank debt, residential mortgages, private sector debt) and set fixed credit-risk weights for each class, ranging from zero to 100 percent; assets with the latter weighting required an equal amount of capital to be held against the risk of default, whereas assets with a zero rating did not require banks to hold any backup reserves. See especially Kapstein, "Between Power and Purpose."

59 This tempers the distinction Kahler and Lake make between two "modes of

international governance": "networks" whereby states coordinate and share regulatory authority, and "hierarchy" whereby states transfer regulatory authority to dominant states. Miles Kahler and David Lake, "Economic Integration, Global Governance: Why So Little Supranationalism?" in Walter Mattli and Ngaire Woods, eds., *The Politics of Global Regulation*, Princeton: Princeton University Press, 2009.

60 Timothy Sinclair, *The New Masters of Capital: American Bond Rating Agencies and the Politics of Creditworthiness*, Ithaca: Cornell University Press, 2005, p. 46.

61 See Eric Newstadt, "Neoliberalism and the Federal Reserve," in Panitch and Konings, *American Empire and the Political Economy of Global Finance*, p. 106–7.

62 Bank of International Settlements, "Strengthening Banking Supervision Worldwide: Recent Initiatives of the Basle Committee on Banking Supervision," Submission for the G7 Heads of Government at the June 1997 Denver Summit, Basel, April 1997, p. 5. The countries were Brazil, Chile, China, the Czech Republic, Hong King, Hungary, India, Indonesia, Korea, Malaysia, Mexico, Poland, Russia, Singapore, and Thailand.

63 Christopher Rude, "The Role of Financial Discipline in Imperial Strategy," *Socialist Register 2005*, London: Merlin, 2004, esp. pp. 90–1.

64 See Porter, *Globalization and Finance*, p. 64; and Bank of International Settlements, "Strengthening Banking Supervision Worldwide," p. 4.

65 For a comprehensive analysis of the "new monetary policy consensus" that gave rise to the push for central bank independence and inflation-targeting regimes in developing countries, see the independent report for the UNDP by Alfredo Saad Filho, "Pro-Poor Monetary and Anti-Inflation Policies: Developing Alternatives to the New Monetary Policy Consensus," Centre for Development Policy and Research Discussion Paper 2405, School of Oriental and African Studies, London, 2005.

66 Volcker and Gyohten, *Changing Fortunes*, p. 181.

67 Baker, *Group of Seven*, p. 79.

68 For an earlier discussion of this in the context of a critique of Robert Cox's "outside-in" approach to the shift in the hierarchy of state apparatuses, see Panitch, "Globalization and the State."

69 See John Williamson, "Did the Washington Consensus Fail?," speech at the Center for Strategic and International Studies, November 6, 2002; and "A Short History of the Washington Consensus," paper presented to the conference on From the Washington Consensus to a New Global Governance, Fundacion CIDOB, Barcelona, September 24–25, 2004, p. 7.

70 Devesh Kapur, John P. Lewis, and Richard Webb, *The World Bank: Its First Half Century*, Washington, DC: Brookings Institution Press, 1997, p. 510.

71 Frieden, *Banking on the World*, p. 65.

72 Harold James, "From Grandmotherliness to Governance: The Evolution of IMF Conditionality," *Finance and Development*, December 1998, p. 45.

73 Sarah. L. Babb and Bruce G. Carruthers, "Conditionality: Forms, Function and History," *Annual Review of Law and Social Science* 4 (2008), p. 19. See also Devesh Kapur and Richard Webb, *Governance-Related Conditionalities of the International*

Financial Institutions, New York: United Nations Conference on Trade and Development, 2000; and Louis Pauly, "What New Architecture? International Financial Institutions and Global Economic Order," *Global Governance* 7 (2001).

74 See the comprehensive survey by Morris Goldstein, "IMF Structural Programs," Institute for International Economics, 2000, esp. pp. 41–2.

75 Benjamin Cohen, "Capital Controls: The Neglected Option," in Geoffrey R. D. Underhill and Xiaoke Zhang, eds., *International Financial Governance under Stress: Global Structures versus National Imperatives*, Cambridge: CUP, 2003, pp. 71–2.

76 See Joel M. Ngugi, "Policing Neo-Liberal Reforms: The Rule of Law as an Enabling and Restrictive Discourse," *University of Pennsylvania Journal of International Economic Law* 26: 3 (2006); as well as Paul Cammack, "Neoliberalism, the World Bank, and the New Politics of Development," in U. Kothari and M. Minogue, eds., *Development Theory and Practice: Critical Perspectives*, London: Palgrave, 2002, pp. 157–78.

77 *World Development Report 1997: The State in a Changing World*, Washington, DC: World Bank, 1997. The quotations here and in the next two paragraphs are from pp. 25, 48–51 and 64–5 (emphasis in the original). See Leo Panitch, "'The State in a Changing World': Social-Democratizing Global Capitalism?" *Monthly Review* 50: 5 (October 1998).

78 *World Development Report 1997*, p. 152.

79 Ben Thirkell-White "The IMF, Good Governance and Middle-Income Countries," *European Journal of Development Research* 15: 1 (2003), p. 99.

80 On the US Treasury's lack of enthusiasm due to its other priorities, see especially the account of the interview with Larry Summers in Rawi Abdelal, *Capital Rules: The Construction of Global Finance*, Cambridge, MA: Harvard University Press, 2007, p. 139. Abdelal's central argument that Europe "made globalization" by taking the lead in pushing for the OECD and IMF rule changes to require capital account liberalization not only downplays the US's structural power in the making of global capitalism, but also ignores the primary responsibility that fell to the US when quick and decisive action was needed to be taken in the face of financial crises, as we shall see in the next chapter.

81 Gowan, *Global Gamble*, pp. 212–3. The Paris Club of international creditors agreed in 1991 to reschedule $30 billion of Polish official debt in two three-year phases, on terms allowing a minimum 50 percent forgiveness of that debt—it could be larger if the creditor chose, as the US did in forgiving 70 percent of the debt it was owed by Poland, provided that Poland remained in compliance with its IMF adjustment agreement. See Jonathan E. Sanford, "Debt Owed to the United States by Foreign Countries: Recent Scheduling and Forgiveness," Congressional Research Service, Library of Congress, November 1993.

82 "The IMF was pretending that it was seeing a lot of reforms in Russia. Russia was pretending to conduct reforms." Boris Fyodorov, Yeltsin's former finance minister, quoted in Michael Gordon, "IMF Urged by Russian Not to Give More Aid," *New York Times*, October 1, 1998. It was Michael Mussa, the IMF's chief economist, who spoke in terms of "lowering the hurdles" for Russia. See Bluestein, *The Chastening:*

Inside the Crisis that Rocked the Global Financial System and Humbled the IMF, New York: Public Affairs, 2001, p. 243.

83 Yves Dezalay and Bryant G. Garth, *The Internationalization of Palace Wars: Lawyers, Economists, and the Contest to Transform Latin American States*, Chicago: University of Chicago Press, 2002, p. 249. Not surprisingly, serious assessments of the World Bank's projects of legal reform in several countries showed a high rate of failure. See Kapur and Webb, *Governance-Related Conditionalities*, p. 11.

84 Quoted in James, "From Grandmotherliness to Governance," p. 46.

85 UNCTAD, *Bilateral Investment Treaties 1959–1999*, Geneva: United Nations, 2000, Figure 1; and UNCTAD Press Release, "Foreign Direct Investment on the Rise," February 9, 1998. A complete BIT database is available at icsid.worldbank.org. See also the useful overview by Mary Hallward-Driemeier, "Do Bilateral Investment Treaties Attract FDI?" World Bank, Working Paper 3121, August 2003; and Simone Ptillo and Muao F. Guillen, "Globalization Pressures and the State: The Worldwide Spread of Central Bank Independence," *American Journal of Sociology* 110: 6 (May 2005), pp. 1,770–1.

86 Lawrence Summers, "Go with the Flow," *Financial Times*, March 11, 1998.

10. The New Imperial Challenge: Managing Crises

1 According to two leading US political scientists who had close ties to the foreign policy establishment in the 1990s, this was a role that "other countries have accepted and, indeed, consented to through decades of past practice . . . This authority, in turn, rests on a perception of the reliable American stewardship of international financial markets." Miles Kahler and David Lake, "Economic Integration, Global Governance: Why So Little Supranationalism?" in Walter Mattli and Ngaire Woods, eds., *The Politics of Global Regulation*, Princeton: Princeton University Press, 2009, p. 267.

2 Alan Greenspan was reappointed by Clinton as Federal Reserve chair in March 1996; Robert Rubin moved from Goldman Sachs to become the first director of Clinton's new National Economic Council in 1993, before becoming Treasury secretary in 1995; while Lawrence Summers, a Harvard economist who was promoted in 1993 from chief economist at the Word Bank to undersecretary for international affairs at the Treasury, became Rubin's deputy secretary in 1995, and then secretary of the Treasury in 1999.

3 See Alan Greenspan, *The Age of Turbulence*, New York: Penguin, 2007, pp. 367–76; Alan Greenspan, "Global Challenges," speech to the Council on Foreign Relations, New York, July 12, 2000; and Richard W. Stevenson, "Anticipate Financial Crises and Prepare, Greenspan Says," *New York Times*, July 13, 2000. On the fundamental pragmatism, rather than commitment to neoclassical intellectual consistency, of G7 finance ministers and central bankers in general, see Baker, *Group of Seven*, pp. 69–70.

4 On Rubin's "whole adult life experience" in financial markets, see Rubin and Weinberg, *In an Uncertain World*, esp. Chapters 2 and 3. The quotation here is from the full transcript of the interview with Rubin for the PBS 2002 documentary *The Commanding Heights*, available at pbs.org.

5   Robert Litan, with Jonathan Roach and a Preface by Robert Rubin, *American Finance for the 21st Century*, Washington, DC: Brookings Institute, 1998, p. 5.

6   Quoted in Blustein, *The Chastening*, p. 295.

7   Carmen M. Reinhart and Kenneth S. Rogoff, "This Time is Different: A Panoramic View of Eight Centuries of Financial Crises," NBER Working Paper No. 13882, March 2008, Table A.3.

8   Pauly, *Who Elected the Bankers?* esp. p.121. See also Michael Bordo, Ashoka Mody, and Nienke Oomes, "Keeping the Capital Flowing: The Role of the IMF," IMF Working Paper WP/04/197, October 2004; and Barry Eichengreen and Richard Portes, "Managing the Next Mexico," in Peter Kenen, ed., *From Halifax to Lyon: What Has Been Done about Crisis Management?*, Princeton: International Finance Section, Department of Economics, Princeton University, 1996.

9   Rubin, *In an Uncertain World*, p. 18

10 See William R. Cline, *International Debt Reexamined*, Washington, DC: Institute for International Economics, 1995.

11 See Barry Eichengreen, "Strengthening the International Financial Architecture: Where Do We Stand?" *Asean Economic Bulletin* 17: 2 (August 2000).

12 Quoted in Stephen Grenville, "Capital Flows and Crises," in Gregory Noble and John Ravenhill, eds., *The Asian Crisis and the Architecture of Global Finance*, Cambridge: CUP, 2000, pp. 37–45.

13 See Dani Rodrik, "The Social Costs of Foreign Exchange Reserves," National Bureau of Economic Research, Working Paper 11952, January 2006, Figure 1.

14 See Jeffrey A. Winters, "The Determinants of Financial Crisis in Asia," in T. J. Pempel, ed., *The Politics of the Asian Economic Crisis*, Ithaca: Cornell University Press, 1999, esp. pp. 84–5.

15 See C. Randall Henning, *The Exchange Stabilization Fund: Slush Money or War Chest?* Washington, DC: Institute for International Economics, 1999, esp. pp. 24–9.

16 Quoted in Pauly, *Who Elected the Bankers?* p. 120.

17 J. Bradford DeLong and Barry Eichengreen, "Between Meltdown and Moral Hazard: The International Monetary and Financial Policies of the Clinton Administration," in J. A. Frankel and Peter R. Orszag, eds., *American Policy in the 1990s*, Cambridge, MA: MIT Press, 2002, pp. 196–7.

18 Ibid.

19 These were the words used to describe Mexico in a Reuters story in September 1992 by Janet Duncan, "Mexico Old IMF Hand 10 Years After Debt Crisis." See also Sebastian Edwards, "Capital Inflows into Latin America: A Stop-Go Story?" NBER Working Paper 6441, March 1998.

20 See John Weiss, "Trade Liberalization in Mexico in the 1980s: Concepts, Measures and Short-Run Effects, *Review of World Economics* 128: 4 (1992); Guillermo Ortiz Martinez, "What Lessons Does the Mexican Crisis Hold for Recovery in Asia?" *Finance and Development* (IMF) 32: 2 (June 1998); James D. Cockcroft, *Mexico's Hope*, New York: Monthly Review Press, 1998, Table 11, p. 171; and World Development Indicators, available at databank.worldbank.org.

21 This move was designed to prove the Clinton administration's commitment to strong dollar and anti-inflation policies. But its timing coincided with the questions being raised in financial markets about whether the Mexican government would relax its monetary and fiscal discipline as the concession to democracy required to elect the governing PRI party's candidate when the "sexenio"—the six-year presidential term—came to an end in the fall. The Zapatista uprising in Chiapas (which began the day of NAFTA's introduction on January 1, 1994) was followed just a few months later by the assassination of the leading PRI presidential candidate. The hopes of the Treasury and Fed that capital inflows to Mexico would resume soon after the presidential election in the autumn were shattered after an attempt at a managed devaluation of the peso failed to reassure international financial markets, and instead induced a massive outflow of capital. See DeLong and Eichengreen, "Between Meltdown and Moral Hazard," pp. 197–11; as well as the excellent account by Arminio Fraga, "Crisis Prevention and Management: Lessons from Mexico," in Peter Kenen, ed., *From Halifax to Lyon: What Has Been Done about Crisis Management*, Princeton: International Finance Section, Department of Economics, Princeton University, 1996.

22 Michel Camdessus, "Argentina and the Challenge of Globalization," Address to the Academy of Economic Science, Buenos Aires, May 27, 1996, available at imf.org; on Gingras's use of the term, see Rubin, *In an Uncertain World*, p. 16.

23 US Federal Reserve, "Transcript of Federal Open Market Committee Telephone Conference," January 13, 1995, p. 7. Available at www.federalreserve.gov.

24 See Henning, *Exchange Stabilization Fund*, pp. 62–5.

25 Rubin, *In an Uncertain World*, p. 25. For Greenspan's expectation that "there will be a considerable amount of posturing, and it will pass," see the FOMC "Transcript," p. 7.

26 See Nora Claudia Lustig, "Mexico in Crisis, the US to the Rescue," *UCLA Journal of International Law and Foreign Affairs* 2: 1 (Spring/Summer 1997); Henning, *Exchange Stabilization Fund*, pp. 64–6; Pauly, *Who Elected the Bankers?* pp. 124–5.

27 Saori N. Katada, *Banking on Stability: Japan and the Cross-Pacific Dynamics of International Financial Crisis Management*, Ann Arbor: University of Michigan Press, 2001, p. 163.

28 Blustein, *The Chastening*, pp. 172–3.

29 Quoted ibid., p. 174.

30 Lustig, "Mexico in Crisis, the US to the Rescue," p. 27.

31 Rubin, *In an Uncertain World*, p. 35.

32 Ibid., p. 34.

33 Shahid Javed Burki and Sebastian Edwards, *Latin America after Mexico: Quickening the Pace*, Washington, DC: World Bank, 1995, p. 1.

34 DeLong and Eichengreen, "Between Meltdown and Moral Hazard," p. 219.

35 See Grenville, "Capital Flows and Crises," Table 2.1, p. 38; Pempel, *Politics of the Asian Financial Crisis*, Table 1.1, p. 8; and especially Graciela Kaminsky and Carmen Reinhardt, "Bank Lending and Contagion: Evidence from the Asian Crisis," available at home.gwu.edu.

36 See Mitchell Bernard, "East Asia's Tumbling Dominoes: Financial Crises and the Myth of the Regional Model," in Leo Panitch and Colin Leys, eds., *Socialist Register*

1999, London: Merlin Press, 1999, pp. 185, 189, 191. The articulation between the local and the global in Thailand (which was the center of US regional operations during the Vietnam War) was rooted in the way Japanese industrial capital used Thailand as a central export platform. When Thailand became one of the main victims of the debt crisis induced by the Volcker shock in the 1980s, it was subjected to a classic IMF structural-adjustment program. But coming as this did just at the time of the readjustment of the yen-dollar relationship in the mid 1980s, a massive inflow of Japanese industrial capital and a shift to mono-crop agribusiness produced a dramatic rise in Thai exports (which were increasing at an annual rate of almost 20 percent by the early 1990s).

37 See IMF, *Crisis in Asia: Regional and Global Implications*, Washington, DC: December 1997, Table 1, p. 6.

38 Blustein, *The Chastening*, pp. 66–7; Bernard, "East Asia's Tumbling Dominoes," pp. 184–5.

39 Rubin, *In an Uncertain World*, p. 12.

40 Quoted in Bluestein, *The Chastening*, p. 78.

41 Morris Goldstein, "IMF Structural Programs," Institute for International Economics, 2000, p. 11. See also Kaminsky and Reinhardt, "Bank Lending and Contagion," pp. 9–10; and Barry Eichengreen, "The International Monetary Fund in the Wake of the Asian Crisis," in Noble and Ravenhill, *Asian Crisis*, p. 172.

42 Rubin, *In an Uncertain World*, p. 221.

43 Blustein, *The Chastening*, pp. 162, 166.

44 "The Asian SWAT Team from Washington," *Business Week*, February 23, 1998.

45 Katada, *Banking on Stability*, pp. 204–7. See also Jennifer A. Amyx, "Political Impediments to Far-Reaching Banking Reforms in Japan: Implications for Asia," in Noble and Ravenhill, *Asian Crisis*, pp. 146–7.

46 Rubin, *In an Uncertain World*, p. 38.

47 These were the very words of a senior administration official quoted in the *New York Times*, December 10, 1997.

48 Quoted by Blustein from an interview with Rubin on PBS's *News Hour*, January 13, 1998. See also Rubin, *In an Uncertain World*, pp. 230–1.

49 See especially Stephen Haggard and Sylvia Maxwell, "The Political Economy of Financial Internationalization in the Developing World," *International Organization* 50: 1 (Winter 1996), pp. 56–60. The quote from the IMF's staff member is in Blustein, *The Chastening*, p. 143

50 CNBC, January 8, 1998.

51 Gowan, *Global Gamble*, p. 114 (emphasis in original).

52 See especially Bruce Cumings, "The Asian Crisis, Democracy, and the End of Late Development," in Pempel, *The Politics of the Asian Financial Crisis*.

53 Seongjin Jeong, "The Social Structure of Accumulation in South Korea: Upgrading or Crumbling?" *Review of Radical Political Economics* 29: 4 (Fall 1997), Table 7, p. 102.

54 Baeksong Song, *State Form and State Strategy: The Case of the Kim Dae Jung Regime in South Korea*, PhD dissertation, University of Newcastle-upon-Tyne, June 2004, pp. 78–9.

55 On the labour legislation, see Song, *State Form and State Strategy*, pp. 94–6.

56 The first quote is from the US executive director to the IMF, Karin Lissakers, cited in Blustein, *The Chastening*, p. 144; the second is from Rubin, *In an Uncertain World*, p. 233.

57 For the myopic strong-versus-weak-states thesis being advanced just at this time, see Peter Evans, "The Eclipse of the State? Reflections on Stateness in an Era of Globalization," *World Politics* 50 (October 1997); and Linda Weiss, *The Myth of the Powerless State*, Ithaca: Cornell University Press, 1998. See the critique by Martin Hardt-Lansberg and Paul Burkett, "Economic Crisis and Restructuring in South Korea: Beyond the Free Market–Statist Debate," *Critical Asian Studies* 33: 3 (2001).

58 Cumings, "Asian Crisis," pp. 25–6. Cumings has no doubt that "the highest officials were lying through their teeth" about the size of Korea's reserves; Blustein, on the other hand, is more inclined to the view that it was because they "were so confused" that they produced "wildly disparate figures during the course of the crisis" (*The Chastening*, pp. 130–1).

59 The account here draws on Blustein, *The Chastening*, pp. 190–8.

60 This is what the Korean envoy to Washington had asked the Treasury to do. As he related the exchange to Blustein, Summers "played a little poker face on me. He said, 'You know our system. Our government cannot tell banks what to do.' I said, 'Well, if you cannot tell your banks would you please tell the Japanese to tell *their* banks.' That is something he said he would consider" (Blustein, *The Chastening*, p. 192–3).

61 Ibid., p. 202.

62 The quotes here are from the *New York Times*, December 10, 1997, and the *Wall Street Journal*, November 4, 1998.

63 Baeksong Song, *State Form and State Strategy*, pp. 98–9, 125–6.

64 Songok Han Thornton, "The 'Miracle' Revisited: The De-Radicalization of Korean Political Culture," *New Political Science* 27: 2 (June 2005), pp. 170–1.

65 Terence C. Halliday and Bruce G. Carruthers, "The Recursivity of Law: Global Norm-Making and National Law-Making in the Globalization of Corporate Insolvency Regimes," *American Journal of Sociology* 112: 4 (January 2007), pp. 1,155–7.

66 Quoted in Ben Steil and Robert Litan, *Financial Statecraft: The Role of Financial Markets in American Foreign Policy*, New Haven: Yale University Press, 2006, p. 139. The tensions were so great, according to the NSC's chief Asia specialist, Sandra Kristoff, that "there were nearly fisticuffs" between Treasury and NSC officials, while the Treasury's Robert Boorstin characterized the tussle this way: "They thought we were a bunch of ignoramuses poaching on their turf, and we thought they were willing to give any amount of money to anyone under the naive assumption that it would actually stabilize the country."

67 Goldstein, "IMF Structural Programs," pp. 38, 60–1.

68 Justin Robertson, "Reconsidering American Interests in Emerging Market Crises: An Unanticipated Outcome to the Asian Financial Crisis," *Review of International Political Economy* 14: 2 (May 2007), pp. 291–2. See also Justin Robertson, *US-Asia Economic Relations: A Political Economy of Crisis and the Rise of New Business Actors*, London: Routledge, 2008.

69 Rubin, *In an Uncertain World*, p. 274.

70 Quoted in Tett, *Saving the Sun*, pp. 131–2.

71 Ibid., p. 135 (emphasis in original).

72 Ibid., pp. 143–9. See also Volcker and Gyohten, *Changing Fortunes*, pp. 29–30, 263-4, 280.

73 Robert Rubin, "Strengthening the Architecture of the International Financial System," Brookings Institute, April 14, 1998.

74 Blustein, *The Chastening*, p. 246.

75 Rubin, *In an Uncertain World*, p. 279.

76 Stanley Fischer, "Farewell to the IMF Executive Board," August 30, 2001. Available at imf.org.

77 See Roger Lowenstein, *When Genius Failed: The Rise and Fall of Long-Term Capital Management*, New York: Random House, 2000.

78 *The Financial Crisis Inquiry Report*, National Commission on the Causes of the Financial and Economic Crisis in the United States, New York: Public Affairs, 2011, p. 57.

79 McDonough interview, PBS, *The Commanding Heights*. See also his statement before the House Committee on Banking and Financial Services, 105th Congress, 2nd Session, October 1, 1998.

80 Martin Wolf, "Back to the Future," *Financial Times*, October 14, 1998.

81 Paul Krugman, "Let's Not Panic—Yet," *New York Times*, August 30, 1998. Another article two days later by the chief economist of Morgan Stanley, Stephen Roach, supported this, saying that "central banks and the IMF need to focus squarely on crisis containment and put tangential considerations aside . . . I had long felt that the Federal Reserve's next move should be to ease interest rates; now I believe it should reduce rates to stem the crisis." Stephen Roach, "Is Global Collapse At Hand?" *New York Times*, September 1, 1998.

82 Remarks by Chairman Alan Greenspan at the Haas Annual Business Faculty Research Dialogue, University of California, Berkeley, California, September 4, 1998. See also Greenspan, *Age of Turbulence*, pp. 192–3.

83 See *Financial Crisis Inquiry Report*, pp. 56–7; and David E. Marshall, "The Crisis of 1998 and the Role of the Central Bank," Federal Reserve Bank of Chicago, *Economic Perspectives* 25: 2 (Q1, 2001).

84 Barry Eichengreen, *Towards a New International Architecture*, Washington, DC: Institute for International Economics, 1999, p. 154.

85 Litan and Rauch, *American Finance for the 21st Century*, p. 5. As Robert Rubin explained in his Preface, this study was prepared in response to a directive in the 1994 Reigle-Neal Interstate Banking Act that the secretary of the Treasury should assess and report on the strengths and weaknesses of the US financial system. An advisory commission was appointed in 1995 consisting of people with experience in financial services and experts outside government, with Litan and Rauch brought in to draft the study in close consultation with Rubin, Summers, and others on the Treasury's staff. The subsequent quotations are from pp. 5–10, 34–6, 42–5, 59–61, 82–6, and 132 of this report.

86 This was how Rubin described, in his Preface to *American Finance for the 21st Century*, the main point of the draft legislation the Treasury initially sent to Congress in June 1997.

87 See Leslie Wayne, "Politics Again Leaves US Financial Overhaul in Limbo," *New York Times*, October 5, 1998.

88 Michael M. Weinstein, "Economic Scene: Keeping Tabs on the Levels of Risk at the Nation's Banks," *New York Times*, October 8, 1998.

89 Donald Mackenzie, "Opening the Black Boxes of Global Finance," *Review of International Political Economy* 12: 4 (December 2005), p. 569.

90 Sheila Bair, "Godzilla in the Mist: How Increased Reporting and Disclosure Could Help Allay Fears About the OTC Derivatives Market," Remarks at International Conference on Derivatives Instruments, University of London, September 28, 1994.

91 Anthony Faiola, Ellen Nakashima, and Jill Drew, "What Went Wrong," *Washington Post*, October 15, 2008. See also Brooksley Born, "International Regulatory Responses to Derivatives Crises: The Role of the US Commodity Futures Trading Commission," *Northwestern Journal of International Law and Business* 21: 3 (2001); Damien Cave, "Risky Business," *Salon*, February 5, 2002.

92 Joseph Bauman, Managing Director of Bank of America, prepared statement on behalf of the International Swaps and Derivatives Association to the House Subcommittee on Risk Management and Specialty Crops, June 10, 1998.

93 Lawrence H. Summers, Alan Greenspan, Arthur Levitt and William J. Rainer, "Over-the-Counter Derivatives Markets and the Commodity Exchange Act," Report of the President's Working Group on Financial Markets, November 1999.

94 It would be mistaken to portray this in terms of Wall Street executives inside the state having less autonomy in this respect than Harvard academics. In his 2003 memoir, Robert Rubin claims that his experience at Goldman Sachs had taught him that there were "situations where derivatives put additional pressure on volatile markets" and that "many people who used derivatives didn't fully understand the risks they were taking." Indeed when he had asked the commercial and investment banks at the height of the Korean crisis "how much exposure they had to South Korea by way of derivative instruments, apart from their direct loans," it was clear most of them had only "a very imprecise idea, and some took a week to find out." Rubin says that Summers "thought I was overly concerned with the risk of derivatives," but does not explain why his deputy's views prevailed. Rubin, *In an Uncertain World*, pp. 238, 287–8.

95 "How IMF Policies Brought the World to the Verge of a Global Meltdown" was the title Stiglitz gave to his chapter on the Asian crisis in his *Globalization and Its Discontents*, New York: Norton, 2002. By the fall of 1998, World Bank criticisms that IMF economists had no sense of the political and cultural conditions of the countries to which they applied their template austerity requirements and structural reforms, and that the US Treasury was pressuring the World Bank to become more of a short-term financing agency, were being regularly leaked onto the pages on the *New York Times*. See for instance Paul Lewis, "World Bank Worried by Pressure For Quick-Fix Fiscal Action,"

New York Times, October 5, 1998. ("Here's another $50 billion to throw at the crisis" was how "a senior World Bank official" was quoted as characterizing Summers's approach to the Bank.)

96 See Robert Reich, *Locked in the Cabinet*, New York: Vintage, 1997. For an early and penetrating critique of Reich's progressive competitiveness strategy, see Manfred Bienefeld, "Capitalism and the Nation State in the Dog Days of the Twentieth Century," *Socialist Register 1994*, London: Merlin, 1994.

97 Jacob S. Hacker and Paul Pierson, *Off Center: The Republican Revolution and the Erosion of American Democracy*, New Haven: Yale University Press, 2006, p. 169. See also Taylor E. Dark, *The Unions and the Democrats*, Ithaca: Cornell University Press, 1999, esp. Chapter 8; and Kim Moody, *US Labor in Trouble and Transition*, New York: Verso, 2007, esp. Chapter 7.

98 Jelle Visser, "Union Membership Statistics in 24 Countries," *Monthly Labor Review*, January 2006, Table 3, p. 45.

99 See Thomas Pickety and Emanuel Saez, "Income Inequality in the United States," *Quarterly Journal of Economics* 143: 1 (February 2003). Available at econ.berkeley.edu.

100 Louis Hyman, *Debtor Nation: The History of America in Red Ink*, Princeton, NJ: Princeton University Press, 2011, pp. 252–4.

101 Gretchen Morgenson and Joshua Rosner, *Reckless Endangerment: How Outsized Ambition, Greed and Corruption Led to Economic Armageddon*, New York: Times Books, 2011, pp. 1–2.

102 A 1992 Federal Reserve study came to be especially widely cited by those advancing this, and was equally strongly criticized by those opposing it. See Alicia H. Munnell, Lynne E. Browne, James McEneany, and Geoffrey M. B. Tootell, "Mortgage Lending in Boston: Interpreting HMDA Data," Working Paper, Federal Reserve Bank of Boston, 1992.

103 Litan and Rauch, *American Finance for the 21st Century*, pp. 172–3.

104 ibid., pp. 66–7.

105 John Sweeney, quoted in Moody, *US Labor in Trouble and Transition*, New York: Verso, 2007, p. 133.

106 The Seattle protest took place in the wake of the exposure of the secretive OECD negotiations to "constitutionalize" investors' rights through a Multilateral Agreement on Investment, which led to this prospective agreement being aborted. See Tony Clarke and Maude Barlow, *MAI: The Multilateral Agreement on Investment and the Threat to Canadian Sovereignty*, Toronto: Stoddart, 1997; Stephen Clarkson, *Uncle Sam and Us: Globalization, Neoconservatism, and the Canadian State*, Toronto: University of Toronto Press, 2002, esp. pp. 47ff.

11. A World After Its Own Image

1 Gillian Tett, "Why Buy-Out Wizards Need to Get Wise to the Cultural Risks," *Financial Times*, November 24, 2006.

2 For Marx's formulation of his classic thesis in 1848 on the bourgeoisie creating "a

world after its own image," see *The Communist Manifesto*, London: Pluto, 2008, pp. 38–9. For Andre Gunder Frank's formulation, over a century later, of the counter-thesis, see his "The Development of Underdevelopment," *Monthly Review*, 18: 4 (September 1966).

3 UNCTADSTAT, "Inward and Outward Foreign Investment Flows, Annual 1970–2000." Available at unctadstat.unctad.org.

4 Charles T. Kelley, Jr., Mark Y. D. Wang, Gordon Bitko, Michael S. Chase, Aaron Kofner, Julia F. Lowell, James C. Mulvenon, David S. Ortiz, and Kevin L. Pollpeter, "High-Technology Manufacturing and US Competitiveness," Technical Report prepared for the Office of Science and Technology Policy, Rand Corporation, March 2004, p. 130.

5 National Science Board, Science and Engineering Indicators, 2004, Appendix, Table 6–5. Available at nsf.gov.

6 Martin Hart-Landsberg and Paul Burkett, "China and the Dynamics of International Accumulation: Causes and Consequences of Global Restructuring," *Historical Materialism* 14: 3 (2006), p. 4.

7 Asian Development Bank, *Emerging Asian Regionalism: A Partnership for Shared Prosperity*, Manila: ADB, 2008, pp. 8, 16, 23.

8 Francisco H. G. Ferreira and Martin Ravallion, "Global Poverty and Inequality: A Review of the Evidence," World Bank, Policy Research Working Paper 4623, May 2008, pp. 10–14. See also Branko Milanovic, "An Even Higher Global Inequality than Previously Thought," World Bank, Carnegie Endowment for International Peace, MPRA Paper No. 6676, Washington, December 2007. Available at mpra.ub.uni-muenchen.de.

9 Quoted in Baker, *Group of Seven*, p. 212.

10 This term was initially coined by G7 policymakers in the wake of the Mexican crisis. See especially Kenen, *From Halifax to Lyon*.

11 "[M]uch of the world's financial regulatory expertise, though difficult to quantify, is concentrated in the United States and United Kingdom. What [have] come to be known globally as 'best practices' in supervision and regulation usually emanate from these countries (from public regulatory apparatuses, but also from the self-regulatory practices of private entities)." Beth Simmons, "The International Politics of Harmonization," *International Organization* 55: 3 (2001), p. 594.

12 Rubin, *In an Uncertain World*, p. 262.

13 Cumings, "Asian Crisis," p. 26.

14 Rubin, "Strengthening the Architecture of the International Financial System."

15 Lawrence H. Summers, "Distinguished Lecture on Economics in Government: Reflections on Managing Global Integration," *Journal of Economic Perspectives* 13: 2 (Spring 1999).

16 Summers, "Go with the Flow," *Financial Times*, March 11, 1998.

17 These reports are available at imf.org.

18 See John Nolan, "Emerging Market Debt and Vulture Hedge Funds: Free-Ridership, Legal and Emerging Market Remedies," Financial Policy Forum, September 29, 2001.

19 See Horst Kohler and James Wolfensohn, "The IMF and the World Bank Group: An Enhanced Partnership for Sustainable Growth and Poverty Reduction," September 5, 2000.

20 Paul Cammack, "Making Poverty Work" in *Socialist Register 2002*, London: Merlin, 2001. See also Marcus Taylor, "Opening the World Bank: International Organizations and the Contradictions of Global Capitalism," *Historical Materialism* 13: 1 (2005).

21 George Soros, "Capitalism's Last Chance," *Foreign Policy*, Winter 1998/99.

22 Eichengreen, *Towards a New International Architecture*, p. 9.

23 IMF Quarterly Report on the Assessments of Standards and Codes, June 2002. See also Susanne Soederberg, *The Politics of the New International Financial Architecture*, London: Zed Books, 2004, esp. Chapter 5.

24 James R. Barth, Gerard Caprio, Jr., and Ross Levine, *Rethinking Bank Regulation*, Cambridge: CUP, 2006, p. 116. Of course, the extent to which authorities would enforce corrective action if banks did not comply was another question. Despite the US pressing other countries to follow the lead it took with the Financial Deposit Insurance Corporation Improvement Act of 1991 (which mandated "specific and progressively more severe actions to be taken against an institution as its capital deteriorates below specific thresholds"), ten years later seventy-nine had done so, but seventy-four had not. Moreover, over thirty countries had still not adopted either US or International Accounting Standards; in sixty-one countries supervisors could not take legal action against external auditors for negligence, and in thirty-six countries off-balance-sheet items were not required to be publicly disclosed. See *Rethinking Bank Regulation*, pp. 124–4, 143–5.

25 Ben Thirkell-White, "International Financial Architecture and the Limits of Neoliberal Hegemony," *New Political Economy* 12: 1 (March 2007), p. 33.

26 Quoted in Robertson, "Reconsidering American Interests," p. 290.

27 Robertson, *US-Asia Economic Relations*, p. 171.

28 *World Investment Report 2007*, UNCTAD, Geneva, 2008, Table 1.8, p. 14.

29 Benjamin J. Cohen, "Capital Controls: Why Do Governments Hesitate?" in Leslie Elliott Armijo, ed., *Debating the Global Financial Architecture*, Albany: SUNY Press, 2002, pp. 107, 109.

30 Baker, *Group of Seven*, p. 212.

31 See Soederberg, *Politics of the New International Financial Architecture*, 2004, pp. 86–8.

32 This also led to the perception that the G20 would "just be a mechanism to foster support for existing policies favored by the G7." Tony Porter and Duncan Wood, "Reform without Representation: The International and Transnational Dialogue on the Global Financial Architecture," in Armijo, ed., *Debating the Global Financial Architecture*, p. 250.

33 For the latter argument, see Robert Wade, "The Coming Fight over Capital Flows," *Foreign Affairs*, Winter 1998/99; for the former, see Rawi Abdelal, *Capital Rules: The Construction of Global Finance*, Cambridge, MA: Harvard University Press, 2007.

34 *World Investment Report 2007*, UNCTAD, Geneva, 2008, Table 1.9, p. 20; UNCTADSTAT, "Inward and Outward Foreign Direct Investment"; and Kevin B.

Barefoot and Raymond J. Mataloni, Jr., "US Multinational Companies Operations in the United States and Abroad in 2008," *US Survey of Current Business*, August 2010.

35 A European Commission official summed this up as follows: "We had different positions and it is the US position that apparently has won." Quoted in Michael Peel, "Accord Puts Common World Standards Drive Back on Track," *Financial Times*, November 19, 1999. See the outstanding analysis of how the "internationalization of accounting standards has taken place as their Americanization," in Thomas Sablowksi, "Accounting for Financial Capital: American Hegemony and the Conflict Over International Accounting Standards," in Panitch and Konings, *American Empire and the Political Economy of Global Finance*, p. 172.

36 See Peter Gowan, "Making Sense of NATO's War on Yugoslavia," *Socialist Register 1999*, London: Merlin, 1999.

37 Interviews by the authors with officials at the UK Treasury, London, October 29, 2002. One senior official spoke in terms of the UK Treasury playing "its traditional role of interpreting the US view to the world," but admitted that "if the US doesn't want to play, nothing happens." He added that, from the UK Treasury's perspective, the US Treasury was "as determining of the IMF and the World Bank as they want to be. The US doesn't get their own way all the time, and depends on working things through the IMF staff and the IMF agenda, but when it cares enough, it does. The UK, for example, is expert on fifty countries while the US is on 150 countries . . . and can go to the IMF staff to initiate decisions with incredible resources. The US is enormously important."

38 Interviews by the authors with officials in the international banking supervision section of the Deutsche Bundesbank, Frankfurt, October 15, 2002.

39 M. M. G. Fase and W. F. V. Vanthoor, "The Federal Reserve System Discussed: A Comparative Analysis," SUERF, Vienna, 2003, esp. p. 20.

40 Interviews by the authors with officials at the UK Treasury, London, October 29, 2002.

41 The sources for the data here, in addition to the World Bank, World Development Indicators, and databank.worldbank.org, are Andrew W. Hodge, "BEA Briefing: Comparing NIPA and S&P 500 Profits," *Survey of Current Business*, March 2011; and Marilyn Ibarra-Catonsville, "Direct Investment Positions for 2009," *Survey of Current Business*, July 2010.

42 For the data on global finance, see the IMF's *Global Financial Stability Report*, various years; the BIS *Quarterly Review* and "Triennial Central Bank Survey of Foreign Exchange and Derivatives Market Activity in 2007—Final Results," Bank for International Settlements, December 2007; McKinsey Global Institute, *The New Power Brokers: Gaining Clout in Turbulent Markets*, July 2008, and *Mapping Global Capital Markets*, October 2008; and International Finance Services, "Financial Market Trends Europe and US," March 2008, esp. Table 2, p. 2. For a recent useful overview, see esp. Chapter 8 of Gerard Dumenil and Dominique Levy, *The Crisis of Neoliberalism*, Cambridge, MA: Harvard University Press, 2011.

43 Philip D. Wooldridge, Dietrich Domanski, and Anna Cobau, "Changing Links

between Mature and Emerging Financial Markets," *BIS Quarterly Review*, September 2003, p. 45.

44 Donald J. Mathieson, Jorge Roldos, Ramana Ramaswamy, and Anna Ilyina, *Emerging Local Securities and Derivatives Markets*, Washington, DC: IMF, 2004, p. v.

45 Wooldridge et al., "Changing Links," p. 48.

46 Yilmaz Akyuz, "Capital Flows to Developing Countries in a Historical Perspective," South Centre Research Paper 37, Geneva, March 2011, p. 24.

47 Costas Lapavitsas, "Financialization Embroils Developing Countries," *Papelas de Europa* 19 (2009), p. 122. Lapavitsas shows that, by 2006, consumer loans as a proportion of total loans by Mexico's five largest banks had increased approximately six-fold relative to what they had been before their foreign takeover between 1999 and 2002 (Table 2, p. 139). He also shows that in Turkey debt as percentage of disposable household income exploded after the foreign bank takeovers from 7 percent in 2003 to 30 percent in 2007 (Figure 10, p. 135).

48 Although much of this involved "intra-regional carry-trade activities," it was also the case that "a very large proportion of South-South capital flows have been in direct investment, and much of these are intra-regional." Akyuz, "Capital Flows to Developing Countries," p. 22.

49 Richard Kozul-Wright and Paul Rayment, "Globalization Reloaded," UNCTAD Discussion Paper No. 167, January 2004, Table 3, p. 32; US Bureau of Labor Statistics, "International Labor Comparisons," available at bls.gov; Erin Lett and Judith Bannister, "China's Manufacturing Employment and Compensation Costs: 2002–2006," *Monthly Labour Review*, April, 2009.

50 See Timothy Sturgeon, Johannes Van Biesebroeck, and Gary Gereffi, "Value Chains, Networks and Clusters: Reframing the Global Automotive Industry" *Journal of Economic Geography* 8: 3 (2008), pp. 297–321.

51 Stephen Hymer, 'The "Multinational Firm and the Law of Uneven Development', in J. Bhawgwati, ed., *Economic and the World Order from the 1970s to the 1990s*, New York: Free Press, 1972.

52 Jason Dedrick, Kenneth L. Kraemer, and Greg Linden, "Who Profits from Innovation in Global Value Chains? A Study of the iPod and Notebook PCs," Industry Studies, Alfred P. Sloan Foundation, Boston, May 2008.

53 Peter F. Cowhey and Jonathon D. Aronson, *Transforming Global Information and Communication Markets: The Political Economy of Innovations*, Cambridge, MA: MIT Press, 2009, p.15. Cowhey and Aronson see American high-tech leadership as having been renewed since the early 1980s, thereby consolidating American postwar technological dominance: "Since 1945 the US market has been the most consistent agenda-setter for the global market. Its policy choices set everyone else's strategic choices" (p. 97).

54 OECD, Main Science and Technology Indicators, vol. 2006, issue 1.

55 Block, "Swimming Against the Current," p. 11.

56 See "Global 500 2010, Market Value by Country and Sector," *Financial Times*. Available at ft.com. The ranking is by market value as of 2008, but using revenue or income would not change the order significantly.

57   Barefoot and Mataloni, Jr., "US Multinational Companies," pp. 208–9.

58   *World Investment Report 2009*, UNCTAD, Geneva, 2009, Appendix A, Table A.1.9, p. 225.

59   This data is drawn from "Financial Market Trends Europe and US," International Finance Services London, March 2008, esp. Table 2, p. 2.

60   We are indebted to Sean Starrs for these calculations, based on Thompson Financial Services data.

61   "Federal Reserve Board Flow of Funds Accounts," Data Download Program. Available at federalreserve.gov.

62   See Greta R. Krippner, "The Financialization of the American Economy," *Socio-Economic Review* 3 (2005); and Julie Froud, Colin Haslam, Sukhdev Johal, and Karel William, "Cars After Financialisation: A Case Study in Financial Under-Performance, Constraints and Consequences," *Competition and Change* 6: 1 (2002).

63   See the perceptive analysis of this by Robert Rowthorn, "Manufacturing in the World Economy," *Economie Appliquee* 4 (1997).

64   See especially James Harrigan, "The Impact of the Asian Crisis on US Industry: An Almost-Free Lunch," Federal Reserve Bank of New York, *Economic Policy Review*, September 2000.

65   World Bank, World Development Indicators.

66   In fact, the volume of American exports after 1487 grew faster than for any of the other G7 countries, while by 2007 US imports were at 14.4 percent of the global total—almost twice as large as Germany's 7.5 percent, and over twice as large as China's 6.8 percent. This data is derived from UNCTADSTAT, "Trade in Goods and Services" tables (not included in the trade statistics here are US MNC's sales abroad, which at $5.5 trillion in 2007 were five times greater than US exports), as well as OECD, *Economic Outlook* 76, Statistical Annex, Table 38.

67   NIPA Table 1.1 and Angus Maddison, *The World Economy: A Millennial Perspective*, Paris: OECD, 2001.

68   Susan Fleck, John Glaser, and Shawn Sprague, "The Compensation-Productivity Gap: A Visual Essay," *Monthly Labour Review*, January 2011.

69   Bureau of Economic Analysis, NIPA Table 1.12.

70   Simon Clark, Ambereen Choudhury, and Gavin Finch, "Banks Bring Jobs to London as Finance Pays Most Tax in UK," *Bloomberg News*, March 23, 2011.

71   FDIC, *Historical Banking Statistics*, Table CB05. Available at fdic.gov.

72   Lee Branstetter and Nicholas Lardy, "China's Embrace of Globalization," in Loren Brandt and Thomas G. Rawski, eds., *China's Great Economic Transformation*, Cambridge, UK: CUP, 2008, pp. 650, 656.

73   PBS, "News Hour with Jim Lehrer," November 18, 1999. Available at pbs.org.

74   Quoted in Branstetter and Lardy, "China's Embrace of Globalization," p. 650.

75   Charlene Barshefsky, "US Trade Policy in China, Hearings before the Senate Finance Committee on the Status of China's Application to Join the World Trade Organization," April 13, 1999.

76   Branstetter and Lardy, "China's Embrace of Globalization," p. 658.

77 Derived from WTO, International Trade Statistics 2011, Appendix tables A1 and A14 and World Bank, World Development Indicators.

78 Martin Hart-Landsberg "The US Economy and China: Capitalism, Class, and Crisis," *Monthly Review*, February 2010.

79 Loren Brandt, Thomas G. Rawski, and John Sutton, "China's Industrial Development," in Brandt and Rawski, *China's Great Economic Transformation*, p. 574.

80 Albert G. Z. Hu and Gary H. Jefferson, "Science and Technology in China," in Brandt and Rawski, *China's Great Economic Transformation*, esp. pp. 307–8.

81 The data in this paragraph is drawn from the World Bank's World Development Indicators.

82 George Shultz, Foreword to K. C. Fung, J. Lau, and Joseph S. Lee, *US Direct Investment in China*, Washington: AEI Press, 2004, p. xi.

83 See especially Barry Naughton, *The Chinese Economy: Transitions and Growth*, Cambridge, MA: MIT Press, 2007.

84 "FDI to Asia Booms Fuelled by Hong Kong," UNCTAD Press Release, September 18, 2001.

85 Christine P. W. Wong and Richard M. Bird, "China's Fiscal System: A Work in Progress," in Brandt and Rawski, *China's Great Economic Transformation*, p. 432.

86 Stephan Haggard and Yasheng Huang, "The Political Economy of Private-Sector Development in China," in Brandt and Rawski, *China's Great Economic Transformation*, p. 368. For the "systematic discrimination against Chinese indigenous firms," see also Branstetter and Lardy, "China's Embrace of Globalization," p. 649.

87 See Hu and Jefferson, "Science and Technology in China," p. 319. It is the strategic importance of US investments in high-tech sectors that is not recognized in more general surveys such as Lee Branstetter and C. Fritz Foley, "Facts and Fallacies about US FDI in China," Working Paper 13470, Cambridge, MA: NBER, 2007. Available at nber.org/papers/w13470.

88 It also exceeded the total for India (24,000), South Korea (26,000), and Taiwan (23,000). National Science Foundation, Division of Science Resource Statistics, Survey of Earned Doctorates, Science and Engineering Indicators, 2010, Table 2–6.

89 Dezalay and Garth, *Dealing in Virtue*, p. 265.

90 Donald Clarke, Peter Murrell, and Susan Whiting, "The Role of Law in China's Economic Development," in Brandt and Rawski, *China's Great Economic Transformation*, p. 400.

91 "China's transition to a capitalist state has been carried out through a remarkable marriage of central power and decentralized authority." Richard Walker and Daniel Buck, "The Chinese Road," *New Left Review* II/46 (July–August 2007).

92 Peter Kwong, citing a report by the China Rights Forum, summarizes the relationship between the Party elite and the owners and managers of business as follows: "[O]nly 5 per cent of China's 20,000 richest people have made it on merit. More than 90 per cent are related to senior government or Communist Party officials . . . China's new 'princelings' took over China's most strategic and profitable industries: banking, transportation, power generation, natural resources, media, and weapons. Once in

management positions, they get loans from government-controlled banks, acquire foreign partners, and list their companies on Hong Kong or New York stock exchanges to raise more capital." Peter Kwong, "The Chinese Face of Neoliberalism," *Counterpunch*, October 7–8, 2006.

93 Official attitudes to private property expanded from its being considered a "complement" to the state sector (Constitution, 1982), to a "supplement" to the state sector (13th Congress of the CPP, 1987), to an "important component of the economy" (15th Congress, 1997), to its developing "side by side" with the publicly owned sector (2001) and "actively encouraged" (2004). Clarke, Murrell, and Whiting, "The Role of Law in China's Economic Development," in Brandt and Rawski, *China's Great Economic Transformation*, p. 380.

94 Haggard and Huang, "Political Economy of Private-Sector Development in China," p. 338.

95 The overall share of SOEs and other publicly controlled enterprises in new fixed investment in 2003 was still 74 percent (two-thirds of the remainder was undertaken by foreign-invested enterprises). Key strategic industries such as steel remained in state hands (though there was great variation in firm size, productivity, and profitability, the output of crude steel increased by 339 percent between 1995 and 2006, while employment fell by 18 percent, implying a more than five-fold increase in output per worker, accompanied by an improvement in quality). See Brandt, Rawski, and Sutton, "China's Industrial Development," Table 15.3, p. 588, Table 15.5, p. 594, Table 15.6, p. 597; and Dwight H. Perkins and Thomas G. Rawski, "Forecasting China's Economic Growth to 2025," in Brandt and Rawski, *China's Great Economic Transformation*, p. 863.

96 Tang Xiangyang, "State Monopolies Dominate China's Top 500," *Economic Observer*, September 9, 2009. Available at eeo.com.cn. The data is collected by the China Enterprise Confederation and China Enterprise Directors Association, and modeled after the *Fortune 500*.

97 See John Whalley and Xian Xin, "China's FDI and non-FDI Economies and the Sustainability of High Chinese Growth," *China Economic Review* 21 (2010); and Martin Hart-Landsberg, "The US Economy and China: Capitalism, Class, and Crisis," *Monthly Review*, February 2010.

98 Cited in Wendy Dobson and A. E. Safarian, "The Transition from Imitation to Innovation: An Enquiry into China's Evolving Institutions and Firm Capabilities," Rotman Institute for International Business, Working Paper Series, No. 11, March 2008, p. 6.

99 See John Whalley and Xian Xin, "China's FDI and non-FDI Economies and the Sustainability of Future High Chinese Growth," *National Bureau of Economic Research*, Working Paper Series, No. 12249, 2006; George J. Gilboy, "The Myth Behind China's Miracle," *Foreign Affairs*, July–August 2004; and Brandt, Rawski and Sutton, "China's Industrial Development," Table 15.1, p. 574.

100 Indeed, one major study concluded that "the current model of technology import and imitation cannot in the long run sustain China's technological advance. As China narrows the gap with the world technology frontier, opportunities for easy gains from

imitating will dissipate." Hu and Jefferson, "Science and Technology in China," esp. p. 332. See also Dale Wen and Minqi Li, "China: Hyper-Development and Environmental Crisis," in Leo Panitch and Colin Leys, eds., *Socialist Register 2007,* London: Merlin Press 2006. Claims about China's challenge to US military dominance should also be discounted: leaving issues of quality and technology aside, US military expenditures in 2008 were 4.9 percent of GDP and China's 1.4 percent. In actual expenditures, the US spent close to $700 billion and China $60 billion, and even if China's official numbers are doubled, as the Pentagon suggests, that still leaves China's expenditures at only 17 percent of the US's. Gordon Fairclough, "China Slows Increase in Defense Spending," *Wall Street Journal,* March 5, 2010.

101 Ching Kwan Lee, *Against the Law: Labor Protests in China's Rustbelt and Sunbelt,* Berkeley: University of California Press, 2007, p. 71.

102 In 2004, only 10 percent of the Chinese precariat had medical insurance, less than half were paid regularly, over half were never paid overtime, and two-thirds worked without any weekly day of rest. At the same time, employment in state-owned enterprises peaked in 1995, and over the next decade fell by 48 million (30 million of those being laid off and the rest transferred to TVEs). See Eli Friedman and Ching Kwan Lee, "Remaking the World of Chinese Labour: A 30-Year Retrospective," *British Journal of Industrial Relations* 48: 3 (September 2010), pp. 510–16; as well as Fang Cai, Albert Park, and Yaohui Zhao, "The Chinese Labor Market in the Reform Era," and Loren Brandt, Chang-tai Hsieh, and Xiaodong Zhu, "Growth and Structural Transformation in China," both in Brandt and Rawski, *China's Great Economic Transformation,* Table 6.1, p. 168, and Table 17.1, p. 690, respectively.

103 Ching Kwan Lee, *Against the Law,* p. 10. See also Friedman and Lee, "Remaking the World of Chinese Labour," pp. 515–17. The number of arbitrated cases went from under 20,000 in 1994 to over 120,000 in 1999, 226,00 in 2003, and reached half a million in 2007.

104 Both the European Union Chamber of Commerce in China and the American Chamber of Commerce in Shanghai (the two largest foreign investor organizations in China), in their detailed recommendations on the 2007 Draft Labor Contract Law to protect employees' rights and interests, threatened to withdraw their investments if this altered the balance of class power. The EU, referring to plants leaving Europe because of competitive pressures, warned that "if China chooses to implement the draft law on labor contracts, it will undoubtedly face a similar challenge." The Americans similarly threatened that it "might have negative effects on China's investment environment." And at a seminar on the draft law, a representative of the Shanghai Association of Human Resources Management in Multinational Companies asserted: "If this kind of law is going to be implemented, we will withdraw our investments." See *China Labour Bulletin.* Available at www.clb.org.hk.

105 Ho-fung Hung, "Sinomania: Global Crisis, China's Crisis," *Socialist Register 2012,* London: Merlin, 2011.

106 There are many problems in interpreting the data, but that there has been a major increase in inequality in China is not disputed. For recent analyses with comparisons to other countries, see Jiandong Chen, Dai Dai, Ming Pu, Wenxuan Hou, and Qiaobin Fen, "The Trend of the Gini Coefficient of China," Brooks World Poverty Institute, University of Manchester, January 2010. A recent OECD study ("OECD Economic Survey—China," February 2010) provides a lower indicator of inequality than the Chinese Academy of Sciences does, but still assesses Chinese inequality as being higher than the US; it also argues that income inequality in China peaked in 2005, and has since stopped increasing.

107 Sean Starrs, "China's Integration into the American-Centered Global Political Economy," CRC Research Report, Department of Political Science, York University, 2009.

108 Paul Masson, Wendy Dobson, and Robert Lafrance, "China's Integration into the Global Financial System," *Bank of Canada Review*, Summer 2008, p. 22.

109 Ibid., p. 27.

110 It was notable, for instance, that even Niall Ferguson fueled such expectations despite his understanding of the "symbiotic economic relationship" between China and the US, which he dubbed "Chimerica." See especially his "Empire Falls" essay in *Vanity Fair*, October 2006.

12. American Crisis/Global Crisis

1 Rubin, *In an Uncertain World*, p. 297.

2 *The Financial Crisis Inquiry Report*, New York: Public Affairs, 2011, pp. 354, 531 n. 5.

3 Quoted in ibid., p. 354.

4 Like Paul Volcker before him, Geithner's progress through the ranks was the closest thing in the US to that of a successful career civil servant. Geithner (whose father was a Ford Foundation executive in Asia) was only in his twenties when he joined the Treasury in 1988 as assistant Treasury attaché in the US embassy in Tokyo. He rose rapidly through the Treasury in the 1990s, and moved briefly to the IMF after the change in administrations before being appointed as president of the New York Federal Reserve in 2003.

5 "Remarks by Treasury Secretary Tim Geithner to the International Monetary Conference," Atlanta, Georgia, US Treasury Press Center, June 6, 2011.

6 See the excellent analyses by Yilmaz Akyuz and Korkat Boratav, "The Making of the Turkish Financial Crisis"; and Arturo O'Connell, "The Recent Crisis—and Recovery—of the Argentine Economy," both in Gerald Epstein, ed., *Financialization of the World Economy*, Northampton, MA: Edward Elgar, 2005.

7 In the wake of a 35 percent devaluation of the Turkish lira and overnight bank lending rates that reached 5,000 percent in February 2001, the IMF provided an $8 billion loan which was tied to the privatization and foreign ownership of banks, telecommunications, and airlines, as well as the accelerated liberalization of capital flows alongside greater central bank independence. It was aided in this by Turkish authorities

"working diligently to ensure the reform was consistent with EU requisites." Korsan Cevdet, "Turkey: Risk-Conscious Foreign Firms and the Maturing Domestic Banking Sector," in Justin Robertson, *Power and Politics After Financial Crises: Rethinking Foreign Opportunities in Emerging Markets*, New York: Palgrave Macmillan, 2008, p. 241.

8   Paul Blustein, *And the Money Kept Rolling In (and Out): Wall Street, the IMF and the Bankrupting of Argentina*, New York: Public Affairs, 2005, pp. 147–53, 177–9. A broader IMF scheme, which O'Neill also initiated—"so that we can work with governments that, in effect, need to go through a Chapter 11 reorganization"—was for an international bankruptcy law. Although strongly promoted by the famously neoliberal Anne Krueger, at the time the second-in-command at the IMF, it also bore no fruit in the face of a distinct lack of enthusiasm by international banks as well as other governments.

9   Interviews by the authors with senior officials in the international banking supervision section of the Deutsche Bundesbank, Frankfurt, October 15, 2002. See also the Report from the President, Federal Reserve Bank of New York, 2002 Annual Report, pp. 5–8.

10 Blustein, *And the Money Kept Rolling In (and Out)*, p. 175; see also pp. 161–4.

11 Ruth Felder, "From Bretton Woods to Neoliberal Reforms: The International Financial Institutions and American Power," in Panitch and Konings, eds., *American Empire and the Political Economy of Global Finance*, p. 193. See also Maria Pia Riggirozzi, "Argentina: State Capacity and Leverage in External Negotiations," in Robertson, *Power and Politics*; although, unlike Felder, she goes much too far in accepting the false polarity between states and markets.

12 See O'Connell, "Recent Crisis"; as well as Emilia Castorina, "The Contradictions of Democratic Neoliberalism in Argentina," *Socialist Register 2008*, London: Merlin, 2007.

13 Barry Eichengreen, "International Economic Policy: Was There a Bush Doctrine?" NBER Working Paper 13831, March 2008, p. 27.

14 Quoted in Stephanie Bell-Kelton, "Behind Closed Doors: The Political Economy of Central Banking in the United States," *International Journal of Political Economy* 35: 1 (Spring 2006), p. 19.

15 The quotations here are from Paul Volcker's speech at the Toronto Board of Trade, October 2, 2002, published as "International Financial Markets: The Prospects for Growth and Stability," in *At the Global Crossroads: The Sylvia Ostry Foundation Lectures*, Montreal & Kingston: McGill–Queens University Press, 2003, pp. 85–98. Volcker observed that the total size of the Argentine banking system in the mid 1990s was $40 billion (equivalent to the second-largest bank in Pittsburgh), which most investment bankers would think was "too small to survive in this modern, turbulent, globalized financial world." Insisting on facing "the fact that major parts of this world simply don't have the institutions" to cope with the inherent volatility of international financial markets, he thus drew the lesson from the Argentine crisis that greater foreign ownership of emerging markets' banks was needed. But in calling for this, Volcker was not facing the fact that, by 2000 (i.e. before the onset of the financial crisis), thirty-nine banks in Argentina, accounting for 73 percent of total bank assets, had already become foreign-owned. See O'Connell, "Recent Crisis," p. 16.

16 See Susanne Soederberg, "A Critique of the Diagnosis and Cure for 'Enronitis': The Sarbanes-Oxley Act and Neoliberal Governance of Corporate America," *Critical Sociology* 34: 5 (2008).

17 There is much confusion in the literature regarding the distinction between mortgage-backed securities and derivatives. The major difference is that the former are really just a collection of fragmented mortgage bonds, and the collateralized debts associated with them actually form the value of those securities. For most traders, the term "derivative" is usually used for a financial instrument that is functionally separate from the underlying asset.

18 *Financial Crisis Inquiry Report*, pp. 64–5.

19 Frederic S. Mishkin, "Over the Cliff: From the Subprime to the Global Financial Crisis," *Journal of Economic Perspectives* 25: 1 (2011), p. 55. A 2005 paper by Rhaguram Rajan, the director of the IMF's research department, was especially prescient in this regard: "Has Financial Development Made the World Riskier?," paper prepared for the symposium sponsored by the Federal Reserve Bank of Kansas City on *The Greenspan Era: Lessons for the Future*, Jackson Hole, Wyoming, August 25–7, 2005.

20 Alan Greenspan and James Kennedy, "Sources and Uses of Equity Extracted from Homes," Finance and Economics discussion Series 2007–20, Federal Reserve Board, March 2007, p. 10.

21 *Financial Crisis Inquiry Report*, pp. 13–14.

22 See ibid., p. 70, Figure 5.2.

23 For both the Nader quote and the data here, see Viral A. Acharya, *Guaranteed To Fail: Fannie Mae, Freddie Mac and the Debacle of Mortgage Finance*, Princeton: Princeton University Press, 2011, pp. 20–2.

24 Alan Greenspan, "Consumer Finance," remarks by Chairman Alan Greenspan at the Federal Reserve Fourth Annual Community Affairs Research Conference, Washington, DC, April 8, 2005.

25 Moreover, because US FDI was so large, and the returns on it so much higher than on securities, total receipts to the US on assets abroad were higher than what was paid out on foreign assets in the US. For this argument, and the quotation used here, see Ricardo Housmann and Federico Sturzenegger, "US and Global Imbalances: Can Dark Matter Prevent a Big Bang?" Working Paper, Kennedy School of Government, November 13, 2005. See also Herman Schwartz, *Subprime Nation: American Power, American Capital and the Housing Bubble*, Ithaca: Cornell University Press, 2009.

26 The data is readily available from the US Bureau of Economic Analysis, and the Federal Reserve Board Flow of Funds Accounts, Data Download Program.

27 This argument was most strongly advanced by Robert Brenner, *The Boom and the Bubble: The US in the World Economy*, New York: Verso, 2002, but was much more widely held. For our critique at the time, see Sam Gindin and Leo Panitch, "Rethinking Crisis," *Monthly Review* 54: 6 (November 2002), pp. 34–59.

28 Alan Greenspan, "Monetary Policy Report to the Congress," statement before the Committee on Banking, Housing, and Urban Affairs, US Senate, February 16, 2005. See also Karen Weaver, "US Asset-Backed Securities Market: Review and Outlook,"

in *Global Securitization and Structured Finance*, Deutsche Bank, 2008. Available at globalsecuritisation.com.

29 Deborah Solomon, "Questions for Paul O'Neill: Market Leader," *New York Times*, March 30, 2008.

30 Ben Bernanke, "GSE Portfolios, Systemic Risk and Affordable Housing," speech to the Independent Community Bankers of America's Annual Convention, Honolulu, March 6, 2007.

31 Both quotes are from Gretchen Morgenson, "The Bank Run We Knew So Little About," *New York Times*, April 3, 2011.

32 Vikas Bajaj, "Central Banks Intervene to Calm Volatile Markets," *New York Times*, August 1, 2007. For the Bush speech, see Gillian Tett, *Fool's Gold*, London: Little, Brown, 2009, p. 227.

33 Quoted in Peter Baker, "A Professor and a Banker Bury Old Dogma on Markets," *New York Times*, September 20, 2008. See Ben Bernanke, "Non-Monetary Effects of the Financial Crisis in the Propagation of the Great Depression," *American Economic Review* 73: 3 (June 1983); and *Essays on the Great Depression*, Princeton: Princeton University Press, 2000.

34 See Bank for International Settlements, "The International Interbank Market: A Descriptive Study," *BIS Papers* 8, Monetary and Economic Department, July 1983; and David Gaffen, "The Meaning of LIBOR," *Wall Street Journal*, September 7, 2007.

35 The leading borrowers in the months to come were Citibank ($3.5 billion in September), Deutsche Bank ($2.4 billion in November) and Calyon of France ($2 billion in December). See Morgenson, "The Bank Run We Knew So little About"; Jody Shenn, "Bank of China New York Branch Was Second-Largest Fed Borrower in Aug. 2007," *Bloomberg*, March 31, 2011; and Bradley Keoun and Craig Torres, "Foreign Banks Tapped Fed's Secret Lifeline Most at Crisis Peak," *Bloomberg*, April 1, 2011.

36 Michael Shedlock, "Banks Worldwide Engage in Global Coordinated Panic," *Seeking Alpha*, December 14, 2007. This was undertaken around the same time as the Fed also launched a Term Auction Facility program to allocate funds to US depository institutions against a wide variety of collateral. See *The Financial Crisis Inquiry Report*, pp. 274–6.

37 Carrick Mollenkamp, Deborah Solomon, and Robin Sidel, "Rescue Readied By Banks Is Bet to Spur Market," *Wall Street Journal*, October 15, 2007. What primarily emerged from this was the Master Liquidity Enhancement Conduit, which sought to create market demand for asset-backed securities to prevent the unraveling of SIV portfolios, but this did little to contain the crisis.

38 Ben Bernanke, "Addressing Weaknesses in the Global Financial Markets: The Report of the President's Working Group on Financial Markets," speech given to *World Affairs Council of Greater Richmond's Virginia Global Ambassador Award Luncheon*, April 10, 2008.

39 See *Financial Crisis Inquiry Report*, pp. 276–8. Monoline bond insurers (institutions which guarantee payments on municipal and other bonds so as to promote their

liquidity) played a crucial role in the transmission of crisis tendencies. Monolines guaranteed about $2.5 trillion worth of public and private bonds (100 to 150 times the size of their capital base), allowing banks to create additional liabilities—including a parallel, highly leveraged market of swap contracts.

40 The Fed's new Primary Dealers Credit Facility, which immediately made $200 billion available to investment banks, was also designed to ensure the continued functioning of the long-established system whereby two major Wall Street "clearing banks" (Bank of New York Mellon and J. P. Morgan Chase) spread the Fed's liquidity to other banks in the US and abroad.

41 In the months following the Bear Stearns collapse, the Fed used its new programs to accept $219 billion in risky assets from financial institutions. And on one day in mid May alone, the Fed not only provided J. P. Morgan with $10 billion as part of its revolving credit line for its takeover of Bear Stearns, but also provided Bank of New York Mellon with over $4 billion to support Barclays in the UK, as well as Countrywide in the US. This data is derived from "Primary, Secondary and Other Credit Extensions Outstanding on Friday, May 16, 2008 by Remaining Term," one of the 29,000 documents the Fed made available under court order in the spring of 2011.

42 Willem Buiter, "The Fed as the Market Maker of Last Resort: Better Late than Never," *Financial Times*, March 12, 2008.

43 See Chris Giles, "Central Banks Become Lender of Only Resort," *Financial Times*, October 3, 2008; Ben Bernanke, "Addressing Weaknesses in the Global Financial Markets: The Report of the President's Working Group on Financial Markets," speech given to World Affairs Council of Greater Richmond, April 10, 2008; and "Board of Governors of the Federal Reserve System: Press Releases," September 14, 2008.

44 Fannie and Freddie were put under a government "conservatorship" directed by the new Federal Housing Finance Agency, with their obligations uploaded to the Treasury's balance sheet. The creation of a program of governmental demand for Freddie and Fannie debt (culminating in March 2009 with the Fed's purchase of $700 billion of their debt) further blurred the distinction between GSE issues, government obligations like Treasury bonds, and indeed the direct expansion of the money supply.

45 By 2008, Lehman's over-the-counter derivatives business alone was composed of 900,000 contracts (including 150,000 with Deutsche Bank, Union Bank of Switzerland, and J. P. Morgan), while its debt-to-capital leverage ratio had reached 40-to-1. With its counterparties pulling out, the panic in the commercial paper market was such that, as the bankruptcy lawyer for Lehman later went so far as to say, "the biggest corporations in America thought they were finished." *Financial Crisis Inquiry Report*, p. 355.

46 Geithner had been more successful three years earlier, in September 2005, when he had summoned the fourteen largest Wall Street banks to a meeting at the New York Fed for the first time since the 1998 LTCM crisis, and was able to get them all to agree to overhaul their back-office procedures for confirming trades on credit derivatives. See Timothy Geithner, Callum McCarthy, and Annette Nazareth, "Safer Strategy for Credit Products Explosion," *Financial Times*, September 27, 2006. In September 2008,

under heavy pressure from the US Treasury, Barclays was on the verge of absorbing Lehman's as Morgan had done with Bear Stearns, but it drew back in the face of the British Financial Services Authority's refusal to allow Barclay's to assume Lehman's obligations and the US Treasury's refusal to allow the Fed to guarantee that it would cover them. See Tett, *Fool's Gold*, pp. 186–8.

47 *Financial Crisis Inquiry Report*, p. 354.

48 Over the previous year, Goldman Sachs in particular had not only stopped buying mortgage-backed securities on its own account while still reaping fees by selling them to others (in a manner reminiscent of its behaviour in the 1970 commercial paper crisis), but had also demanded that AIG put up massive amounts of collateral to back up its credit default swaps with Goldman. *Financial Crisis Inquiry Report*, pp. 265–74.

49 *Financial Crisis Inquiry Report*, Figure 20.4, p. 377.

50 This data is derived from an internal New York Fed email from the Credit Risk Management Division, titled "9-25-08 Final PDCF Numbers," one of the 29,000 documents the Fed made available under court order in the spring of 2011.

51 Bradler Keoun and Craig Torres, "Foreign Banks Tapped Fed's Secret Lifeline Most at Crisis Peak," *Bloomberg*, April 1, 2011.

52 Bob Ivy, "Fed's Biggest Foreign-Bank Bailout Kept US Municipal Finance on Track," *Bloomberg*, April 6, 2011.

53 Linda Goldberg and David Skeie, "Why Did US Branches of Foreign Banks Borrow at the Discount Window?" Available at libertystreeteconomics.newyorkfed.org. See also Linda S. Goldberg, "Is the International Role of the Dollar Changing?" *Current Issues in Economics and Finance* (Federal Reserve Bank of New York), 16: 1 (January 2010), p. 6.

54 See David Stout, "Paulson Gives Way on CEO Pay," *New York Times*, September 24, 2008 (emphasis added); and Simon Bowers, "Wall Street Man," *Guardian*, September 26, 2008. Paulson received $38.3 million in salary, stock, and options in the year before joining the Treasury, plus a mid-year $18.7 million bonus on his departure, as well as an estimated $200 million tax break on the sale of his almost $500 million shares in Goldman Sachs (a sale legally required in order to avoid "conflict of interest" in his new job).

55 Philip Hampton and John Kingman, "Mandate to Protect Taxpayers' Investment," *Financial Times*, November 13, 2008. See the account of this in Julie Froud, Michael Moran, Adriana Nilsson, and Karel Williams, "Opportunity Lost: Mystification, Elite Politics and Financial Reform in the UK," *Socialist Register 2011*, London: Merlin, 2010.

56 A particularly graphic example of this socialization of losses was the guarantees provided (outside the TARP program) for Citigroup's mortgage debt portfolio by the Treasury, FDIC, and Federal Reserve. The bank would be responsible for the first $29 billion of losses, but only for 10 percent after that, which in effect meant a state guarantee of over $300 billion. See Heidi N. Moore, "Citigroup Bailout: Outrageous or Courageous," *Wall Street Journal*, November 24, 2008; and Government Accountability Office, "Financial Assistance: Ongoing Challenges and Guiding Principles Related

to Government Assistance For Private Sector Companies," GAO Report to Congressional Committees, August 2010, esp. p. 16.

57 See Atif Mian, Amir Sufi, and Francesco Trebbi, "Foreclosures, House Prices, and the Real Economy," *NBER Working Paper* 16685, January 2011, p. 32.

58 The data on household credit here is from Federal Reserve Board Flow of Funds Accounts, Data Download Program. The data on sales is from US Census Bureau's "Monthly and Annual Retail Trade" report.

59 Jeffrey White, "On Crisis, Europe to US: 'I Told You So,'" *Christian Science Monitor*, October 10, 2008.

60 "Bush Proud US Economic Woes Can Still Depress World Markets," *The Onion* Issue 43-45, (November 2007). p. 6.

61 See, for instance, Michael Mackenzie, "Outlook for Government Bond Traders Brightens," *Financial Times*, February 17, 2009.

62 The total official reserve holdings of Treasuries increased steadily from $1.6 trillion in August 2007 to $3.1 trillion by the end of 2010. China's portion alone doubled from $500 billion to well over $1 trillion, finally surpassing Japan's. Treasury International Capital System, Securities (b) Special Data Series, "Major Foreign Holders of Treasury Securities." Available at treasury.gov.

63 The figures in this paragraph are drawn from World Bank, World Development Indicators. Available at databank.worldbank.org.

64 David H. McCormick, undersecretary for international relations at the US Treasury, *Washington Post*, November 10, 2008.

65 Set up after the Asian crisis to allow greater interaction between finance ministry deputies, central bankers, and other regulators, primarily among the G7 states, the Financial Stability Forum, now called the Board, had its membership expanded to include the G20 countries. See Eric Helleiner and Stefano Pagliari, "Towards a New Bretton Woods? The First G20 Leaders' Summit and the Regulation of Global Finance," *New Political Economy* 14: 2 (June 2009).

66 G20 Declaration, "Summit on Financial Markets and the World Economy," p. 4.

67 See Toby Helm and Heather Stewart, "Germany and France Reject Brown's Global Economic Recovery Plan," *Guardian*, March 14, 2009.

68 See especially the outstanding comparative analysis by two ILO economists, Sher Verick and Iyanatul Islam, "The Great Recession of 2008–2009: Causes, Consequences and Policy Responses," Institute for the Study of Labour, Discussion Paper No. 4934, Bonn, May 2010.

69 Veena Jha, "The Effects of Fiscal Stimulus Packages on Employment," Employment Working Paper No. 34, International Labour Office, Geneva, 2009.

70 Henry M. Paulson, Jr., *On the Brink: Inside the Race to Stop the Collapse of the Global Financial System*, New York: Business Plus, 2010, pp. 13–14.

71 Martin Wolf, "Why a Successful US Bank Rescue Is Still So Far Away," *Financial Times*, March 24, 2009.

72 Quoted in Andrew Ward, "Obama Urges Restraint over Bonus Penalties," *Financial Times*, March 24, 2009, emphasis added.

73   See Stephen Brill, "What's a Bailed-Out Banker Worth?" *New York Times Magazine*, January 3, 2010.

74   With the great help of what the state had taken off their books, the nineteen firms that were put through the stress test had by 2011 increased their common equity by more than $300 billion over 2008, and reduced their average leverage ratios from 16-to-1 to 11-to-1. The implementation of the detailed plan the Fed required of those banks that did not meet the stress test, involving raising additional capital, would soon put all these banks in the position to gradually pay off their government loans and buy back their stock.

75   See especially the report chaired by Volcker: Working Group on Financial Reform, *Financial Reform: A Framework for Financial Stability*, Washington, DC, January 15, 2009. Available at fic.wharton.upenn.edu.

76   Quoted in Anna Fifield, "Obama in Tough Talk to 'Fat Cat' Bankers," *Financial Times*, December 15, 2009.

77   "Glass–Steagall Lite," *Economist*, January 2010.

78   Jay Newton-Small, "How Barney Frank Forged a Financial Reform Bill," *Time*, June 26, 2010.

79   See the New York Fed's own page on discount window operations. Available at newyorkfed.org.

80   See Thomas Cooley and Ingo Walter, "The Architecture of Financial Regulation," in Myron Scholes, Viral V. Acharya, Thomas F. Cooley, and Matthew P. Richardson, *Regulating Wall Street: The Dodd-Frank Act and the New Architecture of Global Finance*, Hoboken, NJ: Wiley, 2011, p. 45. The Act's new "Special Resolution Regime," which set out provisions to deal with the collapse of a SIFI, focused on the need for SIFIs to write "living wills" (that is, complex plans prepared in advance to ensure an orderly wind-down of operations), so as to allow creditors and equity-holders to take losses without destroying the system, and generally to make it easier for the Fed to try to contain financial crisis.

81   Eric Helleiner and Stefano Pagliari, "The End of Self-Regulation?" in Eric Helleiner, Stefano Pagliari, and Hubert Zimmermann, eds., *Global Finance in Crisis: The Politics of International Regulatory Change*, London: Routledge, 2010, pp. 85–6.

82   Louise Story, "A Secretive Banking Elite Rules Trading in Derivatives," *New York Times*, December 11, 2010.

83   US Department of the Treasury, "Fact Sheet: Notice of Proposed Determination on Foreign Exchange Swaps and Forwards," April 29, 2011. See also Victoria McGrane and Andrew Ackerman, "Treasury Carves Rule Exemption," *Wall Street Journal*, April 30, 2011.

84   See Securities and Exchange Commission, Response of the Office of Chief Counsel Division of Corporation Finance, November 23, 2010. Available at sec.gov.

85   "Remarks by Treasury Secretary Tim Geithner to the International Monetary Conference," Atlanta, Georgia, US Treasury Press Center, June 6, 2011. The International Monetary Conference is an annual meeting of leading bankers from twenty-seven countries, with the American Bankers Association serving as its secretariat.

86   Federal Reserve Press Release, Banking and Consumer Regulatory Policy Division, June 10, 2011.

87   See Aaron Lucchetti, "The Regulator Down the Hall," *Wall Street Journal*, June 20, 2011; as well as Caroline Salas and Bradley Keoun, "New York Fed's Dahlgren Overhauls Bank Supervision to Beef Up Oversight," *Bloomberg*, March 31, 2011. For the lessons the Fed drew for this exercise based on its earlier "stress tests," see Beverley Hirtle, Til Schuermann, and Kevin Stiroh, "Macroprudential Supervision of Financial Institutions: Lessons from the SCAP," *Federal Reserve of New York Staff Reports*, no. 409, November 2009.

88   The aim of quantitative easing was less to control medium- and long-term market rates, although this was how the program was sold to the public, than to stabilize market valuations of securities and sustain interbank markets. Thus, while QE1 in November 2008 involved the purchase of both Treasury bonds and GSE securities ($300 billion and $200 billion respectively), the essence of the project was the socialization of bank losses and risk. The QE2 purchase of Treasury bond securities ($600 billion) two years later had the similar effect of increasing private banks' reserve holdings, but with bank balance sheets now significantly improved, the Fed was now able to manipulate the interest it paid on the reserves that the banks held with it. See Alan S. Blinder, "Quantitative Easing: Entrance and Exit Strategies," Federal Reserve Bank of St. Louis *Review*, November–December 2010, esp. p. 469.

89   See Kenneth D. Garbade and John E. Kambhu, "Why Is the US Treasury Contemplating Becoming a Lender of Last Resort for Treasury Securities?" Federal Reserve Bank of New York, Staff Report no. 223, October 2005.

90   See Jeff Sommer, "Why Are Investors Still Lining Up for Bonds?," *New York Times*, May 29, 2011.

91   Li Daokui, quoted in Mark MacKinnon, "China Sees Yuan Becoming Third Global Currency," *Globe and Mail*, June 4, 2011.

92   Just as this book was being completed, Charles Goodhardt published *The Basel Committee on Banking Supervision: A History of the Early Years, 1974–97*, Cambridge, UK: CUP, 2011.

93   See Walter W. Eubanks, "The Status of the Basel III Capital Adequacy Accord," Congressional Research Service, October 28, 2010. The biggest source of contention during the negotiations centered around types of capital that would be considered top-quality reserve holdings, and the imposition of a 40 percent cap on the use of highly-rated securities as liquid assets.

94   Tony Porter, "Third Time Lucky or Out after Three Strikes? The Political Significance of the Basel III Transnational Standards for Bank Regulation," paper prepared for presentation at the Canadian Political Science Association meeting, May 18, 2011, p. 2.

95   The quotations in this paragraph are from Andrew Walters, "Chinese Attitudes towards Global Regulatory Co-operation: Revisionist or Status Quo," in Helleiner, Pagliari and Zimmermann, *Global Finance in Crisis*, pp. 154, 162, 168.

96   For a particularly scathing attack on Geithner's June 2011 speech to the International

Monetary Conference in this respect, see Simon Johnson, "The Banking Emperor Has No Clothes," *New York Times Economix Blog*, June 9, 2011.

97 See Tom Braithwaite, Brooke Masters, and Jeremy Grant, "Financial Regulation: A Shield Asunder," *Financial Times*, May 20, 2011. See also *An Alternative Report on UK Banking Reform: A Public Interest Report from CRESC*, Manchester: University of Manchester Centre for Research on Socio-Cultural Change, 2009.

98 See Jack Ewing and Liz Alderman, "Banker With A Long Shadow: How Deutsche's Chief Pulls Strings in Europe," *New York Times*, June 12, 2011.

99 Bradley Keoun and Phil Kuntz, "Wall Street Aristocracy Got $1.2 Trillion in Secret Loans," *Bloomberg*, August 22, 2011; Eric Dash, "Profits Falling, Banks Confront a Leaner Future," *New York Times*, August 28, 2011.

100 The relatively few consumers who were able to refinance their debt at lower rates made little difference to total consumption in the context of widespread economic insecurity. In the four years after the crisis hit in the fall of 2007, real consumption increased by only 1.1 percent, which on a per capita basis in fact represented a decline. See US Bureau of Economic Analysis, National Income and Product Accounts, Tables 6.16d and 2.3.3.

101 For a useful discussion of this structural problem, see Maria N. Ivanova, "Consumerism and the Crisis: Whither 'the American Dream'?" *Critical Sociology* 37: 3 (2011).

Conclusion

1 Marx and Engels, *Communist Manifesto*, pp. 38–42.

2 Niall Ferguson, *Colossus: The Rise and Fall of the American Empire*, New York: Penguin, 2005, pp. viii, xxvii; see also his "Empire Falls," *Vanity Fair*, October 2006. For an excellent account of "Ferguson's metamorphoses in the last decade—from cheer-leader, successively, of empire, Anglobalisation and Chimerica to exponent of collapse-theory and retailer of emollient tales about the glorious past—[which] have highlighted broad political and cultural shifts more accurately than his writings," see the review of *Civilization* (Ferguson's latest tome) by Pankaj Mishra, "Watch This Man," *London Review of Books* 33: 1 (3 November 2011), pp. 10–12.

3 The G20 Toronto Summit Declaration, Toronto, June 26–27, 2010, p. 7.

4 See William Greider, "Debt Jubilee, American Style," *Nation*, November 14, 2011, pp. 11–17.

5 Hal Weltzman, "Caterpillar Chief Attacks US," *Financial Times*, August 29, 2011.

6 See Ben Bernanke, "The Near- and Longer-Term Prospects for the US Economy," speech at the Federal Reserve Bank of Kansas City Economic Symposium, Jackson Hole, August 26, 2011; and "Bernanke Warns over Washington Wrangling," *Financial Times*, August 26, 2011.

7 Daniel Kruger, "Downgrade Doesn't Matter as Bond Investors Show Faith in Fed after S&P Cut," *Bloomberg*, August 10, 2011.

8 BBC News, "China State Media Agency Xinhua Criticises US on Debt," July 29, 2011.

9 Quoted in Sumana Ramanan, "Jobs, Trade for US Dominate Day 1," *Sunday Hindustan Times*, November 7, 2010.

10 Saurabh Srivastava, quoted in Thomas Friedman, "It's Morning in India," *New York Times*, October 31, 2010.

11 Alex Barker and Peter Speigel, "Geithner Set to Join European Meeting," *Financial Times*, September 13, 2011.

12 Louise Story and Matthew Saltmarsh, "Europeans Talk of Sharp Change in Fiscal Affairs," *New York Times*, September 5, 2011.

13 World Development Indicators and Global Development Finance. Available at data-bank.worldbank.org.

14 See Ho-Fung Hung, "America's Head Servant," *New Left Review* II/60 (November–December 2009); and R. Taggart Murphy, "A Loyal Retainer? Japan, Capitalism, and the Perpetuation of American Hegemony," in *Socialist Register 2011*, London: Merlin, 2011.

15 See Anita Chan, "Labor Unrest and Role of Unions," *China Daily*, June 18, 2010.

16 See the discussion in Chapter 3, above, of "An American Proposal," *Fortune*, May 1942.

17 Alain Badiou has recently put this very well: "There has been a lot of talk recently about the 'real economy' (the production and circulation of goods), and what I suppose has to be called the 'unreal economy,' which is supposedly the root of all evil, given that its agents have become 'irresponsible,' 'irrational' and 'predatory.' They greedily recycled what had become a shapeless mass of shares, securitizations and money, and then they panicked. The distinction was absurd, and was usually contra-dicted two lines later by the very different metaphor that described financial circulation and speculation as the 'bloodstream' of the economy. Can the heart and the blood be divorced from the living reality of a body?" Alain Badiou, *The Communist Hypothesis*, Verso: London, 2010, p. 95.

18 Kevin Hope, "New PM Faces a Long List of Greek Priorities," *Financial Times*, November 11, 2011. It was quite wrong to see the appointment of Lucas Papademos or Mario Monti as presaging a turn to direct rule by the bankers (see Michael Roberts, "Italy and Greece: Rule by the Bankers," available at thenextrecession.wordpress.com). They were rather typical centrist technocrats whose deep ties to the American empire were all the more valuable for their relative autonomy from narrow capitalist interests. Previous to his elevation to the Greek Premiership, Papademos was an economic adviser to the PASOK government who had studied at MIT, taught at Columbia, and briefly served as senior economist for the Federal Reserve Bank of Boston, before being made chief economist of the Bank of Greece, and later deputy governor of the European Central Bank. After a long academic career in Italy (but with an economics PhD from Yale), Monti served in key economic posts at the European Commission, where he handled competition cases against Microsoft, General Electric, Honeywell, and the German *landesbanken* - even though he also has been an active member of the Bilderberg Group and the Trilateral Commission, as well as an adviser to Goldman Sachs and Coca-Cola.

19 Shavid Javed Burki and Sebastian Edwards, *Latin America After Mexico: Quickening the Pace*, Washington, DC: World Bank, 1995, p. 1. The use of *Alice, Through the Looking Glass* here was rather eerie, in light of the use made of it in a volume of the *Socialist*

Register published a few months earlier to make a rather different point: "Think of the Red Queen's Garden as capitalism. The relentless search for markets and profits brings about faster and faster changes in production and space, industry and commerce, occupation and locale, with profound effects on the organisation of classes and states. It is through this ferocious process of extension and change that capitalism preserves itself, remains capitalism, stays the same system . . . Now think of Alice, frantically running alongside the Red Queen, as the labour *movement*, or the social *movements*, or the broadly defined 'Left'. For all the running they have made in this century, for all the mobilisation and reform, even the moments of revolution and national liberation, the world today is most certainly still very much capitalist, indeed it would seem ever more so . . . [T]he institutions of the Left, not least the once powerful Communist and Social Democratic parties, increasingly could not even keep pace and lost more and more initiative to the forces of capitalist change. Their original ambition *to get somewhere else*, to a social order beyond capitalism—that is, to socialism, however conceived—more or less gradually gave way to attempts at adaptation and accommodation to the dynamics of capitalist change." Panitch, "Globalization and the State."

20 See the excellent critique of John Holloway's *Change the World Without Taking Power: The Meaning of Revolution Today*, London: Pluto, 2005, by Michael Lebowitz, "Holloway's Scream: Full of Sound and Fury," *Historical Materialism* 13: 4 (2005).

21 Perry Anderson, *Lineages of the Absolutist State*, London: NLB, 1974, p. 11.

22 See Leo Panitch and Sam Gindin, "Transcending Pessimism: Rekindling Socialist Imagination," in *Socialist Register 2000*, London: Merlin, 1999; Leo Panitch, *Renewing Socialism: Democracy, Strategy, and Imagination*, second edn., London: Merlin, 2008; and Greg Albo, Leo Panitch and Sam Gindin, *In and Out of Crisis: The Global Financial Meltdown and Left Alternatives*, Oakland: PM Press, 2010.

Index